Play From Birth to Twelve

Second Edition

Play From Birth to Twelve

Contexts, Perspectives, and Meanings

Second Edition

Edited by

Doris Pronin Fromberg and Doris Bergen

Routledge
Taylor & Francis Group
New York   London

Routledge is an imprint of the
Taylor & Francis Group, an informa business

Routledge
Taylor & Francis Group
270 Madison Avenue
New York, NY 10016

Routledge
Taylor & Francis Group
2 Park Square
Milton Park, Abingdon
Oxon OX14 4RN

© 2006 by Taylor & Francis Group, LLC
Routledge is an imprint of Taylor & Francis Group, an Informa business

Printed in the United States of America on acid-free paper
10 9 8 7 6 5 4 3 2 1

International Standard Book Number-10: 0-415-95112-7 (Softcover) 0-415-95111-9 (Hardcover)
International Standard Book Number-13: 978-0-415-95112-8 (Softcover) 978-0-415-95111-1 (Hardcover)

Library of Congress Cataloging-in-Publication Data

Play from birth to twelve : contexts, perspectives, and meanings / [edited by] Doris Pronin Fromberg, Doris Bergen.-- 2nd ed.
    p. cm.
  Rev. ed. of: Play from birth to twelve and beyond / edited by Doris Pronin Fromberg. 1998.
  Includes bibliographical references and index.
  ISBN 0-415-95111-9 (hb : alk. paper) -- ISBN 0-415-95112-7 (pb : alk. paper)
  1. Play. 2. Child development. 3. Play--Social aspects. I. Fromberg, Doris Pronin, 1937- II. Bergen, Doris. III. Play from birth to twelve and beyond.

LB1137.P5545 2006
372.21--dc22
                                                2005036288

Visit the Taylor & Francis Web site at
http://www.taylorandfrancis.com

and the Routledge Web site at
http://www.routledge-ny.com

We dedicate this book to the Dorises' husbands,
Mel Fromberg and Joel Fink,
who continued to endure many hours of free-play time alone
and many piles of papers in their homes
while their wives were working at playing.

.

Contents

Preface

Play is pervasive, infusing human activity throughout the life span. In particular, it serves to characterize childhood, the period from birth to age 12. Since the 1970s, many additions to the knowledge base on childhood play have been published in popular and scholarly literature. This literature has documented the study of play in varied contexts, explored it from numerous perspectives, and imbued it with a range of meanings. The revised second edition of this book assembles and integrates this information, discusses disparate and diverse components, highlights the underlying dynamic processes of play, and provides a forum from which new questions may emerge and new methods of inquiry may develop. The place of new technologies and the future of play in the context of contemporary society also are discussed. New chapters have been developed and selected chapters from the first edition have been updated and revised.

To accomplish this intellectually challenging task, a distinguished group of authors who have made strong scholarly contributions to the study of play from a range of perspectives have written chapters that are designed to be especially useful to educators, other human service professionals, and policy makers. This work can serve as a resource for students or teachers of the arts and humanities, social sciences, and various professional fields. Anthropologists, child development specialists, educators, psychologists, sociologists, community planners, play advocates, communication specialists, and human service professionals will all find this book to be useful. Beyond illuminating the meanings of play from these various perspectives, there is information that can serve to legitimize and advocate for play throughout childhood. If readers can learn about the value of play and consider the contexts in which it takes place, the perspectives on its qualities, and the meanings embedded in its practice, their lives will also be enriched, as will those of the children with whom they share their life space.

There is validity in taking play seriously (and playfully) as an intellectual construct. Moreover, there are important social, emotional, aesthetic, and cultural meanings embedded in play. This exploration of the knowledge base about play reconceptualizes the construct as one that is connected and integrated with its past, its present, and its future. The editors of this edition, each in her own way, had become seduced by the elusive and essential power of play in her own life as well as being attracted to play as a subject of study. As a child growing up in New York City, Doris Fromberg remembers social group play as a cement sidewalk activity with other children, an indoor activity with one or two children, and as a solitary activity. Ball games on the city street stand out as an involving, highly self-motivated, time-consuming, repetitive, skill-building process. She remembers stoop ball, in which she could gain points by bouncing the ball against the edge of the cement step, avoiding the riser. She remembers Chinese handball, in which the brick wall of a small apartment building served as a target surface and the cement sidewalk panels served as each player's separate area. She remembers lots of games of potsie or hopscotch or skelly, in which chalkmarked sections of sidewalk served as the playing field for tossing or flicking bottle caps or other markers into successive squares. Endless hours of playing cards began at 4 years of age with such games as war, casino, slapjack, rummy, gin rummy, poker, canasta, and an irretrievable version of bridge. Checkers at 4 years of age, chess at 5, Monopoly at 6, Sorry, then Ouija, and other board games followed. All of these games included an element of competition.

With those boys who had train sets, she spent time setting up the terrain and mostly watching the repetitive circuits. In middle childhood, she occasionally played marbles and territory with the boys. "Territory," in retrospect, was practice in knife-throwing, and the game of marbles was practice in aiming (as were ball games in general).

Throughout childhood, there were also girl-owned dolls and playing house, often with elaborate props and fantasies that created an empowered world in which children alone could function without adults, a sort of country idyll, similar to the Catskill Mountains bungalow colonies that some children visited in the summer. Another fantasy-based activity took place in the backyards of houses that children annexed as their private thoroughfare. Small groups of children imagined adventures that included punishing and tying up the children who lived around the corner ("the enemy"). These adventures were born and died in the realm of imagination. In middle childhood, children would take long excursions in which they explored empty lots and watched the action at the car barns of the trolley/bus company depot while spinning stories about other times and places. They watched insects, mostly ants and earthworms, and built barriers and habitats for them. Both boys and girls engaged in these games, the boys during middle childhood moving away from the chalkmarked games into roadway-sited punchball or stickball.

Solitary play extended the doll-play fantasy with props, including building a bomb shelter under the kitchen table, building with small wooden blocks and Lincoln Logs, playing with plasticene, drawing and painting, knitting with a "horse rein," and sitting on the windowsill while watching the traffic and imagining herself in other times and places. Although adults might classify some of these activities as arts and crafts or sports, they felt like play because they were self-chosen, self-paced, absorbing, and satisfying. These were activities in which, without reflecting about the feelings, she felt competent or reasonably challenged. They transcended the moment and felt timeless rather than rushed.

As a child, she never reflected on her play. She just filled her time with it. She began to distinguish play from work when she was required to follow the kindergarten teacher's model of drawing a person and acquiesced to her mother's exhortation to practice the piano.

The play experiences of Doris Bergen occurred in a range of contexts. As a child, she lived in two Midwestern cities (St. Louis and Cleveland), a southern rural setting (near Jackson, Mississippi), and a small town in Ohio. Her city play included many of those ball and rule games described by her coeditor, and she especially recalls using the steps and walls for ball playing and the street games such as kick-the-can, usually played in the evening with all the neighborhood. Her favorite recess game was colored eggs, in which the pavement depressions around the fenced-in schoolyard served as the "nests." It was in the city where she first learned to ride a two-wheeled bike, without her parents' knowledge, and she remembers how pleased she was when she could show them that she was ready to get a bike of her own.

The move to the South provided a whole new set of play experiences, including the chance to get the bike that she could ride on the country roads. She recalls her paper-doll play with the one girl who lived close enough to come over to play and such outdoor activities as swinging in the yard and exploring. She also got her first pet playmates: chickens and a dog. (In recently conducted interviews with adults who had lived on farms as children, she learned that pet playmates are common among children living in rural areas.)

She remembers her shock upon moving to the small Ohio town to find that, although the children played some games with names similar to those she played in the city, the rules were often different. For example, the game of marbles in the city was played on pavement and the point of the game was to knock one's own marbles out of the circle drawn on the pavement. In the small town, the game was played on the grass and the point was to throw your marble to hit the other player's marble. What a surprise!

One of her favorite play experiences during her small-town life was the cooperative digging of a large hole in the dirt of the lot between her house and the next one. With the child who lived in the other house (and occasionally other neighborhood children), she and her brother spent hours digging this gigantic hole, which became a house, a fort, a dugout, and a battlefield shelter at various times in its existence. She now wonders at the tolerance of the adults in the neighborhood, who allowed this unsightly hole to exist for a few years while it enriched their children's play lives.

Her indoor play consisted of much building with blocks, making structures such as a drive-in movie theater into which many small cars could drive, and schools and houses. These scenarios were played in many elaborate forms. The fact that she played quite often with her younger brother may have influenced her play, which had an extensive spatial component. She still loves to play with blocks!

Board games of many types were also favorites, most of which were played by her whole family. Both of her parents provided good models of play, and she recalls many happy times playing games with them. She recalls very little play going on in school, however. The one kind of "play" at school she remembers (which she detested and now categorizes as "work disguised as play") was academic "games" she was forced to "play" in class. The one she hated most was the arithmetic competition game, in which two people had to compete at the chalkboard to see who could get the right answer the fastest. She still panics when she has to do a timed math problem. Such is the influence of early experiences!

The play experiences described by the editors may sound familiar to the reader, although translated into distinctive games, terrain, and opportunities. The contexts, perspectives, and meanings of play to be discussed in this book are presented with the hope that readers may better understand their own play experiences and link them to those of children.

We acknowledge the enthusiastic vision and support of Taylor & Francis editor Catherine Bernard. Through our work on these editions, we learned so much from the authors; thus, we also thank the authors who dared to take up the challenge, to think about play in new ways, and to write about how play enriches children's lives.

Introduction

DORIS PRONIN FROMBERG AND DORIS BERGEN

Since the mid-1970s, the phenomenon of play has been a topic of great research interest. Researchers from a number of disciplines have conducted studies of play and based their work on diverse theories and a range of definitional categories. When researchers have looked at play as primarily an individual phenomenon they have structured their study very differently from when their interest has been in play as a cultural phenomenon (Sutton-Smith, 1981). Psychologists and educators, for example, have usually focused on individual aspects, such as the relationship between cognition and play or the adult–child or child–child interaction aspects of play. Anthropologists, sociologists, folklorists, and sociolinguists have been interested in sociocultural aspects, such as the communicative meaning of play within various cultural contexts.

Another difference in approaches to the study of play is whether the questions of interest are about what play is (content) or why it occurs (motive) (Ellis, 1973). If researchers are studying the content of play, they might use observed category structures in their analysis, such as the types and stages of sociodramatic play. If the processes of play are of most interest, investigators might structure the study to observe antecedents, sequences, contexts, and outcomes, such as how children initiate and conclude rough-and-tumble play.

The editors of this book have chosen to look at play through its contexts, perspectives, and meanings because these are three elements present in every type of play.

Perspectives

Various "classical" theorists and researchers have interpreted play from different perspectives and used a range of definitional categories. Psychologists and educators usually have focused on individual aspects of play, such as the relationship of play to children's cognitive, linguistic, social, and creative (associative fluency and imagery) development (Garvey, 1977; Piaget, 1962; Smilansky, 1968). Anthropologists, folklorists, and sociolinguists have been more interested in sociocultural aspects of play, such as the communicative meaning of play within varied contexts (Huizinga, 1955; Schechner, 1985; Schwartzman, 1978; Slaughter & Dombrowski, 1989; Sutton-Smith, 1997, 2001). In investigations of naturally occurring play among animals as well as human beings, ethologists have focused on both the content of play and why play occurs (Ellis, 1998; Fagen, 1995; Panksepp, 1998; Smith, 1995).

Whether play represents an individual or a social phenomenon may be a less important distinction for understanding it than considering its permeable nature. In effect, play interacts with, parallels, represents, and integrates physical, social, emotional, aesthetic, and cognitive experiences. From a developmental viewpoint, play increases in complexity within these integrated developmental domain perspectives. Social play, for example, becomes more complex, less prop-dependent, more varied and verbal. From a physical domain perspective, skills increasingly become more complex, and the line between play and not-play becomes more clearly defined in an activity such as rough-and-tumble play. Similarly, the relationships among fantasy, creativity, and irrationality become more clearly defined. Regardless of the developmental perspective, the meanings of play remain fluid and shift in relation to particular perspectives for viewing the play and the situational contexts in which players find themselves.

When analyses are set aside, play is a self-evident activity to most people. In particular, it serves to characterize childhood, the period from birth to age 12. But although usually associated with childhood, it is pervasive throughout the life span. Studied from the perspectives of many disciplines, play does not end at a particular age but continues to emerge, and occasionally erupt, in shifting forms throughout the life span. That is, students of different disciplines view play from their respective perches, such as historical, philosophical, sociological, psychological, or artistic. While sociologists might document how societies at different times view and participate in play, psychologists might focus on the individual's development of play and artists might be concerned with the creative forces unleashed in playful approaches to representation of the world.

Meanings

The various perspectives from which scholars have studied play and how human beings engage in and experience play suggest that each player constructs different meanings that reflect particular contexts. Scientists, social scientists, and educators have variously defined meaning as "shared awareness" (Penrose, 1994, p. 53), "isomorphism" (Hofstadter, 1979, p. 50), "cross-domain analogy-making" (Hofstadter, 1995, p. 166), and "Central to the development of the meaning system is the event representation (or script), which generalizes from experience of events to provide an interpretation of context" (Nelson, 1985, p. 9).

In the children's play described in the preface, some universal themes of bipolar friends and enemies, dealing with fear or risk, escaping to other times and places, and gaining empowerment through community building are examples of children's meaningful event knowledge that they have built through play.

Meaning as a context-based subject of study is vast, beyond the scope of this volume. The notion of a recursive process that provides an interplay between the meanings for each child (whose personal content base is in the form of event knowledge) and the shared negotiations with other children (who use their own event knowledge) makes possible the synergistic development of sociodramatic play episodes. With respect to play as a skill-building experience, moreover, it is the case that children's development takes place in social negotiation and competence skills, as well as cognitive expansion, elaboration, or flexibility, or physical game playing. Meaning, from these perspectives, therefore, includes both conceptual content and a degree of complexity tempered by commitment and caring. Commitment and caring relate to the self-motivational dynamic of play. Three themes that are evident in meaning making are exploration, power and personal meaning, and imagery.

Contexts

Regardless of city, suburban, or rural settings throughout the world, children play. If they grow up in an agrarian economy and accompany their mothers into the fields, they find ways to play within that environment, and there are reports that mothers who work in such settings also find ways to make the time with their children pass in playful ways (Edwards, 2000). Although the adults in their lives may supply them with toys that seem to direct a single-purpose use or engage them in multiage observations and metaphorical group narratives (Heath, 1983), children find ways to extend their sense of power and possibilities through play. Whether their imagined adventures take them onto a stage with rock stars or into the adventures of Superman, Spiderman, Sponge Bob, Bionicles, or Blues Clues; whether their rough-and-tumble activities are more or less forceful; whether they are building with commercial blocklike materials, rocks and twigs, or discarded boxes, children find ways to imagine, construct, and negotiate with one another. The surface forms of play appear to conform to some powerful underlying patterns. It is these underlying dynamic patterns that make play appear to be self-evident.

Play is a condition that changes in relation to different contexts. The contexts of play are simultaneously influenced by historical events, cultural variations, and personal possibilities. Play can take place in any context and at just about any time. Although opportunities available within different sociocultural contexts may offer different data for the development of event knowledge, the underlying "grammar" of play contributes to each child's integration of particular experiences. Consideration of context makes evident the relativity of play, in that contextual influences often determine whether participants in a culture consider certain behaviors play or not-play. Contexts also have a role in determining who is entitled to play, in that different cultures at certain time periods and in varied settings permit different age, gender, or status groups to play; contexts also provide a basis for judging certain types of play as acceptable or not acceptable.

Relativity

Play may be relatively present in different forms because it functions differently in different contexts; thus, the context codes the activity as play or not-play. Some societies, at different historical periods, for example, permit behaviors often characterized as play only within religious practice. Activities associated with religious rituals and ceremonies, which were performed by religious leaders, priests, or priestesses at an earlier time or in one location, may be recognized as play in other times, places, or cultures (Geertz, 1976; Schechner, 1985).

Some research suggests that children realize the contextual elements that determine play/not-play at an early age. When kindergarten children are able to choose an activity, for example, they code it as play, whereas they code as work the same activity when it is selected for them by an adult (King, 1987). Research indicates that children of this age are able to make quite a fine distinction between contextual elements that determine whether an activity would be called work, play, or learning (Ceglowski, 1997).

Play may also become transformed from the predominance of observation or physical involvement into verbal interaction. Play forms become transformed throughout childhood as the forms are socially redefined as other than play, becoming "recreation" or the "leisure time activity" of adults. Verbalizations and physical action increasingly become internalized, and some types of play become more serious and competitive rather than playful (Bergen, 1998).

Entitlements

Historically, questions and issues have surfaced that concern who could play what activities and what forms of play were acceptable. Riding to hounds, for example, may appear to be leisure activity and the province of the wealthy, whereas using a farm horse to plow has another connotation. With income that exceeds a subsistence level, many who are present-day "royalty" can afford similar leisure activities. Tennis, for example, once the game of kings, has changed and become a gender-neutral activity within the middle class. Children join a variety of groups, teams, and networks to engage in ball games, card games, Lego robotics, and other such play activities.

One of the difficulties in studying play is that, because it is generated within particular contexts, even subtle changes in context can transform play into not-play. Context-based questions include issues such as, who is playing or not playing; with whom are they playing; how are they playing; who decides on the course of events;   and where and when is play taking place?

Manifestations of play, such as the size of gestures, the volume of speech or laughter, and the pace of activity have more or less acceptability in various national cultures, geographic locations within particular cultures, socioeconomic status levels, and times of day and year. Sanctions according to age, gender, class, or ethnic group are also apparent within the forms and expressions of play that particular cultures permitted. People in some cultures or socioeconomic groups might consider that older children or adults who engage in rough-and-tumble play show childlike behavior, for example, while people in other contexts would permit or even encourage such play. Context, of course, has an influence on the perspectives of those whose discipline involves the study of play.

Definitions

Those who have studied play from many perspectives offer a variety of ways to define play. The difficulty lies in the use of the term *play* as both a noun and a verb. As the discussion of context pointed out, play is a *relative* activity. The shifting functions in different settings contribute to researchers' problems in defining play. One definition for example, drawn from a review of research on play in early childhood, states that young children's play is:

Symbolic, in that it represents reality in "as-if" or "what-if" terms
Meaningful, in that it connects or relates experiences
Active, in that children are doing things [including imagining]
Pleasurable, even when children are engaged seriously in activity
Voluntary and *intrinsically motivated*, whether the motives are curiosity, mastery, affiliation, or others
Rule-governed, whether implicitly or explicitly expressed
Episodic, characterized by emerging and shifting goals that develop spontaneously (Fromberg, 2002).

Play has variously been considered a "medium" for learning (Bergen, 1998) and a "condition" (among others) for learning (Fromberg, 2002). Possibly the overriding attribute that is so gratifying and addictive about play is that it is intrinsically motivated, satisfying, and empowering. The experience of "flow," an "optimal" experience, is a compatible image (Csikszentmihalyi, 1999; Csikszentmihalyi & Csikszentmihalyi, 1988). As a dynamic and integrative human activity, it is apparent that play is not at all a simple matter.

The perspectives concerning play in contemporary life take added significance from some of the principles of chaos and complexity theory. As a context-based phenomenon, play is sensitively dependent on initial conditions. This means that chance encounters and brief events, when influenced by the ongoing complexity and volume of daily experiences, can evolve into unrecognizable forms. To this extent, play is also a self-organizing system: when children interact with one another, they influence each other's development, thus creating new renditions of self-organized systems.

Within the broadly based literature of humanistic, scientific, and artistic fields, discussions of play can serve as a way to develop the perspectives included in this volume; these various perspectives serve to bracket a definition of play. This book documents, therefore, an emergent, richly textured definition of play that reflects the broad range of meanings that play has in childhood experiences.

Exploration Contrasted with Play

Power is the central distinction between exploration and play, although both experiences may look playful to an observer. A widely held view (Hutt, 1976, p. 211) suggests that exploration deals with how objects or interpersonal situations function (What can it/they do?). Play, in contrast, deals with what the player can do (What can I do?). A related interpretation is that exploration is an opportunity to learn about perceptual properties, whereas play is an occasion for learning about the functional properties of objects (Collard, 1979, p. 52). Children at play have the power to control a situation in proactive ways.

Power and Personal Meaning

The personal experience of play as a creative force in human life takes on added significance in contemporary life. The 21st century in the United States provides a context that includes new technologies and theories that are shifting human paradigms for understanding the world. Complexity and chaos theories, for example, are contemporary ways of looking at knowledge and experience in general as dynamic, complex, and predictably unpredictable in wholesomely chaotic ways. Human beings who can be flexible connection makers can function more comfortably within such a worldview than can linear thinkers. Mirroring aspects of social pretend play, such contemporary theories add credence to the importance of play in human experience.

There are, therefore, both personal and cultural meanings that reflect play. It is important to look at issues concerning the respective personal meanings which boys and girls take out of and bring to play activities. It is also important to look at the personal meanings that children who have specific learning challenges take out of and bring to play activities. Within this discussion of power and personal meanings, the nature of competition and losing surfaces. What is the point, for example, at which competition sours play or success sweetens play? Framed in this way, this issue represents a look at a *phase transition* between one state and another. From the perspective of complexity theory, learning takes place at the point of transformation from one phase to another.

Personal meanings may relate to the different perspectives from which each player perceives the experience. For some girls, for example, joy from winning may be tempered by the empathy they feel for a disappointed loser. Affiliative motives may also come into play in another way. In public winning, there may be some degree of feeling separated from others. Some boys in the United States, in contrast, may learn a societal message that winning, with its accompanying destruction of others or a sense of being set apart, is preferable. Other cultures create games in which the difficulty lies in avoiding winning by assuring that all participants finish on an equal footing (Bruner, 1980).

What, one might ask, does the child card player or video game player learn when he or she continues to lose more than win? Consider the continuum of covarying empowerment experiences in relation to the development of self-motivated play skills: Power can range from children being totally in control to their loss of control. Practice can range from children persevering to becoming controlled by obsession. This continuum between the self-motivated power to choose and the loss of control parallels the continuum between engaging in the practice of play and the loss of personal control.

These kinds of issues may, in part, tie the personal meanings of this empowerment continuum with sociocultural and political influences. Within sociodramatic play or other forms of fantasy play, for example, girls may be able to be more competitive even if they are the target of attention as a winner, because they are protected by the play frame from social isolation or marginalization. Sociodramatic play also is a collaborative, small-group activity.

Ethnic distinctions may also confound the inclusion–exclusion issue. Such relative meanings also emerge out of particular sociocultural contexts and values. Although people of color and girls in competitive sports or professions, for example, have become more prevalent in the United States in recent years, a fully egalitarian transformation awaits the future. For a child who also carries a physical or verbal challenge into the play arena, the sense of inclusion or exclusion also has important personal connotations.

Imagery

For the excluded child, imagination also is an important support system. It can transport the child to other times and places that may be happy, vengeful, or comforting. For the child who has physical challenges, imagery can serve as a vehicle for transcending, even alleviating, the challenging or difficult moment.

The personal use of imagery can act as a social commodity for any child as well as contributing to success in games and pretending within a play framework. In physical activity, for example, winning athletes, performers, and visual artists are able to "psych themselves" into a state of fluent imagery that helps them perform. In sociodramatic activity, children extend the richness of their play through imagery building and sharing the evolution of script building with other children. In both instances, there is an intensity of interest and a submersion within the rules of the game. Imagery and self-concept, within these contexts, together influence the development of the play and, in turn, become confirmed or disconfirmed. Play, therefore, serves not only to use event knowledge but offers an opportunity to add to the players' repertoire of event knowledge and new meanings.

Overview of the Book

The book is organized into six parts. Part I, "Perspectives on Play Development" looks at the development of play behaviors and experiences across childhood and considers various influences on that development. Chapters focus on the development of play from birth to 12 years of age as well as over the life span. The authors also consider the specific perspectives on the development of play in relation to language, the influence of gender, and as a vehicle for expression of feelings.

Part II, "Meanings of Play," focuses on the variety of types of play, such as sociodramatic play, play with objects, constructive play, rough-and-tumble play, games with rules, and the nature of humor in play.

Part III, "Educational Contexts of Play," focuses on play and learning, and how play may be expressed in school settings. Its role in literacy, logico-mathematical, and scientific development is considered, and the influence of technology on play is discussed. Play and assessment relationships are also considered.

Part IV, "Social and Physical Contexts for Play," focuses on the diverse contexts in which play occurs viewed from historical and cultural contexts, urban and outdoor settings, and in special environments such as health care, family, and clinical locations.

Part V, "Particular Meanings Embedded in Play," focuses on a number of special issues connected with play. These issues include the role of fantasy and imagination, sociocultural and gender influences, understanding violent play, and how play supports education within an unpredictable world.

The book concludes with an "Epilogue" that discusses possible emerging and future perspectives, meanings, and contexts for play. It provides a look at the future of play in a postmodern world in which roles, agents, relationships, functions, and advocates may become delineated in fresh ways. The place of present and emerging technology is a significant influence on trends in play and issues of advocacy concerning children's play.

References

Bergen, D. (1998). *Readings from play as a learning medium*. Olney, MD: Association for Childhood Education International.

Bruner, J. S. (1980). *Under five in Britain*. Ypsilanti, MI: NIL High/Scope.

Ceglowski, D. (1997). Understanding and building upon children's perceptions of play activities in early childhood programs. *Early Childhood Education Journal, 25*(2), 107–112.

Collard, R. R. (1979), Exploration and play. In B. Sutton-Smith (Ed.), *Play and learning* (pp. 45–68). New York: Gardner.

Csikszentmihalyi, M. (1999). *Finding flow: The psychology of engagement with everyday life*. New York: Basic Books.

Csikszentmihalyi, M., & Csikszentmihalyi, I. S. (Eds.). (1988). *Optimal experience: Psychological studies in flow consciousness*. New York: Cambridge University Press.

Edwards, C. P. (2000). Children's play in cross-cultural perspective: A new look at the six cultures study. *Cross-Cultural Research 34*, 318–338.

Ellis, M. J. (1973). *Why people play*. Englewood Cliffs, NJ: Prentice-Hall.

Ellis, M. J. (1998). Play and the origin of species. In D. Bergen, (Ed.). Readings from Play as a medium for development and learning (pp. 29–31). Olney, MD: Association for Childhood Education International.

Fagen, R. (1995). Animal play, games of angels, biology, and Brian. In A. D. Pellegrini (Ed.), *The future of play theory* (pp. 23–44). Albany: State University of New York Press.

Fromberg, D. P. (2002). *Play and meaning in early childhood education*. Boston: Allyn & Bacon.

Garvey, C. (1977). *Play*. Cambridge, MA: Harvard University Press.

Geertz, C. (1979). Deep play: A description of the Balinese cockfight. In J. S. Bruner, A. Jolly, & K. Sylva (Eds.), *Play—Its role in development and evolution* (pp. 656–674). New York: Basic Books.

Heath, S. B. (1983). *Ways with words: Language, life, and work in communities and classrooms*. New York: Cambridge University Press.

Hofstadter, D. R. (1979). *Gödel, Escher, Bach: An eternal golden braid*. New York: Basic Books. (Original work published 1976)

Hofstadter, D. R. & The Fluid Analogies Research Group (1995). *Fluid concepts and creative analogies: Computer models of the fundamental mechanisms of thought*. New York: Basic Books.

Huizinga, J. (1955). *Homo ludens: A study of the play elements of culture*. Boston: Beacon.

Hutt, C. (1976). Exploration and play in children. In J. S. Bruner, A. Jolly, & K. Sylva (Eds.), *Play—Its role in development and evolution* (pp. 202–215). New York: Basic Books.

King, N. R. (1987). Elementary school play: Theory and research. In J. H. Block & N. R. King (Eds.), *School play* (pp. 143–165). New York: Garland.

Nelson, K. (1985). *Making sense: The acquisition of shared meaning*. New York: Academic.

Panksepp, J. (1998). Attention deficit hyperactivity disorders, psychostimulants, and intolerance of childhood playfulness: A tragedy in the making? *Current Directions in Psychological Science 7* (3), 91–98.

Penrose, R. (1994). *Shadows of the mind: A search for the missing science of consciousness*. New York: Oxford University Press.

Piaget, J. (1962). *Play, dreams, and imitation in childhood* (C. Gattegno & M. E Hodgson, Trans.). New York: W W Norton.

Schechner, R. (1985). *Between theater and anthropology*. Philadelphia: University of Pennsylvania Press.

Schwartzman, H. (1978). *Transformations: The anthropology of children's play*. New York: Plenum.

Slaughter, D., & Dombrowski, J. (1989). Cultural continuities and discontinuities: Impact on social and pretend play. In M. N. Bloch & A. D. Pellegrini (Eds.), *The ecological context of children's play* (pp. 282–310). Norwood, NJ: Ablex.

Smilansky, S. (1968). *The effects of sociodramatic play on disadvantaged preschool children*. New York: Wiley.

Smith, P. K. (1995). Play, ethology, and education: A personal account. In A. D. Pellegrini (Ed.), *The future of play theory* (pp. 3–22). Albany: State University of New York Press.

Sutton-Smith, B. (1981). *A history of children's play*. Philadelphia: University of Pennsylvania.

Sutton-Smith, B. (1997). *The ambiguity of play*. Cambridge, MA: Harvard University Press.

Sutton-Smith, B. (2001). Emotional breaches in play and narrative. In A. Goncu & E. L. Klein (Eds.), *Children in play, story, and school* (pp. 161–176). New York: Guilford Press.

I

Perspectives on Play Development

Introduction

Most observers of children would agree that the nature of play changes over the course of children's development and that these changes occur in orderly stages. The early theorists' categorizations of various types of play at different age levels formed the framework for the perception of play as a developmental phenomenon (Rubin, 1982). Early researchers categorized the play they observed in young children into age-related stages (e.g., Parten, 1932/1971). Later theorists described the stages of play development in specific domains (Erikson, 1976; Piaget, 1976; Vygotsky, 1976, 1978). Play development is related to cognitive and moral reasoning; language cognition and social understanding; and social–emotional mastery. Many researchers have attempted to verify the theoretical stages of play in precise and detailed studies.

The conceptualization of play as a developmental phenomenon has resulted in the systematic study of trends in types of play exhibited at various ages, in diagnostic practices that identify developmental problems when these types of play do not occur as expected, and in recommendations for interventions to enhance play development (Bergen, 1998). The systematic study of play development has also made explicit individual and cultural differences that may occur in the sequence, transitions, and content of play. Even in the dominant culture, a number of assumptions about the qualitative differences that occur in play at various ages and stages have recently been called into question. Although adults usually characterize pretend play, for example, as a phenomenon of early childhood, researchers report finding that pretense continues to be an important activity throughout childhood (Bergen, 2003; Bergen, Liu, & Liu, 1994).The settings in which it occurs (home, backyard) during later childhood differ from the more public settings (preschool, school) of the early childhood years, however, and the activities are usually more private. Although adults usually characterize solitary play as a phenomenon of young children, this type of play seems to have a mature as well as an immature form (Rubin, Fein, & Vanderberg, 1983).

For most children, play is as effortless as breathing and as varied as the images in a kaleidoscope. Their development of proficient use of language, social competence, complex thinking, and creative problem solving seems to occur in parallel and integrative ways in concert with their play development.

The chapters in Part I describe the knowledge base that has been accumulated through the study of typical play development. The descriptions of the "typical" development of play during three age periods provide a basis for discussing specific developmental domain issues. The specific domains include cognitive and language facets of play development, and the connections between play, gender identity, and emotional development within the context of the life span.

References

Bergen, D. (1998). *Readings from play as a learning medium.* Olney, MD: Association for Childhood Education International.

Bergen, D. (2003). *College students' memories of their childhood play: A ten year comparison.* Paper presented at the annual conference of the National Association for the Education of Young Children, Chicago.

Bergen, D., Liu, W., & Liu, G. (1994). *Chinese and American college students' memories of childhood play: A comparison.* Paper presented at the conference of the Association for the Study of Play, Atlanta, GA.

Erikson, E. (1976). Play and actuality. In J. S. Bruner, A. Jolly, & K. Sylva (Eds.), *Play—Its role in development and evolution* (pp. 668–703). New York: Basic Books.

Parten, M. (1971). Social play among preschool children. In R. E. Herron & B. Sutton-Smith (Eds.), *Child's play* (pp. 83–95). New York: Wiley. (Original work published 1932)

Piaget, J. (1976). *The grasp of consciousness.* Cambridge, MA: Harvard University Press.

Rubin, K. H. (1982). Non-social play in preschoolers: Necessary evil? *Child Development, 53,* 651–657.

Rubin, K. H., Fein, G. G., & Vanderberg, B. (1983). Play. In E. M. Hetherington (Ed.), *Handbook of child psychology: Socialization, personality, and social development* (pp. 693–774). New York: Wiley.

Vygotsky, L. S. (1976). Play and its role in the mental development of the child. In J. S. Bruner, A. Jolly, & K. Sylva (Eds.), *Play—Its role in development and evolution* (pp. 537–554). New York: Basic Books.

Vygotsky, L. S. (1978). *Mind in society: The development of higher psychological processes* (M. Cole, V. John-Steiner, S. Scribner, & E. Souberman, Eds.). Cambridge, MA: Harvard University Press.

1
Play Development from Birth to Age Four

BARBARA P. GARNER AND DORIS BERGEN

Play is a ubiquitous activity of young children. Exploratory and sensorimotor types of play are primary during the early infancy period, and during the first years of life symbolic play begins and reciprocal social games emerge. These early play behaviors form the basis for play throughout life (Bergen, 1998). As significant developmental changes occur during the first four years of life in children's social, emotional, physical, and cognitive domains, concomitant progressive changes occur in play.

Defining and Categorizing Infant Play

Researchers investigating play have embraced many methods and theoretical orientations; thus, a result has often been a lack of consensus regarding definitions, categories, and views of the developmental progression of play. Observations of play in solitary or social contexts and in a laboratory or a naturalistic setting may yield varying definitions; in particular, during infancy these definitions are amorphous and flexible. One prevalent quality of play during early childhood, for example, asserts that play is a pleasurable and intrinsically motivated activity (Fromberg, 1992). Using this definition, it is possible to define as play many behaviors that infants show. For example, although adults might define as work infants' struggle to balance and begin to stand or walk independently, infants appear to have intrinsic motivations for achieving these motor skills and show expressions of pleasure in achieving them. Thus, this motor practice appears to be play for infants. Although scholars have not often defined it that way, they do give evidence of the high motivation infants show for mastery of motor skills (Adolph, 1997).

There are various categories that can delineate infants' play. Researchers such as Wachs (1993) have usually noted a high proportion of object play, which they have variously called practice, exploratory, manipulative, or functional play, as well as much social play related to peer and adult–child interactions. They have focused studies on comparisons of social play with or without objects, and social play with familiar or unfamiliar objects or people, while giving little attention to motor practice play in infancy. There also has been much research about the beginnings of pretend play, perhaps because researchers often link it to advances in cognitive development (e.g., Youngblade & Dunn, 1996). During infancy, however, these categories of play frequently overlap. For example, toddlers engaged in exploratory play may be practicing newly acquired motor skills in the presence of familiar peers. Similarly, when they imitate each other's motor behaviors, the activity may be both practice play and social play, and the practice of emerging motor skills may be seen as play, exploration, or work. Because infants are not able to label their play, it may be especially difficult for researchers to identify pretense when observing certain motor actions.

Throughout infancy, developmental changes in other domains encourage and change the kinds and levels of play. Changes in physical development, for example, result in changes in coordinated motor play. As children acquire gross motor skills that allow mobility, they can expand their exploration of the environment, and advanced fine motor skill promotes exploration through greater manipulation of objects. As cognitive concepts develop, infants begin to see relations between individual action patterns, and as they combine these, relational and functional play increases. When representational/symbolic thinking advances, pretense emerges and develops. As social development changes from a symbiotic view of self to recognition of a separate self, peer interactions in play begin and progress rapidly. This discussion of types of infant and toddler play uses some of the more commonly used categories; however, two facts must be kept in mind: (1) the influences on play development of rapid developmental changes in other domains, and (2) the difficulty of categorizing play into discrete types during this age period.

Categorizing Infant and Toddler Play

Scholars often categorize the many play behaviors of very young children as object play, motor play, social play, and symbolic/pretend play.

Play with Objects

Object play in the first few months of life is limited if not absent. Infants' reflexive grasp may permit a chance contact with an object that allows the child to explore the object momentarily, but this is fleeting and is certainly not the primary mode of play during the newborn period. Over the first few months of life, infant object play consists of practice play that is focused on the body; that is, the body itself is the object of play. Infants repeat over and over again the motor behaviors that cause an interesting event to occur. Piaget (1962a, 1962b) called this period of development primary circular reactions, and pointed out infants' intrinsic motivation to perform them. By 4 months of age, infants' interests begin to shift away from primary focus on the body to things external to the body, such as objects and people. Exploring objects is something that infants seem uniquely motivated to do. At first, they indiscriminately engage in mouthing, banging, and shaking objects, food, and people. Later in the first year, differentiation occurs, and infants shake rattles, bang toys, and mouth bottles and food (Uzgiris & Hunt, 1975).

Between 4 and 12 months, the achievement of motor developmental milestones allows infants to access more interesting events in their environment. For example, with the ability to sit, infants are able to have visual guidance in reaching to grasp objects and bring their hands to midline for object exploration. Between 7 and 12 months, infants' manipulative skill increases to the point where they can use both hands independently for exploration. In response to a review of research on object manipulation in infancy that suggested such studies primarily explored cognition or perceptual development rather than developmental trends in object manipulations (Lockman & McHale, 1989), several researchers have investigated the developmental sequence involved in manipulating objects.

One group of researchers who investigated the way infants explore objects (Baldwin, Markman, & Melartin, 1993) indicates that patterns of exploratory play emerge between 9 and 16 months, showing that infants are capable of making inferences about novel objects based on very brief exposures to an exemplar. When given objects with similar appearance and properties, infants immediately used similar patterns of exploration, but their actions on dissimilar objects varied. That is, infants are able to use visually available surface properties to infer the presence of underlying functional properties of objects. By 19 months, infants treat symbolic objects (i.e., pictures) differently from three-dimensional objects; pictures are "looked at" rather than treated as toys by that age (DeLoache, Pierroutsakos, Uttal, Rosengren, & Gottlieb, 1998). Infants' ability to make quick and correct inferences helps explain how their knowledge base expands so rapidly over this period. Knowing that objects have such an impact on infants' cognitive development provides support for the value of environments that are rich in availability of a wide variety of objects for play.

Between 7 and 12 months there is an increase in infants' manipulative skill, and this enables them to use both hands to manipulate an object independently (Kimmerle, Mick, & Michel, 1995). Typically, one hand will stabilize an item and the dominant hand will manipulate it. Simple independent use of both hands was observed as early as 7 months. The specific properties of the object do not seem to matter; infants use each hand independently regardless of whether or not the object has movable parts. As their cognitive development advances, the property of the object comes into play, and the object needs to have movable parts in order for infants to manipulate it. Thus, through their object play infants' concepts of causality and object properties, such as stability and movability, increase. Functional play (i.e., object play with relational goals) increases over a similar time span as infants become more able to combine action patterns. At first, infants will combine the action patterns indiscriminately: a comb may be placed in a bowl or a spoon on top of a truck. Later, they will begin to combine items in typical relational patterns: they will place a spoon in a pot, for example, and then place a lid on the top. Before they are 1 year old, most infants will put items into containers and, by 12 months, many will have learned to dump items out of the container.

Although play changes during the second year, the major focus of play remains object-centered, and such manipulative play is predominant throughout the second year. Mouthing as a form of exploration decreases in frequency and is rarely seen after the second year (Mayes, Carter, & Stubbe, 1993). Infants between 1 and 2 years of age seem to ask, "What can I do with this object?" (Vondra & Belsky, 1989, p. 176). Now infants have entered the cognitive stage of tertiary circular reactions (Piaget, 1962a, 1962b), frequently referred to as the age of experimentation. Indeed, toddlers act like scientists experimenting with what objects can do and learning what they can do with the objects (Gopnik, Meltzer, & Kuhl, 2001). Some researchers regard this as the time when infant activity has changed from exploration to play (Hutt, 1979). Infants from 12 to 18 months delight in toys that react to their actions: pop-up characters, activated by pressing buttons, jacks-in-the-box that pop out when someone pulls a string, and books that emit words or music when toddlers press a button are examples.

As children enter the third year of life, manipulative materials such as clay, finger paints, water play toys, blocks, books, dolls, stuffed animals, and puzzles take on added importance. Young children's sense of mastery increases as they find more and more activities that can be under their control. Manipulative or practice play remains an important part of play for the 3-year-old, but most play now is functional; that is, it is in the service of a self-chosen play goal, rather than being simply exploration of object characteristics.

Motor Play

Few researchers have studied the sequence of motor play during infancy. Although many have investigated motor activities in relation to physical development, rarely have they looked at implications for social and cognitive development. However, motor development is intimately tied to other developmental areas. "Enough research has been done to clearly show that the body plays a fundamental role … [in development and] … there is no such thing as a brain without a body" (Fischer & Hogan, 1989, p. 298). As infant motor skills are developing, practice of these skills takes precedence over all other activities. Although manipulation of objects and interactions with adults and peers increase dramatically during the first year, motor play continues to have an important presence. From ages 9 to 12 months, a great deal of infant play relates to developing physical skills. These infants are learning to pull themselves up, cruise along furniture, stand alone, and many walk independently. Genetic factors, physiological factors such as body build and muscle tone, and environmental experiences all affect the achievement of these milestones (Thelan & Smith, 1994). The age of onset of walking has decreased, perhaps due to parents' lessened use of playpens in recent decades. When infants have opportunities to explore, risk, and try again and again, in an environment that is safe but challenging, they can engage in motor practice play that leads to advanced physical abilities.

Two-year-old children are more physically active than at any other time of life. Interest in large motor activities increases as children's motor abilities improve. The availability of safe climbing structures enhances the opportunity for their gross motor play as well as advances in physical development. The 2-year-old will climb, if not on safe equipment that adults provide, then on anything available, some of which may be dangerous. Toys that children can push and pull encourage practice play in the area of motor activities. Riding toys become important as infants reach the second and third year of life. By their second birthday, most children have developed motor skills to the point where they can run with ease and pleasure. Peers frequently practice running and make a game of imitation that looks like "Do what I do." When young children can jump off the ground with both feet, they regale everyone with "Watch me." Throughout this period, practice of motor skills continues to be an important form of play.

As fine motor control develops, young children engage in activities that practice these newfound skills. When the well-defined pincer grasp develops, for example, a favorite activity is poking fingers into holes, picking up minuscule items from the floor, and using toys that they can activate by a poke. Most children over 1 year are interested in objects that make marks. Although they do not have the refined skills to allow them to have good control of crayons and pencils, they enjoy the practice of making marks and scribbles. By 3 years, many children have increased their fine motor activities and are beginning to cut, paste, and use varied kinds of art materials, such as clay or play dough. Children at this age are still primarily interested in the manipulation of and learning about the medium, however, and they will not yet initiate the creation of a product.

Social Play

Adults and children (both peers and siblings) act as play partners during this early period. Each provides different kinds of interactive play experiences that enhance social play.

Social Play with Adults

Adults, in particular mothers and fathers, are infants' first play partners. During the first few months, adults initiate this play but infants quickly enter into it. Simple exchanges of vocalization are the first games babies play with parents. By 6 weeks infants respond to these overtures with smiles and coos. Adults give many cues to help infants discriminate play from nonplay, for example, in the game of peekaboo (Lillard, 2003). Their play interactions change over the first year and infants' responses change as well. Initially, infants will respond to peekaboo games and tickle games with equal delight. By 8 months, a tickle will not automatically produce laughter as it did previously. Pat-a-cake and peekaboo games increase, and tickle games begin to decrease. By 12 months, tickle games have almost disappeared, and give-and-take games, and point-and-name games have increased. Whatever the game, infants' attention and exploring increase by play with an adult (Lockman & McHale, 1989).

Mothers seem able to adjust their introduction of new toys to their infants' needs by offering new play activities and regulating the intensity of play. When infants are engaged in object play, the quality of play and the sustained amount of play increase when playing with mothers over playing alone (Cielinski, Vaughn, Seifer, & Contresas, 1995). After the 18-month-old period, fathers initiate more play episodes with infants than do mothers (Clark-Stewart, 1977, cited in Bergen, 1998); fathers' play encourages toddlers to engage in symbolic play, although the themes fathers use differ stereotypically with boys and girls (Farver & Wimbarti, 1995). Fathers also tend to engage in more physically rousing play, roughhousing, tossing infants in the air, and run-and-chase games than do mothers. Mothers' play tends to involve a teaching component and to be more verbal than that of fathers. They spend more play time naming objects, labeling, and pointing than they do in physically active play (Hughes, 1991).

Because adult partners seem to offer the benefit of extending and enhancing the quality of infants' play, how mothers are able to scaffold play for their infant has been interesting for researchers' speculation. This may be due to mothers typically operating at one or two levels of pretense higher than that of their toddlers (Adler, 1982). Mothers' views of play may motivate infants and have real consequences for social and cognitive development. A number of parenting behaviors seem to be intuitive. In terms of language development, for example, parents are adept at scaling their language just slightly above infants' capabilities thus increasing infant language competence (Papousek & Papousek, 1982). Mothers and fathers both seem to make adjustments in their play based on the developmental level of the infant. One group of researchers, in the interest of understanding what mothers actually believe about developmental levels of play, had mothers rate the difficulty of play behaviors (Tamis-LeMonda, Damast, & Bornstein, 1994). They found that mothers, based on these ratings, have an excellent concept of the developmental progression of play.

Social Play with Peers

Initially, infants are unaware of self as distinct from others. However, very early in life, they seem to distinguish familiar adults from other infants. Infants exhibit behaviors that look very much like excitement when another infant is present (Fogel, 1979). When seated on their mothers' laps, for example, infants will lean forward and stare intently at other infants. These first social encounters are brief and unsophisticated. First exchanges are often simply looks, followed in a short while by smiles and vocalizations. One line of research on peer interaction addresses whether or not toys or objects that are present increase infants' peer interaction. A number of researchers have data that support the hypothesis that infants under 1 year spend more time interacting when in a setting devoid of objects (Eckerman & Watley, 1977; Vandell & Mueller, 1980). In another study, this finding held true for children under 1 year, but a shift was evident at about 14 months (Jacobson, 1981). At this time, longer interactions were present when infants were in settings with objects available.

Children's interest in peers increases throughout the second year. Early in this year interactions with peers remain largely confined to looking, offering, and taking toys and objects. At 14 months there is a shift in the role of objects and peer interactions. Objects now become important in lengthening the time of interactions. Although social interaction may not originate in an object-centered context, object-centered play seems to enhance infants' ability to engage in extended social interactions (Jacobson, 1981). Young toddlers are able to engage in complementary and reciprocal social interactions. They engage in complementary activities such as run-and-chase and give-and-take (Howes, 1987). Well-acquainted infants often engage in ritual-like interactions. These rituals may be similar to scripts that older preschool children use for social pretend play. The complementary and reciprocal nature of play during the early toddler period may be a prerequisite for children's being able to engage in cooperative social pretend play in the latter part of the toddler years (15 to 36 months). Young children who are in play groups, and who have become familiar with their available peers, begin to show preferences for certain play partners. First friendships are formed, and many are stable into the preschool years (Howes, 1987; Howes & Matheson, 1992; Howes, Unger, & Seidner, 1989).

Symbolic/Pretend Play

Symbolic play is the category of play that scholars have most closely linked to early cognitive development. Very simple pretend play becomes evident at approximately 1 year of age. The onset of pretending appears to be sudden, is universal, and in its earliest form, infants direct it toward themselves (Fein, 1981). Infants may use a brush or comb on their hair, for example, or they may "drink" from a bottle or cup, or hold a play telephone to their ear. Although this type of actor-focused pretend play appears at about 12 months, pretense is not a predominant mode of play in the first year of life. Early pretending is a solitary play activity; social pretend play develops after the first 12 months (Howes & Matheson, 1992; Howes, Unger, & Seidner, 1989). It typically follows a sequence of pretend toward self, pretend toward persona objects (e.g., dolls), and finally pretend toward peers (Tamis-LeMonda & Bornstein, 1991). The dramatic change to social pretense is fleeting at first and accounts for a small percentage of the time that children spend in play (Vondra & Belsky, 1989).

An initial social pretend activity may begin with eye contact with another peer, but the activity does not elicit a response in the peer: young children who make eye contact with another child may pretend to drink from a cup, but the activity does not elicit reciprocal imitation prior to 15 to 16 months. Between 15 and 20 months, toddler peers will imitate the pretend acts and continue eye contact. Both may feed the baby a bottle, for example, rock the baby, or push the baby in a stroller. At about 20 to 24 months, they enhance these activities with social exchanges such as smiles, vocalizations, or offers of the doll to the peer. Between 2 and 2½ years, children participate in the same theme but do not coordinate their activity in any way. Two toddlers may pretend to go to the grocery store, complete with shopping carts, dolls, and purses, but each pretends independently. They do recognize that their behaviors are appropriate to the theme, however, and the participants begin to be able to decide upon the theme rather than having the behavior decide the activity. In the age range of 30 to 36 months, children's increased awareness of social roles will shape their pretend play. At this point, role-taking becomes a part of social pretend play (Howes, Unger, & Seidner, 1989).

The ways in which children use objects in pretense change as their level of pretend play advances. When infants are using objects in solitary pretending, with the initial pretending directed to self, for example, they may use a cloth to pretend to wash their own face. Pretending with the object gradually extends to other objects or people; for example, they may use the cloth to wash a doll's face or their mother's face. As toddlers approach the end of the second year, they make the dolls or stuffed animals assume roles, thus having the objects take an active part in the pretending; for example, they expect dolls to eat pretend food at a pretend birthday party. During the third year, their pretense becomes more elaborate, and dolls or other objects carry out longer scenarios, usually with familiar homelike themes (Hughes, 1991). Pretend play also moves from a simple, one-action pattern to combining action patterns. As evidenced in play with objects, as infants move through the sensorimotor period of development, pretending combines action patterns, or sequences of actions, and more elaborate pretending is possible. Initially infants may comb the doll's hair; later they comb the doll's hair and also wash the doll's face; still later, they comb the doll's hair and wash and dress the doll (Hughes, 1991).

By the time children are between 3 and 4 years, they use replica objects as the actors in sequenced themes. A doll may get ready for a party that she is going to attend with her doll friends, for example, and they will ride in a car to the event, eat food and dance at the party, and return home. Several research studies have linked the ability to string pretend actions together to the advancement of language; for example, children who use two-word sentences typically also sequence two pretend actions (Fensen, 1984). Realistic props enhance early pretending. Children will more readily use a realistic toy phone for pretending than a wooden block shaped vaguely like a phone. As children mature, they begin to use less realistic substitute objects. Children under 3 typically pretend more readily if the substitute object has some resemblance to the real item. They may use a cloth as a pillow, but the 2-year-old would have difficulty using a shoe as a pillow, for example, because shoes are for feet! Between 3 and 4 years, children can readily use even counterconventional substitute objects (Bretherton & Beeghly, 1989).

How Adults Affect Children's Pretend Play

Adults more often have an indirect rather than a direct effect on children's pretend play. Although some mothers actively encourage pretend play (Miller & Garvey, 1984), there is wide variation in how actively parents engage in pretending with young children. Parents do, however, affect children's inclination toward pretending by allowing ample opportunities for practice play; their children also engage on their own in pretend play (Singer, Singer, Desmond, Hirsch, & Nocol, 1988). Parents who engage in discussion and storytelling allow children the opportunity to "frame complex events within organized structures" (Singer et al., 1988, p. 341). These children tend to spend a greater amount of time in fantasy or pretend play than do the children of parents whose interactions are predominantly prescription- and discipline-oriented. By tolerating pretending and providing materials and time for play, parents foster the development of pretending. When parents limit the amount of time young children spend viewing television, they also encourage the development of pretend play (Singer et al., 1988).

Aside from encouraging and providing materials for infants' pretend play, the attachment status of infants to a significant adult seems to have an influence on the amount and kind of play in which children engage (Roggman, Carroll, Pippin, & McCool, 1990). Securely attached infants are more likely to explore the environment when in the presence of their mothers, are more sociable, and are more likely to engage in peer interactions. They show more elaborated, complex, and sustained pretend play, and by age 2 are more persistent in problem solving (Elicker, Englund, & Sroufe, 1993; Hazen, 1989; Pepler & Ross, 1981). Sibling play is also an important factor. A study of toddler pretend play with mothers and older siblings showed more pretend relationships between toddlers and siblings than between mothers and toddlers, especially in regard to role play (Youngblade & Dunn, 1995). The investigators state that early pretend play is related to "the child's developing understanding of others' beliefs and feelings" (p. 1488). They think that siblings may be instrumental in the development of "other minds" (p. 1486).

Effects of Gender on Infant and Toddler Play

Infants' play is quite similar for boys and girls, but by 3 years of age, play preferences are evident. Girls prefer play with dolls and household items, art activities, and dressing up, while boys play with transportation toys and blocks and engage in more large-group and aggressive play. Where these differences come from and when they begin is of interest to parents and researchers alike (Bergen, 1998). Adults' influence on children's sex-typed play is undoubtedly both direct and indirect. Although researchers find few actual gender-related differences among infants, parents tend to begin the socialization process into gender-stereotypic behaviors from birth. The fact that parents provide infants with sex-typed toys has a direct impact on infant play, and thus begins the process of gender-stereotypic activities. Parents also furnish young children's rooms, and those furnishings reflect differences based on gender-appropriate activities and materials (Reingold & Cook, 1975).

Parents also selected gender-stereotypic toys when researchers asked them to interact with their 12- to 24-month-old children (Eisenberg, Wolchick, Hernandez, & Pasternack, 1985). Infants as young as 18 to 23 months have shown preferences for sex-typed toys (Caldera, Huston, & O'Brien, 1989): they were less involved with toys stereotyped for the opposite gender and preferred toys stereotyped for their own gender. Adults indirectly influence infants into gender-stereotypic play by reinforcing play the parents consider appropriate for their children. "Masculine" and "feminine" toys elicit different behaviors from infants and from adults interacting with infants and toys. "Masculine" toys tend to elicit low levels of teaching and low proximity between infants and parents; "feminine" toys elicit closer proximity and more verbal interactions between parents and infants (Caldera, Huston, & O'Brien, 1989).

The question of whether children's playing with gender-stereotypic toys and actions is or is not a beneficial kind of play is inherent in a discussion of gender influences on play. The research on developing androgyny in children, which was prominent in the 1970s, suggested that children and adults need to be able to respond to a situation in adaptable, appropriate ways rather than in gender-stereotypic ways. This should be a topic of interest for further study.

Although it may be expedient to suggest that parental influence on children is the most salient reason that children play with gender stereotypic materials, a cognitive dimension is also involved that must be taken into consideration. Young children have not arrived at gender constancy until they reach about 6 or 7 years of age. These young children may well be using stereotypic play materials provided by their parents to arrive at gender constancy.

Summary

From the newborn period to the age of 4 years, infants' play changes from that of experimenting with how body parts work to developing elaborate and highly complex pretend play. As these changes occur, there is also a complementary change in infants' development in other domains. Deciding whether play causes developmental changes or whether other developmental changes cause changes in play is rather like the chicken-and-egg debate or the nature–nurture controversy. Rather than spending time and energy debating the issue, the question to explore is how each of these, the other developmental domains and play development, interact to enhance both.

Infants' early play allows them to build schemata of what their movements might do to affect the environment, thus allowing infants to have a sense of efficacy. Play with objects encourages manipulative skills, and play with adults and peers encourages and enhances social development. Pretend play enhances cognitive development, increases social interactions, gives young children outlets for fears and frustrations, and provides a foundation for good mental health. Because play stays with individuals across the life span, the foundations for a life well lived are laid in the play of infants.

References

Adler, A. (1927). *The practice and theory of individual psychology*. New York: Harcourt, Brace and World.

Adolph, K. (1997). Learning in the development of infant locomotion. *Monographs of the Society for Research in Child Development, 62*(3, Serial No. 251).

Baldwin, D. A., Markman, E. M., & Melartin, R. L. (1993). Infants' ability to draw inferences about nonobvious object properties: Evidence from exploratory play. *Child Development, 64*, 711–728.

Bergen, D. (1998). *Readings from play as a medium for learning and development*. Olney, MD: Association for Childhood Education International.

Bretherton, I., & Beeghly, M. (1989). Pretense: Acting "as if." In J. J. Lockman & N. L. Hazen (Eds.), *Action in social context: Perspectives on early development* (pp. 239–268). New York: Plenum.

Caldera, Y. M., Huston, A. C., & O'Brien, M. (1989). Social interactions and play patterns of parents and toddlers with feminine, masculine, and neutral toys. *Child Development, 60*, 70–76.

Cielinski, K. L., Vaughn, B. E., Seifer, R., & Contresas, J. (1995). Relations among sustained engagement during play, quality of play and mother–child interaction in samples of children with Downs syndrome and normally developing toddlers. *Infant Behavior and Development, 18*, 163–176.

DeLoache, J. S., Pierroutsakos, S. L., Uttal, D. H., Rosengren, K. S., & Gottlieb, A. (1998). Grasping the nature of pictures. *Psychological Science, 9*(3), 205–210.

Eckerman, C. O., & Watley, J. L. (1977). Toys and social interaction between infant peers. *Child Development, 48*, 1645–1656.

Eisenberg, N., Wolchick, S. A., Hernandez, R., & Pasternack, J. F (1985). Parental socialization of young children's play. *Child Development, 56*, 1506–1513.

Elicker, J., Englund, M., & Sroufe, L. A. (1992). Predicting peer competence and peer relationships in childhood from early parent–child relationships. In R. D. Parke & G. W. Ladd (Eds.), *Family peer relationships: Modes of linkage* (pp. 77–106), Hillsdale, NJ: Lawrence Erlbaum.

Farver, J., & Wimbarti, S. (1995). Paternal participation in toddler' pretend play. *Social Development, 4*, 14-31.

Fein, G. G. (1981). Pretend play in childhood: An integrative review. *Child Development, 52*, 1095–1118.

Fensen, L. (1984). Developmental trends for action and speech in pretend play. In I. Bretherton (Ed.), *Symbolic play: The development of social understanding* (pp. 249–270). New York: Academic.

Fischer, K. W., & Hogan, A. E. (1989). The big picture for infant development: Levels and variations. In J. J. Lockman & N. L. Hazen (Eds.), *Action in social context: Perspectives on early development* (pp. 275–300). New York: Plenum.

Fogel, A. (1979). Peer vs. mother directed behavior in 1- to 3-month-old infants. *Infant Behavior and Development, 2*, 215–226.

Fromberg, D. P. (1992). Play. In C. Seefeldt (Ed.), *Early childhood education: A review of research* (pp. 42–84). New York: Teachers College Press.

Gopnik, A., Meltzoff, A., & Kuhl, P. (2001).*The scientist in the crib: What early learning tells us about the mind.* New York: HarperCollins.

Howes, C. (1987). Peer interaction of young children. *Monographs of the Society for Research in Child Development, 53*(1, Serial No. 217).

Howes, C., & Matheson, C. C. (1992). Sequences in the development of competent play with peers: Social and social pretend play. *Developmental Psychology, 28*, 961–974.

Howes, C., Unger, O., & Seidner, L. B. (1989). Social pretend play in toddlers: Parallels with social play and with solitary pretend. *Child Development, 60*, 77–84.

Hughes, F. P. (1991). *Children, play and development.* Boston: Allyn & Bacon.

Hutt, C. (1979). Exploration and play. In B. Sutton-Smith (Ed.), *Play and learning* (pp. 174–194). New York: Gardner.

Jacobson, J. L. (1981). The role of inanimate objects in early peer interaction. *Child Development, 52*, 618–626.

Kimmerle, M., Mick, L. A., & Michel, G. E (1995). Bimanual role-differentiated toy play during infancy. *Infant Behavior and Development, 18*, 299–307.

Lillard, A. (2003). *Why children don't get confused by others' pretense.* Paper presented at the 33rd Annual Meeting of the Jean Piaget Society, Chicago, IL.

Lockman, J. J., & McHale, J. P. (1989). Object manipulation in infancy: Developmental and contextual determinants. In J. J. Lockman & N. L. Hazen (Eds.), *Action in social context: Perspectives on early development* (pp. 129–167). New York: Plenum.

Mayes, L. C., Carter, A. S., & Stubbe, D. (1993). Individual differences in exploratory behavior in the second year of life. *Infant Behavior and Development, 16*, 269–284.

Miller, P., & Garvey, C. (1984). Mother–baby role play. In I. Bretherton (Ed.), *Symbolic play: The development of social understanding* (pp. 101–130). New York: Academic.

Papousek, H., & Papousek, M. (1982). Vocal imitations in mother–infant dialogues. *Infant Behavior, 5*, 176.

Pepler, D., & Ross, H. S. (1981). The effects of play on convergent and divergent problem-solving. *Child Development, 52*, 1202–1210.

Piaget, J. (1962a). *Play, dreams and imitation in childhood.* London: Routledge & Kegan Paul.

Piaget, J. (1962b). *The origins of intelligence in children.* New York: International Universities Press.

Reingold, H. L., & Cook, K. V. (1975). The contents of boys' and girls' rooms as an index of parents' behavior. *Child Development, 47*, 459–463.

Roggman, L. A., Carroll, K. A., Pippin, E. A., & McCool, D. E. (1990). *Toddler play in relation to social and cognitive competence.* (Report No. PS 018837) Little Rock: University of Arkansas. (ERIC Document Reproduction Service No. ED 320664)

Singer, J. L., & Singer, D. G. (1983). Psychologists look at television: Cognitive, developmental, personality and social policy implications. *American Psychologist, 38*, 826–834.

Singer, J. L., Singer, D. G., Desmond, R., Hirsch, B., & Nocol, A. (1988). Family mediation and children's cognition, aggression, and comprehension of television: A longitudinal study. *Journal of Applied Developmental Psychology, 9*, 329–347.

Sutton-Smith, B. (1979). *Play and learning.* New York: Gardner.

Tamis-LeMonda, C. S., & Bornstein, M. H. (1993). Play and its relation to other mental functions in the child. In M..H. Bornstein & A..W. O'Reilly (Eds.), *The role of play in the development of thought* (New Directions in Child Development series, Vol. 59, pp. 17-28). San Francisco: Jossey-Bass.

Tamis-LeMonda, C. S., Damast, A. M., & Bornstein M. H. (1994). What do mothers know about the developmental nature of play? *Infant Behavior and Development, 17*, 341–435.

Thelen, E., & Smith, L. B., (1994*). A dynamic systems approach to the development of cognition and action.* Cambridge, MA: MIT Press.

Uzgiris, I., & Hunt, J. M. (1975). *Assessment in infancy.* Urbana: University of Illinois Press.

Vandell, D. L., & Mueller, E. C. (1980). Peer play and friendships during the first two years. In H. C. Foot, A. J. Chapman, & J. R. Smith (Eds.), *Friendships and social relations in children* (pp. 181–208). London: John Wiley.

Vondra, J., & Belsky, J. (1989). Exploration and play in social context: Developments from infancy to early childhood. In J. J. Lockman & N. L. Hazen (Eds.), *Action in social context: Perspectives on early development* (pp. 173–203). New York: Plenum.

Wachs, T. (1993). Multidimensional correlates of individual variability in play and exploration. In M.H. Bornstein & A..W. O'Reilly (Eds.), *The role of play in the development of thought* (New Directions for Child Development series, Vol. 59, pp. 43-53). San Francisco: Jossey-Bass.

Youngblade, L. M., & Dunn, J. (1995). Individual differences in young children's pretend play with mother and sibling: Links to relationships and understanding of other people's feelings and beliefs. *Child Development, 66*, 1472–1492.

2

Play Development from Ages Four to Eight

JAMES E. JOHNSON

Critical transformations occur in children's relationships to their social and physical world between 4 and 8 years of age. Most 4-year-olds possess considerable language mastery, an impressive array of social and physical concepts, and rudimentary and preoperational thinking skills. They have acquired sufficient levels of social competence and abilities to regulate attention, affect, and activity to sustain child–child social interactions, nurture budding friendships, and engage in prolonged play episodes alone or with others. Children gradually integrate the parent–child socialization system with the peer socialization system, and the social ecology of home and family increasingly meshes with the cultures of child care and school, neighborhood, and community.

Children at 8 years of age have made gigantic developmental strides. They usually possess rather sophisticated communicative and social skills and often are members of various social groups. Their levels of social cognition enable them not only to perspective-take the perceptions, thoughts, intentions, and feelings of others, but also to coordinate diverse perspectives to construct elementary conceptions of social justice and group organization. Their knowledge base has expanded remarkably in 4 years. They are by now at least beginning, concrete-logical reasoners equipped with reversible thought operations and with a good elementary grasp of various symbolic notational systems. Basic literacy and numeracy as well as other academic attainments are the norm. Moreover, children have more differentiated self-concepts, higher levels of social competence, and more mature friendship relationships. Many children also have well-established impulse control and the ability to delay gratification. Not surprisingly, then, 8-year-olds' play is quite different from that of 4-year-olds.

Play Types and Development

The child development and early education literature has classified play forms in diverse ways. Researchers typically have recognized social, emotional, motor, and cognitive dimensions in their category systems and have given attention to play context and structural properties of play behavior and its functional or motivational characteristics (Bergen, 1988; Frost, Wortham, & Reifel, 2005; Johnson, Christie, & Wardle, 2005). Researchers have further noted that, although one can divide play into types and can attempt to calibrate behaviors in terms of levels of performance, or arrange play types hierarchically into developmental sequences (e.g., functional play, constructive play, dramatic play, and games with rules), play expression is actually more complex and classification somewhat artificial and limiting. Not only do play episodes demand description with multiple categories and subcategories to do justice to the phenomena (e.g., parallel-dramatic play with person and object transformations), there is the need for additional modifiers to capture something about play tempo, intensity, style, and other important qualities. There is also the need to note information about the play setting and context. Moreover, scholars also acknowledge that age-related developmental stages of play (e.g., solitary, parallel, constructive, games with rules) become less useful with older children and beg the question of how development unfolds within each play form. Constructive play is qualitatively different, for example, comparing 4-year-olds with 8-year-olds.

Descriptive and experimental studies of sequences and stages of play development, including observations and interviews with children between 4 and 8 years of age, have yielded an abundance of evidence that significant changes in levels of performance do indeed occur within diverse play types, without necessarily suggesting sequences or stages of play development per se (see von Glasersfeld & Kelley, 1982, for a cogent discussion of differences among the terms *period, phase, stage,* and *level in human development*). Accordingly, the sections that follow represent a typology of play, but not necessarily a developmental hierarchy; this typology is based upon the Consumer Product Safety Commission's manual for making age specifications for toys (Goodson & Bronson, 1985). This typology organizes the play of children between 4 and 8 years of age in a manner that usefully and comprehensively describes the age span under consideration.

Gross Motor/Active Play

From 4 to 5 years and on to 6 years of age, children achieve considerable fine and gross motor mastery together with active play skill and dexterity, allowing for the emergence of newer and more variegated play forms. These children frequently engage in climbing, hopping, running, skipping (especially girls), and chasing (especially boys). Some children ride small bicycles, first with and then without supportive training wheels; many jump rope (primarily girls) and do acrobatics or trapeze tricks. The advance of their fine muscle development contributes to their ability to string beads, cut with scissors, paste, trace, draw, and color; they can also use a computer keyboard.

From 6 to 8 years, children make further strides in physical and active play expression in accord with their growing physical prowess, the result of maturation and experience. They continue their interest and heightened proficiency in outdoor games and other physical play, including rough-and-tumble play. Daredevil play, roughhousing, and risk taking become more prevalent. Capture and escape, hide-and-seek, cops and robbers, tag, and "it" and its variants (dungeon tag, frozen tag) are commonplace. During these years of childhood, they engage in and improve their form in sports, athletics, Roller Blading, skateboarding, ice skating, swimming, aerobics, and acrobatics, as well as various forms of dance. Organized sports and adult-sponsored lessons in ballet or gymnastics, for example, are increasingly the norm.

In the domain of fine motor activity and accomplishment, children of 6 to 8 years exhibit remarkable skill development, from hand games and snapping fingers to constructing model airplanes. This physical and motor development also facilitates other types of play such as collecting, building, and making various objects and structures.

Manipulative/Constructive Play

By 4 years of age most preschool children have reached many developmental milestones with respect to object play, which has progressed in terms of how many objects young children can incorporate into play, and how well children can use these objects. The play has progressed from the simple to the complex as children gain increasing ability to order objects and actions in time and space. As children develop they exhibit less manipulative or functional play that consists of using toys only in an "appropriate" (or expected) manner. There is more constructive play and organized goal-oriented play. Preschoolers become increasingly skilled in building complex structures and in producing recognizable products through drawing, painting, arranging designs, and making small constructions.

By 4 years of age such constructive play is commonplace, often occupying over 50 percent of free play time in preschool settings, especially among girls (Rubin, Fein, & Vandenberg, 1983).

Five- and 6-year-olds continue to engage in considerable amounts of constructive play, particularly in indoor play settings. Their constructive play is distinguished from the play of younger preschool children, however, by its enhanced elaboration and by the higher levels of social collaboration that often accompany it. Moreover, elements of pretense or dramatic play are more likely present. Kindergartners, compared to preschoolers, for instance, more often take to building props as a prelude to sociodramatic play, spending considerable time and showing good persistence and cooperation in setting the stage "just right" for playing grocery store or putting on a circus.

Seven- and 8-year-olds' forms of manipulative and constructive play continue to include blocks as a dominant play activity medium. As is the case with the preschool child, primary-grade school children enjoy (and have fully mastered) the use of Lego blocks, Lincoln Logs, and other assorted playthings that have fitted notches or interlocking pieces. Children of this age generally prefer construction sets with complex interlocking pieces. They also like models that result in detailed, realistic productions. Many enjoy using tiny screws, nuts and bolts, and even hooking up and using battery-powered construction sets (Goodson & Bronson, 1985). They also enjoy measuring and balancing objects, activities that reflect the emergence and consolidation of concrete operational thinking. Object manipulation, experimentation, and construction often occur in social commerce with peers and many times include pretense or gamelike play qualities as well. Thus, while preschoolers enjoy matching and sorting objects, older children become increasingly scientific and experimental and engage in classification by using multiple criteria in combination. Finished products become important.

Imitative/Imaginative/Dramatic Play

Make-believe or pretend play is a major play form during childhood, with its earliest emergence occurring usually in the second year of life as children's symbolic functioning develops (Piaget, 1962). Pretense entails employing a transformational mode or an "as-if" stance toward ostensible reality. When pretending, children are assuming an identity in role enactment, they relate to other persons or objects as if they are other than themselves, or alter time and space in the form of situational transformations. Imitating, imagining, and dramatizing are all part of this kind of play as children represent and relive or reenact their actual experiences using the symbolic, language, and social skills available to them at a given developmental level. The expression and the theorized importance of pretense to the children's development and well-being change a great deal during the period between 4 and 8 years of age.

By the age of 4, the typical child is already quite accomplished at role enactment and the ability to do other-person, object, and situational transformations. It is not uncommon to see children at this age able to take on a whole host of pretend characters, ranging from the common familial and everyday occupational roles witnessed day in and day out, to the more far-fetched superhero and other fictional roles that children observe on television and in other media.

Role enactments frequently take place with other children and show a high degree of reciprocity and social and verbal interaction within the play frame. Fours and 5s reach a high watermark in the kind of overt make-believe of sociodramatic play (Smilansky, 1990) or collaborative pretense. Whether children are in such social groups or alone and playing independently, they display ease in using various props in support of play episodes. In addition to realistic props such as a toy telephone, children freely use substitute objects or invented or imagined objects in play; for example, a block for a telephone. Depending on the episode's play theme, the situational transformations also range considerably from the proximal to the distal. Their pretense, for example, ranges from a typical day at home or at the grocery store to being out in the forest in the middle of the night or traveling to a distant country.

While declines occur in overt social make-believe play after age 5 or 6 years (at least in classroom or playground settings), children continue to exhibit a keen interest in it, even as other play forms gain in popularity. Generally speaking, older children's pretend play demonstrates richer texts, more contoured scripts, and more organized plots than the play of younger children. Play episodes of older children are more differentiated and elaborated, as seen, for example, when children put on a puppet show or a skit, or dramatize a circus, battle, or county fair. Six- to 8-year-olds, unlike 4s and 5s, are capable of a good deal more stage managing and directing or redirecting in their play when giving dramatic performances.

Although primary-grade school children often employ role-play materials appropriate for pre-schoolers, the older children can use a greater quantity of materials as well as more detailed equipment. Children within the 4- to 8-year age span very much enjoy costumes and props, such as cash registers, play money, toy guns, and toy cameras, for a variety of dramatic play roles. They enjoy constructing and are able to make their own props out of blocks, cartons, and other manipulatives. Older children typically desire more detail and prefer more realism in their imaginative play props than do younger children, even though they have the cognitive ability to do without the real McCoy. Furthermore, play objects and materials of primary-grade children often become subjects of collections, crafts, or hobbies, in addition to functioning as props for playing library, store, and war games or taking trips.

Finally, pretense serves different purposes in development from 4 to 8 years of age. For younger children, not only does pretense serve to strengthen various cognitive skills such as perspective taking, narrative competence, and decontextualization abilities, it also supports and promotes emotional and social development, particularly in the area of finding one's place or status in the peer group. Pretense helps children overcome fears and cope with these feelings as they make transitions from home to school; sharing fantasies also can be indispensably useful for making friends (Paley, 1988). With older primary-grade children, collaborative pretense continues to serve these purposes and becomes especially important for trust building and the formation of intimacy in friendship relationships (Howes, Unger, & Matheson, 1992).

Creative Play

Creative play in early and middle childhood develops and finds expression in various domains during the 4- to 8-year age range. Typically, the laurel of "creative" describes children's play when it is a product of their directed thinking or self-regulated behavior, as opposed to nondirected or free-association type thinking, or random or stimulus-dominated patterns of behavior (e.g., scribbling in which one mark on the page simply leads to another). Also, creative behavior usually implies original and aesthetically or technically useful expressions. Unlike creativity in adults, where a societal criterion is imposed, creativity for children usually means that the play or activity is original for this particular child, based on a personal or individual criterion. What is technically or aesthetically useful normally goes uninterpreted for younger children, but becomes more of an issue as children mature and can be expected to be judged according to social norms for creativity. Domains of creative play include arts and crafts, designing miniature play scenes (which may then result in imaginative play), and using musical instruments or audiovisual equipment.

Arts and Crafts

By 4 years of age, children's "creative" drawings and constructions already have moved beyond "acting-on-objects" and "exploration-of-the-medium" to a concern with the product (as opposed only to the process) for defining what is important to the child. Children at this age can usually make at least several color distinctions and possess the fine motor coordination needed to enjoy and create products with paints, finger paints, strings, beads, Magic Markers, scissors, large crayons, pencils, paste, and the like. Although 4-year-olds can make representational products and are proud of them, 5-year-olds' products are more realistic and elaborate. At this age, children can also more easily use watercolor paints, smaller crayons, coloring books, and simple weaving looms. Children who are 6, 7, and 8 years of age can make better use of all the materials and activities enjoyed by younger children in the sense of coming up with more skillful and more finished products. Primary-grade children can also sew and do woodworking and enjoy model building and craft kits involving leather work, papier-mache, simple jewelry, and enameling.

Miniature Play Scenes

Creative play is apparent in the tabletop (or on a floor) microcosms young children recreate by constructing miniature worlds or designing play scenes involving various nonrealistic/unstructured (e.g., pipe cleaners, blocks) or realistic/ structured (e.g., farm set) toys and other toys with small parts.

In imaginative or creative play with miniature worlds, children not only act on objects, and build and produce various configurations with the objects, they also often interject narratives or create stories about the play scenes, either in solitary play or as a form of collective, cooperative play. Children up to 6 years of age show peak interest in this form of imaginative play as they do for sociodramatic play. Preschool children enjoy both familiar play scenes such as garages and farms, and imaginary worlds such as space and military forts. By age 5, children like to plan, construct, and play with miniature worlds, and they can show attention to detail, work various mechanisms, and use simple battery-powered accessories. As interest in sociodramatic play wanes, interest in creative play continues through the primary grade years. Older children, however, prefer very detailed and realistic models in their play with miniature worlds or virtual realities (i.e., computer simulations), and they often combine this form of play with constructive play. Gender differences in the type of material and themes of miniature play, as is the case with sociodramatic play, are usually very pronounced; playing house, using dollhouses, and Barbie dolls are common for girls, for example, while playing with toy soldiers and playing superhero are common for boys.

Musical Instruments

Musical and rhythmic instruments are appropriate for children across a wide age range; and children are able to engage in expressive play with them. During the preschool years children's musical skill increases dramatically. Four-year-olds can carry a tune, recognize melodies, and even sing short, simple songs in their entirety. Language play during the preschool years includes inventing songs and rhymes. Children can keep time with music as they jump, gallop, and run—activities that lead to real dancing around at 5 years of age. They experiment with rhythm instruments and can produce sounds with various musical instruments such as the harmonica, ocarina, horn, and simple recorder. They also use other musical instruments such as drums and xylophones. Primary-grade children begin to learn to play real instruments and read music. They show interest in group singing and can use their own song books. Children, especially girls, use their own records, CDs, or tape players, and begin to show interest in dance lessons. Hence, playful expression and more worklike craft and talent merge.

Cognitive Play

All types of play involve cognition but, as used in this section, this category label refers to games with rules, educational or skill-development toys, and books. Preschoolers and primary-grade children exhibit different types and levels of cognitive play.

Games with Rules

Most younger children cannot play games with rules, even with adult scaffolding. By 4 years of age, however, many children can play when the sit-down games have only a few simple rules, an easy scoring system, few if any reading requirements, and depend on simple chance but not skill or strategy.

Preschool children enjoy matching and lotto-type games with pictures and colors, as well as simple letters and numbers when they are older. Younger preschool children find games with spinners or color cards easier than those that involve dice. Race games, in which the child only has to move the game piece along a preordained path without the option of blocking an opponent's piece, are age-appropriate. Preschoolers can also play games involving simple fine motor ability such as pick-up sticks. Interest in games increases during the primary-grade school years. For the typical 6- and 7-year-old, games must remain rather simple and straightforward with few rules and with little skill or strategy required. Some can learn and do play more sophisticated games such as chess.

Around 8 years of age, however, or when children reach the stage of concrete operations and are capable of formulating and carrying out a plan or strategy, they can enjoy a much wider array of games with rules, including rather sophisticated games based on fantasy or adventure themes. Genuine co-operation and competition then are possible and become important ingredients in games-with-rules play; computer and especially video games are very popular among primary-grade school children. A growing majority of children in this age range play videogames on a regular basis (Children Now, 2001).

Skill-Development Toys

Preschool and primary-grade children use educational toys and games, including electronic devices and computers, and literacy, mathematics, and science toys. Preschoolers enjoy cognitive play centered on naming and classifying the world around them. They enjoy performing copying, naming, matching, and sorting activities in their play. Skill-development materials include those that teach colors, shapes, and simple letter and number concepts. Among other materials, science toys for preschoolers include magnifying glasses, flashlights, prisms, magnets, color mixes, rock and shell collections, simple calculators, and see-through clocks. Many available computer software programs are educational in nature and are developmentally appropriate for preschoolers, eliciting various forms of cognitive (and social) play. By 6 years of age and throughout the primary-grade years, children play with many toys and materials that enhance specific skill development. Older children (6 to 8 years of age) are interested in their own anatomy and in the wider world around them, including other countries and times past. Among many other materials, they may enjoy microscopes, chemistry sets, field binoculars, and more complex software for computers. Electronic sports games are also highly popular around 7 or 8 years of age.

Books

Books elicit the cognitive play of preschoolers and primary-grade children. Preschoolers enjoy looking at books and love having adults read to them. Four-year-olds love ridiculous and silly stories; wild, dramatic, and fantastic stories (including fairy tales); animal books; verse; and stories about everyday life, including some factual books. Five-year-olds as well as 6-year-olds generally prefer realistic and credible stories, poetry, holiday and seasonal stories, and comics. Six-year-olds also enjoy stories about fears and magic, nature, and the elements. By 7 or 8 years of age children can use a table of contents and an index. They also enjoy classics and books about travel, adventure, geography, primitive times, legions, and folktales. They continue to like newspaper comics and show an interest in magazines and store catalogues.

Individual and Group Variations in Play Development

Children around the world have a basic right to their childhood, and play is part of the magic of childhood. Quite remarkable strides in play expression between 4 and 8 years of age occur in all five of the play categories described in this chapter. Enormous differences and changes in various developmental domains characterize the growth of children between 4 and 8 years of age. There is a qualitative difference, for example, in both the cognitive and social cognitive ability of preoperational preschoolers as well as concrete-operational primary grade schoolchildren.

Individual Variation

Systematic individual differences exist in the expression of play between the ages of 4 and 8 years that are related to the status of children's gender, personality, and special needs. In general, for example, boys are more likely to engage in rough-and-tumble play, superhero dramatic play, large block play, play themes that are active or adventuresome with pretend violence or aggression, and in various sports or organized athletic team activities. Girls usually prefer to play in smaller groups and show an interest in a greater variety of toys and play materials, including constructive play and other table activities. Games, crafts, and hobbies are acutely sex-typed during this stretch of ontogenesis, which overlaps with the Freudian latency period of psychosexual development and the Eriksonian stage of industry versus inferiority.

Personality further moderates play differences and may reflect age and gender. Some children prefer more reality-oriented play such as building models, doing puzzles, or reading realistic stories, while other children prefer more fantasy-oriented activity, as seen in their choice of toys, games, books, and dramatic play themes. Still other children are more object-centered, while some are more person-centered in their play. The former are more meticulous and fastidious in attending to the stimulus detail of play objects; the latter are more concerned with peer group reactions, adult attention, and social interaction.

The status of special needs has an impact on play development and expression during the 4- to 8-year age spread. Although, in general, all children have similar interests and needs for play and peer relations, children who have special needs often possess a more limited repertoire of the social and cognitive skills needed for elaborative forms of independent and group play. The condition of special needs often adversely affects the rate and terminal level of development for children in relation to various categories of play. Such children may require interventions to prevent or remediate their situation.

Group Variation

Both socioeconomic status (SES) and cultural differences modulate patterns or regularities in play expressions and sequences from 4 to 8 years of age. SES factors, such as low income or poverty, may set limits on availability and accessibility of high-quality play environments and expensive toys and equipment. Quality of play may suffer as a consequence. Lower levels of play (i.e., exploration, functional play) may predominate over higher forms of play (i.e., constructive, sociodramatic, and games with rules) when children lack experience with basic play materials, adult modeling, or encouragement (Smilansky, 1990).

Cultural factors further interact with SES and individual difference variables to produce variation in play behavior and development from 4 to 8 years. Although structural features of play such as sociality of play, elaboration of language, and imagination may not differ across cultures, play themes and content are often culturally specific. Educational or academic play, such as creative play and cognitive play, may show higher degrees of similarity across developed and developing countries than recreational play with games, books, sports, or dramatic play themes, which are more likely to retain the unique flavor of the specific individual cultures.

Play from 4 to 8 is rich and multifarious and can serve as a window on the child's developmental status, personality, and emotional well-being. Play also promotes and reinforces the child's development in social and cognitive areas. Individual and group differences moderate the dynamic relation of play with development. Socialization agents do not always respect or value the importance of play for children who are making the transition from the preschool to the primary-grade school years. The societal push to rush children through their immaturity poses a threat to the optimization of the potential in play of 4- to 8-year-old children. These attitudes are apparent in many school systems in the United States and in families where parents pressure children toward adult-defined group activities such as organizations, ball leagues, or lessons. Adult overmanagement of children's time and activities can also result in more passive, less robust play. Play, for example, has been eliminated or sharply curtailed when schools drop recess or neglect to provide interesting playground equipment. Perhaps the most serious threat to play during this age period, however, comes from the children themselves when adults do not check their notorious tendencies to reject peers and play in segregated groups.

Clearly, adults have a critical role to play to ensure that all children play up to potential during this age period. Providing quality physical environments is only part of the needed response. Adults must also value play and seek to create favorable, socially inclusive environments for all children that honor the right of each individual child to play. Curricular restructuring that leads to more play-oriented experience in the classroom is another step in the right direction. Some adults view recess and playground time as outside extensions of sound, child-sensitive, activity-based educational programs. As more and more parents and teachers gain insight into the importance of play for children, and understand how adults are often implicated in threats to play, they may eliminate many of the barriers that now exist so that play can flourish for all children from 4 to 8 years of age.

References

Bergen, D. (1988). *Play as a medium for learning and development: A handbook of theory and practice.* Portsmouth, NH: Heinemann.

Children Now. (2001). Available at http://www.childrennow.org/media/video-games/2001/

Frost, J., Wortham, S., & Reifel, S. (2005). *Play and child development* (2nd ed.). Columbus, OH: Merrill Prentice-Hall

Goodson, B. D., & Bronson, M. B. (1985). *Guidelines for relating children's ages to toy characteristics* (Contract No. CPSC85-1089). Washington, D.C.: U.S. Consumer Product Safety Commission.

Howes, C., Unger, 0., & Matheson, C. (1992). *The collaborative construction of pretend: Social pretend play functions.* Albany: State University of New York Press.

Johnson, J. E., Christie, J., & Wardle, F. (2005). *Play, development and early education.* Boston: Allyn & Bacon.

Paley, V. (1988). *The boy who would be a helicopter.* Cambridge, MA: Harvard University Press.

Piaget, J. (1962). *Play, dreams and imitation in childhood.* New York: Norton.

Rubin, K. H., Fein, G. G., & Vandenberg, B. (1983). Play. In P. H. Mussen (Ed.), *Handbook of child psychology: Vol. 4. Socialization, personality, and social development* (4th ed., pp. 693–774). New York: Wiley.

Smilansky, S. (1990). Sociodramatic play: Its relevance to behavior and achievement in school. In E. Klugman & S. Smilansky (Eds.), *Children's play and learning: Perspectives and policy implications* (pp. 18–42). New York: Teachers College Press.

von Glasersfeld, E., & Kelley, M. F. (1982). On the concepts of period, phase, stage, and level. *Human Development, 25,* 152–160.

3

Play Development From Ages Eight to Twelve

M. LEE MANNING

Children's play has been a controversial topic for many years and has been neglected in many schools and homes. Controversy has centered around an appropriate definition, the belief that play contradicts our nation's work ethic, and the mindset that schools and learners, to achieve "excellence," require less play and more work. Some adults might even consider children between 8 and 12 years of age too old to play. While a vast body of research has documented the contribution of play to younger children's cognitive and literacy development and to their social growth (Youngquist & Pataray-Ching, 2004), less research and scholarly opinion has focused attention on the significance of play in the development of 8- to 12-year-olds.

Many unanswered questions exist. Among them: What developmental sequences and experiences do 8- to 12-year-olds undergo? How do gender, socioeconomic status, and attitudes of parents and educators affect play? Do 8- to 12-year-olds even have a right to play? This chapter examines the play of 8- to 12-year-olds, looks at contexts and perspectives such as gender and adults' expectations, and recommends that schools, professional associations, parents, and children's advocacy groups take the stand that children have the right to play.

Definitions

Cooney (2004) maintained that *play* is not an easily defined term because of its complexity in behavior and context. Disagreement sometimes surfaces due to differences in opinion regarding play and work, often resulting in blurred lines between play and work. For example, play means different things to different people. Various definitions (Cooney, 2004; Manning & Boals, 1987; Pellegrini & Galda, 1994; Youngquist & Pataray-Ching, 2004), theories (Rubin & Coplan, 1994; Youngquist & Pataray-Ching, 2004), and characteristics (Daiute, 1989; Rubin & Coplan, 1994) have been offered to explain play.

Youngquist and Pataray-Ching (2004) think play should be highly valued in schools because it contributes to children's cognitive, social, and psychological development. Since some criticisms have been focused toward play, these authors propose that educators should establish a different discourse for play that occurs in school, one that establishes play as educational, meaningful, theoretically driven, and curricularly worthwhile in an academic setting.

While play differs due to age and development, play among 8- to 12-year-olds will likely be:

- symbolic of significant aspects of the child's life experiences
- active in the sense that it requires participation
- voluntary and pleasurable due to some sense of satisfaction or gratification

- meaningful from the perspective of the child's context (for example, 8- to 12-year-olds might consider the play of 3- and 4-year-olds to be unfulfilling).

One view of play includes behaviors whereby one child influences or is influenced by another child (Garvey, 1974, 1990). Such a definition includes the ability of children to play with other children in a cooperative, socially acceptable manner while verbally and nonverbally sharing, taking turns, and responding. Examples of social, nonverbal communication include facial expressions, vocalizations, postures and movements, aggressive or nonaggressive behaviors, and social gestures. Still another characteristic of play among 8- to 12-year-olds includes preparing for the future or attempting to reduce the worry and stress of an upcoming event.

Characteristics of Play Among Eight- to Twelve-Year-Olds

Play is often experimental or exploratory; children try alternatives based on implicit principles of language, the social world, or some other phenomena. Eight- to 12-year-olds, for example, might make up and repeat riddles or might experiment with natural phenomena such as gravity by trying various ways to roll a ball. Children also "play" with other linguistic and physical phenomena (Daiute, 1989). Cohen (2002) maintained that older children and teenagers need developmentally appropriate play. They need time to just hang out or achieve developmental tasks such as figuring out who they are, dealing with the pressures that influence them, and determine areas in which they excel.

Many characteristics of play could be listed, depending on one's definition of play and the age level or maturity of the child participating in the play activity. Characteristics of play in later elementary- and early middle-school-age children include intrinsic motivation, spontaneity, self-imposed goals, and active engagement rather than daydreaming and aimless loafing (Rubin, Fein, & Vandenberg, 1983). As children play, they create a safe context in which to master the communication of meaning, learn to compromise, and allow for exploring issues of trust (Howes, 1992).

Contextual Factors

Several contextual factors affect the play of 8- to 12-year-old children. First, children's developmental maturity affects the types and purposes of their play. Second, socioeconomic status and gender also affect the type, amount, and reasons for play. A child from a more affluent socioeconomic group, for example, might engage in play that represents leisure pursuits, while a child from a less affluent socio-economic group might engage in play related to everyday survival. Girls' play might differ dramatically from boys' play. Likewise, cultural backgrounds may affect children's play. Cultural differences in play have been exhibited by lower-class and middle-class African-American and Euro-American children (Manning & Baruth, 2004). Of course, one must be careful with such generalizations because acculturation differs and crossover might occur in relation to socioeconomic status, gender, or cultural heritage.

Historical Perspectives

Some teachers and parents have been reluctant to acknowledge the contribution of play to children's overall development or to regard it as a worthy part of the middle childhood years. The failure to encourage play at this age perhaps resulted from society's lack of understanding of children and our nation's zealous commitment to the work ethic.

A historical look at play indicates that teachers and parents have often neglected play as a vital entity in children's development. During colonial times, adults considered children's play to be a sign of moral laxity and encouraged children to avoid the frivolity of play in favor of work and study (King,

1979). Those who gave top priority to the role of work in the increasingly industrialized society of the United States, while derogating recreation and leisure, did not recognize the importance and necessity of play. Continuing the play vs. work argument, one commentator has suggested that there is an irreconcilable incompatibility between "child's play" and the characteristics of societal expectations (Vandenberg, 1986). The nation's pragmatic attitudes did not view play as having a payoff or a bottom-line gain and could not accept behaviors that did not provide easily observable benefits.

Today, those who favor an extreme emphasis on academic achievement might consider play to be frivolous, especially for 8- to 12-year-olds in schools and homes. They would perceive an incompatibility between play, schoolwork, and academic achievement. They might also believe that 8- to 12-year-olds, unlike their younger counterparts, are too old for "child's play." These views reflect a trend toward encouraging children to "grow up" at a rapid pace, thereby shortening the childhood years. Perceptive educators and parents with an understanding of child development readily recognize the fallacy of these beliefs. While the types and purposes of play change as children develop, there continues to be a powerful need for play in late childhood.

In fact, some early educators, such as Friedrich Froebel (1782–1852), did consider play to be important for children's development and, even more, the basis for all childhood education (Ransbury, 1982). Likewise, John Dewey (1916) supported play as a worthwhile educational endeavor. Much later, King (1979) summarized contemporary thought by stating that play was necessary for healthy mental, physical, and social development. In some situations, the concept of play appears to have come full circle from a time when adults admonished children to avoid the frivolity of play to a time when people consider play to be an essential aspect of the childhood years (King, 1979).

Manifestations of Play Among Eight- to Twelve-Year-Olds

The physical, cognitive, and psychosocial development of later elementary and early middle school children results in types of play that differ from younger children's play forms.

The Public and the Private

Any legitimate discussion of play among 8- to 12-year-olds must admit the possibility of a discrepancy between the public and the private. In effect, children's authentic play sometimes succumbs to factors beyond their control. Teachers and parents, for example, who fail to understand the value of play, may discourage play by calling it "babyish" and suggesting that the children engage in more "age-appropriate" activities. Therefore, "public" play in 8- to 12-year-olds might be limited due to parents' and teachers' expectations, socioeconomic factors, and gender expectations.

Adults' memories of play indicate a difference between "public" play and "less noticeable" play during the 8- to 12-year-old period. For example, while public play appears to decline, some of this play only becomes more private. Adults report that their play changed during this period, perhaps because other children urged them to "act their age" or because types of play for this age group develop a more private nature. Other adult memories include symbolic play becoming integrated into games with rules, such as competitive board games, and becoming more abstract by transformation into mental games and language play. Other play during this age period includes participation in verbal invention and verbal play such as inventing and participating in riddles, puns, tongue twisters, insults, chants, rhymes, and secret codes that might involve playing with syntax and semantics of language (Bergen, 1988).

Professionals who guide play activities attempt to look beyond physical appearances as they play with children. Considerable developmental diversity exists, after all, among 10- to 12-year-olds, especially considering individual and gender differences, which affect the timing of growth spurts. With this caution firmly in mind, several aspects of play in 8- to 12-year-olds can be explicated.

Gender-Typed Play

As elementary-age children develop gender roles and gender-specific behaviors, they readily identify and show a preference for gender-typed play activities that are culturally sanctioned for their gender. At this age, boys typically involve themselves in physical and independent types of play, while girls choose less physical play types. Boys, more than girls, seem to be aware of gender differences and avoid playing with objects that might be labeled "feminine" (Groos, 1901; Rathus, 2006). Girls participate in more varieties of play than boys. It is important to note, however, that the preference for gender-typed play activities might be changing. Increasingly, softball and soccer teams encourage girls to participate, either on their own teams or on mixed teams. Also, as schools provide gender neutral activities, boys might perceive less stigma from participating in activities traditionally considered feminine.

Physical Play

Eight- to 12-year-old children select increasingly demanding physical play, which gives them a greater opportunity to develop muscle control and coordination. In middle childhood, boys spend more time than girls in large play groups of five or more children and spend more time in physical, competitive play. Girls are more likely to engage in arts and crafts and domestic play. The activities are more closely directed and more structured by adults than are boys' activities. Girls spend more time than boys playing with just one child or with a small group of children (Rathus, 2006). Children's increased physical abilities and improved coordination also allow participation in team sports and other organized activities whereby one's physical ability affects the outcome of the game.

Social Play

Ten- to 12-year-old children, in particular, develop the social skills necessary to participate in complex, cooperative forms of play. The complexity and flexibility of their verbal as well as nonverbal communications contribute to this cooperative potential. They are also able to make friends, interact competently and confidently in social situations, and build on their increasing self-esteem (Manning, 2002). These enhanced social skills allow children to see others' perspectives and allow them to realize the benefits of playing socially and cooperatively. Actual play, which requires social skills, might consist of games, team sports, and organized activities.

Schools often provide play activities that emphasize competition rather than cooperation. Educators sometimes lose sight of play's contributions to learning the social skills necessary for everyday life. Instead, they emphasize competition, perhaps because determining winners and losers is easier than evaluating the improvement of social skills. Regardless of the reason, promoters and advocates of play understand that play for 8- to 12-year-olds should place emphasis on cooperative behaviors rather than on competition. Also, competition may be inappropriate for the females, who often place a priority on cooperation and harmony rather than on competitive efforts.

Outdoor Play

Children, predominantly 10- to 12-year olds, shift allegiance from parents and teachers to peers, and increasingly seek freedom and independence, which results in their playing away from home and, often, away from direct adult supervision. Children might visit ball fields, playgrounds, and recreation centers where others play or where special equipment is available.

Outdoor play has several advantages. Researchers have maintained that outdoor play can stimulate physical–motor development (Henniger, 1993–1994; Pellegrini, 1991), can serve as a positive setting for enhancing social interaction (Pellegrini & Perlmutter, 1988), and can stimulate a variety of play forms (Henniger, 1985). Outdoor play should not be equated with the recess periods of younger children, which often result in little more than a break from classwork. Depending on the school and its ability to provide playground equipment, these breaks may provide little chance for children to learn social skills through games and to improve their physical skills through effective outdoor play environments.

Developers of well-planned and equipped playgrounds have viewed them primarily as an opportunity to develop physical skills through vigorous exercise and play. Educators consider the outdoor setting to be an extension of the classroom, with the same potential for enhancing development (Henniger, 1993–1994). In support of this goal, researchers have recommended that playgrounds include seven play zones: transitional, manipulative/creative, projective/fantasy, focal/ social, social/dramatic, physical, and natural element (Esbensen, 1987; Henniger, 1993–1994). While all these play zones might not be appropriate for all 8- to 12-year-olds, it is important that all learners have equal access to playground zones so that they can make their own choices.

Game Play

Children's increasing cognitive abilities allow more advanced forms of organized games and team activities where rules guide actual behaviors. Although younger children often play together (though, actually, they may only be playing near each other), they also often play alone. Eight- to 12-year-olds might also play alone, either by choice or by necessity; however, their increasing cognitive abilities (especially in those 10 to 12 years of age) allow them to play with others in situations requiring consistent, complex rules.

Depending on their popularity at the time, several types of games are prevalent: steady or constant games such as tag; recurrent or cyclical games such as marbles or hopscotch; and sporadic games such as hula hoop contests, which rise in popularity and then disappear. After 12 years of age, games decline in popularity and are replaced by unstructured play, conversations, and organized play (Bergen, 1988).

Most 8- to 12-year-old children are able to engage in sustained cooperative and competitive social interactions, to plan and carry out longer and longer sequences of purposeful activities, and to exercise self-control and submit voluntarily to restrictions and conventions. These emerging capacities rest on the reciprocal interaction of children's experiences with their physical, cognitive, and psychosocial growth (Garvey, 1990).

Cognitive Play

One of the primary goals of schooling is teaching children skills and strategies associated with literacy and the various curricular areas, each of which is measured by some form of standardized achievement test (Pellegrini & Bohn, 2005). Byrne, Deerr, and Kropp (2003) also considered play to be instrumental in cognitive development. They maintained that Piaget and Vygotsky were among the first to associate play with children's cognitive development. They also believe that play contributes to the ability to learn deliberately, development of symbolic representation, oral language, and introduction of content as well as related literacy skills and concepts.

The cognitive abilities of 10- to 12-year-olds also allow for more advanced forms of play such as word games, riddles, and other literacy related play. Other cognitive characteristics that contribute to their ability to participate in cognitive play include the ability to think hypothetically, reflectively, and abstractly; the ability to engage in propositional thought; and the ability to reason through more than one variable (Manning, 2002). These types of literacy play and play as thought particularly contribute to academic achievement, higher-order thinking skills, and other learning and writing activities (Daiute, 1989).

One researcher contends that play also offers a rich context for children's literacy learning (Vukelich, 1993). Such a contention is especially valid for 8- to 12-year-olds who are experiencing rapid cognitive and psychosocial development. Play environments that foster children's engagement in literacy behaviors lead to significant increases in amounts of literacy activity during play; reading and writing behaviors become more purposeful in literacy enriched play settings; and activities in literacy enriched play become more connected. In concert, such literacy behaviors suggest that an enriching play environment provides children with a significant context for developing additional understandings about reading and writing (Vukelich, 1993).

Technological Play

Many technological advances allow new forms of play. Children can play a wide array of computer games either alone or with another youngster. Software, such as for chess, requires that children think and participate in actual decision making, while other software requires writing and complex thinking. As technological advances become commonplace in our society, children will have greater access to problem-solving programs, CD-ROMs, videodiscs, and simulation programs. Many 8- to 12 year-old children who have benefited from computer use in schools are sufficiently computer literate to "play" with the many technological advances. They also have the cognitive and psychosocial capacity to work alone and to perform the thinking required to benefit from increasingly complex computer games.

Pretend Play

Although the pretend play of earlier years is not seen in school settings, children in this age range engage in much symbolic play at home and in other private or semiprivate environments. In fact, the most salient types of play remembered by many adults are pretend play and games with rules. Research also indicates that there are cross-cultural differences in types of play. Adults in the United States, for example, tend to remember more pretend play activities, while Chinese adults recall more examples of games with rules (Bergen, Liu, & Liu, 1994). The different types of pretend play include use of miniature objects to simulate real-life experiences, building forts and tree houses for various and changing purposes (e.g., a fort one day, a house the next), playing school and house (a favorite activity of 8- to 9-year-olds), and giving plays (more common in 10- to 12-year-olds).

Perspectives on Play Among Eight- to Twelve-Year-Olds

There are various sociocultural perspectives that can affect children's play. Educators and parents, for example, might encourage children to engage in specific play behaviors rather than allow children to choose for themselves. Educators and parents sometimes consider play the antithesis of work and learning. Sociocultural attitudes also can influence the relationship between play and gender; for example, children often select play activities that are culturally sanctioned for their gender. Adults who value, and provide for, well-planned outdoor play also can make a difference in children's play experiences.

Parents Encouraging Specific Play Behavior

Parents tend to reward gender-typical play in their children. Many parents, for example, support active large motor play in boys yet discourage such active play in girls. Some parents reward their daughters for playing with dollhouses and domestic toys but punish them for playing with military toys and vehicles. Some parents reward their sons for playing with military toys and vehicles but punish them for playing with dollhouses and domestic toys (Etaugh & Liss, 1992).

Through societal expectations, most 8- to 12-year-old children acquire some idea of gender-role behaviors. These behaviors sometimes result from personal choice, but sometimes children feel pressured by adults and peers to engage in particular "boy" or "girl" behaviors. Societal and parental expectations can create powerful pressures for females and males to behave in "appropriate" ways and to play with "appropriate" toys. The nature of play as voluntary, pleasurable, and meaningful suggests that children should be allowed to choose the behaviors and toys they want. Enlightened parents encourage play in 8- to 12-year-olds and encourage children to select behaviors and toys that have personal meaning and relevance.

Attitudes of Educators

Just as parents often encourage specific types of play, educators also, perhaps unknowingly, have a significant impact on children's play. Educators of preschool children, for example, usually encourage fantasy play by providing time, materials, and space for fantasy (Pellegrini & Galda, 1994); however, they may consider 8- to 12–year-olds too old for fantasy or may consider that fantasy is unproductive play: in effect, play that does not contribute to academic growth. Some educators consider all play to be a poor expenditure of time or a waste of energy. Since play's benefits are usually not measurable with standardized tests, educators often feel that they should not allow too much time for play, especially when they perceive that it takes away from the kinds of study and other academic pursuits that prepare children for such tests. These harsh criticisms of play may grow more intense when reports suggest schools are failing in their academic mission and when achievement test scores decline. Perceptive educators and scholars acquainted with the benefits of play realize that play contributes to learning and academic achievement and is not a cause of their decline.

While most people probably think early childhood teachers should encourage play, it is also important for teachers of 8- to 12-year-olds to provide developmentally appropriate play. The teacher's role becomes a critical component when play is at the center of the school curriculum. The teacher learns to consider play activities as opportunities in which to be involved and to involve students. Play should be considered a vehicle for through which children can grow and develop the foundational skills necessary for academic success (Cooney, 2004).

Gender and Culture

Societal expectations as well as parents' and educators' opinions influence the relationship of gender and play. There might be a fine line between children's actual choice of behaviors and those dictated by others.

Some research has documented gender differences in children's play behaviors (Bergen, 1994; Garvey, 1990; Pellegrini & Galda, 1994). As our schools become more gender-equitable and gender-conscious, educators need to understand the relationship between gender and play and, whenever possible, provide equitable play opportunities for both girls and boys. Since violent play themes and aggressive actions result in a more powerful person winning and a weaker person losing (Bergen, 1994), this type of competitive play favors boys, who tend to be physically stronger in this age group. A corollary message in this type of play is that males are more likely than females to accept violence as a means of solving problems. In fact, because parents and educators are more accepting of aggression in boys, when girls participate in aggressive behaviors they are more likely to be reprimanded.

Those who have studied rough-and-tumble play found that boys participate in such behaviors more than girls (Garvey, 1990; Pellegrini & Galda, 1994). These differences might result from hormonal or socialization factors. A cross-cultural study supports the finding that rough-and-tumble play reflects cultural differences. Boys among the Ilocano of Luzon, the Mixtecans of Mexico, and the Taira of Okinawa, for example, participate in more boisterous and rowdy play than girls (Garvey, 1990). But in other cultures, such as the Pilaga Indians, girls also often engage in rough play.

Culture, therefore, plays an important part in children's amount and selection of play behaviors. Among intracultural and generational differences, some Asian Americans, for example, might place priority on work over play and might be more insistent that children's behaviors be more gender-specific. Adopting the Confucian ideals of hard work and self-discipline (Manning & Baruth, 2004), these parents and families might view play as unnecessary, especially when they do not understand its relationship to academic achievement.

Right to Play

While the literature has not focused extensively on children's having a "right to play," there has been a proposal that children have this basic right because it contributes to healthy development (Almy, 1984). Current emphasis on narrow perspectives of academic achievement has prohibited widespread acceptance of 8- to 12-year-olds' right to play. The growing recognition, however, of the importance of play in children's general development as well as their academic achievement might underscore the position that play is a right of all children. Recognizing play as a basic right can be a major step toward recognizing play as valuable both in itself as well as because of its contributions to broad cognitive and social growth.

The benefits of play in the lives of 8- to 12-year-old children are too significant to ignore. Play contributes to children's cognitive and psychosocial development, to academic achievement, and to a foundation for thinking, writing, and other forms of literacy. Although those who support the provision of opportunities for children to play have written extensively about children's need for play and its many contributions, a discrepancy continues to exist between "public play environments" and "private play environments." Children's play deserves greater respect. Now is the time for schools, professional associations, parents, and children's advocacy groups to take a stand for children's having a right to play.

References

Almy, M. (1984). A child's right to play. *Young Children, 39*(4), 80.

Bergen, D. (1988). Stages of play development. In D. Bergen (Ed.), *Play as a medium for learning and development* (pp. 49–66). Portsmouth, NH: Heinemann.

Bergen, D. (1994). Should teachers permit or discourage violent play themes? *Childhood Education, 70*(5), 300–301.

Bergen, D., Liu, W., & Liu, G. (1994). *Chinese and American college students' memories of childhood play: A comparison.* Paper presented at the conference of the Association for the Study of Play, Atlanta, GA.

Byrne, M., Deerr, D., & Kropp, L. (2003). Book a play date: The game of promoting school literacy. *American Libraries, 34*(8), 42–44.

Cohen, L. (2002). Promoting play at home. *Independent School, 61*(4), 94–98.

Cooney, M. H. (2004). Is play important? Guatemalan kindergartners' classroom experiences and their parents and teachers' perceptions of learning through play. *Journal of Research in Childhood Education, 18*(4), 261–278.

Daiute, C. (1989). Play as thought: Thinking strategies of young writers. *Harvard Educational Review, 59* (1), 1–23.

Dewey, J. (1916). *Education and democracy.* New York: Macmillan.

Esbensen, S. (1987). *An outdoor classroom.* Ypsilanti, MI: High/Scope Press.

Etaugh, C., & Liss, M. B. (1992). Home, school and playroom: Training grounds for adult gender roles. *Sex Roles, 26*(3–4), 129–147.

Garvey, C. (1974). Some properties of social play. *Merrill-Palmer Quarterly, 20*(3), 163–180.

Garvey, C. (1990). *Play.* Cambridge, MA: Harvard University Press.

Groos, K. (1901). *The play of man.* New York: Appleton.

Henniger, M. L. (1985). Preschool children's play behaviors in an indoor and outdoor environment. In J. L. Frost & S. Sunderlin (Eds.), *When children play* (pp. 145–149). Wheaton, MD: Association for Childhood Education International.

Henniger, M. L. (1993–1994). Enriching the outdoor play experience. *Childhood Education, 70*(2), 87–90.

Howes, C. (1992). *The collaborative construction of pretend.* Albany: State University of New York Press.

King, N. R. (1979). Play: The kindergartener's perspective. *Elementary School Journal, 80*(3), 81–87.

Manning, M. L. (2002). *Developmentally appropriate middle level schools* (2nd ed.). Wheaton, MD: Association for Childhood Education International.

Manning, M. L., & Baruth, L. G. (2004). *Multicultural education of children and adolescents* (4th ed.). Boston: Allyn & Bacon.

Manning, M. L., & Boals, B. M. (1987). In defense of play. *Contemporary Education, 58*(4), 206–210.

Pellegrini, A. (1991). Outdoor recess: Is it really necessary? *Principal, 71*(40), 23.

Pellegrini, A. D., & Bohn, C. M. (2005). The role of recess in children's cognitive performance and school adjustment. *Educational Researcher, 34*(1), 13–19.

Pellegrini, A. D., & Galda, L. (1994). Play. In V. S. Ramachandran (Ed.), *Encyclopedia of human behavior* (pp. 535–543). New York: Academic.

Pellegrini, A., & Perlmutter, J. (1988). Rough and tumble play on the elementary school playground. *Young Children, 43*(2), 14–17.

Ransbury, M. L. (1982). Friedrich Frobel 1782–1852: A reexamination of Froebel's principles of children's learning. *Childhood Education, 59*(2), 104–106.

Rathus, S. A. (2006). *Children and adolescence: Voyages into development* (2nd ed.). Belmont, CA: Thomson/Wadsworth.

Rubin, K. H., & Coplan, R. J. (1994). Play: Developmental stages, functions, and educational support. In T. Husen & T. Postle-thwaite (Eds.), *The international encyclopedia of education* (2nd ed., Vol. 8, pp. 4536–4542). New York: Elsevier.

Rubin, K., Fein, G., & Vandenberg, B. (1983). In E. M. Hetherington (Ed.), *Handbook of child psychology: Vol. 4. Socialization, personality, and social development* (pp. 693–774). New York: Wiley.

Vandenberg, B. (1986). Mere child's play. In K. Blanchard (Ed.), *The many faces of play* (pp. 115–120). Champaign, IL: Human Kinetics.

Vukelich, C. (1993). Play: A context for exploring the functions, features, and meaning of writing with peers. *Language Arts, 70*(1), 386–391.

Youngquist, J., & Pataray-Ching, J. (2004). Revisiting "Play": Analyzing and articulating acts of play. *Early Childhood Education Journal, 31*(3), 171–178.

4
Language and Play
Natural Partners

JANE ILENE FREEMAN DAVIDSON

What is the relationship between language and play? To answer this question, consider two examples of children playing.

It is recess time in first grade. Andrew and Malcolm are sitting on the climber swapping jokes. It is Andrew's turn.

"Knock, knock."

"Who's there?" Malcolm answers. "Banana."

"Banana who?" "Banana." "Banana who?"

"Orange." "Orange who?"

"Orange you glad I didn't say banana."

Both boys burst into gales of laughter. The boys spend the rest of recess exchanging knock knock jokes.

Shakeeta and Carly, both 4 years old, are in the pretend house area of their child care center. Carly announces, "Sister, it's time to get dressed. We're going to the ball." They talk about what they will wear as they don frilly negligees, necklaces, and high heels. Yomi asks, "Can I come too?"

"Yeah," says Shakeeta. "You have to get dressed up."

"No!" corrects Carly. "She's Cinderella. She has to stay home."

Yomi readily takes on the Cinderella role. "You need to yell at me to clean," she tells Shakeeta, "'cause you're the mean stepsister."

Both of these examples show the relation between play and language. In the first the children are using language in a playful way: they are manipulating language to create a humorous pun which serves as the punchline for the joke. In the second example the children are using language to further their play: they use it both in the context of their pretend play—"Sister, it's time to get dressed"—and to plan their play—"You need to yell at me to clean." These examples show clearly the two distinct relationships that exist between language and play: (1) Children can play with the language itself; (2) children can use language as a tool in play. What is the nature of each of these relationships?

Playing with Language

Children will play with all aspects of language, including its sound, meaning, form, and purpose. These aspects are discussed in turn.

Playing with Language Sounds

Children begin playing with language before they can speak. Babies delight in playing with sounds; by moving the tongue and lips and varying the air flow, they produce sounds and interesting vibrations and feelings in the mouth. As the child gets closer to talking, the verbal play will expand to explore the intonation and rhythm of language as well as the speech sounds. The babble of the 9-month-old will often replicate the intonation of adult speech, sounding like a question with a raised tone at the end or like a command with a quality of firmness, while the content is still gibberish. Although the baby explores language for the pleasure of the sounds and feelings, and for the social response it creates, this play with sounds also develops the muscles, vocal skills, and social interaction patterns that will form the basis for language.

Even after children begin to talk they still enjoy playing with the sounds of language. Toddlers and preschoolers will repeat intriguing words, frequently turning them into a chant, or varying the emphasis to create subtle differences. Harriet Johnson recorded the chant of a 2½-year-old after completing a block building:

> Now it's done un un
> Done un un un un. (Garvey, 1990, p. 62)

As children begin to interact with peers, their conversations will often involve this type of chant constructed in a turn-taking verbal interchange. Garvey (1984) recorded the following conversation of 2½-year-olds about the father of Judy's baby:

Judy: Well, someday you can see dada, but not for a long time.
Tom: I have a dada, too. *Judy: I* have a dada, too. *Tom: I* have a *real* dada. *Judy: I* have a special dada.
    Tom: *I* have a real dada. *Judy: I* do too.
Tom: I do too.
Judy: I have a special dada, too. *Tom: I* do too.
Judy: I have a special dada doo. Da daaa (starts to chant). (pp. 160–161)

This playful rhythmic exchange involves a combination of repetition, slight modification, and expansion of one another's statements. As children get older the modifications may be greater from statement to statement, and the silliness often develops sooner and becomes more pronounced.

This type of jointly constructed wordplay is an important form of social interaction among young children. Once they develop a funny pattern they often will use it over and over again in the way that they repeat favorite rhymes.

Playing with the Meaning of Language

In addition to playing with the sounds of language, children will also experiment with the meaning, the structure, and the function of language. When they need to describe something new children will use old words in unique ways. Four-year-old Michael, for example, had been to Sleeping Bear sand dunes. He was impressed with the wavelike hills of rolling sand extending in every direction. A few weeks later he noticed a steep, grassy bank along the side of the road. "Look at the grass dune," he exclaimed. Anyone who has spent time with young children will hear examples of creative word use. A Russian poet similarly documented unique word uses among Russian children (Chukovsky, 1963).

This stretching of words to fit new contexts continues through elementary school as children try to make newly learned words their own, but often they use them in odd ways. An 8-year-old walking through a patch of seaweed along the shallows of a lake, for example, warns his brother, "Watch out for the allergy." He was looking for the word *algae,* but came up with a similar sounding word that he knew only slightly.

Playing with the Forms of Language

As children learn language they often invent new word forms. A 4-year-old brags, "I runned up the slide." A 2-year-old points out the "two snowmans." These children are subconsciously beginning to learn about past tense and plurals. They use this knowledge to create their own past tense form of *run* and to make *snowman* plural. These children will eventually learn the exceptions to the rules of forming past tense and plurals but, for now, playing with forms helps them to understand better how language works.

The above examples of language use arc "play" because they are innovative, self-motivated, and satisfying. Children also construct language in this way. Such language construction, however, is not a conscious act. Michael, for example, does not think, "I wonder what new and interesting way I can describe the grassy bank." Nor did the child mentioned above think about how to say *run* in the past tense. These playful uses of language are natural and unconscious.

Children also play with language in conscious, purposeful ways as they tell jokes, test limits, adapt rhymes, adapt language from books, and narrate stories. These playful ways are discussed in turn.

Joking Around

Children's first jokes are not the formal kind that we tell as adults but, instead, a purposeful misstatement of something they know:

Two-year-old Adam is looking at a farmyard picture with his dad. As Dad points to animals Adam makes the appropriate sounds. He now knows the sound of every animal in the picture. As Dad points to the dog, Adam gets a twinkle in his eye, pauses a minute, and says "Meow!" then begins to giggle. Adam continues to make the wrong sound for each animal and the giggles get louder and louder.

Adam is purposefully playing with language and the concepts behind the language. He is intentionally making the wrong sounds to create a humorous incongruity. Adam is in control of the language; he can play with it and change it to amuse himself. As with Adam, it is typical for children to play with parts of language they have recently mastered. They cement their new knowledge by being able to manipulate it at will.

An older child would not find it amusing to suggest that a dog says "meow!" What types of changes a child finds humorous are a good indication of what knowledge the child has just acquired. Children will play with those aspects of language they have just mastered:

Monica, soon to be five, has been fascinated with names. She will introduce herself with her full name, Monica Rachel Hankins. One day when she enters the child care center she stands by the attendance chart watching the arriving children pick out their name cards and place them on the chart. She repeats the name as it is placed in the chart: Binta, Jackson, Julie. Because she knows Jason's full name she says "Jason Tenson" as he puts his name on the chart. She then tries Jason's last name on Darcy: "Darcy Tenson," she proclaims and giggles. Darcy looks a bit unsure, until Monica makes herself a new name, "Monica Rachel Tenson," then both girls laugh. They go around the class making all their peers into Tensons.

Monica has learned that people have more then one name, and that specific names belong to specific people. She has created incongruity by assigning the wrong names to the people around her. Darcy does not realize at first that Monica's errors are intentional; but once she understands the game she quickly joins in. Playing with names is popular with children. Even in elementary school children delight in exchanging names with each other. Lily will become Crystal, and Crystal will be Lily. They will enjoy the confusion that is caused when they answer to each other's name.

The above examples show how children create their own jokes, but children also enjoy traditional jokes like the knock-knock joke at the beginning of this chapter. When that joke is told by a 4-year-old, rather than a 7-year-old, it sounds something like this:

Knock knock. Who's there? Banana. Banana who? Banana. Banana who? Apple! I didn't say Banana.

Other 4-year-olds will then repeat the joke using other fruit, or putting in other words, such as *refrigerator*. To an adult or an older child the original version is better; the incongruity in using *orange* to mean "aren't you" catches the listener off guard and creates the humor. Younger children, however, are not able to comprehend the double meaning of words (Shultz & Pilon, 1973). An orange is an orange and cannot be anything else. Younger children find both versions funny. To them the incongruity comes from having an orange, apple, or refrigerator at the door, rather than from the play on words. In effect, one researcher suggests, "although adults and older children find incongruity humor funny because it makes sense in some unexpected or improbable way, preschoolers find it funny because it *makes no sense*" (McGhee, 1984, p. 226).

At 7 or 8 years of age children begin to understand the dual meaning of words (McGhee, 1984; Shultz, 1972; Shultz & Horibe, 1974). One author, for example, describes her confusion when her brother told her a moron joke when she was 5 (Geller, 1985). He asked, "Why did the moron tiptoe past the medicine cabinet?" and answered it by saying, "So he wouldn't wake the sleeping pills" (p. 1). A few years later while brushing her teeth, staring at the contents of the medicine cabinet, the double meaning came to her and she began laughing. Her enjoyment of the joke came as much from the thrill of now being able to see both sides, as from the joke itself. Children delight in playing with their newly found ability to see multiple meanings.

Children from 7 to 10 years of age enjoy collecting and sharing jokes based on puns with their friends. The telling of jokes becomes an important social ritual. Swapping jokes often is an ice-breaker with new acquaintances. Outsiders have few advantages when they enter an established play group, but knowing new jokes provides them with a special status and a way to become part of the group.

At this age it is the words in the joke that are most important, rather than the telling of the joke. By 11 years of age, jokes become more narrative. Tellers begin to play with the timing, characterizations, and general presentation style when performing the joke. Their jokes become more similar to those of adults, who not only must say the right words in order to have a good story, but must create an ambience that makes the words funny.

Testing the Limits: Is It All Right to Say That?

Not only are children gaining knowledge about the sounds, meaning, and form of language, they are also coming to understand what types of language are appropriate and when they are appropriate. Thus violating the rules of propriety becomes another common form of language play. A 4-year-old might name her doll "poopy-head" and laugh. The child knows that poopy is a naughty word, so the humor comes from using a word in a place in which it definitely does not belong. A group of preschoolers will find conversation seasoned with bathroom language hilarious. Language can also allow children to try out unacceptable ideas, as in this description from a class of 4-year-olds:

Colton, Wesley, and Ilana are filling containers at the water table. "I am making soup," Ilana explains.
"Yeah," says Wesley. "My soup is hot."
"I know," suggests Colton, "lets pretend it is poison soup." The others agree and work for a while cooking their poison soup. When Mr. Wilder, the teacher, comes over to see what they are doing, they giggle.
"We're making soup," says Colton.

"It's yummy," claims Wesley.

"It smells good," says Mr. Wilder.

"Would you like some?" asks Ilana. Mr. Wilder pretends to eat some. The children all begin to giggle. "You ate poison soup," they tell him.

Poisoning a teacher is a totally unacceptable action, but as children create pretend situations with language they can try it out in a harmless fashion. They have the power of imagining that they could care for themselves without a teacher, but know that in reality this will not happen.

As children get older they continue to push the limits of acceptability with their wordplay. They will use jokes as an excuse to try out "naughty" language and ideas. A first-grader might tell friends the following story:

A boy asked his teacher if he could go to the bathroom. The teacher asked the boy to recite the alphabet first.

"A B C D E F G H I J K L M N O Q R S T U V W X Y Z."

The teachers asks, "Where is the p?" The boy tells her, "It's running down my leg."

The joke offers an excuse for using an off-color word and discussing an unacceptable action. Children can strengthen their knowledge about what behaviors are acceptable by violating these expectations in a humorous way.

As children become older, exchanging witty insults becomes a form of competition, with each child seeing who can come up with a better zinger. The following playful insult was shared by a 12-year-old: "Is that your face or did you just sneeze?" Insult creation becomes a contest of verbal agility. Playing "the dozens," an insult-trading dialogue begun by black teens, relies heavily on sexual insults and innuendo about the other person or the other person's family. "Talking trash" or using slang and bad language to insult your opponent is also a show of verbal agility that may be imitated by older elementary schoolchildren.

Playing with Rhymes

Young children are captivated by the lilting flow and rhythm of rhymes. There are differences between nursery rhymes and other chants (Geller, 1985). Nursery rhymes are a form of language play that parents introduce to their children. Parents might recite "This Little Piggie Went to Market" while washing their baby's toes; they may draw their young children into play with action rhymes such as "Pat-a-cake, pat-a-cake, Baker's Man" (Geller, 1985). These rhymes are repeated from generation to generation because children delight in hearing them over and over. The repetition of words, the rhyming pattern, and the catchy rhythm draw children into reciting the rhymes with their parents and, when they are ready, chanting them on their own.

This enjoyment of rhymes remains as children get older, but beginning in about kindergarten, or earlier if the child has older siblings, the source of the rhymes becomes other children rather than adults; children then will learn a wide variety of rhymes. Opie and Opie (1959) made an extensive collection of children's rhymes and other wordplay lore from the playgrounds of English schools. They traced back many of the rhymes over 200 years, although new groups of children often feel sure that the rhymes are fresh and new. The rhymes have many different purposes. Some rhymes are parts of games. Counting-out chants such as "Eenie Meanie, Mime Moe" are often used to decide who will go first. Jumping rope, ball bouncing, and clapping games also are often accompanied by rhyming chants.

Some chants have no purpose other than to amuse, as is the case with this tangle talk:

One fine day in the middle of the night,/Two dead men got up to fight,/

Back to back they faced each other, /Drew their swords and shot each other./ A paralysed donkey passing by /Kicked a blind man in the eye, /Knocked him through a nine inch wall/ Into a dry ditch and drowned them all. (Opie & Opie, 1959, p. 25)

Rhymes also provide a forum for teasing and trying out off-color language. A group of children might chant the following:

> I see London I see France
> I see someone's Underpants.

In repeating a chant the child does not feel responsible for his or her actions. The word *underpants,* which elementary children consider almost a swearword, is acceptable when repeated here because the rhyme demands it. Often other children will join in, turning the chant into a group action, thus seeming to absolve each child of individual responsibility. While children might not tease other children about seeing their underwear, the rhyme provides a socially accepted way of both using the "bad" language and engaging in teasing.

A whole group of children's chants make fun of, or challenge, people in authority. These are often parodies of other poems or songs, as in this grade-school version of "Deck the Halls."

> Deck the halls with gasoline, (chorus: Fa la la la la, la la la la)
> Light a match and watch it gleam, (chorus)
> Watch the school burn down to ashes. (chorus)
> Aren't you glad you played with matches? (chorus)

Rap is a form of rhyme that offers children both the chance to memorize and repeat more up-to-date, cool rhymes, and a format for creating their own rhymes. Children make up a rap for any number of reasons, such as to immortalize a special event, brag about a success, poke fun at something, or tell a story. When creating rap, children can play with words as well as add hand rhythms and sound effects; they can turn a rhyme into a performance.

Playing with Language from Books

Books provide wonderful language for children's play. Dr. Seuss books and other children's books with strong rhythms and rhymes draw children into chanting along. Some books that have favorite repetitive sections will become so much a part of the child's repertoire that the book's language will be used while playing.

Two-year-old Raymond loves the book *Good Night Moon* by Margaret Wise Brown (1947). The book describes the things in a bedroom, then says "Good night" to each thing. One day, when playing in the house area of his preschool, Raymond began walking around saying, "Good night, bed. Good night, table. Good night, shoe."

Raymond does not make his phrases rhyme as they do in the book, but he has used the repetition of "good night" that holds the rhyming phrases together.

Four-year-old Julieann often reads *Chicka Chicka Boom Boom* (Martin & Archambault, 1989), which is about a group of letters that climb up a coconut tree. It gets so crowded that they all fall down. While going down the slide she chants some favorite lines from the book: "I'll meet you at the top of the coconut tree. Will there be enough room? Chicka chicka BOOM BOOM." Sarah hears Julieann and joins in with the chicka chicka boom boom as she too goes down the slide. Eventually there is a group of four children repeating the phrase from the book as they slide.

The language play allows Julieann to add an extra dimension to her sliding, and it also creates a social event by drawing in her peers. Often, therefore, favorite books provide a body of shared rhymes and language play that a group of children can use as the basis for social interaction.

Playing with Storytelling

Language allows children to create incredible stories, in which they can play with absurd ideas and situations.

> At group time in a preschool class, Ms. Garcia asks the children, "Where have you seen birds?" Most list the usual places you would expect, such as the sky, a tree, and the park. But Julia, who is almost 4 years old, announces, "Last night an eagle flew into my house. It flew around, then it ate my dinner."
> "What a wonderful story," said her teacher.
> "No! It really happened!" Julia insisted.

Julia wants to make her story more real by having others believe that it really did happen. Usually children are willing to accept their inventions as stories, but it is still exciting to use words to make incredible things happen in these stories. Exchanging and building one another's tall tales is popular with children through first grade. As they get older, stretching reality through storytelling continues to be a part of the verbal interaction of children, but their greater skill with words will produce more refined stories. In the same way that the manner in which one tells a joke becomes more important around 11 years, the style of telling stories will also gain importance around this age.

Language as a Tool in Play

Not only do children play with language, they also use language as a tool in their play. When playing pretend, children use language to enact the role they have selected. The mother might say, "Don't bother me now! Can't you see I'm making dinner!?" The shopkeeper might inform the customer, "Those shoes are $200." The doctor might tell the patient, "You need a needle. It will hurt a little." Talking as the character is one way children define their role—by using motherlike language it is easier to become the mother. The character's conversation can also communicate to the other players how the play will go; in the extract at the beginning of this chapter, Carly lets Shakeeta know what she wants to play by having her character say, "Sister, it is time to get dressed. We're going to the ball." A researcher discusses numerous techniques children have for setting the direction of the play while remaining in character (Giffin. 1984). For example, children will also step out of their pretend role to discuss what is happening in the play. In observing pretend play, one will hear children distributing roles: "I'm the mother and you're the sister." They also use language to describe and plan the play: "Let's play sea monster." "Yeah! It will chase us to the boat."

The joy of playing pretend pushes children to stretch their language skills in a number of ways. First, this shifting between contexts of talk takes sophisticated language skills. The requirements of talking effectively in each context are different. To be a character in the play one must use an appropriate tone of voice and the language that fits the role. When planning play it is important to use clear, persuasive language that will sway others to one's point of view.

Second, the language that children use in playing pretend is often similar to the language used in books. When children talk in the role of the play character, they use a more storylike language than when talking as themselves. The booklike nature of pretend play language is particularly obvious when you watch children narrating their play as they manipulate small toy figures. Many researchers feel that this type of play prepares children for understanding stories that are read to them, or that they are beginning to read themselves, and also prepares them to create their own written stories.

Third, dramatic play is one of the first forums in which children begin to talk about language itself. This knowledge about language is a sign of metalinguistic awareness. When Yomi tells Shakeeta, "You need to yell at me to clean, `cause you're the mean stepsister," she is talking about the type of language that fits the role. She is demonstrating awareness of the tone and form of the language as well as its content.

In these ways, strong language skills enhance children's pretend play. Strong language skills are apparent as children show their ability to switch contexts, use story language, and talk about language itself. Playing pretend also provides a forum to develop and strengthen these skills. Strong language skills facilitate the play and play facilitates the development of language skills. Thus, language is a tool in play and play is a tool in the development of language.

Pretend Play in Elementary School

Investigators have written much about the pretend play of children through kindergarten age (Bergen, 1988; Davidson, 1996; Fein, 1981; Rogers & Sawyers, 1988). Little has been written, however, about the pretend play of children once they reach elementary school. Looking at what has been written one might erroneously assume that pretend play ends when children become 7 years of age. In fact, pretend play is still important to elementary school children, it just becomes less visible to the adults around them, as evidenced by the following events:

Carla and Jane, both 10, are making the daily, mile-long walk to elementary school. They appear to be walking and talking. Each girl occasionally pats her own thigh, and their walking turns to a sort of galloping skip from time to time. These small actions are the only physical indication that they are pretending. Their conversation revolves around the pretend horses they are riding and the continuing imaginary story they have created around the horses. The horses live in the woods that border the road. The girls have developed elaborate stories around each horse's herd, history, and temperament. According to the narration, they have been taming the horses over the year. Now they are quite easy to ride on the way to school. At times the conversation turns to schoolwork or other matters, but the horse story is maintained with an occasional, "Whoa," or a mention of another horse glimpsed in the woods.

A casual observer might merely have seen two girls walking to school. The occasional pat to the thigh could be interpreted as checking to be sure lunch money was there and the gallop as just a need for physical activity. Unlike younger children these children do not "dress up" or use large overt actions to define their pretending. Their pretend play has become more verbal; it is language, not action that defines the play of these older children. Planning the play becomes as important, or more important, than the actual enacting of the pretend events. The play story often continues to build from day to day over a period of weeks or months. This move to a more language-based play, with an emphasis on planning and a story line that continues across play periods, is also evident as these older children use Barbies, action figures, Legos, or other small toys to create imaginary stories.

At times the pretend stories of older children are solely a verbal creation. Children might create stories that link them with famous or admired people, perhaps inventing a family composed of television or movie actors and, of course, also including themselves and favored peers. Others might create the ideal sports team, pulling in players from everywhere, and often starring themselves as the quarterback or as the player that makes the incredible winning play. Their least liked peers are likely to drop the crucial pass or make some other game-losing error.

As in the above example, the language-play stories become a part of everyday actions. These girls use language to create play about horses as they walk to school. Another child may use language to become Cinderella while making the bed or doing other tedious chores. Bad guy/good guy themes that include superheroes, soldiers, or aliens might be integrated into games of running and fort building. The fantasy sports teams that children create can enrich pickup ballgames.

In the elementary school years the difference between pretend play and storytelling becomes unclear. The planning of the pretending becomes longer and more involved, often itself becoming a form of storytelling. These children therefore are simultaneously playing with language (using language to create stories) and using it as a tool in their play (using language to further pretend play).

Integrating Language Play during Social Interactions

It is not just in pretend play that language and language play become a more integral part of older children's interactions. In elementary school language use, play takes on an important role in children's play in general and in their particular social interactions. While younger children enjoy just chanting favorite rhymes, elementary school children integrate rhymes into other play activities. Children chant rhymes as they jump rope. The text of the rhyme often dictates the jumper's actions, as in the following:

Teddy Bear Teddy Bear turn around Teddy Bear Teddy Bear touch the ground Teddy Bear Teddy Bear climb the stairs Teddy Bear Teddy Bear say your prayers Teddy Bear Teddy Bear say good night Teddy Bear Teddy Bear turn out the light.

Other rhymes combine the action with a prediction for the future, as in the following:

Anna and Mark sitting under the tree k-i-s-s-i-n-g.
First comes love, then comes marriage
Then comes Anna with a baby carriage.
How many babies will she have?

The players count how many fast jumps Anna can do; the number she reaches is the number of babies she will have. Similar rhymes predict such things as how many kisses the jumper will get or what letter of the alphabet begins the name of the jumper's sweetheart. Children also often use rhymes of this type while on the seesaw or when playing hand-clapping games.

Rhymes also expedite games. Children often use counting-out rhymes like the following to select special roles in games:

One potato Two potato Three potato Four
Five potato Six potato Seven potato more.

The caller points to each child at each successive number. The child who is "more" stops playing. The chanting and counting continue until only one child remains; the child who remains is "It," goes first, or has some other special role in the play.

In many cultures, rhyming wordplay of this type infuses all parts of the social world in elementary school. Opie and Opie (1959) include a lengthy chapter, "Code of Oral Legislation," where they explain that the schoolchild "conducts his [sic] business with his fellows by ritual declarations. His affidavits, promissory notes, claims, deeds of conveyance, receipts, and notices of resignation, are verbal, and are sealed by the utterance of ancient words which are recognized and considered binding by the whole community" (p. 121). Promises are sealed with words such as "Cross my heart and hope to die." Found treasures are claimed by declaring "Finders keepers, loser's weepers." Children use other ritualized language to seal bargains, pledge friendship, claim the right to be first, or excuse themselves from volunteering for an unpleasant task.

Some language rituals, however, have no particular purpose. Seeing a blue Volkswagen Beetle might evoke the following words and accompanying action from one group of children:

Punch buggie blue (the chanter playfully punches his friend)
and no punches back.

Another group might have language rituals that are tied to the beginning of the month, the type of clothing someone is wearing, or some other prompt. These rituals have become an accepted part of the culture of that social group. Having these shared language rituals helps to confirm the cohesiveness of a social group: we belong together because we share the same verbal games.

Social groups use other forms of verbal play to reinforce their solidarity. Groups of children will often form clubs or gangs that have secret passwords or special phrases that only those in the group can understand. Elementary school children enjoy using "secret languages" with peers so others will not understand. These languages often involve complex manipulation of English; pig Latin is one of the most familiar of these secret languages. To speak pig Latin one must take the first consonant, or consonant blend, of the word, move it to the end of the word, and add "ay." This sentence in pig Latin would look like this: "Isthay entencesay may igpay atinlay ouldway ooklay ikelay isthay." Other secret languages may involve saying parts of the word backwards or adding additional sounds to each syllable. To speak any of these languages requires a clear sense of how words are composed, then an ability to alter this composition to fit a new set of rules.

From infancy through school age, play and language create a natural partnership. Children play with language for the joy of it and as a way of strengthening what they know about language. The ways that children play with language skills become more refined and elaborate as their language skills become more refined. Children also use language as a tool to further their play. As children become older, often the separation between playing with language and supporting play with language narrows. Children's language becomes more sophisticated and complex. Language play becomes an integral part of many forms of play and social interaction.

References

Bergen, D. (Ed.). (1988). *Play as a medium for learning and development: A handbook of theory and practice.* Portsmouth, NH: Heinemann.

Brown, M. W (1947). *Good night moon.* New York: Harper & Row.

Chukovsky, K. (1963). *From two to five.* Berkeley: University of California Press.

Davidson, J. (1996). *Emergent literacy and dramatic play in early education.* Albany, NY: Delmar.

Fein, G. (1981). Pretend play: An integrative review. *Child Development, 52,* 1095–1118.

Garvey, C. (1984). *Children's talk.* Cambridge, MA: Harvard University Press.

Garvey, C. (1990). *Play.* Cambridge, MA: Harvard University Press.

Geller, I,. (1985). *Wordplay and language learning for children.* Urbana, IL: National Council of Teachers of English.

Giffin, H. (1984). The coordination of meaning in the creation of shared make-believe reality. In I. Bretherton (Ed.), *Symbolic play: The development o f social understanding* (pp. 73–100). Orlando, FL: Academic.

Martin, B., & Archimbault, J. (1989). *Chicka chicka boom boom.* New York: Simon & Schuster.

McGhee, P. (1984). Play, incongruity, and humor. In T. Yawkey & A. Pellegrini (Eds.), *Child play: Developmental and applied* (pp. 217–234). Hillsdale, NJ: Erlbaum.

Opie, I., & Opie, P. (1959). *The lore and language of schoolchildren.* New York: Oxford University Press.

Rogers, C. S., & Sawyers, J. K. (1988). *Play in the lives of children.* Washington, D.C.: National Association for the Education of Young Children.

Shultz, T R. (1972). A cognitive–developmental analysis of humor. In A. J. Chapman & H. C. Foot (Eds.), *Humour and laughter: Theory, research and applications* (pp. 11–54). Chichester, UK: Wiley.

Shultz, T. R., & Horibe, E (1974). Development of the appreciation of verbal jokes. *Developmental Psychology, 10,* 13–20.

Shultz, T. R., & Pilon, R. (1973). Development of the ability to detect linguistic ambiguity. *Child Development, 44,* 728–733.

5
Gender Identity and Play

MELANIE AYRES AND LESLIE D. LEVÉ

In their first years, children learn to identify themselves and others by their sex. As Fagot and Leinbach described, "self-relevance and the importance society places on our standards and expectations for males and females suffuse the gender distinction with affect, making it what is perhaps the most salient parameter of social categorization for the young child" (1993, p. 205). Thus, it is important to understand when children learn gender labels and how labeling might influence or be influenced by children's play.

Children worldwide engage in gender-specific play, although the structure, degree of peer involvement, and gender negotiation vary by culture (Whiting & Edwards, 1988). By age 3, when children have developed the cognitive skills necessary to identify gender in themselves and others, gender differences in play become increasingly complex, and the nature of children's play changes forever (Fagot & Leinbach, 1993). Environmental factors such as peers, parents, and teachers affect the timing and intensity of the gender identity process and the adoption of functional or dysfunctional behaviors. In this chapter, we discuss processes influencing the development of gender identity and early sex-differentiated play, distinctive characteristics of sex-differentiated play, and typical sex-differentiated behaviors' patterns that emerge in childhood and adolescence.

The Emergence of Gender Identity and Sex-Differentiated Play

It is unclear whether gender identity precedes sex-differentiated play or whether play with same-sex peers influences the development of gender identity. Compounding this, establishing a clear link between children's gender cognitions and behavior has been challenging (Martin & Ruble, 2004). Some researchers have found that children engage in sex-differentiated play before they are able to label themselves or others by gender (Caldera, Huston, & O'Brien, 1989). These findings suggest that children self-label after integrating the cognitive and social information in their environment. However, other researchers contend that self-labeling is an early step in understanding gender and might indicate that a child is beginning to think about the world and behave differently (Maccoby, 1998).

Children are able to label the gender of others early in life. In a study of 2-year-olds, Fagot (1985b) found that most children could accurately label the gender in photographs and answer related questions. Furthermore, boys and girls were equally able to label male and female photographs (Leinbach & Fagot, 1986). Boys who could not provide accurate gender labels played with dolls at roughly equal rates to girls' rates, whereas boys who could accurately label gender rarely played with dolls (Leinbach & Fagot, 1986). This finding suggests that a child's understanding of gender identity and understanding of the gender categorization of toys (e.g., dolls are for girls and action figures are for boys) influences sex-differentiated play.

Gender labeling may also relate to choice of playmates and play patterns. Fagot, Leinbach, and Hagan (1986) found that children who accurately gender labeled headshot photographs played with same-sex playmates significantly more often than did children who could not accurately gender-label the photographs. Moreover, girls who accurately labeled were less aggressive than girls who inaccurately labeled. In a longitudinal study of children aged 18 to 27 months, Fagot and Leinbach (1989) found no differences in play preferences between children who would eventually become early or later labelers. However, at 27 months, when half the children were able to correctly gender label photographs, distinct features emerged in their play. Early labeling boys and girls engaged in more sex-typed toy play, and early labeling girls showed lower levels of aggression and engaged in more communication with adults.

The presence of older children, parenting practices, and the provision of sex-typed toys might also affect children's gender identity and play preferences. For example, some parents encourage stereotyped play through the purchase of certain toys and encouragement in certain play activities (Leaper, 2002; Maccoby, 1998). Thus, preference tests might reflect the current socialization context as much as the child's level of cognitive processing. Future research should further explore how socialization influences might mediate the relationship between children's gender cognition and behavior.

The Developmental Sequence of Play and Gender Identity

Children's developing gender identity is also related to the developmental sequence of their play behaviors. Smilansky (1968) suggested a straightforward system for coding the developmental levels of play:

- *Functional play*: repetitive muscle movements, the main goal of which is the movement of an object
- *Constructive play*: making something from objects
- *Dramatic play*: role-playing or engaging in make-believe or pretend play
- *Games with rules*: recognizing, accepting, and conforming to preestablished rules.

Aside from functional play, all other types of play show the influence of children's developing gender identity. For example, boys are more likely to engage in constructive play (Rubin, Watson, & Jambor, 1978), though that may result from the type of toys available to boys and girls in play settings. Dramatic play increases during the preschool years, with boys and girls taking on very different roles; in particular, boys' pretend play often involves danger, combat, and heroic themes, whereas girls' pretend play often involves social, domestic, and familial themes (Maccoby, 1998). Maccoby also suggested that children experience different "cultures" as they grow up, gender differences in play being one illustration of this. Gender segregation, to which we turn next, is another important aspect of these gender cultures.

Outcomes of the Gender Identity Process

Gender Segregation

Gender segregation begins early and persists throughout the human life span. In most cultures, it is practiced beginning at age 3, although preschools in industrialized countries are rarely organized with the aim of promoting gender segregation. Thus, because gender segregation precedes gender-labeling for some children (Maccoby, 1988), it could be considered both an outcome and a cause of sex stereotyping. The psychological literature is highly speculative concerning the origins of gender-segregated play, which might include sex-differentiated play preferences, sex-differentiated peer socialization influences, and cognitive factors (Maccoby, 1998).

One theory, the behavioral compatibility hypothesis, suggests that children sort themselves into sex-segregated groups in pursuit of different interests and behavioral styles (Goodenough, 1934). There is clear evidence of differences in play preferences, with boys' play often involving more rough-and-tumble play and girls' play involving more collaborative discourse (Maccoby, 2002).

Although individual play preferences are meaningful in many ways, researchers have begun to stress the importance of group-level analyses (Fabes, Martin, & Hanish, 2004; Maccoby, 2002). Researchers have found that same-sex playgroups were more cooperative than mixed-sex playgroups; that socially skilled children chose to play with other socially skilled children, regardless of sex; and that girls in same-sex playgroups were more socially skilled than boys in same-sex playgroups (Serbin, Moller, Powlishta, & Gulko, 1991). These researchers suggested that gender segregation might be related to different behavioral styles rather than to specific toy and activity preferences.

The peer context of play highlights the complexities of examining children's gender segregation. When examining children in same-, other-, and mixed-sex peer groups, other researchers) found that children rarely play exclusively with the other sex, but spent a substantial amount of time playing in mixed-sex playgroups (Fabes et al., 2003). In same-sex playgroups, however, they found that sex differences were exaggerated. In addition, a psychologist found that preschool-aged children responded and changed their behaviors at the instigation of same-sex (but not other-sex) peers (Fagot, 1985a). One explanation for how peer groups influence gender typed behavior has been coined the social dosage effect (Martin & Fabes, 2001): the more children play with same-sex peers, the more they will be influenced by these interactions.

There are also noticeable differences in peer group reactions to cross-gender interactions. Girls who attempt to participate in cross-gender activities are, at worst, ignored (Fagot, 1977; Maccoby, 1988). Boys who attempt to participate in cross-gender activities often receive negative feedback from both boys and girls (Fagot, 1977, 1989). Children's maintenance of gender-group boundaries and issues of power and status are also important in understanding gender segregation and its consequences (Leaper, 1994; Maccoby, 1998).

Regarding the influence of cognitive processes, gender labeling might influence gender segregation (Fagot, 1990). In addition, children (ages 40–81 months old) who had more gender-typed beliefs were more likely to prefer same-sex playmates (Martin, Fabes, Evans, & Wyman, 1999). However, gender labeling and gender-typed schemas were unrelated to gender segregation in younger children with a median age of 35 months (Moller & Serbin, 1996). Thus, cognitive processes are intertwined with socialization influences in ways that affect the gender segregation process.

Gender and Aggression

The level and use of direct aggression, particularly physical aggression, remains one of the most consistently reported play differences in boys and girls. A review of observational studies of aggression found that boys were more aggressive than girls in 67% of the studies (Maccoby & Jacklin, 1974). When this review was reclassified into three age groups (infancy–4, 5–12, and 13 and older), the review author observed that age strongly influenced sex differences in aggression (Block, 1976). Reliable sex differences were present in 37% of the youngest age group, 47% of the grade-school age group, and 57% of the adolescent age group. Similar to these findings, an extensive study of cross-cultural differences in aggression found male aggression increased from infancy through school age (Whiting & Edwards, 1988).

Cultures differ greatly in the level of aggression that children show, but in almost all cultures, boys use more direct techniques to obtain their goals than girls, whereas girls tend to use indirect or relational aggression with peers, such as social exclusion, spreading gossip, and trying to get others to dislike a peer (Crick, Casas, & Mosher, 1997). An observational study of preschoolers found that girls displayed more relational aggression than boys and that all children received more relational aggression from girls than from boys (Ostrov & Keating, 2004). Thus, the sex differences found in aggression might result from differences in the ways that boys and girls communicate their aggression.

One explanation for sex differences in the expression of aggression is that teachers often perpetuate children's sex-stereotypic behavior by reacting differently to assertive and communicative behaviors of boys and girls. On the one hand, researchers found no differences in the frequency or duration of 14-month-old boys' and girls' attempts to communicate or to assert themselves (Fagot, Hagan, Leinbach, & Kronsberg, 1985). On the other hand, teachers responded very differently to boys and girls: They responded to girls' communication attempts more often than to boys' communication attempts and responded to girls' tentative attempts to communicate. However, boys had to use more forceful approaches before teachers would respond. Teachers responded positively and supportively to girls' attempts to communicate, but responded negatively to or diverted boys' attempts to communicate. Moreover, they responded to 10% of girls' assertive behaviors as compared with responding to 41% of boys' assertive behaviors. As toddlers, these children were observed to show sex differences in their behavior, with girls communicating more with adults whereas boys were more aggressive.

Gender and Emotion

Children's gender identity and play styles might also have lasting effects on their emotional expression. Researchers have found that high levels of pretend play in childhood were associated with a high level of regulation of emotion and emotional competence with peers for girls, but not boys (Lindsey & Colwell, 2003). Conversely, they found that physical play was associated with boys', not girls', emotional competence. These findings suggest that emotional competence may be differentially embedded within the play context, with girls' emotional development being intertwined with play activities that involve pretend play and emotional connectedness with peers. Girls as young as age 3 master the interpretation of others' emotional states more readily than boys of the same age (Peterson & Biggs, 2001).

The focus on emotions in the play of girls may partially explain sex differences in depression rates in adolescence and adulthood. Compared to boys, girls have higher levels and sharper increases in emotional behaviors such as depression and anxiety from childhood to adolescence (Angold, Erkanli, Silberg, Eaves, & Costello, 2002). Girls' play preferences and emotional connectedness to peers might make them more vulnerable to such negative emotions as a reaction to stress or relationship problems.

Thus, although the sociocultural environment gives children different messages concerning aggression, emotion, and appropriate means of communicating, children also construct different cognitive schemata regarding the appropriateness of some behaviors. One consequence of this is that, when boys and girls engage in pretend play, boys' play is more likely to have aggressive content, even during cooperative play. These play differences early in life may have consequences for the ways that boys and girls interact in friendships and as intimate partners.

Gender and Intimacy

One concern with gender segregation throughout childhood is that boys and girls will meet in adolescence as virtual strangers, having learned different interaction and coping styles as well as different social skills. Researchers have characterized girls' friendships as more intimate than boys' friendships, which may lead to differing views about relationship intimacy (Leaper & Anderson, 1997). A longitudinal study found that boys and girls differentially interpreted the same pattern of interactions, with girls interpreting negative peer interactions as meaning that peers do not like them, and boys interpreting negative peer interactions as positive Fagot (1994).

Although cross-sex friendships exist throughout childhood, after preschool, they are often hidden from the peer group and occur within the confines of homes or neighborhoods (Gottman, 1994). Such friendships tend to be intense and emotional. Whereas same-sex friendships can be used to work through difficulties, cross-sex friendships offer a different quality to discussions. Boy pairs appear to deal with fears by using mastery that they mediate through fantasy or humor, whereas boy–girl pairs combat fear by using emotional support that they mediate through comfort, soothing, and love. Girl pairs do not seem to discuss fear as much as boys, in part because boys often introduce the fearful topic. When girl pairs discuss fear, they use reassurance to comfort each other.

Conclusion

For many children, childhood is not as gender-segregated as it appears from surveys of school data. Although boys and girls spend a significant amount of time playing with both sexes (Fabes, Martin, & Hanish, 2003), little is known about whether children who have cross-sex friendships are more able to interact with the opposite sex throughout life. There appear to be long-term consequences to the different play styles that develop within boys' and girls' peer groups. However, it is difficult to untangle the etiology of these processes. Do boys and girls segregate because they prefer different styles of play, or does segregation cause the different styles? Does boys' aggression drive girls away and force them to separate? It is likely that all of these explanations have some merit, but we know for certain that the development of gender schemata is intertwined with play and other forms of communication throughout childhood.

Acknowledgments

Much of the research discussed was supported by the following grants to Beverly Fagot (now deceased): HD19739, National Institute of Child Health and Human Development, U.S. PHS; BNS 8615868, National Science Foundation; and MH37911, National Institute of Mental Health, U.S. PHS. This chapter is a revised version of B. J. Fagot & L. D. Leve (1998). Gender identity and play. In D. P. Fromberg & D. Bergen (Eds.), *Play from birth to twelve and beyond: Contexts, perspectives, and meanings* (pp. 187–192) New York: Garland.

References

Angold, A., Erkanli, A., Silberg, J., Eaves, L., & Costello, E. J. (2002). Depression scale scores in 8–17-year-olds: Effects of age and gender. *Journal of Child Psychology & Psychiatry & Allied Disciplines, 43,* 1052–1063.

Block, J. H. (1976). Issues, problems, and pitfalls in assessing sex differences: A critical review of "The psychology of sex differences." *Merrill-Palmer Quarterly, 22,* 283–308.

Caldera, H. J., Huston, A. C., & O'Brien, M. (1989). Social interactions and play patterns of parents and toddlers with feminine, masculine, and neutral toys. *Child Development, 60,* 70–76.

Crick, N. R., Casas, J. F., & Mosher, M. (1997). Relational and overt aggression in preschool. *Developmental Psychology, 33,* 579–588.

Fabes, R. A., Martin, C. L., & Hanish, L. D. (2003). Young children's play qualities in same-, other-, and mixed-sex peer groups. *Child Development, 74,* 921–932.

Fabes, R. A., Martin, C. L., & Hanish, L. D. (2004). The next 50 years: Considering gender as a context for understanding young children's peer relationships. *Merrill-Palmer Quarterly, 50,* 260–273.

Fagot, B. I. (1977). Consequences of moderate cross-gender behavior in preschool children. *Child Development, 48,* 902–907.

Fagot, B. I. (1985a). Beyond the reinforcement principle: Another step toward understanding sex roles. *Developmental Psychology, 21,* 1097–1104.

Fagot, B. I. (1985b). Changes in thinking about early sex role development. *Developmental Review, 5,* 83–89.

Fagot, B. I. (1989). Cross-gender behavior and its consequences for boys. *Italian Journal of Clinical and Cultural Psychology, 1,* 79–84.

Fagot, B. I. (1990, April). A longitudinal study of gender segregation: Infancy to preschool. In E Strayer (Chair), *Determinants of gender differences in peer relations.* Symposium conducted at the International Conference for Infant Studies, Montreal, Canada.

Fagot, B. I. (1994). Gender role learning and preschool education. In T. Husen & T. N. Postlewaite (Eds.), *International encyclopedia of education* (pp. 2449–2452). Oxford, UK: Pergamon.

Fagot, B. I., Hagan, R., Leinbach, M. D., & Kronsberg, S. (1985). Differential reactions to assertive and communicative acts of toddler boys and girls. *Child Development, 56,* 1499–1505.

Fagot, B. I., & Leinbach, M. D. (1989). The young child's gender schema: Environmental input, internal organization. *Child Development, 60,* 663–672.

Fagot, B. I., & Leinbach, M. D. (1993). Gender-role development in young children: From discrimination to labeling. *Developmental Review, 13,* 203–224.

Fagot, B. I., Leinbach, M. D., & Hagan, R. (1986). Gender labeling and the adoption of sex-typed behaviors. *Developmental Psychology, 22,* 440–443.

Goodenough, F (1934). *Developmental psychology: An introduction to the study of human behavior.* New York: Appleton-Century.

Gottman, J. M. (1994). Why can't men and women get along? In D. Canary & L. Stafford (Eds.), *Communication and relational maintenance* (pp. 203–229). San Diego, CA: Academic.

Leaper, C. (1994). Exploring the consequences of gender segregation on social relationships. In C. Leaper (Ed.), *Child gender segregation: Causes and consequences* (pp. 67–86). San Francisco: Jossey-Bass.

Leaper, C. (2002). Parenting girls and boys. In M. H. Bornstein (Ed.), *Handbook of parenting: Vol. 1. Children and parenting* (2nd ed., pp. 127–152). Mahwah, NJ: Erlbaum.

Leaper, C., & Anderson, K. J. (1997). Gender development and heterosexual romantic relationships during adolescence. In S. Shulman & W. A. Collins (Eds.), *Romantic relationships in adolescence: Developmental perspectives* (pp. 85–103). San Francisco: Jossey-Bass.

Leinbach, M. D., & Fagot, B. 1. (1986). Acquisition of gender labeling: A test for toddlers. *Sex Roles, 15,* 655–666.

Lindsey, E. W., & Colwell, M. J. (2003). Preschoolers' emotional competence: Links to pretend and physical play. *Child Study Journal, 33,* 39–52.

Maccoby, E. E. (1988). Gender as a social category. *Developmental Psychology, 24,* 755–765.

Maccoby, E. E. (1998). *The two sexes: Growing up apart, coming together.* Cambridge, MA: Harvard University Press.

Maccoby, E. E. (2002). Gender and group process: A developmental perspective. *Current Directions in Psychological Science, 11,* 54–58.

Maccoby, E. E., & Jacklin, C. N. (1974). *The psychology of sex differences.* Stanford, CA: Stanford University Press.

Martin, C. L., & Fabes, R. A. (2001). The stability and consequences of young children's same-sex peer interactions. *Developmental Psychology, 37,* 431–446.

Martin, C. L., Fabes, R. A., Evans, S. M., & Wyman, H. (1999). Social cognition on the playground: Children's beliefs about playing with girls versus boys and their relations to sex-segregated play. *Journal of Social & Personal Relationships, 16,* 751–771.

Martin, C. L., & Ruble, D. (2004). Children's search for gender cues: Cognitive perspectives on gender development. *Current Directions in Psychological Science, 13,* 67–70.

Moller, L. C., & Serbin, L. A. (1996). Antecedents of toddler gender segregation: Cognitive consonance, gender-typed toy preferences and behavioral compatibility. *Sex Roles, 35,* 445–460.

Ostrov, J. M, & Keating, C. F. (2004). Gender differences in preschool aggression during free play and structured interactions: An observational study. *Social Development, 13,* 255–277.

Peterson, C., & Biggs, M. (2001). "I was really, really, really mad!" Children's use of evaluative devices in narrative emotional events. *Sex Roles, 45,* 801–825.

Rubin, K., Watson, K., & Jambor, T. (1978). Free-play behaviors in preschool and kindergarten children. *Child Development, 49,* 534–536.

Serbin, L. A., Moller, L., Powlishta, K., & Gulko, J. (1991, April). The emergence of gender segregation and behavioral compatibility in toddlers' peer preferences. In C. Leaper (Chair), *Gender differences in relationships.* Symposium conducted at the Society for Research in Child Development, Seattle, WA.

Smilansky, S. (1968). *The effects of sociodramatic play on disadvantaged preschool children.* New York: Wiley.

Whiting, B. B., & Edwards, C. P. (1988). *Children of different worlds: The formation of social behavior.* Cambridge, MA: Harvard University Press.

6

Play as the Language of Children's Feelings

GARRY LANDRETH, LINDA HOMEYER, AND MARY MORRISON

Children possess the capacity for experiencing emotions with great feeling and intensity. When they hurt, they hurt all over. When they are happy, they are completely happy. Children are not able, however, to use a verbal language to adequately express the depth or range of these feelings. Their natural language of communication is play and it is through this medium that they express their emotional reactions. Play is a form of self-expression and symbolic play is a vehicle for expressing feelings; humor also plays an important role in play. These expressions occur within the important limits and boundaries of play relationships. In many ways, therefore, the various dimensions of play also facilitate children's emotional growth and development.

Children are people too, and experience the same kinds of feelings as adults. The difference is in the way they express those feelings. Typically, children lack the verbal facility to express adequately the range of emotional reactions they experience. However, when provided the opportunity in a safe environment, they will communicate the depth of their feelings through play, which is the most natural thing children do. Children do not talk out their concerns and feelings; they play them out.

Play Is the Child's Self-Expression

When adults observe and clinically analyze children's behaviors, play emerges as the unique, singular, central activity of childhood, occurring at all times and in all places; it is the medium through which children project the dimensions of their personalities. The distinctive characteristics of play are described by Freud (1925/1958): "every child at play behaves like an imaginative writer, in that he (sic) creates a world of his own or, more truly, he arranges the things of this world and orders it in a new way that pleases him better" (p. 45). Thus, through play, children express all parts of the self that exist and that they experience at the moment. Expression of only a part of the self would not be self-expression. Play enables children to express themselves completely, without reservation or fear of reprisal, because children at play feel safe. Nothing is held back. This total expression of self through play is described by Landreth (2002) as a process in which children discharge energy, express emotions and thoughts, prepare for life's duties, exert their will, achieve difficult goals, and relieve frustrations.

Everything the child is, does, and becomes may at one time or another be demonstrated through play. Children use toys and materials to express what they cannot verbalize, do things they would otherwise feel uncomfortable doing, and express feelings they might be reprimanded for verbalizing. These expressions of self and the accompanying feelings are played out but not planned out by the child. They occur spontaneously and creatively as the child experiences the freedom inherent in play that is devoid of the trappings of adult-imposed structure. A child's play cannot always be understood on the basis of logic and reality.

Since play is the child's expression of self, the child's play must be understood from the child's frame of reference. Play represents the child's symbolic language of self-expression and can reveal the child's past experiences, reactions to those experiences, feelings about what was experienced, the child's wants and needs, and the child's perception of self (Landreth, 2002). Play can be viewed as the process through which the total self of the child is created, expressed, and recreated.

Symbolic Expression in Play

Play is the child's symbolic language of self-expression, and the symbolism represented in play can be likened to a container of the child's emotions. Piaget (1962) proposed that, through play, children deal in a sensorimotor way with concrete objects that are symbols for something else they have experienced directly or indirectly. Play represents the attempt of children to organize or cope with their experiences. That children unconsciously express happenings, experiences, concerns, and problems in their play can readily be seen in the following case. Six-year-old Brenda had to wear a catheter as a result of complications following surgery. She experienced considerable difficulty in trying to empty the bag appropriately and make the necessary connections to put it back in place. The connections were always leaking and that caused her a great deal of frustration and embarrassment. In her play, she repeatedly played out a story using the doll house and depicting a problem with a leaky sink or some related plumbing problem. With great exasperation, she would call a plumber to come and fix the plumbing. She stopped acting out these scenes when she learned to attach the catheter bag correctly.

Play gives concrete form and expression to the unverbalized inner world of children which may be too frightening for children to express directly. Therefore, a major function of play is the changing through symbolic representation of what may be unmanageable in reality to manageable situations. Telling adults about being abused or even using dolls to act out the abuse experience may be much too threatening to traumatized children. However, when children feel safe and are allowed to direct their own play, they will distance themselves from the frightening or threatening experience by selecting toys that symbolically represent the individuals in the real-life experience. Feelings associated with the experience can then safely emerge and be expressed through the play. This symbolic representation was observed in the case of 5-year-old Jackie, who acted out his abuse and accompanying feelings of helplessness and anger by having an alligator puppet swallow a small child figure. He then smashed the alligator with a mallet many times with obvious anger, and gleefully buried the alligator in the sandbox, announcing, "There, that takes care of him!" In this acting-out process, toys are like the child's words and play is the language of expression. Thus Jackie expressed a great deal more intensity of emotion than his words would indicate.

From a psychoanalytic perspective, authors describe play as reflecting inner life, tensions, and the child's response to life's challenges (Solnit, Cohen, & Neubauer, 1993). They view play as allowing children to review their current situation, explore new possibilities, experiment with new solutions, and develop new integrations. Play allows children to experience being in control of that which they may not be able to control in reality. Since children do not easily express their emotions verbally, play enables the child to master the conflict or trauma therefore providing the child with pleasure and relief from internal pressures (Freud, 1905/1960).

The process of play provides healing from hurts, releases emotions, dissolves tension, and gives vent to pent-up urges toward self-expression. The activity of play is one of the most important ways in which children learn that they can safely express their feelings without reprisal or rejection from others (Sweeney, 1997). By acting out a frightening or traumatic experience or situation symbolically, releasing and expressing associated pent-up feelings, and by returning to that event again and again through play and perhaps changing or reversing the outcome in play activity, the child moves toward an inner resolution and then is better able to cope with or adjust to the problem. Through this process of self-expression in play, children resolve conflicts and liberate themselves from overwhelming feelings by reconstructing the conflictual experiences and expressing their feelings in symbolic play.

This process of symbolic representation was readily observed in the play of 5-year-old Trisha, who witnessed her 6-month-old baby brother stop breathing, turn blue, and die in her mother's arms. Following this experience, Trisha repeatedly placed her arm beside her mother's arm and compared their color, remarking, "I'm darker than you." Indeed, she was darker than her mother, having inherited the dark skin of a father she had never seen. This was Trisha's way of expressing her fear of dying, which was very real for her because her skin was darker than her mother's. In play therapy, Trisha repeatedly acted out a scene of an airplane crashing and burning, followed by her arranging small cars around a small box. Her words as she described her activity did not indicate any particular fear or anxiety, but her play behavior certainly did. To the play therapist, the airplane crashing and burning represented bodies burning, turning dark like Trisha's skin, and the cars arranged around the box represented Trisha's enactment of a funeral and a coffin. This was undoubtedly a scene of fear and anxiety. Such free play allows the expression of feelings and attitudes that have been waiting to be released. Once these feelings are expressed, children can deal with them in ways that are more emotionally healthy. Symbolic play provides a safe vehicle for children to express emotions, since the emotion itself or the target of the emotion is disguised through the symbolism.

How Children Express Feelings in Play

Children use play to express how they feel about themselves and their world, both their current perceptions and how they would like it to be. Children use play to relax tension and anxiety, discharge aggression, express conflict, and turn the unmanageable into the manageable (Sweeney, 1997). Play also expresses delight, joy, surprise, and contentment.

As children play, they express and experience their emotions (Landreth, 2002). Children externalize their feelings through play, thus experiencing feelings in the more concrete form of the substance of play. As children control the substance and direction of their play, they develop a sense of mastery and control. In the above example, Trisha was able to express her fear of death through her play. She was also able to work through her understanding of her baby brother's death and the funeral that followed and since her words did not indicate the fear and anxiety she was obviously experiencing it was imperative for her to have the opportunity to play out her true feelings

Children purposively select play media to express their feelings and emotions. For this reason it is appropriate for them to have access to a wide variety of toys. They can easily express nurturing play, for example, through the use of baby dolls, bottles, and blankets. Many children express nurturing toward self and others through cooking and feeding, so pots, pans, spoons, cups, plates, and the like are useful. Plastic food items are helpful, but not necessary; children thoroughly enjoy cooking with sand, water, or both, and serve the results with complete genuineness.

Many of these nurturing toys are useful for the child who needs to regress to an earlier age. Kevin, age 3 years, played out how he felt about his newly arrived baby brother. While cooking himself muffins of sand and water, Kevin sucked on a baby bottle. He was expressing his desire to be like a baby again, to receive special attention, and to have his every need met.

Children have expressed aggressive feelings through dinosaurs, wild animals, rubber knives, a bop bag, toy soldiers, and musical instruments. Cardboard blocks are also useful for this purpose. Building a tower and repeatedly knocking it over can be a very satisfying, and appropriate, way for an angry child to express self. As children use these toys to shoot, bite, hit, and stab, they can release their aggressive feelings, allowing the child to move toward more self-enhancing, positive feelings.

Medical equipment with doctor and nurse figures allow children to confront fears and concerns about doctors, medical procedures, and hospitalizations. Children also use the doctor's medical kit for healing and nurturing play.

Children who have had the freedom to express strong negative emotions typically move on to express more positive feelings. This seems to be largely the result of feelings having become more clear after repeated expressions in play; subsequently, feelings of confidence and courage can emerge (Moustakas, 1959). Often the stressors in children's lives may not have changed, but when they experience the opportunity to express themselves through the natural medium of play communication, they are able to move on to other healthy and age-appropriate uses of play.

Sociodramatic Play

In sociodramatic play the child uses toys and other items as props to assist in the acting out of specific roles and a wide variety of experiences (Calabrese, 2003). Role-playing allows children to enter the world of the adult and portray situations that they may not completely understand. During sociodramatic play children are in control of the content, may assume any number of roles, and change the outcome, while simultaneously experiencing the various feelings and levels of intensity attached to each. Roles that children select may be the opposite of their own personality. This allows children the opportunity to break out of the limitations that confine them in reality and to experience the expression of a much wider range of feelings (Landreth, 1993). An aggressive child may take the part of a caring and gentle caretaker; a confident, outgoing child may play the role of a quiet, much younger child; a compliant child may take the role of a bossy older sibling. Such reversals are quite common in children's play. Role reversal allows the observer an open window into children's perception of their world. While children generally exaggerate personality characteristics during role reversal, they clearly communicate how they feel about that person (Hughes, 1991). Thus, one might observe in children's play a teacher who belittles or a parent who shames.

In addition to developmental purposes, sociodramatic play serves a major function in the emotional/feeling development of children. Research indicates that the benefits of role-playing for children include a greater sense of happiness, ability to self-regulate, sensitivity, and emotional awareness (Elias & Berk, 2002).

Sociodramatic pretending allows children to act out various relationship roles, switching easily from one role to another. Or, as children interact with assumed roles, they are able to experience emotional responses to each role and can decide to continue in that role, change the role, or select an entirely different role. This process also develops problem-solving skills as children review the current situation, explore other possibilities, try out new solutions, and select the one that fits best (Solnit et al., 1993).

Testing Limits as a Way of Expressing Feelings

An often misunderstood area of feeling expression in play is children's use of limit-testing behavior. The innate growth potential in children cannot be fully maximized in settings where children feel insecure. Limits on behavior provide a structure to the environment and the relationship in which children can feel secure. When there are no boundaries and limitations on behavior, children feel insecure and often experience feelings of anxiety; they feel neither safe nor accepted. Some children have difficulty controlling their own impulsiveness and so need the security of limits, which provide them with an opportunity to gain control of their own behavior and promote feelings of self-acceptance and adequacy. Limits, therefore, help to assure the emotional security of children. When children discover where the boundaries are in a relationship or setting and experience consistent adherence to those boundaries, they feel secure because there is predictability (Landreth, 2002).

When children push the boundaries or attempt to break established limits in a play relationship, they may, among other things, be expressing feelings of anxiety, fear, anger, insecurity, or in effect expressing a need for consistency and predictability in their lives. Another possibility is that they are expressing a need to feel accepted and are attempting to find out if the person they are is accepted in spite of their behavior. When viewed in this context, a child's attempt to shoot the adult with a dart gun or hit the adult with a block takes on an entirely new dimension, one that calls for the adult's understanding of the child's feeling rather than the typical attempt to stop the behavior. Some children can only be certain of the adult's unconditional acceptance by testing the adult with the most unacceptable aspects of their personality.

Humor in Play

Although some early work addressed humor (e.g., Freud, 1925/1958, 1905/1960), until recently children's humor was not a major area of study. However, research now indicates that children select various forms of humor according to their developmental level (Socha & Kelly, 1994). Severely abused and neglected children often must be taught to play and do not use humor until later stages of therapy (Allan, 1988). Conversely, children who are more advanced in the development of humor have been found to be more talkative, have larger vocabularies, and have the ability to be more expressive (Cohen, 1987); thus, these children are more likely to express a wide range of feelings in their play. Some researchers have found that children's humor increased self-control, enabled children to indirectly deal with difficulties and feelings, maximized positive feelings, minimized negative feelings, and reduced anxiety and fear (Tower & Singer, 1980). These results are readily observable in children's play.

Children use humor in many of the same ways they use play and often in conjunction with play as a means through which to express other feelings. Children may use humor with others in the midst of play to provide a buffer between self and another person or experience they find uncomfortable or embarrassing. Aggressive humor is used in play by children to release tension and allow emotional relief, thus developing the ability to control aggressive impulses.

Infectious laughter, group glee, and the spontaneous eruption of laughter among children at play are delightful to witness. Group glee may begin with one child or all the children at the same time. A wave of giggles, often accompanied by jumping up and down and hand clapping, usually lasts only 9 or 10 seconds (Garvey, 1977). This group experience of being in tune with each other and resonating with the same emotion provides children with opportunities for expressing deep emotional satisfaction that comes from emotional identification with others.

The child's world is a world of great emotional intensity and diverse feelings that can only be fully expressed through their spontaneously generated play. Left to their own devices, children will play, for that is their most natural form of intrinsic expression. Whether or not the meaning of their play is important is not dependent on the understanding of observers. When adults do not interfere, children play out feelings and reactions in the ways they choose. This playing out process is a natural coping mechanism for children, which allows them to release and explore emotions in a step-by-step process as they feel safe to do so. Therefore, not interfering with children's play is perhaps the most caring and sensitive thing adults can do.

References

Allan, J. (1988). *Inscapes of the child's world: Jungian counseling in schools and clinics*. Dallas, TX: Spring.

Calabrese, M. (2003). Developing quality sociodramatic play for young children. *Education 123* (3), 606–610.

Cohen, D. (1987). *The development of play*. New York: New York University Press.

Elias, C. L., & Berk, L. E. (2002). Self-regulation in young children: Is there a role for sociodramatic play? Early *Childhood Research Quarterly 17*(2), 216–238.

Freud, S. (1958). The relation of the poet to daydreaming. In B. Nelson (Ed.) and J. Riviere (Trans.), *On creativity and the unconscious* (pp. 44–54). New York: Harper & Row. (Original work published 1925)

Freud, S. (1960). *Jokes and their relation to the unconscious.* New York: Norton. (Original work published 1905)

Garvey, C. (1977). *Play.* Cambridge, MA: Harvard University Press.

Hughes, F. P. (1991). *Children, play, and development.* Boston: Allyn & Bacon.

Landreth, G. (1993). Self-expressive communication. In C. Schaefer (Ed.), *Therapeutic Powers of Play* (pp. 41–63). Northvale, NJ: Jason Aronson.

Landreth, G. (2002). *Play therapy: The art of the relationship.* Muncie, IN: Accelerated Development.

Lee, A. C. (1997). Psychoanalytic play therapy. In K. J. O'Connor & L. M. Braverman (Eds.), *Play therapy theory and practice and comparative presentation* (pp. 46–78). New York: Wiley.

Moustakas, C. (1959). *Psychotherapy with children.* New York: Harper & Row.

Piaget, J. (1962). *Play, dreams, and imitation in childhood.* New York: Routledge.

Socha, T. J., & Kelly, B. (1994). Children making "fun": Humorous communication, impression management, and moral development. *Child Study Journal, 24*(3).

Solnit, A., Cohen, D., & Neubauer, P. (1993). Introduction. In A. Solnit, D. Cohen, & P. Neubauer (Eds.), *The many meanings of play: A psychoanalytic perspective* (pp. 1–5). New Haven, CT: Yale University Press.

Sweeney, D. S. (1997). *Counseling children through the world of play.* Eugene, OR: Wipf and Stock..

Tower, R. B., & Singer, J. L. (1980). Imagination, interest, and joy in early childhood: Some theoretical considerations and empirical findings. In P. E. McGee & A. J. Chapman (Eds.), *Children's humor* (pp. 27–58). New York: Wiley.

7

Play in the Context of Life-Span Human Development

Thinking about play in the context of life-span human development requires one to examine play not only in childhood and adolescence but throughout adulthood as well. Although scholars disagree on whether the play of children and leisure of adults have the same meanings, and, hence, whether they can even be compared, a life-span perspective would suggest that childhood play shapes later-life leisure and later-life leisure shapes childhood play

While theories of human development across the life span have roots in several different models or philosophies of human growth and behavior, such as mechanistic, organismic, contextual, and constructionist (Cavanaugh, 2004; Gubrium & Holstein, 1999; Lerner, 1998), a number of assumptions are common to life-span and life-course perspectives. Two of these assumptions are of special interest: (1) Development occurs continually from conception to death, and (2) development occurs in the interaction of internal (biological and psychological) and external (sociocultural and historical) factors and forces. Situating play in the context of life-span human development suggests that the forms and meanings of, and opportunities for, play must be conceptualized as dynamic. Play changes across time(s) as individuals construct, produce, and interact within their society, culture, and historical context.

Development as a Lifelong Process

The idea that development continues beyond the years of childhood and adolescence became a central assumption in the thinking of psychologists and sociologists in the United States in the mid-20th century. During this time, increased longevity led to older adults comprising a greater proportion of the population. The evidence from longitudinal studies suggested that adulthood was not simply a continuation or expansion of the same abilities and issues of childhood and youth (Featherman, 1983); rather, investigators identified developmental issues, changes, and tasks unique to the adult years and observed increasing differentiation within and heterogeneity among individuals.

The belief that development is a lifelong process raises a number of conceptual and philosophical issues. One of these is: Where is development anchored? To put the question in the context of this chapter: Does play in childhood or in end-of-life leisure primarily influence development and construction of meaning? What a life-span perspective suggests is that both early and later play shape development. The so-called stages of life are not discrete periods; rather, the developmental tasks and changes at any given point in life are influenced by experiences of the past, shaped by present experiences, and responsive to the future normative expectations of every age.

Development as an Interactive Process

The interactive process of growth is a second assumption common to life-span perspectives. As a greater proportion of individuals survived into the sixth and seventh decades, longitudinal studies became available. More sophisticated data analysis technologies evolved and scholars recognized that it was no longer appropriate to describe development solely in terms of internal processes or social forces. Rather, a life-span perspective required scholars to situate the active individual in sociocultural and historical contexts and to see human beings as both shaped by and shapers of their contexts; that is, as active agents who negotiate or construct their life course (Gubrium & Holstein, 1999). In addition, in order to understand development, researchers had to take into account both internal and external factors that suggested consideration of multiple types of time, including chronological age, historical time, and time of measurement (Schaie, 1994).

Chronological Age

Chronological age, or years since birth, represents an individual's capabilities or level of functioning. Chronological age marks maturation or the internal readiness of the individual to engage in activities; for example, to run, skip, communicate verbally, kick a ball, and understand riddles. Because there is the belief that chronological age is a marker of ability, it is also the standard for granting rights and privileges (both formal and informal) and assigning expectations and responsibilities. Chronological age is used as a marker, for example, when an individual tries to join a youth sports league; when others expect that one should share toys; or when others state that one is "too old" to play.

There are those, however, who question whether chronological age should be a marker of adult development (Giele, 1980) and whether patterns of age-related change can even be identified (Riegel, 1976). Today there is increasing flexibility in individual lives; for example, in decisions concerning if, when, and how work, spousal, and parental roles are taken on. This flexibility grows out of the increasing complexity and differentiation in society (e.g., in occupational roles because of economic and technological development; and in family roles because of the availability of birth control). It also is indicative of individuals' agency, that is, the extent to which individuals regulate and produce the direction of their development (Kleiber, 1999; Lerner & Busch-Rossnagel, 1981). Hence, development across adulthood is much less ordered and age-related than it once was (Giele, 1980). In fact, one psychologist maintains that development is not predictable and, at most, is probabilistic (Reigel, 1976).

Chronological age also indicates the birth cohort to which an individual belongs. The birth cohort represents historical time. It signifies when an individual is born and at what age individual members of the cohort group might experience various social events, changes, and opportunities. Researchers continue to document the importance of this factor for patterns of growth and development (Elder, Modell, & Parke, 1993). A woman who was born and went through school before Title IX, for example, is less likely to play sports or be involved in physical activities as an adult: lack of opportunity in childhood to develop needed motor skills during crucial developmental stages and attitudes against females' involvement in such activity would have kept her away from sports. Conversely, girls who entered school after Title IX was implemented in 1972 had new opportunities for play, growth, and development.

Measurement of Time

Time of measurement is the third type of time to consider from a life-span perspective. Time of measurement refers to current or contemporary time; that is, what is happening in the environment of an individual may have an impact on his or her behavior at the time a researcher observes or measures the behavior or activity. Media coverage of eating disorders among girls involved in gymnastics, for example, may cause some parents to discourage their daughters' pursuit of this sport, which subsequently affects girls' physical skill development and opportunity structure.

In sum, considering play in the context of life-span human development includes examining the influence of dynamic and interactive dimensions. This dynamism, however, does not mean that there is no continuity in development. In fact, scholarship suggests tremendous consistency in activities, identity, and personality across adulthood (Atchley, 1993; McCrae & Costa, 1988). One explanation for such continuity is that, with advancing age, individuals are increasingly aware of who they are and who they want to be, and of their likes and dislikes, strengths, and abilities.

The play and leisure activities in which people engage provide both a statement of and feedback for the self. While being expansive or experimenting with many different activities allows individuals to "figure out" and construct an identity, narrowing one's focus and sticking with familiar activities or experiences allows individuals to maintain a valued identity in the face of the changing abilities and opportunity structures that accompany aging. Hence, continuity is a means of adaptation. Further, there is an environmental pressure for consistency in self-presentation. People expect continuity from one another, because continuity of self helps others maintain their self-integrity (Atchley, 1993). In addition, some see too much change as an indication of an unstable, weak, or ill personality—a sign that the individual may need clinical treatment.

When looking at play in the context of life-span development, therefore, both change and continuity take place and influence its meanings, motivations, forms, and opportunities. While every age has its own lucid meanings and forms, some meanings and characteristics of play transcend age (Freysinger & Kelly, 2004; Kleiber, 1999).

Change and Continuity in Play's Meanings Across the Life Span

Those practices or activities that people commonly call play in childhood and youth, they typically refer to as leisure in adulthood. Many contend that this is an arbitrary distinction, as play and leisure share, or are defined by, several common dimensions. These dimensions include voluntariness, lack of necessity, or freedom of choice; personal expression or engagement; and motivation that is more intrinsic than extrinsic. In addition, individuals experience both play and leisure as enjoyable or pleasurable (Barnett, 1987; Freysinger & Kelly, 2004). These commonalities suggest that play and leisure are qualities of action, defined by how people do or experience something other than what they do or the time in which they do it.

There is no agreement, however, on the comparability of play and leisure. Conceiving of leisure as a relational practice, there are those who contend that the play of children and the leisure of adults cannot be compared and, in fact, exist in opposition to each other (Rojek, 1985). Behind this contention is a notion of the self as a construct of socialization; that is, the self develops in interactions with both specific (e.g., mother, father) and generalized (e.g., social institutions, such as school, work, social norms) others at a given time in history.

Many adults assume that children's play is selfless because children are selves in the making; openness, unpredictability, and volatility characterize children's play. According to this view, "Children can find literally anything to play with, and they return to it afresh again and again. This inventiveness is the inventiveness of selflessness. Under it, the whole world can inspire dizzy pleasure one moment, and harbour hectic anxiety the next" (Rojek, 1986, p. 174).

> While society allows children such license, there are expectations that adults highly monitor and control their play, and that it is thoroughly self-conscious or self-constructed. This view states that, in fact, adult leisure is organized to exclude the distinctive features of the child's play world

(formlessness, frankness, lack of seriousness, and irrationality) or, instead, to tolerate them only in their mimetic forms. The private self, that dominates modern leisure relations, engages in communal pursuits as a participant or a spectator. He [sic] always acts as an individual body, who is separate and distinct from others, with a life outside the leisure life. In the development of the self, the play world, with its exaggerated emotional polarities and pervasive sense of boundless immediacy is left behind. (Rojek, 1985, pp. 174–175)

That is, because adults are enculturated beings, selflessness is not possible in adulthood. The "play" of adults must be legitimated or permissible fun and pleasure (Freud, 1930/1979). And yet, "some of the most exciting and dangerous situations in adult leisure occur when social controls and discipline break down" (Freud, 1930/1979, p. 180) that is, when individuals manipulate or defy social rules so that selflessness may reemerge. This is consistent with studies of leisure meaning, which have found that high self-expression and low role constraint, or intrinsic motivation and a perception of freedom of choice, distinguish this type of leisure that is high in joy, pleasure, or positive affect. Scholars have labeled this type of experience "pure leisure" (Neulinger, 1981; Samdahl, 1988). It is pure, perhaps, because it comes closest to recapturing the selflessness of childhood play.

Change and Continuity in Life-Span Motivations for Play

Stability and change in motivations for play or leisure across the life span have been the focus of much research. A life-span perspective reveals that motivations are constructed in the interaction of the individual and her or his sociocultural and historical contexts. According to one viewpoint, as human societies become more civilized, life becomes increasingly routinized and predictable relative to the past (Elias & Dunning, 1969). Further, civilized societies expect humans to control the expression of strong, passionate emotions in everyday life, particularly in public settings, though others would argue that such control often extends into private realms of life as well (Foucault, 1983). Such lack of spontaneity and emotional expression results in feelings of monotony and leads to a sense of staleness or lifelessness. To restore "mental tonus" or vitality, adults need to experience; and release strong, passionate emotions, and society needs them to do so in safe and nondestructive ways. Within this context, "mimetic" leisure has developed as an outlet for the expression of excitement (Elias & Dunning, 1969). Rock concerts, spectator sports, theater, and Mardi Gras serve as examples of public contexts within which people can play and safely generate, experience, and resolve emotional tension or excitement.

Emotional Expression in Play

The control of emotional expression is very much age-related. In fact, it seems that one of the indicators of maturity or "being grown-up" is self-control. Self-control may well be antithetical to play and leisure, as both require an ability and willingness to step back or disengage from everyday reality in terms of social norms and expectations in order to express the self fully (Kleiber, 1999; Samdahl, 1988).

Other authors conceptualize leisure as varying according to the intensity of expressive involvement, with solitude being very low in expressive involvement and verbal or physical aggression, sexual activity, and competitive games and sports very high in expressive involvement (Gordon, Gaitz, & Scott, 1976). The social context sanctions the intensity of emotional expression and leisure motivations in terms of the attainment of goals or value themes, such as achievement, acceptance, compliance, and self-control. These value themes emerge out of a complex of culturally defined, idealized aspects of human life

Value themes intersect with stages of life, which emerge from the interaction of physical maturation, cognitive elaboration, social-role acquisitions and relinquishments, and economic resources across the life span.

Some researchers have found that engagement in highly expressive leisure activities declines with age (Gordon et al., 1976). However, while involvement in external (to the home), high-intensity activities ("sensual transcendence") decreased with age, participation in homebound, moderate-level activities, such as creative and developmental activity, remained stable across the age groups (Gordon et al., 1976). The cross-sectional design of this research and the point in time at which it took place (1969–1970) cautions application of the findings to today's adults because more recent research indicates that when the opportunity and support exist, older adults do participate in "high intensity" activities (Freysinger & Kelly, 2004). At the same time, it suggests the need for research that considers the historical embeddedness of play and leisure. Such a contextual approach to research has rarely been incorporated into the work of psychologists and sociologists in North America.

Age-Related and Gender Forces in Emotional Expression

A number of age-related forces may influence an individual's ability and willingness to engage in highly expressive leisure. On the individual level, there is the belief that a sense of basic trust in self and others lays the groundwork for security in self-expression (Erikson, 1963). An individual who has feelings of shame or inferiority that lead to exaggerated feelings of self-consciousness is likely to have a limited capacity for self-expression. In addition, on the social level, there are very real consequences for ignoring both formal and informal sanctions that control affective expression and behavior. For instance, there are formal laws defining what is a disturbance of the peace, as well as gender and age norms regarding appropriate emotional expression for females and males, the young and the old. Age, for example, is often a stronger basis for perceived acceptability of participation in a physical activity than skill, interest, or ability (Ostrow & Dzewaltowski, 1986). Therefore, expectations that older adults have of themselves (because of social norms during childhood as well as current attitudes and media images) and that others have of them influence both opportunity for and interest in participation in highly expressive leisure.

The intrinsic motivation possible for players is also age-related. Specifically, younger and single adults have reported that daily life is more dominated by extrinsically motivated experiences, while older, family-oriented adults report feeling more intrinsically motivated (Graef, Csikszentmihalyi, & Giannino, 1983). According to Kleiber (1999), there are both emergent and continuing motivational influences on the leisure chosen by individuals. The two are related because emergent motivation is often the source of continuing motivation. Emergent motivation is important up through young adulthood and evolves out of new environmental interaction. Continuing motivation develops out of interests that are pursued beyond those circumstances within which they were extrinsically rewarded. Thus, continuing motivation becomes progressively more important with age. A life-span perspective on human development offers some explanations for this difference in motivational orientation.

Both internal processes in the form of changing ego issues or psychosocial crises (Erikson, 1963) and external forces in the form of opportunity and age-related social roles (Riley & Riley, 1994) influence development. Many social roles (e.g., student, worker) function within a system of external sanctions and rewards that regulate entry into, performance in, and movement onto other social roles. The expectations attached to social roles may well mitigate against freedom of choice, spontaneity, and creativity; that is, against play and playfulness. Being a "good parent," for example, requires the ability to provide for the basic economic needs of the family and to defer gratification. To acquire and maintain employment, employers expect an individual to be predictable, responsible, and compliant.

That is, to prepare for adulthood and establish themselves as adults, individuals enact social roles that emphasize extrinsic rewards. Research has found, however, that emphasis on extrinsic motivators decreases intrinsic motivation, which subsequently negatively affects feelings of competence and psychological well-being or happiness. Investigators confirm, for example, that entry into school brings a decrease in creativity among children (Graef et al., 1983). As children progress through the educational system, motivation becomes increasingly extrinsic (Harter, 1981; Maehr, 1983). Hence, the challenge becomes "how to integrate deeply rewarding enjoyable feelings which usually are experienced in leisure settings into the fabric of everyday life" so that life is not "split into useless play and senseless work" (Maehr, 1983, p. 167).

Social roles are not the only factor shaping play or leisure and development across the life span. Psychosocial or ego development also influences this development. Given that the psychosocial issue of young adulthood is intimacy versus isolation (Erikson, 1963), for example, leisure interests are likely to include forms and contexts that are conducive to the establishment and maintenance of an intimate relationship with a significant other (Kelly & Godbey, 1992; Kleiber, 1999). Research with adults has found that affiliative or relational needs are central motivators for, and meanings of, leisure among adults 36 to 43 years of age (Freysinger, 1995).

There is a reorientation of motivation in middle and later adulthood that parallels the psychosocial crises of generativity versus stagnation and integrity versus despair (Erikson, 1963; Kleiber, 1999), as well as a greater tendency toward interiority (Neugarten, 1977). Extrinsic rewards, competitiveness, and a future orientation do not enhance successful adaptation in adulthood, as such motivations are antithetical to the development of generativity, integrity, and interiority. Leisure, however, may support such development.

One definition of leisure describes processes of subjective disengagement and engagement; that is, a stepping back from arbitrary or external demands, an opening up to possibility, and an engagement in more personally meaningful activity (Kleiber, 1999). Adults, for example, may be employed in routine, repetitive work with little responsibility. They may be highly dissatisfied with this situation but stay with it because they do not perceive that other options are available and they need the income to support a family. While finding little joy in their employment, they may develop and pursue an avocation that provides opportunities for creativity, personal expression, and a sense of competence and mastery (Freysinger, 1995). A father, for example, may find himself in middle adulthood estranged from his teenage son because he spent most of his time when he was younger working overtime or at two jobs in order to support his family; leisure becomes a way to establish a relationship with his son because it is a context for sharing interests (Freysinger, 1995). Therefore, leisure potentially has developmental value because it is both a means of adjusting to life as it is and a context for self-enhancement through the facilitation of intrinsic motivation or the realization of developmental issues (Kleiber, 1999). It is a context for escape from and adaptation to negative life events and the stress and challenges they present (Iwasaki & Schneider, 2003; Kimball & Freysinger, 2003; Kleiber, 1999).

Research on leisure motivations and satisfactions in adulthood reveal two continuous themes: affiliation or community and agency or self-determination (Freysinger, 1995; Kelly, Steinkamp, & Kelly, 1986; Kleiber, 1999). The theme of affiliation includes issues of social integration (e.g., development and maintenance of friendships), family affirmation and satisfaction, and development of children. Agency includes motivations for self-expression, learning and development, challenge and accomplishment, and recognition and credibility. Feeling connected with others and gaining and maintaining a sense of mastery and competence are not motivations exclusive to adulthood. They appear to be basic human motivations that are central motivations for play and leisure across the life span. However, the types or forms of activity that individuals pursue to realize these motivations are likely to change across the course of life; the forms of play are also powerfully shaped by gender, race/ethnicity, and social class as well as age. Further, individuals are not passive; that is, they do not simply accept social norms and customs. They also resist and challenge, and leisure is a context within which researchers have documented such resistance (Freysinger & Flannery, 1992; Shaw, 2001; Wearing, 1995).

Change and Continuity in Play Across the Life Span

In forms of play across the life span change and continuity are often difficult to identify because the form of activity may remain the same while the type of engagement and satisfactions sought in and motivations for the activity change. A young child, for example, may engage in sports for the fun of bodily movement and physical expression (Harris, 1994). With age, motivations may change to emulation of sports stars the child sees on cereal boxes and television commercials. In high school, motivation for participation in sports may be to gain status among peers and popularity with the opposite sex (Freysinger & Kelly, 2004). In college, sports are a source of scholarships, prestige, and perhaps career opportunities. In young adulthood the individual may join a recreational sports league to meet others in the new city where she or he moved for a first job. Parents may find that their children's involvement in sports may motivate their own continued involvement (Kleiber, 1999). In later life, participation may continue through Senior Olympics and master's games, which provide a sense of competence and mastery as well as social integration (Schreck, 1990). That is, one can maintain engagement in the same form of play or leisure, but how and why one participates may change.

Nonetheless, reiterating the theme of continuity and change, Kelly (1983) has proposed a core-and-balance model of leisure activity. His research suggests that a core of activities that remain fairly stable or consistent across the course of life characterizes individuals' leisure. Such activities tend to be convenient and inexpensive (e.g., reading the newspaper and watching television) and family and friend oriented (e.g., intimacy and socializing). At the same time, individuals report a balance of activities that change across the life span as time, interests, and abilities change because of shifting social roles, opportunities, developmental orientations, and physical aging. That is, change in forms of play and participation with age varies in relation to the type of activity. Research indicates that involvement in activities requiring physical skill and exertion (e.g., competitive and outdoor sports) levels off and then shows a gradual decline with age. It is not until late old age (over 75 years), though, that a marked decline is visible. Other research has found little difference or even increased involvement in certain types of activity with age (Freysinger & Ray, 1994; Smale & Dupuis, 1993). The cross-sectional design of most of this research makes any definite statements about change in level of activity participation impossible. It is clear, however, that certain factors influence change in the forms of play in which individuals engage across the course of life.

Health is an important factor shaping type and level of activity involvement. Health, not chronological age, is the key factor in physical activity participation across the life span (Kelly, Steinkamp, & Kelly, 1986). Previous experience also influences subsequent participation; that is, if individuals pursued a hobby as children, they are more likely to participate in that activity as adults. Most importantly, examining age within the context of other factors adds to an understanding of activity participation across the life span. In a longitudinal study of predictors of activity involvement in young and middle adulthood, for example, researchers found that previous involvement, such as high school activity, was not a significant predictor of activity participation for either women or men in young adulthood, but young adulthood activity involvement was a significant predictor of women's (but not men's) activity participation in middle adulthood (Freysinger & Ray, 1994).

In fact, research consistently has found that gender shapes forms of play and leisure in which individuals engage. There is disagreement as to why such differences exist. One explanation is that play and leisure differ by gender because the distribution of opportunities and power at all levels of society varies systematically by gender (Henderson, Bialeschki, Shaw, & Freysinger, 1996). This power differential leads to different experiences of self and social roles. In the family context, for example, while both women and men may be parents, gender influences how they enact the parental role and how they experience leisure.

For example, mothers more than fathers play with their children regardless of the children's age and their own employment status (Horna, 1989; Larson & Gillman, 1997); and fathers report a gain in parental satisfaction from sharing their leisure with children, while mothers do not (Freysinger, 1994). At the same time, even though mothers and fathers report similar goals for their children's play and leisure (Shaw & Dawson, 2001), fathers also report greater dissatisfaction with having their leisure constricted by parental obligations than do mothers (Wearing & McArthur, 1988). However, not only gender makes a difference. Because of discrimination, the meanings of children's and family leisure and the importance parents place on leisure for their children vary by race (Philipp, 1999) and sexual orientation of the parents as well (Bialeschki & Pearce, 1997).

Recent research makes apparent that identities such as gender, race/ethnicity, sexual orientation, as well as social class construct individuals' sense of themselves and their play and leisure interests, skills, motivations, and satisfactions or benefits (Henderson et al., 1996). Similarly, these identities shape power and social relations, the experience of age, of individual development, and thus opportunities for play and leisure (Freysinger, 1993; Freysinger & Harris, 2006). As previously noted, individuals are not passive receptacles for social forces. Play and leisure are also contexts in which individuals challenge and sometimes transform age, gender, race, and class norms (Freysinger & Flannery, 1992; Wearing, 1990). While life-span perspectives on play require researchers and practitioners to understand the complexity of play and development, an awareness that age and play are political issues is, for the most part, missing from life-span research.

A life-span perspective on play suggests that play's meanings, motivations, and forms are grounded within the context of the interaction of internal (biological and psychological) and external (social and cultural) factors and forces that change across time and with historical events—and that individuals are active in negotiating and directing their development. Recent critical scholarship also indicates that play and leisure may be contexts where individuals resist and transform social relations and practices. Both continuity and change in the motivations for and forms of play across the life span emerge out of such interactions. Research design, such as cross-sectional versus longitudinal, and the focus of analysis—for example, general activity or specific forms of play and leisure—influence the conclusions that researchers have made. Play across the life span is very much situated in a specific historical time and the economic, political, religious, and social reality of the day. Finally, in North America, play and leisure have rarely been examined as practices constructed in social relations. Looking at play and leisure in this way not only provides insight into these concepts but into the meaning of age and development as well.

References

Atchley, R. C. (1993). Continuity theory and the evolution of activity in later life. In J. R. Kelly (Ed.), *Activity and aging* (pp. 5–16). Thousand Oaks, CA: Sage.

Barnett, L. A. (1987). Play. In A. Graefe & S. Parker (Eds.), *Recreation and leisure: An introductory handbook* (pp. 131–136). State College, PA: Venture.

Bialeschki, M. D., & Pearce, K. (1997). "I don't want a lifestyle, I want a life!" The effect of role negotiation on the leisure of lesbian mothers. *Journal of Leisure Research, 29*(1), 113–132.

Cavanaugh, J. C. (2004). *Adult development and aging* (3rd ed.). Belmont, CA: Wadsworth.

Elder, G. H., Modell, J., & Parke, R. D.(1993). *Children in time and place: Developmental and historical insights.* New York: Cambridge University Press.

Elias, N., & Dunning, E. (1969). The quest for excitement in leisure. *Society and Leisure, 2*, 50–85.

Erikson, E. H. (1963). *Childhood and society*. New York: Norton.

Featherman, D. (1983). The lifespan perspective and social science research. In P. O. Baltes & O. G. Brim (Eds.), *Life-span development and behavior* (pp. 237–251). New York: Academic.

Foucault, W. (1983). The subject and power. In H. Dreyfus & P. Rabinow (Eds.), *Michel Foucault: Beyond structuralism and hermeneutics* (pp. 208–220). Chicago: University of Chicago Press.

Freud, S. (1979). *Civilization and its discontents* (J. Riviere, Trans.). London: Hogarth. (Original work published 1930)

Freysinger, V. J. (1993). The community, programs, and opportunities: Population diversity. In J. R. Kelly (Ed.), *Activity and Aging* (pp. 211–230). Newbury Park, CA: Sage.

Freysinger, V. J. (1994). Leisure with children and parental satisfaction: Further evidence of a sex difference in the experience of adult roles and leisure. *Journal of Leisure Research, 26,* 212–226.

Freysinger, V. J. (1995). The dialectics of leisure and development for women and men in mid-life: An interpretive study. *Journal of Leisure Research, 27,* 61–84.

Freysinger, V. J., & Flannery, D. (1992). Women's leisure: Affiliation, self-determination, empowerment and resistance. *Society and Leisure, 15*(1), 303–322.

Freysinger, V. J., & Harris, O. (2006). Race and leisure. In C. Rojek, S. M. Shaw, & A. Veal (Eds.), *Handbook of Leisure Studies.* Basingstoke, UK: Palgrave.

Freysinger, V. J., & Kelly, J. R. (2004). *21st century leisure: Current issues.* State College, PA: Venture.

Freysinger, V. J., & Ray, R. O. (1994). The activity involvement of women and men in young and middle adulthood: A panel study. *Leisure Sciences, 16,* 193–217.

Giele, J. Z. (1980). Adulthood as a transcendence of age and sex. In N. J. Smelser & E. H. Erikson (Eds.), *Themes of work and love in adulthood* (pp. 151–173). Cambridge, MA: Harvard University Press.

Gordon, C., Gaitz, C. M., & Scott, J. (1976). Leisure and lives: Personal expressivity across the lifespan. In R. H. Binstock & E. Shanas (Eds.), *Handbook of aging and the social sciences* (pp. 310–341). New York: Van Nostrand-Reinhold.

Graef, K., Caikszentmihalyi, M., & Giannino, S. (1983). Measuring intrinsic motivation in everyday life. *Leisure Studies, 2,* 155–168.

Gubrium, J. F., & Holstein, J. A. (1999). Constructionist perspectives on aging. In V. L. Bengston & K. W. Schaie (Eds.), *Handbook of theories of aging* (pp. 287–305). New York: Springer.

Harris, A. R. (1994). *Children 's perceptions of fun in organized youth sport settings.* Unpublished master's thesis, Miami University, Oxford, OH.

Harter, S. (1981). The development of competence motivation in the mastery of cognitive and physical skills: Is there still a place for joy? In G. Roberts & D. Landers (Eds.), *Psychology of motor behavior and sport* (pp. 3–29). Champaign, IL: Human Kinetics.

Henderson, K. A., Bialeschki, M. D., Shaw, S. M., & Freysinger, V. J. (1996). *Both gains and gaps: Feminist perspectives on women's leisure.* State College, PA: Venture.

Horna, J. L. (1989). The leisure component of the parental role. *Journal of Leisure Research, 21,* 228–241.

Iwasaki, Y., & Schneider, I. E. (2003). Leisure, stress, and coping: An evolving area of inquiry. *Leisure Sciences, 25*(2–3), 107–115.

Kelly, J. R. (1983). *Leisure identities and interactions.* London: George Allen & Unwin.

Kelly, J. R., & Godbey, G. (1992). *The sociology of leisure.* State College, PA: Venture.

Kelly, J. R., Steinkamp, M. W., & Kelly, J. R. (1986). Later life leisure: How they play in Peoria. *Gerontologist, 26,* 531–537.

Kimball, A., & Freysinger, V. J. (2003). Leisure, stress, and coping: The sport participation of collegiate student-athletes. *Leisure Sciences, 25*(2–3), 115–152.

Kleiber, D. A. (1999). *Leisure experience and human development: A dialectical interpretation.* New York: Basic Books.

Larson, R. W., & Gillman, S. A. (1997). Divergent experiences of family leisure: Mothers, fathers, and young adolescents. *Journal of Leisure Research, 29*(1), 78–98.

Lerner, R. M. (Ed.) (1998). *Theoretical models of human development.* New York: Wiley.

Lerner, R. M., & Busch-Rossnagel, N. (Eds.). (1981). *Individuals as producers of their own development.* New York: Academic Press.

Maehr, M. L. (1983). On doing well in science: Why Johnny no longer excels, why Sarah never did. In S. Paris, G. Olson, & H. Stevenson (Eds.), *Learning and motivation in the classroom* (pp. 179–210). Hillsdale, NJ: Erlbaum.

McCrae, R. R., & Costa, P. T. (1988). Age, personality and spontaneous self-concept. *Journal of Gerontology, 43,* S177–S185.

Neugarten, B. I. (1977). Personality and aging. In J. E. Birren & K. W. Schaie (Eds.), *Handbook of the psychology of aging* (pp. 626–649). New York: Academic.

Neulinger, J. C. (1987). *The psychology of leisure* (2nd ed.). Springfield, IL: Charles C. Thomas.

Ostrow, A. C., & Dzewaltowski, D. A. (1986). Older adults' perceptions of physical activity participation based on age-role and sex-role appropriateness. *Research Quarterly for Exercise and Sport, 57,* 286–295.

Philipp, S. (1999). Are we welcome? African American racial acceptance in leisure activities and the importance placed on children's leisure. *Journal of Leisure Research, 31*(4), 385–404.

Riegel, K. (1976, October). The dialectics of human development. *Developmental Psychology, 31*(10), 689–700.

Riley, M. W., & Riley, J. W. (Eds.). (1994). *Age and structural lag: Society's failure to provide meaningful opportunities in work, family, and leisure.* New York: Norton.

Rojek, C. (1985). *Capitalism and leisure theory.* London: Tavistock.

Samdahl, D. (1988). A symbolic interactionist model of leisure: Theoretical and empirical support. *Leisure Sciences, 10,* 27–39.

Schaie, K. W. (1994). Developmental designs revisited. In S. H. Cohen & H. W. Reese (Eds.), *Lifespan development psychology: Methodological innovations* (pp. 45–64). Hillsdale, NJ: Erlbaum Associates.

Schreck, M. A. (1990). *Factors influencing participation in Senior Olympic competition.* Unpublished master's thesis, Miami University, Oxford, OH.

Shaw, S. M. (2001). Conceptualizing resistance: Women's leisure as political practice. *Journal of Leisure Research, 33*(2), 186–202.

Shaw, S. M., & Dawson, D. (2001). Purposive leisure: Examining parental discourses on family activities. *Journal of Leisure Sciences, 23,* 217-231.

Smale, B. J. A., & Dupuis, S. L. (1993). The relationships between leisure activity participation and psychological well-being across the lifespan. *Journal of Applied Recreation, 44,* 948–967.

Wearing, B. (1990). Beyond the ideology of motherhood: Leisure as resistance. *Australian and New Zealand Journal o f Sociology, 26,* 36–58.

Wearing, B. (1995). Leisure and resistance in an ageing society. *Leisure Studies, 14,* 263–279.

Wearing, B., & McArthur, M. (1988). The family that plays together stays together: Or does it? *Australian and New Zealand Journal o f Sex, Marriage, and Family, 9,* 150–158.

II
Meanings of Play

Introduction

This section focuses on a variety of types of play ranging from play with objects, play with others in sociodramatic play, play with rules, play from children's perspectives, and their play with humor. Play takes many forms because children are likely to play in a range of diverse settings to which they bring their experiences and in which they share experiences with others. Children also begin to perceive their own play and the play of others. While children's perspectives of play are a central and ongoing feature of play, adults' perspectives can either limit or extend the scope of children's experiences. Chapter authors consider how children engage in and understand play

The personal meaning of play varies for each individual. Each brings idiosyncratic meanings to play and constructs personal meanings from play. Social interaction transforms the nature of performances and the children's meanings through the ways that children engage in group play. Within sociodramatic play episodes, for example, children may scaffold each other's participation within a shared script. In a parallel way, play offers the potential to create instant community among former strangers or enhance the experience of community among friends.

Other representational forms, such as exploration and creativity, while encompassing playful elements, are not play per se, but may reflect proximity to the *phase transitions* that have the potential to easily transform into play. They might be considered mind-sets or approaches to life events. Exploration, from one perspective, is when children attempt to find out what something can do or how it works, whereas play is their proactive attempt to see what they can do with it (Hutt, 1976). Constrained by their event knowledge and the context of a particular setting, their representations will be more or less accurate and accessible.

Humor, however, is a type of mind-set that requires a playful frame of mind. In contrast, play might be humorous or whimsical, but it might also be serious. Children may exhibit humor and whimsy in their play. Their humor provides an important window into their understanding of concepts and language, permits them to express their exuberance in glee and their hostility in insults, and helps them learn the pragmatics of community-appropriate social interaction. These meaningful potentials for play in human life touch on what it means to be a human being in the world.

Reference

Hutt, C. (1976). Exploration and play in children. In J. S. Bruner, A. Jolly, & K. Sylva (Eds.), *Play—Its role in development and evolution* (pp. 202–215). New York: Basic Books.

8
The Meanings in Play with Objects

SHIRLEY K. MORGENTHALER

Play with objects is a pervasive activity of children from a very early age. This play involves objects of both large and small size and of simple and complex character. Contexts also influence the types of object play that can be observed and the meanings children attribute to the play. Although the meanings of object play may differ across individual children, there are a number of age/stage differences in object play that have been observed.

Age-Related Characteristics of Object Play

The object play of infants and toddlers is of a different character than that of older children, although both manipulative and symbolic object play occurs at every age. Numerous studies have documented the developmental stages of object play.

Infants and Toddlers

Object play of very young children is often solitary or imitative in nature, but it may engage the interest and activity of an adult who will actively extend and expand that play. Infants use parts of their bodies, such as fingers, toes, or nose, as objects for their early play. With adult encouragement, this play is often elaborated and transformed into a social game, such as "Where's your nose (eye, toe)?"

Object play of toddlers is primarily exploratory and manipulative. Toddlers begin to include story-based or imaginative manipulation and imitation in their play, however, and to use props to imitate simple adult roles, such as "mommy," and daily activities, such as rocking baby. Props are usually quite realistic. Toddlers may find something to carry that represents a briefcase to play "mommy" or "daddy," for example, or they may remove pots and pans from cabinets to play "mealtime" or "cooking." Although most toddler object play has a realistic basis and is manipulative rather than symbolic, toddlers do begin to use objects symbolically in their play (Fenson, 1986). In so doing, they are building the foundation for symbolic functioning as a cognitive process.

During the second year of life, children are engaged in activities which move their play through a series of increasingly symbolic stages. Fenson (1986) labels these stages *decentration, decontextualization*, and *integration*. In decentration, the toddler moves from self-focus in the use of objects toward a focus on the object as both the recipient and the initiator of make-believe actions. *Decontextualization* refers to the level of similarity between the play object and its make-believe function. At 1 year, there is usually a high degree of similarity between the object and its make-believe role, while by age 2 that similarity has usually diminished. With the stage of *integration*, the child moves from disconnected to interrelated themes in object play, again with age level difference in the degree of relatedness between play themes and the objects used as symbolic tools.

Ages Three to Five

Children between 3 and 5 continue the use of objects as symbolic tools, elaborating and extending that play into social contexts with playmates. Peer social play is initially turn taking in nature, however, rather than being cooperative or collaborative play. Sociodramatic play, in which children use objects as props to develop story episodes that involve other children, is seen increasingly as children progress through this stage. Children's play with blocks, in which each block structure is given a meaning and function, also becomes important. Play with trucks, cars, dolls, and housekeeping materials may be solitary or social. If it is social, it will continue as long as each player agrees to the meanings assigned to the objects (Winnicott, 1971/1982). Thus, this age period is the first in which children develop skills in sharing the meanings embedded in their object play.

During the preschool years, children's construction with objects begins to take on increasingly elaborate forms. This construction includes play with blocks (Hirsch, 1974), and play with three-dimensional materials such as clay, play dough, and collage materials. In this play with objects, the objects become elements in a larger whole toward which the child is building (Monighan-Nourot, Van Hoorn, & Scales, 1987).

Ages Six to Eight

Primary-age children (ages 6 to 8) are adept at cooperative play and skilled at negotiating the meanings and functions of play objects with other children in order to create shared meanings. As objects are used for group play, they still may be a manipulative resource but they are primarily used as props for story- or fantasy-based play. Miniature objects such as Barbie-like dolls (with girls) and action/adventure dolls (with boys) become the props for both story and fantasy play. As children manipulate these objects, they negotiate the story line for those objects (Winnicott, 1971/1982). In the primary years children continue to use objects for individual play, either as fantasy materials or as props in manipulative play; however, small objects such as dollhouse figures, construction toys, stuffed animals, or even game board pieces become the material for story episodes in children's pretense. Because this play is often more internal (thinking about) than external (acting out), adults must engage in careful observation and sensitive interpretation if they are to understand the meanings of such play (Singer & Singer, 1990, 2005).

Ages Nine to Twelve

Intermediate-age children from 9 to 12 also use objects both manipulatively or dramatically. The dramatic or story-based play of these children becomes quite elaborate and intricate and the same theme may go on for days. Themes may be drawn from books, television and movies, or from the everyday life of their expanded world. They may also engage in intricate play by having miniature replica objects taking the roles of the actors. In this type of play, children focus on the inherent properties of the objects and often attempt to create new structures and realities with combinations of objects. This play may also be with complex computer games, intricate board games, or action/adventure and Barbie-like doll play (Ko, 2002; Singer & Singer, 1990, 2005).

Theoretical Views of Play with Objects

The role of objects in shaping play has been discussed from a variety of theoretical perspectives. These include the psychoanalytic view, which focuses on the emotional or larger personal meanings of the objects and the play; the pragmatic view, in which objects are the means of meeting functional ends; the developmental/cognitive view, which focuses on ways play with objects fosters the reasoning, problem-solving, and other cognitive functioning of the child; and the sociocultural view, which examines the meaning embedded in the social and cultural contexts of children's play with objects.

The Psychoanalytic View

Psychoanalytic theory views the object as a tool for the mastery of feelings and emotions. This perspective focuses on story-based play and the internal processes involved in such play. In addition, it stresses the study of the individual in the play, rather than the social context and general meaning of such play. This psychoanalytic (or psychodynamic) view of play emphasizes the larger personal meaning of the play, and the psychoanalyst attempts to draw conclusions about the child's emotional struggles from the emotional quality of the play. Erikson's (1977) analysis of play exemplifies this perspective.

From this viewpoint, children use objects in play to facilitate the mastery of emotions and feelings; this is regarded as personally therapeutic. It is the child, however, who must give meaning to the play. Children who engage in object play for the mastery of emotions often engage in what appears to be regressive play; that is, play that they may have mastered in a prior stage of development. This "regression" is viewed as a part of the therapeutic nature of such play (Axline, 1969; Bromfield, 1997). All parents of a second child have seen the older child engage in "baby" play, for example, taking on the actions and qualities of babyhood, often with the objects of babyhood, such as bottles, pacifiers, and blankets. This play can help the child master the emotional challenge of coping with the new situation where parental attention must be shared with a sibling.

Play therapists observe object play in the counseling room and use their observations to interpret the meanings of such play in their therapy. This requires great skill; the play therapist avoids assigning meaning beyond the child's intent. That is not to say that children may not reveal meanings they do not yet understand through their object play, because that also occurs. The skilled therapist, however, is able to discern such meanings and help the child to see them without projecting meanings beyond those present for the child (Kissell, 1990; Schaefer, 1985).

All children engage, from time to time, in play which has psychodynamic meanings. To ignore this perspective of object play would be a serious omission, but to imbue all forms of object play with psychodynamic meaning would be an error of overgeneralization (Hughes, 1999).

The Pragmatic View

The pragmatic view focuses on the outer activity and function of object play. For the most part, proponents of this view are not interested in the larger meanings of such play, but see the objects used in play as having a pragmatic function and purpose. In this view, objects are the means to functional ends. Thus, the game pieces of a popular board game, the sticks or other props of an active outdoor game, or the child-size cooking utensils of classroom or playroom housekeeping play are used in ways that the characteristics of the objects afford (Wachs, 1985). That is, the attributes of the objects, such as responsivity to manipulation, influence the nature of children's object play. The combined set of stimulus properties that prompt positive levels of object interaction has been called "high affordance" (Wachs, 1985). From this perspective, children's interest in the object as play material depends on its level of affordance. The materials designed and used by Montessori (1912/1973; 2004) are examples of object affordance, because the object itself is supposed to elicit certain child actions. The Montessori environment provides many objects that can be used in functional ways; thus, it is designed from a pragmatic perspective. Adult interactions with children are minimal in the environment because the objects themselves are expected to provide the stimuli for interaction.

The Developmental/Cognitive View

This perspective looks to play with objects as the means for fostering the cognitive functioning of the child. It focuses on the cognitive mastery of reasoning and problem-solving strategies that are enhanced by object play. A developmental/cognitive perspective sees object play as helping the child to reach forward toward mental or developmental challenges which are not yet a part of the child's day-to-day repertoire. It is this perspective which Jean Piaget used in his analysis of the child's play with objects (Flavell, Miller, & Miller, 2002; Piaget, 1962).

Children's play with parquetry blocks or tangrams exemplifies play with objects for the purpose of cognitive mastery. The manipulation of individual pieces in order to reproduce design patterns or to create original designs requires reasoning and problem-solving strategies to be employed and enhanced through the play. Adults' ability to observe and encourage without intruding on the reasoning aspect of this form of object play is crucial to children's development of internal problem-solving strategies.

The Sociocultural View

The sociocultural view examines the social and cultural contexts of children's play with objects. From this perspective, play with objects takes on a shared meaning between players, imbuing it with social significance (Hughes, 1999). Make-believe play with simple props provides children with the raw materials for social interactions and "group productivity" (Rosen, 1974). It is this perspective which Dewey (1966) used in his discussions of the child's entry into the culture through social play. Singer and Singer (2005) discuss the development of the imagination as a sociocultural phenomenon in children. Their concern is that the culture of the electronic age negatively impacts the development of imagination in children.

Children's dramatic play with dress-up and housekeeping objects and artifacts, for example, is most often carried out in a shared social setting. In this form of object play, children negotiate shared meanings through their questions, directives to fellow players, and ongoing dialogue (Rocissano, 1982). Adults' provision of appropriate dramatic play props provides the "stage" for these shared meanings to be negotiated through play and social interaction (Bailey, 2002). Adult involvement beyond observation and awareness is usually not supportive of children's need for social negotiation of meaning with peers. At the same time, adult involvement in the play of young children can provide a model for play with both novel and familiar materials (Gottfried & Brown, 1986).

Although all of these theoretical perspectives view play with objects as having meanings, they differ in their emphasis on the domains of meaning and the importance of object play for symbolic development. Each perspective, however, has given rise to explorations of the structures and processes present in children's play with objects.

Structures and Processes of Object Play

Children's play with objects involves a variety of processes and structures the experiences of children. Objects may be used functionally or fantastically. Objects may support external or internal processes. They may be largely manipulative props, or they may be dramatic, story-based props. The size of objects and their inherent structures may also affect the processes of play. The objects used in play may be a variety of sizes, ranging from diminutive pieces that require mastery of fine motor skills to the larger-than-life objects of the playground, which stress the use of gross motor skills.

Functional or Dramatic

Object play may focus on the manipulation of the functions of the object. Children may repetitively use board game pieces, sorting and classification toys, blocks, or even computer-generated representational objects to master motor or cognitive functions (Mergen, 1982). Object play may also focus on the dramatic properties of objects, providing the vehicle for story-based play (Koste, 1995; Sies, 1922).

When children use the computer mouse to "paint" a picture, they are manipulating the representation of a paint brush to master the movements needed to satisfactorily complete a picture. When they manipulate blocks and small classification toys, they may be using the objects to master either the motoric challenges involved, or the cognitive challenges of space, pattern, or relationships. When children use objects as story vehicles in dramatic play, their use of the object becomes dramatic and can transforms the object into the story prop which it represents.

Realistic or Imaginative

Object play may be realistic or imaginative. Children may focus on the real properties of the objects as they play or they may go beyond the literal qualities to assign imaginative properties and roles to objects (Gowen, 1995). For the most part, very young children use objects realistically and literally (Fenson, 1986). As children's ability to pretend increases, they begin to assign imaginative roles and properties to objects in their play. Preschool and primary children readily engage in this type of imaginative object play. Simple objects may become space ships, furniture, or people as children pretend. Children's imaginative play can also extend to outdoor playground spaces (Factor, 2004).

Intermediate children, on the other hand, tend to return to the literal or realistic qualities of props in their play with objects (Hughes, 1999; Piaget, 1962). Detailed replica objects such as Barbie-like dolls and the action/adventure toys popular with intermediate boys fall into this category. That is, the figures must have clothes, furniture, vehicles, and equipment that are similar to the real objects. While there are imaginative themes expressed in this play, it requires these realistic aspects in order to be satisfying to the players. Replicas of transportation toys, for example, become the vehicles for space travel and dollhouses require intricate and realistic furniture. Doll players at this age level require many more props and changes of clothing than they needed at earlier ages. Action figure players have similar requirements for realistic props, such as replicas of actual gun or airplane models, to engage in hero or superhero activities. Often children of this age spend more time arranging and discussing the plans for the imaginary play than in actual pretend with them. They also especially enjoy computer simulations, such as "SimCity," that involve building their own "world" or "Gameboy" simulations that allow them to practice mastery and domination of their world.

There is a wide difference in the imaginative quality of children's play. Some of this variation is related to the ages of children, while some of the variation is related to children's play interests and intellectual interests (Singer & Singer, 1990). It may also be that some of the variation is due to the availability and complexity of play objects to support imaginative play (Rubin, 1977).

Internal and External Processes

Play with objects focuses on both internal and external processes. Adults are more likely to observe the external processes initially and may not be aware of the internal processes, especially when children are very young. There are almost always internal processes involved in the play with objects, however, with the possible exception of manipulative play that has a very repetitive or "doodling" quality. Even then, children may be playing out an internal theme.

A child who is repeatedly practicing a basketball throw, for example, may be imagining a game being played in which he or she is the "star." Similarly, a child who is manipulating small, doll-like figures may be creating an elaborate scenario for a family event, such as a birthday party or vacation trip. As children develop the ability to think logically and systematically in middle childhood, they also develop the ability for internal play (Singer & Singer, 1990). While objects may be involved as catalysts for the play, they more often serve as the external stimuli for a primarily internal process.

Influence of Physical Size Characteristics

Objects of play come in varied sizes ranging from life-size to minute. Large objects include the child-size objects of the housekeeping or block areas of preschool classrooms, the large beads or sandbox toys of toddler environments, and the larger-than-life "stage coaches" or "ships" of the intermediate child's playground. These large objects may present physical challenges and encourage psychological victories as children use them to master, maneuver, and dominate materials which are and feel larger than life to them.

Play objects may be very small, and children also love these. Smaller-than-life materials include the diminutive objects of dollhouse play, the table-sized objects of manipulative play, the miniature pieces of board games, and the accessories of Barbie-like dolls, action/adventure toys, and transformers and robots. These objects enable children to focus on their emotional and cognitive mastery of the manipulation, allowing an intricacy of domination and a complexity of control not possible with larger objects. Very small cars and trucks, the endurance of dollhouse play, and the numerous "small worlds" (e.g., farm, zoo, shop, train sets) are examples of the inherent interest children have in miniature objects. Children's fascination with such miniatures and the duration of their play with them attest to the powerful appeal of these small objects. Symbolic play, in particular, becomes miniaturized as children grow older (Bergen, 1988).

Methods of Inquiry for Play with Objects

Although much has been studied about children's object play, there is still much to be learned. The challenge for adults interested in appreciating or guiding children's play with objects lies in the interpretation of the meanings of such play.

Direct questions often are not productive for gaining information, and adults must employ indirect (from the child's perspective) methods of inquiry. Thus, observation and subsequent analysis of these observations may provide more objective data for study and interpretation than testing or experimentation. Several scales and observational inventories have been developed for this purpose (Johnson, Christie, & Wardle, 2005; Johnson, Christie, & Yawkey, 1987).

To learn more about children's play with objects, adults can use systematic observation and analysis of the play within the varied contexts in which it occurs.

Observation of children's activity is one method of inquiry that may be useful for understanding children's play with objects. To fully use this method, careful and intentional observation is required, and the adult must observe without intruding. When children are playing with objects, they may see mere awareness of an adult observer as an intrusion. To avoid this, the adult may concurrently engage in "adult" activities near where the child is playing; this legitimizes the adult's proximity to the play. However, systematic observations should only be conducted after receiving permission from the child's parents. Parents who wish to observe their child's play often engage in activities at home such as washing dishes, ironing, gardening, or caring for another child. Teachers may also do routine classroom activities as they focus their observations on particular children. The goal of nonparticipant observation is to observe the play without intruding, for an intrusion will change the nature of the play and not allow the results the observer desires.

Analysis of the observations can focus on the use of specific objects by children. This requires that the adult determine which structures and processes are being used by children involved in object play. They can determine whether the play is function- or fantasy-based, assess whether the play is primarily manipulative or story-based/dramatic, ascertain to what extent the play involves the working out of internal processes, and how it is influenced by the physical characteristics of the objects.

Another method of inquiry into object play is the extrapolation of the meanings of such object play. That is, the adult can consider which of the various theoretical views of play with objects best helps in interpreting the meanings of the play. This is the approach used in the various forms of play therapy (Axline, 1969; Hughes, 1999). Each of the theoretical views of play with objects attaches different types of meanings to such play. As adult observers begin to understand those various theoretical perspectives, they can also deepen their understanding of the meanings of a child's play with objects.

It is important to note, however, that any analysis of the meanings of object play also requires a knowledge of the child and of the context of the play. Parents may have the advantage in that they have the most information about the child's perspective on a day-to-day basis, and can thereby postulate meaning more accurately than adults who have a more limited experience with the child. Educators and other adult professionals, however, may have a more detached perspective, which will be helpful in supporting and interpreting children's play in a more objective and impartial manner, because they can look at the play from a broader range of theoretical perspectives in the context of development and learning.

Contexts for the Study of Play with Objects

Children's play with objects must be viewed in the larger context of their overall activities. Only as one begins to understand the child's activity holistically can the meaning of play with objects be fully appreciated and understood. For the child, objects may function as inspiration for fantasy play, or as touchstones back to reality during fantasy play. It is the adult's task to determine, as much as is possible, the meanings of object play within the contexts of the child's life. To do so enriches the adult's understanding of the child as a whole, and supports the adult's interactions with the child in sympathetic and knowledgeable ways.

Although naturalistic observations give the broader contextual view, staged observations and interviews of children help to ascertain internal meanings. Including these methods of inquiry can help to more fully explore contextual influences on the meanings of play with objects.

Influences of Specific Contexts on Object Play

As with other types of research, the mere fact of study may influence the outcome. Even objectively oriented observers enter the observation with a sense of expected results, which make them see what they want to see.

The type of settings in which play is observed can also have a profound influence on the outcomes of a study. Staged settings, because of their selective nature, may produce results that inadvertently support the biases of the person setting the stage. Open-ended and naturalistic settings, on the other hand, provide the opportunity to observe children's object play in the context chosen by them, thus most closely honoring their perspective. These settings, because they are not completely controlled by the adult observer, add the challenge of unpredictability and novelty to the study. But because even natural settings have constraints designed by the adults in that setting (e.g., toys available, rules of behavior), the researcher must always be careful about recording the setting characteristics and examining the results in the light of those characteristics (Fein & Rivkin, 1986).

Influences of Individual Learning Styles on Object Play

Important contributions to an understanding of the meanings of children's object play come from a variety of related fields, drawn from the various theoretical views discussed earlier. Others are inherent in an understanding of developmental issues and individual differences among children. Yet another important source is the literature on learning styles and the processes by which children acquire and utilize new information.

Children engage in play with objects in a variety of ways, somewhat dependent on development but also dependent on learning styles and internal learning structures. While most of the information about learning styles focuses on intermediate children or even older individuals, informed and careful observation and interpretation of children's play with objects can result in a better understanding of the learning styles of even very young children (Morgenthaler, 1989).

Children who will later be identified as visual learners tend, even as infants, to focus on the visual qualities of the objects of their play. Children who will later be called auditory learners are more likely to note the auditory or noise-making qualities of the objects of their play. Kinesthetic learners, on the other hand, tend to focus even as young children on the manipulative, the textural, or the movement options of objects. Already as infants, they may attempt to mouth or to bend objects as a part of their exploration of the objects. They may exhibit an early focus on the texture of play objects or on the movement of multipieced objects. It may also be that kinesthetic learners are the most engrossed with the pull and push toys of toddlerhood (Dunn & Dunn, 1992; Dunn, Dunn & Perrin, 1994).

Assumptions that May Influence Interpretations of Play Meanings

One assumption that does not facilitate understanding of the meanings of object play is that the play adults observe accurately shows the level of maturity of the child's play. Sometimes, when children are engaged in simple experimentation and manipulation, adults assume that this is the highest level of play in which the child can engage. It may not be the case that the child is incapable of more mature play, but merely that the child's current activity is specific and literal, perhaps due to contextual influences at that time. Adults may make the faulty assumption that brief observation of object play can provide a window into the thinking and developmental level of the child. While this may be true at times, it is not always true. The adult must have an extensive observational base, understand the context, and have a base of knowledge of the individual child in order to draw such a conclusion.

Careful and informed observation of the object play is needed in order to understand that play. If adults do not observe children's object play carefully, they may inappropriately interpret the play and assign maturity or inaccurate meaning that will not facilitate the adult's interactions with the child. The child may be manipulating materials from a board game, for example, creating patterns which appear intricate and complex to the adult. This complexity may be intended, but it may also be accidental and serendipitous at that moment. In fact, as the child discovers the pattern or complexity in the process of object manipulation, that meaning may be extended and elaborated. The adult needs to refrain from assigning intentionality to activity which is exploratory in nature.

The adult must determine whether the play in question is, in fact, cognitive play, and be able to distinguish between play which uses objects primarily as psychodynamic tools for emotional resolution from that in which the child is using objects for cognitive integration of ideas. These different uses are difficult to determine without knowing the child and being able to theorize a purpose for the play. Of course, both purposes may coexist as well.

Another assumption that does not facilitate understanding of play meaning is that observational data have a direct one-to-one correspondence with meanings. Rather, these observations must be informed by an understanding of the child, the context, and the various theoretical perspectives on play with objects.

A phenomenon which both facilitates understanding and hinders understanding is the emphasis on object play as functionally related to its future utility. Object play is very often respected by adults because it is seen as a type of preparatory play that readies children for more abstract cognitive tasks. This is both helpful and problematic.

From one perspective, respecting object play as an important activity of children is always desirable. On the other hand, to respect object play only for its cognitive contributions is too narrow an approach. Play with objects often has emotional or psychological benefits, and it has social and cultural benefits as well, in addition to pragmatic benefits. To assign it primarily cognitive importance does not respect the other meanings that play with objects has for children at a given point in time. The full appreciation of the power of object play requires an awareness and understanding of all its varied natures and meanings, as well as a willingness to take the time to understand the unique utilization that a particular child may be employing in a given play episode.

Adults can allow and facilitate play with objects for primarily manipulative or pragmatic purposes. Adults need to be sensitive to children's simple, natural needs to experiment and to try activity at a variety of levels. Not all object play needs to be interpreted or analyzed for its larger meanings. Knowing that a range of potentially larger meanings is possible, however, allows adults to appreciate and facilitate play in helpful ways, even if that facilitation is simply expressed as giving permission or encouragement to the child to manipulate and experiment.

The appreciation and understanding of children's play with objects are important ingredients in the comprehensive understanding of a child's perspectives and developmental progress. Each of the views of the meanings of object play adds to an understanding of the child's use of objects to acquire meanings. Looking at the variety of structures and processes involved in the child's implementation of objects for play purposes aids the understanding of object play, and knowing which strategy or method of inquiry to employ for a given purpose is an important consideration for the full appreciation of that play.

Appreciating the impact of the child's learning style preferences will also affect adults' discernment of the nuances of the child's play. Becoming aware of the power of both positive and negative assumptions on the comprehension of meanings of object play will guard against false conclusions in the actual attempt to understand that play. It is critical for adults to appreciate all of the ways in which children employ objects in their play. The ability of children to use objects in an array of ways for a variety of purposes enriches the impact of that play on their cognitive, physical, social, and emotional development. To allow or assume less is to limit the power of that play and full understanding of it. The ability of adults to appreciate play may also be related to their willingness to continue to play themselves. The preservation of adult playfulness is important for the awareness and understanding of children's play.

References

Axline, V. (1969). *Play therapy*. New York: Ballantine Books.

Bailey, R. (2002). Children's play and social intelligence. *Early Years: Journal of International Research and Development, 22*(2), 163–173.

Bergen, D. (Ed.). (1988). Stages of play development. In D. Bergen (Ed.), *Play as a medium for learning and development* (pp. 49–66). Portsmouth, NH: Heinemann.

Bromfield, R. (1997). *Playing for real: Exploring the world of child therapy and the inner worlds of children*. Northvale: NJ: Jason Aaronson.

Dewey, J. (1966). *Democracy and education*. New York: Free Press.

Dunn, R. S., & Dunn, K. J. (1992). *Teaching elementary students through their individual learning styles: Practical approaches for grades 3–6*. Boston, MA: Allyn & Bacon.

Dunn, R. S., Dunn, K. J., & Perrin, J. (1994). *Teaching elementary students through their individual learning styles: Practical approaches for grades K–2*. Boston, MA: Allyn and Bacon.

Erikson, E. H. (1977). *Toys and reason*. New York: Norton.

Factor, J. (2004). Tree stumps, manhole covers and rubbish tins: The invisible play-lines of a primary school playground. *Childhood, 11*(2), 142–154.

Fein, G., & Rivkin, M. (1986). *The young child at play: Reviews of research* vol. 4. Washington, D.C.: National Association for the Education of Young Children.

Fenson, L. (1986). The developmental progression of play. In A.W. Gottfried & C.W. Brown. (Eds.), *The contribution of play materials and parental involvement to children's development* (pp. 53–66). Lexington, MA: Heath.

Flavell, J. H., Miller, P., & Miller, S. (2002). *Cognitive Development*. Englewood Cliffs, NJ: Prentice Hall.

Gottfried, A. W., & Brown, C. (1986). *Play interactions: The contribution of play materials and parental involvement in children's development*. Lexington, MA: Lexington Books.

Gowen, J. C. (1995). Research in review: The early development of symbolic play. *Young Children, 50*(3), 75–84.

Hirsch, E. S. (1974). *The block book*. Washington, D.C.: National Association for the Education of Young Children.

Hughes, F. P. (1999). *Children, play, and development*. Boston, MA: Allyn & Bacon.

Johnson, J. E., Christie, J. F., & Wardle, F. (2005). *Play development and early education*. New York: Longman.

Johnson, J. E., Christie, J. F., & Yawkey, T. D. (1987). *Play and early childhood development*. New York: HarperCollins.

Kissell, S. (1990). *Play therapy: A strategic approach*. Springfield, IL: Charles C. Thomas.

Ko, S. (2002). An empirical analysis of children's thinking and learning in a computer game context. *Educational psychology, 22*(2), 219–233.

Koste, V. G. (1995). *Dramatic play in childhood: Rehearsal for life*. Portsmouth, NH: Heinemann.

Mergen, B. (1982). *Play and playthings: A reference guide*. Westport, CT: Greenwood Press.

Monighan-Nourot, P., Scales, B., & Van Hoorn, J. (1987). *Looking at children's play: A bridge between theory and practice*. New York: Teachers College Press.

Montessori, M. (1912/1973). *The Montessori Method*. Cambridge, MA: Bentley.

Montessori, M. (2004). *The Montessori Method: The origins of educational innovation*. G. L. Gutek (Ed.). Lanham, MD: Rowman & Littlefield.

Morgenthaler, S. K. (1989). A question of answer-finding. *Lutheran Education, 129*, 83–86.

Piaget, J. (1962). *Play, Dreams, and Imitation*. New York: Norton.

Rocissano, L. (1982). The emergence of social conventional behavior: Evidence from early object play. *Social Cognition. 1*(1) 50–69.

Rosen, C. E. (1974). The effects of sociodramatic play on problem-solving behavior among culturally disadvantaged preschool children. *Child Development. 45*, 920–927.

Rubin, K. H. (1977). Play behaviors of young children. *Young Children, 32*, 16–24.

Schaefer, C. E. (1985). Play therapy. *Early Child Development and Care. 19*, 95–108.

Singer, D. G., & Singer, J. L. (2005). *Imagination and play in the electronic age*. Cambridge, MA: Harvard University Press.

Singer, D. G., & Singer, J. L. (1990). *The house of make-believe: Children's play and the developing imagination*. Cambridge, MA: Harvard University Press.

Sies, A. C. (1922). *Spontaneous and supervised play in childhood*. New York: Macmillan.

Wachs, T. C. (1985). Home stimulation and cognitive development. In C. C. Brown & A. W. Gottfrieds (Eds.), *Play interactions: The role of toys and parental involvement in children's development* (pp. 142–152). Skillman, NJ: Johnson & Johnson.

Winnicott, D. W. (1982). *Playing and reality*. New York: Tavistock. (Original work published 1971)

9

Social and Nonsocial Play

ROBERT J. COPLAN, KENNETH H. RUBIN, AND LEANNE C. FINDLAY

In this chapter, we distinguish between structural and contextual features of play, broadly defined. For example, from a structural perspective, theorists have distinguished among functional, constructive, and dramatic behaviors, as well as games with rules (e.g., Piaget, 1962; Smilansky, 1968). These structural forms of play occur in a variety of social contexts. In this chapter we examine both ends of the social participation spectrum, exploring both social play (activities that take place when two or more partners interact with one another in both literal and nonliteral fashions) and nonsocial play (solitary activities in the presence of peers). We define both social and nonsocial play and address questions such as these: Why are these forms of behavior of developmental significance? How does one assess social and nonsocial play? and What are the predictors, concomitants, and outcomes associated with individual differences in social and nonsocial play? It is argued herein that social play provides a unique and important context for young children's social, social–cognitive, and emotional development, and that some forms of nonsocial play can reflect psychosocial maladaptation, whereas others may be developmentally benign.

Defining Social and Nonsocial Play

Rubin, Fein, and Vandenberg (1983) defined *play* in terms of the following characteristics: (1) Play is not governed by appetitive drives, compliance with social demands, or by inducements external to the behavior itself; instead play is intrinsically motivated. (2) Play is spontaneous, free from external sanctions, and its goals are self-imposed. (3) Play asks, "What can I do with this object or person?" (this differentiates play from exploration which asks, "What is this object/person and what can it/he/she do?"). (4) Play is not a serious rendition of an activity or a behavior it resembles; instead it consists of activities that can be labeled as *pretense* (i.e., play must comprise nonliterality). (5) Play is free from externally imposed rules (this distinguishes play from games-with-rules. (6) Play involves active engagement (this distinguishes play from daydreaming, lounging, and aimless loafing).

Given these definitional criteria, we admit that the following discussion of social and nonsocial play spreads well beyond the boundaries of the above-noted definition. Nevertheless, our terminology is accepted in the current Zeitgeist of research pertaining to play, and we will return to the original definitional criteria during the course of this chapter.

To state the obvious, that which distinguishes *social* play from other forms of play involves the notion of interaction with others. Social play occurs among dyads and larger groups. It occurs when the child (1) is motivated to engage others in playful activities; (2) is able to regulate emotional arousal; (3) possesses the skills necessarily to initiate interactions with another child; such that (4) the social overtures are accepted in kind. Accordingly, social play compromises the associated constructs of social participation, social competence, and sociability, and typically involves two (or more) children participating in functional-sensorimotor, constructive, dramatic activities, and games-with-rules. It also comprises active conversations between children as they go about interacting with each other, negotiating play roles and game rules.

In contrast, for the purposes of this chapter, *nonsocial* play is defined as the display of solitary activities and behaviors *in the presence of other potential play partners*. An important component of this definition involves the presence of other people, which infers the opportunity to engage in social interaction and group-oriented play. Thus, from this perspective, a child who is playing quietly alone in his or her room at home would not be engaging in nonsocial play, per se, as there are no play partners in the immediate vicinity.

Social Participation

In the 1920s, several attempts were made to develop comprehensive taxonomies for describing children's social interactions with peers. Andrus (1924) and Verry (1923), for example, systematically observed nursery school children and created various categories for social and nonsocial play. Verry (1923) included the categories of "treating playmates as objects" and "cooperating within the group" in her various types of social attitudes. A few years later, Bott (1928) developed a coding scheme which included the category of "occupied with other children." Within this category, the behaviors of talking, watching, interference, imitation, and cooperation were distinguished.

Parten's (1932) observational framework is perhaps the best known of the early social participation taxonomies. In her now classic study, Parten defined two categories of socially interactive play. During *associative play*, the child interacts with other children and may be using similar materials; however, there is no real cooperation or division of labor. *Cooperative play* consists of a group activity organized for the purpose of carrying out some plan of action or attaining some goal. Play partners coordinate their behaviors and take particular roles in pursuit of the common goal. In studies postdating the 1970s, associative play and cooperative play were combined as *social play*.

Parten also defined four categories comprising *nonsocial* or "*semi*"-social play activities. These included: (1) *Unoccupied behavior*—the demonstration of a marked absence of focus or intent (e.g., child stares blankly into space or wanders aimlessly); (2) *Onlooker behavior*—the observation of others' activities without an attempt to enter into the peers' activity; (3) *Solitary play*—playing apart from other children (at a distance greater than 3 feet) and paying little or no attention to others; and (4) *Parallel play*—the child plays *beside* (i.e., within 3 feet) but not *with* other children.

The legacy of Parten's (1932) taxonomy of social participation is that is continues to be used in studies that bear no striking resemblance to those originally published in the 1930s. Contemporary researchers have refined the original scale for purposes of examining developmental, cultural, and individual differences in children's social and nonsocial "play," broadly defined.

The Developmental Significance of Social Play

Theorists have been positing the developmental significance of peer interaction for over 50 years (see Rubin, Coplan, Chen, Buskirk, & Wojslawowicz, 2005, for a recent review). The early work of Piaget (e.g., 1926, 1932), Mead (1934), and Sullivan (1953) emphasized the importance of peer involvement for children's social development. Piaget suggested that peer interaction provides children with an important and unique learning environment. In particular, exposure to instances of interpersonal differences of opinion and thought with one's peers (as opposed to interactions with adults), and opportunities for discussion and negotiation about these differences, were viewed as aiding children in the acquisition and development of sensitive perspective-taking skills in interpersonal relationships.

Mead (1934) echoed Piaget's emphasis on the importance of the development of perspective taking through peer interaction; however, he also stressed the significance of peer interaction in the development of the self-system. In particular, Mead believed that exchanges among peers, in the contexts of cooperation, competition, conflict, and friendly discussion, allowed the child to gain an understanding of the self as both subject and object. According to the notion of the "looking glass self," Mead suggested that children experienced themselves indirectly through the responses of their peers. Finally, Sullivan (1953) proposed that peer relationships are essential for the development of skills for cooperation, compromise, empathy, and altruism. Sullivan emphasized the importance of "chumships," or special relationships, for the emergence of these concepts. The underlying thread connecting these theorists is the emphasis on experiences within the peer group, and its role in the acquisition, maintenance, and practice of important social skills.

It was assumed that peer interaction and particularly social play, as defined above, was of developmental significance. Researchers have long since provided support for this conjecture (e.g., Azmitia, Lippman, & Ittel, 1999; Hogan & Tudge, 1999). These theoretical positions and the empirical support of them take on somewhat different meaning when one ponders the question, "What about those who rarely engage others in social play?" We address this question below.

Assessing Social and Nonsocial Play

There currently exist many different measures designed to assess social and nonsocial play and its related constructs. These measures can be characterized in terms of the source of information regarding children's play behaviors: (1) outside sources; and (2) direct observation.

Outside Source Assessments Outside source assessment procedures involve asking "expert" informants, such as peers, parents, and teachers, to rate or nominate children's social inclinations. There are several advantages to using paper-and-pencil rating scales or nomination techniques. To begin with, outside source assessment is comparatively quick and inexpensive. As well, parents, classmates, and teachers have the potential to observe children in many different circumstances and for long periods of time; thus, they can make inferences about specific children's "everyday" behaviors.

The disadvantage of outside source observation methods center on the use of untrained observers for the purpose of data collection. There may be some bias in their ratings of the children's characteristic social behavior patterns. More importantly, however, because they are untrained, they may not be able to identify specific and detailed aspects of behaviors. This may be particularly germane when assessing social and nonsocial play, as distinctions are made between very fine-grained components of behaviors.

Perhaps as a result, although there are a plethora of measures designed to examine related constructs (i.e., children's social competence, personality, temperament, classroom behaviors), there are relatively few teacher and parent rating scale measures designed specifically to assess social and nonsocial play. In the last few years, several measures have evolved, including the Preschool Play Behavior scale (Coplan & Rubin, 1998), the Penn Interactive Peer Play scale (Fantuzzo, Coolahan, Mendez, McDermott, & Sutton-Smith, 1998), and the Teacher Behavior Rating scale (Hart et al., 2000). However, the most common method used to assess young children's social and nonsocial play has been through the use of direct behavioral observations.

Direct Observations Direct observation techniques involve the systematic recording of children's behaviors. There are several advantages to observational techniques: First, the behaviors observed are face valid. Second, blind observers reduce biases in the coding process. That is, coders are not influenced by their past knowledge of a child's behaviors. Finally, coders can be trained to observe and record very specific and detailed behaviors.

Disadvantages of observational techniques include obvious costs in time and personnel. Also, coders may be limited in the contexts, settings, and time frames during which they can observe behavior. Methodological advances in both time- and event-sampling techniques, however, have increased the generalizibility of direct observational techniques.

There currently exist several observational coding schemes designed to assess social and nonsocial play and their related constructs (see Gitlin-Weiner, Sandgrund, & Schaefer, 2000, for a review). The social aspects of children's play have been investigated using time sampling (e.g., Spinrad et al., 2004); event samples (e.g., Harrist, Zaia, Bates, Dodge & Pettit, 1997); and scan samples (e.g., Ladd & Profilet, 1996). These coding schemes have been employed to observe social and nonsocial play in laboratory playrooms (e.g., Rubin, Cheah, & Fox, 2001), classrooms (e.g., Coplan, Gavinski-Molina, Lagace-Seguin, & Wichmann, 2001), and on the playground (e.g., Hart, 1993). In our work, we have made frequent use of the Play Observation scale (POS, Rubin, 2001). This measure is described in more detail below.

The Play Observation Scale The Play Observation scale (POS; Rubin, 2001) was developed in the 1970s to allow observations to be made of the structural components of play (as defined by Piaget, 1932; Smilansky, 1968) as they were nested in the social participation contexts described by Parten (1932). Early work focused on developmental, normative observations of preschool, kindergarten, and elementary school children during "free play" (e.g., Rubin, Hymel, & Mills, 1989; Rubin, Maioni, & Hornung, 1976; Rubin, Watson, & Jambor, 1978). The POS employs a time sampling methodology within which 10-second segments are coded for both social participation (e.g., solitary, parallel, group) and the cognitive quality of children's play (e.g., functional-sensorimotor, constructive, dramatic, games-with-rules). Several additional free play behaviors are assessed, including instances of unoccupied behavior, onlooking, exploration, peer conversation, anxious behaviors, hovering, transitional behavior, rough-and-tumble play, and aggression. The POS coding taxonomy is illustrated in Figure 9.1.

The use of the POS in our laboratories (e.g., Coplan, Bowker, & Cooper, 2003; Coplan, Prakash, O'Neil, & Armer, 2004; Coplan, Wichmann, & Lagace-Seguin, 2001; Rubin, Burgess, & Hastings, 2002; Rubin, Chen, McDougall, Bowker, & McKinnon, 1995) and in many others (e.g., Fox, Henderson, Rubin, Calkins, & Schmidt, 2001; Guralnick, Hammond, & Connor, 2003; Henderson, Marshall, Fox, & Rubin, 2004; Lloyd & Howe, 2003) has allowed for a clearer understanding of children's social play and nonsocial play behaviors.

The POS has been particularly influential in allowing for a detailed assessment of children's nonsocial play. Using the POS, we have combined aspects of Parten's nonsocial participation categories to create three distinct subtypes of nonsocial play behaviors (e.g., Coplan, Rubin, Fox, & Calkins, 1994). Thus, for example, *reticent behavior* is identified by the frequent production of onlooking behaviors (prolonged watching of other children without accompanying play) or being unoccupied (wandering aimlessly, staring off into space). *Solitary-passive* play includes the quiescent exploration of objects and/or constructive activity while playing alone. Finally, *solitary-active* play is characterized by repeated sensorimotor actions with or without objects (functional activities) or by solitary dramatizing. As described below, each of these different forms of nonsocial play appear to have different meanings, reflect different developmental pathways, and are associated with decidedly different psychosocial outcomes.

Individual Differences in Social and Nonsocial Play

It is well documented that with increasing age, children are more likely to engage in social play (see Rubin, Bukowski, & Parker, 1998 for a review). However, there also exist marked individual differences in the degree to which children are socially initiative and willing to participate in peer play. In recent years, it has become increasingly clear that individual differences in children's social and

Name of Child :_____ Age _____

Time Sample

	:10	:20	:30	:40	:50	:60	
uncodable							
out of room							
transitional							
unoccupied							
onlooker							
Solitary Behaviors:							
Occupied							
Constructive							
Exploratory							
Functional							
Dramatic							
Games							
Parallel Behaviors:							
Occupied							
Constructive							
Exploratory							
Functional							
Dramatic							
Games							
Group Behaviors:							
Occupied							
Constructive							
Exploratory							
Functional							
Dramatic							
Games							
Peer Conversation							
Double Coded Behaviors:							
Anxious Behaviors							
Hovering							
Aggression							
Rough-and-Tumble							

Conversation/Interacting With: 1_____ 2_____ 3_____ 4_____ 5_____ 6_____

Figure 9.1 Sample of Play Observation Scale Coding Sheet

nonsocial play patterns are influenced by children's dispositional characteristics (temperament, sex), social motivations, and social competence. Indeed, play patterns are also influenced by the cultures within which children live. In this regard, the display of social play and different forms of nonsocial play can be considered marker variables for psychosocial adjustment in childhood.

Temperament and Biological Influences There is growing support for a link between biology and social play. This link can be accessed through the study of temperamental characteristics that serve as biologically based precursors to the display of different play styles. For example, Kagan (e.g., Kagan, Reznick, & Snidman, 1999; Kagan & Saudino, 2001) has distinguished between *inhibited* and *uninhibited* children. The former group can be characterized as being quiet, hypervigilant, and restrained while they experience novel situations. The latter group, alternatively, reacts with spontaneity, as if they do not distinguish between novel and familiar situations. Inhibited children, compared to their uninhibited counterparts, have higher and more stable heart rates, larger pupil diameters, greater motor tension, and higher levels of morning cortisol (see Sanson, Hemphill, & Smart, 2004, for a recent review). These data are viewed as supporting the notion that inhibited children have a biologically predispositioned low threshold for arousal in the face of novelty.

Several researchers have argued that physiological mechanisms of emotional regulation are important components of children's dispositions to engage others in interactions or to withdraw from them (e.g., Eisenberg, Shepard, Fabes, Murphy, & Guthrie, 1998; Fabes, Hanish, Martin, & Eisenberg, 2002; Gunnar, Sebanc, Tout, Donzella, & van Dulmen, 2003; Henderson et al., 2004). These physiological mechanisms include patterns of hemispheric imbalance (as measured by EEG activation) and vagal tone (a measure of parasympathetic control over heart rate) (Fox, Rubin, et al, 1995; Schmidt, Calkins, Rubin, & Coplan, 1997; Porges & Doussard-Roosevelt, 1997; Schmidt & Schulkin, 1999). For example, Fox, Henderson et al. (2001) found that stable, inhibited children displayed greater right frontal EEG activity at 9 months and 4 years of age than did the uninhibited group, and were also rated more fearful, shy, and less sociable by their mothers. By comparison, a group of children who displayed inhibited behavior at 4 months of age, but whose behavior was not consistent over time (i.e., who were no longer reportedly inhibited at 24 or 48 months of age), did not show such EEG assymetry. These findings suggest a strong role of brain overactivity in social behavior, namely anxiety in social situations.

Parental Influences

Other influences on children's inclinations to engage primarily in social or nonsocial play are parent–child relationships and parenting behaviors. Conceptually, psychologists have predicted that when insecure anxious-resistant ("C") children find themselves in group settings with peers, they should attempt to avoid rejection through the demonstration of passive, adult-dependent behavior and withdrawal from social interaction (Renken, Egeland, Marvinney, Sroufe, & Mangelsdorf, 1989; Sroufe & Waters, 1977). Empirical support derives from data indicating that infants who experience an anxious-resistant (C) attachment relationship appear to be socially withdrawn at age 7 (Renken et al., 1989). Additional support for both concurrent and predictive associations between insecure attachment and social withdrawal comes from more recent studies (e.g., Booth, Rose-Krasner, McKinnon, & Rubin, 1994; Rubin, Booth, Rose-Krasnor, & Mills, 1995).

Precursors to social play are also predicted by the parent–child attachment relationship in infancy. For example, secure attachment status in infancy is predictive in early childhood of more elaborate play styles, more positive social engagement, and less behavioral inhibition than insecure attachment relationships (e.g., Burgess, Marshall, Rubin, & Fox, 2003; Rose-Krasner, Rubin, Booth & Coplan, 1996). As well, securely attached 4-year-olds are more likely to engage peers in social play than their insecurely attached agemates (Booth et al., 1994).

Insofar as parenting styles and behaviors are concerned, *authoritative* parents (high in control and warmth) are likely to raise well-adjusted children who are socially responsible and competent, friendly, cooperative, and prosocial with peers (Baumrind, 1967, 1971). In contrast, *authoritarian* parents (harsh, coercive, and low in warmth) are likely to have children who are socially incompetent, aggressive, or socially withdrawn (Baumrind, 1967, 1971, 1991; Dishion, 1990, Lamborn, Mounts, Steinberg, & Dornbusch, 1991; Mize & Pettit, 1997).

More recently, researchers have begun to focus on the role of parental *overprotection* and *over-intrusion* (Mills & Rubin, 1998; Rubin, Burgess, & Hastings, 2002; Rubin, Cheah, & Fox, 2001; Rubin, Nelson, Hastings, & Asendorpf, 1999). Overprotective parents overmanage situations for their child and discourage child independence. It is believed that this pattern of parental responses interferes with children's abilities to develop their own coping skills for handling socially stressful situations. Such children would be less likely to engage in social play. For example, Rubin, Nelson et al. (1999) found that maternally rated child shyness at age 2 was negatively related to both mother's and father's encouragement of independence at age 4, indicating that parents' perceptions of their child's shyness influences their social strategies, which may limit the child's opportunities to develop coping strategies for their social wariness.

Transactional Processes Given that both biological and environmental factors influence children's social and nonsocial play, the interplay between biological processes and parenting strategies also warrants investigation. Rubin and colleagues developed a theoretical model that considers pathways to social/nonsocial play styles and adjustment (or maladjustment) which are jointly influenced by child characteristics, parental socialization practices, and the quality of relationships within and outside the family (e.g., Rubin & Burgess, 2002; Rubin & Lollis, 1988; Rubin & Mills, 1991).

Results from several recent studies have suggested that these transactional processes are critical factors in determining peer-related outcomes (Rubin, Burgess, & Hastings, 2002; Rubin, Nelson, Hastings, & Asendorpf,1999; Spangler & Schieche, 1998). For instance, Spangler and Schieche (1998) found that insecurely attached infants who were behaviorally inhibited had higher salivary cortisol levels, indicating that it is a combination of attachment and temperament that leads to changes in physiological stimulation during a novel situation. Rubin, Burgess, and Hastings (2002) also found an interaction between temperament and parenting in predicting children's play behavior. Dispositionally based behavioral inhibition at 2 years predicted socially reticent behavior at 4 years only for those children whose mothers were overprotective and intrusive.

Developmental Outcomes of Social and Nonsocial Play

Social Play and Adjustment Returning to our earlier discussion of play, it is of significance that social pretense, or sociodramatic play, has generally been regarded as a marker of social competence, positive adjustment, and well-being during the period of early childhood (e.g., Howes, 1992; Rubin, Bukowski, & Parker, 1998; Rubin, Fein, & Vanderberg, 1983). The frequent production of sociodramatic play during the preschool and kindergarten years is associated with the development of language skills, early literacy, creativity, theory of mind, self-regulation, and school achievement (e.g., Elias & Berk, 1993; Levy, Wolfgang, & Koorland, 1992; Schwebel, Rosen, & Singer, 1999; Singer & Lythcott, 2002).

There have been relatively few longitudinal studies of the developmental course of children's social play, broadly defined. An exception to this was the Waterloo Longitudinal Project (WLP), initiated originally in 1980 to examine the stability and predictive outcomes of children's social and nonsocial play (e.g., Rubin, 1982, 1985; Rubin, Hymel, & Mills,1989; Rubin, Hymel, Mills, & Rose-Krasner, 1991; Rubin, Chen, & Hymel, 1993; Rubin, Booth, Rose-Krasner, & Mills,1995).

Results from the WLP indicated that social play is relatively stable from preschool through to adolescence (e.g., Rubin, 1993; Rubin & Both, 1989; Rubin, Hymel, & Mills, 1989). Moreover, observed social play in early childhood predicted positive feelings of self worth and was *negatively* associated with feelings of loneliness in late childhood (e.g., Rubin, Hymel, & Mills, 1989). Similar results were found following the participants into adolescence. Rubin and colleagues (Rubin, Coplan, Fox, & Calkins, 1995) followed a sample of children from the WLP into high school (age 14 years). Results indicated that an aggregate of observed social play and peer rated social competence at age 7 years significantly predicted higher self-regard and felt group security, and lower self-reported loneliness in adolescence.

Overall, social play is generally associated with social adjustment. However, there is some evidence to suggest that the frequent display of social play, in and of itself, does not "guarantee" social adjustment. For example, Rubin, Booth, Rose-Krasner, & Mills (1995) found that social play in early childhood was not only predictive of positive outcomes in adolescence, but also predicted deviant behaviors (i.e., drug and alcohol use).

Children's emotion regulation appears to play a key role here. Whereas the ability to regulate negative emotions is related to social competence and peer acceptance (e.g., Eisenberg, et al., 2004; Eisenberg, Pidada, & Liew, 2001) the inability to regulate affect is associated with socially incompetent behavior (e.g., Calkins, Gill, Johnson, & Smith, 1999). More specifically, Rubin, Coplan, Fox, and Calkins (1995) found that an extreme group of socially interactive preschoolers who were also emotionally *dysregulated* (i.e., temperamentally highly reactive and difficult to soothe), were rated by mothers as having more externalizing problems than comparison groups of extremely socially interactive but well-regulated children and average children. Thus, not all young children who display a high frequency of social play grow up to be competent, well-adjusted, teenagers.

Nonsocial Play and Adjustment It had been previously accepted that noninteractive children are at risk for later maladjustment difficulties in later childhood and adolescence (see Rubin, Burgess, Kennedy, & Stewart, 2003, for a review). However, results from recent research indicate that the relations between nonsocial play types and psychosocial adjustment in childhood are quite complex. In fact, different forms of nonsocial play appear to reflect different underlying psychological mechanisms, and are associated with decidedly difference outcomes.

To begin with, *reticent behavior* (i.e., onlooking behaviors and being unoccupied) is thought to indicate temperamental shyness and social fearfulness (e.g., Coplan, Rubin, Fox, & Calkins, 1994). A child frequently displaying reticent behavior is thought to be caught in an approach-avoidance conflict (Asendorpf, 1990), wanting to engage in social interactions with peers but simultaneoulsy desiring to avoid others because of a fear of social interaction.

There is strong emprirical support for this conceptualization. To begin with, the display of reticent behavior in childhood has been related to a constellation of psychophysiological variables (e.g., greater right frontal EEG activation, higher levels of morning cortisol) that similarly underlie the construct of behavioral inhibition (e.g., Henderson et al., 2004; Schmidt, Fox, Rubin, & Sternberg, 1997). Moreover, reticent behavior in childhood has also been associated with temperamental shyness, the overt display of anxious behaviors, internalizing problems, social incompetence, low self-worth, and peer exclusion (Coplan, 2000; Coplan, Findlay, & Nelson, 2004; Coplan, Gavinski-Molina, Lagace-Seguin, & Wichmann, 2001; Coplan, Prakash, O'Neil, & Armer, 2004; Coplan & Rubin, 1998; Coplan, Rubin, Fox, & Calkins, 1994; Fox et al., 2001; Hart et al., 2000; Henderson, Marshall, Fox, & Rubin, 2004; Rubin, Burgess, & Hastings, 2002; Rubin, Chen et al., 1995).

In contrast, solitary-active play (i.e., solitary-functional and solitary-dramatic play) is thought to reflect social immaturity and impulsiveness (Rubin, 1982). Although it occurs rather infrequently during free play (approximately 3% of the time), Rubin (1982) speculated that solitary-active behavior is quite negatively salient to the peer group, even in early childhood, and that children who engage in solitary-active behaviors are actually playing alone because they are being isolated by others. In support of this notion, solitary-active behavior in childhood has been associated with peer rejection, poor social problem solving, impulsivity, externalizing problems, and academic difficulties (Coplan, 2000; Coplan, Rubin et al., 1994; Coplan & Rubin, 1998; Coplan, Wichmann, & Lagace-Seguin, 2001; Rubin, 1982).

It is interesting to note here that the same *structural* form of social play can have very different meanings when displayed in different contexts. Thus, as mentioned earlier, although sociodramatic play (group pretense) is generally viewed as a index of social competence and social adjustment, *solitary*-dramatic behavior, in the presence of peers, appears to reflect impulsivity and social immaturity; it is also associated with externalizing (or acting-out) problems in early childhood.

Finally, solitary-passive play (i.e., solitary-exploratory and solitary-constructive play) has been generally thought to reflect unsociability, or a preference for playing alone (Rubin & Asendorpf, 1993). Children who frequently display solitary-passive behaviors are thought to possess the necessary skills to interact socially, but not to evidence a strong desire for peer play (Rubin, 1982). Empirical support for this characterization came from a series of studies indicating that solitary-passive behavior (in early childhood) was not associated with indices of psychosocial maladaptation (e.g., Coplan, 2000; Coplan, Rubin, Fox, & Calkins, 1994; Coplan & Rubin, 1998; Rubin, 1982).

However, results from recent studies have called into question the meaning of solitary-passive play in early childhood (e.g., Lloyd & Howe, 2003; Spinrad et al., 2004). For example, Coplan and colleagues (2001) reported that observed solitary-passive play in kindergarteners was associated with temperamental shyness and indices of maladjustment for boys but not girls. Coplan and colleagues (2004) found that although children rated as unsociable were less often observed to initiate social interactions with peers and were viewed by teachers as more socially withdrawn, they were not significantly more likely to display solitary-passive behavior.

Thus, there is evidence to suggest that solitary-passive play itself may have varying psychological and emotional meanings, and may be frequently displayed by different types of children for different reasons. Direct evidence for this has been provided by Henderson, Marshall, Fox, & Rubin (2004). In a longitudinal study, they found that a subset of preschool children who displayed frequent solitary-passive play had a lower resting heart period and were more likely to have been shy and inhibited when they were toddlers. This suggests that some children who frequently displayed solitary-passive behavior tended to be shy, but coped sufficiently with their approach-avoidance conflicts in order to at least play quietly in the presence of peers. In contrast, other children who frequently displayed solitary-passive play had a higher resting heart period and were neither previously shy nor inhibited as toddlers. Thus, some children who display frequent solitary-passive play do not appear to be anxious or distressed. Further research is clearly required in this area, particularly to explore the long term longitudinal outcomes associated with this type of nonsocial play.

Summary and Future Directions

The goal of this essay was to explore the constructs of young children's social and nonsocial play within the context of peer interactions. Clearly, *social* play provides children with a unique and important environment for development. Through social play and associated interactions with peers, children are exposed to a domain where they can acquire important social-cognitive and interpersonal skills. Social play allows children to acquire an understanding of other children's perspectives, and leads to a greater understanding of cooperation, negotiation, and conflict resolution. Moreover, children who experience a consistently impoverished quality of social play and social interaction are at risk for later social maladjustment. Thus, social play can be construed as representing a "safe-haven" for children to learn about themselves and others, and to acquire skills and knowledge that will assist them throughout their lifetimes.

In contrast, the different forms of *nonsocial* play appear to have different meanings and are associated with different outcomes. Some children appear to play alone (displaying reticent behavior) because they are shy and anxious, lacking in social competence, and experiencing internalizing problems. Other children seem to play alone (displaying solitary-active behavior) because they are immature, impulsive, and excluded by peers, and display externalizing problems. Finally, although some children likely play alone because of a lack of interest in social interaction, such children may not display a particular type of nonsocial play.

Additional longitudinal work should explore the meanings and implications of social and nosocial play into middle childhood and adolescence. Moreover, a deeper understanding is required of the role of children's relationships (i.e., with parents and peers) in the developmental trajectories associated with the frequent display of social or nonsocial play. Finally, the vast majority of research related to social and nonsocial play has been conducted in Western cultures. There is likely significant cultural variation in the meanings of different forms of solitude. Thus, there are many avenues for future researchers to explore related to the nature and utcomes of social play and nonsocial play.

References

Andrus, R. (1924). *A tentative inventory of the habits of children from two to four years of age.* Columbia University, Teachers College, Contributions to Education, No. 160.

Asendorpf, J. B. (1990). Beyond social withdrawal: Shyness, unsociability and peer avoidance. *Human Development, 33,* 250–259.

Azmitia, M., Lippman, D. N., & Ittel, A. (1999). On the relation of personal experience to early adolescents' reasoning about best friendship deterioration. *Social Development, 8,* 275–291.

Baumrind, D. (1967). Child care patterns anteceding three patterns of preschool behavior. *Genetic Psychology Monographs, 75,* 43–88.

Baumrind, D. (1971). Current patterns of parental authority. *Developmental Psychology Monographs, 4* (No. 1, Pt. 2).

Baumrind, D. (1991). To nurture nature. *Behavioral and Brain Sciences, 14,* 386.

Bott, H. (1928). Observation of play activities of three- year-old children. *Genetic Psychology Monographs, 4,* 44–88.

Booth, C. L., Rose-Krasnor, L., McKinnon, J., & Rubin, K. H. (1994). Predicting social adjustment in middle childhood: The role of preschool attachment security and maternal style. *Social Development, 3,* 189–204.

Burgess, K. B., Marshall, P. J., Rubin, K. H., & Fox, N. A. (2003). Infant attachment and temperament as predictors of subsequent externalizing problems and cardiac physiology. *Journal of Child Psychology and Psychiatry and Allied Disciplines, 44,* 819–831.

Calkins, S. D., Gill,, K. L., Johnson, M. C., & Smith, C. L. (1999). Emotional reactivity and emotional regulation strategies as predictors of social behavior with peers during toddlerhood. *Social Development, 8,* 310–334.

Coplan, R. J. (2000). Assessing nonsocial play in early childhood: Conceptual and methodological approaches. In A. Sandgrund & K. Gitlin-Weiner (Eds.), *Play diagnosis and assessment* (2nd ed., pp. 563–598). New York: Wiley.

Coplan, R. J., Bowker, A., & Cooper, S. M. (2003). Parenting daily hassles, child temperament and social adjustment in preschool. *Early Childhood Research Quarterly, 18,* 376–395.

Coplan, R. J., Findlay, L. C., & Nelson, L. J. (2004). Characteristics of preschoolers with lower perceived competence. *Journal of Abnormal Child Psychology, 32,* 399–408.

Coplan, R. J., Gavinski-Molina, M. H., Lagace-Seguin, D. G., & Wichmann, C. (2001). When girls versus boys play alone: Nonsocial play and adjustment in kindergarten. *Developmental Psychology, 37,* 464–474.

Coplan, R. J., Prakash, K., O'Neil, K., & Armer, M. (2004). Do you "want" to play? Distinguishing between conflicted shyness and social disinterest in early childhood. *Developmental Psychology, 40,* 244–258.

Coplan, R. J., & Rubin, K. H. (1998). Exploring and assessing nonsocial play in the preschool: The development and validation of the Preschool Play Behavior Scale. *Social Development, 7,* 72–91.

Coplan, R. J., Rubin, K. H., Fox, N. A., & Calkins, S. D. (1994). Being alone, playing alone, and acting alone: Distinguishing among reticence and passive and active solitude in young children. *Child Development, 65,* 129–137.

Coplan, R. J., Wichmann, C., & Lagace-Seguin, D. (2001). Solitary-active play: A marker variable for maladjustment in the preschool? *Journal of Research in Childhood Education, 15,* 164–172.

Dishion, T. J. (1990). The family ecology of boys' peer relations in middle childhood. *Child Development, 61,* 874–892.

Eisenberg, N., Pidada, S., & Liew, J. (2001). The relations of regulation and negative emotionality to Indonesian children's social functioning. *Child Development, 72,* 1747–1763.

Eisenberg, N., Shepard, S. A., Fabes, R. A., Murphy, B. C., & Guthrie, I. K. (1998). Shyness and children's emotionality, regulation, and coping: Contemporaneous, longitudinal, and across-context relations. *Child Development, 69,* 767–790.

Eisenberg, N., Spinrad, T. L., Fabes, R. A., Reiser, M., Cumberland, A., Shepard, S. A., et al. (2004). The relations of effortful control and impulsivity to children's resiliency and adjustment. *Child Development, 75,* 25–46.

Elias, C. L., & Berk, L. E. (1993). Self-regulation in young children: Is there a role for sociodramatic play? *Early Childhood Research Quarterly, 17,* 216–238.

Fabes, R. A., Hanish, L. D., Martin, C. L., & Eisenberg, N. (2002). Young children's negative emotionality and social isolation: A latent growth curve analysis. *Merrill-Palmer Quarterly, 48*, 284–307.

Fantuzzo, J., Coolahan, K., Mendez, J., McDermott, P., & Sutton-Smith, B. (1998). Contextually-relevant validation of peer play constructs with African American Head Start children: Penn Interactive Peer Play Scale. *Early Childhood Research Quarterly, 13*, 411–431.

Fox, N. A., Henderson, H. A., Rubin, K. H., Calkins, S. D., & Schmidt, L. A. (2001). Stability and instability of behavioral inhibition and exuberance: Psychophysiological and behavioral factors influencing change and continuity across the first four years of life. *Child Development, 72*, 1–21.

Fox, N. A., Rubin, K. H., Calkins, S. D., Marshall, T. R., Coplan, R. J., Porges, S. W., & Long, J. (1995). Frontal activation asymmetry and social competence at four years of age: Left frontal hyper and hypo activation as correlates of social behavior in preschool children. *Child Development, 66*, 1770–1784.

Giltin-Weiner, K., Sandgrund, A., & Schaefer, C. (2000). *Play diagnosis and assessment* (2nd ed.). New York: Wiley.

Gulranick, M. J., Hammond, M. A., & Connor, R. T. (2003). Subtypes of nonsocial play: Comparisons between young children with and without developmental delays. *American Journal of Mental Retardation, 108*, 347–362.

Gunnar, M. R., Sebanc, A. M., Tout, K., Donzella, B., & van Dulmen, M. M. H., (2003). Peer rejection, temperament, and cortisol activity in preschoolers. *Developmental Psychobiology, 43*, 346–358.

Harrist, A. W., Zaia, A. F., Bates, J. E., Dodge, K. A., & Pettit, G. S. (1997). Subtypes of social withdrawal in early childhood: Sociometric status and social-cognitive differences across four years. *Child Development, 68*, 278–294.

Hart, C. H. (1993). *Children on playgrounds: Research perspectives and applications*. New York: State University of New York Press.

Hart, C. H., Yang, C., Nelson, L. J., Robinson, C. C., Olsen, J. A., Nelson, D. A., Porter, C. L., Jin, S., Olsen, S. F., & Wu, P. (2000). Peer acceptance in early childhood and subtypes of socially withdrawn behavior in China, Russia, and the United States. *International Journal of Behavioural Development, 24*, 73–81.

Henderson, H., Marshall, P., Fox, N. A., & Rubin, K. H. (2004). Converging psychophysiological and behavioral evidence for subtypes of social withdrawal in preschoolers. *Child Development, 75*, 251–263.

Hogan, D. M., & Tudge, T. R. H. (1999). Implications of Vygotsky's theory for peer learning. In A. King & A. M. O'Donnell (Eds.), *Cognitive perspectives on peer learning: The Rutgers invitational symposium on education series* (pp. 39–65). Mahwah, NJ: Lawrence Erlbaum.

Howes, C. (1992). *The collaborative construction of pretend*. New York: State University of New York Press.

Kagan J., Reznick, J. S., & Snidman, N. (1999). Biological basis of childhood shyness. In D. Muir & A. Slater (Eds), *The Blackwell reader in development psychology* (pp. 65–78). Malden, MA: Blackwell.

Kagan, J., & Saudino, J. (2001). Behavioral inhibition and related temperaments. In J. K. Hewitt & R. N. Emde (Eds.), *Infancy to early childhood: Genetic and environmental influences on developmental change* (pp. 111–119). London: Oxford University Press.

Ladd, G. W., & Profilet, S. M. (1996). The Child Behavior Scale: A teacher-report measure of young children's aggressive, withdrawn, and prosocial behaviors. *Developmental Psychology, 32*, 1008–1024.

Lamborn, S. D., Mounts, N. S., Steinberg, L., & Dornbusch, S. M. (1991). Patterns of competence and adjustment among adolescents from authoritative, authoritarian, indulgent and neglectful families. *Child Development, 62*, 1049–1065.

Levy, A. K., Wolfgang, C. H., & Koorland, M. A. (1992). Sociodramatic play as a method for enhancing the language performance of kindergarten age students. *Early Childhood Research Quarterly, 7*, 245–262.

Lloyd, B., & Howe, N. (2003). Solitary play and convergent and divergent thinking skills in preschool children. *Early Childhood Research Quarterly, 18*, 22–41.

Mead, G. H. (1934). *Mind, self, and society*. Chicago: University of Chicago Press.

Mills, R. S. L., & Rubin, K. H. (1998). Are behavioural and psychological control both differentially associated with childhood aggression and social withdrawal? *Canadian Journal of Behavioural Science, 30*, 132–136.

Mize, J., & Pettit, G. S. (1997). Mothers' social coaching, mother–child relationship style, and children's peer competence: Is the medium the message? *Child Development, 68*, 12–332.

Parten, M. B. (1932). Social participation among preschool children. *Journal of Abnormal Psychology, 27*(2), 243–269.

Piaget, J. (1926). *The language and thought of the child*. London: Routledge & Kegan Paul.

Piaget, J. (1932). *The moral judgment of the child*. Glencoe, IL: Free Press.

Piaget, J. (1962). *Play, dreams, and imitation in childhood*. New York: Norton.

Porges, S. W., & Doussard-Roosevelt, J .A. (1997). Early physiological patterns and later behavior. In M. D. Franzen & H. W. Reese (Eds.), *Biological and neuropsychological mechanisms: Life-span developmental psychology* (pp. 163–179). Hillsdale, NJ: Lawrence Erlbaum.

Renken, B., Egeland, B., Marvinney, D., Sroufe, L.A., & Mangelsdorf, S. (1989). Early childhood antecedents of aggression and passive withdrawal in early elementary school. *Journal of Personality, 57*, 257–281.

Rose-Krasner, L., Rubin, K. H. Booth, C. L., & Coplan, R. J. (1996). The relation of maternal directiveness and child attachment security to social competence in preschoolers. *International Journal of Behavioral Development, 19*, 309–325.

Rubin, K. H. (1982). Non-social play in preschoolers: Necessary evil? *Child Development, 53*, 651–657.

Rubin, K. H. (1985). Socially withdrawn children: An "at risk" population. In B. H. Schneider, K. H. Rubin, & J. E. Ledingham (Eds.), *Peer relations and social skills in childhood: Issues in assessment and training* (pp. 125–139). New York: Springer-Verlag.

Rubin, K.H. (1993). The Waterloo Longitudinal Project: Correlates and consequences of social withdrawal from childhood to adolescence. In K. H. Rubin & J. Asendorpf (Eds.), *Social withdrawal, inhibition, and shyness in childhood* (pp. 291–314). Hillsdale, NJ: Lawrence Erlbaum.

Rubin, K. H. (2001). *The Play Observation Scale (POS)*. College Park, MD: University of Maryland..

Rubin, K. H., & Asendorpf, J. B. (1993). Social withdrawal, inhibition, and shyness in childhood: Conceptual and definitional issues. In J. B. Asendorpf & K. H. Rubin (Eds.), *Social withdrawal, inhibition, and shyness in childhood* (pp. 3–17). Hillsdale, NJ: Lawrence Erlbaum.

Rubin, K.H., & Both, L. (1989). Iris pigmentation and sociability in childhood: A re-examination. *Developmental Psychology, 22,* 717–726.

Rubin, K. H., Booth, C., Rose-Krasner, L. & Mills, R. S. L. (1995). Social relationships and social skills: A conceptual and empirical analysis. In S. Shulman (Ed.) *Close relationships and socioemotional development* (pp. 63–94). Westport, CT: Ablex.

Rubin, K. H., Bukowski, W., & Parker, J. G. (1998). Interactions, relationships, and groups. In W. Damon (Ed. in chief) & N. Eisenberg (Vol. Ed.), *Handbook of child psychology: Vol 3. Social, emotional and personality development* (5th ed., pp. 619–700). New York: Wiley.

Rubin, K. H., & Burgess, K. B. (2002). Parents of aggressive and withdrawn children. In M. H. Bornstein (Ed.), *Handbook of parenting: Vol. 1. Children and parenting* (2nd ed., pp. 383–418). Mahwah, NJ: Lawrence Erlbaum.

Rubin, K. H., Burgess, K. B., & Hastings, P. D. (2002). Stability and social-behavioral consequences of toddlers' inhibited temperament and parenting behaviors. *Child Development, 73,* 483–495.

Rubin, K. H., Burgess, K. B., Kennedy, A. E., & Stewart, S. L. (2003). Social withdrawal in childhood. In R. A. Barkley & E. J. Mash (Eds.), *Child psychopathology* (2nd ed.), (pp. 372–406). New York: Guilford Press.

Rubin, K. H., Cheah, C. S. L., & Fox, N. (2001). Emotion regulation, parenting and display of social reticence in preschoolers. *Early Education and Development, 12,* 97–115.

Rubin, K.H., Chen, X., & Hymel, S. (1993). Socioemotional characteristics of withdrawn and aggressive children. *Merrill-Palmer Quarterly, 39,* 518–534.

Rubin, K.H., Chen, X., McDougal, P., Bowker, A., & McKinnon, J. (1995). The Waterloo Longitudinal Project: Predicting internalizing and externalizing problems in adolescence. *Development and Psychopathology, 7,* 751–764.

Rubin, K.H., Coplan, R.J., Chen, X., Buskirk, A., & Wojslawowicz, J. (2005). Peer relationships in childhood. In M. Bornstein & M. Lamb (Eds.), *Developmental psychology: An advanced textbook* (5th ed.), (pp. 469–512). Hillsdale, NJ: Erlbaum.

Rubin, K. H., Coplan, R. J., Fox, N. A., & Calkins, S. D. (1995). Emotionality, emotion regulation, and preschoolers' social adaptation. *Development and Psychopathology, 7,* 49–62.

Rubin, K. H., Fein, G., & Vandenberg, B. (1983). Play. In E. M. Hetherington (Ed.), *Handbook of child psychology: Vol 4. Socialization, personality, and social development.* New York: Wiley.

Rubin, K. H., Hymel, S., & Mills, R. S. L. (1989). Sociability and social withdrawal in childhood: Stability and outcomes. *Journal of Personality, 57,* 238–255.

Rubin, K. H., Hymel, S., Mills, R. S. L., & Rose-Krasner, L. (1991). Conceptualizing different pathways to and from social isolation in childhood. In D. Cicchetti & S. Toth (Eds.), *The Rochester symposium on developmental psychology: Vol 2. Internalizing and extending expressions of dysfunction* (pp. 91–122). New York: Cambridge University Press.

Rubin, K. H., & Lollis, S. P. (1988). Origins and consequences of social withdrawal. In R. Nezworski & J. Belsky (Eds.), *Clinical implications of attachment* (pp. 219–252). Hillsdale, NJ: Lawrence Erlbaum.

Rubin, K. H., Maioni, T. L., & Hornung, M. (1976). Free play behaviors in middle- and lower-class preschoolers: Parten and Piaget revisited. *Child Development, 47,* 414–419.

Rubin, K. H., & Mills, R. S. (1991). Conceptualizing developmental pathways to internalizing disorders in childhood. *Canadian Journal of Behavioural Science, 23,* 300–317.

Rubin, K. H., Nelson, L. J., Hastings, P., & Asendorpf, J. (1999). Transaction between parents' perceptions of their children's shyness and their parenting styles. *International Journal of Behavioral Development, 23,* 937–957.

Rubin, K. H., Watson, K. S., & Jambor, T. W. (1978). Free-play behaviors in preschool and kindergarten children. *Child Development, 49,* 534–536.

Sanson, A., Hemphill, S. A., & Smart, D. (2004). Connections between temperament and social development: A review. *Social Development, 13,* 142–170.

Schmidt, L. A., Fox, N. A., Rubin, K. H., & Sternberg, E. M. (1997). Behavioral and neuroendocrine responses in shy children. *Developmental Psychobiology, 30,* 127–140.

Schmidt, L. A., & Schulkin, J. (1999). *Extreme fear, shyness, and social phobia: Origins, biological mechanisms, and clinical outcomes.* New York: Oxford University Press.

Schwebel, D. C., Rosen, C. S., & Singer, J. L. (1999). Preschoolers' pretend play and theory of mind: The role of jointly constructed pretence. *British Journal of Developmental Psychology, 17,* 333–348.

Singer, J. L., & Lythcott, M. A. (2002). Fostering school achievement and creativity through sociodramatic play in the classroom. *Research in the Schools, 9,* 43–52.

Smilansky, S. (1968*). The effects of sociodramatic play on disadvantaged preschool children.* New York: Wiley.

Spangler, G., & Schieche, M. (1998). Emotional and adrenocortical responses of infants to the strange situation: The differential function of emotional expression. *International Journal of Behavioral Development, 22,* 681–706.

Spinrad, T. L., Eisenberg, N., Harris, E., Hanish, L., Fabes, R. A., Kupanoff, K., Ringwald, S., & Holmes, J. (2004). The relation of children's everyday nonsocial peer play behavior to their emotionality, regulation, and social functioning. *Developmental Psychology, 40,* 67–80.

Sroufe, L. A., & Waters, E. (1977). Heart rate as a convergent measure in clinical and developmental research. *Merrill-Palmer Quarterly, 23,* 3–27.

Sullivan, H. S. (1953). *The interpersonal theory of psychiatry.* New York: Norton.

Verry, E. E. (1923). *A study of mental and social attitudes in the free play of preschool children.* Unpublished master's thesis, State University of Iowa.

10
Sociodramatic Play Pretending Together

PATRICIA MONIGHAN NOUROT

When teachers of young children get together to tell stories about their work, the content of their talks often consists of anecdotes about children's sociodramatic play. Adults marvel at the detail of the characters, settings, and action children derive from the "real" world, delight in the imaginative leaps and connections that define children's ongoing make-believe worlds, and both applaud and lament children's social negotiation techniques. Children collectively spinning a story and stopping along the way to adjust their "frame" or just to check in with one another. Adults watch, sometimes with held breath, as children make moral decisions about who does what and how ideas get to be played, and their hearts respond to the emotional power of the characters and stories that children evoke. Pretend dramatic play reveals the essence of early childhood and privileges those who teach young children to a bird's-eye view of the landscape of imagination created in the hearts and minds of those in their care.

Studying Sociodramatic Play

Researchers in early childhood education have long studied dramatic and sociodramatic play in the lives of young children and their teachers. Early research focused on the affective and psychodynamic aspects of such play, viewing it as a therapeutic tool for working through childhood fears and unconscious emotions, mastering conflict, and fulfilling wishes (Erikson, 1963/1977; Fraiberg, 1959; Gould, 1972; Hartley, Frank, & Goldenson, 1957; Isaacs, 1933). Some contemporary early childhood educators have continued this tradition, drawing on dramatic play to reveal the emotional lives of young children they observe and teach (Ariel, 2002; Fein & Kinney, 1994; ; Katch, 2001; Koplow, 1996; Landreth, 2002; Paley, 1990, 1992). Others have examined sociodramatic play through cognitive lenses. Jean Piaget (1962) described the interaction of imitation and play in children's construction of symbolic thought. Others drew upon his descriptions to devise a scheme for facilitating dramatic and sociodramatic play (Smilansky, 1968, 1990; Smilansky & Shefatya, 1990). They defined two overarching characteristics of such play. The first element is play that children imitate from their experiences in the "real" world, such as a remembered setting, a character's expression or gestures, action, and talk. The second is imagination, or make-believe, which frames play in a pretend context. These two major dramatic play elements include:

- *Role-Play*, imitating the action or verbalization of a character other than the self;
- *Pretending with objects*; using toys, unstructured materials (cloth, sticks, boxes), gesture, or verbal declaration to represent the object;
- *Pretend actions and situations*, using gesture or verbalization to represent actions and/or situations; and
- *Persistence within the imaginary play frame* to create a play episode or event. (Smilansky, 1968, 1990; Smilansky & Shefatya 1990).
- For sociodramatic play, they add two additional criteria:
- Interaction with one or more play partners; and
- Verbal communication among play partners regarding the play event (Smilansky & Shefatya, 1990).

Both dramatic and sociodramatic play encompass a broad range of physical, cognitive, social, emotional, and moral characteristics in the repertoires of children, and both include spontaneity and improvisation (Bergen, 1998, 2002; Bodrova & Leong, 2003; Coohalan, Fantuzzo, Mendez, & McDermott, 2000; Fromberg, 1999, 2002; Frost, Wortham, & Reifel, 2005; Johnson, 1998; Jones, 2003; Roskos & Christie, 2004; Sawyer,1997; Scarlett, Nadeau,Salonius-Pasternak, & Ponte, 2005; J. Singer & Lythcott, 2004; Van Hoorn, Nourot, Scales, & Alward, 2003

Some research has focused more closely on some of the components of sociodramatic play delineated above. Script theory, for example, looks at the schemata children derive from the experiences that they bring to their dramatic play (Corsaro, 1983; Fromberg, 2002; Nelson & Seidman, 1984). Some address scripts that adults use to scaffold play (Neeley, Neeley, Justen, & Tipton-Sumner, 2001; Perry, 2001; Sheridan, Foley, & Radlinski, 1995; Wolfberg, 1999).

Some of these scripts are characterized by the mundane: "event scripts" for bedtime rituals, meal-time routines, going to the doctor, going to church. Others express the social–emotional scripts of daily lives: Grandma's disciplinary techniques; baby sister's invasion of the play space; teenage laments about rules and responsibilities. Content and roles vary by culture and adult perceptions of children's play (Ballenger, 1999; Bowman, 2004; Derman-Sparks & Ramsey, 2005; Joshi, 2005; Roopnarine, Shin, Donovan, & Suppal, 2000).

> Still other scripts may be derived from media or storybooks, with characters and plots shaped by children's interpretations of these outside story forms. These interpretations vary predictably by gender in ways that have been documented by researchers who have studied children's play and imagination (Dyson, 1997, 2003; Katch, 2001; Nicopoulou, 1997, 1998; Nicolopoulou, Scales, & Weintraub, 1994). For example, both the boys and the girls draw images from popular culture (including material transmitted by television, video, and children's books), but what is interesting is that they do so selectively. They have already developed a differential sensitivity and preference for the elements presented to them by their cultural environment; they appropriate different elements and find ways to weave them into distinctive imaginative styles. For example, whereas the girls are particularly fond of princes and princesses and other fairy-tale characters, the boys favor cartoon action heroes such as Superman, He-Man, Teenage Mutant Turtles and so on. (Nicolopoulou et al., 1994, p. 112)

As such, children play what they know, and fuse cognitive and affective dimensions of their lives using both imitated images and fantasy constructions.

Representing Ideas and Feelings in Play

Children appear to become more skilled at detailed representations and the use of abstract symbols with their continued experience as dramatic players (Bergen, 2002; Gowen, 1995; Howes, Unger, &

Matheson, 1992; Singer & Singer, 2004; Uttal et al., 1998). They add elements of make-believe to their "event scripts" through symbolic representation of objects, settings, and characters, as well as conduct ongoing improvisational theater governed by both implicit and explicit rules as they play (Ariel, 2002; Curran 1999; Fromberg, 2002; Sawyer, 1997).

Imagination and make-believe are manifested in an even deeper way through the distortions and paradoxes evident in sociodramatic play events. From one viewpoint these represent children's evolving but "imperfect" understanding of the worlds they represent. From more interpretive viewpoints these distortions and paradoxes express children's propensity to construct mythic forms of meaning outside the boundaries of reality (Ariel, 2002; Egan, 1988; Vandenberg, 2004), or their selective interpretation and even parody of adult roles and behaviors (Gaskins, Miller, & Corsaro, 1992; Nicolopoulou, 1997; Sutton-Smith, 1997). Adults may flatter themselves in assuming that children seek to emulate adult behavior when children may simply be making fun of what they observe adults doing (Schwartzman, 1978).

Framing a Play Script

Metacommunication or metaplay takes place when players communicate to one another the message that "This is play," and then communicate about the content and flow of that play (Bateson, 1972; Sutton-Smith, 1997; Vandenberg, 2004). Much like the processes implicit in improvisational jazz (Oldfather & West, 1994), children signal and respond to one another that what they are doing (or planning to do) is not really what it appears to be, but is instead the delicious paradox humans frame as play. This process is illustrated in the following example, in which Emelia, Mark, and Ethan are playing with a castle they have built from blocks:

> Emelia (to Ethan): You be the crocodile and I'll be the prince.
> Ethan: Here's a net for them to climb up. (He places strands of string along the castle "wall.") Here's a higher part.
> Mark: He goes here, and then here, here, here (moving his toy figure up the wall of the castle).
> Ethan: Here's the horse. The race can start now! Get the king!

Once this make-believe frame is cast around the "play world" (Huizinga, 1950) of children, the metacognitive processes in metaplay weave in and out of the play enactment. These negotiations may occur in both directing, or explicit modes and enacting, or implicit modes of play. In the explicit directing mode children "step out" of the play frame to make suggestions and elaborate on the ongoing script, frequently marking these negotiations with language such as tag questions to establish agreement (Corsaro, 1985; Gaskins, Miller, & Corsaro, 1992). This process in sociodramatic play, mutual intersubjectivity, in which play partners adjust to the perspectives of one another, creates and sustains common ground for their play frame as it flows and expands (Ariel, 2002; Davidson, 1998; Goncu, 1993; Reifel & Yeatman, 1993; Sawyer, 1997; Vandenberg, 2004). For example,

> Ellen and Marcus are playing "camping"in the block area making a tent and campfire from blocks and cloth, and are carrying packs and pretend food from the playhouse.
> Ellen: Let's pretend it started to rain, and we had to go into the tent, OK? (She covers her head with her hands and begins to rush toward the tent.)
> Marcus (agreeing): It started to rain real, real hard, and our boots got muddy. (He covers his head with his hands and begins to walk stiffly, as if sloshing through mud.)

Players might agree to *reframe* or *elaborate* a play script by simply repeating the statement or esture, or extending the idea by adding a new element, as Marcus did. *Countersuggestions* may also follow a particular form in metaplay exchanges within playgroups. These forms may range from overt *contradiction*: "No, it's hot at our camping place"—to *temporizing*—"It was raining, but we were already in our tent `cause it was night."

After these negotiations occur outside the play frame, children reenter their play worlds to enact the elaborated theme or plot. Similar negotiations might occur over character roles, possession of objects (both real and pretend), and the setting of the play (Ariel, 2002; Curran, 1999; Farver, 1992; Fromberg, 2002; Giffin, 1984; Goncu, 1993; Perry, 2001; Sawyer, 1997; Van Hoorn et al., 2003).

In contrast, metaplay in the enactment mode is implicit and more subtle than in the directing mode since children do not step out of the play frame to negotiate. In one sense this form of metaplay may be more sophisticated because it involves using the pretend character role to manipulate and control the play frame from within the script, requiring skill in representing the perspectives of others (Ariel, 2002; Berk, 1994; Curran, 1999; Giffin, 1984; Mead, 1934; Sawyer, 1997), as follows:

> Four-year-old Marney implicitly elaborates the flow of play within her role as the mother:
> Marney (to Elise, who is sitting at the housekeeping corner table): Now darling, it's time to get your coat and go to the bus.
> Ring, ring. Oh hello, teacher. (She picks up a block and holds it to her ear as a phone.)
> Elise (prompts sotto voce): Not teacher, police.
> Marney: Okay. Hello, is this the police? The bridge is flooded? So no school bus? Thank you. Goodbye.
> (to Elise) The river is flooded some more. We have to move our stuff upstairs. (She picks up a chair and makes stair-climbing movements with her feet.)
> Elise (imitates her action, and adds): How will we get food, Mommy?

Such metaplay choreography within the enactment mode draws upon the young child's skills at coordinating multiple perspectives. She represents not only her own perspective as a player in the flood drama, but that of her role as mother within the play, and then the complementary perspectives of both the police on the phone and her "daughter" Elise in relation to the requirements of her role. The children use symbolic representational skills to create a make-believe telephone and make-believe stairs through objects and gesture. The process of representing multiple selves in such play contributes to children's representations of the feelings, beliefs, and intentions of others, and of how roles and rules are coordinated in social contexts. (Astington, 1993; Curran 1999; Lillard & Curenton, 1999; Van Hoorn et al., 2003).

Play Script Strategies

Giffin (1984) proposes a five-element continuum of play negotiation and coordination techniques that range from the overt explicit proposals in the directing mode ("Let's pretend…") to subtle more implicit messages within the enactment mode, such as Marney's messages about the flow of pretend action in the above example. Make-believe orchestration strategies that vary in the degree to which players make the pretend frame explicit exist in between the out-of-frame and in-frame contexts. These include:

1. *Implicit pretend*, in which players make proposals about actions or roles without prefacing them with "Let's pretend" or "Let's say" (a strategy occurring outside the pretend frame in the directing mode).
2. *Prompting*, which is a momentary "step" outside the play frame to prompt another player's performance in a pretend role. Elise's sotto voce correction of Marney's greeting from "teacher" to "police" is an example within this mode.
3. *Storytelling* is marked by a characteristic singsong cadence and the word *and*. It frequently gives

background and detail to the characters and situation of the play worlds, interpreting motives or providing histories of the make-believe events, such as, "And the mom and the dad had to leave the baby home."

4. *Underscoring* is verbal accompaniment to action, more like self-guiding speech than other-guiding speech, such as Mark's saying, "He goes here, here, here" as he moves his toy figure up the wall of the pretend castle.

5. *Ulterior conversation* occurs fully in the enactment mode. Players intentionally propose new elements to the play action not previously present by clarifying characters' histories or intentions within the pretend frame. Marney's comment to Elise, "It's time to get your coat and go to the bus," is an example of this orchestration strategy.

Strategies within the enactment mode, in which the rules of pretend remain implicit and negotiation about play occurs within characters' roles, are characteristic of older children, who skillfully interweave rationales for action into the flow of pretend play (Ariel, 2002; Curran, 1999).

Scaffolding Metaplay Negotiations

The shared histories of children who are frequent playmates may make negotiations about the play frame go more smoothly as they establish patterns of control, compromise, and reciprocity (Howes et al., 1992; Perry, 2001; Ramsey, 1998; Reifel & Yeatman, 1993). Shared scripts may also come from events outside the microsphere of the classroom, especially traumatic or confusing ones, such as the winter floods played out in the example above, or from powerful characters and action sequences derived from children's literature, media, or community events, thus ensuring that children's schemes for enactment have many qualities in common (Ariel, 2002; Dyson, 1997, 2003; Farver, 1992; Fromberg, 2002; Hughes, 2003; Katch, 2001; Levin, 1998; Lin & Reifel, 1999; Wanigarayake, 2001). "Uneven" friendships between dominant and subordinate children, however, may leave little room for true negotiation, and may alert teachers to the need for their orchestration of particular aspects of sociodramatic play (Paley, 1992; Trawick-Smith, 1992, 1994; Van Hoorn et al., 2003; Wolfberg, 1999).

Metaplay and Cognitive Development

Researchers have linked complex sociodramatic play with many other aspects of development and learning in early childhood, including the construction of creative ideas, language and literacy, abstract reasoning, memory, hypothesis formation, classification, problem solving, narrative organization, and the development of a "theory of mind" (Bergen, 2002; Davidson, 1998; Fein, Ardeila-Ray, & Groth, 2000; Fromberg, 1999; Jarrell, 1998; Kim, 1999; Lillard, 1998; Neves & Reifel, 2002; Roskos & Christie, 2004; Singer & Lythcott, 2004; Singer & Singer, 2004; Smilansky, 1990; Stone & Christie, 1996; Wyver & Spence, 1999). Some researchers contend that the metaplay aspects of sociodramatic play are responsible for many of the cognitive advances associated with complex sociodramatic play reported in the research literature, rather than being due to the play enactment itself (Williamson & Silvern, 1992). It seems very difficult, however, to separate the metaplay elaboration that occurs within play enactment from the flow of play itself, and the nonverbal from the verbal negotiation strategies that take place. The personal histories, cultural and linguistic backgrounds, roles, and power relationships within the play frames further contextualize and complicate the picture of metaplay (Hughes, 2003; King, 1992; Meyers, Klein, & Genishi, 1994; Orellana, 1994; Perry, 2001, 2003; Reifel, Hoke, Pape, & Wisneski, 2004; Roopnarine et al., 2000; Schwartzman, 1978; Sutton-Smith, 1997).

This discussion of communication during play in the service of pretend has focused on the complex social choreography that rests on the interaction of contextual elements. Some of this research described the instrumental value of communication within and about play for children's language, social, and cognitive development. The reverse of this relationship, the role of pretend in the service of communication, elucidates yet another perspective on the function of play and imagination in early childhood and the value of these human capacities for future development and learning, particularly in the ways that boys and girls play, which is discussed in a later section of this chapter (Fagot & Leve, 1998; Honig, 1998; Katch, 2001; Paley, 1984; Ramsey, 1998; Sheldon, 1992).

Finding the Story in Sociodramatic Play

Why is the appeal to mutual pretend or story making so powerful and effective for children? Some theorists make a strong case for the power of imagination and fantasy play to lead the development of thought in early childhood, because they bring adults closer to the truly passionate concerns of young children (Egan, 1988, 1999; Singer & Singer, 2004; Vygotsky, 1978). A teacher–researcher identifies fantasy, friendship, and fairness as the major concerns of preschool children (Paley, 1986). These theorists all point to the affective quality of the "logic" of narrative and find its origin in the social nature of the construction of reality (Ariel, 2002; Bakhtin, 1981; Bruner, 1986; Egan, 1988, 1999; Fein & Kinney, 1994; Sutton-Smith, 1997; Vygotsky, 1978).

In contrast to the view that fantasy somehow undermines the "real purpose of education to create logical, rational thinkers," this view points to fantasy in the play and story of early childhood as the element that "gives rationality life and energy" (Egan, 1988, p. 44). The aspect of sociodramatic play that extends characters, creatures, and events into the realm of the impossible is a primary form of logic that encompasses ambiguity and paradox, and stretches the landscape of the known world into new dimensions and possibilities. This viewpoint is echoed by Jerome Bruner (1986) when he describes meaning-making as the essence of human mental activity and the ways in which narrative forms are intrinsic to the ordering of experience.

"Mythic thinking," in which paradox and ambiguity are integral to making meaning in the world, forms the foundation for noncontradictory forms of logic that appear in middle childhood. Rather than beginning with the known world of the child's everyday life and gradually expanding horizons into the probable and then the fantastic, young children's grasp on reality begins by first exploring its outer limits (Egan, 1988). Therefore, sense and nonsense, the everyday and the fantastic, and the safe and the frightening form dramatic tensions that define the borders of physical, social, and emotional reality. These borders offer frames for children to find their own places, or their own selves, within the scope of their fantasy landscapes. Thought and feeling necessarily merge in these efforts to make sense of life through the stories that children compose and enact in sociodramatic play (Fein & Kinney, 1994; Sutton-Smith, 1997).

> Very generally we may say that young children's experiences of the world are such that they have very little sense of the limits, the boundaries, the contexts, in which much of their experience is meaningful. And they have an urge to make sense of their experience, asking endless questions, eager to learn. The story is the linguistic unit, that, as it were, brings its boundaries with it. Within the story, as within the game, the world is limited, the context is created and given and so the events of a story can be grasped and their meaning understood more readily than can the events in a less hospitable, imprecisely bounded world. (Egan, 1988, p. 100)

Kieran Egan (1988, 1999) explicates three other aspects of the role of fantasy in early childhood that illuminate sociodramatic play: (1) the oral nature of the peer culture in early childhood; (2) the importance of binary opposites in creating dramatic tension in play themes; and (3) the sense of magic and ecstasy revealed in social pretend play. He contends that an essential feature of the union of affect and cognition in early childhood is the oral nature of children's culture He finds parallels between cultures that depend on oral rather than literate communication, and children's fantasy play:

We live in a world of nature, but have invented techniques, developed over uncounted millennia for stimulating a vivid mental life that draws members of a society together by strong affective bonds. For children in our society, too, these techniques create mental worlds distinct from the natural world around us, mental worlds charged with vividness and emotional intensity. (Egan, 1988, p. 85)

Dramatic play is the earliest form of oral storying, a linguistic form that comes fully equipped with its own context. As each aspect of the play-story unfolds, the players clarify and elaborate its meaning by its relationships to other parts. In dramatic play these stories are "told" to the self; in sociodramatic play meanings are situated, communicated, and negotiated in the peer culture (Ariel, 2002; Corsaro, 1985, 1992; Howes & Wishard, 2004; Lancy, 2002; Paley, 1990; Perry, 2001). In doing so, children refine their memory skills, charged with emotion and cast in a story form; they explore metaphor and poetic representation; and they create the social bonds that give life and structure to the peer culture of childhood (Berk, 1994; Dyson; 2003; Gallas, 1994, 2003; Paley, 1999).

The binary oppositions frequently noted in children's dramatic play themes (Bettelheim, 1976; Corsaro, 1985; Egan, 1988; Garvey, 1990; Paley, 1988), such as big/little; love/hate; good guy/bad guy; death/rebirth; threat/security; and lost/found, reflect a characteristic of children's early organization of meaning that helps them discriminate features of their physical and social worlds. Tensions between fantasy and reality mapped by children in their imaginative play contribute to a clarified sense of self, framing ideas of character, plot, and setting through bipolar opposition, and then mediating between these "poles" to enrichment and elaboration of story schemata. These bipolar tensions also support shared scripts and conceptions of roles, settings, and events that facilitate negotiation in sociodramatic play. Children want passionately for play to continue despite the potential pitfalls of differing ideas about characters or events in the play, and realize that sharing understandings about the figures and dramas facilitate play's smooth progress (Bruner, 1986).

Play, particularly sociodramatic play, is the vehicle for young children to make sense of the world and their experiences, and to negotiate these meanings with others. But this is not the whole picture. The joyful engagement of children in social pretend play creates a kind of ecstasy that characterizes the creative process throughout life (Ackerman,1999; Csikszentmihalyi, 1993; Nachmanovitch, 1990; Sutton-Smith, 1997). Social pretend play also evokes "magic," or the exploration of the borders of human experience that characterizes the probing of the mysteries of life found in intellectual and aesthetic disciplines (Kaku, 1994; Zukav, 1979). Play is fun, and as such is valued for its human expression (Elkind, 2003; Sutton-Smith, 1997).

Play at the Leading Edge of Development

This reaching beyond the known in play calls forth theories about the importance of play in leading the development of thought in early childhood (Bodrova & Leong, 2003; Nicopoulou, 1997; Rubin, Fein & Vandenberg, 1983; Vygotsky, 1976, 1978). Play leads development in the early years because it creates the "zone of proximal development" (ZPD) in which children stretch beyond their usual level of functioning in play with their peers (Vygotsky, 1976). This developmental stretch occurs because of the power of relationship in sociodramatic play, although sometimes the effects of these stretches of imagination are viewed as negative rather than positive by adults (Katch, 2001; Van Hoorn et al., 2003). The sense of ecstasy and magic that pervades the mutual exploration of the boundaries of possibility is a powerful motivator to move beyond one's own view to encompass the perspectives of others, a quality consistently found in descriptions of "master players" (Jones & Reynolds, 1992). In this way children develop self-regulation in concert with abstract thinking during pretend play (Bodrova & Leong, 2003; Bronson, 2000; Lewis, 1995).

The Social Nature of All Play

Lev Vygotsky (1978) makes a case that all play is essentially social. Even the Legos, blocks, sticks, toy vehicles, and character dolls used by solitary dramatic players encompass the social meanings of that child's culture (Ariel, 2002; Honig, 1998; Hughes, 2003; Levin, 1998; Oravec, 2000; Reynolds, 2002; Roopnarine et al., 2000; Schwartzman, 1978; Seiter, 1995). An imaginary interlocutor may be more agreeable to one's play agenda but contributes the development of perspective through role taking all the same (Kohlberg & Fein, 1987; Mead, 1934).

All play also has rules (Vygotsky, 1978), and the role of binary opposites in fantasy play may serve to scaffold these rules, as do the shared play events and personal histories, culture, and languages of pretend partners (Curran, 1999; Egan, 1988; Haight & Miller, 1993; Howes & Wishard, 2004; Katch, 2001; King, 1992; Orellana, 1994; Wolfberg, 1999). For example, knowing the characteristics of the bad guy and the good guy, the lost and the finders, the princesses and the princes as accepted within the classroom peer culture allows play to proceed with implicit rules (Nicolopoulou et al., 1994; Paley, 1995). When players violate these rules, enacted play may come to a halt and metaplay negotiation outside the play frame begins. For example:

> Amy and Ruth are playing "Star Wars" on the climbing structure. Amy has taken the role of Princess Leia. Ruth wants to take the same role. Amy suggests that Ruth could be "Princess Leia's sister," and Ruth agrees. Ruth goes to the shelf and selects a large straw hat with ribbons that tie. She asks a participating parent, "Will you tie this on for me?" The adult ties the hat, and Ruth returns to the "spaceship." Amy turns and comments, "Princess Leia doesn't have a hat." "I know," responds Ruth. "And neither does her sister!" retorts Amy. Ruth reluctantly takes off the hat and returns it to the shelf. She picks up an apron and holds it to her waist, commenting, "Princess Leia's sister needs this to cook!" (Monighan-Nourot ,Van Hoorn, Scales, & Almy, 1987, p. 82)

The reflection on rules encompassed in metaplay forms a bridge from the oral culture of early childhood to the oral-and-literate culture of middle childhood and later development (Egan, 1988). In play, too, the emphasis shifts from the implicit rules and explicit fantasy of sociodramatic play to the explicit rules and implicit fantasy of games with rules in middle childhood (Vygotsky, 1976).

Personal Styles in Play

The rules for social behavior throughout development also govern the entry, exit, and production of play events that encompass the human issues of identity, status, power, and control. Sociocultural contexts influence rule-governed behavior by defining the relative roles of different groups (Ballenger,1999; Farver & Shin, 1997; Hughes, 2003; Katch, 2001; Lin & Reifel, 1999; Ramsey, 1998; Roopnarine, et al., 2000; Trawick-Smith, 1994).

Gender Influences on Sociodramatic Play

Gender is one important aspect of implicit rule making in the peer culture of children's play. Boys and girls have distinctive play styles characterized by particular roles, themes, and actions, and these differences are apparent early in the preschool years (Ariel, 2002; Fagot & Leve, 1998; Honig, 1998; Hughes, 2003; Katch, 2001; Levin, 1998; Lin & Reifel, 1999; Nicolopoulou et al., 1994; Pellegrini, 1998; Ramsey, 1998; Sutton-Smith, 1997).

Researchers of story-play found that girls structured ordered stories around social relationships, frequently family ones, depicting characters in the home, and routines of family life (Nicolopoulou et al., 1994). They found that even animals, and exotic characters such as witches and princesses, inhabited a stable world marked by order and family. Moreover, girls structured plots that maintained or restored order following a threat or destruction. Boys' stories, in contrast, focused on disorder, unpredictability, and transitory relationships. While both boys and girls depicted active violence, boys' violence was more frequent and detailed than girls' themes. Both boys and girls incorporated themes of danger and disorder but girls neutralized them, or downplayed their importance, while boys elaborated and intensified threats.

In expressing these meanings boys and girls draw upon images of both the larger cultural context and the immediate culture of the classroom to shape their identities as boys and girls (Bronfenbrenner, 1979; Dyson, 1997, 2003; Katch, 2001; Levin, 1998). They are distinct from one another through the use of imaginative conventions. The bipolarity of the symbolic styles that emerge between groups of boys and girls through their play illustrates the view that children frame a stable sense of self by creating axes that explore the boundaries of the possible and locate the self within that range (Egan, 1988).

In another gender contrast, the assertive language of preschool girls differs from that of their male playmates. A researcher characterizes the "directing" and assertive behavior of preschool girls as "double voice discourse," in which the perspective of the play partner is implicit in the language used to advance one's own agenda (Sheldon, 1992). Inviting the interlocutor into a pretense frame to gain one's position is a frequently effective strategy that meshes self-assertion with an appeal for reciprocity, cooperation, and solidarity, as the following example demonstrates:

Lucy (4.9) picks up the phone, enthusiastically proposing a phone conversation. Karla (5.0) is busy driving the car.
Lucy: Hey, I think I'll call a party. Now 'tend you heard your telephone ring.
Ding dong ding dong.
Karla: Pretend I wasn't there.
Lucy: All right—but you got your telephone anyway. All right? Karla: Yeah.
Lucy: Ding dong. Ding dong. Ding dong. Ding dong.
Karla: (No response, continues to drive the car.)
Lucy (exasperated that Karla hasn't answered): Pretend you got it. Pretend you got it,.
Karla: No, pretend I wasn't home.
Lucy: Pretend you were. (Tone of exasperation, pleading.)
Karla: Okay. (Leaves car with a sigh and picks up phone). (Sheldon, 1992, p. 107)

Each play partner uses pretense to overcome her companion's resistance. Such a strategy furthers the movement of the play within the play frame and, at the same time, offers play partners the opportunity to present alternatives in a "Yes, but" format.

In contrast, single-voice discourse, used more frequently by boys than by girls, leaves the play partner with fewer options to maintain his or her power or control in the negotiation by demanding a unilateral voice, as follows:

Four players are playing with the toy plastic sea animals in the block corner. They range in age from 6.8 to 7.11 years old.
Brian: I want a squid.
Damon (to Brian): Let's put all these inside the cage.
(Amos leaves with two sea animals from the collection on the rug.)
Brian (taking what he wants from the collection): This, a squid, and a sperm whale.
Damon: Hey, guys, the animals need water right now…
Brian: Go make your own cage! Go make your own cage!
Damon: I thought we'd be together in one cage.
Brian: No. No! (Ritz, 1994, p. 44)

The researcher concluded that the double-voice strategy is both more effective in achieving one's goals and allows play to continue more harmoniously and for a longer time than the single-voice strategy because it interweaves self-interest and communal interest through shared make-believe (Ritz, 1994, p. 44). She draws parallels between this strategy that very young girls use effectively and the negotiation strategies labeled by others as "soft" or "mutual gains approach" (Fisher & Ury, 1981).

Insiders and Outsiders to Sociodramatic Play

Researchers who have studied the development of peer culture in classrooms with young children also identify the complex interactions that occur in children's efforts to gain access to play events and, conversely, to protect their "interactive space" from intruders (Corsaro, 1985; Gaskins, Miller, & Corsaro, 1992; Kantor, Elgas & Fernie, 1993; Katch, 2001; Paley, 1990; Perry 2001). Social status within the peer culture leads to disputes and bargaining over the possession of territory, such as the blocks area or the slide; materials, such as capes or sticks; and coveted roles. Metaplay negotiations within the play frame and out of the play frame center on these issues, and create the patterns of tensions, alliance, control, and exploitation that characterize the peer culture of any social group (Trawick-Smith, 2001; Van Hoorn et al., 2003).

Teacher Influences on Sociodramatic Play

Play orchestration strategies that facilitate communication about access to play, turn-taking, and alternatives that may expand the borders of possibility in pretend frames are well described by teachers and researchers in the field (Brown & Marchant, 2002; Fromberg, 2002; Isenberg & Jalongo, 2001; Katch, 2001; Reynolds & Jones, 1997; Trawick-Smith, 1994; Van Hoorn et al., 2003). Indirect scaffolds for play in the environment, such as providing adequate space, ample time, and the appropriate kinds and amounts of materials, form one level of orchestration (Christie & Stone, 1999; Fromberg 2002; Isenberg & Jalongo, 2001; Perry, 2001; Reynolds & Jones, 1997; Roskos & Neuman, 1998; Van Hoorn et al., 2003). More directly, teachers guide play enactments, help to elaborate fantasy, and help children negotiate "warrants" for play participation. Teachers' roles range from the stage manager to the very direct play tutoring advocated by Sara Smilansky (1968) for children whose engagement in sociodramatic play is minimal. In all cases, teachers' skills as keen observers, and their respect for children's feelings, intellect, language, and culture, help them manage the complex choreography of both individuals and the group (Ballenger, 1999; Bowman, 2004; Howes & Wishard, 2004; Wolfberg, 1999).

An educator, Vivian Paley (1992), brings to the forefront the powerful and controversial issues that situate sociodramatic play in the peer culture of the early childhood classroom. She believes that the patterns of inclusion and exclusion established early in children's lives have profound and lasting effects on their future development, as follows:

> "Are you my friend?" the little ones ask in nursery school, not knowing. The responses are also questions. If yes, then what? And if I push you away, how does that feel?
>
> By kindergarten, however, a structure begins to be revealed and will soon be carved in stone. Certain children will have the right to limit the social experiences of their classmates. Henceforth, a ruling class will notify others of their acceptability, and the outsiders learn to anticipate the sting of rejection. Long after hitting and namecalling have been outlawed by the teachers, a more damaging phenomenon is allowed to take root, spreading like a weed from grade to grade. (Paley, 1992, p. 3)

Permission to control, dominate, and exploit is implicit in the long-standing tradition of early childhood education that holds teachers apart from the dance of the peer culture expressed on the stage of dramatic play. Vivian Paley (1992) challenges teachers to imagine what would happen if they interrupted the forces that sanction insiders' exclusion of outsiders. In early childhood the trust and control of the boundaries of behavior are still within the hands of the teacher, and their influence is profound: "Equal participation is, of course, the cornerstone of most classrooms. This notion usually involves everything except free play, which is generally considered a private matter. Yet, in truth, free acceptance in play, partnerships, and teams is what matters most to any child" (p. 21). This educator's new social order, the classroom rule that states, "You can't say you can't play," is a courageous step on a path fraught with difficulty. Teachers who have experimented with the idea express mixed feelings. Like the idea of controlling war play and violence in sociodramatic play themes, the idea of leaving play frames open to all brings up fundamental questions about the traditional views of sanctity of imagination, fantasy, and social relationships in childhood. Such questions require a close look at sociodramatic play with full awareness of its richness and potential for human thinking, feeling, storying, and interacting with others.

As teachers carefully observe and interpret the play of children in their care, awareness of all facets of play events is paramount. As Vivian Paley reminds us, first and foremost are children's feelings about themselves as they play and negotiate with peers within and about play scripts and roles. Teachers may well ask themselves if strategies such as providing a well-chosen prop, suggesting an additional role, or helping sustain play by entering the pretend frame will foster a more inclusive play event. Alternatively, establishing a rule such as, "You can't say you can't play," also requires the teacher to be a keen observer and active participant in helping children expand and elaborate their play scripts and in helping to sustain their play. Perhaps there are times when the highly engaged play of one group of children needs to be protected and would-be interlopers guided to create new play events. In each situation, the teacher's understanding of children's histories, the developing peer culture of the classroom, and children's feelings and ideas call for an interpretive stance. From this stance, an adult's decisions to participate or not participate in orchestrating children's play are based on the particular children and particular context. The artistry of play orchestration is alive in each moment of its creation.

Sociodramatic play in early childhood is a rich, complex, and many-splendored phenomenon. It draws upon children's capacities for constructing meaning, framing stories, and making sense of their worlds in ways that enrich the development of the individual and the group simultaneously. Such play provides the matrix for understanding and representing the perspectives of others and for opportunities to compromise and also to stand firm in one's beliefs and intentions.

For teachers of young children, sociodramatic play offers a unique privilege and a formidable responsibility. The privilege is to enter the magical worlds that children create in their pretense together; the responsibility is to help each child reach his or her potential in the powerful realm of shared make-believe.

References

Ackerman, D. (1999). *Deep play.* New York: Random House.

Ariel, S. (2002). *Children's imaginative play: A visit to wonderland.* Westport, CT: Praeger.

Astington, J. (1993). *The child's discovery of the mind.* Cambridge, MA: Harvard University Press.

Bakhtin, M. (1981). Discourse in the novel. In M. Holmquist (Ed.) & C. Emerson & M. Holquist (Trans.) *The dialogic imagination: Four essays by M.M. Bakhtin* (pp. 259–420). Austin: University of Texas Press. (Original work published 1934–1935)

Ballenger, C. (1999). *Teaching other people's children: Literacy and learning in a bilingual classroom.* New York: Teachers College Press.

Bateson, G. A. (1972). *Steps to an ecology of mind.* New York: Ballantine.

Bergen, D. (Ed.). (1998). Play as a context for humor development. In D. Fromberg & D. Bergen (Eds.), *Play from birth to twelve and beyond: Contexts, perspectives, and meanings* (pp. 324–347). New York: Garland.

Bergen, D. (2002). The role of pretend play in children's cognitive development. *Early Childhood Research and Practice, 4*(1), accessed on line at http://www.ecrp.uiuc.edu/v4n1/bergen

Berk, L. (1994). Research in review: Vygotsky's theory: The importance of make-believe play. *Young Children, 50*(1), 30–39.

Bettelheim, B. (1976). *The uses of enchantment: The meaning and importance of fairy tales*. New York: Knopf.

Bodrova, E., & Leong, D. (2003). Chopsticks and counting chips: Do play and foundational skills need to compete for the teacher's attention in an early childhood classroom? *Young Children, 58*(3) 10–17.

Bowman, B. (2004). Play in the multicultural world of children; Implications for adults. In E. Zigler, D. Singer, S. Bishop-Josef (Eds.), *Children's play: The roots of reading* (pp. 125–142).Washington, DC: Zero to Three Press.

Bronfenbrenner, U. (1979). *The ecology of human development: Experiments by nature and design*. Cambridge, MA: Harvard University Press.

Bronson, M. (2000). Research in review: Recognizing and supporting the development of self-regulation in young children. *Young Children, 55*(2), 32–37.

Brown, C. R., & Marchant, C. (Eds.). (2002). *Play in practice: Case studies in young children's play*. St Paul, MN: Redleaf Press

Bruner, J. (1986). *Actual minds, possible worlds*. Cambridge, MA: Harvard University Press.

Christie, J. (1998). Play: A medium for literacy development. In D. Fromberg & D. Bergen (Eds.), *Play from birth to twelve and beyond: Contexts, perspectives, and meanings* (pp. 50–55). New York: Garland.

Christie, J. G. & Stone, S. J. (1999). Collaborative literacy activity in print-enriched play centers: Exploring the "zone" in same-age and multiage groupings. *Journal of Literacy Research, 3*, 109-131.

Coolahan, D., Fantuzzo, J., Mendez, J., & McDermott, P. (2000). Preschool peer interactions and readiness to learn: Relationships between classroom peer play and learning behaviors and conduct. *Journal of Educational Psychology, 92*, 458–465.

Corsaro, W (1983). Script recognition, articulation, and expansion in children's role play. *Discourse Processes, 6*, 1–19.

Corsaro, W. (1985). *Friendship and the peer culture in the early years*. Norwood, NJ: Ablex.

Corsaro, W. (1992). *Interpretive approaches to children's socialization*. San Francisco: Jossey-Bass.

Csikszentmihalyi, M. (1993). *The evolving self: A psychology for the third millennium*. New York: HarperCollins.

Curran, J. M. (1999). Constraints of pretend play; Implicit and explicit rules. *Journal of Research in Childhood Education, 14*(1), 47–55.

Davidson, J. (1998). Language and play: natural partners. In D. Fromberg & D. Bergen (Eds.), *Play from birth to twelve and beyond: Contexts, perspectives, and meanings* (pp. 175–184). New York: Garland.

Derman-Sparks, L., & Ramsey, P. (2005). A framework for culturally relevant, multicultural, and antibias education in the twenty-first century. In J. P. Roopnarine & J. Johnson (Eds.), *Approaches to Early Childhood Education*, 4th ed. (pp. 107–124). Upper Saddle River, NJ: Merrill/Prentice Hall.

Dyson, A. H. (1997). *Writing Superheroes: Contemporary childhood, popular culture, and classroom literacy*. New York: Teachers College Press.

Dyson, A. H. (2003). *The brothers and sisters learn to write: Popular literacies in childhood and school cultures*. New York; Teachers College Press.

Egan, K. (1988). *Primary understanding: Education in early childhood*. New York: Routledge.

Egan, K. (1999). *Children's minds, talking rabbits and clock work oranges: Essays on education*. New York: Teachers College Press.

Elkind, D. (2003). Thanks for the memory; The lasting value of play. *Young Children, 58*(3), 46–51.

Erikson, E. (1977). *Childhood and society* (2nd ed.). New York: Norton. (Original work published 1963)

Fagot, B., & Leve, L. (1998). Gender identity and play. In D. Fromberg & D. Bergen (Eds.), *Play from birth to twelve and beyond: Contexts, perspectives, and meanings* (pp 187–192). New York: Garland.

Farver, J. (1992). Communicating shared meaning in social pretend play. *Early Childhood Research Quarterly, 7*(4), 501–516.

Farver, J., & Shin, Y. (1997). Social pretend play in Korean and Anglo-American preschoolers. *Child Development, 68*, 544–556.

Fein, G., Ardeila-Ray, A., & Groth, L. (2000). The narrative connection: Stories and literacy. In K. Roskos & J. Christie (Eds.), *Play and literacy in early childhood: Research from multiple perspectives* (pp. 27–43). Mahwah, NJ: Lawrence Erlbaum.

Fein, G. G., & Kinney, P. (1994). He's a nice alligator: Observations on the affective organization of pretense. In A. Slade and D. Wolf (Eds.), *Children at play: Clinical and developmental studies of play* (pp. 188–204). New York: Oxford University Press.

Fisher, R., & Ury, W (1981*). Getting to yes: Negotiating agreement without giving in*. Boston: Houghton Mifflin.

Fraiberg, S. (1959). *The magic years: Understanding and handling the problems of early childhood*. New York: Charles Scribner's Sons.

Fromberg, D. (1999). A review of research on play. In C. Seefeldt (Ed.), *The early childhood curriculum: A review of current research*, 3rd ed. (pp. 27–53). New York: Teachers College Press.

Fromberg, D. (2002). *Play and meaning in early childhood education*. Boston, MA: Allyn & Bacon.

Frost, J., Wortham, S., & Reifel, S. (2005). *Play and child development* (3rd ed.). Upper Saddle River, NJ: Merrill/Prentice Hall.

Garvey, C. (1990). *Play*. Cambridge, MA: Harvard University Press. (Original work published 1977)

Gaskins, S., Miller, P., & Corsaro, W (1992). Theoretical and methodological perspectives in the interpretive study of children. *New Directions in Child Development, S8*(Suppl.), 5–23.

Giffin, H. (1984). The coordination of meaning in the creation of a shared make-believe reality. In I. Bretherton (Ed.), *Symbolic play: The development of social understanding* (pp. 73–100). New York: Academic

Goncu, A. (1993). Development of intersubjectivity in the dyadic play of preschoolers. *Early Childhood Research Quarterly, 8*, 99–116.

Gould, R. (1972). *Child studies through fantasy*. New York: Quadrangle.

Gowen, J. W. (1995). Research and review: Early development of symbolic play. *Young Children, 50*(3), 75–83.

Griffin, E. (1982). *Island of childhood: Education in the special world of the nursery school*. New York: Teachers College Press.

Haight, W. L., & Miller, P. J. (1993). *Pretending at home: Early development in sociocultural context*. Albany: State University of New York Press.

Hartley, R. E., Frank, L., & Goldenson, R. M. (1957). *The complete book of children's play*. New York: Crowell.

Honig, A. (1998). Sociocultural influences on gender role behaviors in children's play. In D. Fromberg & D. Bergen (Eds.), *Play from birth to twelve and beyond: Contexts, perspectives, and meanings* (pp. 338–347). New York: Garland.

Howes, C., Unger, O., & Matheson, C. (1992). *The collaborative construction of pretend: Social pretend play functions*. Albany: State University of New York Press.

Howes, C., & Wishard, A. (2004). Revisiting shared meaning: Looking through the lens of culture and linking shared pretend play through protonarrative development to emergent literacy. In E. Zigler, D. Singer, & S. Bishop-Josef (Eds.), *Children's play: The roots of reading* (pp. 143–158).Washington DC: Zero to Three Press.

Hughes, F. (2003). Sensitivity to the social and cultural contexts of the play of young children. In J. Isenberg & M. Jalongo (Eds.), *Major trends and issues in early childhood education: Challenges, controversies, and insights* (2nd ed., pp. 126–135). New York; Teachers College Press.

Huizinga, J. (1950). *Homo ludens: A study of the play element in culture*. London: Routledge & Kegan Paul.

Isenberg, J., & Jalongo, M. (2001*). Creative expression and play in early childhood curriculum* (3rd ed.). Columbus, OH: Merrill.

Jarrell, R. (1998). Play and its influence on the development of young children's mathematical thinking. In D. Fromberg & D. Bergen (Eds*.), Play from birth to twelve and beyond: Contexts, perspectives, and meanings* (pp. 56–68). New York: Garland.

Johnson, J. (1998). Play development from ages four to eight. In D. Fromberg & D. Bergen (Eds.), *Play from birth to twelve and beyond: Contexts, perspectives, and meanings* (pp. 146–153). New York: Garland.

Jones. E. (2003). Viewpoint; Playing to get smart. *Young Children, 58*(3), 32–37.

Jones, E., & Reynolds, G. (1992). *The play's the thing: Teachers' roles in children's play*. New York: Teachers College Press.

Joshi, A. (2005).Understanding Asian Indian families: Facilitating meaningful home-school relations. *Young Children, 60,* 75–79.

Kaku, M. (1994). *Hyperspace: A scientific odyssey through parallel universes, time warps, and the 10th dimension*. New York: Doubleday.

Kantor, R., Elgas, P., & Fernie, D. (1993). Cultural knowledge and social competence within a preschool peer culture group. *Early Childhood Research Quarterly, 8*(2), 125–148.

Katch, J. (2001). *Under deadman's skin: Discovering the meaning of children's violent play*. Boston, MA: Beacon Press.

Kim, S. Y. (1999). The effects of storytelling and pretend play on cognitive processes, short-term and long-term narrative recall. *Child Study Journal, 29*(3), 175–191.

King, N. (1992). The impact of context on the play of young children. In S. Kessler & B. Swadener (Eds.), *Reconceptualizing the early childhood curriculum* (pp. 43–61). New York: Teachers College Press.

Kohlberg, L., & Fein, G. (1987). Play and constructive work as contributors to development. In L. Kohlberg et al. (Eds.), *Child psychology and childhood education* (pp. 392–449). New York: Longman.

Koplow, L. (Ed.). (1996). *Unsmiling faces: How preschools can heal*. New York: Teachers College Press.

Lancy, D. (2002). Cultural constraints on children's play. In J. L. Roopnarine (Ed.), *Play and culture studies: Vol. 4. Conceptual, social-cognitive,and contextual issues in the fields of play* (pp. 53–62). Westport, CT: Ablex.

Landreth, G. L. (2002). *Play therapy; The art of the relationship* (2nd ed.). New York: Brunner-Routledge.

Levin, N. (1998). *Remote control childhood? Combating the hazards of media culture*. Washington DC: National Association for the Education of Young Children.

Lewis, C. (1995). *Educating hearts and minds: Reflections on Japanese preschool and elementary education*. New York: Cambridge University Press.

Lillard, A. (1998). Playing with theory of mind. In O. Saracho & B. Spodek (Eds.), *Multiple perspectives on play in early childhood education* (pp. 11–33). Albany, NY: State University of New York Press.

Lillard, A., & Curenton, S. (1999). Do young children understand what others feel, want and know? Research in review. *Young Children, 54*(5), 52–57.

Lin, S. H., & Reifel, S. (1999). Context and meanings in Taiwanese Kindergarten play.In *Play and culture studies: Vol 2. Play contexts revisited* (pp. 151–176). Stamford, CT: Ablex.

Mead, G. H. (1934). *Mind, self and society*. Chicago: University of Chicago Press.

Meyers, C., Klein, E., & Genishi, C. (1994). Peer relationships among 4 preschool second language learners in "small group time." *Early Childhood Research Quarterly, 9*(6), 1–85.

Monighan-Nourot, P., Scales, B., Van Hoorn, J., & Almy, M. (1987*). Looking at children's play: The bridge between theory and practice*. New York: Teachers College Press.

Nachmanovitch, S. (1990). *Free play: The power of improvisation in life and the arts*. New York: Putnam.

Neeley, P. M., Neeley, R. A., Justen, J. E., III, & Tipton-Sumner, C. (2001). Scripted play as a language intervention strategy for preschoolers with developmental disabilities. *Early Childhood Education Journal, 28*(4), 243–246.

Nelson, K., & Seidman, S. (1984). *Playing with scripts*. In I. Bretherton (Ed.), *Symbolic play: The development of social understanding* (pp. 45–71). New York: Academic.

Nicolopoulou, A. (1991). Play, cognitive development, and the social world: The research perspective. In B. Scales, M. Almy, A. Nicolopoulou, & S. Ervin Tripp (Eds.), *Play and the social context of development in early care and education* (pp. 129–142). New York: Teachers College Press.

Nicopoulou, A. (1997). World making and identity formation in children's narrative play-acting. In B. D. Cox & C. Lightfoot (Eds), *Sociogenetic perspectives on internalization* (pp. 157–187). Mahwah, NJ: Erlbaum.

Nicolopoulou, A., Scales, B., & Weintraub, J. (1994). Gender differences and symbolic imagination in the stories of four-year olds. In A. H. Dyson & C. Genishi (Eds.), *The need for story: Cultural diversity in classroom and community* (pp. 102–123). Urbana, IL: National Council of Teachers of English.

Nourot, P. M. (1997). Playing with play in four dimensions. In J. Isenberg & M. Jalongo (Eds.), *Major trends and issues in early childhood education: Challenges, controversies and insights* (pp. 123–148). New York: Teachers College Press.

Oldfather, P., & West, J. (1994). Qualitative research as jazz. *Educational Researcher, 23*(8), 22–26.

Oravec, J. (2000). Interactive toys and children's education: Strategies for Educators and parents. *Childhood Education, 7*(3), 81–85.

Orellana, M. (1994). Appropriating the voice of the superheroes: Three preschoolers' bilingual language uses in play. *Early Childhood Research Quarterly, 9*(2), 171–193.

Paley, V. G. (1984). *Boys and girls: Superheroes in the doll corner.* Chicago: University of Chicago Press.

Paley, V. G. (1986). *Mollie is three.* Chicago: University of Chicago Press.

Paley, V. G. (1988). *Bad guys don't have birthdays.* Chicago: University of Chicago Press.

Paley, V. G. (1990). *The boy who would be a helicopter: The uses of storytelling in the classroom.* Cambridge, MA: Harvard University Press.

Paley, V. G. (1992). *You can't say you can't play.* Cambridge, MA: Harvard University Press.

Paley, V. G. (1995). *Kwanzaa and me.* Cambridge, MA: Harvard University Press.

Paley, V. G. (1999). *The kindness of children.* Cambridge MA: Harvard University Press.

Pellegrini, A. (1998). Rough and tumble play from childhood through adolescence: Different perspectives. In D. Fromberg & D. Bergen (Eds.), *Play from birth to twelve and beyond: Contexts, perspectives, and meanings* (pp. 401–408). New York: Garland.

Perry, J. (2001) *Outdoor play: Teaching strategies with young children.* New York: Teachers College Press.

Perry, J. (2003). Making sense of outdoor play. *Young Children, 58*(3) 26–31.

Piaget, J. (1962). *Play, dreams and imitation in childhood.* New York: Norton.

Ramsey, P. (1998). Diversity and play: Influences of race, culture,class, and gender. In D. Fromberg & D. Bergen (Eds.), *Play from birth to twelve and beyond: Contexts, perspectives, and meanings* (pp. 23–33). New York: Garland.

Reifel, S., Hoke, P., Pape, D., & Wisneski, D. (2004). From context to texts: DAP hermeneutics, and reading classroom play. *Social contexts of early education, and reconceptualizing play.* II. *Advances in Early Education and Day Care, 13*, 209–220.

Reifel, S., & Yeatman, J. (1993). From category to context: Reconsidering classroom play. *Early Childhood Research Quarterly, 8*, 347–367.

Reynolds, G. (2002). The welcoming place. In C. R. Brown & C. Marchant (Eds.), *Play in practice: Case studies in young children's play* (pp. 87–104). St Paul, MN: Redleaf Press.

Reynold, G., & Jones, E. (1997). *Master players: Learning from children at play.* New York: Teachers College Press.

Ritz, K. (1994). *Peer conflict in a multi-age setting.* Unpublished master's thesis, Sonoma State University, Rohnert Park, CA.

Roopnarine, J. L., Shin, M., Donovan, B., & Suppal, P. (2000). Sociocultural contexts of dramatic play; Implications for early education. In *Play and literacy in early childhood: Research from multiple perspectives* (pp. 205–220). Mahwah, NJ: Lawrence Erlbaum.

Roskos, K. (2000). Through the bioecological lens: Some observations of literacy in play as a proximal process. In K. Roskos & J. Christie (Eds.), *Play and literacy in early childhood: Research from multiple perspectives* (pp. 125–138). Mahwah, NJ: Lawrence Erlbaum.

Roskos, K., & Christie J. (Eds.). (2000). Afterword. In *Play and literacy in early childhood: Research from multiple perspectives* (pp. 231–240). Mahwah, NJ: Lawrence Erlbaum.

Roskos, K., & Christie J.(2004). Examing the play–literacy interface: A critical review and future directions. In E. Zigler, D. Singer, & S. Bishop-Josef (Eds.), *Children's play: The roots of reading* (pp. 95–124).Washington D.C.: Zero to Three Press.

Roskos, K., & Neuman, S. (1998). Play as an opportunity for literacy. In O. Saracho & B. Spodek (Eds.), *Multiple perspectives on play in early childhood education* (pp. 100–115). Albany, NY: State University of New York Press.

Rubin, K., Fein, G., & Vandenberg, B. (1983). Play. In E. M. Hetherington & P. H. Mussen (Series Ed.) (Eds.), *Handbook of child psychology: Vol. 4. Socialization, personality, and social development* (pp. 698–774). New York: Wiley.

Sawyer, K. (1997). *Pretend play as improvisation: Conversation in the preschool classroom.* Mahwah, NJ: Lawrence Erlbaum.

Scarlett, W. G., Naudeau, S., Salonius-Pasternak, D., & Ponte, I. (2005). *Children's play.* Thousand Oaks, CA: Sage Publications.

Schwartzman, H. B. (1976). Children's play: A sideways glance at make-believe. In D. F. Laney & B. A. Tindall (Eds.), *The anthropological study of play: Problems and prospects* (pp. 208–215). Cornwall, NY: Leisure Press.

Schwartzman, H. B. (1978*). Transformations: The anthropology of children's play.* New York: Plenum.

Seiter, E. (1995). *Sold separately: Parents and children in consumer culture.* New Brunswick, NJ: Rutgers University Press.

Sheridan, M., Foley, G., & Radlinski, S. (1995*). Using the supportive play model: Individualized intervention in early childhood practice.* New York: Teachers College Press.

Sheldon, A. (1992). Conflict talk: Sociolinguistic challenges to self-assertion and how young girls meet them. *Merrill Palmer Quarterly, 38*(1), 95–117.

Singer, D. G., & Singer, J. L. (2004). Encouraging school readiness through guided pretend games. In E. Zigler, D. Singer, & S. Bishop-Josef (Eds.), *Children's play: The roots of reading* (pp. 175–188).Washington, DC: Zero to Three Press.

Singer, J., & Lythcott, M. (2004) Fostering school achievement and creativity through sociodramtic play in the classroom. In E. Zigler, D. Singer, & S. Bishop-Josef (Eds.), *Children's play: The roots of reading* (pp. 77–94). Washington, DC: Zero to Three Press.

Smilansky, S. (1968). *The effects of sociodramatic play on disadvantaged preschool children.* New York: Wiley.

Smilansky, S. (1990). Sociodramatic play: Its relevance to behavior and achievement in school. In E. Klugman & S. Smilansky (Eds.), *Children's play and learning: Perspectives and policy implications* (pp. 18–42). New York: Teachers College Press.

Smilansky, S., & Shefatya, L. (1990). *Facilitating play: A medium for promoting cogntive, socioemotional, and academic development in young children.* Gaithersburg, MD: Psychosocial and Educational Publications.

Stone, S. J., & Christie, J. F. (1996). Collaborative literacy learning during sociodramatic play in a multiage (K-2) primary classroom. *Journal of Research in Childhood Education, 10*(2), 123–133.

Sutton-Smith, B. (1997). *The ambiguity of play.* Cambridge, MA: Harvard University Press.

Trawick-Smith, J. (1992). A descriptive study of persuasive preschool children: How they get others to do what they want.*Early Childhood Research Quarterly, 7*(1), 95–114.

Trawick-Smith, J. (1994*). Interactions in the classroom: Facilitating play in the early years.* Columbus, OH: Merrill

Trawick-Smith, J. (2001). Play and the curriculum. In J. Frost, S. Wortham, & S. Reifel (Eds.), *Play and child development* (pp. 294–339). Upper Saddle River, NJ: Merrill/Prentice-Hall.

Uttal, D., Marzolf, D., Pierroutsakos, S., Smith, C., Troseth, G., Scudder, K., & DeLoache, J. (1998). Seeing through symbols: The development of children's understanding of symbolic relations. In O. Saracho & B. Spodek (Eds.), *Multiple perspectives on play in early childhood education* (pp. 59–79). Albany, NY: State University of New York Press.

Vandenberg, B. (2004). Real and not real: A vital developmental dichotomy. In E. Zigler, D. Singer, & S. Bishop-Josef (Eds.), *Children's play: The roots of reading* (pp. 49–58). Washington DC: Zero to Three Press.

Van Hoorn, J., Nourot, P. M., Scales, B., & Alward, K. (2003*). Play at the center of the curriculum* (3rd ed.). Columbus, OH: Merrill.

Vygotsky, L. S. (1976). Play and its role in the mental development of the child. In J. S. Bruner, A. Jolly, & K. Sylva (Eds.), *Play: Its role in development and evolution* (pp. 537–554). New York: Basic Books.

Vygotsky, L. S. (1978). *Mind in society: Development of higher psychological processes.* Cambridge, MA: Harvard University Press.

Wanigarayake, M. (2001). From playing with guns to playing with rice: The challenges of working with refugee children: An Australian perspective. *Childhood Education, 77*(5), 289–294.

Williamson, P., & Silvern, S. (1992). "You can't be grandma; you a boy": Events within the thematic fantasy play context that contribute to story comprehension. *Early Childhood Research Quarterly, 7*(1), 75–94.

Wolfberg, P. (1999). *Play and imagination in children with autism.* New York: Teachers College Press.

Wyver, S. R., & Spence, S. H. (1999). play and divergent problem solving: Evidence supporting a reciprocal relationship. *Early Education and Development, 10*(4), 419–444.

Zukav, G. (1979). *The dancing Wu Li masters: An overview of the new physics.* New York: Macmillan.

11
Constructive Play

GEORGE FORMAN

Children's play with construction materials can render patterns, objects, functional systems, and pretend sequences. Study of constructive play reveals a child's developmental level, how children learn, and the precursors to later cognitive structures. Methods of study should include a microanalysis of the process of play. Adults can support constructive play by protecting the time it takes, by asking children to design before they build, and by establishing a social dynamic that encourages risk taking. Animated computer graphics have created microworlds that give children new methods to reflect on their constructive play. Children's museums also have provided new learning environments that enhance the educational value of constructive play. These new learning environments require their own forms of evaluation.

Constructive Play Defined

Researchers have studied play from many perspectives and have defined various categories, including constructive play. One way to look at constructive play is to think of it as a set of questions about the value of play materials that children use to build or construct something. These play materials include any elements that can be put together or shaped into structures, such as Lego bricks, Lasy blocks, Zoobs™, Constructo straws, clay, pipe cleaners, wooden blocks, and even natural objects such as blades of grass for weaving patterns and pebbles for making designs. We should also include electronic objects, such as movable icons that can be assembled on a computer screen (Colella, Klopfer, & Resnick, 2001; Harel & Papert, 1991; Kafai & Resnick, 1996).

Construction itself has its own complex definitions. Fundamentally, the builder(s) construct from basic elements. These basic elements are reiterated in number, arranged in a plane, oriented at a point, and even sequenced across time to yield some product that embodies a goal of these processes. The constructions can be static or dynamic, that is, the construction can be a stationary product or an animated product. A block tower is static, for example, while an animated cartoon on a computer is dynamic.

Computer animation is an example of constructive play that does not employ three-dimensional objects (Kafai, 1996). Psychologically, the cognitive demands and educational value of building a block tower with movable computer icons, given that the computer is programmed to make the tower fall when it violates the laws of physics, is eqivalent to an example of constructive play. Animating a sequence of wing positions that simulate bird flight when run in real time on a computer is also a case of construction.

Children engage in constructive play when they are trying to make something, from a drawing, to a Lasy system that works, to a mosaic pattern that appeals. It will be helpful, however, to distinguish between several types of products in constructive play: the pattern, the object, the system, and the sequence.

Making Patterns

Children can construct mosaic patterns with parquetry blocks or computer icons. These patterns may have no particular referent in the outside world. The goal is pure symmetry, variations on symmetry, repeated motifs, and other parameters of aesthetics. These are an important form of constructive play. As children mature, they translate their play with patterns into the notations of mathematics, music, and computer language (Gargarian, 1996; Sinclair, Stambak, Lezine, Rayna, & Verba, 1989). Constructive play with spatial patterns occurs when children focus on the spatial relationship of the medium's elements to each other, rather than to the semantic relationship of the elements to some imagined or sighted object outside the medium itself. The constructive play in this context looks more self-referential and nonsymbolic. The placement of one element is determined by the placement of a previous element. The child's objective is primarily the extension and elaboration of a spatial rule, such as fitting together wooden pieces that do not make identifiable pictures (Forman, Laughlin, & Sweeney, 1971). Of particular note is that children prefer to make patterns instead of recognizable objects when they play with computer graphics (Papert, 1993; Wright & Shade, 1994).

Objects

Children can build cars with plastic elements, birdhouses with wooden pieces, and miniature playground equipment with pipe cleaners and cardboard. These objects do have referents in the world outside the medium in which the children work. Object construction play gives observers insight into how children learn to represent and to make meanings (Reifel & Greenfield, 1982; Smith & Franklin, 1979).

Constructive play to make objects is determined by the child's reflective thinking about something external to the medium. Paradoxically, these objects may be patterns, such as a child trying to make a good-looking snowflake from parquetry blocks. It is the psychological stance toward the media elements that distinguishes play-to-construct-patterns from play-to-construct-objects. When constructing patterns, children are intrigued with the regularities, repetitions, and permutations of element relations, independent of what they represent. When constructing objects, children will correct an arrangement of elements if it does not look like the reference object, even if this correction yields an arrangement that violates patternlike rules of symmetry and motif (Forman, 1994).

Systems

Children can build working systems, such as a waterwheel that spins, a miniature Ferris wheel that allows the seats to remain upright, or a fanciful mousetrap that catches three mice at once. The cognitive demands of systems are greater than for the construction of most static objects. Building a clockwork with gears, for example, requires a great deal of thinking about patterns of reversed direction, spatial configuration, and relative size (Metz, 1985). Constructive play to make systems adds the demand of building a working set of elements. Elements are not only attached, but also articulated (movable); the articulations often need to be constrained in definite ways. The system, such as a miniature machine, needs to stay intact while its parts move. Watching children build systems provides observers, therefore, with special insights into children's cognitive development, such as their increasing ability to deal with compound movement, gear ratios, principles of leverage, and torque (Forman, 1986).

Sequences

Children can construct sequences of action by arranging computer elements. such as using the Widget Workshop™ computer program to build a whimsical device that sorts random objects into three piles according to height, or make a robot that intelligently navigates a maze using Lego/LOGO blocks (Granott, 1991).

Constructive play with a temporal sequence is somewhat new to the research literature, primarily because the best medium for this type of play, computer animation, is itself rather new. Constructing sequences requires that children go beyond what is possible and consider what is reasonable. A machine or cartoon might move in a well-oiled manner, but children need to ask if it performs the work in a sequence that guarantees the desired product or produces it in an efficient manner. The difference between a sequence and a system is really the difference between a general system (building a toy car that rolls) and a specific sequential application of a system that requires an ordered set of actions (driving the toy car through the miniature village from the train station to the town hall).

Children can approach all of these cases with a playful attitude. That is, they need not build something in a ritualized manner. They are not making their fortieth origami bird for the Christmas tree. They are varying the means, rearranging parts just to see how they look, and inventing new sequences to inspect and then to approve or reject. It is this element of variation during construction that makes it play. The children are taking a metacognitive attitude toward the process (see Fromberg, 1999). Rather than being worried about finishing the product, they have taken one step back and asked, "What is the form of the process?" In other words, during constructive play, as opposed to construction, the children are reflecting on the process and on their own assumptions about what processes are appropriate. It is in this category, constructive play, that observers most often confuse play and work. Placing elements together to get the job done is not play. Placing elements together to see if the arrangement might get the job done is play. The "what-if" attitude defines the act as play and places it in an entirely different epistemic stance to cognition and development (Garvey, 1977; Hutt, 1976).

Why Look at Constructive Play?

Constructive play provides a window into children's thinking. A child trying to build a waterwheel might orient the paddle blades more like a ceiling fan (same plane as the hub) than like a paddle wheel (at right angles to the hub). When he or she plays with this construction in the water, however, he or she reorients the paddle blades. Therefore, constructive play, in this instance, can provide a window through which to watch the processes by which children learn to modify part of a structure they are using. The fact that this architectural problem arises in the context of self-regulated play provides observers with an authentic sighting of childhood thinking. The thinking is not mediated or scaffolded by adults in this instance; it bears witness to how children invent solutions based upon their own reflections on prior attempts.

In addition to solitary play with objects, observers can study constructive play in small group contexts and in the context of adult scaffolding. These kinds of studies answer the Vygotskian question of how specific learning with a more competent person can improve general development of the individual. No simple conclusions are possible regarding the quality of play with materials alone versus play with more competent person. Both prepared environments and competent play partners can provoke the individual child to engage an interesting problem. Both situations bear the mark of a more competent peer, either in the sensitive way adults lay out materials to engage the child's mind or the sensitive way an adult asks the child to describe his or her play at a slightly higher level of abstraction (Pellegrini, 1986).

The Importance of Playful Construction

If a child becomes too goal-oriented, construction ceases to be play. A child trying to complete a bridge from Erector set pieces can become frustrated when the bridge falls down for the third time. His or her attitude can visibly shift from a lighthearted, "What if I do this?" attitude to a "Why won't it do that?" attitude. This shift from "I" to "it" is the death knell for constructive play (Forman & Hill, 1984). In other words, the playful child is content to change what he or she does, just to see what it yields. The task-oriented child is determined to achieve a particular goal.

There is a psychological difference between acting to make something happen and acting to see if something might happen. Play rides on the back of tentativeness. When children are tentative, they know that they do not know, but they have a theory about what might work. The tentative act is an attempt to find out, not an attempt to make something happen. This tentativeness is an essence of constructive play and distinguishes it from construction.

The playful child may keep the goal in mind, but not always in the foreground. The playful child understands that free-flowing exploration can be of great service to later success with the ultimate goal. This attitude toward construction requires a type of dual thinking. The playful period is not goal-directed now, but helpful to goal direction later. Finding the optimal balance between play and problem solving, therefore, places great cognitive demands on the player.

Factors That Support the Play Attitude toward Construction

As obvious as it might sound, the most essential condition to support constructive play is the child's sense of the schedule. Play does not survive when children feel rushed; constructive play must be nurtured by time. Children distracted by the minute hand on a clock will not allow themselves to become immersed in the autonomous flow of play. Teachers who value constructive play need to allow more time for it.

While longer periods are necessary for constructive play, they are not sufficient. Adults can support constructive play by asking children to design before they construct. Design, like play, is essentially a "what-if" proposition (Fromberg, 1999). During design, children can change their minds without suffering the consequences of making a system that does not physically work. The separation of performance from particular goal states is also an essential aspect of play.

The wrong social dynamic among children can also destroy a playful attitude toward construction. It is common, for example, for children to work in twos and threes when designing microworlds on the computer. If one member of the group, however, is both expert and condescending, the other children will back away from taking risks (see Wright & Shade, 1994). Risk taking and the suspension of evaluation are critical to generative, constructive play.

Interest in Constructive Play

The interest in constructive play has derived in part from several findings in the child education and development literature. First, researchers have found a high level of thinking when children participate in rich problem-solving environments with minimal direct instruction from an adult (DeVries & Kohlberg, 1987). Second, problem solving requires a period of divergent in addition to convergent thinking in order to progress. Third, children learn more completely and with greater understanding when they engage in the design and construction of their own invented systems (Resnick & Ocko, 1991). Fourth, there has been a shift in educational objectives from learning facts to learning how to organize facts into personal systems of meaning (Turkle & Papert, 1991); this metacognitive attitude has more resemblance to playing around with relationships than it does with learning the elements themselves. Fifth, the school emphasis on intuitive theories has created a great interest in construction as a variation on science education. Today's teachers have developed academic rationales for the purchase of constructive material to build simple machines, computer simulations, ecosystems, and mathematical patterns. Their comfort with these academic rationales comes in part from their recognition of the logic and planning involved when children play with construction material (Forman & Hill, 1984).

The Developmental Importance of Constructive Play

The study of constructive play fits the Piagetian perspective that, generally speaking, cognitive development beyond age 7 draws from constructive play before age 7. The logicomathematical structures of cognition in middle childhood have their analogue in self-regulated play with objects in the first years of life (Forman, 1982b; Kamii, Miyakawa, & Yasushito, 2004). Suppose a child is trying to use two 8-inch long rectangular blocks to span a 12-inch gap between two stacks (e.g., "keep the rain off the little doll in there between the stacks."). The two long blocks collapse inward when both are placed end to end to close the gap. So he spreads the two blocks apart so they won't fall down, but now there is a small space between the inside ends of the two blocks (e.g."the rain will fall on the doll below."). To cover the hole in the roof he places a four inch block across the small gap, but the extra weight causes the two long blocks to fall inward on top of the little doll. If this child overlearns that he should not place the smaller block on top of the longer blocks, he will never invent the solution of placing two smaller blocks as counterweights on top and at the outside ends of the longer blocks. The solution requires the child to unlearn something he learned, or to negate an negation. The demands of this construction are high, but once the problem is solved the child's success marks an advance in logical thinking, the logic of negations (Fosnot, Forman, Edwards, & Goldhaber, 1988).

Methods for Studying Constructive Play

Constructive play is a process, and should be studied as such. Category checklists for different levels of constructive play will too often miss the subtle framing that defines an act as playful. The checklist uses a definition for a category that is, of necessity, decontextualized from the manifest content. This definition is written to increase the agreement rate between independent raters observing the same play episode. This checklist, however, will overly constrain the researcher's ability to understand the relationship between behavior and thought. Thinking invariably occurs in context and should be studied in situ (Granott & Mascolo, 2003; Turkle & Papert, 1991). A preferred approach to study, called microanalysis, involves a careful documentation and subsequent analysis of the flow of behavioral acts.

In microanalysis the researcher first captures, in some form of notation, the sequence of acts, verbalizations, changes of mind, and transformation of materials in a connected temporal flow. The researcher then analyzes and rewrites the construction process from the premises of the theory that drove the analysis. In a study of block play, for example, the author filmed children making spontaneous clusters with geometric blocks (Forman, 1982a). The notation system captured every placement, rotation, change of position, and choice of block that the children made across time, and included a description of the block as a spatial array. From this microanalysis the author discovered that the movements of blocks (banging identical blocks together at the midline) presage the stationary construction of blocks on the table (two identical blocks placed side by side on the table). The block constructions, even without clear representational status for cars and trains, therefore, are symbolic expressions of the earlier gestures. The block structures are a type of "atemporalization" of action and thus are symbols. From these data, this author contends, as did Piaget (1954), that constructive play with geometric objects provides a base for higher mathematics and logical relations that are based on action rather than language.

Constructive Play in a Virtual World

As mentioned earlier, building virtual physical systems on a computer screen has all. the requisite attributes of construction and participants can engage in a playful mode. The computer can offer the user a virtual physical world to explore when adults have it programmed to treat object icons as physical objects that tilt and fall, maintain their shape as users move them, and conform to laws of friction, solid obstruction, elasticity, and so forth. Such electronic worlds are called microworlds (Char & Forman, 1994; Pea & Sheingold, 1987).

One of the first market successes was a computer program called the Bill Budge Pinball Construction Kit by Electronic Arts. Children could design a pinball rolling board filled with bumpers, magnets, drop holes, and flippers, then propel a virtual ball into this electronic space to watch the ball bounce, career, and be hit by flippers that the children activated. The children could change the Newtonian parameters of gravitation, kick, and elasticity to study the effects of these changes on ball play.

Microworlds allow the child to predict a result during the design process and observe its effects when the ball is released. The computer allows the children to easily edit the space, stretch it, add bumpers, eliminate dead spaces that trap the ball, and so forth. Because the computer makes it so easy to vary the pinball rolling space, the children are free to play around with their creative ideas. If they had to physically build these spaces, the effort involved in making only one space would be so great that the children would not risk a playful stance toward the task. For constructive play to occur, players need to be able to easily vary the process. Otherwise, the players would have to plan and debug the plan from a more conceptual and analytical stance than from a "Let's see what happens" stance.

Herein lies the paradox. While it is important for children to play around, learning environments that make it easy to vary the process could encourage a type of mindless "push-and-see" attitude. If it takes no effort to make a change when one does not get the desired effect, then why not just start anywhere and, by the process of elimination, create the desired effect in time? How can scholars cite the value of constructive play in microworlds if the play is mindless? If it is too difficult to vary the process, however, children will become so premeditated and locked into one plan that they will not explore alternative solutions and expressions. The process seems to be caught between the fluidity of random play and the rigidity of premeditated plans. The study of constructive play, therefore, needs to establish the look and the source of a balance between these extremes.

Classroom use of computers provides a good site to study how educators provide this balance between playing and planning. The new use of LOGO in classrooms combines the open environment of turtle geometry with the structure of specified problems to solve. The work by Juda Schwartz (Harvard University) on the "Geometric Supposer" (Sunburst Software) is a case in point. The software asks children to derive the regularities that explain a certain set of geometric conditions, but they can easily vary angle, line, and relationship in a microworld that instantly draws upon their ideas. The educators require students to document their initial period of experimenting with options. The "play," therefore, becomes an object of reflection and, over time, becomes less random while at the same time maintains fluidity. This is the stuff of expertise, which is the balance between planning and fluency.

The more advanced versions of microworlds, such as Working Model by Knowledge Revolution, produce mathematical equations for the physics involved in the movements of a simulated machine. This role of the computer, to take the child's constructions and translate them automatically into equations, rather than the other way round, is an advance in educational practice (see Forman, 1988a, 1988b). Children then can learn the formal notations of mathematics through spontaneous play on a computer screen, much as they learned their native language in a social context with adults.

The Merger of Constructive Play and Computation

Children like to build little machines with moving parts and tiny motors. Now they can add personality to their constructions by adding behaviors to their machines. With the advent of Mindstorms™ children can program their Lego™ machines to move forward on the slap of their hands, to avoid a bright light, to go in reverse when hitting a barrier, and to lift a robotic arm after a given time. The Mindstorm blocks can be programmed by the child. So constructive play enters the world of computation.

Not only does such a medium provide children with a rich problem solving environment, it also embodies computational thinking such as "if x, then y" and quantifiers such as "after 10 seconds" and "after six revolutions." Constructive play blends with constructionism or "learning by making" (see Harel & Papert, 1991; Kafai & Resnick, 1996). The formal language of programming has been embodied in the playful explorations of children trying to make their little machines do something intelligent.

Conclusion

Play with elements that players assemble into patterns, objects, systems, and sequences is an extremely rich source of information about children's development. Indeed, our everyday parlance alludes to the objects that children use in constructive play, such as in the phrase "DNA molecules are the building blocks of life." The architect Frank Lloyd Wright attested to the importance of a set of Froebel building blocks his aunt bought him at the Chicago World's Fair when he was young and their influence on his sense of design much later in life. Blocks, puzzles, and now computer constructions provide children with physical analogues to complex thoughts, a culture of mind embodied in the structure of these materials (Minsky, 1986). The fact that these materials lend themselves to a playful mode of exploration makes their value even greater.

References

Char, C., & Forman, G. (1994). Interactive technology and the young child: A look to the future. In D. Shade & J. Wright (Eds.), *Technology and young children* (pp. 178–186). Washington, DC: National Association for the Education of Young Children.

Colella, V. S,, Klopfer, E. & Resnick, M. (2001). *Adventures in modeling: Exploring complex, dynamic systems with StarLogo*. New York: Teachers College Press.

DeVries, R., & Kohlberg, L. (1987). *Programs of early education: The constructivist view*. New York: Longman.

Forman, G. (1982a) A search for the origins of equivalence concepts through a microanalysis of block play. In G. Forman (Ed.), *Action and thought: From sensorimotor schemes to symbolic operations* (pp. 97–136). New York: Academic.

Forman, G. (Ed.). (1982b). *Action and thought: From sensorimotor schemes to symbolic operations*. New York: Academic.

Forman, G. (1986). Observations of young children solving problems with computers and robots. *Journal of Research in Childhood Education, 1*(2), 61–75.

Forman, G. (1988a). Making intuitive thoughts explicit through future technology. In G. Forman & P. Pufall (Eds.), *Constructivism in the computer age* (pp. 83–101). Norwood, NJ: Ablex.

Forman, G. (1988b). The importance of automatic translation for the representational development of young children: Get a code of my act. *Genetic Epistemologist, 21*(1), 5–10.

Forman, G. (1994). Different media, different languages. In L. Katz & B. Cesarone (Eds.), *Reflections on the Reggio Emilia approach* (pp. 41–54). Urbana, IL: ERIC Clearinghouse on Elementary and Early Childhood Education.

Forman, G., & Hill, E (1984). *Constructive play: Applying Piaget in the preschool*. Menlo Park, CA : Addison-Wesley.

Forman, G., Laughlin, F., & Sweeney, M. (1971). The development of jigsaw puzzle solving in preschool children: An information processing approach. *DARCEE Papers and Reports, 5*(8), 38. Nashville, TN: Kennedy Center for Research.

Fosnot, C., Forman, G., Edwards, C., & Goldhaber, J. (1988). The development of the balance concept and its enhancement through stopped action video feedback. *Journal of Applied Developmental Psychology, 9*(1), 1–26.

Fromberg, D. (1999) A review of research on play. In C. Seefeldt (Ed.), *The early childhood curriculum: Current findings in theory and practice, 3rd ed.* (pp. 27–53). New York: Teachers College Press.

Gargarian, G. (1996).The Art of Design. In Kafai, Y. & Resnick, M. (Eds.), *Constructionism in practice: Designing, thinking, and learning in a digital world* (pp. 125–159). Mahwah, NJ: Lawrence Erlbaum.

Garvey, C. (1977). *Play*. Cambridge, MA: Harvard University Press.

Granott, N. (1991). Puzzled minds and weird creatures: Phases in the spontaneous process of knowledge construction. In I. Harel & S. Papert (Eds.), *Constructionism* (pp. 295–310). Norwood, NJ: Ablex.

Granott, N., & Mascolo, M. F. (2003, June). *Change mechanisms in microdevelopment: Progress through individual synthesis, joint regulation, and backward transitions.* Symposium presented at the 33rd Meeting of the Jean Piaget Society

Harel, I., & Papert, S. (Eds.). (1991). *Constructionism.* Norwood, NJ: Ablex.

Hutt, C. (1976). Exploration and play in children. In J. S. Bruner, A. Jolly, & K. Sylva (Eds.), *Play: Its role in development and evolution* (pp. 202–215). New York: Basic Books.

Kafai,Y. (1996). Electronic play worlds. In Y. Kafai, & M. Resnick (Eds.), *Constructionism in practice: Designing, thinking, and learning in a digital world* (pp. 97–123). Mahwah, NJ: Lawrence Erlbaum..

Kafai, Y. & Resnick, M. (Eds.). (1996). *Constructionism in practice: Designing, thinking, and learning in a digital world.* Mahwah, NJ: Lawrence Erlbaum.

Kamii, C., Miyakawa,Y., & Yasuhito, K. (2004, Fall) The development of logico-mathematical knowledge in a block-building activity at ages 1–4 . *Journal of Research in Childhood Education Online, 19*(1), 44–57.

Metz, K. (1985). The development of children's problem solving in a gears task: A problem space perspective. *Cognitive Science, 9* (3), 431–471.

Minsky, M. (1986). *Society of mind.* New York: Simon & Schuster.

Papert, S. (1993). *The children's machine: Rethinking school in the age of the computer.* New York: Basic Books.

Pea. R. D., & Sheingold, K. (1987). *Mirrors of minds: Patterns of experience in educational computing.* Norwood, NJ: Ablex.

Pellegrini, A. D. (1986). The effects of play centers on preschoolers' explicit language. In G. Fein & M. Rivkin (Eds.), *The young child at play* (pp. 40–48). Washington, DC: National Association for the Education of Young Children.

Piaget, J. (1954). *The construction of reality in the child* (M. Cook, Trans). New York: Basic Books. (Original work published 1937)

Reifel, S., & Greenfield, P. (1982). Structural development in a symbolic medium: The representational use of block constructions. In G. Forman (Ed.), Action and thought: *From sensorimotor schemes in symbolic operations* (pp. 203–234). New York: Academic.

Resnick, M., & Ocko, S. (1991). Lego/LOGO: Learning through and about design. In I. Harel & S. Papert (Eds.), *Constructionism* (pp. 141–150). Norwood, NJ: Ablex.

Sinclair, H., Stambak, M., Lezine, I., Rayna, S., & Verba, M. (1989). *Infants and objects: The creativity of cognitive development.* New York: Academic.

Smith, M., & Franklin, M. B. (Eds.). (1979). *Symbolic functioning in childhood.* Hillsdale, NJ: Lawrence Erlbaum.

Turkle, S., & Papert, S. (1991). Epistemological pluralism and the revaluation of the concrete. In I. Harel & S. Papert (Eds.), *Constructionism* (pp. 161–192). Norwood, NJ: Ablex.

Wright, J. L., & Shade, D. D. (Eds.). (1994). *Young children: Active learning in a technological age.* Washington, DC: National Association for the Education of Young Children.

12

Rough-and-Tumble Play
from Childhood through Adolescence
Differing Perspectives

ANTHONY D. PELLEGRINI

The Controversy Surrounding Rough-and-Tumble Play

Educators and researchers often take for granted the value of play in the lives of children. Some educators view play as the quintessence of developmentally appropriate practice (Bredekamp, 1987). Researchers, too, have treated play as a hallowed developmental process, essential to a variety of social and cognitive processes (see Bruner, Jolly, & Sylva, 1976; Pellegrini & Galda, 1993; Smith, 1982, 1988 for discussion). However, these researchers view play as a natural process by which children come to know their worlds.

There has been some dissonance since the mid- to late 1980s, however. First, the empirical record supporting the unequivocal value of play is weak (Pellegrini, 2002; Smith, 1988). Second, some adults have voiced concern over the role of certain forms of play in children's lives. Specifically, children's play with "war toys" and their play fighting, or rough-and-tumble play (R&T), have been the subject of wide and heated debate. On the one hand, the "antis" (those opposed to war toys and R&T) generally view these forms of play as encouraging children's antisocial behavior and advocate policies to discourage them. Supporters of these forms of play, on the other hand, see them as merely children's expression of fantasy that adults, particularly female teachers, do not understand (Sutton-Smith, 1988). A number of papers refer to war toys (Smith, 1994; Sutton-Smith, 1988; Wegener-Spohring, 1994). The related topic, R&T and its role in children's development, has also been a subject of research.

To understand the construct R&T properly, it is crucial to define it in relation to aggression as the two are frequently confused. As part of this definition, the differing developmental trajectories of R&T and aggression will also be discussed. The following section will address the ways in which R&T and aggression predict social–cognitive status in primary and middle school youngsters. As part of this discussion, there will be a discussion of a darker side to R&T, the ways in which some youngsters use R&T as an aggressive tactic to bully their classmates.

Defining R&T in Relation to Aggression

Often R&T is confused with aggression because at some levels they resemble each other. Upon close inspection, however, they are clearly different (for a fuller discussion see Pellegrini, 2002; Smith, Smees,

& Pellegrini, 2004). Categories of behavior, like aggression and R&T, can be classified, or defined, along the following dimensions: individual behaviors, consequences, structure, and ecology.

Individual Behaviors

Beginning with individual behaviors, numerous factor and analytic studies have differentiated R&T and aggression behaviorally (Blurton Jones, 1972; Smith & Connolly, 1972, 1980) in some reliable ways. The assumption here is that behaviors with similar meaning, for example, will reliably co-occur and form a meaningful whole, or category. R&T is composed of these behaviors: run, chase, flee, wrestle, and open-hand hit. Aggression, in contrast, is typified by a different set of behaviors: closed-hand hits, shoves, pushes, and kicks. R&T and aggression also differ in their expression of affect. Smiles generally accompany R&T while frowns, or crying, accompany aggression.

Consequences

Classes of behavior can also be differentiated in terms of consequences, or behaviors that follow those that are of interest. Behaviors that follow a focal behavior (in this case, the focal behavior is R&T) describe the function or meaning of the behavior. R&T and aggression are different because they have different consequences and functions. When R&T bouts end, for example, children often stay together and begin cooperative social games (Pellegrini, 1988). Aggression, on the other hand, usually leads to one of the participants trying to separate from the other (Humphreys & Smith, 1984). Thus, R&T may have a peer-affiliative function while aggression does not. Longer-term, or more distal, consequences of R&T and aggression are also evident. These will be discussed in the section on developmental trajectories.

Structure

The structure of R&T is also different from that of aggression (Humphreys & Smith, 1984). For example, the structure of roles that typify each class of behaviors differ. In R&T, youngsters alternate roles, such as chaser and chasee. In some cases, stronger or bigger players "self-handicap" so as to sustain play. An older child, for example, may pretend to fall while trying to escape from a pursuer, thus enabling the younger child to "capture" him or her. Self-handicapping enables children of different levels of strength and physical prowess to play together.

Role alteration is a hallmark of other forms of play, such as dramatic play where children often change or negotiate roles repeatedly in the course of an episode (Garvey, 1990). Role alternation seems to play an important part in children's social perspective taking; taking different play roles, both in fantasy (Burns & Brainerd, 1979) and R&T (Pellegrini, 1993; Pellegrini & Smith, 1998), enables children to take different perspectives. Aggression, on the other hand, is typified by unilateral roles: aggressors do not switch roles with their victims. Thus, the social perspective-taking function is absent in aggression.

Ecology

Ecological factors also influence the expression of R&T. It tends to occur in spacious areas, such as the outdoors (Smith & Connolly, 1980), and on those parts of playgrounds with soft, grassy surfaces (Pellegrini, 2005). That R&T is physically vigorous and involves running, falling, and wrestling means that it is more likely to occur in areas that can support this sort of behavior, compared to more confined areas.

School policy variables, such as adult tolerance for R&T and the amount of time permitted between outdoor play breaks, also relate to the observed amount of physically vigorous behavior, including R&T (Pellegrini, 2005). Some schools have an explicit policy forbidding children to engage in any form of play fighting, because adults typically (and incorrectly!) assume that it will escalate into "real" fighting.

School policy related to the timing of free play and recess periods affects R&T as well as other forms of physically vigorous behavior. When children spend longer rather than shorter periods indoors involved in sedentary activities before recess, their outdoor play is more physically active and socially interactive (Pellegrini, 2005; Pellegrini, Huberty, & Jones, 1995). Correspondingly, high levels of physical activity often lead to aggression (DeRossier, Cillessen, Coie, & Dodge, 1994). Thus, long confinement before recess probably has the effect of increasing both types of physical activity.

Aggression does not, however, vary according to playground location (Pellegrini, 2002); it is likely to occur anywhere. Where toys and play are present, however, the cause of aggression often stems from children's disputes over objects (Smith & Connolly, 1980). As is the case with R&T, school policy can influence aggression to the extent that an explicit policy discouraging aggression and other forms of bullying does reduce aggression (Olweus, 1993; Smith & Thompson, 1991).

Although research has indicated that, under close scrutiny, it is evident that R&T and aggression are distinct constructs, many teachers and playground supervisors do not differentiate R&T from aggression, but rather, categorize all vigorous physical interaction as aggression. It may be necessary, from a policy perspective, to "educate" these caregivers about the difference between the two because, while R&T leads children into a very positive developmental trajectory, this is not the case for aggression.

Developmental Trajectories and Differences in Expression

The distinction between R&T and aggression is further evidenced by the fact that each has a different developmental trajectory. R&T, like other forms of play (Fagen, 1981; Fein, 1981; Pellegrini & Smith, 1998), follows an inverted-U developmental function. It accounts for about 5% of the free play of preschoolers, increases to 10 to 17% of the play of elementary school children, and declines in middle school to about 5% (Humphreys & Smith, 1984; Pellegrini, 2003; Pellegrini & Smith, 1998). Aggression, on the other hand, is stable from childhood through adolescence (Olweus, 1979); the trajectory is flat.

Gender Differences

There are also differences in the individual expression of R&T and aggression, most notably in the differential expression of each by boys and girls. Boys exhibit more R&T *and* aggression than do girls (Maccoby, 1998). These differences have been observed cross-culturally (Whiting & Edwards, 1973) and among most nonhuman primates (Humphreys & Smith, 1984). These gender differences are not *individual* differences per se but are probably due to both hormonal and socialization events (Maccoby, 1998). Among the factors that may influence boys' expression of vigorous and rough play at higher rates than girls are hormonal events, such as higher levels of testosterone during the development of the fetus; socialization pressures, such as the selection of certain toys and games; and permission to engage in active play. Gender differences in play are further reinforced in sexually segregated peer groups—a robust characteristic of young children's peer groups (Maccoby, 1998; Pellegrini, 2004).

Individual Differences

There are, however, individual differences in the expression of R&T by children of the same sex. Primary school boys who are both sociometrically rejected by their peers (that is, they are rated as disliked by more of their peers than they are liked), and physically aggressive tend to engage in R&T at rates similar to other boys. Their R&T, however, co-occurs with aggression. That is, rates of aggression and R&T are significantly intercorrelated for rejected, physically aggressive boys (Pellegrini, 1988). Further, the R&T of these boys tends to escalate into aggression; that is, when an R&T bout ends, aggression is likely to follow (Pellegrini, 1988). Boys who are aggressive and rejected in the primary grades retain this status as they move into adolescence. In adolescence, however, these boys engage in a particularly rough form of R&T and tend to use R&T to bully their peers (Pellegrini, 2003). While rates of R&T decline markedly for most adolescent boys, the R&T of rejected boys remains relatively high and continuous in relation to aggression (Pellegrini, 2002).

Attention Deficit Hyperactivity Disorder (ADHD) is another individual difference that relates to children's expression of aggression. ADHD is a commonly diagnosed (some would say too commonly diagnosed) syndrome where children (also mostly boys) exhibit high levels of physical activity and/or low levels of attention. (Pellegrini, 2005; Pellegrini & Horvat, 1995) These children often exhibit aggression as well as R&T.

This syndrome also seems to be exacerbated or inhibited by certain environments. It may be that in extreme cases, ADHD is primarily a biological problem, but in most cases it is probably the interaction between individual biological differences and environment. A moderately active kindergarten boy, for example, might be considered a problem in a classroom where adults expect children to sit quietly most of the day. In a classroom where the stress is on social interaction among peers, this same child would probably not be a problem.

Thus, for most children during the middle childhood period, especially boys, R&T is a playful construct, the exception being in rejected/aggressive boys. As most boys move into adolescence, R&T declines dramatically. Those boys who continue to engage in R&T, however, tend to be aggressive and to use R&T in antisocial ways. Thus, R&T relates to social–cognitive outcomes during childhood and early adolescence.

R&T as a Predictor of Social–Cognitive Status

Longitudinal studies offer data on some ways in which R&T predicts social–cognitive status during childhood and early adolescence (for summaries see Pellegrini, 2002; Pellegrini & Smith, 1998).

R&T in the Primary School Years

During the primary school years, the consequences of children's R&T depends on their sociometric status, or the degree to which they are liked and disliked by their peers. For popular boys, R&T predicts peer popularity, engagement in cooperative games, and social problem solving (Pellegrini & Smith, 1998). For boys rejected by their peers, R&T is correlated with aggression and does not predict positive social–cognitive outcomes. During childhood for most boys, therefore, R&T is a positive predictor of social cognitive status. R&T does not have these positive benefits for rejected boys; indeed, it predicts antisocial behavior.

These results have important implications for school policy. They clearly suggest that the R&T of *most* boys does not escalate to aggression. Indeed, it is related to a number of positive outcomes. Thus, school policy that discourages R&T needs to be reconsidered. Of course, for those children who are rejected and aggressive, their aggression and associated behaviors cannot be tolerated. Numerous social skills training programs are available to help aggressive children (Coie & Koeppl, 1990).

R&T in Adolescence

Early adolescence witnesses a dramatic shift in the role of R&T: its rate decreases dramatically after the primary school years. This decrease probably reflects boys' increasing concerns with heterosexual relationships (Pellegrini, 2003). Whereas primary school boys play in groups composed predominantly of other boys, young adolescent boys spend more of their free time in groups composed of both boys and girls and, therefore, do not engage in activities such as R&T that do not include girls.

Those adolescent boys who continue to engage in R&T tend to be antisocial and unpopular with their peers (Pellegrini, 2002). It seems that these boys use R&T as an opportunity to target weaker boys and then "victimize up." It may be the case that these "tough" boys, bullies, sample a variety of probable targets for their aggression through R&T overtures. When they find weaker boys who succumb to their aggression, they probably continue to victimize them. In this way, what starts off ostensibly as play typically ends with aggressive boys turning R&T into aggression, especially toward boys they consider to be weaker.

It is probably the case that these "bullies" are using R&T as a way to exhibit dominance to their peers (Pellegrini, 2003). This explanation is supported by the observation that adolescence is a period during which dominance is in considerable flux (Fagen, 1981). As a result of rapid change in body size and changes in schools (from primary to secondary) and peer groups, youngsters must renegotiate their peer status. Bullies may be using physical aggression as a basis for peer affiliation, whereas other, well-adjusted boys use other means, such as academics and sport.

It may be the case that most boys use R&T in childhood as a way to learn and practice social skills necessary for other sorts of cooperative interaction, such as social games. As they mature and the presence of R&T diminishes, they use those skills learned and practiced in R&T for other forms of interaction. The longitudinal relationship between R&T and cooperative games noted above illustrates this point. In effect, for many boys, R&T may be a bridge between the social fantasy play characteristic of preschool age and the social games with rules typical of middle childhood. They continue to structure their play with alternating roles and physically vigorous behaviors, while the goals of the play become subject to the rules that larger social groups enforce.

Asking Youngsters about R&T

Thus far, indirect methods of study have established the value, or function, of R&T in childhood and adolescence. Researchers have correlated one set of behaviors (R&T) with other behaviors, such as aggression, or related R&T behaviors to various tasks, such as sociometric nominations or contrived social problems, and then made inferences about the meaning of those relations. Interviewing children is a more direct method of assessing the meaning and function of R&T. Questionnaires can ask about R&T in general, or children can view filmed episodes of R&T and aggressive bouts and then answer questions about those bouts. Researchers have used variants of both of these procedures.

Some researchers have used questionnaire procedures with children in the United Kingdom and Italy (Costabile et al, 1991; Smith, Smees, Pellegrini, 2004). They asked children a series of questions about their perceptions of R&T and aggression; for example, the frequency with which they engage in R&T, the identity of their partners in R&T, and their reasons for engaging in R&T. These studies, like the behavioral studies discussed above, clearly show that children differentiate R&T from aggression and can give reasons supporting their judgments. Generally, and not surprisingly, children say they engage in R&T because it is fun.

The videotape methodology has taken two forms. Children more commonly view videotapes of the R&T and aggression of unfamiliar children. In this case, again, children clearly differentiate R&T from aggression and can give numerous reasons for doing so (Pellegrini, 1988).

It should be noted, however, that individual differences also crop up here. Rejected children, compared to popular children, neither are very accurate in their discrimination nor do they give as many reasons for their decisions. This difference may be due to a social information-processing deficit (Dodge & Frame, 1982). Briefly, these researchers have suggested that rejected children simply do not accurately process ambiguous, provocative interactions such as R&T (Dodge & Frame, 1982). When they see an ambiguous/provocative event that can be either playful or aggressive, they tend to attribute aggressive intent to it; thus, they see R&T as aggression.

There is another explanation for rejected children's poor performance on these discrimination tasks. It may be that these children, as general "problem children" in school, take on a negative stance when they are being interviewed. As a way to project this negative image to the interviewer, they label R&T

bouts as aggressive (thus the aggressive bias) and minimally comply with requests to give reasons for their responses (thus the low number of attributes given to differentiate R&T from aggression). In short, their responses may be a way of expressing defiance/noncompliance to an adult in school.

This purposeful, rather than deficient, explanation is consistent with other research showing that rejected boys are also very purposeful in their choice of R&T partners. For a particularly rough variant of R&T, but not other forms of social interaction, rejected boys (who are also considered to be "tough" by their peers) initiate interactions with boys who are weaker than themselves; peers also consider these targets to be "victims." These R&T bouts typically escalate into aggression at a greater-than-chance probability (Pellegrini & Smith, 1998). Thus, "tough" boys may use R&T as a pretext for victimizing less dominant boys, especially during early adolescence (Pellegrini, 2003).

Another, less commonly used, videotape method involves showing children and their teachers aggressive and R&T bouts in which they and their classmates were participants (Pellegrini, 2003; Smith, Smees, Pellegrini, & Menisini, 2004). Individual children who participated in the R&T bouts viewed the films on the same day as the bouts and again two weeks later; their classmates and teachers viewed the films at the same intervals. Researchers predicted that teachers' interpretations would be at odds with children's. From previous findings (Sutton-Smith, 1988), the researchers knew that teachers tended to be biased against the R&T, considering it aggression.

Instead, researchers found that participants agreed with each other on the meaning of the event, in effect, whether it was R&T or aggression. This agreement was stable across a two-week period. Nonparticipating peers and teachers also agreed with each other, but their interpretations were significantly different from those of the participants. For example, if participants would agree that a bout was play, nonparticipants and teachers would be more likely to agree with each other in saying the same bout was aggression.

What does this mean? At a very simple level it means that different people have different interpretations of the same ambiguous events. To understand ambiguous events, such as R&T, one may require a participant's point of view. Participant status, however, may be a proxy for something else. It may be the case that these participants are also friends and have a different sort of relationship between them than do nonparticipants. Friends tend to engage in R&T with each other more than with peers who are not friends (Humphreys & Smith, 1984). Friends also have a more accurate understanding of each other than do nonfriends (Hartup, 1983). Thus, it may be that R&T participants agree with each other because they are friends.

These results have very clear implications for both research and educational policy. Researchers should make provision for the differing interpretations of ambiguous provocation events, such as R&T, when they interview children. From a policy perspective, these results suggest that to understand potentially ambiguous forms of behavior, such as aggression and R&T, teachers and school administrators should interview participants and their friends and not rely on what bystanders say.

This chapter outlined the ways in which one form of play, R&T, differs from aggression. As part of this exposition, the review of evidence showed that R&T and aggression have very different developmental histories, and consequently, very different impacts on children's social cognitive status. R&T is quite "normal" and actually a "good" form of play for young children, particularly prevalent among boys. R&T is "good" because it predicts cooperative interaction, popularity, and social problem solving. It may also be the case that engaging in R&T affords an opportunity to practice encoding and decoding social information. Further, the role alternation characteristic of R&T play during childhood is then used during adolescence in other forms of reciprocal social interaction, such as cooperative games.

An interesting developmental shift occurs in adolescence (Pellegrini, 2003). R&T no longer has positive implications for social cognitive development. During this period, R&T is used primarily by bullies victimizing their weaker peers. Thus, this is an interesting case of a set of behaviors serving different functions for different youngsters—rejected versus popular—at different periods (childhood vs. adolescence). This form of play is not all good for all children.

Another important conclusion from this work is that not all children seem to need this specific form of play in order to develop. R&T is a particularly male phenomenon and many boys seem to use it in the service of their social–cognitive development. Girls generally do not engage in R&T but also develop into well-functioning social beings. Girls use other strategies to become socially competent; they engage in social pretense play at high rates, compared to boys, which suggests that this form of play, not R&T, is important for their social–cognitive development.

In short, not all children must travel the same developmental path to competence. This sort of behavioral flexibility seems crucial in light of the fact that children, as a species, are reared in a variety of conditions. To flourish in these different niches, children must adopt different strategies. Thus, educators should beware of advice that one "royal road" leads to anything. There are numerous roads.

References

Blurton Jones, N. (1972). Categories of child interaction. In N. Blurton Jones (Ed.), *Ethological studies in child behavior* (pp. 92–129). Cambridge, UK: Cambridge University Press.

Bredekamp, S. (1987). *Developmentally appropriate practice in early childhood programs serving children from birth through age 8*. Washington, DC: National Association for the Education of Young Children.

Bruner, J., Jolly, A., & Sylva, K. (Eds.). (1976). *Play: Its role in development and evolution*. New York: Basic Books.

Burns, S., & Brainerd, C. (1979). Effects of constructive and dramatic play on perspective taking in young children. *Developmental Psychology, 15*, 512–521.

Coie, J., & Koeppl, G. (1990). Adapting intervention to the problems of aggressive and disturbed rejected children. In S. Asher & J. Coie (Eds.), *Peer rejection in childhood* (pp. 309–337). New York: Cambridge University Press.

Costabile, A., Smith, P. K., Matheson, L., Aston, J., Hunter, T., & Boulton, M. (1991). Cross-national comparisons of how children distinguish play from serious fighting. *Developmental Psychology, 27*, 881–887.

DeRossier, M., Cillessen, T., Coie, J., & Dodge, K. (1994). Group social context and children's aggressive behavior. *Child Development, 65*, 1068–1079.

Dodge, K., & Frame, C. (1982). Social cognitive deficits and biases in aggressive boys. *Child Development, 53*, 620–635.

Fagen, R. (1981). *Animal play*. New York:; Oxford University Press.

Fein, G. (1981). Pretend play in childhood: An integrative review. *Child Development, 52*, 1095–1118.

Garvey, C. (1990). *Play*. Cambridge, MA: Harvard University Press.

Hartup, W. W. (1983). Peer relations. In E. M. Hetherington (Ed.), *Handbook of child psychology* (Vol. 4, pp. 103–196). New York: Wiley.

Humphreys, A., & Smith, P. K. (1984). Rough-and-tumble play in preschool and the playground. In P. K. Smith (Ed.), *Play in animals and humans* (pp. 241–266). Oxford: Basil Blackwell.

Maccoby, E. E. (1998). *The two sexes: Growing up apart, coming together*. Cambridge, MA: Harvard University Press.

Olweus, D. (1979). Stability and aggressive patterns in males: A review. *Psychological Bulletin, 86*, 852–875.

Olweus, D. (1993). Bullies on playgrounds. In C. Hart (Ed.), *Children on playgrounds* (pp. 85–128). Albany: State University of New York Press.

Pellegrini, A. D. (1988). Elementary school children's rough-and-tumble play and social competence. *Developmental Psychology, 24*, 802–806.

Pellegrini, A. D. (1993). Boys' rough-and-tumble play, social competence, and group composition. *British Journal of Developmental Psychology, 11*, 237–248.

Pellegrini, A. D. (2002).Rough-and-tumble play from childhood through adolescence: Development and possible functions. In C. H. Hart & P. K. Smith (Eds.), *Handbook of childhood social development* (pp. 438–454). Oxford, UK: Blackwell.

Pellegrini, A. D. (2003). Perceptions and functions of play and real fighting in early adolescence. *Child Development, 74*, 1552–1533.

Pellegrini, A. D. (2004). Sexual segregation in childhood: A review of evidence for two hypotheses. *Animal Behaviour, 68*, 435–443.

Pellegrini, A. D. (2005). *Recess: Its role in education and development*. Mahwah, NJ: Erlbaum.

Pellegrini, A. D., & Galda, L. (1993). Ten years after: A re-examination of the relations between symbolic play and literacy. *Reading Research Quarterly, 28*(2), 162–175.

Pellegrini, A. D., & Horvat, M. (1995). A developmental contextual critique of attention deficit hyperactivity disorder. *Educational Researcher, 24*(1), 13–20.

Pellegrini, A. D., Huberty, P. D., & Jones, L. (1995). The effects of recess timing on children's playground and classroom behavior. *American Educational Research Journal, 32*, 845-864.

Pellegrini, A. D., & Smith, P. K. (1998). Physical activity play: The nature and function of a neglected aspect of play. *Child Development, 69*, 577–598.

Smith, P. K. (1982). Does play matter? Functional and evolutionary aspects of animal and human play. *The Behavioral and Brain Sciences, 5*, 139–184.

Smith, P. K. (1988). Children's play and its role in early development: A re-evaluation of the "play ethos." In A. D. Pellegrini (Ed.), *Psychological bases for early education* (pp. 229–244) Chichester, UK: Wiley.

Smith, P. K. (1994). The war play debate. In J. Goldstein (Ed.), *Toys, play, and child development* (pp. 67–84). New York: Cambridge University Press.

Smith, P. K., & Connolly, K. (1972). Patterns of play and social interaction in preschool children. In N. Blurton Jones (Ed.), *Ethological studies in child behavior* (pp. 65–96). Cambridge, UK: Cambridge University Press.

Smith, P. K., & Connolly, K. (1980). *The ecology of preschool behavior.* Cambridge, UK: Cambridge University Press.

Smith, P. K., Smees, R., Pellegrini, A. D., & Menisini, E. (2004). Play fighting and real fighting: Using video playback methodology with young children. *Aggressive Behavior, 30,* 164–173.

Smith, P. K., & Thompson, D. (Eds.). (1991). *Practical approaches to bullying.* London: David Fulton.

Sutton-Smith, B. (1988). War toys and childhood aggression. *Play and Culture, 1,* 57–69.

Wegener-Spohring, G. (1994). War toys and aggressive play scenes. In J. Goldstein (Ed.), *Toys, play, and child development* (pp. 85–109). New York: Cambridge University Press.

Whiting, B., & Edwards, C. (1973). A cross-cultural analysis of sex differences in behavior of children age 3 through 11. *Journal of Social Psychology, 91,* 171–188.

13
Games with Rules

RHETA DEVRIES

Games with rules are a form of play involving competitive interindividual relationships in the context of regulations as to possibilities and prohibitions, with sanctions for violations. While various writers (Baldwin, 1897/1973; Mead, 1934/1962) have considered the role of games with rules in psychological development, it is to Piaget that we owe the greatest debt for elaborating their psychological significance in the child's development. In his book (1945/1963) Piaget discussed games with rules as the third in a succession of types of structure in children's activities. Let us consider the developmental context of group games according to Piaget.

The Developmental Context of Group Games

The first structure, practice play, appears in the first months of life as the infant continues to exercise actions already mastered simply for pleasure. Examples in later childhood include throwing pebbles in a lake, throwing a ball, lacing and unlacing shoes, and jumping back and forth over a puddle. While such practice play diminishes in frequency over childhood, it reappears whenever there is a new acquisition, even in adulthood. Practice play begins to evolve into symbolic play during the second year of life when the infant loses interest in practicing something already mastered and becomes interested in imitating the content of actions. Examples include imitation of one's own familiar actions out of context, such as sleeping or eating, and extends eventually to exact imitations of reality; for example, instead of simply using a piece of wood for a boat, really making a boat with a hollowed-out space, masts, sails, and seats. Practice play declines after the age of 4 years when the child becomes more interested in activities involving adaptation to reality. It does not disappear altogether, however, and continues into adult activities of fantasies and dramatic productions.

Both practice play and symbolic play evolve into games with rules, beginning between ages 4 and 7 years and especially belonging to ages 7 to 11 years. In the case of practice play, actions are socialized. Piaget (1945/1963, p. 143) gives the example of three 5-year-olds whose play at jumping from stairs evolves into rules as they agree to try to jump as far as they can from the same step, and decide that anyone who falls loses. In the case of symbolic play, symbols can be socialized into a system of rules. Piaget (1945/1963, pp. 143–144) gives the example of some shepherd boys who cut hazel branches in a Y shape and pretended these were cows, with the two tips of the Y representing horns and the lower part the body, with spots on top and loosened bark on bottom for the belly. This symbolism evolved into a game with rules: the cows had to be balanced horn to horn, after which the competition was to push them by the base of the Y to see which one fell on its back and therefore lost.

Piaget (1932/1965) developed in much more detail the evolution of games with rules in his book, *The Moral Judgment of the Child*. His description of stages in the practice of rules and consciousness of rules in the game of marbles provides an account of development that is still important and applicable to children's play more than 60 years later.

Stages in the Game of Marbles

Piaget's approach was to pretend he had forgotten how to play marbles and to ask children (ages approximately 6 to 14 years) to instruct him so that he could play with them. In this way, he was able to learn children's conceptions of the rules. He brought pairs of children together to play the game by themselves in order further to observe their practice of rules with one another, and he then interviewed children as to their consciousness about various aspects of rules, for example, whether they could invent rules, the origin of the rules, and so forth. He also observed younger children with marbles.

Let us consider the results with regard to the practice of rules. Piaget found four stages or levels in children's play. The first stage is motor and individual play, occurring before the age of 2 years, when the child simply uses the marbles to explore their properties (for example, by dropping them one by one onto a carpet) or in symbolic play (for example, "cooking" them in a toy saucepan). While the child in these activities imposes some regularities on the marbles, these cannot be called rules because they are asocial and entail no obligation to engage in these actions.

The second stage is egocentric play, occurring between about 2 and 5 years of age, when the child tries to learn other people's rules and submits to their authority. While social in intent, the child's rules are not thoroughly social in action. That is, the child imitates observable actions of players but cannot at first think about the opposed intentions of players. Play is thus not competitive, and the child at this stage often says that everybody won. While children play side by side, they do not unify their rules and often play by different rules, without noticing or without considering this important.

The third stage is incipient cooperation, appearing between 7 and 8 years of age (although we certainly observe this much earlier, even in some 4-year-olds, among children with considerable experience in playing games). The hallmark of this stage is, paradoxically, the emergence of a competitive attitude. Rules now rest on mutual agreement and reciprocity. The desire to unify rules leads children to see the necessity of coordinating with others in deciding on what the rules are to be, following them, and agreeing on their consequences. At the beginning of this stage, children still may have incomplete rule systems and cooperation may exist more in intention than successful action. What is important is that children are consciously trying to coordinate with others. At the end of this stage, the child understands fully the necessity of rules as the basis for agreement on how to play. When asked, for example, why there are rules in the game of marbles, one 11-year-old answered, "So as not to be always quarrelling you must have rules, and then play properly [stick to them]" (Piaget, 1932/1965, pp. 66, 71). Thus, the feeling of obligation to obey rules is motivated not by external coercion, as in the second stage, but by self-regulated cooperation.

The fourth stage is codification of rules, beginning at 11 to 12 years of age among Piaget's subjects (although we observe this stage much earlier among children experienced with games). At this stage, children are not only interested in cooperation but also in anticipating all possible instances of conflict of interest, and providing a codified set of rules to regulate play. Children elaborate the game in a very complex way and, when disagreements arise about rules, players know how to come to agreement. One 13-year-old acknowledged that people sometimes play differently, but said that when there are conflicting ideas, "You ask each other what you want to do." Asked what happens if they cannot agree, he said, "We scrap for a bit and then we fix things up" (Piaget, 1932/1965, p. 49). At this stage, the relation to others is autonomous, since the regulation by rules is mutual self-regulation (see Piaget, 1932/1965, for further details on this research on marbles). This general outline of progress in the practice of rules in marbles has parallels in all other games with rules.

Stages in Playing Guess-Which-Hand the-Penny-Is-In

Another game studied systematically is guess-which-hand-the-penny-is-in (where one player puts his or her hands behind his or her back, grasps a penny in one fist, and presents both fists for the opponent to guess which hand it is in). Working with children ages 3 to 7, the researcher found it easy to engage them immediately simply by showing them a penny and inviting them to guess which hand the penny was in. With a penny in both hands (so children were always successful for about 10 guesses), the researcher was able to observe children's spontaneous approaches to finding the penny, especially with regard to whether they guessed the same hand each time, alternated from left to right, or shifted their guesses in an irregular way. After about 10 guesses, the researcher left the pennies on the floor behind her and continued to play with both fists empty, enabling her to observe the child's reactions to not finding the penny. Taking up both pennies again she guaranteed that the child's last guess was successful. She then gave a penny to the child and invited him or her to hide it so the researcher could guess.

This game is especially good for assessing whether, or to what degree, a child is able to take the perspective of the other in the game. As Piaget found with marbles, young children at first only imitate what is observable to them in others' physical actions. Not yet aware of the possibility of deceptiveness and secrecy (requiring the ability to think about others' intentions), some see the game as one in which one person simply gives the penny to another. With this idea of the game, they enact the hider's role by simply holding out a palm with the penny. Others see the game as one in which one person puts the penny in a fist, with the object being for the other to find the penny; with this conception of the game, the young child may offer only one fist, or hold one fist forward suggestively, even becoming irritated if the other does not point to the fist with the penny. Clearly, a competitive attitude is missing. When a competitive attitude emerges, the child still does not necessarily take adequately into account the other's perspective. For example, while not wanting the other to find the penny, the child may unconsciously provide clues to the location of the penny by presenting a limp empty fist, changing the location of the penny before putting hands behind the back, bringing out fists while obviously still getting a good grip on the penny, and so forth. Earlier levels of play of this game involve perseverating in guessing or hiding in the same hand, or, at a somewhat more advanced level, moving or guessing the location in a regular left-right-left-right alternation. More advanced play is characterized by irregular shifting in guessing and hiding. (For a more detailed discussion of the systematic study of this game, see DeVries, 1970; summarized in DeVries & Kohlberg, 1990; Kamii & DeVries, 1980).

Stages in Playing Tic-Tac-Toe

Similarly, DeVries and Fernie (1990) recount the results of systematic study of the videotaped play of tic-tac-toe among children 3 to 9 years of age. Using a board and movable plastic Xs and Os, and working with children one at a time, Fernie asked children if they knew how to play and learned their conceptions of the game. If they did not know how to play, he explained the rules. After playing a series of about 10 games, Fernie then interviewed the children as to their conceptions of the game and what would be "good moves" in several standard situations. An observer made a record of the exact sequence of plays in each game, and children's play was analyzed in detail with regard to whether they followed the rules, used blocking or two-way strategies, and so forth. An assessment from verbal and nonverbal behaviors was made as to whether the child had a competitive attitude.

Findings in this study parallel those of Piaget. Level 1 of motor and individual play was observed when children simply stack Xs and Os, throw them, and use them as props for pretense. Three sublevels of level 1 egocentric play are described, from 1A, schematic imitation of some aspects of the game (simply putting pieces in spaces without taking turns), to 1B, taking turns (and no longer going out of turn to complete a line), to 1C, knowing that the goal of the game is a straight line (and no longer believing a crooked line is adequate). Level 2 of cooperative play has three sublevels, with level 2A signaled by the emergence of a competitive attitude, although children do not yet think of logical strategies by which to try to win. Level 2B emerges with the strategy of blocking used only some of the time when necessary (by playing in a space that, if filled by the opponent's piece, would complete a line, as a means to trying to win). Preoccupied with this newly invented strategy, however, the child blocks at times without noticing the possibility of a win by playing a different space. Level 3A involves the consolidation of defensive strategies that include blocking most of the time when necessary in order to avoid losing. At level 3B, the child constructs the temporal aspect of the game, reflected in recognizing that the first line wins without attempting to continue playing when the opponent completes a line. At level 4A, the child coordinates an advanced offensive strategy through using two-way setups, trying to guarantee a win by setting up the situation so that the possibility to make three in a line exists in two directions at the same time. The child sometimes loses sight, however, of a possibility to win when preoccupied with how to arrange a two-way setup. Finally, at level 4B, the child coordinates strategies by shifting flexibly, when necessary, between two-way setups and blocking. (For a more detailed presentation of the systematic study of this game, see DeVries & Fernie, 1990; summarized in DeVries & Kohlberg, 1990).

Education through Games with Rules

Kamii and DeVries (1980) took seriously Piaget's work on games with rules and proposed the inclusion of group games in constructivist programs of early education that aim to promote children's development. In their book, *Group Games in Early Education: Implications of Piaget's Theory*, they (Kamii & DeVries, 1980; also, DeVries & Kohlberg, 1990) discuss the educational rationale for games with rules as educational activities. Games with rules can be justified as educational because they promote children's sociomoral and intellectual development.

Sociomoral Development in Games with Rules

The sociomoral objective of constructivist teaching is long-term progress in the structure or stage of moral reasoning, not just in the specific content of moral rules or even behavior conforming to moral rules. That is, as Kohlberg (1987) has argued, our aim should focus not in an isolated way just on teaching moral rules or moral behaviors, but on facilitating the construction of inner moral convictions about what is good and necessary in one's relations with others. If one focuses only on promoting conformity to heteronomous rules given ready-made to children, conforming behavior may reflect only superficial knowledge of social expectation without personal commitment to the moral value itself.

The broad constructivist sociomoral goal is for children to develop autonomous feelings of obligation (or moral necessity) about relations with others that are not just dictates accepted from adults. Rather, a feeling of moral necessity reflects an internal system of personal convictions. Such a personal system is autonomous insofar as it leads to beliefs and behavior that are self-regulated rather than other-regulated. It is cooperative insofar as it reflects a view of the self as part of a system of reciprocal social relations.

From the point of view of promoting children's autonomy, group games contribute by providing a context in which children can voluntarily accept and submit themselves to rules. Children are free to exercise their autonomy by choosing to play and choosing to follow rules. Rules in games are different from the set of obligations adults must impose in daily living, such as eating certain foods, going to bed at a certain time, and not playing with certain delicate objects. Rules in everyday living are fully formed and given to the child ready-made. The child usually cannot understand the reasons for these rules and thus can only abide by them out of obedience to the authority of adults. That is, he or she cannot follow them out of an internal feeling of commitment to their necessity.

Autonomous adoption of sociomoral rules is prevented to the extent that the child is bound by a heteronomous attitude. That is, when children think and act in terms of what they perceive to be the requirements of others, they are not likely to submit these to the reflection that leads to understood and self-accepted values. The loosening of the heteronomous attitude requires experiences in which children can exercise autonomy by choosing to follow or not follow rules, reflecting on the consequences, and gradually growing to understand the reasons for rules that are rooted in maintaining desired relations with others.

In a game with rules, the adult authority and system of rules is temporarily suspended. Players can practice cooperation among equals when adult authority is put aside in favor of rules to which adults, too, must conform. When the adult participates as one player among others, adult authority can be more easily suspended in the minds of children, and this opportunity for interacting with the adult on a more equal basis is particularly good for the loosening of children's heteronomous attitudes. In daily living, it is difficult for the adult to tolerate a child's breaking a rule. In games, however, rules are not so sacred. In games, adult authority can decrease while children's power increases. When power is equalized, coercion ceases to be the regulating force, and autonomous cooperation can begin.

In games, therefore, children find conditions in which they can willingly adapt to society. Children thus have the opportunity to exercise autonomy in freely regulating their actions with others in relation to rules. They experience the consequences of failing to follow a rule when others protest and the game comes to a halt; they can then decide whether to change their behavior or, with the help of the teacher or another child, change the rule. This leads to dawning awareness of the necessity of collective agreement to the continuation of a mutually satisfying experience. In a game, children thus have the possibility of creating, in part, the rules and values by which they regulate their behavior.

In a game with rules, society intervenes in the experience of the individual, offering a situation in which the child can adapt to external social rules and construct feelings of obligation to them. From the point of view of promoting children's cooperation, games with rules contribute by providing a context, a minisociety, in which children can autonomously relate to others according to rules. Interest in the game leads to interest in others. Interest in playing with others according to the rules leads to efforts to coordinate individual actions with those of others. Self-regulation thus evolves into mutual adaptation, that is, the mutual accommodation and mutual adjustment of cooperation. Interest in the end, playing the game, brings an interest in the means, cooperation, by which to have fun in the game.

Games uniquely promote attitudes of reciprocity that lead to feelings of moral necessity, which is the core of sociomoral development. These feelings of obligation arise not out of obedience, but out of a feeling of personal necessity. Feelings of moral necessity about relations with others develop in games as children confront issues of fairness, individual rights, and the reasons for rules. They can practice mutual respect, which is a defining characteristic of cooperation and democratic principles.

A competitive game is especially conducive to moral development because opposed intentions must be coordinated within a broader context of cooperation. That is, competition can only exist when players cooperate in agreeing on the rules, enforcing them, abiding by them, and accepting their consequences even when unfavorable to themselves. The game cannot occur unless players cooperate by coordinating their points of view. When players have different conceptions of how a game should be played, the game may stop; this creates a situation in which children have the opportunity to confront the different perspective of someone else, decenter, and negotiate an agreement. Seen in this light, the competitive aspect is, in fact, subordinate to the cooperative aspect. Following mutually agreed-upon rules puts everyone on an equal basis in a social system regulated by the players themselves. Playing a group game is thus a useful point of departure for promoting children's sociomoral progress (see DeVries & Zan, 1994, for elaboration of the constructivist sociomoral atmosphere of which playing games with rules is only one part. See also DeVries & Kohlberg, 1990, for a discussion of the contribution of games with rules to children's personality development.)

Research on Children's Sociomoral Development in the Context of a Game

In a comparative study of three kindergarten classrooms reflecting different educational paradigms (constructivist, behaviorist, and eclectic), I used the context of a game to assess children's sociomoral development. A teacher-made board game was used in which players rolled a die to determine how many spaces to move along a path from start to finish. Pairs of children were taught to play this simple game with its rules for turn taking, going back to the nearest picture of a haunted house upon landing on a ghost, and going back to start when the opponent lands on the space one occupies. During the teaching session, the experimenter played alongside the children. Several days later, the same pair of children was invited to play the game again, but this time without the adult's participation. The goal was to learn how children engage and negotiate with each other (self-regulate) when no adult controls or influences them. Microanalysis of videotapes utilized Selman's (Selman & Schultz, 1990) conceptualization of developmental levels of interpersonal understanding.

Briefly, to summarize the results, children from the constructivist program were more actively engaged with one another. They had more friendly, shared experiences with each other, and not only negotiated more but negotiated more successfully. They used significantly more strategies reflecting consideration for the other's point of view and made efforts to achieve mutually satisfactory interaction. In harmonious interactions, these children were also more reciprocal; for example, sharing secrets and recalling past shared experiences, than children from the other two classrooms (who engaged in much more impulsive silliness). Children from the constructivist classroom also used a greater variety of different strategies and resolved more conflicts than children from the behaviorist and eclectic classrooms. Children from the behaviorist classroom tended to try to resolve conflicts by overwhelming the other person physically or emotionally and, in general, related in less complex ways. (See DeVries, Reese-Learned, & Morgan, 1991, for details of this study; and see DeVries, Haney, & Zan, 1991, for a description of the study of the sociomoral atmosphere of these three classrooms.)

Intellectual Development in Games with Rules

Descriptions of stages given above reflect intellectual development in children's play of games as studied systematically by researchers. Kamii and DeVries (1980) studied how children play games in constructivist classrooms where teachers facilitated children's play. Working with teachers to develop an approach to using games with rules, they videotaped instances of games and analyzed what children and teachers did. This work led to the conclusion that the cognitive advantages of games with rules vary, depending on the type of game, its idiosyncratic characteristics, and the ways in which children use it.

Kamii and DeVries (1980) categorize group games into eight types (aiming, racing, chasing, hiding, guessing, games involving verbal commands, card games, and board games), giving many examples of each of these types with cognitive rationales. Aiming games, for example, are good for the structuring of space because children think about spatial relationships when they try to figure out how to hit a target.

Not all games with rules are educational. Recreational games include those that provide no intellectual challenge to children. A particular game may be educational for some children but not others. Kamii and DeVries (1980) discuss criteria for educational games and present principles of teaching group games. Detailed accounts of how teachers use seven specific games are provided, with comments on teachers' strategies.

Children's play of games with rules is important for their intellectual, sociomoral, and personality development. Psychological research reveals stages in play that signal developmental progress. Educational research reveals how teachers can use games with rules as an important component of constructivist education that aims to promote children's development. Program comparison research reveals that young children in constructivist classrooms who play games on a regular basis are more advanced in their interpersonal understanding and ability to negotiate and resolve conflicts with peers. These findings suggest that games with rules should be seriously considered as an important part of early education.

References

Baldwin, J. M. (1973). *Social and ethical interpretations in mental development.* New York: Arno. (Original work published 1897)

DeVries, R. (1970). The development of roletaking in young, bright, average, and retarded children as reflected in social guessing game behavior. *Child Development, 41*(3), 759–770.

DeVries, R., & Fernie, D. (1990). Stages in children's play of tic tac toe. *Journal of Research in Childhood Education, 4*(2), 98–111.

DeVries, R., Haney, J., & Zan, B. (1991). Sociomoral atmosphere in direct-instruction, eclectic, and constructivist kindergartens: A study of teachers' interpersonal understanding. *Early Childhood Research Quarterly, 6,* 449–471.

DeVries, R., & Kohlberg, L. (1990). *Constructivist early education: Overview and comparison with other programs* (2nd ed.). Washington, DC: National Association for the Education of Young Children.

DeVries, R., Reese-Learned, H., & Morgan, P. (1991). Sociomoral development in direct-instruction, eclectic, and constructivist kindergartens: A study of children's enacted interpersonal understanding. *Early Childhood Research Quarterly, 6,* 473–517.

DeVries, R., & Zan, B. (1994). *Moral classrooms, moral children: Creating a constructivist atmosphere in early education.* New York: Teachers College Press.

Kamii, C., & DeVries, R. (1980). *Group games in early education: Implications of Piaget's theory.* Washington, DC: National Association for the Education of Young Children.

Kohlberg, L. (1987). *Child psychology and childhood education: A cognitive–developmental view.* New York: Longman.

Mead, G. H. (1962). *Mind, self, and society.* Chicago: University of Chicago Press. (Original work published 1934)

Piaget, J. (1963). *Play, dreams, and imitation in childhood.* New York: Norton. (Original work published 1945)

Piaget, J. (1965). *The moral judgment of the child.* New York: Basic Books. (Original work published 1932)

Selman, R., & Shultz, L. (1990). *Making a friend in youth.* Chicago: University of Chicago Press.

14
Play as Children See It

NANCY W. WILTZ AND GRETA G. FEIN

Scholars have spent hours, decades, and even centuries debating a definition of play. There are also those who bemoan the debate as if a term for which there is no consensus should not be taken seriously (Berlyne, 1960). But the definitional status of play is not different from that of other terms that receive serious attention from scientists and educators. Terms like *aggression, love, teaching*, and *learning*, to name but a few, also lack widely shared, rigorous definitions. Yet these terms signify large ideas that are understood in some fashion across cultures, across centuries, and by individuals of disparate status, ages, and experience. Play is one of those large ideas that touch a strand of human experience beginning in childhood and, perhaps in different forms, continuing throughout life. Formal definitional variations reflect scholarly discipline, ideology, and cultural preferences (Sutton-Smith, 1995).

As Sutton-Smith (1995) has argued so persuasively, folk ideas about play are richly laced with cultural "rhetorics" that reflect the preoccupations for a particular historical and social era (Sutton-Smith, 1995). Play cannot be understood without regard to its ideological context which then shades and shapes what an observer or participant sees or feels. It is even possible that these rhetorics change with age and vary with social status. It is only recently that investigators have asked what children, teachers, and parents mean when they use this term.

Definitions of play also have practical consequences. With the endorsement of Developmentally Appropriate Practices (DAP) by the National Association of Young Children (Bredekamp & Copple, 1997), play received formal professional recognition as a core component and educational tool in early childhood practice. Although not without its critics, DAP has received widespread approval from the field. Areas of disagreement have less to do with play per se than with matters such as the role of teacher-directed small-group activities (Fowell & Lawton, 1992). However, how play serves educational purposes depends mightily on how it is used in the classroom. It is in this area that there may be major disagreements. Play in a general sense, as an underlying pedagogical attitude, has different implications from play in a particular sense, as a set of specific pedagogical strategies or curriculum plans.

The encouragement and cultivation of a child-centered play curriculum in preschools and kindergartens has several implications. Naïve observers easily agree on the occurrence of play even when they define it differently (Smith & Vollstedt, 1985). Some observers dismiss such a curriculum as just play, a way little ones keep busy. Better informed observers might see play as contributing primarily to children's social skills, especially their ability to function in a group (Elias & Berk, 2002). Skilled teachers might view play as "the glue that binds together all other pursuits, including the early teaching of reading and writing (Paley, 2004, p. 8). In any case, the contribution of play to intellectual competence is often neglected. While the contribution of play to aspects of development is an important issue, the second implication, which has received far too little attention, is that children also define and evaluate play.

How children themselves perceive the place of play in their homes and classrooms provides adults with a context for viewing and evaluating the home and school experiences. At an early age children use the term *play* to describe their own and others' activities. What do they mean when they do so? Answers to this question have been explored in studies representing different theoretical traditions. Because these traditions have something useful to say about the meaning of play as viewed by players, they are viewed in the following sections. The first section considers studies that ask children the seemingly simple question: What happens when you go to school? Of interest is whether play enters into children's school scripts and, if it does, where it goes. Do children's responses reveal their emotional and motivational judgments of schools and, if so, how are these judgments expressed?

From script-oriented research, the second and third sections turn to studies that deal more specifically with the distinction between work and play. These studies view work and play as sociocultural concepts that children acquire at an early age. Studies of children's views of work and play examine the criteria children use to separate these concepts and how these criteria change with age. Finally, there is a summary of recent data about children's retrospective accounts of play, especially pretend play. What are the highlights of these memories? How are they organized? How do children of different ages remember their play as preschoolers?

Play in School: A Script Theory Perspective

One approach to understanding and documenting children's perspectives depends on the assumption that individuals create cognitive "scripts" to organize daily experiences (Nelson, 1978; Schank & Abelson, 1977). Each script has a skeletal sequential structure stored in long-term memory, with slots reserved for the details of what happens, when, and to whom, which are filled as needed with appropriate information (Schank & Abelson, 1977). Using this theory, children view what goes on at school, for example, as a series of events that make up the school day (Fivush, 1984; Nelson & Gruendel, 1981; Wiltz, 1997; Wiltz & Klein, 2001). Play is simply one of those events organized in memory as a general event representation that is then used to anticipate, understand, and interpret recurring events (Light, 1987; Mandler, 1983; Schank & Abelson, 1977). Children respond to questions about activities they engage in at school with general statements about playing, working, helping, making things, having lunch, taking naps, and going home. Some children mention some of these events and other children mention others; some children cite more events and others cite fewer. Yet almost all children mention play.

A prototypical script theory response from a 4-year-old who was asked, "What happens when you come to school?" goes as follows:

Ben: I play. And I play with some toys and I play with my friends. Then we go outside and then we come in for snack. Then I wait for my mom and she picks me up.

It is not surprising that play figures prominently in preschoolers' accounts of what happens in school. Typical preschool classrooms provide areas and materials for various types of play (e.g., block centers, areas for manipulation of toys, housekeeping areas, dramatic play corners, large-motor play areas) and daily schedules provide periods of time for both indoor and early school settings.

One investigator asked 30 kindergarten children on the second day, the second week, the fourth week, and the 10th week of school, "What happens when you go to school?" (Fivush, 1984). At all four meetings the interviewer also asked what had happened at school the previous day and mentioned specific events that had occurred. At the fourth and final interview, the researcher asked the children to recall the first day of school. Fivush (1984) found that 5-year-old children had a general representation of the kindergarten routine by the second day of school, which remained stable over time, but that children had difficulty recalling specific episodes from the previous day. The content of children's reports over the semester became more elaborate, and the lists of specific events that occurred at a particular time and place in the routine became increasingly more complex and showed remarkable consistency over time. Play was mentioned more than any other activity. On the second day of school, 85% of the children talked about play, and by the 10th week, 100% did so. Details of what constituted play were not explored, but play became a part of the kindergartners' scripts from the second day of school on.

Beyond Script Theory

Script theorists agree that knowledge is organized around the structure and routine of daily activities, a process that begins at or near birth and continues throughout life. Several researchers have moved beyond this theory by examining how children organize different aspects of the school day. In these studies, sequence is less important than types of activity.

One group of researchers asked 14 3- to 6-year-old children in a full-day child care program, "Tell us what you do at school each day" (Garza, Briley, & Reifel, 1985; Reifel, 1988; Reifel, Briley, & Garza, 1986). Children listed a consistent core of classroom activities, including doing jobs, reading stories, lunching, napping, listening to music, going to the gym, going home, and playing. Even the youngest children included play as a part of their overall structure of day care, using simple statements such as, "We play" (Reifel et al., 1986, p. 85). Older children included riding scooters, playing outside, working on puzzles, playing with toys, playing games, and playing with mud in their responses. These researchers generated two main categories of play types that accounted for 93% of the responses: (1) nonsocial play with materials included pretense (e.g., feeding dolls and playing house) and manipulation of materials (e.g., riding scooters); and (2) social play included dramatic play (e.g., make-believe or pretending) and games with rules (e.g., duck-duck-goose).

More recent studies also found that children report a core of school activities consistent with previous research (Klein, 2001; Klein, Kantor, & Fernie, 1988). Wiltz and Klein (1994, 1995, 1996) asked 3-, 4-, and 5-year-old children what they did at school. Two broad categories: structured (teacher-controlled) and unstructured (child-controlled) activities emerged. Structured activities were subdivided into three areas: curriculum, function, and construction. Curriculum activities related to the academic areas of school, were primarily teacher directed, and included such things as singing, reading, and math. Functional activities involved routine tasks such as eating lunch, doing jobs, or napping. Construction activities were primarily teacher guided and involved making things. Lists of structured versus unstructured activities increased steadily with age, from 55% for the 3-year-olds, to 61% for the 4-year-olds, to 80% for the 5-year-olds, and culminating at 90% for the 6-year-olds. The most dramatic increases appeared in the curriculum category, where 3-year-olds mentioned activities like writing stories and singing, while 6-year olds talked about doing math, reading, and taking spelling tests.

Unstructured activities fell into two main categories: creative play which included activities such as outside play, dressing up, and playing house; and play with toys, which incorporated play with blocks, cars, trucks, and stuffed animals. In direct contrast to structured activities, both categories of play steadily declined with age, with a dramatic drop as children entered formal school. Three-year-olds mentioned play more frequently than 5-year-olds, and first graders equated play at school only with recess. According to these children a sharp curriculum shift occurs at 5 years of age.

Previous research supports several conclusions. First, even preschool children respond with an understanding of classroom activities beyond their mere sequencing. Second, older children relate school events in greater and more vivid detail than do younger ones (Fivush, 1984; Reifel et al, 1986: Wiltz & Klein, 1994). Third, children's reports accurately reflect the diminishing role of play in the kindergarten curriculum. Children's accounts of their school day reveal extensive substantive knowledge of the school world and the place of play within it (Corsaro, 1986).

How Children View Play: A Reflective Perspective

Researchers have tried to investigate what the term *play* means to children. When children say they are playing, what do they think they are doing? Why do some children list going to the bathroom and time-out as school events, whereas others do not; why do some children talk about positive internal states, whereas others talk about negative ones? Script theory provides a structure to describe how children remember events, but it does not tell us why children remember this rather than that; it does not describe the motivational forces that cause children to evaluate these events. Nor does it provide many clues to the ways in which the emotional tone of events affects children's remembrances (Fein, 1987).

Consider the following responses by 4-year-olds to the questions, "What happens when you go to school?"

Reb: You feel happy. (pause. "What else?") Ohhh, you play a lot. If you need to, you can go to the bathroom.
Art: I get in trouble. When I get in trouble when I play, I go in time out....
Al: ...sometimes I play with Dan when...when he's at school, and I play every single game he plays, and sometimes I don't and sometimes I do.
Ceci: Oh, we have to listen to the teacher's words and play....

Note that none of the four children quoted above use the term *play* in exactly the same way. To Reb, play involves autonomy and personal decision making ("If you need to..."); Ceci also sets up a strong contrast between play and what "we have to" do. To Art it can be an occasion to get into trouble; for Al, play is being with a special friend. When children report school happenings, the same terms may not report exactly the same events.

In an effort to explain why children view play activities as they do, one must look further into their accounts of the play environment. In one of our studies, we asked 26 4-year-old children, "What happens when you come to school?" The children came from 10 different community schools and child care centers. These results are shown separately for boys and girls in Table 14.1. Interestingly, only half the children offered a script that we defined as two or more distinction activities regardless of accuracy of ordering. Far more children, 65 percent, mentioned play as one of the happenings, whether or not there were any others.

Table 14.1 Children's Responses To: What Happens When You Come to School?

Response Type	Girls $N = 13$	Boys $N = 13$
Script-like sequences	6	7
Play	9	8
Routines	6	8
Other activities (e.g., drawing)	2	4
Behavioral states	6	6
Linguistic forms reference		
I, we	8	10
You, they	5	3
Timeless verbs	12	13

In our analysis of children's responses, we also paid special attention to the emotional/motivational implication of what the children shared. The most provocative data came from what we call "behavior states," a category meant to gather children's observations about their own and others' mental and emotional states. We included in this category comments on desired behavior and disciplinary actions. Of the 12 children whose comments were scored in this category, only two made positive comments: "I feel happy" and "I give my mom a hug." For 10 children, the report had a negative tone. Among the most poignant accounts was a child who reported, "When I get in trouble, I have to sit in the thinking chair." One child complained that the "Kids scream and shout." Another confessed, "Sometimes I forget"; and still another listed her faults; "I don't listen, I don't come when I'm sick. I got paint on my dress...." And, of course, these comments were unrelated to whether the children listed play as a school activity. In itself, play in the preschool may not mean a positive learning environment.

Where these childhood concerns come from is not clear. Some parents may be anxious about the child's school behavior and overly stress faults and comportment. In some cases, the teachers might be critical and demanding. It is even possible that were we to observe these children, they would seem to be happy and comfortable but still talk about unpleasant moments in the school day. Several interpretations of these data are possible. In one, the children are veridical reporters of the emotional climate of the classroom. In another, the children reflect parental pressures to be mature and they try very hard to comply; their reports reflect strenuous efforts to follow their parent's wishes. In still another, the children's reports should be discounted because they simply reflect salient recent events rather than atypical events.

In most schools and homes, children are scolded and criticized, but these events are relatively infrequent and brief, even though they are unpleasant and likely to be remembered. Research in this area is much too new to evaluate the merits of these alternatives. Nevertheless, it is clear that children's reports of the school day provide provocative information about the context within which play occurs.

In a study of 122 4-year-olds in high and low quality child care settings, children's responses to what they did at day care varied greatly, but their most common answer was "play" (Wiltz, 1997; Wiltz & Klein, 2001). Fifty 3- to 6-year-olds were asked, "Do you play at school?" (Wiltz & Klein, 1994). Eight of the nine 3-year-olds agreed that they did. The 4- and 5-year olds also acknowledged that they played at school, but they elaborated on their experiences during playtime or about what and how they played. First-graders, however, reported that they only played at recess. King (1983) also found that recess was the only sanctioned school activity that all school-age children agreed was play. The fact that recess is an activity normally done outside the classroom is one way that play is separated from the work of school.

Moreover, children as young as 3 have a mental picture of play as a part of their child care experience, but only 5- and 6-year-olds make references to games with rules as play (Reifel, 1988). Preschoolers also identify something as "just play" if they themselves decide on the activity and the ways in which to use materials, time, and space. "Learning play" in the nursery school exists only within adult defined frameworks (Romero, 1989).

Work and Play

The normal, day-to-day sequence of events in the classrooms of young children includes not only the things children do, but also the people with whom they interact. The social dimensions of school also provide rules for the classroom, and, in later life, rules for the workplace. Children's views of the distinction between work and play provide another way of understanding play's place in the world of childhood. In a series of studies, kindergarten children who responded to open-ended questions about experiences at school spontaneously used the categories of work and play to describe and define their daily classroom actions (King, 1979, 1990).

King (1979, 1990) studied four profoundly different kindergarten classrooms, two child-centered and two teacher-directed. Her study revealed that children describe most of their classroom experiences as work. Whereas the relationship between work and play in culture is not clear, anthropologists have begun to critically question the work/play dichotomy of Western societies. In a cross-cultural study of 50 Chinese and 50 U. S. kindergarteners, Zhang and Sigel (1994) found that American children focused on having fun at school while Chinese children were more concerned with learning. The more those children in the United States played, the more they wanted to play. Thirty-three percent of the U. S. youngsters longed to play more while only 8% of the Chinese children desired more playtime. Within the constraints of the Dutch kindergarten curriculum, free play was found to be an important educational tool for "stimulating general cognitive development, at least among four- to five-year-olds" (Leseman, Rollenberg, & Rispens, 2001, p. 382).

In several studies of how children view school, the categories of work and play emerged as significant factors (Fein, 1985; King, 1979; LeCompte, 1980; Reifel, 1988, Wiltz, 1997). Prior to entry into kindergarten children view school as a place where they do what other people want them to do (LeCompte, 1980). Kindergarteners associate learning, mandatory events, and teacher-controlled activities with work, while voluntary, self-chosen activities where the teacher is not involved are considered play (King, 1979). Kindergarten, first-, second- and third-grader children view work as extrinsically oriented and internally obligatory, while play is "fun" (Fein, 1985). Researchers report that preschool children are able to classify work and play activities (Fein, 1985; Hennessey & Berger, 1993; Romero, 1989, 1991). When asked, "Do you ever work at school?" 3-year-olds unanimously agree that they do not work at school, while 4- and 5-year-olds disagree, defining work as activities such as playing, coloring, drawing, and making pictures (Wiltz, 1993). When Romero (1991) asked 4-year-old children to choose whether they had played or worked in school the previous day and gave them a list to choose from, the children classified more classroom activities as work than as play.

Hennessey and Berger (1993) used an innovative procedure to study children's notions of work and play. Twenty-seven children listened to stories that contrasted two activities that needed to done, one "fun" and one "not-so-fun." They were then shown two paper dolls, asked to decide which of the dolls was working and which was playing, and to award a sticker to the doll they believed deserved a reward. Most preschoolers awarded stickers to the doll they believe to be playing, and when asked which of the dolls really liked what he or she was doing, they were also significantly more apt to choose the doll that was playing. Chi-square analysis revealed that "not-so-fun" activities were consistently labeled as work. While these children were able to distinguish between work and play tasks, they saw no reason to reward the doll that was working over the doll that was playing.

The criteria children use to differentiate work from play change as children mature (King, 1979; Wiltz & Klein, 1994). Younger children focus on the social context of their activities and label all required activities work and all voluntary activities play. Repeated documentation indicates that 4- and 5-year-old children describe most of their classroom experiences as work, defining the activity as play only if it is voluntary, if there is an absence of obligation, if it is child controlled, and if the teacher is not involved (Fein, 1985; King, 1979: LeCompte, 1980). School age children use the psychological context of activities as their primary criterion. Activities that are tedious or hard are called work while pleasurable activities are called play (King, 1982). Whereas kindergartners label as work activities that are not clearly play, as children move through the elementary grades, activities that are not clearly work are recategorized as play. First- and second-graders offer an interesting compromise by characterizing some activities as "in between" work and play (Wing, 1995).

In attempting to understand the relationships between work and play, one cannot assume that play is necessarily the opposite of work. There is a discontinuity, however, between preschool where play is emphasized, and public school kindergarten, where work is the major construct (Fernie, 1988). Children at younger and younger ages seem to be developing a sense of the differences between the two (Romero, 1991; Wiltz & Klein, 1994), perhaps because the academic curriculum is beginning earlier and earlier. Paley (2004) suggests that academics is not "the villain in our midst" (p. 46); instead it is the *time* we are subtracting from play.

Play in the Elementary School

Based on observations and interviews, King (1982, 1983, 1986) posits three distinct types of play in the elementary school classroom: instrumental play, real play, and illicit play. Instrumental play includes activities that are required, controlled, and evaluated by the teacher, such as watching a movie, writing poems, listening to a story, doing a science experiment, or drawing an mural. Elementary school children enjoy all these activities even though they are not voluntary and serve academic goals beyond the participants' pure enjoyment.

Real play includes voluntary and self-directed activities, such as during recess. Most all children say they like recess and many think it is the best part of school (King, 1983; Wiltz & Klein, 1994). Recess provides children with an opportunity to indulge in exuberant play, develop autonomy and self-expression, freely organize their time, choose their playmates, and plan, select, and carry out their own activities without adult intervention. Even in preschool, children value outdoor play as a favorite activity, and 82.5% perceive outdoor play as a social activity (Cullen, 1993).

The third type of play, illicit play, is defined as unauthorized, surreptitious interactions during classroom events (King, 1982, 1983). It includes actions like whispering, passing notes, making faces, and giggling. Children are aware that this type of play is against the rules. They are careful to conceal it and use it in nondisruptive ways. Illicit play not only provides children with a resistance to the dominant social structure, but it allows them to develop autonomy within the classroom organization (King, 1983). Preschool children also engage in illicit play. During dramatic play periods, children enforced play rules when the teachers were nearby and disregarded them when teachers were not around (Romero, 1989, 1991).

Illicit play also occurs in the kindergarten during snack time. Interviews with 21 kindergartners during snack time revealed that play activities included "playing with your drink," "pretending," "telling a joke," "fooling around," and "goofing." Although "goofing and "fooling around" were only recorded in 57 of 386 episodes, these types of illicit play led to verbal reprimands from the teacher if children were caught in the act. These behaviors were exclusively performed by boys, and, in fact, 40 of the illicit play episodes were performed by five of the most popular boys in the class (Romero, 1989, 1991).

In the research discussed thus far, investigators explored children's views of the distinction between work and play. If the children's views are lined up against Sutton-Smith's (1995) six rhetorics, how do the children come out? To the degree that the youngest children stress the obligatory nature of work and the voluntary nature of play, the children would seem to be operating within the *rhetoric of power*. Some children stress the social aspects of play: whom one plays with rather than who controls the activity. These children operate within the *rhetoric of identity*. The oldest children pay more attention to the pleasures of play in a way similar to the *rhetoric of frivolity*. No child mentioned that play was good for children or that they played because it improved them in some way. Sutton-Smith's *rhetoric of power* has not influenced children of these ages. There appear to be no efforts to systematically analyze these relationships, but from a sociocultural perspective, one would expect that as children get older, they would increasingly express the dominant rhetoric of their culture.

Children's Views of Pretend Play

From Piaget (1962) comes the idea that three different cognitive forms of play emerge during the first six years of life: "Practice games, symbolic games, and games with rules, while constructional games constitute the transition from all three to adapted behaviours" (p.110).

What do children think is happening when they engage in one of these forms? Researchers have asked this question for only one of these forms: pretense. There have been two ways of studying children's understanding of their own pretense, one drawn from theory of mind research, and the other from children's memories of their pretend play.

Theory of Mind Research

One virtue of theory of mind research is that children are being queried directly. One problem is that the experimental paradigms used are highly constraining and depend on the child's understanding of the question that the experimenter is presenting. At issue is whether or not children can envision a mind—their own or others—capable of thinking about events that are not happening, may never have happened, and even may never happen. In the simplest case, how do children understand what happens mentally when someone pretends that a banana is a telephone? Most theorists assume that pretense involves a mental representation, or perhaps, a "representation of a representation." When children talk into the tip of the banana, they are "thinking" of a telephone. Do children understand that pretense involves the mental representation of an object or event that is concurrently known not to be, in fact, present? Where children stand on this issue bears upon their "theory of mind."

Most of the research that deals with this issue presents children with a hypothetical situation (Lillard, 1993). In one task, 4- and 5-year-olds were shown a troll doll and told, "This is Luna, and she's from the land of the trolls. Luna doesn't know what a rabbit is—she's never seen a rabbit before—but she's hopping up and down like a rabbit. Rabbits hop like that." To ensure that the children heard the premises the interviewer asked, "Does she know what a rabbit is?" and "Is she hopping like a rabbit?" If the children answered correctly, the third question was, "Would you say she's pretending to be a rabbit, or she's not pretending to be a rabbit?" Follow-up questions were, "Why do you say that? And "If you . . . said, 'Hey Luna! What are you doing?' what would she say?"

It is not surprising that preschoolers do poorly on this task. In fact, the premises are so intricate, it is conceivable that many adults would lose the subtle contrast between "like a rabbit" and "pretending to be a rabbit." In other words, the task requires a high level of comprehension monitoring in order to catch the shift from an observer's perspective ("like a rabbit") to a participants' perspective ("pretending to be a rabbit"). If one adopts the observer perspective throughout, there is no contradiction, because presumably one can observe someone doing something that the observer then characterizes as pretense. For the younger children, therefore, this may be a question about an observer's mind and not a question about Luna's mind.

A second problem comes from the supposition that these preschoolers are so sophisticated that they can imagine a creature from another universe that truly knows nothing about a familiar animal. They must be able to imagine such a mind for the task to make sense. If preschoolers can imagine such a naïve mind—a mind that does not know what the children themselves know—they will have a far greater appreciation of other minds than the task itself assesses. An "uninformed mind" task is used as the setting for a "pretend mind" task.

Custer (1996) designed a simpler task that investigated the question: Do 3- and 4-year-olds understand that mental representations are involved in pretense, memory, and false belief? In this task, the children might view pictures of a child who was pretending that a fish was hooked at the end of a fishing line, when there was actually a boot at the end of the line. The children first viewed the picture of the hooked boot and then viewed alternative "thought" pictures placed over the protagonist's head. One thought picture depicted the real situation (catching a boot), and the other depicted the pretend situation (catching a fish). The latter choice was the correct one because it depicted how the situation would be depicted if the protagonist were pretending. On this task, 3-year-olds did extremely well, with 11 of the 18 children correct on all trials. Thus, young children might understand the representational nature of pretense.

Memory Research

A somewhat different approach is to ask the children to reminisce about their own pretend behavior. Ultimately, one would want to ask 3- and 4-year-olds to explain how they play, but in one study we asked 25 5- to 6-year-olds (N = 13 girls) and 25 7- to 8-year-olds (N = 12 girls) to tell us how they pretended when they were 4 and how they pretend now. Of course we cannot be sure that their accounts are accurate playbacks of what happened at 4 years of age; however, almost all children, regardless of age, recalled playing pretend games at age 4. No child described pretend episodes that occurred in nursery school even though most children had attended. In fact, most of the play took place at home, in the yard or bedroom, away from adult scrutiny. Some of their accounts were so vivid that they conveyed the excitement and pleasure of the activity. Here is an especially vivid account of the pretense that a 5-year-old claims to have played at the age of 4:

> I played cops and robbers. My uncle James, we used to play cops and robbers. I was the little one and I used to go to the store and act like I be stealing something, and he used to take my hands and put them behind my back and tie something to the back of my hand and I couldn't break out. Then he used to tie me against the tree with a rope and I couldn't break out and then he be hitting me with sticks. Not that hard. Then he said he's going to do that again and I said no and then I go do it again and he can't catch me. I be hiding under the car.

Keep in mind that this 5-year-old is offering a vivid account of a *pretend* scenario that happened sometime in the past. The child is in the present, representing events about a previously represented event. Further, the events are "act like." The narrator makes it clear that even being hit with sticks was "not hard." In pretense, children act, speak, dress up, and in as many other ways they can think of, present themselves as the pretend characters they seek to be. However, these actions, statements, and clothing are not meant to be replicas of the real thing. They are exaggerations, abbreviations, and highlighted caricatures of whatever the children know and feel about what they are representing. To an adult, some childhood memories are unsettling. Why would children pretend that cops tied up robbers and beat them? Keep in mind, however, that the memories reveal what children play on their own time and in their own spaces. Another 5-year-old described the following pretense:

Mar: My brother keep making me wash the dishes, set the table, and my other brother telling me to wash the floor and wash the stairs.
Interviewer: And what did you do?
Mar: I done it all.
Interviewer: In your game, what did you pretend to be?
Mar: Cinderella.

Some memories of pretense reveal personal and painful pasts. A second-grader reported, "I pretend like when I lived with my grandparents again that I used to pretend that they were the bad guys . . . and we used to play that my parents and our grandparents were the robbers and we were the cops and we used to tie them up and everything. The interviewer asked, "Why did you play your grandparents were robbers?" The child answered, Because [in real life] she was mean to our parents when they were our age, so we pretend like they're the bad guys."

Some children simply gave a popular label for the pretense theme (house, school), whereas others told the stories that they played. Some children described particular roles; one child described how she and her friend set out blankets to get a suntan: "We're pretending we are womens." Another said, "We pretend my sister is my sister and we go to school and that we have babies." Superheroes were overrepresented, but some children spontaneously described episodes of thematic fantasy play built around Jack the Giant Killer, Hansel and Gretel, Pinocchio, and other characters.

Table 14.2 Memories of Pretense: Percentage of Children Who Mention Roles and Scenes

	Roles		Scenes	
	At 4	Now	At 4	Now
5–6-year-olds				
Girls	62	36	60	45
Boys	73	82	64	27
7–8-year-olds				
Girls	75	63	58	58
Boys	50	60	42	25

Of 50 children, 44 admitted to pretending when they were 4, a figure that did not differ by age. A different picture, however, emerged in response to the question of whether they played pretense now. For the younger children, all but two said they did. But 8 of the 25 older children, denied playing pretend games, and of these, 6 were boys. One third-grader explained, "I'm too old to play like that … people say that pretend is baby stuff."

The proportion of children at each age level who mentioned roles and scenes is shown in Table 14.2. Five- and six-year old boys are big role-players, and most of their roles are superhero or fantasy figures. But when children talk about past self-directed pretense, they often describe scenes. This tendency shows a marked drop in accounts of their current play, which are fairly sophisticated accounts of mimed activity.

Some children describe object-substitution pretense, playing ball games such a football, kickball or basketball without a ball. One third-grader described playing pretend kickball with his brother. "My brother was throwing the ball and I act like I kick it and ran to all the fake bases." One child pretended that he had a television in his room, another described running around the house as if he were riding a bike, and another talked about pretending that dolls were people.

What do these data tell us about children's understanding of pretense? A major theme in reminiscences of early play was the storylike character of the children's accounts. Many described enactments or theatrical renditions of stories, some conventional and some quite unique. In a sense, these enactments "represented" things, actions, and relationships. No child referred explicitly to a pretending mind; no child explicitly described pretense as an inner mental experience. They liberally used the terms *like, as if,* and *pretend* interchangeably, as if these terms adequately captured the phenomenon. As Lillard (1993) believes, children even at these ages might not consider pretense as a matter of "mental representations."

Another interpretation is that this way of thinking about pretense might better characterize psychological theories than the theories of "folk" culture. One kindergarten child described playing with his dog: "We play going to the woods and we saw a fox. Casey grabbed it and pounced on it." Just think of the questions we would like to have asked, but did not. Does Casey know what a fox is? Did Casey think he was pouncing on a fox? Was he pretending? Such questions should be asked in the context of a reported scene. If Lillard is correct the child will answer yes to the last two questions. If Custer (1996) is correct, the child will answer no. We think that the child will find the questions puzzling because, after all, he said, "we play." Perhaps it is only psychologists who think about representational minds; others may simply represent the representations of representations of others and themselves, in effect, play without reflectivity.

The Debate Continues

Most children in Western culture think that play should be fun, active, spontaneous, free, unconstrained, self-initiated, and natural (Frost & Klein, 1979; Stevens, 1978); whereas at the same time, the seriousness, purposefulness, and intensity of play contribute to its role as a vehicle of learning during childhood. Play is a context or frame (Bateson, 1955), with an emphasis on process rather than goals. Play's major characteristics are active involvement, intrinsic motivation, attention to process rather than product, nonliterality, freedom from external rules, and self-reference rather than object-reference (Rubin, Fein, & Vandenberg, 1983).

Not everyone subscribes to the notion that play contributes to child development. For example, the value of play "in the life of the children . . . is perhaps something of little importance which he undertakes for the lack of something better to do" (Montessori, 1936/1956, p. 122). Some would argue that play provides children with opportunities to imitate and practice culturally appropriate adult roles (Schwartzman, 1978a). Others make a case that play involves social invention and therefore is a more original, creative process (Fein, 1987). Still others take the position that, during play, some children learn to create their own worlds within the adult-imposed physical and social world of school (Gracey, 1975). Kindergartners note that "Play is at a different time; it is easy. Play is fun" (LeCompte, 1980, p. 123). Experiences described in this way, as fun, spontaneous, and improvisational, suggest an apparent lack of externally imposed rules (Schwartzman, 1978b). Children seem to know what play is, and they know that "play is not working" (LeCompte, 1980, p. 123).

The seeming dichotomy between work and play helps educators develop curricula that organize schools into routine, controlled workplaces that serve society. Education, then, is a part of the socialization process that takes place in the school (Apple & King, 1978; Gracey, 1975; Tyler, 1986; Weinstein, 1983). The dichotomy continues. Play complements and supports the work ethic of the school. Play provides a relief from the drudgery of work, and after periods of relaxation or physical exercise, adults expect children to return to work refreshed. Play serves as a reward, a prize, a compensation for those who are obedient, who complete assigned tasks, and who follow the rules. Likewise, the loss of recreational privileges serves to punish disruptive, disobedient children or those who do not finish their work (King, 1983).

Spontaneous, flowing play is not what one sees children do in school. Play in school is play in a workplace, confined to particular times, relegated to specific areas, limited to certain materials, and controlled by teachers. This is not memorable play that children describe with relish and delight many years later. Children's descriptions of their school day and their play enrich researchers' understanding of their experiences in early schooling, at play, and the role of each in development. Although these reminiscences may also be unreliable, they provide another source of information about how children perceive school.

References

Apple, M. W., & King, N. R. (1978). What do schools teach? In G. Willis (Ed.). *Concepts and cases in curriculum criticism* (pp. 444–465). Berkeley, CA: McCutchan.

Bateson, G. (1955). A theory of play and fantasy. In N. S. Kline (Ed.), *Approaches to the study of human personality:Vol. 2. Psychiatric research reports* (pp. 39–51). Washington, DC: American Psychiatric Association.

Berlyne, D. (1960). *Conflict, arousal, and curiosity.* New York: McGraw-Hill.

Bredekamp, S., & Copple, C. (Eds.). (1997*). Developmentally appropriate practice in early childhood programs.* Washington, DC: National Association for the Education of Young Children.

Corsaro, W. A. (1986). Discourse processes within peer culture: From a constructivist to an interpretive approach to childhood socialization. In P. A. Adler & P. Adler (Eds.), *Sociological studies of child Development* (Vol. 1, pp. 81–101). Greenwich, CT: JAI Press.

Cullen, J. (1993). Preschool children's use and perceptions of outdoor play areas. *Early Child Development and Care, 89,* 45–56.

Custer, W. L. (1996). A comparison of young children's understanding of contradictory representations in pretense, memory, and belief. *Child Development, 67*(2), 678–688.

Elias, C. L., & Berk. L. E. (2002). Self-regulation in young children: Is there a role for sociodramatic play? *Early Childhood Research Quarterly, 17*(2), 216–238.

Fein, G. G. (1985). Learning in play: Surface of thinking and feeling. In J. L. Frost & S. Sunderlin (Eds.), *When Children Play* (pp. 45–53). Wheaton, MD: Association for Childhood Education International.

Fein, G. G. (1987). Pretend play, creativity, and consciousness. In D. Gorlitz & J. Wohlwill (Eds.), *Curiosity, imagination, and play* (pp. 281–304). Hillsdale, NJ: Lawrence Erlbaum.

Fernie, D., Kantor, R., Klein, E., Meyer, C., & Elgas, P. (1988). Becoming students and becoming ethnographers in a preschool. *Journal of Research in Childhood Education, 3,* 132–141.

Fivush, R. (1984). Learning about school: The development of kindergartners' school scripts. *Child Development, 55*(5), 1697–1709.

Fowell, N., & Lawton, J. (1992). An alternative view of appropriate practice in early childhood education. *Early Childhood Research Quarterly, 7,* 53–73.

Frost, J. L., & Klein, B. L. (1979). *Children's play and playgrounds.* Boston: Allyn & Bacon.

Garza, M., Briley, S., & Reifel, S. (1985). Children's views of play. In J. L. Frost & S. Sunderlin (Eds.), *When children play* (pp. 31–37). Wheaton, MD: Association for Childhood International.

Gracey, H. L. (1975). Learning the student role: Kindergarten as academic boot camp. In H. R. Stub (Ed.), *The sociology of education: A sourcebook* (3rd ed., pp. 82–95). Homewood, IL: Dorsey.

Hennessey, B. A., & Berger, A. R. (1993, March). *Children's conceptions of work and play: Exploring an alternative to the discounting principle.* Poster presented at the Society for Research in Child Development, New Orleans, LA.

King, N. R. (1979). Play: The kindergartner's perspective. *The Elementary School Journal, 80*(2), 81–87.

King, N. R. (1982). Children's play as a form of resistance in the classroom. *Journal of Education 164*(3), 320–329.

King, N. R. (1983). Play in the workplace. In M. W. Apple & L. Weis (Eds.), *Ideology and practice in schooling* (pp. 262–280). Philadelphia, PA: Temple University Press.

King, N. R. (1986). When educators study play in schools. *Journal of Curriculum and Supervision, 1*(3), 233–246.

King, N. R. (1990). Economics and control in everyday school life. In M. W. Apple (Ed.), *Ideology and curriculum* (pp. 43–60). Boston, MA: Routledge & Kegan Paul.

Klein, E. L. (2001). Children's perspective on their experiences in early education an child-care settings. In S. Golbeck (Ed.), *Psychological perspectives on early childhood education: reframing dilemmas in research and practice* (pp.131–149). Mahwah, NJ: Lawrence Erlbaum.

Klein, E. L., Kantor, R., & Fernie, D. E. (1988). What do young children know about school? *Young Children, 43*(5), 32–39.

LeCompte, M. D. (1980). The civilizing of children: How young children learn to become students. *Journal of Thought, 15*(3), 105–127.

Leseman, P. M., Rollenberg, L., & Rispens, J. (2001). Playing and working in kindergarten: Cognitive co-construction in two educational situations. *Early Childhood Research Quarterly, 16*(3), 363–384.

Light, P. (1987). Taking roles. In J. Bruner & H. Haste (Eds.), *Making sense: The child's constructions of the world* (pp. 41–61). London: Methuen.

Lillard, A. S. (1993). Young children's conceptualization of pretense: Action or mental representational state? *Child Development, 64,* 372–386.

Mandler, J. E. (1983). Structural invariants in development. In L. S. Liben (Ed.), *Piaget and the foundations of knowledge* (pp. 97–124). Hillsdale, NJ: Lawrence Erlbaum.

Montessori, M. (1956). *The child in the family.* New York: Avon. (Original work published 1936)

Nelson, K. (1978). How children represent knowledge of their world in and out of language: A preliminary report. In R. S. Siegler (Ed.), *Children's thinking: What develops?* (pp. 255–273). Hillsdale, NJ: Lawrence Erlbaum.

Nelson, K. (1993). Events, narrative, memory: What develops? In K. Nelson (Ed.), *Memory and affect in development. The Minnesota Symposia on Child Psychology* (Vol. 26, pp. 1–24). Hillsdale, NJ: Lawrence Erlbaum.

Nelson, K., & Gruendel, J. (1981). Generalized event representations: Basic building blocks of cognitive development. In M. E. Lamb & A. L. Brown (Eds.), *Advances in Developmental Psychology* (Vol. 1, pp. 131–158). Hillsdale, NJ: Lawrence Erlbaum.

Paley, V. G. (2004). *A child's work: The importance of fantasy play.* Chicago: University of Chicago Press.

Piaget, J. (1962). *Play, dreams and imitation in childhood.* New York: Norton.

Reifel, S. (1988). Children's thinking about their early education experiences. *Theory into Practice, 27*(1), 62–66.

Reifel, S., Briley, S., & Garza, M. (1986). Play at child care: Event knowledge at ages three to six. In K. Blanchard (Ed.), *The many faces of play* (Vol. 9, pp. 80–91). Association for the Anthropological Study of Play. Champaign, IL: Human Kinetics.

Romero, M. (1989). Work and play in the nursery school. *Educational Policy, 3*(4), 401–419.

Rubin, K., Fein, G., & Vandenburg, B. (1983). Play. In P. Mussen (Ed.), *Manual of child psychology* (Vol. 3, pp. 693–774). New York: Wiley.

Schank, R. C., & Abelson, R. P. (1977). *Scripts, plans, goals and understanding.* Hillsdale, NJ: Lawrence Erlbaum.

Schwartzman, H. B. (1978a). *Transformations: The anthropology of children's play.* New York: Plenum Press.

Schwartzman, H. B. (1978b). The dichotomy of work and play. In M. A. Salter (Ed.), *Play: Anthropological perspectives* (pp. 185–249). West Point, NY: Leisure Press.

Smith, P. K., & Vollstedt, R. (1985). On defining play: An empirical study of the relationship between play and various play criteria. *Child Development, 56,* 1042–1050.

Stevens, P. (1978). Play and work: A false dichotomy? In H. B. Schwartzman (Ed.), *Play and culture: 1978 Proceedings of the Association for Antrhopological Study of Play* (pp. 316–324). West Point, NY: Leisure Press.

Sutton-Smith, B. (1995). The persuasive rhetorics of play. In A. Pellegrini (Ed.), *The future of play theory: Chapters in honor of Brian Sutton-Smith* (pp. 275–295). Albany: State University of New York Press.

Tyler, L. (1986). Meaning and schooling. *Theory into Practice, 25*(1), 53–57.

Weinstein, R. S. (1983). Student perceptions of schooling. *Elementary School Journal, 83*(4), 287–312.

Wiltz, N. W. (1997). *Four year-olds' perceptions of their experiences in high and low quality child care.* Unpublished doctoral dissertation, University of Maryland at College Park.

Wiltz, N. W., & Klein, E. L. (1994, April). *What did you do at school today? Activities in child care from the child's point of view.* Paper presented at the Annual Meeting, American Educational Research Association, New Orleans, LA.

Wiltz, N. W., & Klein, E. L. (1995, March). *Young children's perceptions of activities in child care*. Paper presented at the Biennial Meeting, Society for Research in Child Development.

Wiltz, N. W., & Klein, E. L. (1996). Children's understanding of the structure of activities in child care settings. *Making a difference for children, families and communities: Partnerships among researchers, practitioners and policymakers*. Summary of Conference Proceedings, Head Start's Third National Research Conference, Washington, DC.

Wiltz, N. W., & Klein, E. K. (2001). "What do you do in child care?" Children's perceptions of high and low quality classrooms. *Early Childhood Research Quarterly, 16*(2), 209–236.

Wing, L. A. (1995). Play is not the work of the child: Young children's perceptions of work and play. *Early Childhood Research Quarterly, 10*(2), 223–247.

Zhang, X., & Sigel, I. (1994, April). *Two kindergarten programs and children's perceptions of school—A cross-cultural study*. Paper presented at the Annual Meeting of the American Educational Research Association, New Orleans, LA.

15

Play as a Context for Humor Development

DORIS BERGEN

Although play and humor are closely connected conceptually, in that both are enjoyable, reality bending, and internally motivated and controlled, there continues to be only a small body of research on the ways they are related and the means by which playful contexts might facilitate humor development. Some theorists who focus on explaining humor development have described possible connections between early play and humor and hypothesized that they arise from similar sources. A few researchers have described factors in play contexts, such as adult and peer interactions that affect humor expression and appreciation, and have given suggestions for fostering children's humor development. On the other hand, theorists and researchers who focus their work on play have primarily focused on how play is related to development of children's thinking and problem solving, social–moral interactions, emotional control, language, motor coordination, and the learning of literacy, math, science, and other academic content. A few play researchers have identified qualities of humor in the personality construct of "playfulness." However, the research literature still has only snatches of information about the play–humor connection, and much still remains to be learned about this important relationship. Thus, there is a need to explore systematically the development of children's sense of humor within the context where it might be mostly likely to flower—that of play.

Because humor researchers often conduct their studies in play-oriented environments such as preschools and playgrounds, they have provided some insights into the social and environmental factors that are present when children express humor in their play. Researchers who study play, however, usually have not examined the affective quality of the play events they study. Based on most research reports on play, one would conclude that play is a somber event. If researchers gave some systematic attention to children's humor that occurs in the play contexts that they observe, they could add an important dimension to knowledge of the play–humor connection.

Research on Humor Development

The study of children's humor has followed a pattern relatively similar to that of the study of play, in that there was an interest in this topic during the 1920s and 1930s, a dearth of studies for almost 50 years after that, and a resurgence of interest since the mid-1970s. The overall number of studies of children's humor has been small, however, in comparison to the many studies of adult humor and of child play.

The early studies of humor (as well as the early studies of play) were primarily naturalistic ones conducted in university laboratory nursery environments (e.g., Brackett, 1934; Ding & Jersild, 1932,

Gregg,1928; Jones,1926; Justin, 1932). Because the researchers used naturalistic observation of humor instances that occurred in the play-oriented environments of these nurseries, they typically described the play context when reporting their results. They explored questions such as what types of humor were observed during the children's play times, how often different manifestations of humor were observed at those times, and what factors in the setting influenced humorous expression. One researcher, for example, investigated the relationship of laughter to a number of other variables and found it was associated with active play situations, surprising events, and peer interactions (Justin, 1932). This researcher also found that girls' humor was more subdued than boys', with girls showing more smiling and boys more laughing, which she attributed to early socialization expectations. Another researcher found, however, that during play time, laughter was exhibited about equally by boys and girls (Brackett, 1934).

During the 1970s and 1980s, studies of children's humor focused primarily on its relationship to cognitive development, especially on children's perception of humorous incongruity, and on qualities of the social environment that might affect humor production or responsiveness, such as the effects of peer presence. Many of these studies were conducted in experimental settings, although some also used preschool or school classroom and playground environments. The study results indicate that typical types and stages of humor can be reliably observed; that the sequence of humor development shows relationships to that of other developmental domains; and that both physical and social contexts affect the types and amount of humor expressed and appreciated.

Types of Humor Children Exhibit

A number of researchers have recorded and categorized the types of humor exhibited by children in home and school settings (e.g., Aimard, 1992; Bergen, 1989, 1998, 2001, 2003a, 2003b; Bernstein, 1986; Frabrizi & Pollio, 1987; Klein, 1985; McGhee & Lloyd, 1982, Varga, 2001). Their research findings indicate that infants respond to humorous situations initiated by adults, and toddlers begin to initiate their own versions of humor. In fact, "the majority of toddler's humor is self-generated" (McGhee, 1979, p. 2). Even 2-year-olds begin to show iconoclastic humor, which seems to be deliberately designed to gain some control in social interactions (Aimard, 1992). There is some progression in types, with young children most enjoying the humor of unexpected actions and language, while children of 7or 8 enjoy hearing and telling conventional riddles and jokes that convey a range of meanings. By age 12, most children are able to comprehend and use jokes that convey complex meanings as long as the content is within their range of experience. Children enjoy types of humor that are also appreciated by adolescents and adults, although the sophistication of content and complexity of meaning are, of course, much greater at older ages. There is some evidence that gifted children's humor development occurs at a faster pace than that of typically developing children (Bergen, 2004, 2005). Table 15.1 gives examples of humor types found in the author's studies of children age 2 to 12 (Bergen, 1989, 2001, 2002; Bergen & Brown, 1994).

Researchers have used both experimental and observational methods to study particular types of humor (e.g., riddles or jokes), and have compared this development with cognitive or social factors. They have explored age level as well as gender differences.

Cognitive Aspects of Human Development

Not surprisingly, researchers interested in cognitive dimensions note that older and younger subjects often find different types of humor funny and, within the same type of humor (e.g., riddles), researchers see some differences in level of understanding. They have been particularly interested in the development of riddles and jokes as indicators of children's understanding of incongruity humor,

Table 15.1 Humor Types with Examples

Humor Category/Type	Examples
Expressed joy in mastery and movement play	Tickling games, tag or other chasing; trial-and-error actions/manipulative play
Clowning	Making faces, very exaggerated movements or voice, with child monitoring of "effect" on audience
Verbal/behavioral teasing, iconoclastic humor (mockery, resisting control)	Using provoking action words, such as calling sister "Baby, Baby," deliberately holding toy out of sibling's reach, or dropping food from high chair and faking surprise to adult
Discovering incongruous objects/actions/events	Observing and reacting with surprise and laughter to a picture of a cat wearing a dress
Performing incongruous actions/pretend/fantasy	Putting boxes on feet and acting as if they are the shoes of a clown
Sound Play	Chanting or singing nonsense words such as ringo, dingo, bingo
Reproduction/elaboration of story/song/poetry pattern	Repeating familiar song but changing words, such as "I hate you" instead of "I love you"
Word play with multiple meanings	Covering the dog with a blanket and saying, "Now he's hot dog"
Describing impossible events or incongruities	Telling a "tall tale" about growing as tall as the ceiling and jumping over the house
Riddling patterns or "preriddles"	Asking "Why does the turtle cross the road? And answering "To go to bed."
Conventional riddling	Asking "What do you call a yo-yo that only goes up? and answering "A yo-yo."
Joking or playing jokes	Putting "trick" candles (that won't go out) on a birthday cake
Self-disparagement/displacement	After making a mistake in a game, saying, "My brain must be on vacation"

which is defined as "conflict between what a person expects and what is actually experienced" (Pien & Rothbart, 1976, p. 966). In general, older children show more ability to express and understand the complexities of humor. One study found, for example, that 6-year-olds laugh at incongruity in jokes even if there is no resolution of the incongruity, but that older children enjoy jokes with resolvable incongruity more (Shultz & Horibe, 1974). This finding was disputed, however, when another study did not find an age difference in children's appreciation of incongruity resolution humor (Pien & Rothbart, 1976).

Before they master the riddle concept, children of 5 or 6 often tell and laugh at "preriddles," which have the form of riddles but not the incongruous point (Bernstein, 1986). One study suggests that children first comprehend conceptual–trick riddles (i.e., ones that violate knowledge of what the reality should be).

At later ages children understand those based on language ambiguity and absurd situations (Yalisove, 1978). Another researcher found, however, that most riddles told by children are of only moderate complexity and those with lexical ambiguity are in the majority (70%), with jokes becoming the more popular type of verbal humor by age 12 (Bowes, 1981). In middle childhood, language play is a common vehicle for humor; children engage in gibberish rhymes, puns based on sound similarities, "catching" others with trick repetitive patterns, tangle talk, verbal duels, and tongue twisters (Kirschenblatt-Gimblett, 1979; Opie & Opie, 1959). Children can often tell a good riddle or joke before being able to explain the conceptual incongruity or word play that makes the humor funny (Bergen, 1998).

Other cognitive researchers have studied the relationship of stages of logical thought to humor understanding. One researcher found that children who had recently mastered the concept of conservation were the ones who most appreciated humor that violated this concept (McGhee, 1976). Two other studies were less clear about the relationship of cognitive processes to humor. One found that both conservers and nonconservers understood cognitive incongruity in a humor stimulus based on the concept of qualitative identity (Klein, 1985). Another research team reported that they were not able to demonstrate a straightforward relationship between conservation stage and humor, although at some ages and for certain types of riddles, conservation abilities and humor did seem to be related, so they concluded that "the role of logical thinking in the development of children's riddle enjoyment and comprehension was not clearly demonstrated" (Whitt & Prentice, 1977, p. 135).

Although age differences in cognitive level of humor were evident in typically developing children aged 5 to 6, 8 to 9, 11 to 12 (Bergen, 1998), there were no differences in groups of gifted children age 8 to 9, 10 to 12 on comprehension of incongruity humor and ability to provide appropriate word play answers to riddle stems (Bergen, 2005). Gifted children are also more able to understand both verbal and visual (cartoon) humor than are typically developing children (Klavir & Gorodetsky, 2001). There remains a need for more study of the precise connections between humor and cognitive processes.

Social Aspects of Humor

Researchers interested in social aspects of humor have conducted experimental studies of effects of same- and cross-gender peers on humor expression, and found that elementary school-age children find humor funnier and laugh more when a peer is present (Chapman, 1975; Chapman & Chapman, 1974; Chapman & Wright, 1976). Other studies found girls were more likely to be influenced by the social setting (e.g., Chapman, 1973), and preschool boys were more likely to laugh at aggressive humor than were girls (King & King, 1973). Preschoolers' laughter at humor was also affected by the actions of models (laughing and nonlaughing) (Brown, Wheeler, & Cash, 1980).

Other indicators that the social situation facilitates humor come from naturalistic observations in early childhood and elementary classrooms. A study of toddler and preschool children's humor found that the presence of peers initiated more boisterous humor (Bergen, 2002). Other observational studies with preschoolers indicated that 95% of humor occurred in the presence of peers or adults (Bainum, Lounsbury, & Pollio, 1984) and that the size and gender composition of groups affected the expression of group "glee" Sherman, 1977). The use of hyperbole (tall tales) in children's language humor was also evident in one study of preschoolers (Varga, 2001). In elementary settings, boys have been observed as expressing more humor, while girls tended to be the responders to boys' humor (Canzler, 1980; Masten, 1986). A "good" sense of humor may also be a facilitator of social acceptance; 4th-grade children who rated their peers high on sense of humor, for example, also rated those peers as less socially distant (Sherman, 1988). One age difference found in an observational study conducted in 3rd-, 7th-, and 11th-grade classrooms found that children were more likely to show disruptive humor at middle school age (Fabrizi & Pollio, 1987).

Even though there are some typical cognitive stage based responses to humor, there are also indicators of individual differences in humor expression and appreciation levels among subjects of the same age, and these differences moderate the effects of social factors. One set of studies, for example, found differences in humor responsiveness both for social conditions and for individual conceptual tempo, with reflexive children showing more understanding than impulsive children, but impulsive children showing more intense appreciation (Brodzinsky & Rightmyer, 1980; Brodzinsky, Tew, & Palkovitz, 1979). Another study indicated that the communicative competence of the individuals was a major factor in amount of humor expression (Carson, Skarpness, Schultz, & McGhee, 1986). Thus, depending on cognitive and motivational characteristics, children of similar age may respond differently to varied themes of humor (Pinderhughes & Zigler, 1985).

Although many questions remain to be answered, overall the results of research on humor development suggest that there are three types of competence that may be related to its development: intellectual ability, social relations with peers, and mastery motivation (Masten, 1986; see Honig, 1988, for further review of humor development research).

Research on Play–Humor Connections

Since the mid-1980s, there have been only a few researchers specifically intent on investigating the connections that might be found between humor and play. Some of them have studied the personality construct of playfulness, examining the extent that qualities of humor (e.g., manifest joy, sense of humor) relate to overall playfulness qualities (e.g., Barnett & Kleiber, 1982; Barnett & Fiscella, 1985; Lieberman, 1977; Steele, 1981). These researchers have found that the presence of humor qualities is highly related to children's overall "playfulness" rating. There are also some gender differences, with adults rating boys as having more playful components (exuberance, teasing, clowning) than girls (Barnett & Fiscella, 1985).

A number of the researchers whose primary interest has been in social facilitation of humor but who conducted their studies in preschool school and school settings (discussed earlier) also noted how characteristics of the setting related to play, such as presence of peers and adults as play facilitators and play group size factors (e.g., Bainum et al., 1984; Groch, 1974; Sherman, 1975). In general, however, present research provides only glimpses of how various play-related factors may affect humor development. Ratings of preschool children who were high in creativity (based partly on their pretend play activity) did not predict their expression of humor in middle school, but ratings of creativity after the age of 6 years did predict their later humor initiation levels (McGhee, 1979). Play requiring gross motor skills, in comparison to fine motor play, was also related to later sense of humor. Both boys and girls who showed more verbal and dominating behaviors at younger ages appeared to have a greater sense of humor at later ages. They apparently learned as they grew older that they could gain peer attention and approval "within the playful framework of humour" (McGhee, 1979, p. 233). Although this early longitudinal study showed mother distance related to girl's later humor (McGhee, 1979), two cross-sectional studies of children's sense of humor have suggested that the presence of interactive, playful adult models may encourage humor expression and appreciation in preschool- and elementary-age levels (Bergen, 1989; Bergen & Brown, 1994).

The existing body of humor research gives information on a number of aspects of the play–humor connection, but it remains surprising that so few studies of play include information about humor observed within the play contexts. Humor is rarely one of the behaviors coded in play-based observations or experiments. So little is humor mentioned in the play literature, in fact, that a thorough reader of this literature might conclude that humor is rarely evident during play! This is particularly strange because there is a strong theoretical link between humor and play, as well as evidence that both teachers and parents are aware that much child humor is exhibited during play events with peers and with play-oriented adults (Bergen, 1998, 2001).

Play Connections to Theories of Humor Development

Theorists have explained humor development and its connections to play in a number of ways. While some of them have addressed the connection only incidentally, others have tried to explain how play and humor development are directly connected.

The Perspective of Psychoanalytic Theory

One theoretical explanation of the role of play in the course of humor development has come from psychoanalytic theory (Freud, 1905/1960). Although this theory emphasizes adult use of jokes to express unconscious emotions and relieve tension, the theory also connects early emotional development to humor, particularly in regard to children's emerging ability to "joke." The theorist states, "Before there is such a thing as a joke, there is something we may describe as 'play' or as 'a jest'" (p. 156). In this view, there are two types of humor, verbal and conceptual, with verbal humor beginning earlier. In the first stage, called "play," young children of about age 2 begin "learning to make use of words and to put thought together…to practice their capacities" (p. 157). Their pleasure comes from repeating similar sounds, putting together strings of words, and performing repetitive acts with objects; that is, it is based on "the child's peculiar pleasure in constant repetition" (p. 281). Because early humor behaviors do not have the intent of communicating meaning, they are not the same as later expressions of humor; thus, they are "play." This definition of play is similar to the concept of "practice play" (Piaget, 1962).

From the psychoanalytic perspective, at about age 4 children begin to use humor to convey meaning. This occurs both because children's critical faculties have developed and because they have learned that "reasonableness" rather than "absurdity" is preferred by the adults in their lives. Thus, "jesting" becomes the primary humor mode. In jesting, children begin to use some joking techniques that convey meaning, but they are not conveying unique or even "new" meaning. Although "all the technical methods of jokes are already employed" (Freud, 1905/1960, p. 158), the true joke, in which children of about age 7 begin to display "sense in nonsense," must have meaning that is freshly enhanced by the use of a joke. "If what a jest says possesses substance and value, it turns into a joke" (p. 161).

Another psychoanalytically oriented theorist extended the theory to describe how children's developmental stages are reflected in their humor (Wolfenstein, 1954). Their humor serves to counter the general distress of being a child in a world of adults and to master the anxieties triggered at various developmental age levels. This view explains, for example, why toddlers find "wrong name" play humorous when they are establishing their own self-identity, why preschoolers engage in gender-reversal humor when their gender identity is being confirmed, and why elementary children use "dumb" jokes to show their achievement of learning competence.

Older children's humor is also related to the developmental themes of their lives, in particular to issues around aggression and sexuality. Many early jokes are crude because children have not yet learned the subtleties of humor expression, and they often seem cruel because they are not couched in the language of appropriate conventions. With increasing age, however, children become adept at disguising hostile and sexual elements within a "joke facade" (Wolfenstein, 1954). During the age period from 7 to 11, children gain facility both in telling conventional riddles and jokes and in inventing their own spontaneous jokes. By age 12, children have learned most humor conventions, which enable them to understand the socially shared emotional meanings and humorous intent of other joke tellers. This understanding of shared social intent results in ability to express "laughter not only at distortions of reality, but also at the derision of the social world" (Bariaud, 1989, p. 42) and marks their transition to the adult stage of humor. This transition to adultlike joke telling takes some time, and during the transition children may tell jokelike riddles unsuccessfully because they leave out some point that is essential to the joke's meaning. They also may be able to tell the riddle or joke correctly but cannot explain the socially derisive or sexual meaning. These examples, told by 10-year-olds (Bergen & Brown, 1994, 1996; Bergen, 1998, p. 329), show the transitional stage:

Why did the elephant take toilet paper to the party?
  Because he was a party pooper.
(Reason why it is funny: Because it's a joke.)

Why is a pool table green?
  You would be green too if someone hit your balls around.
(Reason why it is funny: It just made me laugh.)

In Bergen's study (2005), riddles that denigrated particular groups were also evident.

How do you know a toothbrush came from Kentucky? Anywhere else it is called a teeth-brush!
  (Child's explanation: Kentuckian's only have one tooth so you say toothbrush there.)

Who are the most overweight superheroes? Fat Man and Blobbin
   (Child's explanation: "It makes names goofy. Instead of F put in B.")

This explanation of a hostile meaning conveyed effectively within a joke facade was told by a 12-year-old in one of these studies:

We think "insult" jokes are funny, like:

Your mother's so dumb she tried to alphabetize M and M's.
   Your mother's so dumb she tripped over the cordless phone. (And on and on…)
(Reason why it is funny: It's stupid humor; you use it when you are trying to insult someone in a funny way.)

Thus, from the psychoanalytic viewpoint, a "good" sense of humor can convey a range of emotions, including highly negative ones that could never be expressed directly. The ability to engage in joking that conveys complex, meaning-laden emotions is the end product of a process that begins with the exuberant, repetitive mastery play of young children. Perhaps these "unacceptable" meanings are allowed to be expressed in adult jokes because, at some level, they still connote the playful context from which they were initially generated.

The Perspectives of Sociological/ Anthropological, Communication, and Information Processing/Arousal Theory

Children thus learn the cues for "This is humor" in the same manner that they learn the cues for "This is play," and often these cues are the same. Both come from early adult-initiated interactions with children that signal "This is play/This is humor." Parents signal both play and humor by giving infants cues such as exaggerated facial expressions, high-pitched and emphasized voice quality, intense play gazes, and smiles and laughter, for example, in social games such as peekaboo or "gonna get you" (Stern, 1974; Sutton-Smith, 1979). Infants of about 4 months are already able to distinguish playful modes used by adults from those that signal seriousness, and they respond with smiles, laughter, excitement, and other positive affect (Pien & Rothbart, 1980). In fact, "playful interpretation of incongruous events depends on the development of an infant's play capacity" (p. 5).

However, if the cues signaling that the interaction is nonliteral are difficult for the child to understand, if the adult increases the child's arousal level too quickly or intensely, or if the adult is an unfamiliar person, children may see these cues as fear-producing rather than as humorous (Sroufe & Wunsch, 1972). Research based in arousal theory has shown that children adjust their arousal level to meet the play context demands (Shultz, 1972); thus, when they are able to be in control of their humor response levels, they exhibit the most enjoyment. That is, humor is most evident when the challenge level, is optimal for the child and there is a context that is both safe and playful.

From this theoretical perspective, children's ability to develop a good sense of humor is based on their early adult–child play experiences, because these experiences transmit the essential metacommunication "This is humor." The implication of this view is that the human capacity to become socially skilled users of humor depends on their incorporation of this message.

The Perspective of Cognitive Theory

Another source of understanding of humor development is derived from Jean Piaget's (1962) cognitive theory. Although this theorist recorded instances of his own young children initiating humor-inducing actions, he did not address the play–humor connection in detail. Other theorists and researchers, however, have drawn upon cognitive theory and information processing theory to explore how children's humor arises from their increasing ability to perceive cognitive incongruities.

Reacting to incongruity is not the same as reacting to novelty. It is a more complex cognitive process "because an incongruous stimulus is *mis*expected…while a novel stimulus is unexpected" (Pien & Rothbart, 1980, p. 3). Even young children have expectations of what *should* happen that conflict with what they experience. These authors make a strong case for adult–child social play during the first year of life because it is one way that children's initial understanding of incongruity can be facilitated. They argue that incongruity humor begins at about 4 months of age, before the development of symbolic play, and that it "involves only the recognition of incongruity and playful interpretation" (p. 3).

Other theorists, however, have focused on the importance of symbolic play for humor development (e.g., McGhee, 1979; Tower & Singer, 1980). Explanations for humor development from this perspective typically pinpoint humor as beginning when children are able to engage in pretend play. As children progress from sensorimotor to symbolic thinking, they become able to represent actions and thoughts with pretend play and to act "as if." This ability is seen as essential for humor development, as evidenced in these authors' view that the "most extensive and complex forms of humor development and humor appreciation may be related to the 'as if' and imaginative character of symbolic play" (Tower & Singer, 1980, p. 29). These authors speculate that "children who play at make-believe can later enjoy humour and express their joy" (p. 39).

Children's increasing cognitive ability to perceive incongruity is the basis of one Piagetian based theory of humor development (McGhee, p. 9). In this view, there are four stages of increasing sophistication in incongruity detection. In stage 1, beginning about age 2, children find humor in observing incongruous actions of objects, people, or animals. For example, "facemaking" or watching an animal character perform unusual physical actions on television is likely to make children laugh. They also perform such actions themselves by putting objects in unusual places (e.g., making a carrot their "nose"). Examples from one of the author's studies follow (Bergen, 1998, p.339):

C., age three: He put a doll's baseball cap on his head and laughed.
R., age two: She laughed when her slipper flew off her foot.

In stage 2, children of 2 to 4 typically find incongruous language and labeling of objects and events humorous, but there is variation in when this stage begins, depending on how well developed the child's language is. Adult–child games such as "Where's your …" suddenly become funny when the child points to the wrong place and laughs. The syntactic and semantic structures and rules of language are much used for humor; for example, two children may engage in turn-taking play, each saying a more preposterous sentence, such as, "I'll eat a cookie; I'll eat a pie, I'll eat a house, I'll eat an elephant!"

During the preschool years, children need relatively broad cues to interpret the incongruous humor of others while they "know" the incongruity embedded in the humor they devise. One author indicates that one of the best evidences that children really know information well is their ability to generate humor by giving "incorrect" laughing responses to questions on well-known information (Chukovsky, 1963). Adults are sometimes surprised, for example, when young children say things such as "The cow says meow" or "The cat says moo" and then laugh heartily, or older children make up wordplay or parodies to songs or stories that they know well. The adults may not be aware that this behavior is evidence of children's increasing ability to devise incongruities to express humor. Another example illustrates this (Bergen, 1992).

C, age three: When C. was finishing eating lunch, Mother said she was going to the store and he could come too. He said, "And C. can come too, and Dad can come too, and Fluffy can come too, and cheese can come too, and bread can come too… " (Many repetitions of pattern, with laughter).

Stage 3, humor derived from conceptual incongruity, becomes a major mode of humor by age 6.

Children often display this ability through the telling of riddles that have conceptual incongruities. The transitional stage, in which children use a riddling pattern without the conceptual meaning present, usually occurs at about age 4 to 6. These "preriddles" (at which young children laughing "appropriately" at nonmeaningful riddle patterns) show children's lack of understanding that conceptual incongruity is essential for this humor. One such example is the laughter of kindergarten children to the answer "To be a baby" when responding to a version of the riddle "Why did the chicken cross the road?" (Ramsey & Reid, 1988, p. 218). Another preriddle example is the following (Bergen & Brown, 1996):

Why did the frog cross the road? To get to the pond.
    (Reason why it is funny: I made it up and my mom laughs at it. Every time I do it my mom laughs.)

Even when children laugh correctly at a riddle that has conceptual incongruity, however, they may not really understand its meaning, as shown in the explanations given by various children for why this set of riddle variations is funny (Bergen & Brown, 1996; Bergen, 1998, p. 332):

What is black and white and red all over? A newspaper.
    (Reason why it is funny: I don't know.)

A suntanned zebra.
    (Reason why it is funny: Thinking about a zebra with a suntan makes me laugh.)

As children move toward formal reasoning and have expectations about what should happen logically, violations of these expectations appear humorous. Children who have multiple classification skills and ability to detect lexical ambiguity are adept users of conceptual incongruity and word play, as some of these examples show (Bergen & Brown, 1996):

Where are elephants found?
    You can't find them because they never get lost.
(Reason why it is funny: Elephants are big; they can always be seen.)

What can be served but cannot be eaten? A volleyball.
    (Reason why it is funny: It sounds like you're serving food to eat but it tricks you.)

A recent, more sophisticated example of cognitive incongruity was provided by a gifted 10 year-old (Bergen, 2005).

A skeleton walks into a bar and orders a drink and a mop
    (Child explanation: "It takes a while to get it—you have to think about it and visualize it.")

This last stage of cognitive incongruity humor, wordplay with multiple meanings, begins about age 7, and is the primary mode of elementary-age children's humor (McGhee, 1979). Authors of humorous children's books are well aware of children's ability to understand conceptual incongruity and multiple meanings and they use that knowledge to create the humorous situations in their books. Elementary-age children can usually explain why riddles or jokes are funny by using explanations that correctly point out the wordplay—but not always, as the following examples show (Bergen & Brown, 1996):

Why are Saturday and Sunday strong days?
    Because the rest are week days.
    (Reason why it is funny: I don't know, it just is.)

Where do sick boats go? To the dock.
(Reason why it is funny: The word's got two meanings.)

Elementary children's multiple meanings are often designed to be shocking, which gives support to the view that the "joke facade" permits such meanings to be expressed. These riddles provide examples (Bergen & Brown, 1996):

Why did the condom fly across the room? Because it got pissed off.
(Reason why it is funny: It's just weird.)

Children's humor also stays "up to date," as these recent word play riddles that incorporate present day celebrity names illustrate (Bergen, 2005).

What did Bugs Bunny say to Michael Jordan? What's up Jock?
(Child's explanation: "It's a play on words")

Who is the worst to play cards with? Derek Cheater (Jeeter)
(Child's explanation: "The rhymes make sense.")

One of the best ways for adults to learn what children really do understand is by seeing what types of humor are enjoyable to them. In particular, observing children's response to humor with conceptual incongruities and multiple meanings is an excellent way to determine their understanding of subtle information distinctions. This joke, for example, from a 12-year-old, shows a more sophisticated level of understanding (Bergen & Brown, 1996):

A guy is driving a truck full of penguins to the zoo when his truck breaks down. He asks another guy, "Will you take these penguins to the zoo?" and he gives him twenty dollars. When the truck is fixed the guy goes to the zoo and sees the other guy leaving with the penguins still in the car. That guy says, "I had money left so now I'm taking them to the movies." (Reason why it is funny: Because the guy who picked up the penguins thought that the first guy meant for him to take them to the zoo for pleasure, not to drop them off to stay.)

The cognitive-humor stage perspective shows the progress of children's humor from their enjoyment of incongruous actions and language within the play frames of their early childhood experience to the sophistication of the multiple meanings of wordplay. As McGhee stated, "Humor is the logical result of an extension of playful forms of behavior to the more abstract intellectual sphere of ideas" (1979, p. 103.

McGhee has continued to make his ideas more explicit, elaborating on some of his earlier stages (2002). For example, he outlines a number of substages during the the earliest years, including: Laughter without humor (birth to 6 months); laughter at the attachment figure (6 to 12 to 15 months); and treating an object as a different object (12 to 15 months to 3 to 5 years). By preschool age he states that children show the following: misnaming objects or actions; opposites—a special case of misnaming; playing with word sounds; nonsense/real-word combinations; distortion of features of objects, people or animals; and gender reversal. From ages 5 to 7, he identifies the pre-riddle stage and at ages 6 to 11, he states that the riddles and jokes stage and the use of the joke façade occur. McGhee also recommends that children's humor comprehension and expression should be enhanced by helping them learn ways to look at the world from a humorous perspective. One method he suggests is asking them try to think of the "punchlines" for riddles. In a study by this author (Bergen, 2005), gifted children were asked to do this. The riddles were given in order from ones with more familiar to less familiar terms and scored on the basis of how many hints the child needed to get the answer. Mean scores ranged from 2.9 for the first riddle to 1.4 for the last riddle. Only 1% of the children did not get the first one after the hints (What day of the week is best to make eggs? Friday) but 23% did not get the last one (What kind of furniture is used in math class? Multiplication table). Apparently the "tables" are not called that in many classrooms at the present time. The task of trying to figure out an answer to a riddle seemed to be a new one to many children, and thus, there appeared to be a learning curve for those children who got the idea. Correlations between riddle 2 and the other riddles were significant, showing that getting riddle 2 made it more likely that the child would get 3, 4, and 5. Solving riddle 4 was also significantly related to the riddle 3 score and 5 was related to 4.

Play and Humor as Separate Conceptual Entities

The theories discussed all suggest that play and humor seem to be closely connected behaviors originating from similar sources; however, the question remains as to how they become differentiated and varied in the nature of their connectedness. Young children's humor is closely connected not only to play, of course, but also to emotional growth, communicative and metacommunicative competence, and increasing ability to recognize incongruity. One hypothesis is that, although humor and play both originate at the time that children develop the capability for symbolic activity, they become differentiated as children's "as-if" abilities develop. Because both pretend play and humor require the ability to be free of reality and to act in an "as-if" mode, they are initially closely linked. That is, "Humor develops as the child's playfulness extends to recently mastered ideas and images, as well as overt play with objects" (McGhee, 1979, p. 61). Not all play is connected to humor, however, because it requires the child to imagine that the objects he or she is playing with "do something that he knows is nonsense, absurd, or impossible" (p. 61). "In humor, as in pretend play, there is a certain 'distancing' from the norms of reality, and a combination of being fooled and complicity required from the other" (Bariaud, 1989, p. 21). That is, the "as-if" stance is evidenced in the ability of children to understand that incongruities expressed in humorous action are not "incorrect" but of a "pretend" nature.

Although humor may share a similar origination point with pretend play, one theorist says pretense becomes differentiated when it splits into two strands, which she called "serious" make-believe and "joking" make-believe (Wolfenstein, 1954). The difference is that serious pretend intends to create a world that differs from the children's actual world primarily because it is governed by children (as the actual world is not). In joking pretend, on the other hand, children are not acting "as if" the pretend world is real, but rather, they deliberately continue to distort reality through "silliness" or "nonsense." Thus, in the "joking" pretend world, children emphasize incongruity, but in the "real" pretend world, they imagine that the world they have created makes sense. "Joking pretend play involves inventing fictitious deformations of the world, of others and of oneself. This fiction is not there for purposes of reverie, but to trigger laughter" (Bariaud, 1989, p. 23). This joking pretend is also the probable root of what adult humor researchers call "nonsense" humor (Ruch, 1993). Interestingly, the two major adult forms of humor that researchers have studied are "nonsense" and "incongruity" humor.

Observations of the humor of young children are rich with examples of joking pretend, which typically arise as children are playing together in a "real" pretend situation and something triggers a change to repetitive wordplay or sound play, "silly" and exaggerated actions, or deliberate distortions of meaning. One reason that humor may not be observed in many play situations in preschool or school may be that teachers encourage "serious" make-believe but discourage "joking" make-believe because they are concerned about its "out-of-bounds" nature (Bergen, 1992). An example from a study of humor within play settings provides these examples (Bergen, 2001):

> Lucy (4½ years old) in one 10 minute record engaged in clowning (hopping in a "silly" manner and looking to see the effect), teasing (poking and hugging another child who was engaged in

an activity), verbal/sound play (saying "baby, baby, baby" in an increasing loud manner), and "joking" make-believe (pretending to "comb" the hair of the "baby" with a wooden rod and pretending to feed her in an exaggerated manner). During most of this variety of activities, Lucy was giggling or laughing expansively. The teacher intervened once to ask Lucy not to annoy the other child.

Shane and his friends (all age 4½ to 5) were sitting at the table awaiting materials to be used in making an animal creation, but when they got the first material, a square of wax paper, one of the boys performed an incongruous act by beginning to "kiss" the paper. Then all the boys kissed their paper, laughing and looking around to get the teacher's reaction. Later the boys engaged in verbal pattern/sound play when yellow butter was provided for the activity. Patrick said, "Yellow is smello" and Shane replied, "Red is bread" and hilarious laughter ensued. Then Jamie engaged in a series of food-related humor, the last of which was making "Yum, yum" and chewing noises very loudly while he was eating his sandwich. Everyone at the table was laughing until the teacher said, "Jamie, don't play with your food!"

Playful Methods of Facilitating Children's Humor Development

Whether children initially learn that certain things they do are funny through solitary fantasy play (McGhee, 1979) or accidentally through social interactions with adults who "react" to their funny actions or words (Bariaud, 1989; Singer, 1973) is another question of interest. It is probable that internal cognitive processes and external interactions with the social world both contribute to humor development. The audience does seem to be essential, however, because "the feeling of funniness is more apparent when the child, using language, becomes able to exploit his personal incongruous invention to fool others and at the same time to lead them into an upsidedown world with their complicity" (Bariaud, 1989, p. 22).

For play and humor to develop optimally, an important message that adults must convey during play interactions with infants and young children is that the play frame is a safe environment. The cues that signal "This is play/This is humor" must clearly communicate that it is safe for children to exhibit a "what-if" attitude (i.e., behavior may be more unusual or risk-taking because there are no "real" consequences). The nature of adults' responses to children's humor attempts is also likely to have an influence on how much children engage in humorous behavior and the types of humor they express. The presence of "playfulness" in parents and teachers, for example, seems to be related to the children's expressions of humor (Bergen, 1989, 1998).

Ways that adults facilitate humor in children include performing as models of humor (e.g., telling funny stories or using cues that help children know they are joking); selecting materials or activities that encourage humor appreciation (e.g., tapes of silly songs, sound-play games); eliciting humor expression from children (e.g., asking them if they know any riddles); and responding to children's humor attempts (e.g., laughing at riddles even if they have been heard numerous times). Most importantly, because humor initially arises from playful "as-if" situations, adult provision of a safe climate in which humor expression and appreciation are valued and welcome is essential for children at all age levels (Bergen, 1992).

Thus, although the research evidence is limited, whether humor development will flourish as an expanded part of children's behavioral repertoire does seem to depend partly on the facilitating actions of adults in the environment who give the cues that help children know the distinctions between what is real and what is a humorous contradiction to reality. Further, the evidence that, as they grow older, boys and girls are similar in their understanding of humor but increasingly differ in humor expression (with boys expressing more) suggests that adults also give "permission" for socially and culturally appropriate humor expression.

While the theoretical basis for connecting play and humor is not new, it is relatively strong. In contrast, research evidence regarding the nature of the play contexts that foster humor development continues to be sparse. The limited research base that does exist indicates that play-based social interactions, language and sound play, pretend play, and adult and peer models of playfulness all contribute to humor development. Cognitive, emotional, and social developmental domains, especially as expressed in early play behavior, appear to be related to the stages of humor development and its modes of expression and appreciation. It is also likely that there are personality variables that make both "playfulness" and a "sense of humor" more prevalent in some children and adults (Bergen, 1998, 2005).

Both humor and play are pervasive parts of the human experience. They enhance the quality of life for adults as well as children, and they are present in rituals that ameliorate traumatic events. What is play without laughter, without joy? How can humor exist without playfulness? From personal experience, this author knows that the play–humor connection is very important to explore. Moreover, it is fun to explore!

Riddle: What is the difference between a researcher who studies play and one who studies humor?

Answer (choose one or make up your own): One finds the humor in play and one finds the play in humor.

One is full of play and the other is playful.

Nothing, both must be humored and played up to.

Riddle: How many researchers are needed to study the play–humor connection?

Answer (choose one or make up your own): One hundred—one to conduct the study and 99 to convince Congress to fund it.

One, as long as the subject is taken seriously.

Guess the answer to this riddle:

Who is Batman's favorite humorist?

 Hint 1: It's the name of a type of humor

 Hint 2: It's the name of a character in his show

 Hint 3: The answer is in the directions

References

Aimard, P. (1992). Genèse de l'humour. *Devenir, 4*(3), 27–40.

Bainum, C. K., Lounsbury, K. R., & Pollio, H. R. (1984). The development of laughing and smiling in nursery school children. *Child Development, 55,* 1946–1957.

Bariaud, F. (1989). Age differences in children's humor. *Journal of Children in Contemporary Society, 20*(1–2), 15–45.

Barnett, L. A., & Fiscella, J. (1985). A child by any other name…A comparison of the playfulness of gifted and nongifted children. *Gifted Child Quarterly, 29*(2), 61–66.

Barnett, M. A., & Kleiber, D. A. (1982). Playfulness and the early play environment. *Journal of Genetic Psychology, 144*(2), 153–164.

Bateson, G. (1956). The message "This is play." In B. Schaffner (Ed.), *Group processes: Transactions of the second conference* (pp. 145–241). New York: Josiah Macy, Jr. Foundation

Bergen, D. (1989). An educology of children's humour: Characteristics of young children's expression of humour in home settings as observed by parents. *International Journal o f Educology, 3*(2), 124–135.

Bergen, D. (1990, August). *Young children's humor at home and school: Using parents and teachers as participant observers.* Paper presented at the International Humor Conference, Sheffield, UK.

Bergen, D. (1992). Teaching strategies: Using humor to facilitate learning. *Childhood Education, 68*(4), 105–106.

Bergen, D. (1993, September). *Structures and strategies in humor expression: Changes in cognitive and social–emotional meaning from ages two to twelve.* Paper presented at the International Humor Conference, Luxembourg.

Bergen, D. (1998a). Development of the sense of humor. In W. Ruch (Ed.), *The sense of humor: Explorations of a personality characteristic* (pp. 329–358). Berlin: Mouton deGruyter.

Bergen, D. (2001). Finding the humor in play. In J. Rooparine (Ed.), *Play and culture studies, Vol. 4: Conceptual, social–cognitive, and contextual issues in the fields of play.* Stanford, CT: Ablex.

Bergen, D. (2002). The role of pretend play in children's cognitive development. *Early Childhood Research & Practice* [Online], 4(1). Available: http//ecrp.uiuc.edu/v4n2/bergen.html

Bergen, D. (2003a). Humor, play, and child development. In A.Klein (Ed.) *Humor in children's lives.* New York: Greenwood Press.

Bergen, D. (2003b). Theories of pretense, mental representation, and humor development: Answers and questions. In B. Spodek & O. Saracho (Eds.), *Contemporary perspectives in early childhood education.* Greenwich, CT: Information Age.

Bergen, D. (2005, June). *Gifted children's humor preferences, sense of humor, and comprehension of riddles.* Presentation at International Humor Conference, Youngstown, OH.

Bergen, D., & Brown, J. (1994, June). *Sense of humor of children at three age levels: 5–6, 8–9, and 11–12.* Paper presented at the International Humor Conference, Ithaca, NY.

Bergen, D., & Brown, J. (1996). Sense of humor development: A longitudinal study. Manuscript.

Bernstein, D. (1986). The development of humor: Implications for assessment and intervention. *Topics in Language Disorders, 6*(4), 65–71.

Bowes, J. (1981). Some cognitive and social correlates of children's fluency in riddletelling. *Current Psychological Research, 1,* 9–19.

Brackett, C. W (1934). Laughing and crying of preschool children. *Child Development Monographs,* 14.

Brodzinsky, D. M., & Rightmyer, J. (1980). Individual differences in children's humour development. In P. McGhee & A. Chapman (Eds.), *Children's humour* (pp. 181–212). Chichester, UK: Wiley.

Brodzinsky, D. M., Tew, J. D., & Palkovitz, R. (1979). Control of humorous affect in relation to children's conceptual tempo. *Developmental Psychology, 15*(3), 275–279.

Brown, G. E., Wheeler, K. J., & Cash, M. (1980). The effects of a laughing versus a nonlaughing model on humor responses in preschool children. *Journal of Experimental Child Psychology, 29,* 334–339.

Canzler, H. (1980, April). *Humor and the primary child* (ERIC Document Reproduction No. ED 191 583).

Carson, D. K., Skarpness, L. R., Schultz, N. W, & McGhee, P E. (1986). Temperament and communicative competence as predictors of young children's humor. *Merrill Palmer Quarterly, 32*(4), 415–426.

Chapman, A. J. (1973). Social facilitation of laughter in children. *Journal of Experimental Social Psychology, 9,* 528–541.

Chapman, A. ,J. (1975). Humorous laughter in children. *Journal of Personality and Social Psychology, 31*(1), 42–49.

Chapman, A. J., & Chapman, W A. (1974). Responsiveness to humor: Its dependency upon a companion's humorous smiling and laughter. *Journal of Psychology, 88,* 245–252.

Chapman, A. J., & Wright, D. S. (1976). So cial enhancement of laughter: An experimental analysis of some companion variables. *Journal of Experimental Child Psychology, 21,* 201–218.

Chukovsky, K. (1963). *From two to five.* Berkeley: University of California Press.

Ding, G. F., & Jersild, A. H. (1932). A study of the laughing and smiling of preschool children. *Journal of Genetic Psychology, 40 ,*452–472.

Fabrizi, M. S., & Pollio, H. R. (1987). A naturalistic study of humorous activity in a third, seventh, and eleventh grade classroom. *Merrill-Palmer Quarterly, 33*(1), 107–128.

Freud, S. (1960). *Jokes and their relation to the unconscious.* New York: Norton. (Original work published 1905)

Gregg, A. (1928). *An observational study of humor in three-year-olds.* Unpublished master's thesis, Columbia University, New York.

Groch, A. S. (1974). Joking and appreciation of humor in nursery school children. *Child Development, 45,* 1098–1102.

Honig, A. (1988). Humor development in children. *Young Children, 43*(4), 60–73.

Jones, M. C. (1926). The development of early behavior patterns in young children. *Pedagogical Seminary, 33,* 537–585.

Justin, E (1932). A genetic study of laughter-provoking stimuli. *Child Development, 3,* 114–136.

King, P. V., & King, J. F. (1973). A children's humor test. *Psychological Reports, 33,* 632.

Kirschenblatt-Gimblett, B. (1979). Speech play and verbal art. In B. Sutton-Smith (Ed.), *Play and learning* (pp. 219–238). New York: Gardner.

Klavir, R. & Gorodetsky, M. (2001). The processing of analogous problems in the verbal and visual-humorous (cartoons) modalities by gifted/average children. *Gifted Child Quarterly, 45*(3), 205–215.

Klein, A. J. (1985). Humor comprehension and humor appreciation of cognitively oriented humor: A study of kindergarten children. *Child Development, 15*(4), 223–235.

Lieberman, J. N. (1977). *Playfulness: Its relationship to imagination and creativity.* New York: Academic.

Masten, A. S. (1986). Humor and competence in school-aged children. *Child Development, 57,* 461–473.

McGhee, P. (1971). Cognitive development and children's comprehension of humor. *Child Development, 42,* 123–138.

McGhee, P. (1976). Sex differences in children's humor. *Journal of Communication, 26,* 176–189.

McGhee, P. (1979). *Humor: Its origin and development.* San Francisco: Freeman. McGhee, P. (1988). *Humor and children.* New York: Haworth.

McGhee, P. (2002). *Understanding and promoting the development of children's humor: A guide for parents and teachers.* Dubuque, IA: Kendall-Hunt.

McGhee, P., & Chapman, A. J. (Eds.). (1980). *Children's humour.* New York: Wiley.

McGhee, P., & Lloyd, S. (1982). Behavioral characteristics associated with the development of humor in young children. *Journal of Genetic Psychology, 41,* 2532–2559.

Opie, I., & Opie, P (1959). *The lore and language of schoolchildren.* Oxford: Oxford University Press.

Panksepp, J. (2000). The riddle of laughter: Neural and psychoevolutionary underpinnings of joy. *Current Directions in Psychological Science, 9*(6), 183–186.

Piaget, J. (1962). *Play, dreams and imitation in childhood.* New York: Norton.

Pien, D., & Rothbart, M. K. (1976). Incongruity and resolution in children's humor: A reexamination. *Child Development, 47*, 966–977.

Pien, D., & Rothbart, M. (1980). Incongruity humour, play, and self-regulation of arousal in young children. In P. McGhee & A. J. Chapman (Eds.), *Children's humour* (pp. 1–26). New York: Wiley.

Pinderhughes, E. E., & Zigler, E. (1985). Cognitive and motivational determinants of children's humor responses. *Journal of Research in Personality, 19*, 185–196.

Ramsey, P, & Reid, R. (1988). Play environments for preschoolers and kindergarteners. In D. Bergen (Ed.), *Play as a medium for learning and development* (pp. 213–239). Portsmouth, NH: Heinemann.

Ruch, W (1993). Exhilaration and humor. In M. Lewis & J. M. Haviland (Eds.), *The handbook of emotions* (pp. 605–676). New York: Guilford.

Sherman, L. S. (1975). An ecological study of glee in small groups of preschool children. *Child Development, 46*, 53–61.

Sherman, L. S. (1977). Ecological determinants of gleeful behaviours in two nursery school environments. In A. Chapman & H. Foot (Eds.), *It's a funny thing, humour* (pp. 357–360). New York: Pergamon.

Sherman, L. S. (1988). Humor and social distance in elementary school children. *Humor: International Journal of Humor Research, 1*, 389–404.

Shultz, T. R. (1972). The role of incongruity and resolution in children's appreciation of cartoon humor. *Journal of Experimental Child Psychology, 13*, 456–477.

Shultz, T. R. (1974). Development of the appreciation of riddles. *Child Development, 4* (5), 100–105.

Shultz, T. R., & Horibe, F. (1974). Development of the appreciation of verbal jokes. *Developmental Psychology, 10*, 13–20.

Singer, J. L. (Ed.) (1973). *The child's world of make-believe.* New York: Academic Press.

Sroufe, L. A., & Wunsch, J. P (1972). The development of laughter in the first year of life. *Child Development, 43*, 1326–1344.

Steele, C. (1981). Play variables as related to cognitive constructs in three- to six-year olds. *Journal of Research and Development in Education, 14*(3), 58–72.

Stern, D. N. (1974). Mother and infant at play: The dyadic interaction involving facial, vocal, and gaze behaviors. In M. Lewis & I. Rosenblum (Eds.), *The effect of the infant on its caregiver* (pp. 187–213). New York: Wiley.

Sutton-Smith, B. (1979). Epilogues: Play as performance. In B. Sutton-Smith (Ed.), *Play and learning* (pp. 295–322). New York: Gardner.

Tower, R. B., & Singer, J. L. (1980). Imagination, interest, and joy in early childhood: Some theoretical considerations and empirical findings. In P. McGhee & A. J. Chapman (Eds.), *Children's humour* (pp. 27–57). New York: John Wiley.

Varga, D. (2001). Hyperbole and humor in children's language play. *Journal of Research in Childhood Education, 14*(2),142–146.

Whitt, J. K., & Prentice, N. M. (1977). Cognitive processes in the development of children's enjoyment and comprehension of joking riddles. *Developmental Psychology, 13*(2), 129–136.

Wolfenstein, M. (1954). *Children's humor: A psychological analysis.* Glencoe, IL: Free Press.

Yalisove, D. (1978). The effects of riddle structure on children's comprehension of riddles. *Developmental Psychology, 14*, 173–180.

III
Educational Contexts for Play

Introduction

This section focuses on the varied educational contexts in which play and learning occur, and how play may facilitate learning. Within the relatively new paradigms of chaos and complexity theory, and theory of mind research, there is discussion of the place of play as a present-time human experience and its implications for future generativity and creativity. In addition, recent brain research and theory provides insights into how children's brains are engaged in the process of meaningful play. From the various visions that each chapter offers, the coherence and integration of play in human life stand out as significant.

Authors of chapters in this section consider how play interfaces with various educational contexts that promote children's literacy development, logico-mathematical knowledge, and discovery of scientific insights. The chapters suggest how learning can be supported through children's playful interactions within these various curriculum content areas, and support the view that play is an excellent learning medium. Perspectives on technological developments in contemporary life are also included because they revise some historical realities and expectancies concerning children's play. Technology, for example, offers the potential for either sharpening or dulling children's playful construction of knowledge. The chapters address a number of aspects of the technology and learning contexts and they give suggestions for optimum use of technology to enhance learning. The role of play in facilitating valid assessments of the abilities of children with special learning needs is another important topic addressed in this section because the use of play in assessment is an ongoing issue in the contemporary educational climate. Finally, a chapter considers how play can remain in the classroom in the present era of emphasis on standardized assessments. These assessment issues related to educational contexts for play are especially important for discussion in a period of pervasive standardized testing.

16
Play's Pathways to Meaning
A Dynamic Theory of Play

DORIS PRONIN FROMBERG

This chapter considers play from two perspectives. First, children at play provide evidence of how they construct meaning (learning).[1] Second, play is a condition for learning. Adults can see how children construct meaning, especially when children engage in sociodramatic play. Therefore, there is a particular focus on the process and practice of sociodramatic play.

After looking at how sociodramatic play functions, there is a discussion of how theory of mind studies have contributed to illuminating children's development. Then, the additional consideration of processes described in dynamical systems theory culminates in a proposed dynamic theory of play and meaning.

Sociodramatic Play

Sociodramatic play takes place when two or more human beings engage in pretense and negotiate with one another about how to conduct the pretense. Players communicate with words, sounds, posture, and gestures. However, when they negotiate about the pretense, they step outside the play framework to decide who will do what, such as become a parent, physician, teenager, storekeeper, or pilot. During the negotiation process, metacommunication, players plan before pretending. Then, the process of pretending typically begins seamlessly within the play framework as the players "become" the characters and build the play imagery together.

Throughout the play, there is an ongoing choreography that moves back and forth between planning and pretending. The play imagery that they build together is a form of collaborative oral playwriting during which the players serve as audience, voice, and oral coeditors for one another.

Metacommunication and Imagery

Metacommunication and imagery weave their way throughout the sociodramatic play episodes which do not necessarily follow a beginning-middle-end format but might, indeed, be episodic. Nevertheless, there are distinctive implicit rules underlying the explicit play that take on many different forms, depending on the past experiences that the players bring to the play. *Event knowledge* is the term scholars use to refer to the past experiences that players bring to their play. It is possible to see how players represent different event knowledge when considering an example of pretense. In effect, as one child "becomes" a role, other children might respond in ways that reflect a particular life experience, as follows:

Child 1: "Wah! My leg is broken."
Child 2: "Stop moving. I need to put on this bandage."
A Different Child 2: "I've told you not to jump off the roof. Bad, bad. Now I have to get some splints."
A Different Child 2: "Don't move. I'm calling 911."
A Different Child 2: "Poor baby. There, there."

Different children, or the same child at a different time, might respond in numerous ways to a similar theme. Each interaction includes a combination of each child's event knowledge (past experience) and the influence of the other player(s). Their interaction, regardless of the nature of the responses, demonstrates that the players have an implicit agreement that this collaborative, oral playwriting is relevant and meaningful to them.

Predictable Unpredictability During Sociodramatic Play

The predictability of the play script is that children engage in the imagery within the same theme. The unpredictability of the script is the particular prior experience (event knowledge) or personal imagination that each child may represent while playing the respective roles, as presented in the example above. Also, without predictability, any player may involve other play roles in their script.

The synergy that takes place as children move between irregular cycles of metacommunication (enplotting) and imagery (enacting) is a predictable *process* that underlies sociodramatic play. The unpredictable nature of the play, however, lies in the multiple surface forms (content imagery), the play *product* so to speak, through which children represent their experiences. The interactive plots of sociodramatic play represent their understandings and motives, and adults can assess what children understand and intend by observing the play. Beyond revealing their understandings, and their facility with language, children also reveal their problem solving skills, attitudes, and their social competence.

Script Theory: Building Meaning During Representations in Sociodramatic Play

Script theory[2] defines the implicit rules that underlie sociodramatic play. Script theory refers to children's capacity to enter one another's oral scripts on the basis of minimal clues or plans (Nelson et al., 1986; Schank & Abelson, 1977). Young children instantly become the roles that they play within the emerging scripts. They engage in different degrees of oral script development, depending on their developmental age and language skills. In this sense, sociodramatic play is a form of representation in which script theory is apparent; the rules of the play consist of children engaging in the fluctuating processes of metacommunication and building imagery together during the play.

The content of the imagery that children enact during their sociodramatic play reflects the event knowledge that each child brings. However, beyond what each child brings to the play, their collaboration during the play is an opportunity for them to learn from one another as each child embellishes the play process with their distinctive experiences, attainments, and language skills.

Script theory, the underlying play grammar system that emerges during sociodramatic play, is a nonlinear system. The capacity to communicate pretense through play signals appears to be a part of the brain "wiring" (or potential) of normal children. Indeed, research on brain development suggests that neural connections within the brain function in a nonlinear manner (Fromberg, 2002; Gallagher, 2005). The neural connections develop when children have opportunities to interact with one another. Within this interaction, it is apparent that there is a *transformational relationship* between the underlying rules of play (metacommunication) and the variety of surface forms of imagery that the players create with one another.

Theory of Mind[3]

When children play together, they also reveal their understanding of others' motives, thoughts, and concerns. Scholars refer to this decentering process as the development of a theory of mind. In effect, children become able to imagine that others have thoughts, motives, feelings, and desires that may coincide with or differ from their own. Theory of mind involves the *transformational relationship* between self-awareness (metacognition) and awareness of the thoughts, beliefs, and motives of others.

Just as children develop an implicit grammar of play, they develop an implicit self-aware understanding that they have thoughts, beliefs, intentions, and feelings, and infer that others also have these experiences. Scholars believe that children begin to develop a theory of mind between the ages of 2 and 4 years. (It is noteworthy that sociodramatic play also typically begins during the second year of life.) Theory of mind researchers study how children represent real and imaginary thought, and how they think about thinking, motives, beliefs, false beliefs, and deception (Astington, 1993; Astington & Pelletier, 1999; Bartsch & Wellman, 1995; Leslie, 1995). Their work points to the isomorphism between children's narrative structures in sociodramatic play scripts and youngsters' developing theory of mind (Garvey, 1993; Harris, 2000; Harris & Kavanaugh, 1993; Leslie, 1995).

During their play, children develop mental models, the imagery that they enact together. These mental models make it possible for them to behave as-if they were the roles that they become and have expectations that the other players will behave in a predictable relation to the players that they have become. Thus, there is a covenant between *as-if* and *if-then*; in effect, if I am this role then I can predict that you will behave within the scope of the play framework that we have negotiated. In effect, they represent implicit meaning in explicit forms.

A child's theory of mind is apparent in parallel situations. For example, when children lie to adults, it is apparent that they have made a prediction about the adult's expected, preferred reaction. When 4-year-olds choose to engage in unacceptable play behavior, they will evade observation or relabel the behavior for the adult in what they perceive to be acceptable terms. When toddlers or preschoolers playfully tease adults with a clearly "wrong" response, it is apparent that they have developed a working theory of mind (Wolfenstein, 1954). Young children, therefore, reveal their theory of mind as a system of relationships between underlying images and the many meaningful surface forms that represent these images.

Both script theory and theory of mind demonstrate the nonlinear nature of meaning. The transformational generative process of constructing meaning offers support for learning, the acquisition of meaning, as a nonlinear process. Dynamical systems theory, that includes chaos and complexity theory, is another contemporary theory that mirrors the transformational relationship between an implicit grammar that players can represent in a variety of explicit ways. Within complexity theory, the notion of phase transitions stands out as an essential model of how learning takes place.

Phase Transitions within Dynamical Systems Theory/Chaos and Complexity Theory[4]

Phase transition refers to the "bridge" between one state and another, the transition system that includes the time before insight and the crossing over to meaning. It is possible to envision the synapses within the brain as analogous connectors of meaning.

Phase transitions are apparent in everyday experiences. For example, as children carefully watch events take place, they try to capture the precise instant when a light switches on or when heated water begins to bubble and boil, to know how far they need to move a magnet before it will no longer attract a key, and identify the exact spot to stand on the see-saw in order to tip it to the other side

A phase transition, like the fulcrum on the see-saw, is that turning point when one state changes into another, such as moving from up to down; turning from on to off; shifting from calm to turbulent; and moving from in to out; changing from a liquid to a gas; transmuting from a milling group to a mob; defining a puzzle then finding its solution; being naïve and then knowledgeable; and so forth. Effective teachers try to create the learning conditions, including play, within which phase transitions can take place.

There is a dynamic phase transition in play between reality and pretense; metacommunication and representation; and enplotment and enactment. *Phase transitions are areas of opportunity for teacher or peer intervention; they are the moments during which meaningful, extended, and expanded development for children may take place.*

Phase transitions serve as "attractors" that draw children to a change of focus. For example, when children identify or change a play theme or direction, they appear to grant a "warrant" that signals an agreement to proceed together (Cook-Gumperz, cited in Van Hoorn, Nourot, Scales, & Alward, 2003, p.244). The boundary between two or more attractors in a dynamical system serves as a threshold of a kind that seems to govern so many ordinary processes, from the breaking of materials to the making of decisions (Gleick, 1987, p. 233).

The phase transition process helps children to bridge nonmeaning and meaning. Phase transitions also help children to become aware of other peoples' meanings and move toward building a theory of mind.

Learning takes place during phase transitions, the "tipping points" between one state of being and another, ignorance and knowledge, or self-involvement and caring. Teachers who respect the power of play in children's learning attempt to tip the oscillating balance between irrelevance and meaning, boredom and engagement. They help children negotiate freedom and independence, and responsibility and impulsivity, by sensitively scaffolding rather than controlling for its own sake. Dynamical systems theory, including chaos and complexity theory, along with script theory, confirms the generally predictable but specifically unpredictable nature of children's play and construction of meaning.

A Dynamic Theory of Play and Meaning

There is a confluence of script theory, theory of mind, and dynamical systems theory. These parallel theories have in common nonlinear relationships between underlying forms, rules, images, and attractors, and the variety of emergent surface forms. There is a transformational, generative relationship between the distinctive underlying forms that can be represented in a variety of surface forms. Therefore, the theories share predictable unpredictability, and depend upon children's experiences. The three theoretical perspectives focus on the dynamic, nonlinear nature of meaning. The commonality among these theories adds credibility to the practice of nonlinear early education.

Comparing these theories highlights the power of nonlinear processes and lets us build a nonlinear model of teaching practice on a nonlinear, dynamic theory of play and meaning. Matching teaching to learning processes from a nonlinear perspective can help children feel and be competent in an unpredictable world.

However, attempting to grasp the nonlinear processes that play and meaning share is like trying to catch water in your hands. Instead, we need to capture "snapshots" of the flow. The section that follows outlines some "snapshots" of nonlinear models that deal with relationships between underlying forms and their surface representations:

Underlying Forms	Surface Variety
A musical scale offers a limited number of notes	but there are many ways in which the notes can be related to one another in their sequence or through different rhythms.
An underlying alphabet	changes into different meanings as the letters are combined to create different words.
An underlying set of grammatical rules	change into different meanings as words proceed in different orders.
Children use an underlying set of rules during play	to represent a variety of emergent meanings.
An underlying set of images in the physical world, dynamic themes such as cyclical change or synergy,	take unpredictable forms within different physical or social environments.

In these examples, the deep forms are predictable, and the surface forms are unpredictable. *It is within the transformation (phase transition) between the deep and surface forms that meaning occurs.* When children engage in sociodramatic play, they demonstrate their capacity to use the underlying sociodramatic play structures (script theory) to represent their variety of experiences in both predictable and emergent ways. Their interactions during play demonstrate that children have developed an awareness of their own thinking and motives, and the thinking and motives of others, in effect, a theory of mind.

Taken together, research findings about the influence of play on learning and development along with nonlinear theories such as script theory; theory of mind; and chaos and complexity theory, provide a dynamic image of physical, social, and person meaning. Educators who support children's use of dynamic play can extend and enrich children's development of meaning. *Teachers of young children must therefore bridge the distance between adults' and children's knowledge in ways that children perceive as meaningful* (Dewey, 1933).

It is uniformity that does not serve education. The predictable in early learning is its predictable unpredictability. The dynamic theory of play and meaning celebrates ambiguity, predictable unpredictability, and the place of meaning at the core of education. Within the dynamic processes of play and meaning, children demonstrate their power as agents in their own learning. Children's collaborative oral playwriting within sociodramatic play, noted earlier, is a notable form of ongoing, self-directed literacy development.

The dynamic theory of play and meaning coincides with neuroscientists' current findings about the dynamic, holistic ways in which the human brain functions (Calvin, 1996; Jensen, 1998; Shore, 1997; Sylwester, 1995). Neuroscientists have found that the human brain functions as a network of connections, particularly during problem solving and learning. They have accepted that the brain solves problems holistically, as do young children at play. Rich experiences in the form of variety, feedback, and secure and supportive early encounters optimize brain functions.

As children interact with the physical world, other children, and adults, they experience phase transitions that lead to fresh perceptions. Children perceive new meaning as first-time figures emerge from a background of familiar experiences. Their brains process these fluid experiences in fractal,[5] holistic ways. Children use and expand their event knowledge as they develop oral scripts with others. The feedback that children receive during interactions with the physical world and others during play, and during their other daily life experiences, helps them to develop a theory of mind. *Play serves as a lymphatic system for the development of meaning through the holistic processes of the brain.*

We have an opportunity to rethink and transform the nature of teacher and child relationships and communication when we study the processes by which events shift, changes take place, and children make new connections. *The teacher within this dynamic theoretical perspective can become a creator of experiences that generate transitions from unfamiliar to familiar meaning.*

Concluding Statement

Meaning is the significant center of children's sociodramatic play as well as their education. Children feel powerful when they play; personal power grows out of the dynamic political and cultural context in which young children develop.

Young children's sociodramatic play, in which their meanings predominate and in which they employ their personal power, is a significant integrative force in children's development. Their play influences their development of social competence, language, cognition, and some degree of creativity (Fromberg, 1999).

The dynamics of script theory and narrative structures; dynamical systems theory, including chaos and complexity theory; and theory of mind, share predictable unpredictability. The varied surface forms of children's play demonstrate an underlying grammar of play. These theoretical perspectives parallel recent research concerning how the human brain develops.

An integrated theory of play as a dynamical, nonlinear phenomenon is past due. It is time to recognize the importance of phase transitions as the learning points in script theory, a major process that pervades human functioning, learning, and growth. When we focus on the processes by which events shift, changes take place, and children make new connections, we have an opportunity to rethink and transform the nature of teacher and child relationships and communication. *The teacher within this dynamic theoretical perspective becomes a creator of phase transition experiences.*

This chapter has invited you to consider that a dynamic theory of play and meaning can influence a holistic, nonlinear approach to early childhood education. Our society's unpredictable future necessitates the retention—even cultivation—of children's nonlinear strengths as players and as creators of meaning. When educators match children's learning strengths by focusing nonlinear early education on meaningful themes, children can also learn linear skills in functional, intuitive, and intrinsically motivated ways

These theories support the contention that play is a living model of how children develop meaning and solve problems. Therefore, the challenge for teachers is to schedule and provide for play. The challenge for teachers also is to plan for teaching that supports learning that is nonlinear. Teachers have the potential to actively engage children in their own learning when teachers plan with dynamic themes in mind, from a holistic standpoint, and with a focus on children's construction and acquisition of meanings through direct experiences. Such a match between how children learn and how teachers teach helps children to learn in ways that are intellectually satisfying, personally supportive, engaging, and worthwhile.

Notes

1. Like music, [meaning] is a direct experience. …When you understand something, you understand its meaning. Meaning is the center of human experience and the shared center of learning and play. It is an internal, personal experience. More than just concepts or ideas alone, meaning also consists of emotions and motives. Some meaning involves more powerful or weaker emotion; human beings grasp specific meanings with different degrees of perceptual strength or motivation. Motivation is both an emotional and cognitive reaction to meaning, and it influences how much attention we pay to particular experiences. Therefore, meaning is not "delivered "(in linear terms). Rather, it develops in nonlinear, unpredictable ways when children engage in focused interactions with others and the physical world…. Nonlinear learning consists of diverse connections that are evident in children's sociodramatic play (when children act out imaginary events with other children or an adult). (Fromberg, 2002, p. 5)

    Meaning also develops through imagery and the use of analogy and metaphor. We use metaphor and analogy when we recognize part of a familiar image in a new encounter, thereby facilitating meaningful recognition and connection. For example, hugging a doll or pillow is analogous to hugging a person, an applied metaphor. In some ways, the analogue (doll or pillow) is similar to the person (the referent), and in some ways it is different…."Metaphor involves the transformation of one thing seen as another" (Belth, 1993, p.48). Imagery and metaphor form a basis for meaningful thinking. The imagery in metaphor is dynamic and flexible (Prawat, 1999) as well as "unpredictable" (Belth, 1993, p. 48). (Fromberg, 2002, p. 6)

The pretense within sociodramatic play embodies analogy and metaphor when children simulate roles and substitute props for real objects.
2. Script theory comes mainly from the work of psychologists (Nelson et al., 1986) who have collaborated with linguists and specialists in artificial intelligence (Schank & Abelson, 1977).
3. Studies of theory of mind come from the fields of child development and cognitive science (Astington, 1993; Astington & Pelletier, 1999); Bartsch & Wellman, 1995; Harris & Kavanaugh, 1993; Rosengren, Johnson & Harris, 2000).
4. Dynamical systems theory, including chaos and complexity theory, involves the *relationship* between predictably unpredictable phenomena in physical, social, and aesthetic experiences. This theory grew from work in the physical sciences (Gleick, 1987; Holte, 1990) and expanded to encompass the social sciences (Robertson & Combs, 1995; Waldrop, 1992), including the nature of play (Fromberg, 1999; VanderVen, 1998). Educators have theorized about nonlinear relationships in models of learning (Belth, 1970; Fromberg, 1977, 1995, 2002; McLuhan, 1963).
5. Fractals describe self-similar patterns that appear on smaller to larger size scales as do networks of neurons in the brain.

Acknowledgment

Parts of this chapter have been adapted from D. P. Fromberg, (2002). *Play and meaning in early childhood education.* Boston: Allyn & Bacon, pp. 33–53.

References

Astington, J. S. (1993). *The child's discovery of mind.* Cambridge, MA: Harvard University Press.

Astington, J. E., & Pelletier, J. (1999). *Theory of mind and representational understanding in early childhood education.* Presentation at annual meeting of the American Educational Research Association, Montreal, Canada.

Bartsch, K., & Wellman, H. M. (1995). *Children talk about the mind.* New York: Oxford University Press.

Belth, M. (1993). *Metaphor and thinking* (F. T. Johansen, Ed.). Lanham, MD: University Press of America.

Calvin, W. H. (1996). *How brains think: Evolving intelligence, then and now.* New York: Basic Books.

Dewey, J. (1933). *How we think.* Boston: D.C. Heath.

Fromberg, D. P. (1977). *Early childhood education: A perceptual models curriculum.* New York: Wiley.

Fromberg, D. P. (1995). *The full-day kindergarten: Planning and practicing a dynamic themes curriculum* (2nd ed.). New York: Teachers College Press.

Fromberg, D. P. (1999). A review of research on play. In C. Seefeldt (Ed.), *The early childhood curriculum: Current findings in theory and practice,* 3rd ed. (pp. 27–53). New York: Teachers College Press.

Fromberg, D. P. (2002). *Play and meaning in early childhood education.* Boston: Allyn & Bacon.

Gallagher, K. C. (2005). Brain research and early childhood development. *Young Children, 60*(4), 12–20.

Garvey, C. (1993). Diversity in the conversational repertoire: the case of conflicts and social pretending. *Cognition and Instruction, 11*(3&4), 251–264.

Gleick, J. (1987). *Chaos.* New York: Viking.

Harris, P. L. (2000). On not falling down to earth: Children's metaphysical questions. In K. S. Rosengren, C. N. Johnson, & P. L. Harris (Eds.), *Imagining the impossible: Magical, scientific, and religious thinking in children* (pp. 157–178). Cambridge, UK: Cambridge University Press.

Harris, P. L., & Kavanaugh, R. D. (1993). Young children's understanding of pretense. *Monographs of the Society for Research in Child Development No. 231, 58*(1).

Holte, J. (Ed.). (1990). *Chaos: The new science.* St. Peter, MN: Gustavus Adolphus College.

Jensen, E. (1998). *Teaching with the brain in mind.* Alexandria, VA: Association for Supervision and Curriculum Development.

King, N. (1992). The impact of context on the play of young children. In S. Kessler & B. Swadener (Eds.), *Reconceptualizing the early childhood curriculum* (pp. 42–61). New York: Teachers College Press.

Leslie, A. M. (1995). Pretending and believing: Issues in the theory of ToMM. In J. Mehler & S. Franck (Eds.), *COGNITION on cognition* (pp. 193–220). Cambridge, MA: MIT Press.

McLuhan, M. (1963). We need a new picture of knowledge. In A. Frazier (Ed.), *New insights and the curriculum* (pp. 57-70). Washington, DC: Association for Supervision and Curriculum Development.

Nelson, K., (1985). *Making sense: The acquisition of shared meaning.* Orlando, FL: Academic Press.

Perner, J. (1991). *Understanding and the representational world.* Cambridge, MA: MIT Press.

Prawat, R. S. (1999). Dewey, Peirce, and the learning process. *American Educational Research Journal, 36*(1), 47–76.

Robertson, R., & Combs, A. (Eds.). (1995). *Chaos theory in psychology and the life sciences.* Mahwah, NJ: Lawrence Erlbaum.

Rosengren, K. S., Johnson, C. N., & Harris, P. L. (Eds.). *Imagining the impossible: Magical, scientific, and religious thinking in children.* Cambridge, UK: Cambridge University Press.

Schank, R., & Abelson, R. (1977). *Scripts, plans, goals and understanding: An inquiry into human knowledge structures.* Hinsdale, NJ: Lawrence Erlbaum.

Shore, R. (1997). *Rethinking the brain: New insights into early development.* New York: Families and Work Institute.

Sylwester, R. (1995). *A celebration of neurons: An educator's guide to the human brain.* Alexandria, VA: Association for Supervision and Curriculum Development.

Van Hoorn, J., Nourot, P. M., Scales, B., & Alward, K. R. (2003). *Play at the center of the curriculum* (3rd. ed.). Upper Saddle River, NJ: Prentice–Hall/Merrill.

VanderVen, K. (1998). Play, Proteus, and paradox: Education for a chaotic and supersymmetric world. In D. P. Fromberg & D. Bergen (Eds.), *Play from birth to twelve and beyond: Contexts, perspectives, and meanings* (pp. 119–132). New York: Garland.

Waldrop, M. M. (1992). *Complexity: The emerging science at the edge of order and chaos.* New York: Simon & Schuster.

Wolfenstein, M. (1954). *Children's humor: A psychological analysis.* Glencoe, IL: Free Press.

17

Adult Influences on Play

The Vygotskian Approach

ELENA BODROVA AND DEBORAH J. LEONG

Contexts for Play

In the cultural–historical approach developed by Vygotsky and his colleagues and students, "play" as currently understood is a relatively late phenomenon in human history (Elkonin, 1978). In primitive societies, when children functioned as equals with adults in such tasks as helping to gather food or tend animals, modern play did not exist. Play at that time was primarily pragmatic in that it sharpened needed skills and could not be differentiated from the actual adult activities. Children used carpentry tools to make objects, for example, and hunted with miniature bows and arrows.

Modern play is nonpragmatic in that it does not prepare the child for specific skills or activities, but prepares the child's mind for the learning tasks of today as well as future tasks that humans cannot yet imagine (Elkonin, 2005). Modern play emerged as society evolved, as professional skills required more and more training, and as the information to be learned became more complicated and demanding. Not only does the modern training process take more time than in the past, but it is also based on more advanced psychological abilities. Until children develop sufficient underlying skills and abilities, they will not be able to acquire the knowledge base and skills necessary for this highly industrialized and technical society. Children who are 7 years of age, for example, cannot be taught how to program a computer system even by the most gifted teacher unless the child has an extensive background of numerical skills and the logical understandings that are the prerequisites for understanding programming.

Vygotskians argue that, while formal schooling provides the training for these advanced psychological processes, play produces important prerequisites for them (Vygotsky, 1966/1977). Children's observable play provides the means for acquiring and practicing underlying skills in preparation for learning the more advanced and technical ones later. Much human learning, for example, requires literacy. Play prepares the child for literacy by providing practice and opportunities to master the making and manipulation of symbols and representations. Until children can think and draw using symbols, they will not be able to learn to read (Vygotsky, 1997).

As is true of other mental processes in the Vygotskian approach, play is something that is coconstructed and not invented by the child alone (Vygotsky, 1930/1978). Coconstruction involves interaction with another person, either another child or an adult. Adults historically have supported play in different ways depending on whether play was pragmatic or not. In addition, the adult role in play depends on the child's age, play stage, and the abilities of other children. When children are younger, the older person takes on a larger role in the play; for example, labeling what the child is doing. As the child matures, the adult will be a coequal in developing the plot or may follow the child's lead, responding to the child's directives.

The Definition of Play in the Vygotskian Approach

For behavior to be classified as "play," it must have specific characteristics that include creating an imaginary situation having defined roles with implicit rules, and using language. First, play must create an imaginary situation in which children pretend "as if." As children mature, these imaginary situations become more elaborate and are shared between partners. You can tell if this imaginary situation has emerged when children play with objects in novel, unconventional ways or use language to change the function of an object, for example, "Let's pretend the spoon is a magic wand."

Play's second characteristic is that it has defined roles with implicit rules for acting in each role. A child will play being the teacher, which implies that he or she must act in a specific way that is different from when he or she is acting as the student. The role is identified aloud to the other participants in the play. The rules for acting out the role are not necessarily spelled out, but can be seen when a child violates them. When the "teacher" brings a "baby" to school, for example, other children will protest that the teacher doesn't have a baby. Only when the "teacher" says "I'm a mommy and a teacher" would this violation be allowed. Children can adjust their roles or take another role that implies that the rules have also changed.

Finally, play must involve language. The child must be able to label the role and describe the imaginary situation. The child is either talking to other children, negotiating roles and the imaginary situation, or the child can be engaged in self-directed speech. Children use language to help create and maintain the play. Thus a child who is trying on hats would not necessarily be considered "playing" unless the child says or can explain, "I'm playing hat store and I'm going to buy myself a nice hat to go to a party." Without the language, the child is only exploring the material, not playing. Both language and the contents of children's play offer observable opportunities to assess the developmental level of play.

The Importance of Play in Development

Vygotskians define development by means of two levels on which a child can perform at any given time (Vygotsky, 1966/1977). The lower level is what the child can do independently, without help from anyone. The upper level of the child's ability is what that same child can do with assistance from another person either directly or indirectly.

The Zone of Proximal Development

The zone of proximal development (ZPD) is the distance between the lower and upper levels. It defines where the child's learning happens. The ZPD is a dynamic structure because as the child masters skills that were previously assisted, new skills emerge at the upper level of the zone. Most of the examples of the ZPD given in Western literature show adults or peers in the classroom providing assistance. For Vygotsky, however, the ZPD extends to informal settings, such as play interactions with adults, siblings, and peers.

For many behaviors, play provides support at the highest levels of the ZPD. The same 5-year-old, for example, who cannot stop interrupting the teacher and talks during group time, when playing school with another child can hold up his or her hand and pretend to be a "model student." As the child's self-regulatory skills develop through play, it is possible to expect that in the future this child will be able to stop interrupting during group time. Play facilitates the transition to more mature functioning in the following ways: (1) It forces children to renounce reactive behavior; (2) promotes symbolic thinking; and (3) provides a context to practice planning and self-regulation.

Setting Limits on Behavior

One of the distinctive features of the Vygotskian approach to play is the belief that the play situation actually sets limits on a child's behavior instead of setting the child "free" or promoting totally spontaneous behavior (Berk, 1995; Berk & Winsler, 1995). To engage in play, children must act in a specific way that is agreed upon by other children. If the children are playing bus, for example, there is a driver and passengers. Not everyone can be a bus driver, and all of the participants have specific behaviors they perform. The driver, for example, announces the stops, opens the door, takes tickets, and drives; the passengers enter and leave from a specific place, buy tickets, give the tickets to the driver, and sit down. The "passenger" who starts opening the bus door or pretends to drive will be chastised by the other children, who will note, "You can't do that. You aren't the driver."

For Vygotsky, therefore, play has very specific roles and rules (Vygotsky, 1966/1977). To be "in" the play you must renounce your immediate spontaneous wishes and conform to the way you are supposed to act and play. Children, however, change and renegotiate these roles and rules, so play does not become a rigid script that the actors follow. Neither is it a mosaic of unrelated actions and episodes with each child's spontaneous interests acted out without any coordination. So strong is the desire to integrate each child's separate actions into a whole that preschool children will assign a special role to a younger child who is not able to invent his or her own. This allows the little one to participate without disrupting the play of others.

Promoting Symbolic Thinking

Another feature of play is that it facilitates the separation of thought from actions and objects (Vygotsky, 1934/1962, 1930/1978). Children act in accordance with internal ideas or symbols rather than external reality. They pretend that the wooden block is a telephone or a boat; they are not dependent on having the actual object. In the early stages of play, children will treat the block in the same way they would a telephone. As children's play matures, they use language to substitute for action; it is enough, for example, to say, "Let's pretend that this is the phone." Overt actions become more and more abbreviated, and symbolic thought in the form of language begins to represent the constellation of actions and behaviors associated with a specific role.

Children create a fantasy world that may have objects that do not exist in reality. Through language they create a shared fantasy with another child and act out their fantasy. This ability to depart from reality and function in a world of imagination and symbols is the first step toward the development of abstract symbolic thought.

Practicing Planning and Self-Regulation

Another important aspect of self-regulation in play is the ability to plan, monitor, and reflect on one's own behavior (Elkonin, 1978). These regulatory skills set the stage for the later development of metacognitive skills when children plan, monitor, and reflect on thinking. For Vygotskians, children who do not practice planning, monitoring, and reflecting on their overt behaviors will not be able to use these processes in their mental actions.

During play, children must reflect on their own plans—what they want to do, and think about how to make these plans merge with the themes and plans of the other partners. For example, David wants to be the garage mechanic, but his friend Linda has already started playing hospital with another child. David has to revise his initial idea of the garage and his role of mechanic into becoming the ambulance driver so he can still wear the tool belt, fix the car, drive, and yet keep interacting with his friends.

The Role of Adults in the Development of Play

Adults have both a direct and an indirect influence on children's play.

Adults Influence Child Play in Both an Indirect and a Direct Way

Adults influence play indirectly by setting up the environment, choosing toys and props, and encouraging children to play together: "Why don't you play with Susan?" Adults also provide experiences that become the fodder for play themes. For example, a field trip or book about zoo animals leads to playing zoo.

For Vygotskians, adults may also directly influence child play, particularly in the case of toddlers and young preschoolers who may lack necessary skills. Teachers may model, for example, how to play with a toy, take turns, settle disputes, and then describe to a partner what one is going to do: "I'm going to be the zebra and you are the lion." As a rule, as children progress toward more advanced levels of play, the need for adult intervention decreases.

Infants and Toddlers: Preparation for Play

Vygotskians do not use the word *play* to describe many of the interactions infants and toddlers have with objects and people. This is different from Western views, where the word *play* is used more broadly. Because infants explore objects using sensorimotor actions, not involving any symbolic representation, Vygotskians do not consider this to be play. Infants can use objects in a nonconventional way, not because they are pretending, but because they do not know how to use the object.

Preparation for play occurs in infancy. The most important thing about the interactions that occur in infancy is the establishment of a warm, caring relationship with a caregiver. This attachment becomes the foundation of all later learning, which for Vygotskians always takes place in a social context. Thus, the baby learns how to use objects as well as how to interact with others. Learning to manipulate objects and to interact with others about these objects are precursors to being able to use objects in pretend play. In addition, infants acquire language, which is the third characteristic of play through interaction with others.

The role of adults during infancy is to establish the attachment and to interact with the baby using toys, books, and other objects. But adults should not rely on objects alone as the primary way to stimulate development: without interaction with another person around these objects, the infant will not acquire mature levels of play later on. It would be better, therefore, to have fewer toys but more interaction with people who demonstrate various ways to use those toys.

Toddlerhood is the period when the first elements of play emerge in the child's behavior, but these elements are not organized into a structure as they are at the preschool ages. Toddlers start using objects in a pretend way, although most of their play is determined by the conventional use of objects. The toddler will also take on some roles, but these are usually determined by the characteristics of the objects. Putting on an apron, for example, makes you "Mommy," but this role is not elaborated with speech and action; the apron is enough. Finally, toddlers are in the process of mastering language and they begin to use it to label what they are doing.

The adult role when interacting with toddlers is to help the child see the potential imaginary situation, the roles and implicit rules, the uses of language to describe action, and the ways to facilitate social interaction with peers. The teacher, for example, sees the toddler wearing the apron and says, "Oh, I see you are cooking something. Can I have a piece of pie?" Toddlers may need help using objects in an unconventional way. The teacher might say, "We can pretend there is a pie here." Teachers facilitate social interaction with others by indicating how another child's play can be incorporated into the situation. The teacher might say to a toddler playing alone, "Josh, I see you're driving a truck. Could you drive to the store to get some more flour and milk, and help us make more pies?"

Play in Preschool

During the preschool years, play evolves into its most mature form. By the time they are 4 and 5 years of age, children learn to create elaborate imaginary play situations that involve complex roles and extended scenarios. Play themes are begun one day and reworked the next. Preschoolers are able to negotiate roles so that the ideas of a number of partners can be integrated into the whole theme. They use language to describe the actions and roles to be played out. These are discussed in detail, and the actual playing out of the actions and roles begins to take a secondary role to the planning and discussion that precedes it. By the time children are 6 years of age, the actual overt actions can become abbreviated, with the discussion and preparation to play occupying most of the children's time.

Play as a coconstructed activity is not meant to imply that all of the partners must be physically present. Vygotskians describe a special kind of play, "director's play," when the child pretends alone, playing all of the parts as if there were other people involved. The preschooler plays as if there are imaginary partners there. For example, Joan is having a tea party all by herself. She talks to the animals and then runs to an empty chair and pretends to talk to Joan, the hostess. She changes her voice when she is the visitor and then jumps up and pretends she is the hostess again. She is engaged in what some psychologists would call solitary play (e.g., Parten, 1932), but all the signs of mature play are actually present. Vygotskians consider this play on a par with mature play with others.

For Vygotskians, movement to this mature level of play does not happen naturally when a child turns 5 or 6 years of age. Preschoolers learn from others how to play at this mature level. When children interact in mixed-age groups with older children who have mature play, the social context will scaffold the play of the younger children. Playing with an older sibling, an older neighborhood friend, or more mature schoolmate, therefore, will provide the ZPD necessary for development. When children do not have these older children to play with, adults may have to provide the missing scaffolding. This does not mean that the teacher should play in the playhouse like a child, but rather that the teacher should make suggestions or organize activities so that the more mature behavior can emerge.

When a child's play is at the immature level, such as putting shoes in and out of a cupboard, teachers take a more active role by labeling the child's actions and helping the child to define a role. If a child flits from play area to play area without becoming engaged in play, the teacher must find ways to help this child maintain interest to engage in an extended role for longer and longer periods of time. When a child cannot interact with others without fighting, the teacher must intervene to facilitate that child's as well as the other children's interactions.

For Vygotskians, the most beneficial times for teachers to facilitate and scaffold play is during the planning stages and at the end of the play time, when children will plan for the next day's play. Adult monitoring during the entire play time may only be necessary for specific children or groups of children who are having trouble sustaining their interactions. As children begin, the teacher's presence can prompt more discussion and richness of possible roles than the children may be able to initiate on their own. Sensitivity is needed because the teacher will not want to direct the children's play, but just make suggestions that will expand and encourage more pretending. Teachers may have to explain how different people's ideas can be woven into the same play. This planning is not rigid and, as the play evolves, children need to know that they can modify and change their plans.

The ending of a play period is as important as the beginning for Vygotskians. By planning the next day's play, children begin to learn the self-regulation skills necessary for later development. Teachers can facilitate this development by eliciting plans, setting aside props for the next day, or making notes on paper with the children so they can have a reminder of what they wanted to do. This becomes the basis of the next day's discussion. Once again, the teacher should make clear to the children that these are just ideas that they are free to change and modify on the next day. This extended play provides more opportunities to create more complete mental images and to use more complex mental processes.

Play in Elementary School

The fantasy play that emerges in preschool does not die in elementary school, but loses its leading role in cognitive and social development. Vygotskians believe that children still engage in fantasy play well through the elementary grades.

During elementary school, games, another type of play, become the more dominant type of interaction. Like Piaget (1932), Vygotsky believed that rules govern games. For Vygotsky, the existence of rules in fantasy play indicates that games are a natural extension of the earlier types of play. In games, the imaginary situation is hidden, and the rules are explicit: "For example, playing chess creates an imaginary situation. Why? Because the knight, king, queen, and so forth can only move in a specified way; because covering and taking pieces are purely chess concepts. Although in the chess game there is no direct substitute for real life relationships, it is a kind of imaginary situation nevertheless" (Vygotsky, 1930/1978, p. 95).

Games are the context in which children learn more about rules: how to follow the rules, negotiate rules, and reestablish rules. This means that children continue to practice self-regulation in this naturally motivating context. Children can only learn self-regulation by practicing regulating themselves and others, just as they did in fantasy play.

Adults should take a minor role in the children's game playing during the elementary grades. An appropriate role, for example, would include clarifying rules or giving written rules for such games as chess and checkers. Children today too often engage in sports and games such as Little League and team soccer that are completely dominated by adults, which robs them of important and necessary practice at self-regulation. Just as in the case of play in the preschool years, children learn games best by interacting with peers who are slightly older or more mature.

In the Vygotskian paradigm, play has a unique place in a child's development. Play is not something that all children develop spontaneously. It is learned through interactions with others in a social context. For play to promote the development of cognitive abilities and self-regulation, adults must plan for interactions that are most beneficial and relevant to the child's age and level of play.

References

Berk, L. E. (1995). Vygotsky's theory: The importance of make-believe play. *Young Children, 50*(1), 30–39.

Berk, L., & Winsler, A. (1995). *Scaffolding children's learning: Vygotsky and early childhood education.* Washington, DC: National Association for the Education of Young Children.

Elkonin, D. (1978). *Psikhologija igry* [*The psychology of play*]. Moscow: Pedagogika.

Elkonin, D. (2005). On the historical origin of role play. *Journal of Russian & East European Psychology, 43*(1). (Original work published 1978)

Parten, M. B. (1932). Social participation among preschool children. *Journal of Abnormal and Social Psychology, 27*(2), 243–269.

Piaget, J. (1932). *The moral judgment of the child* (M. Gabain, Trans.). New York: Harcourt, Brace & World.

Vygotsky, L. S. (1962). *Thought and language* (E. Hanfmann & Gertude Vakar, Trans.). Cambridge, MA: MIT Press. (Original work published 1934)

Vygotsky, L. S. (1977). Play and its role in the mental development of the child. In M. Cole (Ed.), *Soviet developmental psychology* (pp. 76–99). White Plains, NY: M. E. Sharpe. (Original work published 1966)

Vygotsky, L. S. (1978). *Mind and society: The development of higher mental processes.* Cambridge, MA: Harvard University Press. (Original work published 1930)

Vygotsky, L. S. (1997). *The history of the development of higher mental functions* (M. J. Hall, Trans., Vol. 4). New York: Plenum Press.

18
Social Play in School

JEFFREY TRAWICK-SMITH

Play is an ideal context for acquiring social skills and language. Play at home and in the neighborhood is sufficiently open-ended and child-directed to allow opportunities for social learning; children can choose when and what to play and with whom, and they can terminate play interactions with peers if they wish. Play at school, however, has distinct features that can limit social development.

Play and Social Competence

Play is useful for acquiring social skills and language, partly because of its symbolic and non-literal qualities. The following play interaction demonstrates this:

> A 4-year-old in preschool is pretending to drive a car constructed from large hollow blocks; another child sits next to her in the passenger seat. "We're going to drive to New York City," she announces. Her playmate disagrees: "Oh, no. It's too crowded there today. Let's go to McDonald's, instead."
>
> "Well, okay," the first child responds. "We'll go to McDonald's. Then we'll go to New York for the show." Her playmate seems satisfied with this plan; they set out on their pretend trip.

As illustrated above, children must regularly negotiate shared symbolic meanings and coordinate ideas and intentions in play (Fein & Kinney, 1994; Fein & Schwartz, 1986; Garvey, 1990; Rubin, Bukowski, & Parker, 1998; Rubin & Coplan, 1998). Often, they must clarify ambiguous personal symbols. When they announce make-believe actions ("We're driving to New York"), for example, they must be ready to explain and defend these representations. Peers may affirm such play suggestions or offer alternative symbolizations ("Let's go to McDonald's, instead."). Original proposals for make-believe may need to be modified to satisfy all players ("We'll go to McDonald's. Then we'll go to New York."). In any case, intricate conversations and negotiations take place as children attempt to reconcile their personal symbolic meanings with those of others. The ambiguous, nonliteral quality of play leads, then, to an inordinate amount of complex interaction and verbalization (Fein & Kinney, 1994; Fein & Schwartz, 1986; Trawick-Smith, 1993, 2000).

As children negotiate in play, they acquire specific sociolinguistic competencies. These include play group entry skills which children utilize to gain admission into games or play enactments already in progress (Corsaro, 1985, 2005). Research suggests that some entry strategies are likely to succeed (e.g., joining a play group unobtrusively and performing an interesting action); others are rarely successful (e.g., asking, "Can I play?"). Children also learn to persuade peers in play (Trawick-Smith,

1993, 2000). They may discover, for example, that one type of persuasive behavior is more effective than another with certain playmates. When playing with bullies, for example, friendly requests work better than aggressive demands. Conflict resolution abilities are acquired in play (Hartup & Abecasis, 2002; Hartup, French, Laursen, Johnston, & Ogawa, 1993). Play disputes provide an optimal context for learning to compromise, be tactful, and avoid violence (Corsaro, 1998; Hazen, Black, & Fleming-Johnson, 1984; Trawick-Smith, 1993). Rubin (1980) has suggested that arguing <u>about</u> play may be more valuable for children, than play itself.

Acquiring these sociolinguistic competencies through play interactions can result in acceptance by peers and the formation of reciprocal friendships (Hartup & Abecasis, 2002; Hartup & Moore, 1990). Skilled players are often better liked and have more friends; such positive peer relationships have been found to predict long-range positive social development and mental health (Hartup & Abecasis, 2002; Hartup & Sancilio, 1986).

Unique Features of School-Based Play

School-based play differs markedly from play at home or in the neighborhood. It has a different structure and interpersonal dynamic. It involves distinct play skills. Adults and sometimes children adopt unique goals for classroom play. These differences can lead to social outcomes which contrast sharply with those of open-ended free play outside of school.

Open- Versus Closed-Field Play

Researchers have distinguished between open- and closed-field play (Hartup et al., 1993; Tomada, Schneider, & Fonzi, 2002). Open-field play takes place in relatively unrestricted social contexts; examples include spontaneous interactions in the neighborhood, where children are free to choose when to play and with whom. Closed-field play is socially confined or controlled. School-based cooperative learning groups, competitive games, or teacher-assigned dramatic play activities are examples; in these settings children may be unable to choose their playmates or to terminate play interchanges.

Differences between home and school play can be observed most clearly in children's arguments. The *neighborhood-based* narrative in Example 18.1 illustrates the social interactions in open-field play.

Example 18.1 Two 7-year-old children are climbing into a cardboard box and rolling down a hill in their neighborhood. An argument erupts.

Child A: Let's say this is our cave and we have to hide in it. Hunters are coming, all right? And so we have to hide.
Child B: No! Let's just play. (Climbs into the box and rolls down the hill alone.)
Child A: Jamal! No! Don't roll down! This is the cave all right?
Child B: (Ignores Child A; drags the box back up to the top of the hill.)
Child A: I'm not going to play. I don't want you to roll it down. (Begins to walk away.)
Child B: We could say it's a cave that can roll down, all right, Alonzo? (Laughs) It could be a cave that rolls down.
Child A: (Laughs) That's pretty funny. The cave rolls down. It'll be a rolling cave. Come on. (Climbs into the box with Child B and continues to play.)

Open-field play, as represented in this example, can be discontinued suddenly, at any time, by any participant. When conflicts become too strong, as in Example 18.1, above, an individual player can separate from play interactions. Since children are usually committed to maintaining play in progress, they will make efforts to assure that activities do not dissolve in conflict. Child B, sensing that his playmate will leave because of an argument, initiates a carefully crafted compromise to keep the play alive ("It's a cave that can roll down..."). It may be hypothesized that in open-field play children are more likely to be persuasive rather than demanding, in order to compromise, and to resolve disputes without aggression. They are apt to adopt positive peer-group entry strategies rather than barging in; there is a possibility of not being admitted in an open-field context. Generally, children in open-field play will seek to "manage their conflicts in ways that minimize risk to their interactions." (Hartup et al., 1993, p. 446) So, open-field play affords rich opportunities to exercise interpersonal skills.

The social interactions in the *school-based* play narrative in Example 18.2 contrast with those in Example 18.1.

Example 18.2 A teacher has assigned two 5-year-old children to the dramatic play area during their kindergarten center time. Following a field trip to a local medical facility, the teacher has created a pretend hospital in this space. The children are dressing dolls; one suggests a new medical-related play theme.

Child C: Our babies are sick all right, Cheryl? So, we need to drive them to the hospital now.
Child D: They're not sick. They're just... um... they're sleeping.
Child C: (In a loud, angry tone) Cheryl! These babies go to the doctor! We need to take them! This is the hospital, see? Hurry! Before snack! (Snatches the doll out of Child D's hands.)
Child D: No, Samantha! Give it to me! (Turns and shouts across the room to a teacher.) Mrs. DeSoto! Samantha took my doll!
Teacher: (Moving over quickly) Cheryl, you seem very angry!
Child D: (In a loud voice) Samantha took my doll!
Child C: (In a loud voice) We need to take the babies to the hospital!
Teacher: Let's calm down a minute and talk in quieter voices. What can we do about this problem?
Child D: I want my doll.
Teacher: Okay. Samantha, you shouldn't just grab Cheryl's doll. Can you give it back to her please?
Child C: (Hands Child D the doll) Okay, but I want to play the babies are sick.
Teacher: You could pretend that you each take your own baby to the hospital. I could play the doctor, if you want. (Begins to play out a hospital theme)

The school-based, closed-field play of Example 18.2 is thematically, temporally, and interpersonally bound. The teacher regulates how and what children play, with whom, and for how long. These limitations may restrict play development and hamper positive peer interactions.

In contrast, play at home, illustrated in Example 18.1, is relatively unbound; children in the neighborhood are free to choose playmates and play themes. They may play as long as they wish (or at least until dinner); they can opt to stop playing altogether if conflicts become too intense.

Such is not the case in closed-field interactions. Children need not work as hard in these contexts to maintain play. Child C in Example 18.2 is not required to soften her demands to preserve interactions. Her playmate must remain in the area and at her disposal; snatching a toy carries less interpersonal risk.

Research supports the thesis that closed-field play involves less positive social interaction. Hartup and colleagues (1993) found that pairs of school-aged friends—who in open-field settings had displayed remarkable conflict resolution abilities—argued more frequently and more intensely in play settings which were closed. These authors conclude that children in closed-field play have less to lose by being bossy, aggressive, or otherwise aversive.

Openness and closedness of play represent a continuum. A neighborhood game can be relatively closed (e.g., a parent may insist that a child play with a younger sibling); school play can be comparatively open (e.g., a teacher might provide pure free choice of activities and play partners within a preschool).

It is proposed here, however, that typical school-based play is relatively closed, when compared with other play contexts. Children in classrooms are often confined in their choice of play partners to a small, finite group of peers with whom they are expected to play and get along. The narrowness of playmate choices is exacerbated by three common classroom practices:

1. Teachers will sometimes assign children to particular centers and certain groups of peers during free play or center time. This "assign and rotate" system of managing free play has come under criticism, but is nonetheless common in kindergartens or primary grade classrooms (Trawick-Smith, 1994).
2. Teachers will set a policy that all children must include all other children in play groups; the "you can't say you can't play" rule advocated by Paley (1992) is an example. In this case there is no freedom to terminate interactions.
3. Teachers implement "match-making" strategies to bring less socially competent children together with prosocial models. An example would be assigning a withdrawn and outgoing child to play together in the class library. Here, adults select children's play partners. These efforts have clear benefits; their cost, however, is interpersonal restriction.

Time-Bound Classroom Play

Play in school is distinctly time bound. There is usually a designated period for play activities in classrooms; in kindergartens and elementary schools play time is being threatened by growing expectations for teacher-directed academic instruction. Some kindergarten teachers have reported, for example, providing 10 minutes or less of free choice time in school (Hatch & Freeman, 1988). Such temporal restraints on play are problematic for several reasons. Play, like art or writing, cannot be performed on demand; children play when the time is right. (Can play which is required at the wrong time still be considered play?) Play themes take time. Games, pretend enactments, even rough and tumble activities are complex. They progress in stages; these include planning, implementation, and closure (Garvey, 1990).

Of concern in this chapter is the effect of time constraint on social interactions. Play takes longer if it is to be socially meaningful and useful. Children spend an inordinate amount of time engaged in joint planning for play (Craig-Unkefer & Kaiser, 2002; Forbes, Katz, Paul, & Lubin, 1982; Garvey, 1990). In preschool symbolic play, for example, children must create together make-believe themes and roles. They also must decide which peers get to play along. For this reason, it has been recommended that blocks of 30 to 50 minutes be allowed for play in school (Johnson, Christie, & Yawkey, 1999). Even this may not be enough. One study found that 5- year-olds who were afforded adequate play time spent an average of 30 minutes just setting up and organizing pretend play themes before actually playing (Trawick-Smith, 1993).

Conflicts in play take time to resolve. Several researchers have documented long chains of arguments and counterarguments that occur in disputes (Chen, Fein, & Tam, 2001; Forbes et al., 1982; Markell & Asher, 1984). Prosocial resolutions may take longer than less positive ones. Angry hitting or screaming are delivered more quickly than elaborate persuasive behaviors, for example (Trawick-Smith, 1992). In play example 18.2, above, temporal urgency may have caused Child C's harsh demands. She likely felt compelled to rush her play demands without the usual negotiation and planning, since play time would soon end ("Hurry. Before snack!") It is possible that she would have used more elaborate and positive persuasive strategies if time had permitted.

Thematically Bound Classroom Play

With threats to play coming on every side and a movement in United States education toward "cognitive child labor" (Sutton-Smith, 1983, p. 13), many teachers have felt driven to make outrageous claims about play's contributions to academic achievement. There is great pressure to make play something that it is not. One approach has been to make play part of the content of the curriculum; all classroom play spaces are designed, in this method, around central educational themes. When preschool children are taught about transportation, for example, the dramatic play center is transformed into a train station, the block area is filled with toy vehicles. In another effort to legitimize play, playful experiences are recast as literacy events (Christie, Enz, & Vukelich, 1997). Play spaces are saturated with books and writing implements (Trawick-Smith, 2004). If play helps children to read and write, teachers imagine that play detractors surely will be silenced.

The net effect of these strategies can be to distract children from the important work of play. The imaginative qualities and interpersonal meanings of play are threatened in such thematically bound contexts. A child who has been spanked with a belt by his mother on a particular morning may need to play something other than train engineer in the dramatic play center. Another child with ego needs for feelings of power and mastery, may do better playing a magical princess, rather than a customer trying to decode print on a pretend train schedule. Adult-devised play themes may dissuade children from pursuing their own play needs.

Of interest is how thematically bound play influences peer relations. Teachers create thematic play experiences by using a preponderance of realistic props and materials. To elicit children's grocery store play, for example, teachers have provided shopping lists, cash registers, and empty food containers. This realism tends to limit interpersonal interaction. The uses of realistic props do not require as much explanation or justification and do not demand the same level of agreement among players. The forms and functions of a shopping list or a grocery cart are obvious, therefore no on-going negotiations are needed about what these represent. In contrast, transforming a wooden rod into a fire hose requires some debate, since children can imagine so many alternative symbolizations. One child may propose that the object is a hose, while another may suggest a magic wand. Children must reconcile such different personal symbols if cooperative play is to continue.

Research verifies that toy realism can be socially limiting. One study found that children verbalized and interacted far less when playing with realistic than with nonrealistic materials (Trawick-Smith, 1993). These limiting effects may be seen in Example 18.2, above, as Child C confines her play pursuits to themes suggested by teacher-selected play props. Her rigid insistence on hospital play leads to hopeless conflict. Would she have been more likely to compromise or negotiate had expectations for hospital play not been so fully dictated by the play environment? In contrast, the cardboard box in Example 18.1 lends itself to multiple representations. So, negotiation is possible. In fact, lack of realism allows the children to integrate two seemingly disparate play interests—a pretend cave theme and a hill-rolling game.

Adult Facilitated Classroom Play

Play is the one arena where children have a modicum of control over their lives. In play, children run the show; they are powerful and free of adult regulation. This is especially true in neighborhood or home play, though perhaps less so in school.

Teachers will often facilitate play. They justify this practice with a growing body of research suggesting that some children need support in play and that intervention can lead to positive developmental outcomes (Smilansky, 1968; Van Berckelaer-Onnes, 2003). There is a fine line, however, between facilitating and managing play, particularly when teachers sometimes are heavy handed in their interventions (Trawick-Smith, 1994). In an effort to assure that play yields cognitive benefits, teachers will occasionally interrupt play themes with educative questions, directives, or praise statements which are incongruous with activities in progress. For example, they may ask, "What shape is that pan you're cooking with?" or "What is the name of that vegetable you are putting in your soup?" Teachers often issue admonishments for loud and active play or reminders that only certain numbers of children are allowed in particular areas. One researcher observed that the vast majority of teacher interactions in play involved terminating or quieting children's activities (Trawick-Smith, 1987).

 This heavy-handedness is a particular problem in social interactions. Adults usually wish to structure activities and environments for children so as to avoid conflict and assure peaceful peer relations. Teachers may intervene too quickly and intensively, then, when play arguments erupt. They may impose adult solutions to social problems. They may, for example, mandate timed sharing arrangements in disputes over toys, such as, "Alonzo can have the big wheel for five minutes, then Hanna can have it for five minutes." They may quickly separate children when they are arguing, stating, "Sarah, you can't play nicely with Lawanda right now; why don't you come over with me and read a book." These tend to be adult solutions. Would children, left to their own devices, resolve disputes in these ways?

Example 18.2, above, shows how teachers can impose adult resolutions to conflict. This kindergarten teacher insists that children, "calm down and talk in quiet voices." Anyone who is familiar with children's conflict knows that loud expressions of anger are fundamental (though perhaps unpleasant) aspects of resolving play disputes. Like adults, children may need to speak their minds and show their intense feelings before moving on to reconcile disagreements. During neighborhood play, however, children would not hesitate to argue things out.

The teacher of Example 18.2 imposes a solution to the conflict ("pretend you each take your own baby to the hospital"), rather than allowing children to do so. Here she may have deprived students of an opportunity to generate and test their own alternative social strategies. Decision making and problem solving are critical features of overall social competence; children must read social situations, scan their own repertoire of available strategies, and choose those which match the demands of a particular circumstance (Crick & Ladd, 1987; Trawick-Smith, 1992). The imposing interventions of this kindergarten teacher may have obstructed this process.

Children need to get into arguments in order to learn how to resolve them. They must be excluded from groups in order to learn play group entry skills. They must play with disagreeable peers and bullies to broaden their repertoire of social strategies. They must have play ideas rejected so they can learn to become persuasive. When adults intervene too quickly in conflict, these opportunities are lost.

Classroom Play in Primary and Middle Grades

Classroom play in the elementary or middle school years, or what passes for play at these grade levels, is even more closed, time-bound, and teacher-directed. Elementary teachers often provide play centers that line the periphery of their classrooms; however, these are used rarely. Children sit at their desks in the middle of the room and complete mathematics problems or reading assignments. They may use the centers when they finish the "important work of school." Outdoor play is a reward for work completion. So, children in most need of a break from the rigors of academic work, those with a high preference for movement, or who have attentional challenges, for example, are regularly deprived of playground time. Play, when it occurs, is overmanaged by teachers who give children play assignments (an oxymoron?) or rigid time limits for play. Noise and social interaction are usually not tolerated.

By middle school, even the appearance of play has vanished. Recess is a thing of the past for this age group in most countries in the world. Teachers might initiate cooperative learning groups or engage students in active debate or discussion, but nothing approaching the open-ended, socially active quality of early free play is apparent in the modern middle school.

Play, then, in the elementary and middle school years must go underground. It becomes illicit. Elementary school children create imaginative doodles on paper or notebooks during work time.

Older children transform Cuisenaire rods into rocket ships during mathematics lessons. Adolescents create elaborate fantasy worlds during algebra class. Teachers cannot prevent children from playing in these ways, although they sometimes make them feel guilty for doing so.

What can be concluded about school-based play? Typical play in school is more bound than play at home. It can and should be emancipated. Four recommendations for achieving this are:

1. Children should be given the chance to play with whomever they choose during at least a portion of the school day, because such open-field play allows greater opportunity to exercise positive social skills.

2. Play time should be lengthened, because positive interactions in play take longer than negative ones. It may not be enough to make time in school for play. Play may need to become the primary focus of school.

3. Open-ended raw materials should be provided in school, because realistic props and curriculum-bound play themes can restrict conversation and debate. A move to generic play contexts, where children can invent what they will do, may better allow pursuit of personally felt play needs.

4. Teachers should avoid intervening too quickly in play disputes and give over to children the regulation of social interchanges. Certainly a degree of intervention is warranted; some children will need support to play at all. Heavy-handed interventions or those not related to play in progress, however, will distract children from the very important work of play.

References

Chen, D., Fein, G. G., & Tam, H. (2001). Peer conflicts of preschool children: Issues, resolution, incidence, and age-related patterns. *Early Education & Development, 12*, 523–544.

Christie, J., Enz, B., & Vukelich, C. (1997). *Teaching language and literacy: Preschool through the elementary years*. New York: Addison Wesley.

Corsaro, W. A. (2005). *Sociology of childhood* (2nd ed.). Thousand Oaks, CA: Pine Forge Press/Sage.

Craig-Unkefer, L. A., & Kaiser, A. P. (2003). Increasing peer-directed social-communication skills of children enrolled in Head Start. *Journal of Early Intervention, 25*, 229–247.

Crick, N. R., & Ladd, G. W. (1987, April). *Children's perceptions of the consequences of aggressive behavior: Do the ends justify the means?* Paper presented at the biennial meeting of the Society for Research in Child Development, Baltimore.

Fein, G. G., & Kinney, P. (1994). He's a nice alligator: Observations on the affective organization of pretense. In A. Slade (Ed.), *Children at play: Clinical and developmental approaches to meaning and representation* (pp. 188–205). London: Oxford University Press.

Fein, G. G., & Schwartz, S. S. (1986). The social coordination of pretense in preschool children. In G. Fein & M. Rivkin (Eds.), *The young child at play: Reviews of research* (Vol. 4, pp. 95–111). Washington, DC: National Association for the Education of Young Children.

Forbes, D. L., Katz, M. M., Paul, B., & Lubin, D. (1982). Children's plans for joining play: An analysis of structure and function. In D. Forbes & M. T. Greenberg (Eds.), *New directions for child development: Children's planning strategies* (No. 18, pp. 61–79). San Francisco: Jossey-Bass.

Garvey, C. (1990). *Play*. Cambridge, MA: Harvard University Press.

Hartup, W. W., & Abecasis, M. (2002). Friends and enemies. In P. K. Smith & C. Hart (Eds), *Blackwell handbook of childhood social development* (pp. 286–306). Malden, MA: Blackwell.

Hartup, W. W., French, D. C., Laursen, B., Johnston, M. K., & Ogawa, J. R. (1993). Conflict and friendship relations in middle childhood: Behavior in a closed-field setting. *Child Development, 64*, 445–454.

Hartup, W. W., & Moore, S. G. (1990). Early peer relations: Developmental significance and prognostic implications. *Early Childhood Research Quarterly, 5*, 1–17.

Hartup, W. W., & Sancilio, M. F. (1986). Children's friendships. In E. Schopler & G. B. Mesibov (Eds.), *Social behavior in autism*. New York: Plenum.

Hatch, J. A., & Freeman, E. B. (1988). Kindergarten philosophies and practices: Perspectives of teachers, principals, and supervisors. *Early Childhood Research Quarterly, 3*, 151–166.

Hazen, N., Black, B., & Fleming-Johnson, F. (1984). Social acceptance: Strategies children use and how teachers can help learn them. *Young Children, 39*(3), 26–36.

Johnson, J. E., Christie, J. F., & Yawkey, T. D. (1999). *Play and early development*. Glenview, IL: Scott, Foresman.

Markell, R. A., & Asher, S. R. (1984). Children's interactions in dyads: Interpersonal influence and sociometric status. *Child Development, 55*, 1412–1424.

Paley, V. (1992). *You can't say you can't play*. Cambridge, MA: Harvard University Press.

Rubin, K. H. (1980). Fantasy play: Its role in the development of social skills and social cognition. In K. H. Rubin (Ed.), *Children's play* (pp. 69–84). San Francisco: Jossey-Bass.

Rubin, K., Bukowski, W., & Parker, J. G. (1998). Peer interactions, relationships, and groups. In N. Eisenberg (Ed.), *Handbook of child psychology: Social, emotional, and personality* (5th ed., Vol. 3, pp. 619–700). New York: Wiley.

Rubin, K. H., & Coplan, R. J. (1998). Social and emotional development from a cultural perspective. In O. N. Saracho & B. Spodek (Eds), *Multiple perspectives on play in early childhood education* (pp. 144–170). Albany, NY: State University of New York Press.

Smilansky, S. (1968). *The effects of sociodramatic play on disadvantaged preschool children*. New York: Wiley.

Sutton-Smith, B. (1983). One hundred years of change in play research. *Association for the Anthropological Study of Play Newsletter, 9*(2), 13–17.

Tomada, G., Schneider, B. H., & Fonzi, A. (2002). Verbal and nonverbal interactions of four- and five-year-old friends in potential conflict situations. *Journal of Genetic Psychology, 163*, 327–339.

Trawick-Smith, J. (1987). The validity and reliability of an instrument to measure the dramatic play behavior of young children. *ERIC Document #ED 286 654.*.

Trawick-Smith, J. W. (1992). A descriptive study of persuasive preschool children: How they get others to do what they want. *Early Childhood Research Quarterly, 7*, 95–115.

Trawick-Smith, J. (1993, April). *Effects of realistic, nonrealistic, and mixed realism play environments on young children's symbolization, verbalization, and social interaction*. Paper presented at the Annual Meeting of the American Educational Research Association, Atlanta, GA.

Trawick-Smith, J. (1994). *Interactions in the classroom: Facilitating play in the early years*. Columbus, OH: Merrill.

Trawick-Smith, J. (2000, April). *Drawing back the lens on play: A frame analysis of the play of children from Puerto Rico*. Paper presented at the annual meeting of the American Educational Research Association, Atlanta.

Van Berckelaer-Onnes, I. (2003). Promoting early play. *Autism, 7*, 415–423.

19
Play as a Medium for Literacy Development

JAMES F. CHRISTIE

Current theories of literacy acquisition, including emergent literacy and critical theory, maintain that play can have an important role in early reading and writing development. There are links between play and literacy learning which have implications for education. These links suggest guidelines for setting up print-rich classroom play centers and for facilitative teacher involvement in play.

Emergent Literacy and Critical Theory

Beliefs and instructional practices connected with early literacy have changed dramatically over the past decade. Scholars used to believe that children learned very little about reading and writing until age 5 or 6, when they entered school and began to receive formal instruction (Christie, Enz, & Vukelich, 2003). They assumed that children waited for teachers to teach them how to read and write. This instruction typically began with perceptual "readiness" activities, such as visual discrimination exercises, and then moved on to rote drill and worksheets focusing on letter–name recognition, handwriting, and letter–sound relationships. Schools delayed book reading and actual writing until children had mastered these prerequisite skills. Once children started doing "real" reading and writing, their teachers expected them to master conventional forms. During reading, children were supposed to accurately recognize all text items and accurately spell all words when writing.

This traditional view of literacy acquisition has been recently supplanted by two new perspectives: emergent literacy and critical theory. The emergent literacy perspective maintains that children begin to learn about written language much earlier than had previously been believed. Infants and toddlers observe the literacy that surrounds them in everyday life, such as bedtime stories, environmental print (labels on cereal boxes, restaurant signs), and family literacy routines (looking up programs in *TV Guide*, writing down phone messages, making shopping lists). Children then begin to construct their own hypotheses about the function, structure, and conventions of print (Hall, 1987). In this process, young children invent their own "emergent" versions of reading and writing that initially have little resemblance to conventional forms: the story they "read" may be completely different from the one in the book and their writing may look like drawing or scribbles. As children have opportunities to use these emergent forms of literacy in meaningful social situations, their constructions become increasingly similar to conventional reading and writing (Sulzby & Teale, 1991).

Critical theory views literacy acquisition in the broader sociopolitical context of the children's culture (Solsken, 1993). It is concerned with how reading instruction affects the balance of power between different groups in society. According to this view, traditional textbook-based reading instruction benefits the upper classes by conditioning lower-class children to passively accept the status quo. Critical theorists believe that "schools should encourage and foster students' attempts to make sense of their immediate experience by establishing 'voices' that enable them to participate in control of their lives.... The goal...is to have students participate within the production of knowledge, culture, and society" (Shannon,1990, p. 157).

Critical theorists favor pedagogical approaches that give children control over their own literacy learning and that are closely linked to their own cultural experiences.

Early childhood educators who subscribe to these new perspectives believe that early childhood language arts programs should provide children with opportunities to construct their own knowledge about reading and writing. These programs feature print-rich classroom settings, daily storybook reading by the teacher, teacher modeling of the reading/writing process (e.g., language experience charts), and lots of opportunities for children to engage in meaningful reading and writing activities (Christie et al., 2003). In addition, teachers try to connect these classroom activities with children's own cultural experiences outside of school.

Play and Literacy Connections

Sociodramatic play occurs when children take on roles and act out a situation or story (Johnson, Christie, & Wardle, 2005). Several children, for example, might adopt the roles of family members and pretend to prepare and eat dinner. This type of play commonly takes place in classroom "housekeeping" or "theme" centers and can provide an ideal context for the types of literacy learning experiences advocated by these two new perspectives (Roskos & Christie, 2004).

The following episode, which occurred in a university preschool classroom, is an example of how children can incorporate reading and writing into their sociodramatic play.

Several 4-year-olds have agreed to take a make-believe train trip to France. They decide to use an elevated loft in the classroom as their train and begin moving chairs up the stairs to use as passenger seats. Two of the children go to an adjacent center and begin making tickets for the journey, using scribbles to represent writing. Once the tickets are made, they are distributed to every child and collected by the engineer as passengers enter the train. While the children wait for their teacher to finish packing his bag and join them on board, they lean over the loft railing and attempt to read signs that had been made earlier for the train, including "No Smoking," "No Drugs," and "No Ghosts." They have difficulty reading the prohibition against drugs and ask the teacher, "What's that say?" The teacher reads the sign out loud for the children and then climbs on board so that the journey can begin.

This vignette illustrates several ways in which sociodramatic play can promote literacy learning. First, the play scenario allowed children to demonstrate their emerging conceptions about the functional uses of print. They knew that print communicates meaning (evident in the question, "What's that say?") and that it can be used to control behavior (prohibit smoking) and grant access to goods and services (via tickets). Second, the make-believe nature of the play provided an ideal context for experimenting with emergent forms of literacy. It was perfectly acceptable to use scribble writing to produce tickets, and all of the players treated the pretend tickets as if they were real. Thus, play's fantasy component invited risk-taking while adding meaning and significance to children's attempts at reading and writing. Third, the play provided an opportunity for literacy-related social interactions with peers and with the teacher (Neuman & Roskos, 1991; Roskos & Neuman, 1993). The children, for example, worked together to figure out the meaning of the train signs and also sought help from the teacher on the one sign they could not decipher on their own. In this instance, the teacher created what Vygotsky (1978) called a "zone of proximal development," allowing children to engage in a literacy activity (sign reading) that they could not do on their own.

This vignette also illustrates how sociodramatic play can provide links between classroom activities and children's cultural experiences outside of school. Two of the signs that the children had made for their train, "No Smoking" and "No Drugs," reflect community concern over passive smoke and substance abuse. The fact that these signs resemble real signs in the children's own neighborhoods makes them more salient and meaningful.

Educational Implications

Research has shed light on the conditions that encourage children to engage in this type of literacy-related play (Roskos & Christie, 2004). First and foremost, play centers need to be equipped with relevant types of reading and writing materials. The second variable concerns how teachers interact with children during play. If teachers get involved in children's play in a facilitative manner, they can enrich the quality of the play and encourage the children to incorporate emergent forms of reading and writing into their dramatizations.

Table 19.1 presents examples of the literacy materials for a variety of sociodramatic play settings. Note that these props meet the three criteria above and could be supplemented with literacy materials from children's homes and neighborhoods.

Children are more likely to engage in play-related reading and writing activities if materials are present that invite these types of activities (Neuman & Roskos, 1992). Early childhood teachers have been encouraged to set up literacy-enriched play areas which resemble the literacy environments that children encounter at home and in their communities. The kitchen area of a housekeeping center might contain empty product containers (cereal boxes, soft drink cans, catsup bottles), cookbooks, a telephone directory, food coupons, message pads, and pencils. A restaurant center could be equipped with menus, wall signs, pencils, and notepads for taking food orders. These centers would then invite children to incorporate familiar literacy routines into their play.

Time for Play

In addition to theme-related literacy props, one additional resource is needed to ensure that children can take maximum advantage of these literacy-enriched play environments: an adequate amount of

Table 19.1 Literacy-Enriched Play Centers

"Supermarket" Shelf labels for store Areas ("Meat") Product containers Wall signs ("Deli") Pencils, pens, markers notepads	Grocery Store
Bank checks, wall signs	Bank
Pencils, notepads, menus Cookbooks	Restaurant
Pencils, pens, markers Stationery, envelopes, stamps	Post Office
Address labels, wall signs ("Line Starts Here")	Mailboxes
Pencils, pens, markers, appointment book, wall signs ("Waiting Room"), Labels with pets' names, patient charts, prescription forms Magazines (in waiting room)	Veterinarian's Office
Pencils, books, shelf labels for books, ("ABCs," "Animals"), Library wall signs ("Quiet") Library cards, checkout cards for books	
Pencils, pens, markers, tickets Luggage tags, magazines (onboard plane), Air sickness bags with printed instructions, Maps	Airport/Airplane

Source: Based on J. Christie & B. Enz (1992). The effects of literacy play interventions on preschoolers' play patterns and literacy development *Early Education and Development, 3,* 211. Reprinted with permission.

time for play (Christie & Wardle, 1992). Young children need considerable time to plan and act out a sustained play episode. They need to assign roles, make props, organize the setting, solve social problems, and plan the story they are going to enact. In one incident witnessed by this author, a group of 4-year-olds spent more than 45 minutes preparing to play pizza parlor. They sorted pizza ingredients made of felt fabric into containers, rearranged the furniture in the play center, and made a variety of props, including signs and money. The actual making and eating of the pizza took less than 10 minutes! Had the play period only been 30 minutes long, the children would have had to stop and clean up before their drama had even started, and many valuable literacy experiences (sign making, menu reading, and money counting) would have been missed.

Teacher Involvement in Play

Teacher involvement in play can have either positive or negative effects, depending upon timing and the role that the teacher assumes. On the one hand, if teachers observe carefully and link their involvement with children's current play interests, they can enrich and extend play episodes. They also can encourage children to incorporate relevant literacy activities into their ongoing play episodes (Neuman & Roskos, 1993). On the other hand, if teachers take control of the play or try to redirect children toward unrelated literacy activities, the results can be disastrous. Children may begin to think of the activity as work rather than play (King, 1979), and play will often get disrupted (Schrader, 1990). In such situations, children often stop playing altogether.

Research has revealed that there is a continuum of teacher roles in play, ranging from complete noninvolvement to directing what children do during play (Enz & Christie, 1997; Jones & Reynolds, 1992; Roskos & Neuman, 1993). The most effective teacher roles, both in terms of facilitating high-quality play and encouraging play-related literacy activity, lie between these two extremes. Some researchers have found that four teacher roles were effective in enhancing preschoolers' play and literacy activities:

Audience

The teacher watches children as they play, demonstrating that play is an important and worthwhile classroom activity. The teacher also subtly provides support by nodding in approval, verbalizing praise, and making brief comments designed to encourage children to continue their play activities. For example, if the teacher observes that children are using an emergent form of writing (scribbles, letterlike forms, or random strings of letters) in connection with a pretend trip to a store, she or he might compliment their efforts ("That's a nice shopping list that you've written"). This role is most appropriate when children are engrossed in rich, sustained play.

Stage Manager

The teacher supports children's play by responding to their requests for materials, by helping them construct costumes and props, and by assisting in organizing the play set. In the vignette above, the teacher engaged in this role when he helped the children make the regulatory signs for their make-believe train. A stage manager may also make theme related script suggestions to extend the children's ongoing dramatic play ("Why don't you make tickets for the train? Then you can give them to the conductor when you get on board"). As in the audience role, the teacher remains on the sidelines and does not join in the children's play. The stage manager role is often used at the beginning of play periods and during transitions when children are switching to new play themes and activities.

Coplayer

In the coplayer role, the teacher accepts an invitation to play and actually becomes an actor in the children's dramatizations. As a coplayer, the teacher takes a minor role and carefully follows the children's lead, letting them make all the major decisions. For example, the teacher might take the role of a customer in a store dramatization. In this role, the teacher could model using a shopping list, reading product labels, and paying for purchases with a check, provided that these literacy activities fit in with the ongoing play.

Play Leader

Like the coplayer, the play leader joins in and becomes the children's play partner. However, play leaders take a more active role and attempt to alter the course of the play by introducing new elements or plot conflicts. If a grocery store dramatization, for example, is growing stale and boring, the teacher might adopt the role of a customer and exclaim, "It's awfully hard to find anything in this store! The shelves need to be labeled so that we know where things are."

Flexibility is a key element in successful teacher involvement in play. Researchers have found that experienced preschool teachers do not exhibit a dominant play interaction style (Roskos & Neuman, 1993). Instead, these veteran teachers adopt a variety of roles—onlooker, coplayer, and play leader—depending on the children who are playing and type of play that is occurring. Roskos and Neuman (1993) concluded that teachers' ability to switch roles to fit the children's "play agenda" was as important as the interaction styles they used. Ideally, teachers should have a repertoire of play interaction styles and know when it is appropriate to use each one.

Conclusion

Sociodramatic play can be an excellent means for providing children with the types of literacy learning experiences advocated by emergent literacy and critical theory perspectives. Play can give meaning and significance to children's early attempts at literacy, and its "low-risk" atmosphere encourages experimentation with emergent forms of reading and writing. Play can also provide valuable social interactions connected with literacy, both with teachers and peers. It also presents opportunities for bringing culturally relevant literacy materials into the classroom.

When the three resources discussed in this chapter—literacy, enriched settings, adequate time, and facilitative teacher involvement—are in place, sociodramatic play can function as an ideal medium for children to construct their own knowledge about reading and writing. Play makes literacy learning fun and enjoyable, and it guarantees that children's early attempts at reading and writing will be successful. Play also presents teachers with opportunities for "authentic" assessment by allowing children to demonstrate their growing knowledge about the forms and functions of print (Vukelich, 1992). For these reasons, literacy-related play deserves a central role in early childhood language arts programs.

References

Christie, J., Enz, B., & Vukelich, C. (2003). *Teaching language and literacy: Preschool through the elementary grades* (2nd ed.). New York: Allyn & Bacon.

Christie, J., & Wardle, F. (1992). How much time is needed for play? *Young Children, 47*(3), 28–32.

Enz, B., & Christie, J. (1997). Teacher play interaction styles: Effects on play behavior and relationships with teacher training and experience. *International Journal of Early Childhood Education, 2,* 55–69.

Hall, N. (1987). *The emergence of literacy.* Portsmouth, NH: Heinemann.

Johnson, J., Christie, J., & Wardle, F. (2005). *Play, development, and early education.* New York: Allyn & Bacon.

Jones, E., & Reynolds, G. (1992). *Play's the thing: Teachers' roles in children's play.* New York: Teachers College Press.

King, N. (1979). Play: The kindergartners' perspective. *Elementary School Journal, 80,* 81–87.

Neuman, S., & Roskos, K. (1991). Peers as literacy informants: A description of young children's literacy conversations in play. *Early Childhood Research Quarterly, 6,* 233–248.

Neuman, S., & Roskos, K. (1992). Literacy objects as cultural tools: Effects on children's literacy behaviors during play. *Reading Research Quarterly, 27,* 203–223.

Roskos, K., & Christie, J. (2004). Examining the play-literacy interface: A critical review and future directions. In E. Zigler, D. Singer, & S. Bishop-Josef (Eds.), *Children's play: The roots of reading* (pp. 95–123). Washington, DC: Zero to Three Press.

Roskos, K., & Neuman, S. (1993). Descriptive observations of adults' facilitation of literacy in play. *Early Childhood Research Quarterly, 8*, 77–97.

Schrader, C. (1990). Symbolic play as a curricular tool for early literacy development. *Early Childhood Research Quarterly, 5*, 79–103.

Shannon, P. (1990). *The struggle to continue: Progressive reading instruction in the United States*. Portsmouth, NH: Heinemann.

Solsken, J. (1993). *Literacy, gender, and work in families and in school*. Norwood, NJ: Ablex.

Sulzby, E., & Teale, W (1991). Emergent literacy. In R. Barr, M. Kamil, P. Mosenthal, & P. D. Pearson (Eds.), *Handbook of reading research* (Vol. 2, pp. 727–757). New York: Longman.

Vukelich, C. (1992). Play and assessment: Young children's knowledge of the functions of writing. *Childhood Education, 68*, 202–207.

Vygotsky, L. S. (1978). *Mind in society: The development of psychological processes*. Cambridge, MA: Harvard University Press.

20
Play and Mathematics at Ages One to Ten

CONSTANCE KAMII AND YASUHIKO KATO

Mathematics (including arithmetic, algebra, and geometry) is traditionally viewed as part of our cultural heritage that must be transmitted from one generation to another. From a Piagetian point of view, however, mathematics grows out of the logico-mathematical knowledge that each child constructs from within, through his or her own ability to think (Piaget, Inhelder, & Szeminska, 1948/1960; Piaget & Szeminska, 1941/1952). To clarify the nature of mathematics, it is necessary to review the distinction Piaget made among three kinds of knowledge according to their ultimate sources—physical, logico-mathematical, and social-conventional knowledge (1967/1971; 1936/1951).

Physical knowledge is knowledge of objects in the external world. Our knowledge of the color and weight of an object is an example of physical knowledge. Our knowing that a block stays put but a ball may roll away is also an example of physical knowledge, which can be acquired empirically by observation.

Examples of *social-conventional knowledge* are our knowledge of languages, such as English and Spanish, holidays like Thanksgiving, and when to say "Good morning." These were created by convention among people, and the ultimate source of social knowledge is conventions. By contrast, the ultimate source of physical knowledge is objects in the external world.

While physical and social-conventional knowledge have sources outside the individual, *logico-mathematical knowledge* consists of mental relationships that originate in each person's head. If we are presented with a red block and a blue one, for example, we can say that they are different. Each block is observable (physical knowledge), but the difference between them (logico-mathematical knowledge) is not. The proof is that we can also say that the two blocks are similar. If we decide to focus on color, the two objects are different for us, but if we decide to ignore color, the same two blocks become similar. If, on the other hand, we decide to think about the blocks numerically, we can say that there are two. "Different," "similar," and "two" are mental relationships that each person makes, and the ultimate source of logico-mathematical knowledge is each person's head.

If each child mentally creates "two," "three," "four," and so on through his or her own ability to think, each child should be able to coordinate these relationships and create arithmetic. After all, all numbers are created by the operation of +1 (1 + 1 = 2, 2 + 1 = 3, 3 + 1 = 4, and so on). This theory about the nature of logico-mathematical knowledge is supported by countless cross-cultural studies (such as Berry & Dasen, 1974; Dasen, 1977) that proved its universality regardless of nationality, ethnicity, race, or socioeconomic class. The fact that logico-mathematical knowledge originates in each child's head led one of us (CK) to stop using a textbook and workbook in primary mathematics and, instead, provide two kinds of activities--word problems and math games. This way of teaching arithmetic without teaching it in the traditional sense is described in Kamii (1994, 2000, 2004)

The three kinds of knowledge distinguished by Piaget clarify the difference between the traditional view of mathematics and our view based on Piaget's theory. The traditional view is that mathematics is social-conventional knowledge that must be transmitted from one generation to the next. By contrast, our view is that each child can invent mathematics and that the teacher's job is to foster this development from within.

In the preceding discussion, we spoke about physical and logico-mathematical knowledge as if the two developed independently of each other. In reality, the two kinds of knowledge develop together in an inseparable way until the age of about 5 or 6, when the conservation of number (Piaget & Szeminska, 1941/1952) is attained. The conservation of number attests to the differentiation of number as an independent system out of an undifferentiated network of mental relationships.

The inseparable development of physical and logico-mathematical knowledge can often be observed within ten days after birth. Many mothers have reported that, by the time their babies were 10 days old, the babies could tell the difference between a real nipple and a rubber nipple. To become able to make this distinction, babies of course have to come in contact with nipples (physical knowledge, the first column in Figure 20.1), but they also have to categorize "a nipple that feels good" and "one that feels bad" (*classification*, the first column under logico-mathematical knowledge in Figure 20.1). Without this organization, every contact with a nipple would be an independent experience without any relationship to any other experience. This is an example of what Piaget meant when he said that a logico-mathematical framework is indispensable for children's acquisition of physical knowledge.

By age 1, babies are insatiably interested in objects and the relationships they can make with them. Following is an example of what Piaget said about one of his daughters, Lucienne, who was preoccupied with containers, putting things into them, and taking them out. Between 1;2 (28) (one year, 2 months, and 28 days) and 1;3 (6), Lucienne systematically put "grass, earth, pebbles, etc., into all the

	Physical knowledge	Social (conventional) knowledge	Logico-mathematical Knowledge				
			Logico-arithmatical knowledge			Spatio-temporal knowledge	
			Classification	Seriation	Number	Spatial relationships	Temporal relationships
Distinguishing a real nipple from a rubber nipple	X		X				
Putting objects in and out of containers	X		X			X	X
Block building	X	X	X	X	X	X	X
Painting	X	X	X	X	X	X	X
Pretend play	X	X	X	X	X	X	X

Figure 20.1

hollow objects within reach: bowls, pails, boxes, etc. (Piaget, 1937/1954, p. 217)." One day, Lucienne had four or five pebbles in front of her, put them into a bowl one by one, and transferred them into another bowl, one by one. She then transferred these pebbles to another bowl, one by one. Two days later, she piled some metal molds, stones, blades of grass, etc., into a basket, turned it upside down, and dumped everything out all at once.

This is one of the thousands of examples Piaget (1936/1952; 1937/1954; 1945/1951) gave about babies' construction of logico-mathematical knowledge in their play. Lucienne engaged in *classification* (see Figure 20.1) when she collected blades of grass, pebbles, and so on, and looked for hollow objects like bowls, pails, and boxes. Precursors of *number* (see Figure 20.1) could be seen when she transferred the pebbles from one container to another, *one by one*. When she dumped *all of them* out, we could see evidence of *temporal* and *spatial reasoning* (see Figure 20.1). Dumping all the objects out with a single action took much less time than transferring them one by one, and Lucienne figured out that she could do this by turning the basket upside down.

Because space is limited in this chapter, we will focus on arithmetic and not deal with geometry. For arithmetic in grades K through 4 (and beyond), it is possible to conceptualize goals and objectives in terms of aspects of arithmetic such as number and addition. For 1- to 4-year-olds, however, goals and objectives must be conceptualized as the development of logico-mathematical knowledge out of which number will develop. As discussed earlier, babies' and preschoolers' logico-mathematical knowledge is not yet differentiated from their physical knowledge, and their thinking is not yet differentiated into academic subjects like mathematics, science, and social studies. For example, when preschoolers begin to paint, they are engaged not only in art but also in mathematics (two brushes for two colors), science (finding out what happens when colors are mixed and when the finished product is left at school overnight), spatial reasoning (figuring out how paint can run down by itself on the paper on an easel), and representation, which is the foundation for reading and writing. Accordingly, this chapter is divided into two parts—play in relation to the development of logico-mathematical knowledge at ages 1 to 4, and play in relation to arithmetic in grades K through 4.

Play and the Development of Logico-Mathematical Knowledge at Ages One to Four

The importance of the logico-mathematical foundation for number can be seen in a study conducted in two first-grade classrooms in California (Kamii, Rummelsburg, & Kari, 2005). It involved 26 children from low-SES homes who came to first grade without any number concepts. They could count four chips out, but when the teacher hid some of them under her hand asking, "How many am I hiding?" they gave random numbers like "Eight."

Because these 6-year-olds were logico-mathematically at the level of most 3- and 4-year-olds, they were given physical-knowledge games like "Bowling," Ring Toss, and Pick-Up Sticks during the math hour for half of the school year to strengthen their foundation for number. In "Bowling," for example, they were given a tennis ball and 10 empty plastic bottles to arrange in various ways to knock over as many as possible. (A few began to make comments like, "Nine are down because there's only one that's up.") By the middle of the school year, the children gradually demonstrated their ability to play math games such as Piggy Bank. In this game, they had to find two cards that made a total of 5.

By the end of the school year, their ability in mental arithmetic with numbers like 4 + 4 was significantly higher than that of a similar group who had received traditional instruction focusing narrowly on number and addition. The group who played physical-knowledge games was also significantly better in solving word problems like "Let's pretend that I had 12 pieces of candy. If I gave 2 pieces to my mother, 2 pieces to my father, and 2 pieces to my sister, how many pieces would I have left?"

This study confirmed our belief that play in which children *think hard in their own ways with their peers* is superior to lessons and exercises that focus narrowly on number and the addition of small numbers. Logico-mathematical knowledge develops when children *think to solve their own problems and to answer their own questions* (Piaget, 1971/1974). Another way of saying "children think" is to say "they make mental relationships." Since number does not appear as an independent system before the age of 5 or 6 among most middle-class children, we can say that it takes five or six years of mental activity for children to create number concepts.

The early childhood educators who developed the child-development curriculum observed that young children are highly interested in activities like block building, painting, pretend play, listening to stories, raising animals and plants, cooking, sand and water play, and playing with swings and see-saws. Children's interest proves that they are thinking and that the aforementioned activities are therefore developmentally beneficial for them. When an activity becomes too easy, young children go on to something else that is more interesting for them. All these activities can be analyzed from the standpoint of children's development of logico-mathematical knowledge as can be seen in three examples in Figure 20.1 (block building, painting, and pretend play).

As can be seen in Figure 20.1, block building, of course, involves physical knowledge. When children build a hospital or a gas station, social-conventional knowledge comes into play. *Classification* is involved when children look for a triangular block to represent a roof, and *seriation* (the next column) is involved when they look for the longest block, the next longest one, and a short block. When they complain about not having enough blocks because "you took all of them," children engage in *prenumerical* thinking. They make *spatial* and *temporal relationships* (the last two columns) when they choose big and stable blocks first for the bottom of a tall tower and then choose smaller ones for the top part.

Two kinds of play especially appeal to young children and encourage them to *think* and to build logico-mathematical knowledge. One is what we call physical-knowledge activities (Kamii & DeVries, 1978/1993), and the other is group games (Kamii & DeVries, 1980/1996). Each is discussed below.

Physical-Knowledge Activities

In a physical-knowledge activity, children act on objects, mentally and physically, (1) to see what happens, or (2) to produce a desired effect. Dropping an object from a high chair to see what happens is an example of the former. By varying the point of release, babies take pleasure in making *correspondences* between where they let the object go and where it lands. An example of the latter (producing a desired effect) is the use of a lever to make a beanbag fly up (see Figure 20.2).

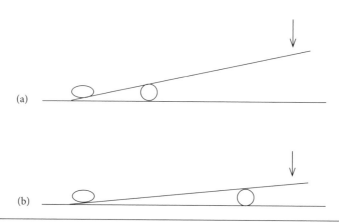

Figure 20.2 Two ways of making a beanbag fly up.

Lever

A lever can be made by laying a wooden board (60 cm long, 12 cm wide) on a tube (30 cm long, 5 cm in diameter). By putting a beanbag on the down end of the board and quickly pushing down the up end, the child can make the beanbag fly up. These actions are easy for 4-year-olds to imitate but very hard for young 2-year-olds (Kamii, Miyakawa, & Kato, in preparation). Most 2- and 3-year-olds figure out that the end of the board to push down is the end that is up, but where to put the beanbag is much harder to decide. Some put it over the tube; others randomly put it at various places on the board; and still others put it on the up end of the board (the same end that they push down).

This kind of physical-knowledge activity, in which children act on objects to produce a desired effect, especially encourages them to think because they can tell immediately whether or not they were successful. If they are unsuccessful, they try to figure out what to do differently to produce a better outcome.

When this activity becomes too easy by age 4, a larger tube and a longer board can be used so that children can jump on the board to make a large beanbag fly up 5 feet or more. In this situation, children have the possibility of thinking about the position of the board in relation to the tube as can be seen in Figure 20.2. After much trial and error, some conclude that the arrangement in Figure 20.2(a) makes the beanbag fly up much higher than the one in Figure 20.2(b).

Block Building and Rolling a Cylinder Down an Incline

In earlier publications, we emphasized the interrelated way in which various aspects of logico-mathematical knowledge develop. In a block-building activity (Kamii, Miyakawa, & Kato, 2004), for example, we gave 20 blocks of various shapes and sizes to 1-, 2-, 3-, and 4-year-olds and individually asked them to build "something tall." One of our findings was that as soon as a child made the *spatial relationship* between a triangular block used as a "roof" and a flat block placed on it, most 2- and 3-year-olds avoided the use of all the triangular blocks. This is an example of new *categories* ("triangular blocks" and "all the others") children made as a result of making a new *spatial relationship*. In another study, we individually encouraged 1- to 3-year-olds to imitate the rolling of a cylindrical block down an incline (Miyakawa, Kamii, & Kato, 2005). The children were given cylindrical and cubic bloks, and until the age of 2 years and 4 months, most of them began by indiscriminately putting both kinds of blocks on the incline and pushed the cubes to make them go down. However, as soon as they made the *spatial relationship* between the roundness of a block and the phenomenon of rolling, the children made the *categories* of "cylinders" and "cubes" and stopped putting cubes on the incline.

Many curricula for young children recommend sorting activities like putting circles and squares in two separate groups. A physical-knowledge activity is much better for the development of logico-mathematical knowledge because *classification* grows naturally out of other mental relationships children make while they play. Sorting activities are not harmful, but children construct richer, more complex mental relationships while they play, with much more pleasure and enthusiasm. In rolling a cylinder down an incline, for example, they begin to vary the angle of the cylinder's position in relation to the fall line before releasing it, so that the cylinder will roll along the fall line and continue to roll on the floor and hit a distant target.

Traditional child development curricula often include activities that resemble physical-knowledge activities. For example, some child development texts recommend a pendulum activity in which children try to hit a target. Such an activity is often found in a chapter on science. Our use of a pendulum is different in that our objective is not that children learn how a pendulum (or a lever) works. Our objective is the development of logico-mathematical knowledge rather than the learning of "science." Therefore, it is much more important for us that children *think and invent new problems to solve* than whether or not they learn to hit a target (or to make a beanbag fly up). Many other examples of physical-knowledge activities can be found in Kamii and DeVries (1978/1993), DeVries (2005), and DeVries, Zan, Hildebrandt, Edmiaston, and Sales (2002).

Group Games

We use the term *group games* in the following sense: "In games,…there are prescribed acts, subject to rules,…and the action proceeds…until it culminates in a given climax; which generally consists of a victory of skill, speed or strength (*Encyclopedia Americana,* 1957, p. 266)."

Some games like bowling, dodge Ball, ring toss, marbles, billiards, and hockey are aiming games that extend physical-knowledge activities (Kamii & DeVries, 1980/1996). Some like musical chairs are parallel-role games in which all the players compete by doing the same thing. Others like hide and seek are complementary-role games in which one player tries to do something, and the others try to prevent his or her success.

Children *think* especially hard when they have to make a decision. In physical-knowledge activities, they think hard to decide what to change to produce a desired effect. In group games, too, they constantly make decisions. In hide and seek, for example, they have to decide where to hide. When they become the seeker, they have to decide where to look first, second, and so on to find the others.

Young children at different levels of development play the same game very differently. musical chairs, hide and seek, and a card game are discussed below to illustrate how much they can develop logico-mathematically by playing these games.

Musical Chairs

In this game, chairs are arranged in a circle or a line, and the players march around the chairs while music is played. When the music stops, all the children run to find a chair to sit on. Since there is one chair less than the number of children, one of the children does not get a chair. This child and a chair are removed from the game before the next round, and the game continues in this way, until the last two players compete to sit on the last remaining chair.

This is the conventional way of playing musical chairs, but this conventional way does not make sense to children up to about 4 years of age for two reasons: (1) Four-year-olds are cognitively incapable of competing in games, and (2) they do not yet have number concepts and cannot understand the teacher's explanation about why there will always be a child who does not get a chair. The teacher can ask all the children in the group to sit in a chair and explain that Suzy did not get a chair because there is one more child than chairs. Regardless of how many times the teacher repeats this explanation, 3- and 4-year-olds usually cannot understand it because number is logico-mathematical knowledge that cannot be made understandable empirically or through verbal explanation.

With 3- and 4-year-olds, therefore, it is best to play musical chairs with as many chairs as children. Such a modification seems nonsensical to adults, but the fact that 3- and 4-year-olds are incapable of competing in any competitive game reinforces the desirability of this modification. Three- and 4-year-olds are usually so egocentric that they are interested only in what *they* are doing, and it does not occur to them to compare their performance with that of others. If they are not interested in comparing their own performance with that of other players, they cannot possibly be interested in winning in a game.

At ages 3 and 4, therefore, the logico-mathematical value of musical chairs does not lie in figuring out how to be close to a chair when the music stops. When 3- and 4-year-olds play musical chairs without competition, they still have to decide what to do when the music starts and stops, and what to do if one does not find a chair immediately. But the greatest value of musical chairs for these children may lie in deciding how to set the chairs up before the game. The teacher does well to ask questions like "How shall we arrange the chairs?" and "How can we make sure we have just enough chairs for everybody?"

Hide and Seek

There are many ways of playing hide and seek, but one way is to have "It" cover his or her eyes and count to a number agreed upon while the others hide themselves. "It" then tries to find the other players, and the last person found is the winner, who becomes the next "It."

Three-year-olds are so egocentric that they often "hide" by merely covering their eyes! They think that if *they* cannot see the other people, other people cannot see them either. They may also hide under a table, unaware that most of their body parts are visible. They are not only egocentric in these ways but so uncompetitive that they cannot wait to be found and yell, "I'm here! Come find me!"

To decide when and how to intervene truly requires judgment and knowledge of young children. At the beginning, it is best to let children play in their own ways and study what makes sense to 2- and 3-year-olds. Their ways of playing may seem nonsensical to us, but they are likely to be thinking seriously in their own ways. For example, they often try to stuff themselves into a carton that is much too small for them and gradually make the *categories* of "spaces that are big enough" and "spaces that are too small."

When children have played hide and seek many times, adult intervention may be desirable to encourage more thinking. For example, if "It" finds one child first, the teacher might ask "It," "How did you know that Johnny was there?" Johnny can benefit from answers like, "He was there last time; so I figured he might be there again," or "His shoes were sticking out."

Animal Rummy

An example of a card game that encourages thinking is animal rummy, which a group of teachers in Japan modified to maximize the logico-mathematical thinking of 4-year-olds. Animal rummy conventionally uses 36 cards showing 9 different kinds of animals (4 monkeys, 4 elephants, 4 cows, etc.; Kamii & DeVries, 1980/1996, p. 65). Six cards are dealt to each player. The remaining deck is turned face down, with the top card beside it, face up, to start the discard pile. The object of the game is to make two sets of three identical cards. Each player begins his or her turn by taking a card either from the discard pile or from the top of the deck. He or she then tries to make a set, if possible, and then discards a card on the discard pile. The person who makes two sets of three identical cards first is the winner.

This game is good for young children's *classificatory thinking*, *numerical thinking*, and *temporal thinking*, but the group of teachers mentioned earlier modified it in the following way: (1) The group is limited to three players so that children can be mentally more active without having to wait for a fourth player to have a turn; (2) Seven cards are dealt to each player instead of six so that each player will have more choices; (3) It is specified that each player align the seven cards received, face up, in front of him- or herself. Making everybody's cards visible made it possible for each player to figure out (a) which animal each player is trying to make a set of and (b) who will be helped if one discards a particular card.

Four-year-olds' ability to make logico-mathematical relationships is limited, and Figure 20.3 shows how two of them decided to take a card (either from the discard pile or the face-down deck). Figure 20.3(a) shows that a low-level 4-year-old decided to take a card from the face-down deck when he had two pigs, and a third pig was on the discard pile! His low level can also be seen in the arrangement of his cards. Neither his two pigs nor his three monkeys were grouped together *spatially*.

By contrast, the 4-year-old in Figure 20.3(b) had grouped two pigs and two dogs together. When he saw a pig on the discard pile, he took it immediately and completed a set of three.

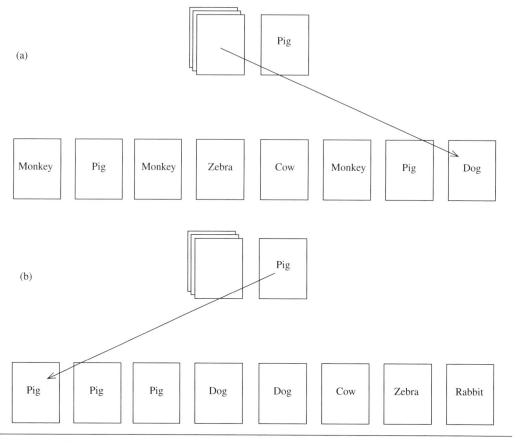

Figure 20.3 Two children's ways of deciding which card to take.

Figure 20.4 shows how two 4-year-olds discarded a card at the end of their turns. Figure 20.4(a) shows a low-level child who discarded one of his two monkeys when it would have been more advantageous to have discarded his rabbit, cow, zebra, or dog. This child was single-mindedly trying to make a set of three pigs and could not think of anything else.

By contrast, the 4-year-old in Figure 20.4(b) had grouped two cows, two pigs, and two zebras together and was all set to discard either his monkey or his dog. He glanced at the next player's cards, saw that his neighbor was collecting monkeys, and decided to discard his dog. This decision illustrates the advantage of playing animal rummy by making all the players' cards visible. Low-level 4-year-olds do not pay any attention to the next player's cards, but higher-level children begin to make *temporal relationships* and are careful not to help the other players.

Play and the Learning of Arithmetic in Grades K through Four

The instructional program described in Kamii's earlier works (1994, 2000, 2004), uses two kinds of activities instead of a textbook and workbookG(1) word problems and (2) math games. Half of the math hour is generally spent on word problems, and the other half is spent playing math games. Since word problems are beyond the scope of this chapter, we will not discuss them in this section.

As stated earlier, every child is capable of *inventing* arithmetic because number concepts are *created* by each child. This is why kindergartners can play path games if they are taught only the social–conventional knowledge about taking turns and advancing by the number of steps indicated by a die.

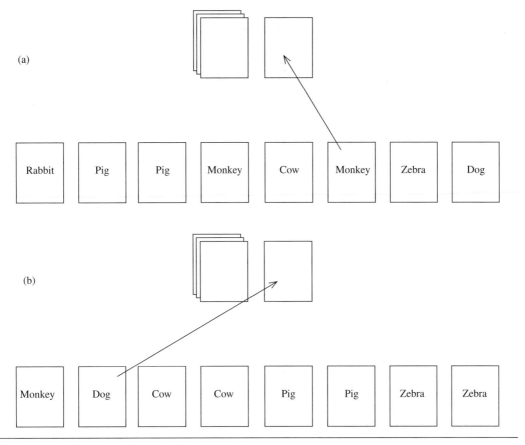

Figure 20.4 Two children's ways of deciding which card to discard.

When they can play path games well with one die, we give a second die and ask, "What can you do with two dice?" Some children immediately know what to do, but others continue to play with one die. Sooner or later, everybody figures out how to play with two dice.

All children begin to add numbers by counting the dots on the dice. After some time, however, they begin to remember sums and stop counting the dots. The cognitively advanced children quickly come to remember the easier sums (e.g., 2 + 1, 3 + 1, 4 + 1, 2 + 2, 3 + 3, and 5 + 5), while the less advanced students continue to count the dots. As they play board games and card games with small numbers day after day, most of them commit all the sums up to 6 + 6 to memory. By the end of first grade, almost all middle-class children come to remember these sums, plus many others such as 7 + 2, 9 + 9, and 2 + 8 (Kamii, 2000).

Card Games

Space permits the description of only three card games here, and the reader is referred to the three aforementioned books for more examples.

Tens with Nine Cards Regular playing cards up to nine are used in this game. The top nine cards are arranged in the middle of the table as shown in Figure 20.5, and the object of the game is to find two cards that make 10. If it were your turn now, you could take 7 + 3, 1 + 9, and 4 + 6. For the next player's turn, you would need to replace the six cards you took with six new cards from the drawing pile. The winner is the person who collected more pairs than anybody else.

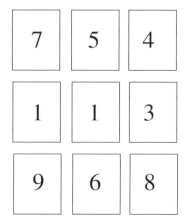

Figure 20.5 The arrangement of cards in "Tens with Nine Cards."

Salute! This is a popular three-person game that can be played with addition and subtraction or with multiplication and division. We present the version with multiplication and division. The cards are dealt to two of the three players, who hold the cards received in one hand, face down. As they both say "Salute!" the two players take the top cards of their respective stacks and hold it next to their ears in such a way that they cannot see their own card but can see the opponent's card. The third player, who can see both cards, multiplies the two numbers and says "Thirty-six," for example. Each of the other two tries to figure out the number on his or her own card by looking at the opponent's card. If the opponent's card shows a 4, the other card must show a 9. The first person to announce the number on his or her card can keep both cards. The game continues until all the cards have been used, and the person who collected more cards is the winner.

This game can be modified according to the children's level of mastery. At the beginning, it is best to use only cards up to four or five so that the players can master the easy combinations before going on to six, then to seven, and so on.

Twenty-Four (Suntext International, 1989) These cards come with three levels of difficulty. Each card has four numbers on it, and the object of the game is to make 24 by using all four of the numbers once, with addition, subtraction, multiplication, or division. An example of a card at the easiest level has 2, 2, 4, and 6 on it. (A possible solution is $4 \times 6 = 24$, $2 : 2 = 1$, $24 \times 1 = 24$.) An example at the middle level of difficulty has 6, 5, 4, and 4, and an example at the most difficult level has 9, 6, 1, and 4. The first person to find a solution and prove its correctness can keep the card. The winner is the player who collects the most cards.

"Twenty-Four" has many versions for many different grade levels that come in different boxes. The easiest version requires only single-digit addition and subtraction. Other games involve multiplication and division with single- and double-digit numbers. For ages 11 and up, one box involves fractions and decimals, and for ages 12 and up there is a box for integers and one for algebra and exponents.

The Value of Games over Worksheets and Timed Tests

Repetition is necessary for mastery of all the operations, but games are much better than worksheets for many reasons. The first advantage is that children play games for the pleasure of playing them while they fill out worksheets to obey the teacher. We never say to children that they *have to* remember sums or products, but remembering happens naturally as the students play math games day after day. They want to play well, and this motivation comes from within.

A second advantage of games is that feedback is immediate in games because children supervise each other. By contrast, worksheets are usually returned the next day, and children cannot remember and do not care about what they did yesterday.

Third, when worksheets are used, truth is decided by the teacher, and children get the message that truth can come only from the teacher. In a game, by contrast, the players decide whether an answer is correct. If a child says that $4 + 3 = 6$, for example, other children try to convince him or her that another answer makes better sense. In logico-mathematical knowledge, children are bound to arrive at truth if they argue long enough because there is absolutely nothing arbitrary in logico-mathematical knowledge.

Fourth, having to write answers interferes with the possibility of remembering sums. Children are much more likely to remember sums when they are free to think "2, 3, = 5," for example, without having to write "5." Some first graders have to take time to think to make a "5" look different from an "S."

Our fifth and final point is that children do not develop sociomorally by sitting alone filling out worksheets. They are well behaved when worksheets are used, but working alone precludes the possibility of sociomoral development. In games, by contrast, children have to interact with others, make decisions together, and learn to resolve conflicts.

Not all teachers give timed tests to encourage children to memorize sums, differences, and products, but many students dread this activity. Too many children memorize sums and products for timed tests but resort to counting when they solve word problems. Children will know sums and products much more solidly if they are allowed to play math games day after day for the pleasure of playing them.

Conclusion

Early childhood educators have long advocated play in the classroom, and many of them have strongly resisted behavioral objectives and direct instruction. We feel, however, that the time has come to analyze play more precisely on the basis of a rigorous scientific theory about how children acquire knowledge and moral values. This chapter focused only on arithmetic and logico-mathematical knowledge, and we would like to point out in conclusion that teachers can make an enormous difference in children's socioemotional development.

To know how to encourage children to think logico-mathematically from one moment to the next, teachers need to have deep and precise knowledge about how this thinking develops. In this chapter, we gave only some examples of what teachers can do. Many more activities and situations remain to be studied to take early childhood education to the next stage of its development.

References

Berry, J. W., & Dasen, P. R. (1974). *Culture and cognition: Readings in cross-cultural psychology.* London: Methuen.

Dasen, P. R. (1977). *Piagetian psychology: Cross-cultural contributions.* New York: Gardner.

DeVries, R. (2005). *Ramps and pathways* (DVD). Cedar Falls, IA: Regents' Center for Early Developmental Education, University of Northern Iowa.

DeVries, R., Zan, B., Hildebrandt, C., Edmiaston, R., & Sales, C. (2002). *Developing constructivist early childhood curriculum.* New York: Teachers College Press.

Encyclopedia Americana (1957). New York: Americana Corporation.

Kamii, C. (1994). *Young children continue to reinvent arithmetic—3rd grade.* New York: Teachers College Press.

Kamii, C. (2000). *Young children reinvent arithmetic.* New York: Teachers College Press. (Original work published 1985.)

Kamii, C. (2004). *Young children continue to reinvent arithmetic—2nd grade.* New York: Teachers College Press. (Original work published 1989.)

Kamii, C., & DeVries, R. (1993). *Physical knowledge in preschool education.* New York: Teachers College Press. (Original work published 1978)

Kamii, C., & DeVries, R. (1996). *Group games in early education.* Washington, D.C.: National Association for the Education of Young Children. (Original work published 1980)

Kamii, C., Miyakawa Y., & Kato, Y. (2004). The development of logico-mathematical knowledge in a block-building activity at ages 1–4. *Journal of Research in Childhood Education, 19*(1), 44–57.

Kamii, C., Rummelsburg, J., & Kari, A. (2005). Teaching arithmetic to low-performing, low-SES first graders. *Journal of Mathematical Behavior, 24,* 39–50.

Kamii, C., Miyakawa, Y., & Kato, T. (in preparation). The development of logico-mathematical thinking in trying to make a lever work at ages 1–4.

Miyakawa, Y., Kamii, C., & Nagahiro, M. (2005). The development of logico-mathematical thinking at ages 1–3 in play with blocks and an incline. *Journal of Research in Childhood Education, 19*(4), 292–301.

Piaget, J. (1951). *Play, dreams, and imitation in childhood.* New York: Norton. (Original work published 1945)

Piaget, J. (1952). *The origins of intelligence in children.* New York: International Universities Press. (Original work published 1936)

Piaget, J. (1954). *The construction of reality in the child.* New York: Basic Books. (Original work published 1937)

Piaget, J. (1971). *Biology and knowledge.* Chicago: University of Chicago Press. (Original work published 1967)

Piaget, J. (1974). *Understanding causality.* New York: Norton. (Original work published 1971)

Piaget, J., Inhelder, B., & Szeminska, A. (1960). *The child's conception of geometry.* New York: Basic Books. (Original work published 1948)

Piaget, J., & Szeminska, A. (1952). *The child's conception of number.* London: Routledge and Kegan Paul. (Original work published 1941)

Suntex International. (1989). *Twenty-four.* Easton, PA: Suntex International.

21
Scientific Inquiry and Exploratory Representational Play

CHRISTOPHER R. WOLFE, R. HAYS CUMMINS, AND CHRISTOPHER A. MYERS

Of Play and Science

At first blush, it may appear that science and play represent two extremes on a continuum. Science, for example, is often characterized by precision of measurement, rigorous methods, mathematical formulations, and skepticism. Play, on the other hand, is typically regarded as carefree, spontaneous, and fun. Upon reflection, however, one soon discovers many relationships between play and science. As readers of these pages will surely recognize, both play and science are complex, multifaceted human activities incorporating sociocultural, cognitive, kinesthetic, and affective dimensions. Science, or more accurately, the sciences, address phenomena as different in scale and substance as astronomy, psychology, and atomic physics. Scientists employ a range of research methods including dissection, field observation, and laboratory experimentation, and construct scientific theories ranging from mathematical models to reliable qualitative generalizations. In a similar vein, play includes games with rules, sociodramatic make-believe, and "roughhousing." As authors approaching the theme of play and science, our task is more than one of identifying and cataloging the web of connections between various aspects of science and play. Instead, we will argue that shared systematic inquiry is the heart of science, and that exploratory representational play in middle childhood plays an important role in the making of a scientist. Toward this end we will speculate about the relationship between scientific inquiry and exploratory representational play from a number of theoretical perspectives, share the musing of an active scientist on the role of play in his development, and consider the educational implications of science play for children.

Research on Play and Science

The literature on science and play is both varied and interesting. One branch of "basic" research examines the relationship between aspects of play and performance on scientific achievement tests (e.g., Cooper & Robinson, 1989) and other tasks. For example, Smith and Dutton (1979) examined the relative usefulness of play opportunities and direct training on 4-year-old children's problem solving. They found that play and training produced approximately equivalent direct transfer for a standard transfer task. However, children who had play opportunities were faster and needed fewer hints than those with direct training in learning an innovative task. In a study of kindergarten children, Li (1978) found that free play and make-believe play yielded more divergent thinking than a control condition on a task requiring the generation of alternative uses of a paper clip. In a transfer task, make-believe play produced more divergent thinking than free play. Similarly, Pepler and Ross (1981) compared the effects of children's playing with convergent and divergent materials (form boards and puzzles) on subsequent convergent and divergent problem solving. They found that the divergent play group performed better on divergent tasks, and the convergent play group employed more strategy-based moves in solving convergent problems.

Tracy (1987) conducted a thoughtful review of the literature on the relationship between spatial abilities, scientific achievement, toy playing habits, and gender roles. She found indirect evidence that socially stereotyped "boy toys" might promote spatial abilities that are employed extensively in some kinds of scientific thinking. In subsequent research, Tracy (1990) found a positive correlation between spatial ability and science achievement scores. However, she failed to find the hypothesized relationships between science achievement and gender, sex role orientation, or toy-playing habits. Thus, although there appears to be a "logical relationship" between gender, toy playing, and science achievement, an empirical relationship has not yet been adequately demonstrated.

Taken collectively these studies suggest a relationship between play, problem solving, and science achievement. While educators must be careful to avoid promoting sex-stereotyped toy-playing habits, there are strong reasons to believe that play is a powerful and underutilized vehicle for elementary science education.

Applying Play to Science Education

Another body of "applied" literature addresses play-oriented curriculum reforms in elementary science education. For example, Fine and Josephson (1984) describe science play activities for kindergarten children in the United States, and von Aufshnaiter and Schwedes (1989) discuss play orientation in elementary physics education in Germany. In a review of the literature on play and science, Severeide and Pizzini (1984) argue that "When teachers incorporate guided play into science activities, children develop fluent and flexible problem-solving skills. In addition, playful learning also tends to increase creativity and general cognitive achievement, and improves aptitude scores," (p. 60). In a similar vein, Henniger (1987) argues that learning science and mathematics through play promotes curiosity, motivation to learn, and divergent thinking. Wassermann (1988) presents a play-debrief-replay model of elementary science education. The first stage is "play" during which the teacher creates the conditions for focused scientific inquiry. Teachers provide materials conducive to hands-on investigations and try to create an atmosphere that promotes generating and testing hypotheses, observation, recording findings, and evaluating results. The next stage is debriefing, in which children and teachers reflect on their experience. "The purpose of Debriefing is to *help pupils extract meaning from their experiences* (Wassermann, 1988, p. 233). Finally, students replay with the same materials to extend their initial inquiries and replicate earlier discoveries. While not a panacea, we believe that the play-debrief-replay curriculum model captures one of the key element of science—the spirit of inquiry.

The Spirit of Inquiry

We believe that *shared systematic inquiry* is at the heart of the scientific endeavor. Scientific inquiry is systematic in the sense that it is well planned and well reasoned, and shared in that it occurs in a highly refined social context. Although science is often a solitary (and even lonely) enterprise, the "rules of evidence" of the scientific community, rather than the whims of the individual scientist, guide scientific inquiry. Moreover, presenting one's results and interpretations to the scientific community is always an important part of the process. Shared systematic inquiry is central to domains as diverse as theoretical physics and experimental psychology. The spirit of inquiry places curiosity and questioning at the heart of what it means to be a scientist. Although scientists spend a great deal of time studying the work of others, a distinguishing characteristic of science is asking questions to which no one has the definitive answer. For a scientist, inquiry means asking questions of nature, and getting answers from empirical evidence.

Exploratory Representational Play

As we have already suggested, play is a construct that subsumes a wide range of behaviors. Others have provided thoughtful definitions of play (e.g., Fromberg & Bergen, 1998). For our purposes, it is sufficient to say that the term play describes activities that are internally motivated, self-directed, spirited, and characterized by some degree of divergent "as if" thinking (Spodek & Saracho, 1987). Although we do not deny that sports, board games, and make-believe may exercise some role in the development of a scientist, our focus on science as a process of shared systematic inquiry leads us to *exploratory representational play* in the latency years (roughly 8 to 12 years old) as a pivotal experience in the development of a scientist.

Defining Exploratory Representational Play

It has been said that psychologists would rather use each other's toothbrushes than use each other's terminology. We add to the fracas by coining the term *exploratory representational play* (ERP). By this we mean intrinsically motivated, self-directed explorations with a significant symbolic or representational dimension. In considering what we mean by ERP it is useful to distinguish it from related concepts. Exploratory representational play is not identical to exploration. Children and adults often engage in explorations that are serious, extrinsically motivated, other-directed, or otherwise outside of what we call play. Eight- to 12-year-old children are capable of engaging in shared systematic inquiry—science. However, shared systematic inquiry need not be "play" in any of the ways described above. Exploratory representational play is different from the exploratory play common among infants and toddlers. Exploratory representational play is primarily goal-directed and cognitive, rather than kinesthetic in nature. Exploratory representational play is representational in the sense of mental representations that are personally meaningful to the individual, and may or may not manifest themselves as drawings or stories.

I (Wolfe) remember an afternoon when I was 9 years old that provides an example of ERP. My cousin and I had been collecting butterflies for some time, and got the notion that we would like to find the chrysalis of a Monarch butterfly. Knowing what we knew about their habits, we explored unfamiliar woods and fields asking ourselves "What do we know about Monarchs?" We recalled that they make their chrysalis on Milkweed plants, and learned to identify Milkweed first by breaking the leaves of a likely suspect (the sap looks and feels like Elmer's glue—great fun). From there, we could easily identify Milkweeds at a distance from their leaves and pods, and constrained our search to fields rather than the woods. We spent hours looking for chrysalises, and if memory serves, found two. We became completely absorbed in the hunt, losing awareness of ourselves as "self" or ego. Although the goal of finding a chrysalis guided our actions that afternoon, our selection and maintenance of that goal was playful. It may seem paradoxical to adults, but although the goal was at the forefront of our thinking, and directed our actions and conversations, the goal itself was less important than the process. Indeed, had the goal not sustained our play, I believe we probably would have found another—and one we may have clung to just as earnestly. Moreover, if someone had fulfilled our goal for us, by handing us a chrysalis, I believe we would have been secretly disappointed.

Exploratory representational play need not take the form of play-in-the-woods (although those were important experiences for these authors). Richard Feynman, the Nobel Prize winning physicist, writes of the laboratory he set up when he was 11 or 12 made from an old wooden packaging box. There he would create electric lamp banks, fix broken radios, and dabble with electrical gadgets. He recalls spending an afternoon trying to find a burned-out resistor in his mother's friend's radio, and notes, "I finally fixed it because I had, and still have, persistence. Once I get on a puzzle, I can't get off. If my mother's friend had said, 'Never mind, it's too much work,' I'd have blown my top, because, I wanted to beat this damn thing, as long as I've gone this far" (Feynman, 1985, p. 9). As we will argue below, ERP is really more closely associated with developing minds than fixing radios.

Theoretical Perspectives on ERP

Exploratory representational play is not the predominate mode of play for older children (see Bergen, 1988, p. 64 for a clear portrait of developmental trends in play). Yet we believe that ERP plays a key role in the development of a scientist. Here we will briefly speculate about the significance of ERP from five theoretical perspectives; Piagetian theory, constructivism, fuzzy-trace theory, Vygotsky's theory, and Csikszentmihayli's notion of flow. In doing so, we are aware of important distinctions and contradictions between these perspectives. However, we believe that each provides a useful lens through which to view the relationship between exploratory representational play in children and shared systematic inquiry in adults.

Piagetian Theory

Assimilation and accommodation are the "twin engines" of intellectual development from a Piagetian perspective. Assimilation refers to processes of incorporating experiences into existing mental frameworks (schema), and accommodation refers to processes of refining schema to suit experiences that do not easily fit into existing schema. Although most of the exploratory play of infants and toddlers consists of assimilation (Piaget, 1962), we believe that ERP is, for the most part, play with accommodation. Exploratory representational play may be characterized as exploring to change one's representation of the world. Trumbull (1990) describes scientists as "people who play with ideas in order to change the complex into the simple" (in Goldhaber, 1994, p. 26). Much the same could be said of ERP. While some Piagetians might argue that ERP is not play at all, we would argue that the "play" comes from playfully selecting goals that challenge existing schema, and from the joy of exploration.

Constructivism

Constructivism represents another useful theoretical lens. From a constructivist perspective, people build mental representations of the world, which serve as the bases of beliefs and actions. Learning is thus a process of constructing mental frameworks, rather than recording facts. A psychologist argues that "effective learning depends on the intentions, self-monitoring, elaborations, and constructions of the individual learner" (Resnick, 1989, p. 2). With the possible exception of self-monitoring, these elements are characteristics of ERP. In ERP, the child constructs and elaborates cognitive structures through the process of exploration. Indeed ERP is "no fun" if everything is known, or readily knowable. For example, a child engaged in the exploratory representational play of hunting for snakes may prefer looking in new places, or for new species, once she or he has reliably mastered a particular situation. These same tendencies are the mental habits of a scientist.

This relationship between scientific inquiry and exploratory representational play highlights weaknesses in traditional methods of instruction, and indicates the importance of discovery-oriented learning in science education (Bruner, 1966; Cummins & Myers, 1992). We agree with Albert Einstein that "it is in fact nothing short of a miracle that modern methods of instruction have not entirely strangled the holy curiosity of inquiry.... It is a very grave mistake to think that the enjoyment of seeing and searching can be promoted by means of coercion and a sense of duty," (quoted in Henniger, 1987, p. 169).

Fuzzy-Trace Theory

Fuzzy-trace theory emphasizes the importance of "getting the gist of it." A relatively new perspective, fuzzy-trace theory has important ramifications for cognitive processes such as learning, reasoning, and memory, and enjoys strong empirical support (Brainerd & Reyna, 1990a, 1990b; Reyna, 1991; Reyna & Brainerd, 1989, 1995; Wolfe, 1995; Wolfe, Reyna, & Brainerd, 2005).

> The basic claim is that when information is encoded, global gist-like patterns, impressions, and essences are encoded along with verbatim information. The result is a multifaceted fuzzy-to-verbatim representation of information. Individual knowledge items are represented along a continuum such that vague, fuzzy-traces coexist with more precise verbatim representations. Moreover, people exhibit a strong preference to reason with the vaguest gist-like representations allowable for a given task. (Wolfe, 1995, p. 86)

Research on cognitive development suggests that young children initially reason with verbatim representations, and as they develop, gain an ability to reason with increasingly fuzzy representations (Reyna & Brainerd, 1991). From a fuzzy-trace perspective, we speculate that exploratory representative play facilitates the encoding of useful and meaningful gist by creating tasks with "the right mix" of familiar and novel components. ERP seems ideally suited for creating and refining intuitions (gist) because it puts children into playful positions of attempting tasks where existing intuitions and verbatim representations are inadequate. Although science is a matter of precision, scientific insight and understanding require the development of useful and appropriate intuitions.

Vygotskian Theory

In recent years, developmental theories constructed by the Russian psychologist Lev Vygotsky in the 1930s have become increasingly influential in the United States. "A basic premise of Vygotsky's theory is that all uniquely human, higher forms of mental activity are jointly constructed and transferred to children through dialogues with other people" (Beck, 1994, p. 30). A key concept in Vygotsky's theory is the "zone of proximal development," which refers to the set of cognitive tasks a child cannot yet perform alone, but which can be completed by the child with a little help from adults or older children. By working on tasks in the zone of proximal development with older children and adults, children create a "cognitive scaffolding" that enables learning and development. Our experience is that ERP is often, although not always, an activity shared with others. We speculate that exploratory representational play creates cognitive scaffolding, because it is generally conducted in a zone of proximal development. Although some Vygotskians may disagree, we speculate that exploratory representational play encourages children to play at tasks at the edges of their current competencies, and thus promotes development—even in the absence of interactions with older peers.

Theory of Flow

Thus far, we have discussed ERP primarily in cognitive terms. Yet we best remember the *feeling* of exploratory representational play. ERP is accompanied with a raw sense of wonder and a deep connection to nature and exploration. Sadly, this feeling of connection is difficult to reproduce in adulthood.

However, on occasion, scientists do feel immersed in the process of discovery. This experience has been characterized as one of "flow" (Csikszentmihayli, 1979, 1990; Csikszentmihayli & LeFever, 1989). Flow is a condition in which task and talent are in harmony. People experiencing flow find their work "takes their full concentration, they feel in control, they lack self-consciousness, and they have goals that lead to immediate feedback" (Bergen, 1988, p. 57).

It is interesting to note that immediate feedback and the same feelings of concentration, control, and self-consciouslessness also characterize the feeling of exploratory representational play. We speculate that these feelings in ERP often motivate children to become scientists. However, we believe that they may do something more. Experiencing the feeling of flow in childhood ERP may be a necessary prerequisite for experiencing flow in adult scientific inquiry. The joy in matching talent to task may well be born of childhood experience. Just as the spirit of inquiry is at the heart of science, it may be that flow is at the heart of the spirit of inquiry.

On Play, Science, and Salvation: Dr. Cummins Reflects—What Takes the Fun Out of It?

If science and play hold in common a sense of wonder and a passion for discovery, why is science education often perceived as tedious and dehumanizing? From our earlier discussions of exploratory representational play, should not scientists and science students feel blessed by the uncommon opportunity to shape their lives around their own questions? In the ideal world, science has many elements of play. Even the rules of research would seem to support fun, just as the rules kids create make their games more satisfying. But for many, play and science exist in separate worlds. Without a sense of play, science may no longer seem worth doing. We are concerned when practicing scientists become disenchanted. Even worse is when children lose heart. How does science lose its sense of play?

Using the same characteristics that define exploratory representational play, we contend that for science education to harness the power of play it must, to some extent, be internally motivated, be characterized by some degree of divergent "as if" thinking, and be personally meaningful. We present three related characteristics of science education that undermine play, then we suggest possible solutions. These three characteristics are intriguing for they may be healthy, even essential, in small doses, but they become drawbacks when they dominate the spirit of inquiry. We will refer to these obstructions to the "flow" of play as "clogs."

Clog 1: Duty and Other Extrinsic Expectations

When external demands become too great, internal motivation is compromised and play becomes work. For science students, duty includes homework that is not personally relevant, rigid expectations from parents and teachers, and grades. Memorizing the bones of the body or the table of periodic elements, for example, would be a meaningless experience for most children if taught without regard for their own interests and understandings. Young investigators are often asked to sacrifice the spirit of inquiry to outside requirements.

Clog 2: Overspecialization and Isolation

Over time, the topics of science have tended to grow narrower and the possibility of meaningful exchanges between professionals—even in related subdisciplines—have grown more remote. This overspecialization has, unfortunately, spilled over into elementary science education. Because personal meaning is derived from a full spectrum of experience, overspecialization and isolation can make it difficult for children to connect their own questions and interests with the curriculum. For example, addressing the question "why is the grass green and the sky blue" requires one to draw upon and integrate a range of scientific disciplines including physics, biochemistry, and the psychology of perception. Overspecialization thus shuts off a wide range of questions that children wish to explore. When the sciences are taught in isolation the spirit of inquiry may be compromised.

Clog 3: Objectivism

Without adequate outlets for subjective exploration, science becomes a poor vehicle for the flow of play. Children who are taught that science is purely objective might reasonably conclude that science has limited ability to inform their lives. This problem is particularly apparent among children who are not part of mainstream culture (Cajete, 1995). For example, when children are asked to write up lab reports (already a rarity) they are generally asked to exclude their own motivations and feelings. This undermines enthusiasm for the spirit of inquiry. Objectivism reduces science to a collection of uninteresting facts rather than a fully human process of creating knowledge.

Antidotes for Change

For creating an environment that supports exploratory representational play, it is important to allow children to pursue and communicate their own investigations. Children naturally wonder where rainbows come from, what smoke is made of, why the sky is blue. Children ask great questions, yet until their questions and investigations are given credibility, children will not perceive themselves as part of the community of science. By writing of their inquiries, explorations, and affective experiences to their peers, children may come to see themselves as fellow investigators, challenging the traditional role of the scientist as a distant source of facts. Peer and adult modeling fosters children's self-confidence and their disposition to be self-initiating problem posers and problem solvers (Brooks & Brooks, 1993). Internally motivated exploratory representations can be personally motivated and externally validated.

Of Science and Play

And so we have come full circle. We began by asserting that the spirit of inquiry is central to science, and that exploratory representational play in childhood lays the foundations for adult scientific inquiry. Yet in our reverie we find that something has been lost. Science is not always true to the spirit of inquiry. Flow is sometimes blocked. Rather than placing science on a pedestal, we feel a longing for the playfulness of those early explorations. But it doesn't have to be this way! As Rachel Carson stated so eloquently (1956):

> A child's world is fresh and new and beautiful, full of wonder and excitement. It is our misfortune that for most of us that clear-eyed vision, that true instinct for what is beautiful and awe-inspiring, is dimmed and even lost before we reach adulthood. If I had influence with the good fairy who is supposed to preside over the christening of all children, I should ask that her gift to each child in the world be a sense of wonder so indestructible that it would last throughout life, as an unfailing antidote against the boredom and disenchantments of later years, the sterile preoccupation with things that are artificial, the alienation from the sources of our strength. (pp. 42–43)

References

Beck, L. E. (1994). Vygotsky's theory: The importance of make-believe play. *Young Children, 49*, 30–39.

Bergen, D. (1988). Stages of play development. In D. Bergen (Ed.), *Play as a medium for learning and development: A handbook of theory and practice.* Portsmouth, NH: Heinemann.

Brainerd, C. J., & Reyna, V. F. (1990a). Gist is the grist: Fuzzy-trace theory and the new intuitionism. *Developmental Review, 10*, 3–47.

Brainerd, C. J., & Reyna, V. F. (1990b). Inclusion Illusions: Fuzzy-trace theory and perceptual salience effects in cognitive development. *Developmental Review, 10,* 365–403.

Brooks, J. G., & Brooks, M. G., (1993). *In search of understanding: The case for constructivist classrooms.* VA: Association for Supervision and Curriculum Development.

Bruner, J. S. (1966). *Toward a theory of instruction.* Cambridge, MA: Harvard University Press.

Cajete, G., (1995). *Look to the mountain: An ecology of indigenous education.* CO: Kidakí Press.

Carson, Rachel (1956). *The sense of wonder.* New York: Harper & Row.

Cooper, S. E., & Robinson, D. A. G. (1989). Childhood play activities of women and men entering engineering and science careers. *The School Counselor, 36,* 338–341.

Csikszentmihalyi, M. (1979). The concept of flow. In B. Sutton-Smith (Ed.), *Play and Learning* (pp. 257–274). New York: Gardner Press.

Csikszentmihalyi, M. (1990). *Flow: The psychology of optimal experience.* New York: HarperCollins.

Csikszentmihalyi, M., & LeFevre, J. (1989). Optimal Experience in Work and Leisure. *Journal of Personality and Social Psychology, 56*(5), 815–822.

Cummins, R. H., & Myers, C. A., (1992). Incorporating sciences in a liberal arts education. *National Honors Report. 13,* 2–5.

Fine, E. H. & Josephson, J. P. (1984). Footprints, fireflies, and flight: Primary science magic. *Childhood Education, 61,* 23–29.

Feynman, R. P. (1985). *Surely you're joking. Mr. Feynman.* New York: Bantam Books.

Fromberg, D. P., & Bergen, D. (1998). Introduction. In D. P. Fromberg & D. Bergen (Eds.), *Play from birth to twelve and beyond: Contexts, perspectives, and meanings* (xv–xvi). New York: Garland.

Goldhaber, J. (1994). If we call it science, then can we let the children play? *Childhood Education, 71,* 24–27.

Henniger, M. L. (1987). Learning mathematics and science through play. *Childhood Education, 64,* 167–171.

Li, A. K. F. (1978). Effects of play on novel responses in kindergarten children. *The Alberta Journal of Educational Research, 24,* 31–36.

Pepler, D. J. & Ross, H. S. (1981). The effects of play on convergent and divergent problem solving. *Child Development, 52,* 1202–1210.

Piaget, J. (1962). *Play, dreams, and imitation in childhood.* New York: Norton.

Resnick, L. B. (1989). Introduction. In Lauren B. Resnick (Ed.), *Knowing, learning, and instruction: Chapters in honor of Robert Glaser* (pp. 1–24). Hillside, NJ: Lawrence Erlbaum.

Reyna, V. F. (1991). Class inclusion, the conjunction fallacy, and other cognitive illusions. *Developmental Review, 11,* 317–336.

Reyna, V. F., & Brainerd, C. J. (1989). Output interference, generic resources, and cognitive development. *Journal of Experimental Child Psychology, 47,* 42–46.

Reyna, V. F., & Brainerd, C. J. (1995). Fuzzy-trace theory: An interim synthesis. *Learning and Individual Differences, 7,* 1–75.

Severeide, R. C., & Pizzini, E. L. (1984). The role of play in science. *Science and Children, 2,* 58–61.

Smith, P. K., & Dutton, S. (1979). Play and training in direct and innovative problem solving. *Child Development, 50,* 830–836.

Spodek, B., & Saracho, O. N. (1987). The challenge of educational play. In D. Bergen (Ed.), *Play as a Medium for Learning and Development: A Handbook of Theory and Practice* (pp. 9–26). Portsmouth, NH: Heinemann.

Tracy, D. M. (1987). Toys, spatial ability, and science and mathematics achievement: Are they related? *Sex Roles, 17,* 115–138.

Tracy, D. M. (1990). Toy-playing behavior, sex-role orientation, spatial ability, and science achievement. *Journal of Research in Science Teaching, 27,* 637–649.

Trumbull, D. (1990). Introduction. In E. Duckworth, J. Easley, D. Hawkins, & J. K. Smith (Eds.), *Science education: A minds-on approach for the elementary years* (pp. 1–20). Hillside, NJ: Lawrence Erlbaum.

Wassermann, S. (1988). Play-debrief-replay: An instructional model for science. *Childhood Education, 2, 2,* 232–234.

Wolfe, C. R. (1995). Information seeking on Bayesian conditional probability problems: A Fuzzy-trace theory account. *Journal of Behavioral Decision Making, 8,* 85–108.

Wolfe, C. R., Reyna, V. F., & Brainerd, C. J. (2005). Fuzzy-trace theory: Implications for transfer in teaching and learning. *Transfer of Learning from a Modern Multidisciplinary Perspective.* (53–88). Greenwich, CT: Information Age Press.

von Aufshnaiter, S., & Schwedes, H. (1989). Play orientation in physics education. *Science Education, 73,* 467–479.

22
Play and Technology
Revised Realities and Potential Perspectives

YASMIN B. KAFAI

Interactive technologies such as video games and digital toys have become a significant part of children's play culture. Video games present virtual worlds in which children can control and interact with fantasy figures and receive feedback responses tailored to their interactions. Feedback and control are two new important features of the interactive play technologies, not previously available. If the nature of the play devices and environments themselves has changed considerably, the growing immersion of interactive technologies in children's living conditions is another important factor (Calvert, 1999). In contrast to most adults, children do not feel threatened by computational media and other programmable devices; they enjoy explorations of and interactions with them. For children growing up today, technology is part of the fabric of their everyday life.

With these changes in living conditions and play devices it is worthwhile examining the reality and potential of interactive technologies for children's play. The following sections present selected research on video games as a case in point for the revised realities of children's play. The social, cognitive, and motivational aspects of video game playing then are examined more closely by looking at the nature of games and their relevance to children's development. The potential of interactive technologies also is discussed by considering constructive aspects of play; one example is children's engagement in making games. The potential perspectives of interactive play environments will be explored by looking at the next generation of electronic building blocks and virtual playgrounds.

Revised Realities of Play: Video Games as the New Electronic Playground

More than any other form of interactive technology, video games have entered children's homes and hearts and have received an enthusiastic reception. The number of hours spent in front of these video screens must be in the order of hundreds of billions. Not only the time spent, but also the energy displayed in playing these games have initiated many discussions among parents, practitioners and researchers about their impact on children's well-being. To understand the impact of video games it is worthwhile to analyze their particular nature in relation to other games that children play.

The psychologist Jean Piaget (1962) offered a classification of game playing that also reflected children's various developmental needs. According to Piaget, most games can be classified as either games of practice, symbolic games, rule-governed games, or games of construction. Children in early infancy engage mostly in games of practice to gain mastery over motor movements. Symbolic play enters at a later age in which "as if" plays a crucial role. In this context, children build their understanding of the world by reenacting situations and telling stories until they feel secure in the mastery of them. The next level is rule-governed games, where children play according to a finite set of rules (often set by others). At this level, children enjoy exploring and discovering a set structure that can be intentionally modified; that is, the rules are negotiable to make the game more enjoyable. Piaget considered games of construction to be the most complex form of game playing as they require children to build representations of the world according to their understanding.

Even though Piaget's classification was developed well before video games entered the playroom, it seems evident that video games combine three different forms of game playing: practice, symbolic, and rule-governed (Gee, 2003). Playing video games requires a great amount of practice before the player gains mastery and can advance to the next level. Video games are a stellar example of the central "as if" quality of play: they not only allow children to be engaged in fantasy worlds but also to accomplish incredible feats, such as fighting monsters, on the screen. In addition, each video game is set up as a world governed by a set of rules, which the player has to uncover to win the game. It is the convergence of these three forms of game playing that makes video games different from traditional toys and games. The mastery of all three levels provides young players with an experience of control and competence previously not available.

This unique combination of features in video games might explain their motivational, cognitive, and social appeal to children. When one researcher observed several video game players and their interests in games, she identified features of role-playing, fantasy, and rule systems as responsible for the games' "holding power". Video games respond to children's developmental needs in interacting with well-defined rule-systems. A further insight of her analysis was that playing video games resonated with different aspects of the players' personalities. Whereas some players were attracted to the fantasy aspects, for others the uncovering of principles designed by someone else or the perfection of performance were the most compelling aspects of video game play (Turkle, 1984, 1995). Other researchers confirmed this analysis by having students play a number of different computer games, rate the games according to attractiveness, and then name their outstanding features (Malone & Lepper, 1987). They found that players rated factors such as challenge, fantasy, curiosity, and control as the main attracting features of games.

Video games appeal on a motivational level and also provide cognitive challenges as well. Sensorimotor skills such as hand–eye coordination are a prerequisite to successful video game play and require hours of practice. There is an abundance of research documenting the spatial reasoning involved in video game playing (Gagnon, 1985; Greenfield, Brannon, & Lohr, 1994; McClurg & Chaille, 1987). Most games are large environments with complicated spatial arrangements not entirely visible on the screen. To successfully move through the different levels, the player needs to build a "mental map" of the video game world—something which takes hours of exploration.

One factor that most clearly appeals to video game players is the uncovering of the rules that govern the screen world. Most of these rules are unknown and not apparent at the beginning of the game playing; many of them also change as the player progresses to higher game levels. A number of cognitive processes are involved in the process of rule detection: trial and error, pattern generation, hypothesis testing, generalization, estimation, and organization of information (Loftus & Loftus, 1983). As players move through the game, they are engaged in analyzing their experiences and the ways they contribute to the mastery of the game. Players might decide to change responses in given situations to develop more successful strategies. Furthermore, many players are not satisfied with just finding one right way to achieve the final game level; instead, many pride themselves in knowing alternative routes or shortcuts to the next level. It is clear that to achieve the final level of a video game requires a great deal of skill and investigation on the part of the player. Deserving of further consideration is that many of these processes are happening simultaneously; as players are mapping out the layout of the video world, they are also uncovering hidden principles and interacting with other game players (Greenfield, 1984).

The high concentration and coordination required for successful video game playing supports a commonly held notion of the antisocial nature of the players. Instead of playing with other children, the new generation of toys requires children to play against themselves (Sutton-Smith, 1986). One could characterize video game playing as a solitary activity because the player is interacting alone with the machine. This view, however, neglects to take into account that video games support a whole culture consisting of movies, magazines, fan clubs, and competitions. In fact, most video games are played in groups, where players exchange tricks and hints for advancing in the game (Gee, 2003). Also, most machine setups allow for two players to compete against each other. Competition and cooperation are other features that make video games attractive for players (Malone & Lepper, 1987).

One of the most distinctive features of the video game culture is that the majority of game players are boys (Provenzo, 1991). There is a consistent pattern of gender differences in interest and achievement in video game playing; few girls play video games and their performance lags behind that of boys (Cassell & Jenkins, 1998). One explanation lies in the spatial skills that are crucial to successful video game play (Greenfield & Cocking, 1996). New research, however, points out that these observed gender differences disappear after extended exposure (Subrahmanyan & Greenfield, 1994). The violent themes and gender stereotypes provided in video games offer a more compelling explanation. One commentator argued that the values embedded in movies, toys, television, and video games are powerful stereotypes for children's thinking. In many commercial video games, the main game figure is usually a male hero whose function is to save a female or obtain a treasure (Kinder, 1991). Many video games include the eternal conflict between evil and good as their main theme. Children find these themes compelling, because it supports their need to understand their own position and place in the social context. Some researchers have speculated that boys are drawn to identify with the characters in video games, whereas girls rather prefer to interact with game figures. This might provide an explanation as to why boys take so easily to video games.

Gailey (1992) has questioned to what extent children experience violence and gender-stereotyping. She analyzed what values video games convey, how child players interpret the play process, and what children get out of the games. One of her findings is that children do not accept the universals provided in video games; they make up their own descriptions. Irrespective of the considerable gender stereotyping found in many video games (portraying women as victims or prizes), girls seem to resolve the dilemma by redefining their roles—placing themselves in managerial roles.

It is clear that video game playing offers children an engagement that challenges them at various levels, including the cognitive, motivational, and social. Video games are the new playground that can provide entrance into a fantasy world in which children can experience control and competence. Children have always been able to create their own fantasy worlds by playing with traditional toys and games. What is new is that this generation of games and toys can "talk back," responding in sophisticated ways to children's interactions, and that players are able to control the flow of the game by their own interventions. The design of characters and themes in many video games replicates gender preferences found for traditional toys. After all, video game worlds—their figures, actions, and contents—are environments constructed by others; by game designers. In early versions, players have very few opportunities to change the features of a purchased video game. It seems, therefore, worthwhile to investigate another variant of interactive technologies: constructive play. The idea of using technology to make video games and further game technology developments will be presented in the following section.

Potential Perspectives of Play: Electronic Play as Constructive Activity

While video games in their current form provide children with new playgrounds, the potential of interactive technologies to provide construction material for play has received far less attention. We know that, as much children enjoy playing games according to given rules, they are also constantly modifying rules and inventing their own. Piaget (1962) claimed that these modifications reflected children's growing understanding of the world. The process of game construction represented for Piaget the ultimate efforts by children to master their environment in creating external representations of the world. Researchers in the digital domain, however, have not considered extensively this constructive aspect of children's play. They have seen the difficulties associated with learning programming, the language of construction for computers, as a major obstacle. It is only in the last decade that some have considered programming computers as an appropriate and feasible activity for children (Papert, 1980, 1993).

Turkle pointed out an interesting parallel between the attractions of playing games and of programming computers. She sees programming as a way for children to build their own worlds. Within this context, children can determine the rules and boundaries governing the game world and become the makers and players of their own games. In contrast, when children play a video game, they are always playing a game programmed by someone else; they are always exploring someone else's world and deciphering someone else's mystery. Turkle concludes that what she called the holding power of playing purchased video games could be applied to the making or programming of video games.

This parallel provided the rationale for investigating game making as a new avenue for children's play with interactive technologies. In a series of studies, one of which may serve as an example for this kind of effort (Kafai, 1995), a group of 10-year-old children made their own video games. The children met everyday over a period of six months to design their own games, creating all their own characters, story lines, and game themes, and interactions. It is worthwhile to take a closer look at the games created by the students and to what extent they represent play preferences known from other games and toys (Kafai, 1996).

All the games included sophisticated graphics, animation, and interaction in their programming. The most distinctive feature, however, is the degree to which gender differences permeate nearly all aspects of game design. Almost all of the boys, for example, created adventure hunts and explorations whereas the girls' games were more evenly divided among adventure, skill/sport, or teaching. The sports theme was selected by a few students who focused on skill aspects such as navigating a maze or spider web, or dunking basketballs. Only two students (girls) chose an educational format, a teaching game, to incorporate the content to be learned. One of the sharpest thematic differences between boys and girls concerned the morality issue of the contest between good and evil, in which one good player fights off the bad guys in order to achieve a goal. In the boys' games the goal is to recover objects or defeat evil creatures to receive a prize. Not one girl incorporated the conquest of good versus evil in her game, whereas five boys chose to do so.

The diversity of genre and gender differences was also reflected in the design of the game world. All game designs centered around the construction of physical spaces. In many instances, game worlds could be described as fantasy places because they were imaginary worlds for the younger players. The majority of boys created fantasy places such as imaginary cities, islands, or countries. Most girls confined their game places and worlds to real-life settings, whereas only one boy did so.

The places or worlds in which the games were situated were populated with an interesting cast of characters. One group contained the game character assigned to the player, the other the supporting cast of game actors. Nearly all the boys chose fantasy figures or assigned a specific gender to the player. Most of the boys also assumed that the player would be male. Some of them had fantasy names by which the gender was more difficult to detect. In contrast, most girls left the player's gender or age open. They addressed the player simply by a generic "you" without any further specifications. One might interpret this choice as involving a more personal identification between the player and the character. The cast of supporting game actors emphasized this result even more; most boys created several characters with fantasy names for the game world in which the player had to interact. Most girls chose one or two figures for their supporting cast. It is apparent in this comparison that the girls had a significantly different take on the roles that the player and actors have in the game.

The feedback provided as a result of the interaction between the player and the game differed as well. Boys' feedback modes were overwhelmingly violent; girls' feedback was overwhelmingly nonviolent. In the case of a wrong answer, most boys chose to end the game in a violent fashion. Their game characters either lost their lives before the game was over or as a result of it. In contrast, almost all the girls programmed different kinds of feedback for a wrong answer. In case of a wrong answer, their player usually continued, but did not receive a reward (or punishment).

Most of the games designers set all of the worlds, including interactions within a narrative context. As students made their games, they also created a story that situated the actors in a fantastic yet meaningful context. Students included additional scenes in which the different actors spoke to each other. The graphics were accompanied by text. A possible explanation for the popularity of the narrative game format is that it allowed students to incorporate fantasy and to decorate their worlds in a more attractive way. This was also one of the features that other researchers identified as appealing to children playing games (Malone & Lepper, 1987).

Making video games emphasized the gender differences found in playing purchased video games, but with an interesting difference: the stories, characters, and worlds of most of the girls differed in kind from those created by most of the boys. The influence of commercially available games was especially strong in the case of boys' games. Many game designers started out with ideas taken from popular video games such as "Super Mario Brothers" or "Pac man." Many of the boys' game implementations included violent aspects, as documented in the design of their feedback to player interactions. The violence is one of the most prominent features in commercial video games (Provenzo, 1991). Boys incorporated this violence into their own game designs; girls did not. In the commercial games female game figures rarely are cast in the main role, and the thematic embedding of video games in hunts and adventures are not to many girls' tastes; they compensated for this by creating their own world in which they included familiar spaces and characters from their households.

The game design activity offered a framework in which both girls and boys could situate their preferred ideas and fantasies. In their choices of game themes and their programming of animation and interactions, the students offered a glimpse into what they found appealing and unappealing in the games and stories they experienced through other media. Making a game and its rules allowed the game designers to be in charge and to determine the player's place and role in the world with all the consequences. These results point toward the potential of new interactive technologies for play in providing the construction tools for making computational toys and games.

Programmable Building Blocks, Computational Game Tool Kits, and Virtual Playgrounds

There is a long tradition of construction tools and toys in children's play history: Fröbelian blocks, Lincoln Logs, Tinker Toys, and Lego bricks. These tools offer children the opportunity to rebuild structures found in the real world and to populate them with their own figures and actions. Even though they are all categorized as construction tools and toys, each set offers distinct building possibilities reflecting technological advances in engineering. Whereas Lincoln Logs clearly favor building wooden cabins, for example, Tinker Toys and Lego bricks allow for a much wider range of structures. The materials of physical construction tool kits define, to a certain extent, the objects to be built.

It is worthwhile to consider for a moment what the computational equivalents or extensions of the traditional building blocks could be. For that reason, the following sections contain some examples of computational construction building blocks and tool kits in different settings. The first section looks at a combination of traditional building blocks and control structures that merge the computational world with the physical world. The second examines a computational game tool kit. The last extends the settings to virtual playgrounds, which allow children to bridge large distances to come together and play. These examples are indicators of what is possible.

Programmable Building Blocks

A first step in the direction of computational construction tool kits is to combine the physical building blocks with computational control elements (Resnick, 1998). Children would be able not only to build mechanical objects and structures but also to have ways of programming and controlling engines and sensors that allow for movements and interactions. Rather than just building architectural structures, children would also become involved in engineering. Lego bricks with sensors and motors that could be connected via wires and controlled through programs would provide such programmable building blocks. Further developments would provide bricks that contain all the computational power. An extension of computational Lego bricks, called the programmable brick, allows control of motors and sensors without being tethered to a personal computer. These programmable bricks allow children to build computational objects that can interact independently with the world. In that sense, each playroom in a house could become a potential game environment with computational elements in it. Children could create a haunted house, for example, by attaching programmable bricks to doors that make creaking sounds when they open and drop spiders whenever people walk into the room. Children also could use programmable bricks to send secret messages via the infrared beam to other children in the room. In addition, they could build creatures with sensors that explore the environment. A computational version of Mr. Potato Head might have eyes that move toward light and a mouth that starts to talk when placed on a head.

Computational Game Tool Kits

This kind of tool kit would allow children to make their own software or video games. The Pinball Construction Set (Greenfield, 1984), for example, provides players with a blank board and all the necessary tools and parts to install flippers, backgrounds, and controllers for their own pinball game. The user can design innumerable versions, and he or she can play the game alone or with others. More generic computational tool kits would allow children to make any kind of game world, characters, and game rules. Children could be provided with sets of rules and actions and could change the parameters to fit the game's needs and children's desires. The sharing of ideas and strategies, already an essential part of the existing video game culture, could continue because children could invite each other to play the games they have designed. The more recent generation of commercial video games now provides game and character editors that allow players to add to the game play and customize the game space.

Virtual Playgrounds

Video games are considered the new electronic playground in which children can control and interact with figures in a world. A step further would be to think about networked video games in which other children could control characters that interact those controlled by others. From the vision of one player with a machine we would move into a world where the computer provides a platform to connect several players for a play experience; they then can interact with each other. Multiuser dungeons, or MUDs, are one example of networked environments that allow children to play with each other even though they are physically located at different places. Early versions of MUDs were text-based virtual reality environments organized around metaphors of physical spaces such as space stations or buildings that users can access from all over the world. Players could assume fantasy characters that explore the space provided and build new structures and objects for other players to find (Bruckman, 2000). Newer networked versions take advantage of three-dimensional graphics and rendering for their characters and buildings.

Video games and electronic toys are the new digital toys and playground for children. Children's play is still the same, but their world and materials with which they grow up have changed. When compared to a set of toys developed by Friedrich Froebel over 150 years ago—woolen balls for toddlers to catch and throw, papers and sticks to be folded in intricate patterns, wooden blocks to create houses and buildings—it becomes clear that the nature of toys, and consequently, the interactions with them, have changed. But play with digital media and in virtual playgrounds can still have the features of make-believe and relate to children's experiences.

Parents, educators, and psychologists need to carefully consider interactive technologies' potential to be both ready-made play worlds provided by adults for children and the materials with which children can create their own worlds. The current reality of interactive technologies tends to undervalue the constructive aspects of play in which children have always engaged. However, electronic building blocks and virtual playgrounds are materials and places as acceptable as wooden blocks, bricks, and sandboxes.

References

Bruckman, A. (2000). Situated support for learning: Storm's weekend with Rachael. *Journal of the Learning Sciences, 9*(3), 329–372.

Calvert, S. (1999). *Children's journeys through the information age.* New York: McGraw-Hill.

Cassell, J., & Jenkins, H. (1998). *From Barbie to Mortal Kombat: Gender and computer games.* Cambridge, MA: MIT Press.

Gailey, C. (1992). Mediated messages: Gender, class, and cosmos in home video games. *Journal of Popular Culture, 15*(2), 5–25.

Gagnon, D. (1985). Video games and spatial skills: An exploratory study. *Educational Communications and Technology Journal, 33,* 263–275.

Gee, J. P. (2003). *What video games have to teach us about learning and literacy.* New York: Palgrave Macmillan.

Greenfield, P. M., Brannon, C., & Lohr, D. (1994). Two-dimensional representation of movement through three-dimensional space: The role of video game expertise. *Journal of Applied Developmental Psychology, 15*(1), 87–104.

Greenfield, P. M. (1984). *Mind and media. The effects of television, video games, and computers.* Cambridge, MA: Harvard University Press.

Greenfield, P. M., & R. R. Cocking (1996). *Interacting with video.* Norwood, NJ: Ablex.

Kafai, Y. (1995). *Minds in play: Computer game design as a context for children's learning.* Hillsdale, NJ: Lawrence Erlbaum.

Kafai, Y. (1996). Electronic playworlds: Gender differences in children's construction of video games. In Y. B. Kafai & M. Resnick (Eds.), *Constructionism in practice* (pp. 97–124) Mahwah, NJ: Lawrence Erlbaum.

Kinder, M. (1991). *Playing with power.* Berkeley: University of California Press.

Loftus, G. R., & Loftus, E. F. (1983). *Minds at play: The psychology of video games.* New York: Basic Books.

Malone, T. W., & Lepper, M. R. (1987). Making learning fun: A taxonomy of intrinsic motivations for learning. In R. E. Snow & M. J. Farr (Eds.), *Aptitude, learning and instruction: Vol. 3. Conative and affective process analysis* (pp. 223–253). Hillsdale, NJ: Lawrence Erlbaum,

McClurg, P. A., & Chaillé, C. (1987). Computer games: Environments for developing spatial cognition? *Journal of Educational Computing Research, 3,* 95–111.

Papert, S. (1993). *The children's machine.* New York: Basic Books.

Papert, S. (1980). *Mindstorms.* New York: Basic Books.

Piaget, J. (1951). *Play, dreams, and imitation in childhood.* New York: Norton.

Provenzo, E. F. (1991). *Video kids: Making sense of Nintendo.* Cambridge, MA: Harvard University Press.

Resnick, M. (1998). Technologies for life-long learning. *Educational Technology Research & Development, 46*(4), 43–55.

Subrahmanyan, K., & Greenfield, P. M. (1994). Effects of video game practice on spatial skills in girls and boys. *Journal of Applied Developmental Psychology, 15*(1), 13–32.

Sutton-Smith, B. (1986). *Toys as culture.* New York: Gardener.

Turkle, S. (1984). *The second self: Computers and the human spirit.* New York: Simon & Schuster.

Turkle, S. (1995). *Life on the screen: Identity in the age of the Internet.* New York: Simon & Schuster.

23

Educational Implications of Play with Computers

STEVEN B. SILVERN

Any examination of the implications of play with computers requires specifying the meaning of the term *play* and describing what children typically do with computers. Those who have studied and theorized about play have conceived of it as being anything from dark, messy, and barbaric (Sutton-Smith, 1981) to a beneficial, voluntary match between challenge and skills unrelated to real-life consequences (Csikszentmihalyi, 1979).

Examination of children's use of computers may entail studying their exploration (Hutt, 1979) rather than their play (Escobedo, 1992). Exploration can be included within a concept of play: in exploration children attempt to find out what an object or material does, whereas in play they attempt to find out what they can do with the object or material (Bergen, 1988). The distinction is primarily temporal because exploration occurs before play (Hutt, 1979). During observations of children's play, however, it is extremely difficult to draw a temporal dividing line between exploration and play. Therefore, knowing that some, though not all, scholars may disagree, this chapter defines play with computers as the players' attempts to find out both what the computers can do and what the players can do with the computers. When children are engaged in computer play, there is a match between challenge and skills that may or may not relate to real-life consequences. Play with computers also may involve play in both antiseptic, socially acceptable environments and in environments that offer darker, more aggressive simulations.

Play in Microworlds

The computer provides a microworld in which children can both imitate and play, for, despite Piaget's (1945/1976) classifications, imitation occurs within a playful frame and observers easily categorize these actions as play behaviors. Microworlds provide a context that challenges children's skills and thoughts. The children might be trying to hit a target, design a pleasing representation, or accomplish a self-imposed task. Early researchers studying the effects of the computer program Logo (Papert, 1980) recognized self-imposed activity in children's attempts to change the color of the screen by filling it up with hundreds of lines (Silvern, 1988). No one observing the laughter and joy exuded by successful children could conclude that the activity was anything other than play. At the same time, no one observing the intense concentration children exhibited as they matched their thoughts to the problem posed could conclude that the children were not learning during their playful interaction with the computer and with each other. There are a number of strategies that schools are currently using to encourage children to enter such computer microworlds, including computer games, the computer as a tool, and the Internet.

Play with Computer Games

Many educators have suggested that electronic games can provide ideal microworlds for children's learning in school (Baird & Silvern, 1990; Kafai, 1995; Silvern, 1985). Computer games challenge the player's abilities to reason, provide nonthreatening environments to encourage exploration, support academic risk taking, and create a demand to learn how to apply school learning (Downes, Arthur, & Beecher, 2001; Ko, 2002). To advance to the next level of play in "The King's Rule" (O'Brien, 1984), for example, the player must supply the guard with the general rule of problem solving being applied at that level. Adventure games like "Winnie the Pooh in the Hundred Acre Wood" and "Mickey's Space Adventure" (Walt Disney Personal Computer Software, 1984a, 1984b) encourage map making as well as solving relational problems. They also expect children to join together to use their combined understandings to try to solve problems.

Even though the prediction that computer games will play a substantive role in children's learning and provide many excellent learning opportunities is a modest one, such games are not now widely used in classrooms, and there is some doubt that they ever will be (Kerawalla & Cook, 2002). Early theorists and later researchers both have recommended that children's learning be based in play and games (Dewey, 1900; Kamii & DeVries, 1980); yet schools are still adamantly resistant to having play as a major component in classrooms (Block & King, 1987). There remains within school an ethic that identifies the appropriate activity for learning as work, hard work, and asserts that children may play games only after work is done, especially as a reward for good work. Within school there is also a dichotomy between play and work, and the majority of classroom activity planners perceive that games are too enjoyable to use as real classroom experiences (Sutton-Smith, 1987).

Play with Computing Tools

Children can also experience computer play in schools by receiving opportunities to use tool applications in playful ways (Ferguson, 2001; Henniger, 1994). Within this vision, children can use drawing or word processing programs for their own ends. In a kindergarten classroom, for example, children can use "Kid Pix 2" to generate pictures that they will write about in their journals (Broderbund, 1994). The creation of the pictures is fanciful and most often demonstrates the playful manipulation of a particular kind of instrument. Children might use word processing programs to experiment and play with writing or use spatial design programs to create structures. An 8-year-old and her friends, for example, used the word processor to create a school newspaper, greeting cards, and advertisements for a scheme to make money. The children even composed a song on the computer that was later used in a school presentation on intercultural relations. These children successfully negotiated with the teacher to engage in these playful literacy creations in place of their typical literacy-related schoolwork. In the same vein, Israeli kindergartners write stories and keep records on the computers in their classrooms as a part of their play activity (Silvern & Levita, 1994). This playful use of computers is certainly being adopted in classrooms and appears to be a dominating function of computers, especially in early childhood classrooms. The challenge for teachers is to keep the computer as a playful instrument and not to use it only as a machine that involves children's doing drill activities.

The Internet as a Microworld Playground

Perhaps the most innovative current play with computers is surfing the Internet computer network (note that even the verb is playful). The Internet provides opportunities for both a "challenge" use (at the game, simulation, and word processing or design level) and a "barbaric" use (finding access to dark, dangerous, and mischief-making information). Thus, children can challenge themselves to find useful and enjoyable information and activities as well as engage in illicit dark imaginings. Even though there are screening devices, adults have not found a good solution to alleviate their concerns about these darker possibilities. Although the Internet can certainly serve as an essential research tool for both children and adults it is also a playground because it fits precisely into the concept of play, answering questions such as "What is this? What can I make it do? What will I find at a particular site? What will be new or surprising?" and "What will I be able to do with it?" Children can think of the Internet as a toy box in which the games and toys inside are concealed by cryptic names. They might ask, for example, "What is in `Susan' or in 'MacTrek'?" Then the children can download applications that have interesting names, to see what is in these various "toy boxes" and to find out what they can do with them. Of course, teachers will want to monitor this play activity closely while still allowing for reasonable exploration. One might imagine children searching for one piece of information and becoming sidetracked by something more interesting, similar to looking for one word in the dictionary and having one's attention diverted by other words. Just as in other forms of play, the "product" may be of less interest than the "process" of exploring, manipulating, and expanding on the activities in the electronic playground of ideas, images, sounds, and games.

Accessing the Internet Playground

It is possible for teachers to easily create an interface (home page) that allows children selected access to the Internet. Because the World Wide Web (WWW) browser can use icons and pictures as "pointers," children who cannot yet read or who do not know English (the lingua franca of the Internet) can use the Internet. This means that users may access data from a huge variety of sources without using memory on the home computer. It also means that data can be readily available for children's play and learning. Text can also be stored as sound, so that by clicking on an icon children can hear the text as they read it or listen instead of reading it. There is a dinosaur museum on the Internet, for example, that displays pictures and information about a dig; the text is available to be heard as well as read.

So much data are available on the Internet that it is difficult to imagine what a child might access. A kindergarten teacher whose class was doing a theme on the arts, for example, "went," with one of the 5-year-olds in the class, to visit the Louvre (an Internet site). Although they never left the classroom, by using the WWW browser, they found the paintings of Monet on the Louvre site. The paintings were conveniently cataloged as early and late, so they did not have to search among the other works to find the paintings they wanted to see. Once they found those paintings, they were able to download them, print them, and save them on disk for later use. The 5-year-old selected the paintings she preferred and talked with other children about the aspects of the paintings that made them attractive to her. She particularly liked *La Promenade* because of the sky. This is but one example of potential play material available in cyberspace; there are samples of art, music, photographs, games, and movies about almost every subject one might imagine. The Internet is a manipulative center (microworld) that contains a vast number of items with which children can play and from which they can learn.

Playing in the Internet Playground

The informational items that have been described might also be found in a book or on a tape, video, or movie. The distinction between these media and the Internet is that the items are permanent and static in traditional media; that is, the information from these media does not lend itself to playful exploration. Although the teacher and child easily could have found the same Monet paintings in library books that reprint his work, once they had found out the characteristics of the painting reproductions, what else could they have done with them? Could they have rearranged them to explore a particular theme? Could they have changed the colors in them to see if the mood or idea of the painting changed?

Could they have found a pattern, copied it, and compared it to other patterns in other paintings, or even repeated the pattern in the same picture? In other words, they could not have manipulated the static media in a playful way to generate new ideas or meanings. The computer clearly allows children to manipulate data in ways that are not possible using other media.

Using the WWW, adults can structure the environment so that children can easily access the kind of data with which they wish to play. They can create a page that takes them to museums or one that permits them to visit other schools. (When this chapter was first published there were approximately 300 elementary schools registered on the Internet, there are now more than 1,130,000). Children can create a page that takes them to virtual reality sites, in which they create a nonreal environment that simulates a form of reality (i.e., pretend play!). One such site is "Addventure," where children follow and add to an endless adventure story. Children can find "Addventure" on the Internet by using the Web browser (http://www.addventure.com/addventure/). Children can experience another aspect of play by "traveling" from site to site. Without leaving the classroom, they can find out what other places are like. If they "visit" another school, they can see what projects those children are working on and try to find ways to be involved in the distant projects. It is possible for children to store their ideas on the WWW so that other children can access those ideas and make suggestions. These forms offer the possibility of children's playing with each other's ideas. Imagine how the culture of one child might influence another child several thousand miles away!

The Downside of Computer Play

The positive aspects of play with computers have been presented in detail. Computers themselves are not good or bad, however, but how humans choose to use them might be. Adults may encourage inappropriate as well as appropriate uses of computers in classrooms (Kelly & Schorger, 2001). It is inappropriate, for example, for teachers to require children to use the computer as an electronic worksheet and then call that activity play. Some software requires children to type in the completion to repetitive, meaningless equations that then blow up space monsters. There are also "run-and-jump" games that require nothing more from children than a facility with pushing buttons. Naturally, adults concerned with appropriate educational activities will avoid using such software, just as they avoid trite books and meaningless drill and practice worksheets.

Rather than using poor technology, or using technology poorly, it would be better not to have children using the technology at all. Adults can choose the way they use technology with children. They need to select software and activities that playfully challenge children's skills. They can arrange for telecommunications events that take children far beyond the here and now into a world of imagination and action that makes other media pale in comparison.

On occasion there have been horror stories about children accessing data that they should not access. There is now software available on the Internet, however, that effectively blocks children from inappropriate sites. Adults can arrange their telecommunications interfaces so that exploration can occur within fairly safe parameters. Adult involvement and interest in what children are doing and their occasional collaboration with children in computer play are also helpful ways to assure that children's computer play will be appropriate.

Extending Play and Learning Worlds

Given the potential that this technology offers, educators now must consider how the computer can enhance school learning and how to use play effectively in schools in the future. It is likely that teachers will begin to realize more fully the rich learning that can occur when children and adults play together in cyberspace. With that recognition, there is a possibility that teachers will make significant changes in the content and activity emphases of their classrooms and give more credence to the role of play in learning. A number of changes may occur, including a change in the boundaries of school, a move from individual learning to cooperative learning, and the opportunity to play with forms and ideas that were not accessible before.

Boundary Changes

There are two ways that school boundaries may change. First, the physical boundaries of school can be transformed as children gain access to the WWW from home and school. Imagine parents and children accessing the school's WWW page from their home. The following scenario might occur:

Dad: What did you do in school today?

Bud: Come on, Dad, turn on the computer and I'll show you. OK, first click on Cyber Elementary School. There, set the pointer to Miss Electra's class. Click on it. See my picture? Click on it.

Dad: Whoa! How many projects did you work on today?

Bud: Three. See, I've got three things on my page. This one's really neat. A school in France is doing a project on cleaning up the environment. They've asked us for pictures that show what kinds of things we are doing. I took a video of our nature trail before we started our pick-up project, while we were cleaning up, and after we finished the project. Click on the nature trail sign and you can see the video. I sent them the video by e-mail today. I hope they like it. Maybe I'll get a message back tomorrow.

Dad: Good idea. What else can we do?

Bud: Well, we can look at the projects of Leslie, Tracey, Shasta, and Yoni. Let's go to their pages and see what they've done.

Dad: Look, this icon here shows that you have mail waiting for you. Hey, the school from France has sent you a message already. Let's see what it says....

Home access to school through the WWW would give parents a more intimate role in their child's school activities. Not only could parents have access to what their child has done, but the parents also could have access to information which teachers, counselors, and administrators might supply. Children and parents could work on projects and play together while enhancing what the child is doing at school.

The second way boundaries will change was also illustrated in the conversation between Dad and Bud. Children will now have access to environments that go beyond the school walls. They will be able to play with the Internet at home as well as at school and to "travel" around the globe searching for new ideas or challenges. There is no longer the need to be limited to the thoughts and actions of those in the immediate environment: it is possible to share in the thoughts of others on the planet and to cooperatively engage them in games or other activities.

Cooperative Learning

The Internet is based on the idea of communication; it goes against the popularly held assumption that each person has to learn a defined set of "facts" in a completely individual way. This isolated learning style is challenged when, every day, individuals can read e-mail and see questions posed and answered by a diverse group of individuals in various parts of the globe. This cooperative learning model can easily find its way into the classroom (Ferguson, 2001). Learning can then be based on the playful manipulation of problems shared with other learners on the Internet. Such a model works on the assumption that problems have multiple possible solutions and that each solution should be evaluated for its worthiness. For example, a child may become enamored of a book of arithmetic puzzles that could have multiple answers. It would be fun for the child to post these puzzles on the WWW page and see the kinds of answers other people provide. Making puzzles for others is another form of play that works well on the Internet. One example of this is the "Great Internet Hunt," only one of many puzzles found on various WWW pages.

Play with Forms

This type of play entails the manipulation of graphic or other media data that have never been available for manipulation before. Children can paint a mustache on the Mona Lisa, for example, or put additional figures in the painting *La Promenade*. These changes are not permanent, so this play with forms is not harmful. Being able to manipulate that which was once inaccessible opens up whole new realms of play. Imagine using a video image and creating a new soundtrack for it! The possibilities for play with forms are bounded only by the child's imagination and the adult's willingness to let formerly static, sometimes sacred, forms be manipulated in play. Schools of the future, therefore, may change not only in place or time but also in content, impact, and reach. Adults and children can adapt the topics and manner of study. The types of learners who are involved together can expand. The overall scope of study can extend throughout the world.

Extending Possibilities

Almost 20 years ago a colleague raised the objection, "I don't see how playing with a turtle is going to change children's thinking." (The "turtle" is used in LOGO programming.) The reply to that objection was a chapter on how thinking differently will change thinking (Silvern & McCary, 1986). A similar question can be posed now: How will play with computers, especially play with the Internet, change children's play and how they learn through play? Will playing differently change playing? Will learning differently change learning?

Having different play "materials" may or may not change the way one thinks (although it would appear that the world would be quite different today if children had not had toy chariots to play with thousands of years ago). Having items to play with that require a different way of thinking, however, can change one's thoughts. Seventy years ago few people ever dreamed of leaving their hometown or using the telephone to talk to someone outside of their city because communicating with people in other places was the purpose of the mail. Forty years ago most individuals considered flying to a destination a big event and used long-distance telephone calls sparingly.

Today, the majority of people in technologized countries think it is normal to fly to other continents and to contact people throughout the world by telephone. How people think and behave is affected by what tools they have to think with.

Today there is the Internet, a thinking tool that is new for the present generation. It appears to be shrinking the world. The messages that used to be sent by mailed letters no longer take weeks to get to a destination; they take seconds. Responses are equally quick. The Internet is expanding people's imagination because images, sounds, and ideas are no longer set in stone; people can adapt and try them in different environments with different people. Play is not limited to the games and players who are immediately present; rather, play can include actions in an imaginary place that exists only in cyberspace with people who are far away. It is possible to play with games that go beyond what is available at the local department store. Unlike chess-by-mail, for example, where each move took days or weeks to complete, one can play with another person thousands of miles away in real time.

The Internet encourages the manipulation of possibilities so that one can find out what the Internet can do and what one can do with the Internet—taking Hutt's (1979) definition into cyberspace). It allows players to test the limits of their capabilities in a match between challenge and skill within a nonthreatening environment, removed from most of the dangers of the real world. That's what play is!

References

Baird, W. E., & Silvern, S. B. (1990). Electronic games: Children controlling the cognitive environment. *Early Child Development and Care, 61,* 43–49.

Bergen, D. (1988). Stages of play development. In D. Bergen (Ed.), *Play as a medium for learning and development: A handbook of theory and practice* (pp. 49–67). Portsmouth, NH: Heinemann.

Block, J. H., & King, N. R. (Eds.). (1987). *School play: A source book.* New York: Garland.

Broderbund Software. (1994). *Kid Pix* [Computer software]. Novato, CA: Author.

Csikszentmihalyi, M. (1979). The concept of flow. In B. Sutton-Smith (Ed.), *Play and learning* (pp. 257–274). New York: Gardner.

Dewey, J. (1900). Froebel's educational principles. *Elementary School Record, 1,* 143–151.

Downes, T., Arthur, L., & Beecher, B. (2001). Effective learning environments for young children using digital resources: An Australian perspective. *Information Technology in Childhood Education Annual,* 139–153.

Escobedo, T. H. (1992). Play in a new medium: Children's talk and graphics at computers. *Play and Culture, 5,* 120–140.

Ferguson, D. (2001). Technology in a constructivist classroom. *Information Technology in Childhood Education Annual,* 45–55.

Henniger, M. L. (1994). Computers and preschool children's play: Are they compatible? *Journal of Computing in Childhood Education, 5(3/4),* 231–239.

Hutt, C. (1979). Exploration and play (#2). In B. Sutton-Smith (Ed.), *Play and learning* (pp. 175–194). New York: Gardner.

Kafai, Y. B. (1995). *Minds in play: Computer game design as a context for children's learning.* Hillsdale, NJ: Lawrence Erlbaum.

Kamii, C., & DeVries, R. (1980). *Group games in early education: Implications of Piaget's theory.* Washington, DC: National Association for the Education of Young Children.

Kelly, L. L., & Schorger, J. R. (2001). Let's play 'puters: Expressive language use at the computer center. *Information Technology in Childhood Education Annual,* 125–138.

Kerawalla, L, & Crook, C. (2002). Children's computer use at home and at school: Context and continuity. *British Educational Research Journal,28,* 751–771.

Ko, S. (2002). An empirical analysis of children's thinking and learning in a computer game context. *Educational Psychology, 22,* 219–233.

O'Brien, T. C. (1984). *The King's Rule* [Computer software]. Pleasantville, NY: Sunburst Communications.

Papert, S. (1980). *Mindstorms: Children, computers, and powerful ideas.* New York: Basic Books.

Piaget, J. (1976). *The grasp of consciousness* (S. Wedgwood, Trans.) Cambridge, MA: Harvard University Press. (Original work published 1974)

Silvern, S. B. (1985). Classroom use of video games. *Educational Research Quarterly, 112,* 10–16.

Silvern, S. B. (1988). Creativity through play with LOGO. *Childhood Education, 64,* 220–224.

Silvern, S. B., & Levita, A. (1994). Word processing in the kindergarten. *Kindergarten Echos, 9,* 147–154. [Published in Hebrew]

Silvern, S. B., & McCary, J. C. (1986). Computers in the educational lives of children: Developmental issues. In J. L. Hoot (Ed.), *Computers in early childhood education: Issues and practices* (pp. 6–21). Englewood Cliffs, NJ: Prentice Hall.

Sutton-Smith, B. (1981). *A history of children's play: The New Zealand Playground 1840–1950.* Philadelphia: University of Pennsylvania Press.

Sutton-Smith, B. (1987). School play: A commentary. In J. H. Block & N. R. King (Eds.), *School play: A source book* (pp. 277–289). New York: Garland.

Walt Disney Personal Computer Software. (1984). *Mickey's Space Adventure* [Computer Software]. Anaheim, CA: Author.

Walt Disney Personal Computer Software. (1984). *Winnie the Pooh in the Hundred Acre Wood* [Computer Software]. Anaheim, CA: Author.

24
The Role of Play in Assessment

MICHELLE GLICK GROSS

Play assessment is a valuable tool for capturing information about the development of children. This chapter[1] describes the ways in which investigators can use play as a paradigm for assessing children's development, provides an overview of prevailing assessment techniques, and discusses some critical points to consider when using play for purposes of assessment. There are differences, however, between the goals and methods of approaches that use play in the assessment of children's development. Play assessment methods may be either structured or unstructured, and can include the use of both videotapes and audiotapes as tools for evaluating and scoring play behaviors. Selection of play assessment measures involves planning and addressing several key decision points.

Theoretical and Research Contexts

Jean Piaget (1962) offers an important theoretical perspective from which to examine the role of play in assessment. He saw children as active explorers and experimenters who use play to gain knowledge through a process of assimilation and accommodation. In so doing, children are able to organize their world and reflect their growing intellect. Piaget described three stages of play development: sensorimotor, symbolic and pretend, and games with rules. Through play, adults can observe these stages of the maturing intellect in much the same way as they observe the changing stages of language and motor behavior.

This Piagetian view of play has been broadened through the research of a number of psychologists and other professionals who have reported linkages and correlations between play behavior and skill development in such areas as language (Beeghley, Hanrahan, Weiss, & Cicchetti, 1985; Casby & Corte, 1987; Fewell & Ogura, 1997; Finn & Fewell, 1994; Lyytinen, Poikkeus, & Laakso, 1997; McCune, 1995; Yoshinaga-Itano, Snyder, & Day, 1998), social skills (Caster, 1984; Johnson, Christie, & Yawkey, 1987), and motor skills (Johnson et al., 1987; Mullan, 1984). Their findings provide a strong reason to examine the development of children in the context of the joyful activity of play. The play environment is both a natural and a valid arena in which to see children exercise their play skills and other developmental attributes.

Observations of the Child at Play

If play is to have a role in child assessment, then it is important for the examiners to be clear on how they will use play. Two approaches to play assessment are described in the professional literature: (1)

play itself as a developmental phenomenon and (2) play as a context for observing the development of skills such as language, motor, social, and cognitive behavior while children are playing.

Play Itself as a Developmental Phenomenon

To assess a child's play itself as a developmental domain is to take the view that play has a discernible, sequential path of maturation. It is possible to assess play skills in ways that are comparable to those used in assessing other domains of development (Belsky & Most, 1981; Fenson, 1985; Hill & McCune-Nicolich, 1981; Piaget, 1962; Sheridan, Foley, & Radlinski, 1995). The scales of play development and the options for coding play described below, for example, are based on the premise that play is a viable phenomenon for understanding and interpreting the child's abilities.

Play as a Context for Observing Development

Play provides children with opportunities to express whatever they wish, whether through bodily movements, actions on objects, words, or simply with facial expressions. Without constrictions on what they do or say, children can be themselves. It is in this context that the behaviors of children tell observers about the children's development. The young girl on a playground who holds onto the monkey bars and swings her body back and forth like a gymnast demonstrates her courage, agility, and strength. The boy who picks up a cookie, feeds it to Barney, and says, "Barney cookie" tells the observer about his understanding of eating and food preferences, in addition to his understanding and use of language symbols and sequencing of words. These simple examples permit others to see the child's competence in many domains. There is no requirement that the child run a specified distance, at a given pace, within a predetermined period of time. Opportunities arise and children can decide how to confront them. Within the context of the play experience, therefore, observers can see how the child uses time and makes decisions, two important applied skills that are valid indicators of intellect.

For those who wish to use the play arena for observing children's developmental skills, some facilitations or manipulations might be useful to elicit the desired behavior. For example, if one wishes to observe children's movements with balls or steps, placing these things in the environment is likely to elicit the behavior. It is quite natural to encourage the demonstration of skills without being intrusive. It is for this reason that play presents a potentially excellent environment for the assessment of children. The observer needs to have patience and a clinical knowledge of development, actually a more in-depth understanding of development than traditional standardized child assessment requires. Play may not be a setting that can assure standard procedures, but it adds a dimension to testing that is seldom captured in traditional child assessment.

The time has come to recognize and value children's play and realize the opportunity it presents for understanding a child's development. It is time for researchers and clinicians to fill the void and report on the usefulness, reliability, and validity of play assessment measures.

Procedures for Assessment of Play Development

Investigators can assess play development, similar to the ways in which they assess language development, by taking a sample of behavior and analyzing that sample for indicators of various concepts. They also can measure it in more structured ways, such as giving a child a specific toy or set of toys and then observing his or her actions, looking for behaviors known to be associated with a particular toy or object.

Free-Play Coding Systems

Several methods of evaluating play skills capitalize on the benefits of assessing children in naturalistic, nonstructured, "free play" settings. As children engage in activities that are part of their regular daily routines, such as free play or center time in an early childhood classroom, observers record and note their play behaviors. The cognitive play categories of Smilansky (1968) and the social categories of Parten (1932) continue to form the basis of most scales used to measure play behaviors in such settings[2] (Farmer-Dougan & Kaszuba, 1999; Levine & Antia, 1997; Lim, 1998; Rubin, 1989; Sluss & Stremmel, 2004)

An alternative measure to code play in natural settings is a system to code nonprompted toy manipulation and play of toddlers with multiple disabilities to serve inclusive classrooms (DiCarlo, Reid, & Stricklin, 2003). When the researchers identified low frequencies of toy play, they implemented and evaluated an intervention designed to increase child access to preferred toys. In another study to evaluate the changes in preschool play over a 1-year period, researchers used the *Manual for Observation of Play in Preschools* that coded both behavioral and verbal play (Culp & Farran, 1989; Farran & Son-Yarbrough, 2001). Behavioral play included play level, partners, and settings. Verbal play categories included codes for listening, talking, and verbalizing with play partners.

The Peer Play scale (Howes, 1980), often used in research studies to assess the peer interactions of young children during free play, is a very useful measure of social play because it includes more categories than the traditional Parten (1932) levels. This enables better pinpointing of levels and more accurate assessment of progress. The scale was used in a large Head Start study to assess child progress (Zill et al., 2001). The scale was expanded and modified in 1992 to better reflect the development of play from the infant through preschool periods (Howes & Matheson, 1992).

Professionals can use rating scales and questionnaires to evaluate children's play skills without imposing structure and formality upon natural activities. Instead of coding play behaviors as they occur, respondents report on characteristics of children's play based on cumulative observations and knowledge about individual children. The Penn Interactive Peer Play scale (Fantuzzo, Manz, Atkins, & Meyers, 1995; Fantuzzo & Hampton, 2000).) is a very promising rating scale that can be used by both teachers and parents to assess peer play in the school and home context. The purpose of the scale is to identify children who exhibit less successful play interactions with their peers and who might benefit from intervention. Parents and teachers rate the frequencies with which they have observed 36 positive and negative social play behaviors during the prior two-month period. The scale was developed in partnership with Head Start teachers and parents and designed to be culturally sensitive and appropriate for use with African-American children enrolled in the program. The measure is being heavily researched, and current findings support its reliability, validity, and use to determine intervention effectiveness (Fantuzzo et al., 2005; Hampton & Fantuzzo, 2003; Milfort & Greenfield, 2002).

The Play Checklist (Heidemann & Hewitt, 1992) is a very simple practitioner-oriented tool specifically designed for use by caregivers. The purpose of the 10-item scale is to help caregivers observe and understand child play skills in order to guide intervention for children who exhibit deficits in their play skills. The checklist manual provides clear information on the importance of play, the development of play, how to use the checklist, and how to plan appropriate interventions. The book and checklist can be valuable tools for teachers of young children, though information on the reliability and validity of the measure and approach is lacking in the literature.

Semistructured Procedures for Assessing Play

At times it is useful to assess the growth of play skills using more structured procedures. The use of standardized procedures, for example, allows one to compare the performance of one child with other children. Such procedures may better reflect the best performance of individuals because their attention is focused on the present activity and they have far fewer opportunities for distraction. Therefore, researchers also have developed scales that are more quantifiable than the various free-play coding systems described above. These formats often meet a specific need, such as a way to compare a group of children with disabilities to children who are developing typically.

One format is to present toys singly or in order and then rate the child's interactions (Largo & Howard, 1979). Another format uses structured observations and parent input to determine developmental scores in both play and language (Westby, 1980). A different set of procedures permits an examiner to give sets of toys to a child, observe and score the developmental sequences of play behavior, and then derive a play age score (Fewell, 1991). Because of the flexibility in the toys and timing, this scale has been used frequently with children under age 3 who have disabilities and others who respond poorly to standardized testing.

Assessment of Skill Development

In addition to assessing children's play competence one can use play as a medium for observing children's communicative, motoric, social, and cognitive development (McCune-Nicolich, 1980; Parten, 1932; Rogers, 1982). Information gained from observations during free-play time can supplement test scores from standardized and structured assessments. Almost every area of development can be assessed through play observation.

Observation of Social and Behavioral Skills

Social and behavioral skills are readily observable in a play setting. Observers can compare how children interact with parents, siblings, teachers, strangers, and peers. These observations can yield important information concerning a child's needs for intervention related to social interaction skills. After observations of mother–child play, for example, a team might suggest strategies for the mother to use to promote turn taking with the child. Through peer play observations, teachers and other professionals can note whether a child needs to learn how to approach other children to join in their play. Researchers are currently investigating the use of free play observations to identify behaviors of toddlers that could predict future diagnoses of Attention Deficit Hyperactivity Disorder (Deutscher & Fewell, 2001).

Observation of Cognitive and Language Skills

Observing children during play also yields valuable information regarding the development of cognition and communication. During play, observers can see children's cognitive skills in problem-solving, mastery motivation, attention, classification, and sequencing (Linder, 1993). To assess language, researchers and clinicians can audiotape and videotape communication samples that occur during play for later transcription and coding. Examples of the types of information that can be collected from these samples include discourse and conversational skills; total number of words; diversity of words; mean length of children's utterances; and their basic use of sentence structures (Crais & Roberts, 2004).

There are many advantages to assessing language using naturalistic samples of behavior. First, personality characteristics of children tend to have less of an impact on performance in naturalistic samples as compared with formal testing situations. For example, shy behavior affects access to studying expressive language. In addition, assessment of language skills during naturalistic observations has the potential to address concerns raised about the cultural fairness of current methods used to identify diverse groups of children with language impairments (Craig & Washington, 2000). Many believe that this method is a more valid indicator of specific language impairment than standardized psychometric measures (Dunn & Flax, 1996).

Observation of Motor Skills

Although observers can easily see both fine and gross motor skills, motor behavior during play is a neglected area of study. In a typical setting with object toys, children use their hands to grasp and pick up objects, put objects inside containers, or hold a crayon. Children sit, climb into chairs, and move from one place to another. A playground provides a perfect setting for observing gross motor skills that require larger spaces. One can observe risk-taking behaviors, walking, running, jumping, climbing, swinging, and throwing and catching balls. Researchers have developed a Playground Skills Test to assess and study the motor skills and proficiency of elementary school children on playgrounds (Butcher, 1991, 1993).

Assessment Instruments

One question that arises is: How does one know what specific skills to look for in each developmental area during the observation of a child at play? The answer to this question varies depending upon the purpose of the observations. A classroom teacher, for example, will want to observe play in order to adapt the curriculum to the needs of the children. An evaluation team, however, may need more specific information about the level of the child's functioning in each domain.

Curriculum Based Assessment Measures

One approach to assessing multiple skills within the context of play is the use of curriculum-based assessment measures, which assess children's performance on goals and objectives used in teaching specific tasks. Teachers have used these for many years, with the teacher doing all the observations and assessments. The Hawaii Early Learning Profile (Furuno et al., 1984) is one curriculum-based measure. The Assessment, Evaluation, and Programming System (AEPS) for Infants and Children is a more recent curriculum-based measure designed to be completed while children engage in play and other everyday activities (Bricker, 2002).

Arena Assessment

Arena assessment provides an alternate approach to assessing skills within the context of play. As early childhood assessment and intervention teams have become transdisciplinary in nature and less discipline-specific, arena assessment has become a popular method (Foley, 1992). In arena assessment, professionals from different disciplines simultaneously assess the child. One team member typically acts as the facilitator and other team members observe the process live in the same room, live through an observation window, or later, while viewing a videotape.

Transdisciplinary teams are beginning to use play-based observational procedures as part of their arena assessments (Bergen, 1994), though the field is only just beginning to collect data regarding the reliability and validity of such methods (Myers & McBride, 1996). The Transdisciplinary Play-Based Assessment (TPBA) is an example of a. well-known procedure. TPBA involves observing aspects of children's development as they interact in structured and unstructured play situations (Linder, 1993). The information collected can be used to identify the child's service needs, develop intervention plans, and evaluate progress. TPBA includes the following assessment situations: unstructured facilitation, child–child interaction, parent–child interaction, motor play, and snack. Thus, it is possible to collect information in the areas of cognition, social–emotional, communication and language, and sensorimotor development. The TPBA provides guidelines with approximate age ranges for the observation of each area (Linder, 1993). Kelly-Vance, Needelman, Troia, and Ryalls (1999) compared the performance of 2-year-olds on the Bayley Scales of Infant Development-II, a standardized measure of cognition and motor development, with scores derived using a modified TPBA procedure. Although scores from the two methods were highly correlated, scores from the play-based approach were significantly higher than scores on the standardized tests. Findings from this study support the use of caution when reporting scores from play assessment methods: These scores may represent child skills and abilities differently from the way they are represented by standardized measures.

Purposes of Observation: Guiding Decision Points

Before beginning observations of play for assessment purposes, investigators decide on the purposes of the observations and how they will be used. Those who evaluate children to decide on their eligibility for special services, for example, may need to collect different types of information and use different types of coding schemes than would classroom teachers or other early intervention team members who need to plan a child's intervention. Another decision is whether or not there is a need for more structured, formal assessment measures in addition to the play assessment. Play assessment yields valuable information, although examiners often consider it supplementary to traditional, standardized tests. The advantages of play assessment include an environment that is familiar to the child, as well as the ability to adapt the situation to children with special needs. Until more is known about the validity and reliability of assessment during play, however, it is likely that standardized assessment will continue to be necessary and appropriate. A combination of multiple forms of assessment, however, provides more useful information than only one form.

Videotaping as an Assessment Method

Investigators also must decide on the method of observation. Are videotaped interactions or live coded behavior more helpful? The use of videotape to assess play skills or other domains of development through play has become increasingly popular.

Advantages of Videotaping Videotaping enables teachers, parents, and researchers to view an observation repeatedly and examine children's progress over time (Linder, 1993; Prizant & Wetherby, 1993; Segal & Webber, 1996). Individuals can visually and auditorily compare the children's behavior from one point in time to another, making it easier to detect subtle differences. In a transdisciplinary model, team members who were unable to complete their evaluations during the time of the assessment can refer to the videotape (Linder, 1993).

Busy classroom teachers who do not have time to observe how children play during the day can videotape different areas of the classroom and then code the behaviors during a less hectic time (Johnson, Christie, & Yawkey, 1987). During the observation itself, videotaping frees up the assessors to respond to parent questions and concerns and give the parent prompts as necessary. It also enables the observation of detailed information that might not be possible during firsthand observation (Johnson et al., 1987). Although children often cannot be encouraged to repeat an unintelligible utterance or an unheard vocalization, the videotape of the session can be easily rewound.

Disadvantages of Videotaping Even though videotaping is a useful tool, its disadvantages need to be considered. First, assessing a child and then scoring behavior from the videotapes is often time consuming. Second, some observational tools may not be appropriate to use when scored from a videotape. Researchers, for example, have found differences in the coding of live and taped observations with groups of children in a playgroup setting (Fagot & Hagan, 1988). Possible differences between the two methods of coding need further investigation. Another disadvantage to videotaping occurs when the camera is visible and novel to the children. The visibility may cause children to change their behavior; they may, for example, point to the camera or act shy. Some parents may resist being videotaped or having their children videotaped (Segal & Webber, 1996). Videotaping equipment tends to be costly and often requires upgrading as technology improves and older equipment becomes outdated. Finally, the individual who does the videotaping needs to be trained to adequately capture what is needed on tape. It is necessary, therefore, to choose the observational tool in advance to plan the kinds of actions and behaviors that must be captured by the videotaping.

How to use and report findings depends on the purpose of the assessment. As mentioned earlier, play observations can be used in diagnosing children, making placement decisions, and also in planning children's intervention services. Play assessment data is often very valuable for researchers who are conducting program evaluations. While investigators often use standardized instruments, play assessment captures children's typical performance rather than their performance in a strange situation

Conclusion

Children's play provides a delightful arena for viewing developmental skills in action. Today's assessment team members can capture the functional use of skills in all domains as children use them while having fun. The opportunity that play provides through an informal process requires the assessor to have good clinical and observational skills and to make decisions about what should be done during the assessment process. Researchers are beginning to provide evidence that the play assessment process, both from the perspectives of assessing play itself as a domain and the assessment of other domains within the play context, is a valid and reliable way to capture and quantify children's developing skills. Because play assessment is still underutilized and in its infancy compared to the use of traditional standardized measures of child development, it is imperative for this research to continue and for practitioners to share and disseminate information regarding its use. Continued research and use of play assessment will push the field forward and allow play assessment to become the norm and a respected part of a child's assessment battery as opposed to being continually considered as an alternative measure of child development.

Notes

1. This chapter is a revision of an earlier version written by Rebecca Fewell and Michelle Glick.
2. Smilansky (1968) identified four categories of cognitive play: functional play, constructive play, dramatic play, and play with rules. The six social play categories of Parten (1932) are as follows: unoccupied behavior, solitary play, onlooker behavior, parallel play, associative play, and cooperative play.

References

Beeghley, M., Hanrahan, A., Weiss, B. W., & Cicchetti, D. (1985). *Development of communication competence in children with Down syndrome.* Paper presented at the biannual meeting of the Society for Research on Child Development, Toronto.

Belsky, J., & Most, R. K. (1981). From exploration to play: A cross-sectional study of infant free play behavior. *Developmental Psychology, 17(5),* 630–639.

Bergen, D. (1994). *Assessment methods for infants and toddlers.* New York: Teachers College Press.

Bricker, D. (2002). *Assessment, evaluation, and programming system (AEPS) for infants and children: Vol. 1. AEPS administration guide* (2nd ed.). Baltimore: Brookes.

Butcher, J. (1991). Development of a playground skills test. *Perceptual and Motor Skills, 72(1),* 259–266.

Butcher, J. (1993). Socialization of children's playground skill. *Perceptual and Motor Skills, 77(3),* 731–738.

Casby, M. H., & Corte, M. D. (1987). Symbolic play performance and early language development. *Journal of Psycholinguistic Research, 16(1),* 21–42.

Caster, T. R. (1984). The young child's play and social and emotional development. In T. D. Yawkey & A. D. Pellegrini (Eds.), *Children's play and play therapy* (pp. 17–29). Lancaster, PA: Technomic.

Craig, H. K., & Washington, J. A. (2000). As assessment battery for identifying language impairments in African American children. *Journal of Speech, Language, & Hearing Research, 43(2),* 366–379.

Crais, .R., & Roberts, J. E. (2004). Assessing communication skills. In M. McLean, M. Wolery, & D. B. Baily, Jr. (Eds.), *Assessing infants and preschoolers with special needs* (3rd ed., pp. 345–411). Upper Saddle River, NJ: Pearson.

Culp, A. M., & Farran, D. C. (1989). Manual for observation of play in preschoolers. Unpublished manuscript. Available from D. C. Farran, Peabody College, Vanderbuildt University, Ashville, TN 37203.

Deutscher, B., & Fewell, R. R. (2001). The development and use of the attention deficit hyperactivity disorder-observational rating scale: Factor analysis and a preliminary investigation of predictive validity. *Journal of Psychoeducational Assessment, 19*, 317–333.

DiCarlo, C. F., Reid, D. H., & Stricklin, S. B. (2003). Increasing toy play among toddlers with multiple disabilities in an inclusive classroom: A more-to-less, child-directed intervention continuum. *Research in Developmental Disabilities, 24*, 195–209.

Dunn, M., & Flax, J. (1996). The use of spontaneous language measures as criteria for identifying children with specific language impairment: An attempt to reconcile clinical and research incongruence. *Journal of Speech and Hearing Research, 39*(3), 643–654.

Fagot, B., & Hagan, R. (1988). Is what we see what we get? Comparisons of taped and live observations. *Behavioral Assessment, 10*(4), 367–374.

Fantuzzo, J. W., & Hampton, V. R. (2000). Penn Interactive Peer Play Scale: A parent and teacher rating system for young children. In K. Gitlin-Weiner, A. Sandgrund, & C. Schaefer (Eds.), *Play diagnosis and assessment* (2nd ed., pp. 599–620).

Fantuzzo, J., Sutton-Smith, B., Coolahan, K. C., Manz, P. H., Canning, S., & Debnam, D. (1995). Assessment of preschool play interaction behaviors in young low-income children: Penn Interactive Peer Play scale. *Early Childhood Research Quarterly, 10*, 105–120.

Fantuzzo, J., Manz, P., Atkins, M., & Meyers, R. (2005). Peer-mediated treatment of socially withdrawn maltreated preschool children: Cultivating natural community resources. *Journal of Clinical Child and Adolescent Psychology, 34*(2), 320–325.

Farmer-Dougan, V., & Kaszuba, T. (1999). Reliability and validity of play-based observations: relationship between the PLAY behavior observation system and standardized measures of cognitive and social skills. *Educational Psychology, 19*(4), 429–440.

Farran, D. C., & Son-Yarbrough, W. (2001). Title I funded preschools as a developmental context for children's play and verbal behaviors. *Early Childhood Research Quarterly, 16*, 245–262.

Fenson, L. (1985). The developmental progression of exploration and play. In C. C. Brown & A. W. Gottfried (Eds.), *Play interactions: The role of toys in children's development* (pp. 31–38). Skillman, NJ: Johnson & Johnson.

Fewell, R. R. (1991). *Play assessment scale.* Unpublished manuscript, University of Miami, School of Medicine.

Fewell, R. R., & Ogura, T. (1997). The relationship between play and communication skills in young children with Down syndrome. *Topics in Early Childhood Special Education, 17*(1), 103–118.

Finn, D. M., & Fewell, R. R. (1994). The use of play assessment to examine the development of communication skills in children who are deaf-blind. *Journal of Visual Impairment and Blindness, 88*(4), 349–356.

Foley, G. M. (1992). Portrait of the arena evaluation: Assessment in the transdisciplinary approach. In E. D. Gibbs, & D. M. Teti (Eds.), *Interdisciplinary assessment of infants: A guide for early intervention professionals* (pp. 271–286). Baltimore: Brookes.

Furuno, S., O'Reilly, K. A., Hosaka, C. M., Inatsuka, T. T., Zeisloft-Falbey, B., & Allman, T. (1984). *HELP checklist.* Palo Alto, CA: Vort.

Hampton, V. R., & Fantuzzo, J. W. (2003). The validity of the Penn Interactive Peer Play scale with urban, low-income kindergarten children. *School Psychology Review, 32*(1), 77–91.

Heidemann, S., & Hewitt, D. (1992). *Pathways to play: Developing play skills in young children.* St. Paul, MN: Redleaf.

Hill, R. M., & McCune-Nicolich, L. (1981). Pretend play and patterns of cognition in Down's syndrome children. *Child Development, 52*(2), 611–617.

Howes, C. (1980). Peer Play Scale as an index of complexity of peer interaction. *Developmental Psychology, 16*(4), 371–372.

Howes, C., & Matheson, C. C. (1992). Sequences in the development of competent play with peers: Social and social pretend play. *Developmental Psychology, 28*(5), 961–974.

Johnson, J. E., Christie, J. F., & Yawkey, T. D. (1987). *Play and early childhood development.* Glenview, IL: Scott, Foresman.

Kelly-Vance, L., Needelman, H., Troia, K., & Ryalls, B. O. (1999). Early childhood assessment: A comparison of the Bayley Scales of Infant Development and play-based assessment in two-year old at-risk children. *Developmental Disabilities Bulletin, 27*(1), 1–15.

Largo, R. H., & Howard, J. A. (1979). Developmental progression in play behavior of children between nine and thirty months. 1: Spontaneous play and imitation. *Developmental Medicine and Child Neurology, 21*(3), 299–310.

Levine, L. M., & Antia, S. D. (1997). The effect of partner hearing status on social and cognitive play. *Journal of Early Intervention, 21*(3), 21–35.

Lim, S. E. A. (1998). Linking play and language in Singapore preschool settings. *Early Child Development and Care, 144*, 21–38.

Linder, T. W. (1993). *Transdisciplinary play-based assessment: A functional approach to working with young children* (Rev. ed.). Baltimore: Brookes.

Lyytinen, P., Poikkeus, A. M., & Laakso, M. L. (1997). Language and symbolic play in toddlers. *International Journal of Behavioral Development, 21*(2), 289–302.

McCune, L. (1995). A normative study of representational play at the transition to language. *Developmental Psychology, 31*(2), 198–206.

McCune-Nicolich, L. (1980). *A manual for analyzing free play.* New Brunswick, NJ: Rutgers University Press.

Milfort, R., & Greenfield, D. B. (2002). Teacher and observer ratings of head start children's social skills. *Early Childhood Research Quarterly, 17*, 581–595.

Mullan, M. R. (1984). Motor development and children's play. In T. D. Yawkey & A. D. Pellegrini (Eds.), *Children's play and play therapy* (pp. 7–15). Lancaster, PA: Technomic.

Myers, C. L., & McBride, S. L. (1996). Transdisciplinary, play-based assessment in early childhood special education: An examination of social validity. *Topics in Early Childhood Special Education, 16*(1), 102–127.

Parten, M. B. (1932). Social participation among pre-school children. *Journal of Abnormal and Social Psychology, 27*, 243–269.

Piaget, J. (1962). *Play, dreams, and imitation in childhood.* New York: Norton.

Prizant, B. M., & Wetherby, A. M. (1993). Communication and language assessment in young children. *Infants and Young Children, 5*(4), 20–34.

Rogers, S. J. (1982). Cognitive characteristics of young children's play. In R. Peiz (Ed.), *Developmental and clinical aspects of young children's play* (pp. 1–13). Monmouth, OR: WESTAT.

Rubin, K. (1989). *The play observation scale.* Waterloo, ON: University of Waterloo.

Segal, M., & Webber, N. T. (1996). Nonstructured play observations: Guidelines, benefits, and caveats. In S. J. Meisels & E. Fenichel (Eds.), *New visions for the developmental assessment of infants and young children* (pp. 207–230). Washington, DC: Zero to Three National Center for Infants, Toddlers, and Families.

Sheridan, M. K., Foley, G. M., & Radlinski, S. H. (1995). *Using the supportive play model.* New York: Teachers College Press.

Sluss, D. J., & Stremmel, A. J. (2004). A sociocultural investigation of the effects of peer interaction on play. *Journal of Research in Childhood Education, 18*(4), 293–305.

Smilansky, S. (1968). *The effects of socio-dramatic play in disadvantaged preschool children.* New York: Wiley.

Westby, C. E. (1980). Assessment of cognitive and language abilities through play. *Language, Speech and Hearing Services in the Schools, 11*(3), 154–168.

Yoshinaga-Itano, C., Snyder, L. S., & Day, D. (1998). The relationship of language and symbolic play in children with hearing loss. *Volta Review, 100*(3), 135–164.

Zill, N., Resnick, G., Kim, K., McKey, R. H., Clark, C., Pai-Samant, S., et al. (2001). Head Start FACES: Longitudinal findings on program performance (Third Progress Report). (ERIC Document Reproduction Services No. ED453969).

25

Reconciling Play and Assessment Standards

How To Leave No Child Behind

DORIS BERGEN

Throughout history, play has been seen as the natural "medium"of childhood, through which learning occurs in physical, social, emotional, language, moral, and cognitive realms (Bergen, 1998). It has been defined in many ways, but in all definitions there are a few characteristics that are usually agreed upon. For example, play requires physical and mental activity, it is enjoyable and thus internally motivated, it is flexible and elaborative rather than static, it allows risk taking without dire consequences, and it permits the creation of "realities" that are under child control and direction. Perhaps because play is such a pervasive characteristic of childhood, many renowned theorists have pondered the meaning of play and hypothesized about its purposes. Most of its purposes have been related to learning outcomes. For example, classical theorists have stated that the purpose of play is:

- to organize and make meaning out of experiences; that is, to construct knowledge (Piaget, 1962);
- to socially construct knowledge and learn self-regulation (Vygotsky, 1967);
- to master and gain control over social and emotional experiences (Erikson, 1977);
- to obtain one's preferred arousal level required for effective performance and maximum learning (Berlyne, 1966); and
- to insure survival of the human species by encouraging flexible thought and ability to adapt to uncertain and changing conditions (Ellis, 1998).

And, more recently, play has been promoted as a way:

- to keep the frontal lobe of the brain challenged with critical thinking and problems to solve between those times of actual crises that might require use of all of the brain's capacities (Sylwester,1995); and
- to enable children to have active experiences that assist in the maturation of executive functioning in the frontal lobe of the brain (Panksepp, 1998).

As other chapters in this book demonstrate, there are many studies supporting conclusions that play makes contributions to learning in a wide range of areas. Present day researchers have built upon the existing knowledge base to delve more deeply into specific questions about how play fosters a range of cognitive processes, such as theory of mind, symbolic representation of objects, understanding of humor, and development of language/literacy (Bergen, 2002a), as well as promoting mathematical, literacy, and other academic skill development (Christie & Roskos, 1999; Wolfgang, Stannard, & Jones, 2001). There is also study of sociocultural learning opportunities embedded in the play of children from diverse ethnic, racial, and national groups (Roopnarine, et al., 1998); and of play's role in facilitating the learning of children who have special needs, such as those with autism (e.g., Greenspan & Breslau-Lewis, 1999). Studies of the relationship of play to brain development (Panksepp, 1998) and of playfulness to coping skills (Barnett, 1998) also provide insights into play's importance. There is also a debate about the growth of "edutainment," which primarily involves the ways computer gaming may influence learning either positively or negatively (Papert, 1996, 1998). A few of the types of learning that can occur during typical types of play are listed in Table 25.1.

One of the most valuable aspects of playful learning is that children develop more positive attitudes toward the learning process. Here are a few of these attitudes (adapted from Honig et al., 1981):"I want to learn," "I know I can learn," "I know I can try new ways to learn," "I want to know many different things," "I'll keep trying to learn even when it is difficult," and "I feel good about myself as a learner." Children who do not develop these positive attitudes toward learning cannot be as successful learners as those who do have such attitudes.

Indeed, the question is not whether play can foster and elaborate children's learning but rather why play's importance in this regard is so often overlooked by policy makers, educational administrators, many parents, and even by some teachers. Recent reports of recess abandonment in order to have more academic task time; sections of the school year reserved primarily for drill and practice test preparation; and the cutting of play and other child choice times from the daily schedule, even in preschools, are all evidence that, as a response to educational assessment pressures and demands to

Table 25.1 Development/Learning Promoted by Play

Physical	Fitness and health as a life practice	Mastery of fundamental movements	Motor coordination for complex tasks	Preparation for actions required for academics and sports	Persistence in practice and focus on increasing skill
Cognitive	Imagination, creativity, ability to risk in thinking	Problem finding and solving	Discrimination, categorization, and concept development	Academic readiness skills	Metacognitive awareness and good learning strategies
Language	Verbal fluency and vocabulary growth	Mastery of language sounds, structures, meanings	Ability to use narrative and inner speech to solve problems	Ability to transform objects symbolically	Pragmatics of communication and metalinguistic awareness
Social	Knowledge of social scripts and appropriate behaviors	Appropriate role taking in learning situations	Practice in leading and following peers as well as adults	Conflict negotiation skills, self control, and empathy	Understanding of social comparisons, cooperation, and competition
Emotional	Appropriate expression of positive and negative emotions	Control of excessive emotions; self-regulation skills	Growth of self-efficacy and self-esteem in learning situations	Ability to use coping skills, such as humor	Gaining concepts of fairness, sharing, respect for others
Academic Readiness	Ability to use concrete materials to explore spatial, logical, and mathematical relationships	Use of a rich range of language and print symbols	Experience with a wide range of media and ability to express self in that wide range	Practice using fine motor skills, coordination, and self-regulation skills	Increased attention to self chosen tasks and persistence in completing them

increase test performance, even the small part of the day that play occupied in educational settings is being lost. What are the reasons for play not being considered by decision makers as a valuable activity that enhances learning? Is it because their definition of standards-based outcomes is so narrowly prescribed at the present time that it is difficult for them to see the many learning outcomes that play facilitates? Could it be a function of the way that such outcomes are being measured as a result of legislative mandates? Could it be that the educational outcomes they desire for all children are not ones that support the emergence of mentally active, flexible, creative, and adaptive problem solvers who hold positive learning attitudes?

Effects of Standards Assessment Requirements on Classroom Practice

In the United States, when the No Child Left Behind Act was passed (NCLBA, 2002), every state was mandated to demonstrate that they had standards-based accountability. That is, each state had to make standards for mathematics, reading, and science explicit for grade levels and also develop or select tests that were aligned to these standards. They had to set performance levels that could identify groups of children who had demonstrated basic, proficient, and advanced achievement as measured by these tests at the designated grade levels. The reading and mathematics tests are to be given every year from grade 3 to 8 and given once in high school (grades 10–12). Science proficiency is to be tested three times: in grades 3 through 5; in grades 6 through 8; and in grades 10 through 12. Further, the test results are to be reported to the public and used to judge the adequacy of student progress in each school. Students of all ability levels and diverse backgrounds must show progress in gaining proficiency and there are sanctions to be implemented against schools that do not demonstrate effectiveness in their testing results. Many states are now requiring testing in these subject areas at every grade level, including kindergarten, in order to have students "prepared" for the high stakes testing, and some states have expanded these requirements to include other subject areas as well. Other legislation has mandated that Head Start children demonstrate their "learning readiness" by acceptable performance on a test NRS, and the effectiveness of programs are to be judged by these children's test performance (Administration for Children and Families, 2004). While the exact nature of standards assessment in other countries of the world vary in their provisions, overall there has been a movement toward such use of standards-based assessments for school "accountability" in many parts of the world.

Because successful and productive adulthood in present day society requires highly educated individuals, having standards for learning at every age level in all subject areas is a defensible policy, and the belief that "every child can learn" is admirable. Indeed, earlier federal initiatives such as Head Start and concerns that national policy should have a goal to "Leave No Child Behind" (Children's Defense Fund, 2005) are important. Moreover, a portion of the goals stated in many standards do focus on helping children become mentally active, flexible, and creative; and acquire adaptive problem solving skills However, difficulties arise when policy-makers decide on what should be the appropriate means for measuring achievement of standards. At present the use of standardized tests predominates.

There are certainly some advantages to the use of such tests. For example, they serve as a way to evaluate a larger number of students (and teachers, schools, states, and countries!) in a fast, relatively cost-efficient way. By providing information that policy makers can use in comparing the test results of groups, they can measure how well various groups are learning the specific test-related content. Most importantly, if the tests are well-aligned with curriculum standards, they can help to identify problem areas that can inform instruction within schools. Even while education groups are attempting to meet these requirements of standards assessment, however, they have also raise voices in opposition to this approach as being too narrow, developmentally inappropriate, discriminatory, and anxiety producing—thus, counterproductive (Association for Childhood Education International, 1991; National School Boards Association, 2004) Problems with standards assessment approaches that have been identified include (but are not limited to) the following:

- *Because tests are representative of specified content standards, they may not reflect the specific curriculum of a particular school.* Thus, if there are curriculum areas (such as music, social studies, art, health, physical education) not currently covered by standards, those areas may begin to get less emphasis in the school. Informal reports from many school personnel indicate that this shift in curriculum emphasis is already occurring. If they are emphasized, student gains in these curriculum areas may be discounted or overlooked because they are less valued.
- *School mandated requirements that teachers "teach to the test" are becoming more and more evident, especially in communities where students' test performance has been compared unfavorably to that of other schools.* Because test questions are samples selected from a broad content body, however, when students are taught the specifics of tests they may perform better on that test, but the evidence that they have learned the entire body of content required in the standard is compromised. That is, the test loses its validity.
- *The assumption that the same group of children are taking the tests each year is not usually accurate because of the constant change in school demographics.* Scores from one year may go down in another year while teaching methods are constant because the mix of students with different abilities, experiences, or cultures have changed. This flux in student class composition is especially problematic for schools in lower socioeconomic areas.
- *Overall school standards may be lowered and curriculum narrowed in order to provide the best success rates on the tests.* This is especially likely when sanctions that reduce school funding may be the consequence of lower test performance.
- *For younger children in particular, demonstration of learning by means of standardized tests may be more difficult than showing learning through performance assessments such as collection of daily work through portfolios.* This is another problem with the validity of such tests; validity may be lower when tests are used with younger children.

While all of these concerns are relevant, at the present time they are not influencing national policy in the United States, nor that of many other countries. Although advocates for broader means of demonstrating standards achievement will continue to try to affect policy, no change is likely in the short term. Testing as the major method of standards assessment is likely to be required for the foreseeable future. Therefore, proponents of play must ask the question of how to reconcile play and assessment standards.

Methods for Reconciling Play and Assessment Standards

There are two major methods for reconciling play and assessment standards. One is to enlarge the standards in every curriculum area to include learning attributes that are particularly fostered by playful experiences. More educational outcomes that measure the emergence of mentally active, flexible, creative, and adaptive problem solvers who also hold positive learning attitudes could be instituted. The case for this can be made on the basis of what is currently being discussed in the economic, business, and technology world, in which the answer to the loss of routine jobs to developing countries is that the creative and innovative talents of the United States work force need to be supported. In order to keep the advantage that the United States has held in these areas, the education of young people has to include the elements that are strongly supported by playful approaches to learning because these approaches are more likely to foster creative ingenuity than are requirements to do well on routine standards assessment. This would require that the narrowly prescribed outcomes of the present standards assessment be greatly expanded to incorporate these more playful outcomes.

Another method that would incorporate playful learning is for the present standards outcomes to be measured in a variety of ways, which might include performance assessments in addition to standardized tests or as a replacement for such tests. Admittedly, the ability to compare groups on test scores would be more difficult; however, these comparisons appear to be more debilitating than enabling to the goals of increasing school evidence of effective performance. The education of legislators about the diverse methods available to measure performance outcomes would be necessary, of course. The many diverse ways of measuring learning outcomes seems to be an important body of knowledge that is unknown to most policy makers. This approach would require educators to analyze the present standards and determine how each of them could be measured by multiple means, including ones that involved playful choice and enactment. Although comparisons of schools would be more complex, there are statistical methods that could show individual growth in competency across time, which is a major goal of NCLB.

Four (Interim) Suggestions for Including Play in the Assessment Standards Preparation Process

The two major methods suggested for making assessment standards more developmentally appropriate and encompassing of playful learning will take time to implement, although there should be a concerted effort to influence policy in those ways. Although these are ideas that might be embraced by many teachers, especially those who are in early childhood classrooms, it may be difficult to implement them any time in the near future. As the negative effects of the present policies become more explicit, perhaps there will be a change in these policy directions. However, until such time, there are four suggestions discussed in the section below and in Figure 25.1 for including play in the preparation of children for the present standards assessment requirements. The suggestions draw on the "Schema of Play and Learning"discussed in earlier works of the author (Bergen, 1998; derived from Neumann, 1971). The schema characterizes the range of play and learning types in relation to the amount of internal control, motivation, and reality that the participants have in the activity. That schema is presented in Figure 25.1.

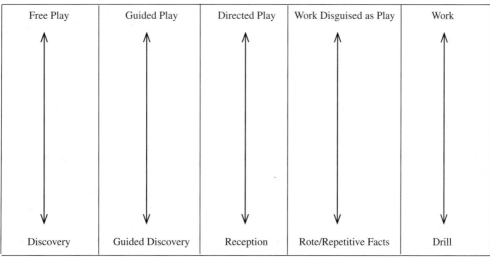

Types of Play*

Free Play	Guided Play	Directed Play	Work Disguised as Play	Work
Discovery	Guided Discovery	Reception	Rote/Repetitive Facts	Drill

Types of Learning*

*Based on amount of internal control, motivation, and reality the activity contains (Neumann, 1971).

Figure 25.1 The Schema for Play and Learning.

   1. *Promoting playful means for learning required material (Work Disguised as Play)*.
When teachers are required to "teach to the test," they have little internal control over the task, minimal motivation to do the task, and no escape from the "real world" demands of testing. However, with the students' help, they can still change much of this activity into "Work Disguised as Play." For task-oriented activities that are not inherently playful but must be done, such as rote memorization, repetitive practice, and anxiety-producing drills, teachers can engage the students in suggesting ways that these tasks can be made more fun. Teachers have often used this strategy in teaching routine material; for example, learning the alphabet song or playing a game to learn one-to-one correspondence. However, rather than having teachers disguise the "test game" as a type of play, they can discuss with the students why this repetitive work must be done and engage students in thinking up some ways to make it more fun. Since creating challenges through play is something that students are experts at, they can help invent playful ways to learn "test taking" and "test facts," which can increase the motivation for practice and also reduce test anxiety. For example, small groups of students could work together, taking turns being the "test giver" and "grader." Games can be invented that require orally stating information in order to win, and students can invent mnemonic songs or stories to help them remember algorithms or categories. The strategy of turning work into play can succeed with students of all age levels, not just with young children. Older students are very adept at turning work into play if they are allowed to do so. Of course, not all test preparation needs to be playful, but having the play option interspersed during the test preparation time period can change the dynamics for both students and teachers.

   2. *Promoting meaningful learning tied to active experiences (Directed Play)*
Much learning requires a common experiential base and if that base is evident, meaningful learning can occur in "Directed Play." To use directed play, the teacher must know what common experiences the students already bring to school or must be sure that those experiences can be provided, either directly or vicariously. Much directed play is tied to active experiences of pretend, in which a "set" may be provided and students then enact roles that have been given to them that can make standards content meaningful. In this type of play, there is at least some internal control, motivation, and reality-bending that the students can access. For example, many reading tests require making inferences or developing concept maps. In class, "plays" that enact those stories and require the players to have read the story, planned the play, and designed inferential questions for the audience to answer can help children learn meaningfully. They can enact a variety of different endings based on the information in the story. Interspersing this playful activity among sessions of individual reading and answering inferential questions would add motivation to the task. Similarly, having concrete materials that students must label with concept names and organize into "shows" that they then explain to other students can make the task of concept mapping more fun. One of the requirements in the fifth grade standards in Ohio, for example, is that students can understand "figurative language." Such understanding comes more easily when students can create such language through storytelling of tall tales, finding or writing poetic expressions, and developing simulations. While directed play activities may seem to be more time consuming than drill and practice, the salience of meaningful learning gained in directed play is often much greater and may lead to better remembrance of such strategies during test taking.

   3. *Promoting structured learning experiences that lead to deep conceptualizations (Guided Play)*
Many standards, especially at upper elementary and middle school grade levels, require students' ability to engage in higher order thinking and deeper conceptualization in order to perform correctly. Thus, "Guided Play," with problem-based projects that include playful qualities and choices for students can greatly assist their ability to analyze and synthesize information. In guided play, the teacher can set up "experiments to be explored" with some guidelines for solving the problems. While this approach is most often seen in science or math, it can be useful in many subject areas. For example, a type of question often on tests is one of "conversion" of units of measurement. When the teacher sets

up a problem center that requires children to playfully explore many units, and students make up problems that test these unit similarities and differences, and then record those results, the children will have a much better experiential base for doing such problems on tests than if they had just seen drawings of the units on workbook or test materials without having had direct experiences playing around with the quantities. Play with table blocks, measuring units, water, room dimensions, and other instances requiring measurement will give students a better base of experience when such questions are encountered on tests because they will understand what the test question really means. The ability to "compare and contrast information" is a standard for second grade in Ohio, for example, and the state recommends helping students to learn how to use graphic organizers such as cluster maps, spider maps, family trees, and hierarchy diagrams. Children can learn these skills through many playful open-ended projects that allow some internal control, motivation, and reality-testing. Students usually can remember such concepts much more strongly if they design the organizers in projects they have chosen rather than having drill and practice on these skills.

4. *Promoting child directed learning experiences that build on individual interests (Free Play)*
While the kind of "Free Play" that teachers encourage in settings for young children is not likely to be prominent in schools, there is still an opportunity for two types of free play to be available and to add a rich dimension to test preparation. One type involves a time for "choices" that is set up on a regular basis in a classroom and is not contingent on having completed "work." During that time period, each student might choose some type of learning in which they have an interest and pursue that learning through books, construction activities, technology, or social interactions. These activities could all be within parameters of certain skills needed for standards performance. A means of reporting what they learned would be needed but it might be through writing, pictures, or other appropriate means. Another type of free play that is unfortunately not seen very much in schools is "mental free play" in which creative "brainstorming" types of discussions are held. These can also be standards-focused but would have the element of "anything goes" initially. The old standby exercise often used with adults, for example, where everyone writes down their ideas, solutions, and important points on sticky notes and pastes them around the room could be useful for many kinds of learning. For example, children could generate solutions to social or self-regulation problems and then find areas for agreement or ways to adapt solutions to meet the ideas of many students. This type of play has the greatest internal control, motivation, and reality-bending-of-actual "worlds" with new rules or practices that children might design. While this type of play might seem far from the kinds of thinking needed for test taking, it often is not. The hardest questions on tests are usually ones with some hypothetical case or problem that students need to think through in order to understand the best solution.

Providing Well-Educated Persons for the "Flat World:" A Play Strategy for Educators

As a recent book title indicates, the educated person for the future must be capable of living in a "Flat World" (Friedman, 2005), in which creativity and adaptability will hold sway throughout the world, and those societies that foster such abilities will reign supreme. There will probably always be societal and educational standards that must be met but these will provide just the minimum for the educated person in the world ahead. The goal of having every child be well educated is an admirable one and the ability to demonstrate one's knowledge, either through tests as we know them today or by other performance means will continue to be important. One of the best things about play is that it allows individuals to expand their abilities in a low-risk way and they can then demonstrate the competence they gain through play in higher-risk situations. To best prepare students for standards assessment, therefore, teachers need to help them to draw on their playful natures as well as on their practiced skills. For consistent, long term achievement, play and learning are closely tied together, for "enjoyment of learning is most likely to be fostered in play environments" (Bergen, 1998, p. 120).

References

Administration for Children and Families (2004). National Reporting System: Author. Retrieved November 2005.

Association for Childhood Education International/Perrone, V. (1991). Position paper. On standardized testing. *Childhood Education, 67*, 12–142.

Barnett, L. (1998). The adaptive powers of being playful. In S. Reifel (Ed.), *Play and culture studies* (Vol. 1, pp. 97–120). Stanford, CT: Ablex..

Bergen, D. (Ed.) (1998). Readings from play as a medium for learning and development. Olney, MD: Association for Childhood Education International.

Bergen, D. (2002a). The role of pretend play in children's cognitive development. *Early Childhood Research & Practice [Online], 4*(1). Available: http//ecrp.uiuc.edu/v4n2/bergen.html

Bergen, D (2002b). Evaluating "brain-based" curricular claims. *Social Education*, 66(6), 376–379

Berlyn, D. E. (1966). Curiosity and exploration. *Science, 153*, 25–33.

Children's Defense Fund (2005). Leave no child behind. Retrieved November 2005 from http://www.childrensdefense.org.

Christie, J., & Roskos, K. (Eds.).(1999). *Literacy and play in the early years: Cognitive, ecological, and sociocultural perspectives*. New York: Lawrence Erlbaum.

Ellis, M. (1998). Play and the origin of the species. In D. Bergen, (Ed.), *Readings from play as a medium for learning and development* (pp. 29–31). Olney, MD: Association for Childhood Education International.

Erikson, E. H. (1977). *Toys and reason*. New York: Norton.

Friedman, T. L. (2005). *The world is flat: A brief history of the 21st century*. New York: Farrar, Straus, & Giroux.

Greenspan, S. I,. & Breslau-Lewis, N. (1999). *Building healthy minds: The six experiences that create intelligence and emotional growth in babies and young children*. Cambridge, MA: Perseus.

Honig, A., Sponseller, D., Bergen, et al. (1981). *Getting involved: Your child's attitude toward learning*. (ACYF Contract No. 105-78-1025). Washington, DC: U.S. Government Printing Office. (017-092-00084-1) (also translated into Spanish)

National School Boards Association (2004). *An overview of student testing and assessment*. Alexandria, VA: Author.

Neumann, E. A. (1971). *The elements of play*. New York: MSS Information Corp.

No Child Left Behind Act of 2001. (2002) Pub. L. No. 107-110, 115 Stat. 1425

Panksepp, J. (1998). Attention deficit hyperactivity disorders, psychostimulants, and intolerance of childhood playfulness: A tragedy in the making? *Current Directions in Psychological Science, 7*(3), 91–98.

Papert, S. (1996). *The connected family: Bridging the digital generation gap*. Marietta, GA: Longstreet Press.

Papert, S. (1998, June, September). Does easy do it? Children, games, and learning. *Game Developer*, 88(5), retrieved November 2005 from http://www.papert.org/works.html.

Piaget, J. (1962) *Play, dreams, and imitation in childhood*. New York: Norton.

Roopnarine, J. L., Lasker, J., Sacks, M. & Stores, M. (1998). The cultural contexts of children's play. In O. N. Saracho & B. Spodek (Eds.), *Multiple perspectives on play in early childhood*. (pp. 194–219). Albany, NY: State University of New York Press.

Sylwester, R. (1995). *A celebration of neurons: An educator's guide to the human brain*. Alexandria, VA: Association for Supervision and Curriculum Development.

Vygotsky, L. (1967). Play and the role of mental development in the child. *Soviet Psychology, 5*, 6–18.

Wolfgang, C. H., Stannard, L. L., & Jones, I. (2001). Block play performance among preschoolers as a predictor of later school achievement in mathematics. *Journal of Research Childhood Education, 15*(2), 173–180.

IV
Social and Physical Contexts for Play

Introduction

The chapters in this section cover a variety of social and physical contexts for play. As an integrative activity in human life, play is an experience in simultaneity and immediacy. The personal meanings that children bring to sociodramatic and pretend play also serve as a lymphatic system that integrates children's diverse experiences, whether linguistic, social, cognitive, or creative (Fromberg, 1999). Play is at once discontinuous, predictably unpredictable, and self-organizing in sometimes episodic ways. In these ways, it is both dynamic and paradoxical. Because the process of delineating specialized views of play in earlier parts occasionally can have the effect of dismantling the uniqueness of play as a dynamic paradox, it is the purpose of this part to focus on the essentially integrative nature of play.

The opening synoptic chapters explore in turn the changing historical contexts as well as the multiple cultural contexts of play. Because play has a quality of extreme sensitivity to environmental factors, any analysis of play quality must consider the physical and social contexts in which play occurs. The physical factors in the environment include the materials and equipment available, the spatial arrangement and dimensions, the organization of time, and the presence of a range of sensory experiences such as texture, color, and sound. The broader ecological environment, such as an urban or rural community or the presence of natural or artificial features, also influence the quality of play. The social environment consists of child–adult and child–peer interactions within the contexts of family, school, community, religious, and other settings. It also includes influences from media, from ethnic and cultural messages, and from the values promoted by all of the social, economic, and political forces in the broader society.

Children are likely to play in any environment, whether or not it is physically safe or culturally circumscribed. The nature of their play, however, will be different if the environment lacks play materials or is emotionally risky. If adults want to facilitate play, they can be models of playfulness and provide interesting and challenging spaces for play. Many environments are conducive to high-quality play because they are designed especially to enhance play development. Natural environments also provide many opportunities for play if children can be safe. Traumatic environments, however, may prevent play or cause it to be minimal or distorted. Without question, play helps children to engage in the outside worlds of people and resources. These interactions have a profound impact on their capacity to cope with challenges and problems as well as successes that occur within or beyond play events.

There are some children, however, for whom both play development and progress in other developmental domains may be more costly acquisitions. If they have disabilities that hinder their active participation, or come from environments where adults do not encourage playful action, they may not have as much ease in meeting developmental challenges. Although most educators and psychologists are sensitive to the basic needs of such children, this sensitivity often has excluded their play lives, perhaps because learning the essential survival skills of daily life has such emphasis. The scholarship on play, however, suggests that all children can have optimal growth opportunities when play and playful learning approaches are integrated with their everyday lives.

The physical settings the chapter authors discuss in this section include play locations found by children in cities; outdoor play in unplanned, natural settings; and park and playground play specifically designed for children. Other authors discuss play at school and in the potentially traumatic setting of hospitals and clinics. In regard to social contexts, the contributors examine the influences of adults on the play of children in both early and middle childhood. These adult–child interactions can occur with parents and other family members, as well as with caregivers and teachers. Important social play interactions also occur with siblings and peers. The distinctive confluence of who plays, where, and when they play, how they play, and their motives for play contributes in complex ways to the children's experiences.

Reference

Fromberg, D. P. (1999). A review of research on play. In C. Seefeldt (Ed.), *The early childhood curriculum: A review of current research,* 3rd ed. (pp. 27–53). New York: Teachers College Press.

26
Play in Historical and Cross-Cultural Contexts

DONNA R. BARNES

From the beginning of history, children have played. They have played alone or with other people, sometimes with adults, more often with other children. Philippe Ariès argues that until the 1600s, European adults and children often played the same games: no distinction was made (Ariès, 1962). Children have played with toys, games, animals, and found objects. Among the earliest toys are dolls, balls, pull or push toys on wheels, and miniature boats. Children have engaged in both indoor and outdoor sports activities. Children have invented, or learned and recited, riddles, rhymes, songs, and verse; they have collected and traded objects that they prize; and they have joined in festivals and special celebrations. Play activities, sometimes varying from culture to culture, are often a function of a child's age, gender, and socioeconomic position, but can be seen as the "natural right" of childhood.

Through play, the serious "work of childhood" occurs. In play activity, children learn to test their strength, their agility, their determination, their capacities to cooperate and to compete, their speed, their cunning, their cognitive, physical, and manipulative skills, their gracefulness, their memories, and their imaginative abilities. Of course, usually children do not realize that they are testing themselves in these ways; rather they think only of the activity and not the larger meaning of the activity.

Parents and childcare providers are interested in the play of children. Educators, librarians, social workers, and pediatricians have professional interests in children's play. Academicians, philosophers, psychologists, sociologists, cultural anthropologists, archaeologists, historians, art historians, theologians, ethicists, and folklorists focus attention on children and their behaviors and toys. Anthropologists, for example, see play as a reflection of a society's economic and political organization, noting that games of strategy are associated with high political organization, while games of physical skill are found in societies at all levels of social organization. Manufacturers of children's toys, clothing, sportswear and equipment, playground equipment, and home furnishings; authors, illustrators, and book publishers; song writers and musicians; computer program designers; television producers, dramatists, and filmmakers; advertising agencies; recreational facilities owners, resort managers, travel agents, and coaches—all have an interest in what children do, what they need and want, and what they can be persuaded to acquire or use.

Playthings

Historical sources in print, artistic representations, and surviving artifacts document the evolution of playthings. Beyond preparation for adult roles, playthings have supported ceremonial purposes, built physical strategies and gaming skills, and stimulated children's imaginations. The sections that follow outline these phenomena.

Evidence of Children's Toys and Games

That children have played with toys and games during varied time periods and in cultures all over the world is known, in part, because museums collect and display these objects. Toys have been found in tombs, such as the wooden and papyrus wooden balls from Egypt that date back to 1400 BC, and game-playing activities are depicted on tomb decorations.

Archaeologists have unearthed ceramic, glass, ivory, and metal toys (or fragments of broken toys) from privies and underground rubbish long since covered by streets and newer construction. (Wood, cloth, and straw toys decompose more rapidly if buried in soil.) Sculpted, woodcut, or painted images of children playing appear on ancient Greek vases, in illuminated manuscripts, on paintings, on folding screens and hanging scrolls, friezes and decorative motifs in buildings. Children are occasionally depicted at play in tapestries or on other textiles. Two woodcuts from the 1491 *Hortus Sanitatis* depict a Nuremberg dollmaker creating dolls with movable limbs.

Literature is replete with references to toys and games, whether in the plays of Aristophanes, or published journals, diaries, memoirs, sermons, and letters of travelers, ambassadors, or missionaries. Oral accounts in the form of folktales, adages, songs and rhymes, frequently told family episodes, and oral history interviews are resources. Court records supply information, especially those fining parents for children´s misdeeds committed while playing boisterously or pilfering. Photographs, films, television tapes, as well as mail order catalogs and newspaper advertisements, illustrate children with toys and games. Occasionally children's toys or games are represented on minted coins or postage stamps.

Dolls and Balls

Dolls are among the oldest known toys for children. Early earthenware examples from ancient Greece indicate attention to hairstyles, breasts, and buttocks, suggesting that the dolls were probably meant as playthings for girls. "The earthenware dolls of the Greeks have survived in some quantity; they were very simply shaped and limbs were articulated by cords at the shoulders and thighs" (King, 1979, p.8).

Dolls have been cuddled, dressed, and chastised by their owners for centuries. Dolls have been cherished confidantes with whom a girl could share her secrets and her fears. For many girls, learning to fashion dolls' clothing was one way to learn and perfect sewing skills; even Queen Victoria sewed for her dolls as a child.

Dolls have also served religious or ceremonial purposes. Since the 18th century when Neapolitan artisans began producing miniature crèche figures (*presepio*) for home celebration of the Advent season, Christian children have arranged figures, including Mary, Joseph, the baby Jesus, shepherds, three kings from the Orient with their camels, and assorted barnyard cows and lambs at Christmas, hearing again the story of Christ's Nativity. In the 17th century, some Dutch Catholic youngsters received doll-like figures of saints as treats on St. Nicholas Day. Hopi children have been given small katsina dolls to remind them of spirit forces operating in the world.

On Boy's Day, May 5th, Japanese boys display their collection of samurai dolls just as their sisters display the dolls representing the Imperial Court on Girl's Day, March 3rd, but these dolls were never meant to be played with in a frivolous manner. They functioned for 1000 years or more as icons of cultural identity and heritage, closely linked to traditions of ancestor worship and veneration.

In 1810, the first manufactured paperdoll, Little Fanny, made her debut in London, but paper dolls in the mid-1700s had been used by dressmakers in London, Paris, Vienna, and Berlin to show fashions to adult women clients.

Balls

Around the world, balls have been made of wood, leather, cloth, wool, yarn, baked clay, polished stone, rubber, and plastic. Closely related to balls are the balloons made from inflatable latex rubber. Prior to the use of rubber, children would blow up, tie, and toss pig bladders, as evidenced in numerous 17th century Dutch genre prints and paintings. Chinese and Japanese children have long played with inflated tissue-paper "balloons." Balloons are often tossed, sometimes attached to a string and allowed to rise on the currents of moving air, and frequently broken with a loud pop. Fragile tubular rubber balloons have been twisted into animal shapes. Twentieth-century children in the United States also came to enjoy helium-filled plastic balloons, often printed with greetings and messages.

Rattles and Drums

Rattles appear in virtually all cultures. Native American peoples made their children rattles of dried gourds or turtle shells. During the time of the pharaohs, Egyptians made rattles of clay. Chinese and Japanese youngsters had rattles made from hollow bamboo tubes whose heads were covered with paper or thin sheets of wood.

Silversmiths working in the Netherlands, Germany, and France during the 16th and 17th centuries created engraved silver rattles for the tinkling amusement and pleasure of children from well-to-do families. Often silver rattles adorned with a piece of coral were used to soothe sore gums when infants were teething.

Children in Africa, Asia, Europe, and the Americas have delighted in drums fashioned of wood, tin, or pottery bodies and covered with tautly drawn animal skin, leather, parchment, or paper. Children have also found that hollow logs, cooking pots, or soldiers' metal helmets turned upside down can be beaten with a stick or spoon to make drumlike noises.

Horses

Hobbyhorses were an early European toy. A realistically carved or stylized horse head affixed to the top of a wooden pole provided a reliable mount for straddling children to imagine themselves riding across the fields, chasing enemies, or racing with friends in moments of derring-do. It is not surprising that hobbyhorses were popular in equestrian-based societies of Europe, when warfare was conducted by both foot soldiers and mounted warrior knights. While girls might have occasionally played with these hobbyhorses, they were much more often the toys of boys.

Seventeenth-century portraits and genre prints from Holland depict boys with hobbyhorses; in one engraving, a boy accompanies his mother to a market toy stand selling hobbyhorses along with drums and dolls. Interestingly, horses remain popular toys for young children, even in 21st-century highly industrialized societies where a child is unlikely to ride a horse either for transportation or in war.

Besides hobbyhorses, rocking horses became popular with children in Europe and the United States in the 19th and 20th centuries. These nursery steeds provide kinesthetic pleasure in their rocking movements. Psychologists suggest genital sexual stimulation might be another component. But rocking horses also serve to stimulate imaginary rides into terrains remote from home.

Toy horses have an even older history. Some have been made of wood, like a painted horse from Benares decorated with calligraphy displayed in 1956 in Santa Fe, New Mexico, as part of a special exhibition, *Decorative Arts of India*. Another Indian horse made of cast bronze with wheels, is characterized as having "all the requirements for a good toy: simple, sturdy, bright, and moveable" (Museum of International Folk Art, 1956, p. 24).

Brightly painted blue and red wooden horses are part of Swedish folk art traditions, often used as Christmas holiday decorations. Other horses have been made of clay or cast metal; numerous tin horses were manufactured in Germany, England, and the United States during the 19th and 20th centuries.

Tin Vehicles and Soldiers

Tin began to assume importance as a toy-making material for mass production early in the 19th century, and model horses were quick favorites. Makers of tin flats in the 18th century had created a number of scenes and situations in which the horse was the most important creature, such as the *Boar Hunt* made by the Hilperts of Nuremberg in 1770. Johann Friedrich Ramm of Luneberg made metal hunting scenes and menageries, while horse-drawn transport was a specialty of Georg Spenkuch of Nuremberg. Early tin fire engines were, of course, horse-drawn, and some continued to be made that way until 1920. The amazing variety of late 19th century horse-drawn transport can be witnessed in the London Museum's famous collection of "penny toys," most of which originated in France and Germany, though some were made in England (King, 1979, p.42). Splendid examples of tin and cast iron horses pulling fire engines, sales carts, and passenger carriages can also be found in the Rotterdam Historical Museum in the Netherlands as well as the collections of the Museum of the City of New York and the Shelburne Museum in Vermont.

Motorized transportation vehicles, as opposed to horse-drawn ones, have been favorites for children in the industrialized world during the 20th century. These range from scale-model miniaturized cars, trucks, fire-engines, police squad cars, ambulances, tractors, railway engines and train cars, ships, airplanes and spaceships to larger vehicles that small children can sit in and operate either by pedaling or engaging a battery drive. Often these vehicles provide opportunities for youngsters to fantasize about travel, or crash accidents, or possible adult work roles. The 2004 "Pedal to the Metal" exhibition at the Shelburne Museum explored the toy's connection to the evolution of American automobile design.

Toy soldiers have a venerable history. Wooden foot soldiers and charioteers have been found in tombs of ancient Egypt. Initially given to princes and sons of noblemen so they might rehearse battle strategies to be used later as adults when they assumed command of armies, toy soldiers were eventually mass produced in lead, tin, or plastic for countless boys.

Cards, Board Games, and Puzzles

Children devise games for themselves or play games taught to them by adults or older children. Sometimes these are card games or board games in which either chance or strategy comes to the forefront. Among the oldest is chess, a strategic war game that goes back to the seventh century A.D.

Game boards and pieces have also been preserved from the early Sumerian and Egyptian civilizations, as well as pictures of games being played. A wall painting in the Tombs of the Queens in Upper Egypt shows Queen Nefertari (the queen of Ramses II who reigned 1304–1237 B.C.) playing the board game *senet*; an Egyptian papyrus of about 1000 B.C. shows a seated gazelle and a lion engaged in the same pastime (Dennis & Wilkinson, 1968, p. viii).

Other favorite international games include checkers, parchesi, dominoes, mah jong, and backgammon. Backgammon was immortalized as *tric trac* by 17th-century Dutch genre painters such as Jan Steen, who show the game being played by adults in homes and taverns.

Playing cards were printed from wood blocks during the medieval period. By the 17th century, the Dutch were printing engraved playing cards on paper stock and exporting them to England, France, Poland, and Scandinavia. Images of adult card players can be found in Dutch art from the time period, and at least one painting by Dirck Hals shows children playing cards. Despite the fact that moralizing writers warned parents against permitting children to play cards or play with dice, various games of chance were popular with Dutch children.

Later, card games for children during the Victorian era tended to be intentionally "educational" with information about authors, rulers, countries, or trades rather than the spades, hearts, clubs, and diamonds used by adult players. But children have enjoyed matching images, besting one another with dares and bets, and playing for points in many card games. Moreover, the temptation to cheat at cards has not been restricted to adult players. Solitaire is an option when there is no one to play with; Go Fish! is a way for the youngest children to begin matching images; playing cards with different designs and images printed on their backs have been traded and collected by children in the United

States; and, when all else fails, playing cards can be carefully balanced into towers and castles and then knocked down.

Jigsaw puzzles have quietly amused children for years. Initially puzzles were devised as educational tools in the mid-18th century by European mapmakers who pasted maps on wood and had them cut into small pieces. However, nowadays simple large-sized geometric shapes, clown faces, or animal figures produced in wood or plastic are used by toddlers who also occasionally put pieces in their mouths when teething. Cardboard puzzles of greater complexity, more elaborate colorful imagery, and considerably smaller interlocking pieces are available to older children (and adults, to whom they were initially marketed at the beginning of the 20th century). Spatial relations skills and patience are strengthened by puzzlers who frequently play alone with jigsaw puzzles.

Construction Activities and Toy Machines

Construction activities with such materials as blocks, Lincoln Logs, Erector sets, and Legos reflect a major genre of playthings. Children use all of these materials to construct small buildings, roadways, and machines. Children have long found ways of stretching a blanket or piece of fabric between the backs of chairs or over fence posts and tree branches to form temporary castles, caves, hideaways, and tents. In these settings, children become warriors, explorers, prospectors, pirates, and other adventurers. More elaborate building schemes have been launched by those youngsters who build tree houses in the woods or in the backyard.

Teaching youngsters to play with machines was typical of industrialized societies. Toy manufacturers in Europe and the United States during the late 19th and early 20th centuries reflected the growth of industrialization occurring in England, France, the Netherlands, Germany, and the United States. Models of steam engines and power-driven lathes were meant to be instructive, not merely diversionary, for boys. Principles of leverage, balance, and gravity were inherent in many toys.

Even toddlers were not immune from construction-related toys. Sturdy wooden hammers, screw drivers, and large-size nuts-and-bolts in the mid-20th century gave way later to lightweight, colorful plastic versions that could not only be manipulated by the budding carpenter seated on the floor, but could also be used as floating bathtub toys.

Communications Technology and Imagination

Child versions of typewriters and printing presses were intended to promote literacy while teaching about equipment used in business offices. Late in the 20th century, children in the United States, Canada, Japan, and Europe entered the computerized electronic age, playing with video and computer games, such as Nintendo, that honed their computer literacy skills. Television programming for children, taking over the role previously served by radio, stereopticons, films, and magic lanterns, has expanded youngsters' knowledge of the world and also exposed them to animated cartoon figures' antics and mayhem. Many children know how to turn on and turn off television sets, VCRs, and DVDs by the time they are 2 years of age; they are not intimidated by the technology. Technologically fearless children are part of the communications revolution.

Even young children learn how to answer the telephone or mobile cellular phone through imitation and the use of small plastic toy versions. Some parents view such play as encouraging mannerly communication; but for children, the early childhood fascination with the telephone is connected to its sound, the fact that using a real telephone seems like such an adult thing to do, and the mystery of hearing the voice of someone you know but cannot see. Sometimes children invent people to talk with on the telephone, just as they relish the opportunities to play make-believe and dress up in fanciful costumes.

Children in the 21st century are manipulating digital cameras and animated computerized imagery, storing images and impressions, and creating stories that can be transmitted electronically for their own amusement and that of family and friends.

Animals as Playthings and Playmates

Live animals have long served children as both playthings and playmates. The Puerto Rican boy who carefully measures out feed and water for his rooster, for example, may view the cock as a pet that can be carried around from time to time by tucking it under his arm. Perhaps the rooster will be trained by the boy to participate in cockfights, with metal spurs attached to his legs to slash away at competitors. Or perhaps the boy views the rooster as livestock that will mate with the hens to produce eggs and more chicks, knowing that the cock will eventually end his days in the stock pot for caldo de pollo. Caring for the rooster is both a form of work, which, with its routine of feeding and watering, requires careful attention to the health and condition of the animal, and a form of play, particularly if the boy talks to the bird, strokes its feathers, imitates its crowing sounds, or chases it around the pen.

Caring for animals, whether sled dogs in Alaska, caged crickets in China, pigeons on the rooftops in Brooklyn, horses in Khazhakstan, milk cows in the Netherlands, golden carp in Japan, wooly llamas in Peru, pigs in New Guinea, elephants in India, reindeer in Lapland, or cats in London—is an activity for children around the world. It is a way to learn responsibility and it is a source of pleasure for children. Images of children enjoying their play with animals are found on ancient Greek vase paintings. A sculpture from ancient Rome, now housed in the Vatican Museum, depicts a young boy with his goose. Medieval European sculpture and paintings depict the infant Christ child playing with a bird. The artistic and literary traditions of children playing with pets are old ones.

Animals are a source of transport, and fun, as well as love and acceptance, for the children who grow up with them. Even prior to the invention of the axle shaft, Roman children enjoyed driving a cart hitched to a small horse (Veyne, 1987). Bedouin boys learn to saddle, cajole, and race camels across the desert, sampling victory and savoring the hot burning sun casting shadows across the sand. Indian boys have learned to drive elephants and decorate them with a magnificently ornamented *howdah* (saddle) and blankets for ceremonial processions in honor of earthly princes and the elephant-headed god Ganesha or various incarnations of Lord Vishnu. Southeast Asian youngsters in Cambodian rice paddies learn to ride the backs of stolid water buffaloes.

Children sometimes interact with animals out of curiosity or out of cruelty. Chasing butterflies with a net, trapping small silvery fish by damming up a rushing stream with rocks, collecting glowing fireflies in a glass jar, following the hare's footprints in the snow, picking lizards from the swaying branch of the hibiscus plant, quietly staring at the redheaded woodpecker making holes in the trunk of a tree, rolling acorns in the direction of a squirrel, and following the swarming bees back to the hive may all be the result of curiosity. Such activities have occurred since time immemorial because children are keenly interested in the natural world.

There is literature that advises adults who wish to introduce children to nature, whether through the crashing waves at the beach or the tiny seeds that sprout among the mosses in the woods (Carson, 1965). Publications for children, such as *Ranger Rick* (National Wildlife Federation), color photographs in the *National Geographic,* and public television broadcasts, such as *Nature,* have also prompted children's fascination with birds, mammals, insects, reptiles, and fish.

Attendance figures at the American Museum of Natural History in New York City, the British Museum of Natural History in London, and zoos and aquariums throughout the world also bespeak children's curiosity about the lives of creatures in the animal world. The animals need not be exotic. The Amsterdam Historical Museum's 2005 exhibition, *Stadse Beesten: City Animals,* focused not only on the animals of the local Artis zoo and domestic pets, but also on the herons, magpies, rats, fleas, mice, and fish found on the city's streets and in its canals.

Many children respond sympathetically to creatures of the natural world as playthings and play-mates; however, some are tormenters of animals. They squash frogs, tease dogs by attaching metal cans to their tails, steal the robin's blue-shelled eggs from its nest, throw sharp-edged rocks at snakes, or hurl cats and mice down a well. But whether responsible caretakers, curious investigators, or cruel tormenters, children play with animals.

Toy Animals

Some children play not with live animals but with stuffed, molded or carved toy animals. In nine-teenth-century America, wooden animals, representing the passenger list of Noah's ark, were thought appropriate play toys on Sundays for Christian children.

Teddy Bears, named in honor of President Theodore Roosevelt's 1902 refusal to shoot a young bear cub, quickly became popular. Miniaturized or nearly life-size stuffed lions, giraffes, monkeys, bears, ponies, rabbits, and pigs have joined cats and dogs as toy animals sold to children. Moreover, from Aesop's fables to the books of Beatrix Potter and Maurice Sendak, children around the world have enjoyed stories about animals, especially those whose behaviors and feelings mirror their own or the foibles of other people. Winnie the Pooh and Paddington Bear are both international favorites. Children have no difficulty imagining themselves in the animals' predicaments.

Imagination and Dramatization

Through observation, Greek children in Socrates' time learned to participate in religious rites and joined other families attending festivals, theater productions, and games. They also had ample op-portunities for the rich, imaginative recreation of the adventures and exploits of heroic gods and goddesses, warriors, kings, and queens during play activities in their own homes and among their friends. Imagining oneself the slayer of sea monsters or the ruler of a rich kingdom might have been enhanced by a wooden sword or piece of cloth used as a royal robe. But, even without such props, Greek children could project themselves onto center stage, given the stories they had heard and the dramas they had seen.

Jewish children during the Hellenistic period were not encouraged to display the athleticism characteristic of the Greeks. Modesty ruled against nude wrestling and dancing. However, stories celebrating the courage of the Maccabees, the skill of David in his encounter with Goliath, and the cleverness of Esther in her dispute with the treacherous Hamen all played a part in the imaginative life of the children of Israel wherever they were found. Music, song, and dramatic storytelling were among their pleasures. Biblical approval had been granted to timbrels, strings, pipes, cymbals, lyres, harps, tambourines, and castanets. Ancient Jewish peoples also taught their children to play the flute, trumpet, and oboe as well as to enjoy the pleasures of song and dance. Dramatizations through music, song, and dance were (and remain) part of the celebratory holiday experiences of Jewish children as they grew up in Canaan, Egypt, and Mesopotamia (America-Israel Culture Foundation, 1968). Storytelling and dramatizations among the people of Canaan formed and kept alive religious convictions. Children heard dramatic stories that originally in the hands of biblical writers were spare of narrative details; the stories aroused young listeners' sense of wonder, curiosity, and imagination. (Chase, 1955/1962).

Children everywhere also enjoy hearing about fairies, leprechauns, ghosts, witches, elves, monsters,, and spirit figures. For some of today's children, these creatures are introduced in books, films, and videos. For others, they are the characters in traditional tales told by storytellers or in puppet shows. Puppetry has been a source of delight for children in India, Indonesia, Japan, England, France, Italy, and the United States for many years. Whether puppets are made of paper, papier-mâché, wood, leather, fur, fabric, or plastic, they are granted a reality and life by child audiences (Baird, 1973). Imaginary or supernatural beings also appear as masked figures in dramas, parades, and festivals. At the end of September in the Ghanian city of Odumasi-Krobo, for example, the seven-day Nmayem festival is held to thank the gods who have provided millet. Talking drums and parading celebrants carrying carved statuettes that illustrate local legends, banners, brilliantly colored clothing and parasols are all part of the festival, which attracts, and enchants, children and adults (Van der Post, 1970, pp. 78–81). Chinese children have long enjoyed tossing firecrackers at the feet of masked dragon or lion dancers ushering in the lunar New Year: with each noisy explosion, they help keep evil spirits at bay.

Children have laughed at the antics of clowns and mimes, marveled at the legerdemain of magicians and jugglers, admired the gravity-defying contortions of acrobats and towering presence of stilt walkers, and have sung and danced to tunes played by musicians who show up from time to time in the streets and marketplaces or at festivals and fairs. Street drama has engaged children's attention from the days when wagon stages, drawn through the streets of medieval European cities, depicted the harrowing maw of Hell, belched smoke and fire, or reenacted the biblical tale of Abraham and Isaac.

Children have not only witnessed street drama and theatrical productions performed for their enchantment, but have played with toy theaters replete with sets, curtains, and actor figures to be moved across the stage. Paper theaters with paper sets and literary characters were popular with in children England, Denmark, Germany, and the Netherlands in the Victorian era. Children around the world have utilized shadow puppets, as well as hand puppets and marionettes, in creating their own plays or staging and reenacting familiar plays, fairy- or folktales. Collections of 19th- and early-20th-century miniature European paper shadow puppet figures are displayed at the Deventer Speelgoed Museum in the Netherlands. Today's child visitors are encouraged to try their hand by utilizing more durable plastic silhouette figures on stage behind a lit fabric screen.

Books

For centuries children enjoyed hearing stories, long before books were printed to be read to them or by them. In the 1640s, Jan Amos Comenius, the Moravian educational theorist, pioneered in the development of illustrated books to teach children to read. *Orbis Pictus* originally taught children the Latin words for common objects and experiences; later his method was applied to vernacular languages. But while Comenius's approach was didactic, it launched a later trend of vernacular language story books with printed illustrations for children. A popular theme was (and continues to be) dolls and toys who come to life. Hans Christian Anderson's *The Steadfast Tin Soldier* of 1838, Carlo Collodi's (1883) *Pinocchio*, Johnny Gruelle's rag doll characters, Raggedy Ann (1918) and her little brother, Raggedy Andy, introduced in 1920, were joined by Margery Williams's stuffed toy, *The Velveteen Rabbit* in 1922. Handsomely illustrated story books have become traditional gifts for children throughout much of the world.

Picture books with printed cloth or virtually indestructible plastic-coated pages, minus text, have been sold for little children who invent their own narrative to accompany the illustrations and who also develop an appetite for reading. Picture books also have featured pop up parts, moving parts, and flaps that open, along with different textures.

Symbolic Representations

Children around the world represent their play in a variety of forms, including singing and making music, dancing, making up stories, engaging in sociodramatic play, role-playing, and drawing with ink, pencils, charcoal, crayons, paints, colored chalks and other media. Perhaps what is most striking is that this impulse to play and draw finds expression even in the harshest of environments, for instance, children produced drawings in the Nazi concentration camps, some of which are on display at the U.S. Holocaust Memorial Museum in Washington, DC.

Navajo children have made drawings with colored sands; colored peas and lentils are used in India; brilliantly colored bird feathers are used by children in New Guinea. Australian Aboriginal children learn to make spirals of traditional geometry using colored rocks and soil. Polish and Ukrainian children draw on eggshells, using dyes and wax, creating *pysanky* (dyed egg shells) for Easter celebrations. Some youngsters draw on their own faces and bodies using dyes, paints, nail polishes, powders, or inks. Some color the skin of their companions. During the Holi festival in Bombay, India, commemorating the triumph of Lord Krishna over the wicked Holika, youngsters squirt each other with colored water and dust-colored powders (Rau, 1969, p. 103). Revelers at Mardi Gras in New Orleans frequently paint their faces; children at city street fairs in the United States often pay small sums to have their faces painted like clowns; and Halloween costuming for small children has often included smudgy beards and moustaches drawn on young faces with burnt corks.

Rituals and Ceremonies

A night of feasting culminates Ganesha's 10-day festival celebrated throughout India in the fall. Spectacular elephant parades in Mysore precede entertainment by traveling performers, professional storytellers, and puppeteers (Rau, 1969).

Children are often trained to participate in highly ritualized cultural ceremonies. These activities are not so much "play" as instances of instilling cultural values via aesthetically satisfying behaviors. Native American youngsters have learned to dance to the drum beat of "fancy dance" displays at pow-wows: their colorful costumes and flashing footwork, often jumping in and out of increasing numbers of hand-held hoops, reflect pride in heritage.

Yet just such rituals are also part of the human capacity for play (Brown, 1963; Huizinga, 1950). Some Japanese girls, for example, are trained in the rituals of the tea ceremony (*cha no yu*) which takes years of study (Steinberg, 1969, pp. 136–150); others learn about the art of flower arrangement (*ikebana*). Balinese youngsters, wearing elaborate headdresses, are taught to dance with stylized movements and play finger cymbals. Balinese girls in Serongga learn to balance on their heads towering food offerings, known as *bebanten*, of fruits, cakes, and rice balls decorated with flowers and carved palm fronds. Teenage girls carry these to the shrine of Batari Durga, the goddess of death. Once presented there, the delicacies are returned to the families who have donated them for consumption at a ceremonial feast (Steinberg, 1970, pp. 86–87). Training to balance these offerings begins at an early age. Mexican children accompany their mothers to the cemetery on November 1st and 2nd to honor deceased relatives on the Day of the Dead (*Dia de los Muertos*). The night-long candlelit vigil features music, offerings of flowers, much laughter, and candies for children shaped as coffins, skulls, and skeletons.

Gendered Play

Often those who have financial or commercial interests in children's activities direct their attention to play that is culturally sanctioned by gender, thereby expanding the potential market for their services and products. But it is not only economic interests that sanction separate play activities for children. Cultures that have fairly strict separation between activities and spheres of interest for adult males and females frequently begin training for that gender separation and future gender roles through the toys and games played by children. The pattern is evident throughout time and across cultures.

The Play of Boys

Ask the Haitian child playing marbles what he is doing and he might tell you that boys (but not girls) compete to win brightly colored glass marbles by well-aimed shots and by wagering. This boy might reveal some of the rules used by other players to decide which shot is best. Perhaps he might also describe the procedure for a boy who has lost his marbles but wants to stay in the game by playing "bokies"; wagering his ability to withstand pain, he places his hands in the ring for others to shoot marbles at his knuckles.

The boy would probably not tell you that boys of different social backgrounds can play marbles together, crossing over social barriers that prevent their interactions on most other occasions. Nor is it likely that the marble player would explain that the verbal exchange, sometimes encouraging and often jocularly insulting, among the male players is a pattern of male interaction that will last through adulthood. Nor would the boy reveal that Haitians believe it good for boys to spend time with other boys in activities that exclude the participation of girls, just as later in life he will spend time with grown men in relaxing activities that exclude adult women. The boy is playing marbles, and to him, that is the significance of the activity; he is playing to win and he is playing because it is fun.

Just as today's Haitian boy plays marbles for the fun of it, so, too, did the children of Ancient Rome who used nuts (Carcopino, 1963). So fond were 17th-century Dutch boys of using baked molded clay balls for marbles that they occasionally played on the smooth gravestones serving as floors in Dutch churches, much to the consternation of fulminating ministers.

In Attic Greece, through training programs in the open-air stadiums and arenas (*palaestra*), boys learned to wrestle, run, throw a javelin, hurl the discus, and broad jump. Stripped, their bodies oiled and coated with sand or soil, they worked out to develop bodily strengths. These skills would serve them well in their eventual adult roles as men who defended their own city-states when these came under enemy attack. Manhood was proven on the battlefield and in athletic competitions. Excellence, honor, and glory—all the rewards and attributes of *arête*—were celebrated in Homeric verse, in drama, and in olympiads.

Even if a boy was not destined to compete athletically at major contests, his physical training was thought to be important. Partly because of the Greek ideal of building sound bodies in which to house sound minds, and partly because adult warfare required men from the ages of 15 to 65 to be prepared to fight, these programs of physical activity were important. Teenage boys were trained rigorously for military service, building upon the physical capacities already developed in childhood. Greek vase paintings show boys with wheeled carts, and scholarship reveals that "Boys played with model warships and were also encouraged to build their own toy boats and carts as well as model horses" (King, 1979, p. 8).

Part of the Greek ideal for education included the importance of athletic games and training (Jaeger, 1939/1960; Kitto, 1951/1962; Marrou, 1964). Similarly, the virtues of courage that physical training was meant to instill were celebrated in Greek mythology and drama (Kingsley, 1855). Comparable patterns of training in weaponry and horsemanship persisted in medieval Europe for boys who were being groomed for knighthood. Competitions, jousts, and other games in the tiltyard served as means for chivalric education and displays of trained competence and courage. Seventeenth-century Dutch boys were expected to play with bows and arrows, whips, and slings to hone skills associated with hunting, a manly prerogative; just as American boys, especially those living in rural areas from the Colonial era through the 20th century, were expected to become adept at shooting guns at targets so they could hunt.

Danger has been a frequent concomitant of boys' play. Testing one's body strength and control, or one's bravery, was not only the hallmark of historic ancient cultures, but also is present in today's boys hitching "free rides" on the back of moving buses, subways, or trams; in audacious competitive displays of skateboard dare-deviltry; and in youngsters' elaborate break dancing on busy city sidewalks.

The Play of Girls

In ancient Greece, little girls often learned to dance and run races, activities thought appropriate for them before they entered puberty. Once reaching early adolescence, however, greater modesty was demanded of them.

Embedded in many childhood activities are preparations for later adult roles. Around the world and throughout many historical eras girls have played with miniature pots and pans and spoons. Whether made of pottery, wood, metal, porcelain, glazed ceramic, or plastic, these toys have allowed girls to imaginatively use implements typical of household domestic utensils and to imitate the behaviors of adult women. Miniaturized pots have been excavated from ancient Egyptian tombs and archaeological sites in Crete. No doubt Greek girls planned imaginary meals featuring olives, dates, bread, and honey more than 30 centuries ago.

Tea sets were popular toys for girls in England and the United States during the 19th and early 20th centuries. Pretending to cook and serve food and drink allowed girls to practice behaviors eventually expected of them as homemakers and hostesses. Bread and jam, muffins and fruitcake, tea with milk or lemon: these were what the young hostess offered her guests, whether the guests were dolls, teddy bears, or an occasional child or adult. Not just food preparation and service but table manners and the rules governing hospitality were learned as miniature meals were envisioned.

Tea sets for girls were manufactured in Europe during the 18th century (since the tea had been imported from India and China into Europe from the 17th century onward) and flourished in the nineteenth century (King, 1979). Not only basic tea sets with teacups and saucers, coffee cups, teapots, sugar bowls, bread and butter plates, and milk mugs, but entire dinner services with gravy boats, serving platters, vegetable bowls, dinner plates, soup bowls, covered soup tureens, and dessert plates were made in England and Germany. Colored patterns for children's sets often paralleled adult models produced by major dishware manufacturers. Porcelain tea sets were also illustrated with engraved images from nursery stories such as "Cinderella."

> The toy tea-set could be used to instruct girls in the elements of social behavior and the number of surviving sets suggests their play was often supervised. Production of... very well made sets appears to have declined in the early twentieth century, possibly because unsupervised play was becoming more common (King, 1979, p. 191).

Similar sets of miniature tableware were produced in limited quantities in Holland during the 17th century and later mass-produced for that country's children in the 18th and 19th centuries. In 1994, the Museum Boijmans-van Beuningen in Rotterdam displayed such a collection of children's tableware in its *poppen-goed* exhibition, organized by the decorative arts department's curator. Toy dishware collections also can be found in the Rotterdam Historical Museum, the West Fries Museum in Hoorn, and the Mr. Simon van Gijn Museum in Dordrecht. An early 17th-century Dutch engraving depicting children at play shows a group of young girls with their miniature cookware (*poppegoed*). Jan Luyken's *poppegoed* image of 1712 echoes the same theme (Barnes, 2004).

The elaborate 17th-century Dutch dolls' houses located now in museums in Amsterdam, Haarlem, and Utrecht were not meant for children but were created for the amusement of a very few wealthy women. However, the creation of miniature tableware displayed in these dolls' houses also reflects the popularity of dishware items for children. By the late 19th and early 20th centuries, dollhouses were common as girls played out domestic chores and imaginatively tried their hands at home decoration and furnishing.

The chores connected to kitchen work were also envisioned for the 19th-century British girl who played with a miniature kitchen range heated by methylated spirits. The child, just like her mother or the family's household servant, was expected to spend hours polishing the stove and its equipment (King, 1979, p. 175). Given adult women's sentiments concerning domestic chores (Davidson, 1982; Strasser, 1982), the girl's "play" at polishing bordered on "work".

Gender-Neutral Play

Since the mid-1960s in the United States and other industrialized Western nations, attention has been focused on children's toys and activities that are not gender-restrictive. Often at the urging of feminists, child development specialists, and early childhood educators (Greenberg, 1978), boys have been encouraged to play in the miniaturized kitchens, learning to wash dishes or set tables or serve food; to push replicas of vacuum cleaners and small brooms and mops across the floor; and to play at shopping for household foodstuffs in child-sized supermarkets.

In the 1990s, the Museum for Children (Museo del Niño) in Old San Juan, Puerto Rico, featured just such a *supermercado* for youngsters, who pushed small shopping carts through the aisles as they made selections from well-known brands of canned beans, milk, juices, and cereals, or from plastic oranges, bananas, and coconuts. Some children played the part of supermarket cashier, ringing up purchases on a cash register at the check-out area.

These activities mirrored the experiences of the adult world's markets and encouraged boys and girls to try out adult roles. Children were provided with similar opportunities to practice consumerism by role playing in the Edwardian grocer's shop with goods on display from the early days of the 20th century or by playing with the model of an English butcher shop featuring three butchers dressing and selling cuts of beef, pork, and lamb, both models now at the Bethnal Children's Museum in London (King, 1979, pp. 188–189). Frugal bargaining and budgeting for 19th-century Dutch youngsters was an objective of the miniaturized toy grocery shop now displayed at the Mr. Simon van Gijn Museum in Dordrecht.

The modern hope has been that boys would learn that homemaking chores are not restricted to women and girls; that they, too, have roles to play in acquiring and preparing foodstuffs and keeping the family living quarters neat and clean. Montessori nursery schools in Europe and the United States, like Japanese elementary schools, have long operated on the principle that it was educationally sound for both boys and girls to keep their classroom tidy, but seldom has that "work" been seen as a form of "play," nor was the lesson typically expanded to males assuming responsibility for household domestic cleaning.

Girls, previously excluded from the block corners by the boys in their nursery schools, have recently been encouraged to build ramps and bridges with blocks; to put pilots' caps on their heads and pedal-drive mock airplanes and helicopters in the schoolyard; and to pick up stethoscopes and announce, "The doctor is in." Here the hope is that girls will not have their adult career options limited to the more traditional roles of mother, nurse, and schoolteacher but will think of engineering, architecture, technology, aeronautics, science, and medicine as possibilities for them in the 21st century.

Resistance to Gender Neutrality

For both boys and girls, the aim recently has been to enlarge children's eventual adult options by expanding the range of toys played with in childhood. Clearly not all parents and not all children respond enthusiastically to these gender-free efforts.

Barbie dolls, first introduced in America in 1959 and now sold around the world, are not sold for boys. Ken, her masculine counterpart, was not offered to boys, but rather was a doll partner for Barbie. (He has since been retired from the product line; as of 2004 the hipper Australian surfer, Blaine, has taken his place.) Young girls who cherish their Barbies could arrange dates, slumber parties, and weddings for Barbie and either Ken or Blaine. They might pay attention to the males' costumes and fashionability, but both male dolls are an "accessory" to Barbie, just as her shoes, muff, and skis are. Barbie's dolls of the world collection, Barbies from the ballet, and the fashion designer Barbies have no male counterparts: they are pure girl fantasy toys meant exclusively for girls. Since 2001, a rival group of multicultural dolls, Bratz, have been marketed to the 'tween age (ages 7–11) girls who share the dolls' passion for fashion (Thompson, 2005, p. 44). On the other hand, the "anatomically correct" G.I. Joe and other "action heroes" are geared for boys; girls are not expected to play with them. Action Man was marketed in 1966 strictly for boys. Boy-appealing Ninja Turtles, Power Rangers, Wrestle Mania, and Rescue Heroes figures followed.

Play in Natural Environments

Contrasting with elaborate cultural rituals are children's imaginative pursuits in natural environments. Children often treat as seasonal adventures the search for edible bounties. Gathering foods as supplemental treats, those not the mainstays of the family diet, are viewed as "play" rather than "work."

Many children around the world are taught by older siblings or adults how to locate and pick fruits, nuts, and edible mushrooms or seaweed that grow in the wild. Czech, Polish, and Russian youngsters search out mushrooms in the forests; when these treasures are brought home, they are cooked in simmering butter or sour cream, treats for the entire family. Micmac children in Maine picked summer-ripe huckleberries long before white settlers arrived in New England. Scotch-Irish youngsters in Appalachia know where the luscious wild blackberries grow and how to avoid snakes that make their homes amidst the brambles. Caribbean island boys are often adept at scaling the trunks of coconut palms to bring down the ripe fruits. Irish children have gathered seaweed used to thicken puddings.

Similarly, children pick wildflowers and vines which they weave into wreaths or garlands, fashion into daisy chains, or bunch together into bouquets to give as gifts or use decoratively. They view these activities as a form of play.

Traditional play activities with natural props have also been present in varied forms throughout history. Children splash in streams or dam them up with stones, shells, or tiles to make small ponds just as Sir John Froissart recollected of his boyhood in medieval England (Rickert, 1964). Children roll large snowballs into snowmen or flop into the snow with their arms outstretched to create angels. Children skate on frozen ponds with the same joy that sent 17th-century Dutch children and adults to the ice as immortalized in Hendrick Avercamp's winter landscapes. Perishable mud balls, snowballs, and sand castles have had short but dramatic lives in the experiences of many of the world's children.

Children who climb trees and swing on branches in Africa, Asia, Europe, or the Americas, swim in the Dead Sea, dive into the Australian surf, fish in Canadian trout streams, or hike through woods are also carrying out time honored behaviors that delight and amuse them. Children have collected seashells, birds' nests and feathers, brightly colored autumn leaves, pine cones, rocks, dried seed pods, wasp nests, and animal bones—often to be saved, frequently to be discarded when the novelty of touching and looking at the detritus of nature wore off.

What could be more natural than a child's own body? Babies and toddlers, no doubt, found their toes and fingers, noses, ears, and penises just as fascinating in pre-Columbian South America or Renaissance Italy or Elizabethan England as they do in Tibet or Toronto today. Children have also explored, admired, and tickled the bodies of brothers, sisters, and friends.

Playgrounds and Parks

For centuries, children have found opportunities to play games in fields, along the shoreline of the beach, or on town streets. However, with an increase in population and subsequent demand for more housing, plus the increase in dangerous vehicular traffic in the 19th and 20th centuries, many large cities began to develop special playgrounds for children or sections of city parks where they might seek amusement. Child welfare reformers' efforts during the Progressive Era did not only extend to curbing child labor, but also to the creation of suitable play spaces which would take children out of harm's way, especially from traffic congestion on the streets and from the possibility of injuries sustained while playing in abandoned buildings or on construction sites. In 1892, Jane Addams initiated a model play yard for children at Hull House in Chicago. The Los Angeles Playground Department was established in 1904 to provide safe places for children to play outdoors. But another agenda behind these efforts was to provide "morally appropriate" recreational activities for energetic youngsters who might otherwise get into street fights, steal from market stalls, and harass adults. Much of the same motivation led in New York City to the formation of the Police Athletic League (PAL) which organizes team sports for city youngsters, especially those living in congested immigrant ghettoes. PAL blocks off certain city streets as outdoor play streets during selected hours of the day. Channeling youthful energy into healthy recreation is considered a deterrent to juvenile delinquency.

In the 1930s, with assistance provided by the WPA, city playgrounds across the United States began to be outfitted with swing sets, teeter-totters, and slides, to be later followed with metal climbing jungle gyms. Here children of varying ages could interact with others from their neighborhood or could play alone on the equipment. Large playgrounds often included a sand box play area and wading pool for little children who needed to be supervised by older siblings or adults; some playgrounds included tennis courts, baseball diamonds, and basketball courts for older youngsters; and some were equipped with swimming pools that required life guards or pool attendants.

Parks, previously considered green oases for urban residents who enjoyed some contact with planted gardens, trees, hedges and the birds and squirrels attracted to these environments, began to have some space set aside specifically for children's playground equipment and activities. Central Park in Manhattan housed a children's zoo. Other parks included hiking trails or bicycle paths, horseshoe pits, skating rinks for ice skating and later, at the end of the 20th century, for inline roller blades, wildlife discovery centers, game tables for chess and checkers, and picnic tables amidst the greenery.

Metal playground equipment set onto cement or asphalt for small children gave way in the last quarter of the 20th century to equipment made of colorful plastic often set atop thick rubber mats so that children who fell were less likely to break bones or sustain bad cuts and bruises. Presumably for the amusement of children, or at least for the amusement of their parents, some playground equipment was made in the form of colorful plastic animals such as dinosaurs, turtles, horses, and frogs. The Adventure Playground was one reaction against the tendency to overstylize or sanitize playgrounds. Based on European patterns after World War II, where youngsters claimed play space in rubble-filled derelict areas of bombed cities, during the 1960s, adults in Europe and America began to see that creative and thoughtful play might involve use of old tires that could be turned into swings or forts and large cement sewer pipes through which children could climb or slither on their bellies.

The Kwanzaa Playground begun in 1993 by community activist Shirley Bowen involved local African-American artists in Columbus, Ohio, who helped design equipment, and local children who selected colors for play equipment and created tiles that form the border around one of the play areas. Community involvement in planning and using the playground represented a significant departure from the usual top-down pattern of city park design.

Boundless Playgrounds is another grassroots movement in the United States beginning to attract worldwide attention. Begun in 1994 by Amy and Peter Barzach in West Hartford, Connecticut as an effort to build barrier-free playgrounds where children of all abilities, including the most severely disabled, could play together on challenging and stimulating equipment, the playground opened in 1996. Among the developmentally advantageous activities are a glider boat swing, fun house mirrors, raised sand tables, and cozy places to interact with other youngsters. The movement has spread across the United States, tapping into volunteers, foundation and government funding sources, child study experts, playground equipment designers, and parents and children with disabilities. If adults now see play as a natural right of childhood, then the Boundless Playground movement is advancing the claim that play is a right of all children.

Many municipal authorities and parents in cities across the United States and Europe are increasingly concerned that children's playgrounds are no longer safe for youngsters because they have been overrun by drug dealers, alcoholic derelicts, prostitutes turning tricks, and homeless people. Society's problem adults turn up in the parks. Even when playgrounds are free from these potentially harmful intruders, they are not always safe for children.

Childhood bullying has been a feature of playground life for several decades. Unsupervised children not only enjoy the pleasures associated with making new friends or learning new games and skills on the playground, they also run the risk of being hasseled by older, stronger, meaner, sneakier, angry vicious kids who, acting alone or in packs, bully the weaker among them. Playgrounds are not always safe or fun for children.

Play Under Adversity

While children everywhere have sought relief and pleasure in play, conditions have not always been favorable for them. African-American young slave children might have been permitted to play with the sons and daughters of their masters or overseers but they were never able to forget the status differences between them; if anyone was going to ride on the back of another child, black children learned quickly enough that they were the "mules" and never the "riders" (Mintz, 2004). Deference was required at all times, even if it meant deliberately loosing foot races.

Children have learned to "make do" with adverse conditions and have played games, or told each other stories, or sung songs in refugee camps; in the overcrowded, fetid ships' holds transporting immigrant families; and in orphanages and dismal workhouses. Prior to the passage of child labor laws, American children working in factories, textile mills, coal mines, cotton fields, or hawking newspapers on the city streets, or selling flowers outside taverns and train stations had little chance to play often, but they found—or made—opportunities to do so whenever possible.

Terminally ill children in pediatric hospitals continue to play with toys and games often to the very ends of their lives. When medicine fails, a teddy bear is still there. Severely physically or mentally disabled youngsters, or those who are hearing impaired or visually impaired, enjoy toys, games, and play activities. By the end of the twentieth century, a wide range of adaptive toys had been devised for use by children at home, at school, and in hospital settings.

Persistence of Toys and Games

Athletic events and childhood games based on physical prowess and skill have been a part of many societies. Ball courts, found among the ruins of the Taino peoples in Puerto Rico and the Mayan people of Mexico, illustrate the widespread popularity of ball games for both adults and children. Throwing balls, kicking balls, rolling balls, catching balls in wooden cups or woven baskets, or hitting them with bats, clubs, rackets, paddles, mallets, or pool cues are activities found in many societies throughout history. A second century Roman child's sarcophagus depicted girls throwing a ball at a wall (Veyne, 1987). Children around the world have used balls and balloons in imaginative ways. Sometimes there have been elaborate rules governing the games which must be mastered by players; sometimes rules are made up on the spot by the ballplayers, who agree to designate what will serve as "home" and where the "goal" will be.

Pieter Bruegel's paintings *Children's Games* and *Battle between Carnival and Lent* document the play of 16th-century Flemish children. While he might have meant to satirize adult behaviors, he provided a splendid compendium of more than a hundred different ways that Flemish children played and amused themselves. Among other activities, Bruegel's children walk on stilts, whip tops, shoot marbles, duel on piggyback, dress up, play leapfrog, ride hobbyhorses, beat on drums, make mud pies, stand on their heads, swing on a rail, and play dice or jacks (see Foot, 1968, especially the chapter "Low Life in High Art").

African-American children who jump rope in double-Dutch patterns or who "do the dozens" with each other, British children who play May I? or Statues, and the world's children who play hide-and-seek, tag, or hopscotch are resorting to old games requiring minimal or no equipment. The persistence of these games, like the persistence of dolls and whistles, tops and toy horses, speaks eloquently of the ability of children to amuse themselves in traditional ways.

Child-Made Toys

Children have often made their own toys. Children have molded clay into birds, horses, and pigs in countless societies. For centuries, boys have whittled wooden animals, mastering knife skills even as they create figures for their own amusement or that of siblings. Native American girls from the Iroquois and Oneida tribes made dolls from cornhusks, just as their European-American counterparts learned to make soft dolls and their clothes from scraps of fabric.

Sometimes children use found objects to create settings for imaginative play. Discarded wine barrels became hiding places, or steeds for waging mock battles for countless European children over the ages. An abandoned automobile can become a space shuttle, racing car, submarine, tank, or airplane cockpit, depending upon the playfulness of its occupant(s).

Twentieth-century city children in the United States have retrieved baby carriage wheels, roller skate wheels, and bicycle wheels and attached them to scrap lumber and discarded wooden packing crates to make box-cars used for racing down hilly streets. Boys in Malawi, Kenya, and Cameroon have salvaged scrap metal and wire to fashion wheeled toys (*galimoto*) for themselves.

In the 18th century, Irish youngsters hollowed and carved turnips, placing a candle inside, to use as a lantern to deter unfriendly spirits on All Hallow's Eve; the pattern was later adopted by children in the United States who carved pumpkin jack o' lanterns for Halloween. Children for centuries have modeled foodstuffs into images; Aristophanes, the fifth century Athenian playwright, spoke of a boy who carved pomegranates in the shape of little frogs (Beaumont, 1994). Small children have used dried raisins, brown sugar, or maple syrup to make happy faces on hot cereal in bowls or on pancakes. And countless toddlers have made moats of mashed potatoes, enclosing gravy and peas, on their dinner plates.

Putting Toys Aside

Children eventually outgrow their toys, if they have not already broken them. Teething rattles are retired, awaiting the family's next newborn. Dolls and wagons, tops and hobby horses might be passed along to younger siblings or friends.

In ancient Greece, the dedication or sacrifice of a child's toys at a temple or shrine dedicated to a god or goddess was a common rite of passage: girls gave up their toys to Artemis, goddess of virginity, when marrying (usually between the ages of 14 and 16) and boys did so at the onset of puberty. Toys, especially broken ones, have been discarded in trash heaps and privies, while wooden ones have ended up in the fireplace or furnace.

Enterprising Dutch youngsters now sell their outgrown toys to other children at a fraction of their original cost on Queen's Day, April 30th, which functions as a special permitless, tax-free market day (*Vrijmarkt*). Having taken fastidious care of their toys, Japanese children in the Netherlands can even "market" the toy with its original packaging. Stoop sales, yard sales, or garage sales are all ways that children in the United States during the last quarter of the 20th century sold used toys, while other children have contributed them to fund-raising rummage sales organized by religious institutions.

Children are sometimes reluctant to put aside their toys and games. Not infrequently, today's adults in the United States, Australia, and Europe display at home or on their desk in the workplace a toy or collection of toys retained as nostalgic mementoes of childhood. Worldwide, museum collections of toys have been built in large part because some adults have not been willing to let go of cherished favorites.

Play and Learning

Children have an astonishing capacity for play and for learning vitally important skills, values, attitudes, and information through play activities. All the more astonishing is the fact that children embrace this learning as part of play, not a product of work.

Moralists have often chastised children for spending too much time at play, and often criticized the children's parents for indulging youngsters with toys. These adults, and there have been some in virtually every period, have viewed children's play as foolish or trivial. They have often worried aloud, sometimes in print or in sermons, in testimony to legislative bodies, or in neighborhood gossip, about the potentially disrespectful, morally corrupting, or sacrilegious attitudes that children might absorb by wasting time rolling hoops, or watching television cartoons, or celebrating Halloween.

Educational theorists—such as Plato (427 BC–c.347 BC) who observed in the *Laws* that children naturally invent games whenever they meet; Aristotle (384 BC–322 BC) who urged a moral connection between the amusements of childhood and the serious tasks of adult life; Vittorino da Feltre (1378–1446) who emphasized the importance of physical activity and games while teaching the children of Gian Francesco Gonzaga, the Marquis of Mantua, during the Italian Renaissance; Desiderius Erasmus of Rotterdam (1466–1536) who argued early in the 16th century that young children should be taught by play; and North America's John Dewey (1859–1952) who clearly understood that creative playful activities were an aid to children acquiring problem-solving skills—have all seen important connections between play and learning, often including academic learning.

Schoolchildren, however, frequently draw distinctions between play and work at school. While they might enjoy playful learning activities in school settings, they seem to recognize that those activities are not meant merely for their pleasure and delight. The instructional games are not "play" in the child's view.

Learning to be a person in the world is a fundamental task for *every* human being, and a lifelong process that begins at birth. Infants and children must learn to find places for themselves in the natural world they inhabit and in the social milieus of their cultural group. Changing economic conditions, technological developments, ideological commitments, political organization, and religious beliefs might all impact on children's specific tasks, but one historical pattern is strikingly clear: Children have always learned and created places for themselves through play.

References

America-Israel Culture Foundation, Inc. (1968). *From the lands of the Bible: Art and artifacts* [Catalog]. New York: Author.

Ariès, P. (1962). *Centuries of childhood: A social history of family life*. (R. Baldick, Trans.). New York: Random House.

Baldwin, P. (1992). *Toy theatres of the world*. London: Zwemmer.

Baird, D. (1973). The art of the puppet. New York: Bonanza/Crown.

Barnes, D. R. (1995). Dutch games: Seventeenth-century Dutch depictions of children's games, toys, and pastimes. In R. L. Clements (Ed.), *Games and great ideas*. Westport, CT: Greenwood.

Barnes, D. R. (2004). *Playing, learning, working in Amsterdam's golden age: Jan Luyken's mirrors of Dutch daily life* [Catalog]. Hempstead, NY: Hofstra Museum.

Beaumont, L. (1994). Child's play in Athens—Ancient Greek children's games. *History Today*, August; retrieved October 25, 2004 from http://www.findarticles.com/p/articles/mi_m1373/is_n8_v44/ai_15700222/print

Brown, I. C. (1963). *Understanding other cultures*. Englewood Cliffs, NJ: Prentice Hall.

Burton, A. (1966). *Children's pleasures*. London: Victoria and Albert Museum.

Carcopino, J. (1963) *Daily life in ancient Rome* (E. O. Lorimer, Trans.). New Haven, CT: Yale University Press. (Original work published 1940)

Carson, R. (1965). *The sense of wonder*. New York: Harper & Row.

Chase, J. E. (1962). *Life and language of the Old Testament.* New York: Norton. (Original work published 1955)

Davidson, C. (1982). *A woman's work is never done: A history of housework in the British Isles, 1650–1950.* London: Chatto & Windus.

Dennis, J. M., & Wilkinson, C. K. (1968). *Chess: East and west, past and present.* New York: Metropolitan Museum of Art.

Durantini, M. F. (1983). *The child in seventeenth-century Dutch painting.*

Foot, T. (1968). *The world of Bruegel, c. 1525–1569.* New York: Time-Life.

Fraser, A. (1972). *A history of toys.* London: Hamlyn. (Original work published 1966)

Greenberg, S. (1978). *Right from the start: A nonsexist guide to child-rearing.* Boston: Houghton-Mifflin.

Gröber, K. (1932). *Children's toys of bygone days.* London: Batsford.

Hadfield, J. (1987). *Victorian delights.* New York: New Amsterdam.

Huizinga, J. (1950). *Homo ludens: A study of the play element in culture.* Boston: Beacon.

Jaeger, W. (1960). *Paideia: The ideals of Greek culture.* New York: Oxford University Press. (Original work published 1939)

Kakar, S. (1985). The child in India. In *Aditi: The living arts of India.* [catalog] Washington, DC: Smithsonian Institution Press.

King, C. L. (1979). *Antique toys and dolls.* New York: Rizzoli.

Kingsley, C. (1855). *The heroes of Greek fairy tales for my children.* Chicago: Donohue & Henneberry.

Kitto, H. D. F. (1962). *The Greeks.* Baltimore: Penguin. (Original work published 1951)

Luyken, J. (1712). *Des menschen begin, midden en einde.* Amsterdam: Weduwe de P. Arentsz and C. van der Sys.

Marrou, H. I. (1964). *A history of education in antiquity.* New York: Mentor.

Mintz, S. (2004). *Huck's raft: A history of American childhood.* Cambridge, MA: Belknap Press/ Harvard University Press.

Museum of International Folk Art. (1956). *Decorative arts of India* [Exhibit catalog]. Santa Fe: Author.

Rau, S. R. (1969). *The cooking of India.* New York: Time-Life.

Rickert, E. (1962). *Chaucer's world.* New York: Columbia University Press. (Original work published 1948)

Schama, S. (1987). In the republic of children. In *The embarrassment of riches: An interpretation of Dutch culture in the golden age.*

Seethi, R. et.al. (1985). *Aditi: The living arts of India.* Washington, D.C.: Smithsonian Institution Press.

Steinberg, R. (1969). *The cooking of Japan.* New York: Time-Life.

Steinberg, R. (1970). *Pacific and Southeast Asian cooking.* New York: Time-Life.

Strasser, S. (1982). *Never done: A history of American housework.* New York: Pantheon.

Thompson, H. (2005). Doll wars. *British Airways Business Life, May,* 40–44.

van der Post, L. (1970). *African cooking.* New York: Time-Life.

Veyne, P. (Ed.). (1987). *A history of private life: from pagan Rome to Byzantium.* (A. Goldhammer, Trans.) Cambridge, MA: Belknap Press/Harvard University Press.

Williams, A. (1977). *Jigsaw puzzles—A brief history.* Retrieved May 2, 2005 from http://www.oldpuzzles.com/history.htm.

Zumthor, P. (1962). *Daily life in Rembrandt's Holland.* (S. W. Taylor, Trans.).

27

Influences of Race, Culture, Social Class, and Gender

Diversity and Play

PATRICIA G. RAMSEY

The population of the United States is becoming increasingly racially and culturally diverse and economically polarized. Moreover, inequities related to these demographic variables as well as those related to gender, and sexual orientation persist despite many reform efforts since the mid-1950s. While these issues may at first glance seem to be distant from young children's play, in fact they profoundly influence children's play themes and the power differentials in their peer relationships. At the same time, play is a potential vehicle for children to explore their differences and commonalities and to create more equitable relationships.

With the exception of gender differences, we know relatively little about how diversity affects play among children from different groups. Most studies on the effects of racial differences focus on children's social contact patterns and attitudes rather than on the quality of their interactions. Researchers who compare children's play across cultural and socioeconomic groups have identified play themes, styles, and rituals of specific groups but have rarely observed what occurs when children from different groups play together. One reason for these gaps in the research is that many children live in neighborhoods and attend schools that are racially, culturally, and economically segregated.

The sections that follow discuss how race, culture, social class, and gender potentially affect play themes and choice of partners, and how these factors, in turn, may influence relationships among members of diverse groups. The final section of this chapter includes suggestions for using play to increase cross-group contacts and to support equitable relationships.

Racial Differences

"Race" has traditionally been used to define groups that share visible physical attributes such as skin color, hair type, and facial features. Recent research, however, has proved that no meaningful biological interracial differences exist and that genetically there is more *intra*race than *inter*race variability (Quintana, 1998). With increasing numbers of interracial births and transracial adoptions, the concept of race has become even more ambiguous and blurred (Root, 1992, 1996). Despite its biological ambiguities and irrelevance, race has been defined by social, economic, and political forces (Omi & Winant, 1986) and used to exclude and subordinate groups throughout the history of the United States. It continues to profoundly affect individuals' status and prospects in this society

(Ogbu, 1991). This system of racial advantage and disadvantage (Tatum, 1992) has persistently worked to provide European Americans with a disproportionate amount of economic wealth and social and political power. People who are identified as whites enjoy the privilege of being part of the "invisible norm" that sets the standards for everyone else's experiences (Levine, 1994; McIntosh, 1995; McLaren, 1994; Sleeter, 1994). Most whites take this benefit for granted and are oblivious to the privilege they enjoy in every detail of their lives (e.g., being able to go into stores and not be followed, seeing a police car and not being afraid). In contrast, people of color, Asian, African, Latino, and Native Americans continue to suffer discrimination in all areas of their lives: housing, employment, and education. Unlike their European-American counterparts, they are usually acutely aware of the inequities of the system.

As they grow up, children absorb these racialized concepts. Despite the myth that children are "color blind," several decades of research have revealed that children notice racial differences early in life. Katz (1976) postulated that children go through the following steps in their acquisition of racial attitudes: First, infants and toddlers seem to notice racial differences and often react with surprise when they see a racially unfamiliar person as observed by Katz and Kofkin (1997). By the ages of 3 and 4, children have a rudimentary concept about race and can easily label and sort people by "racial" traits such as skin coloring and facial features (e.g., Clark & Clark, 1947; Katz, 2003; Porter, 1971; Ramsey, 1991a). At this age they may begin to absorb and repeat evaluative comments about race, although they may not fully understand their implications (Ramsey, 1991a; Van Ausdale & Feagin, 2001).

During elementary school, children elaborate and refine their concepts about race and clarify which characteristics are associated with particular racial groups. For example, they learn that skin color is a permanent characteristic and distinct from temporary changes related to sun exposure. Concurrently, children develop more definite feelings and beliefs about different racial groups, which usually reflect the attitudes they have been exposed to in their communities and may focus on intergroup differences (Doyle & Aboud, 1993). Children at this age also develop their abilities to take others' perspectives and to differentiate individuals in other groups, which potentially lead to the reduction of prejudice (Aboud & Amato, 2001). At the same time, children are also influenced by community values and media images that may foster prejudiced views. Individual differences also play a role. For example, children who tend to form rigid classification systems are more likely to develop and maintain stereotypes (Bigler & Liben, 1993; Bigler, Jones, & Lobliner, 1997).

Children's racial attitudes reflect the system of racial advantages and disadvantages in the United States. Across three decades of research white children have consistently shown stronger same-race preferences than their African-American classmates do (Fox & Jordan, 1973; Katz, 2003; Newman, Liss, & Sherman, 1983; Ramsey & Myers, 1990; Rosenfield & Stephan, 1981; Stabler, Zeig, & Johnson, 1982), and this difference appears to increase with age (Aboud & Amato, 2001). Conversely, black children tend to be more accepting of cross-race peers (Hallinan & Teixeira, 1987; Ramsey & Myers, 1990).

Studies of children's racial contacts reveal some variability. Same-race preference has been observed in some racially mixed preschools and kindergartens, particularly on the part of white children (Finkelstein & Haskins, 1983; Ramsey & Myers, 1990). Several studies and reviews point to a pattern of decreasing cross-race friendship choices during the elementary and secondary years (Epstein. 1986; Schofield, 1981; Ulichny, 1994). However, in one study, third graders in a very racially diverse setting played more with their cross-ethnic peers than the kindergartners did, suggesting that a trajectory toward racial cleavage is not inevitable (Howes & Wu, 1990).

Just bringing children together does not ensure equitable relationships, as children often play out the power differentials that characterize the larger society. In one of the few observational studies of children playing in a racially integrated stetting, Van Ausdale and Feagin (2001) observed many incidents of white preschoolers explicitly rejecting classmates of color on the basis of race (e.g., referring to African-American peers as "dirty" and refusing to play with peers who are not "American") and very few of the reverse. In Australia, MacNaughton found a similar pattern of white preschoolers relegating their black peers to subordinate roles in sociodramatic play (Brown, 1998).

Given that racial differences such as skin color and facial features do not have any functional impact on children's social behaviors and play styles, the racial segregation and hierarchies found in classrooms attest to the impact of growing up in a racialized system. Despite the official ideology of unity and equality, children are absorbing and enacting the reality of social fragmentation and inequity that they observe and experience in their daily lives (e.g., racially segregated neighborhoods and schools, status differences among employees in institutions and workplaces).

Cultural Differences

Racial differences often embody cultural variations that are related to countries of origin and/or living in segregated communities. Lack of familiarity with particular childhood games and rituals may cause members from different groups to see each other's behaviors as strange and possibly threatening (Schofield, 1981) and exacerbate cross-race avoidance (Boulton & Smith, 1993). The following account (paraphrased by Beresin, 1994) of elementary school girls on a playground illustrates how the lack of shared rituals limits the roles and reciprocity of play:

> Five African American girls are playing double Dutch jump rope and chanting a popular rhyme that is a take-off on McDonald's menu. A Chinese immigrant child is trying to learn double Dutch and misses several times despite encouraging instructions from the other girls. A Polish American girl also enters, tries to jump, and also misses. One of her instructors shouts, "I told you not to come down!" At that point the bell rings to end recess and the children rush toward the door.

In this observation the children were trying to play together despite their lack of shared expertise in a particular game. The helpfulness of the African-American girls and the willingness of the two outsiders to try an unfamiliar game suggest that these children are motivated to play together. At this point, however, each group is stuck in particular roles: the African-American girls are instructors and the Chinese- and the Polish-American girls are learners. Thus, the relationship is potentially unstable; over time, the outsiders may become embarrassed and intimidated if they continue to miss, and the patience of their instructors might wear thin.

Cultures are always evolving as they respond to cross-cultural influences and technological changes. However, for each of us our culture does impose "order and meaning on our experiences and allows us to predict how others will behave in certain situations" (Gollnick & Chinn, 1998, p. 4). To understand how cultures function, we need to see them as both explicit and implicit (Garcia, 1990). Language, rituals, tools, edifices, and arts are the explicit manifestations of the implicit beliefs, values, and orientations that define a culture. In the United States, for example, shopping malls are common expressions of our country's passion for consumption, new products, private property, and material success. Both these covert and overt aspects of culture are reflected in children's play, as seen in children's frequent enactments of "going shopping" and references to new clothes and toys.

As with race, certain cultures in this country are endowed with more privilege and power than others. In the United States, English-speaking, middle-class, Christian European Americans are usually considered the norm. Immigrants from all continents (including Europe) have often been pressured to abandon their languages and traditions and to conform to the Anglo-American norms as quickly as possible so that they might fit in and succeed in the mainstream society (Kivel, 2002). Schooling has traditionally focused on "Americanizing" immigrant children (Tyack, 1995). During the period from the 1960s to the 1980s, the ethnic studies and multicultural movements encouraged educators to support children's home languages and cultures. However, the pressure to assimilate has reemerged as seen in efforts to dismantle bilingual education (e.g., California Proposition 227; Crawford, 1999) and the rise in standardized testing.

Even though they have lived in this country for generations, many families of color are also viewed as cultural outsiders. Their languages, literatures, music, and arts are rarely taught in schools, and their children are often judged on how well they adapt to European-American mores. Some schools include a few examples of art and literature from a broader range of cultures, but the underlying values and measures of success reflect the European values of individual achievement and success that do not always fit with other cultural orientations (Gonzalez-Ramos, Zayas, & Cohen, 1998). For example, many Native American children, despite their long-term residence in this country, often feel uncomfortable in schools that emphasize individual achievement, competition, and material success, because these conflict with the interdependent, group oriented values that they have learned in their homes. Norbis (2004) did an in-depth analysis of children's dramatic play in an ethnically mixed kindergarten. She noted that the Latina children, especially those with more limited English-speaking skills, tended to be cast in more subordinate roles, whereas their English-speaking peers usually directed the play.

As they grow up children learn culturally specific social conventions and priorities such as levels of independence and interdependence (e.g., Gonzalez-Ramos, et al., 1998); play patterns (e.g., Farver, Kim, & Lee, 1995; Farver & Shin, 1997; Roopnarine, Lasker, Sacks, & Stores, 1998; Whiting et al., 1988); family responsibilities (Whiting & Edwards, 1988); and ways of expressing emotion (Farver, Kim, & Lee, 1995; Farver, Welles-Nystrom, Frosch, Wimbarti, Hoppe-Graff, 1997; see Roopnarine, Shin, and Donovan, 1999 for a review.) These experiences, in turn, influence children's play themes and social relationships. American children, for example, enact more aggressive themes than their German, Swedish, and Indonesian counterparts (Farver et al., 1997). In another study, Farver and Shin (1997) found that Korean-American children developed dramatic play around family roles, whereas their American counterparts enacted more fantasy themes such as superheroes. Moreover, the American children used more blunt directives to influence their peers; the Korean-American children used more subtle means such as polite requests. Likewise, Norbis (2004) found that Latino American children stressed companionship in their dramatic play, whereas the American children enacted media inspired roles.

Despite these influences, young children usually do not understand the concepts of culture or national origin because they have yet to grasp the significance of country or region (Lambert & Klineberg, 1967; Piaget & Weil, 1951). They do react, however, to the unfamiliar behavior, language, or dress of people from different cultural backgrounds and often express a wariness or derision when confronting such elements as unfamiliar rituals, foods, music, or names. English-speaking children frequently describe someone with an accent that deviates from "standard English" as "talking funny." This discomfort is reinforced when neighborhoods are segregated by ethnicity, and parents restrict their socializing to their own cultural groups. Taken together these factors potentially interfere with the development of cross-cultural friendships (Farver & Shin, 1997) as seen in Doyle's findings (1982) that French-Canadian and English-Canadian children tended to play within their own ethnic groups despite the fact that they were all fluent in both languages and were in the same classroom.

Even when children share a common ethnic and economic background, differences in lifestyles and child-rearing priorities can create some social distance, as seen in the following observations from a middle-class, predominately white kindergarten:

> Karl lives in a household where there is no TV, and his parents go to considerable lengths to ensure that he does not watch any TV at other people's homes. One day in kindergarten, Karl is sitting next to Glen, who tells him with great excitement that he is going to see a Goofy

movie. With considerable animation, Karl answers, "I know what the word goofy means. It means silly. Goofy must be a silly person. I like silly things. Who is this Goofy person?" Glen looks puzzled, then annoyed, and begins to talk with another child.

Although play themes may differ across cultures, the frequency, structure, and type of play may not be that different. A comparison of children in Senegal and the United States found that, despite differences in physical settings and types of play objects (scrounged and handmade materials for the Senegalese children and manufactured ones for children in the United States), both groups engaged in similar types of play (functional, constructive, pretense, gross motor, and dance/music) for about the same percentages of time. The structure of play also may not be culturally specific (Bloch, 1989). Farver (1992) observed that 3-year-olds in Mexico and in the United States enacted play themes that mirrored their daily lives and activities and therefore differed between the two groups. However, the style of play (constructed with spontaneous comments rather than planned scripts) was similar.

Some types of play may require more shared cultural knowledge than others. Several years ago, our family adopted Andrés, who was then 3, from Chile. Daniel, our 6-year-old son, had been adopted from Chile as an infant and was thoroughly assimilated into the peer culture of the United States by the time Andrés came along. The following two observations illustrate how sensorimotor play may facilitate cross-cultural connections better than sociodramatic themes, which usually require shared language or cultural knowledge.

Day 2 (Andrés had been with us for about 48 hours; we are in a park in Santiago, Chile.) Daniel calls to his brother, "Look at this, Andrés!" He then sings out, "Go, go, Power Rangers!" and leaps from a low brick wall. Andrés looks a little bewildered and turns away. "Donde esta la pelota? [Where is the ball?]," he asks and runs off. (Balls were one of the few toys that were available in the foster home where Andrés lived for three years.) Daniel shouts again, "Look, Andrés!" and makes another leap. Meanwhile Andrés is looking under bushes trying to find the ball. Daniel looks down and walks away.

An hour later both boys are in the bathtub. They are blowing bubbles and pouring water over each other and laughing gleefully. Andrés sticks his head in the water and comes up with wet hair. Daniel follows suit, and they both shriek with delight.

Cross-cultural distance also may be aggravated by newcomer status. Children of recent immigrants to this country are often intimidated by their unfamiliar surroundings and by trying to learn how to bridge the gap between their home culture and their new school culture (Igoa, 1995). A few studies have shown that these children engage in less social and pretend play than their culturally dominant peers (Child, 1983; Quisenberry & Christman, 1979; Robinson, 1978). However, these studies have been criticized because they fail to consider the meaning of play in children's home cultures and the challenges of accommodating to two (or more) cultural contexts (Slaughter & Dombrowski, 1989).

I recently observed Saman, a young Pakistani girl in a predominately European-American middle-class kindergarten. Throughout the day, she sat near other students watching them intently but not engaging with them. The other children in turn primarily ignored her, unless the teacher set up a group activity where she had to participate. Although Saman spoke English quite well, she did not seem to understand the peer culture and the nuances of how to enter and sustain interactions. In her brief peer interactions, she often seemed confused and quickly backed away, illustrating how lack of familiarity with particular rituals and behaviors can become a barrier to social play. This observation occurred near the beginning of the year, and Saman may well become an active player as the year progresses. She and other newcomers are not necessarily deficient in their play skills but rather in the process of learning how to function in a new culture.

Social Class Differences

Socioeconomic status is "an encompassing structure...it relates to virtually every aspect of human psychological development and across a considerable period of time" (Gottfried et al., 2003, p. 204). It also interacts with race, culture, and gender, as different groups are disproportionately represented among the wealthy (white males) and among the poor (female-headed households, families of color, recent immigrants). For example, 9.4% of non-Hispanic white children live in poverty as compared to 31.5% of African Americans and 28.6% of Hispanic children (Children's Defense Fund, 2003).

Despite our egalitarian principles, the United States has been moving away from, not toward, more equitable distribution of wealth, especially since the mid-1970s (Huston, 1991; Lott, 2002; McLoyd, 1998a; Thompson & Hupp, 1992). From 1979 to 1997 the average after-tax income of the poorest 20% of the United States population has declined from $10,900 to $10,800, while the average income of the top 1% has grown from $263,700 to $677,900 (Lott, 2002). During the 1980s the numbers of children growing up in very poor (deprived) households and in very affluent (luxurious) households increased, whereas the number of children growing up in "frugal" (i.e., working-class) or "comfortable" (i.e., middle-class) households declined. Currently 16% of all children under the age of 6 in the United States are living below the national poverty level, and one-third of all children will be poor at some point during while they are growing up (Children's Defense Fund, 2004).

Economic circumstances profoundly affect children: some have to struggle with simply surviving; whereas others are preoccupied with overblown materialistic expectations engendered by affluence and consumerism. Being poor in and of itself does not necessarily impair development (Thompson, 1992). Many families face the daunting challenges of poverty with fortitude and protect their children from its most deleterious effects. However, common consequences of growing up in poverty—malnutrition, inadequate health care, exposure to toxins and diseases, unsafe living conditions, neighborhood disorder and violence, homelessness, frequent moves, and poor educational facilities—do pose enormous risks for children (Brooks-Gunn, Duncan, & Maritato, 1997; Jackson, Brooks-Gunn, Huang, Glassman, 2000; Kohen, Brooks-Gunn, Levanthal, Hertzman, 2002; McLoyd, 1998b). Ironically, affluent children, who have access to enormous amounts of material goods, are also at risk. Research has shown that these children tend to be less happy and more at risk for drug and alcohol abuse than their less affluent peers (Csikszentmihalyi, 1999; Csikszentmihalyi & Schneider, 2000; Luthar & Becker, 2002), suggesting that consuming does not bring contentment to children, but rather stimulates new desires.

As with cultural differences, most young children are not consciously aware of social class (Naimark, 1983; Ramsey, 1991b). Nevertheless, children often gravitate toward other children from similar socioeconomic (SES) backgrounds for several reasons. Because childrearing goals and methods reflect the social and economic roles of specific groups (Ogbu, 1983), children's values and behaviors may vary across SES groups. Children from different SES groups may also be less familiar with each other because neighborhoods, churches, social clubs, and preschools are usually economically segregated. In one virtually all-white rural community, the kindergarten and first-grade teachers noticed that children divided themselves along social class lines from the very beginning of school. Not only did the two groups come in from different neighborhoods, but many children had formed friendships while attending their economically segregated preschool programs: federally funded programs for low-income children or tuition-based programs that served primarily middle-income families. Access to resources such as after school dance, art, and sports programs can also make cross-group contacts more strained, as seen in the following observation:

In a third-grade classroom, Andrea and Katy, both middle-SES, and Laurie, low SES, are talking on the playground during recess. Andrea twirls around and says, "This is part of the recital." Katy smiles and says, "Yeah, we're doing that too," and twirls around. "It makes me dizzy, though. I hope that I don't fall down. Does it make you dizzy?" Andrea says, "No, not really," and she twirls around again. The two girls continue twirling and giggling. During this exchange, Laurie looks down at the ground.

Many researchers who have studied social class differences in play have concluded that low-income children engage in less sociodramatic play and are more often on the periphery of the play that occurs in socioeconomically integrated classrooms (Fein & Stork, 1981; Rubin, Maioni, & Horning, 1976; Smilansky, 1968). These studies and findings have been criticized because the settings, observers, and assessment instruments potentially favor middle-class styles of play (McLoyd, 1982).

To avoid making these deficit-oriented assumptions, we need to always consider the sociocultural and economic contexts of children's play (Roopnarine, Lasker, Sacks, & Stores, 1998). Because schools are usually oriented to the values and subject matter of the middle class, low-income children may feel less at home and be more socially constrained than their middle-income peers. For example, role-play props and books that reflect middle-class lifestyles may create a welcoming environment for middle-class children but an alienating one for children who are poor. Furthermore, teachers have often made assumptions about the potential of children based on their social class (Bigelow, 1995; Gollnick & Chinn, 1998; McLoyd, 1998a; Rist, 1970). As a result children are frequently placed in ability groups that parallel their social class (e.g., wealthier children in the highest groups) further aggravating tendencies to stereotype and avoid people in different SES groups. Taken together, these influences may undermine poor children's engagement in play as well as interfere with developing relationships among children from different social class groups.

Young children have a limited understanding of social-class differences (Ramsey, 1991b). However, in preschool and early elementary school, they are developing ideas and attitudes about rich and poor people (Leahy, 1983). Their definitions of "rich" and "poor" shift from depending on concrete material expressions (e.g., housing, clothing) to ones that encompass employment status and some understanding of the economic system. One disturbing developmental trend is that young children often assert that unequal distribution is unfair and that rich people should share their wealth with poor people, but older children are more apt to accept these disparities and to blame people for their poverty (Chafel, 1997; Leahy, 1990, Ramsey, 2004). Thus, the psychological distance between more affluent segments of the society and poor people may increase as children get older. This trend may be exacerbated as children engage in more and more activities that reflect their relative affluence (e.g., sports camps, dance, karate, and art classes) and begin to consider their future roles in the context of those that they see in their families and communities.

Gender Differences

As demonstrated in the previous sections, little is known about how children from different racial, cultural, and class backgrounds actually play together. In contrast, many researchers have studied same-sex and cross-sex play. As with the other dimensions discussed in this chapter, gender also embodies power differentials in our society. Despite many legal reforms, males still dominate the social, political, and economic realms. Children's relationships and play frequently reflect these asymmetries (Maccoby, 1998; Sadker & Sadker, 1995). Boys typically enact more superhero play and use more physical and verbal aggression than girls do (Fabes, Martin, & Hanish, 2003; Farver et al., 1997). These behaviors often lead to disrupting or dominating girls' play as illustrated in the following video clip description:

Reece and Bradley are jumping on a balancing board outside. Nearby Claire and Catherine are dressing two dolls....Suddenly Reese snatches the dolls from Claire and Catherine and puts them in the pram. He and Bradley race the pram past the girls and around the sandpit towards the outside shed. The boys are laughing and clearly enjoying themselves immensely. They race the pram back to the balancing board, onto which they place the dolls. Reece scrambles onto the board and starts jumping. Each 'boing' of the board bring the dolls closer to its edge.… Bradley giggles and watches in anticipation of the fall. (MacNaughton, 2000, p. 154)

In this observation the girls were relegated to passively watching as the boys stole and threatened their dolls. The fact that they did not vociferously protest this interference suggests that this power differential was an accepted norm at least among these children.

This tendency for boys to dominate emerges in many aspects of social interactions. During cross-gender entry attempts, for example, girls are more tentative with boys than they are with girls; boys, however, are more imperative with girls than with boys (Phinney & Rotheram, 1982). Likewise, boys tend to use more aggressive actions in conflicts than girls do (Sheldon, 1990). According to Maccoby (1998), boys are resistant to girls' influence, whereas girls are more open to suggestions from by both boys and girls. Moreover, while girls tend to prefer same-sex partners, some want to join in male-typed activities. In contrast, boys very rarely venture into female-dominated activities and interactions. As a result of all these factors girls tend to be wary of boys and avoid intruding in their spaces or fighting back when boys disrupt their play.

Same-sex preference dominates children's choices of friends at all grades in school (Bigler, 1995). Cross-sex contacts, however, follow a curvilinear pattern: they decrease from preschool to middle school and then increase during adolescence (Epstein, 1986; Paley, 1984; Ramsey, 1995; Swadener & Johnson, 1989). Maccoby (1998) posits several reasons for this seemingly universal pattern of gender cleavage in children's play. First, with early socialization, children learn to enjoy sex-typed activities and behaviors and are drawn to each other when they observe each other's play styles and activity preferences. Preschool girls typically congregate in the art and housekeeping areas, and boys engage in more physically active play with blocks and trucks (MacNaughton, 2000). In elementary schools, boys usually play vigorous physical contact games at recess, whereas many girls play games that require more precise physical skills and social coordination, such as jump rope. Second, according to Maccoby, fantasy play themes are different. Girls enact reciprocal roles (e.g., mother and child; teacher and pupil) that often center on domestic themes; whereas boys frequently play out individual heroic roles that are based on media figures (e.g., batman, power rangers). Another factor is the differences in discourse between the two groups. Girls' conversations tend to be more reciprocal and collaborative (e.g., taking turns talking, agreeing with the other person before adding a new idea); boys use more dominating speech (e.g., direct imperatives, forceful rejections of suggestions). As a result of these differences, children are drawn to same-sex peers because they are more confident of what to expect. Conversely, they avoid cross-sex peers because they are unsure about how they will behave and are more uncertain of their own roles. Fabes et al. (2003) found that, when preschool and kindergarten children played in same-sex groups or dyads, girls and, in particular, boys were more likely to engage in sex-typed activities and behaviors than when they played in mixed-sex groups. Thus, gender segregation and the development of separate and rigid gender cultures are mutually reinforcing.

Sex segregation increases during the elementary years and by the sixth grade it is virtually complete; boys and girls rarely sit together in the cafeteria or play with each other on the playground (Maccoby, 1998). It is continuously reaffirmed by the factors discussed earlier and by children's engagement in "borderwork" between the two groups (Thorne, 1986), such as cross-gender chasing games that sometimes include a threat of kissing or pollution rituals (for example, giving cooties to each other), and invasions in which one group (usually boys) disrupts the play of the other. As they get older, children, especially boys, also learn that peer acceptance depends on conforming to sex-typed roles (Damon, 1977; Sadker & Sadker, 1995). With the increasing separation, those children who enjoy playing with members of the opposite sex find it more difficult to maintain these friendships; children who cross the gender divide are often accused of "liking" someone of the opposite sex or being a member of that group (Thorne, 1986). Therefore, cross-gender friendships in childhood frequently "go underground."

Cross-racial, cross-cultural, cross-SES, and cross-gender contacts may be affected by similar factors. First, children are drawn to peers who are familiar in some way—appearance, language, activity preferences, or play themes. Second, as they spend more time together, they learn what to expect from familiar peers and therefore feel more confident and comfortable and so stay with them. Third, as the groups congeal, they develop their own peer culture that reflects a synthesis of their home, community, and peer cultures. Over time, group loyalty may make it more difficult for children to spend time with other groups, and so the divisions become more rigid. Finally, as children become aware of the racial, cultural, economic, and gender hierarchies that define their worlds, their cross-group discomfort and distance may further increase. Thus, when observing and facilitating children's play, teachers need to always consider how the sociocultural and economic contexts are influencing the themes and dynamics of the play (Roopnarine et al., 1998).

Facilitating Cross-Group Play

Ironically, although these differences may interfere with forming cross-group relationships, play itself may be a means of encouraging cross-group contact. When children are engaged in open-ended and spontaneous play they are creating their own world, which can potentially accommodate everyone and facilitate more equal roles. Yet how do we get children who regard each other as strangers to play with each other in the first place? And how do we encourage them to overcome the power differentials that they observe and experience in their day-to-day lives?

Teacher-facilitated groups is one possible strategy. Reviews of the effects of cooperative learning on cross-group relationships show that cross-racial and cross-ethnic cooperative groups foster strong intergroup friendships as well as more amicable contacts throughout the classroom (Johnson & Johnson, 2000; Slavin, 1995). Not only do children in the same cooperative groups become friends, but their friends get to know each other and, in some cases, become friends. When teachers form mixed-sex collaborative groups, boys and girls are able to work together on absorbing tasks (Thorne, 1986). Thus, group collaboration provides opportunities for children from different backgrounds to see each other, at least momentarily, as competent and familiar individuals and to develop some common ground. Slavin (1995) observed that relationships started in cooperative groups often continue and extend to other activities. However, cooperative groups must be organized and monitored so that they do not simply re-create the same hierarchies that exist in the larger society (e.g., dominance of white academically proficient males).

Teachers can also use the physical environment and materials to encourage children to play with a wider group of peers. One common technique is to arrange the room to bring groups of children who usually play separately into closer proximity. Two kindergarten teachers constructed an "Outer Space" center in what were formerly the housekeeping and block areas (Theokas, Ramsey, & Sweeney, 1993). They found that the number of cross-sex contacts increased markedly during the period of time that the space center was available. Moreover, as they spent more time together, the boys and girls developed some common play themes and played together more cooperatively. However, a close reading of the observations revealed a small but persistent pattern of male dominance in both planning and executing different activities, highlighting the need to help children learn new roles and ways of seeing themselves in the world as argued by MacNaughton (2000).

Likewise, a novel or desirable activity may lure children into mixed-group situations. New toys in the sandbox, for example, might offer children a shared play medium that does not require a common language. Likewise, the challenge of figuring out a computer program or game can encourage children to collaborate even if they do not know each other well. To make these kinds of interventions work, teachers may need to assign children to these activities so that they do not just gravitate to their usual friends. Moreover, they need to be sure that the materials do not favor one group over another. If some children, for example, have access to computers at home and others do not, then new computer games may widen rather than bridge the gap.

Another strategy is to try to develop more common ground among children from different backgrounds. One kindergarten teacher noticed that the children from low-income families were frequently left out of conversations that focused on the latest toy fads. She raised some money and bought a few of these toys for the classroom, so that all children could have access to them. Although this intervention did not address the more basic and enduring social class divisions, the teacher found that it did reduce the numbers of conversations divided by social class. In another predominately white classroom, three Cambodian children were on the social periphery. The teacher, with the help of the children and their parents, created a learning center with lots of books, pictures, art, and information about Cambodia. The Cambodian children introduced the materials to their peers and, as the "experts," enjoyed a great deal more social contact and visibility. Moreover, other children began to build "Cambodian houses" in blocks and cook "Cambodian food" in the role-play area, based on photographs and books and cooking experiences provided by the parents. Thus, these activities not only encouraged the Cambodian children to become more socially active and assertive, they also served to expand all the children's play themes.

Because play is spontaneous, fluid, and infinitely malleable, many cultural themes can be woven into it. Moreover, it has the potential to break down the distinctions between insiders and outsiders and to equalize relationships. Teachers who want to use play to facilitate cross-group contacts may need to set up particular situations (as described earlier in this section) or to assign children to areas in order to overcome their tendency to congregate with familiar peers. This practice does not mean that teachers then try to direct the play (assigning roles or suggesting themes). Rather, they provide materials, props, and stories, along with some novel toys to attract attention; then they step back and let the children create their world and weave together themes as the play unfolds, as seen in the observation below.

> I walked into a kindergarten classroom and two girls rushed over to me and said, "Look at our McDonald's!" They had set up a counter with a toy cash register and had laid out the food behind it—tacos, sushi, rice, grapes, salad, and several kinds of breads (plastic foods available from most early-childhood catalogues). On the two tables were chopsticks and forks. A stuffed dog had been squeezed into a coat hanger and was sticking out from the wall. I asked what it was and one of the girls cheerily answered, "The piñata for the birthday parties."

We cannot ignore the segregation and inequities that prevail in the United States. Early in their lives, children learn to divide the world by race, culture, social class, and gender; many experience the privileges and hardships inherent in these divisions. These differences are often reflected in children's play and peer relationships, and societal hierarchies are sometimes re-created in classrooms. We must be sure that we do not define play in ways that render some children "deficient," but rather we must embrace "more culturally contextualized constructions of meaning of play for the acquisition of skills relative to the social and cognitive demands of individual cultures" (Roopnarine, Shin, & Donovan, 1999, p. 211). Moreover, while play cannot change the external realities of children's lives, we can help children use it as a vehicle for exploring and enjoying their differences and similarities and for creating and seeing the possibilities of a more just world where everyone is an equally valued participant.

References

Aboud, F. E., & Amato, M. (2001). Developmental and socialization influences on intergroup bias. In R. Brown & S. L. Gaerther (Eds.), *Blackwell handbook of social psychology: Intergroup processes* (pp. 65–85). Oxford, UK: Blackwell.

Beresin, A. R. (1994, April). *Until the bell rings: The play cultures at recess.* Paper presented at the annual meeting of the American Educational Research Association, New Orleans, LA.

Bigelow, B. (1995). Dumb kids, smart kids, and social class. *Rethinking Schools, 10*(2), 12–13.

Bigler, R. S. (1995). The role of classification skill in moderating environmental influences on children's gender stereotyping: A study of the functional use of gender in the classroom. *Child Development, 66*, 1072–1087.

Bigler, R. S., Jones, L. C., & Lobliner, D. B. (1997). Social categorization and the formation of intergroup attitudes in children. *Child Development, 68*(3), 530–543.

Bigler, R. S., & Liben, L. S. (1993). A cognitive–developmental approach to racial stereotyping and reconstructive memory in Euro-American children. *Child Development, 64*, 1507–1518.

Bloch, M. N. (1989). Young boys' and girls' play at home and in the community: A cultural–ecological framework. In M. N. Bloch & A. D. Pelligrini (Eds.), *The ecological context of children's play* (pp. 120–154). Norwood, NJ: Ablex.

Boulton, M. J., & Smith, P K. (1993). Ethnic, gender partner, activity preference in mixed-race schools in the U. K.: Playground observations. In C. H. Hart (Ed.), *Children on playgrounds: Research perspectives and applications* (pp. 210–237). Albany: State University of New York Press.

Brooks-Gunn, J., Duncan, G. J. & Maritato, N. (1997). Poor families, poor outcomes: The well-being of children and youth. In G. J. Duncan & J. Brooks-Gunn (Eds.), *Consequences of growing up poor* (pp. 1–17). New York: Russell Sage.

Brown, B. (1998). *Unlearning discrimination in the early years.* Stratford, UK: Trentham Books.

Chafel, J. A. (1997). Children's views of poverty: A review of research and implications for teaching. *The Educational Forum, 61*, 360–371.

Child, E. (1983). Play and culture: A study of English and Asian children. *Leisure Studies, 2*, 169–186.

Children's Defense Fund (2003). *2002 Facts on Child Poverty in America.* http://www.children'sdefense,org/familyincome/childpoverty/basicfacts.asp

Children's Defense Fund (2004) Key facts about American children. http://www.childrensdefense.org/data/keyfacts.asp

Clark, K. B., & Clark, M. P. (1947). Racial identification and preference in Negro children. In T. M. Newcomb & E. L. Hartley (Eds.), *Readings in social psychology* (pp. 169–178). New York: Holt, Rinehart & Winston.

Crawford, J. (1999). *Bilingual education: History, politics, theory, and practice* (4th ed.). Los Angeles: Bilingual Education Services.

Csikszentmihalyi, M. (1999). If we are so rich, why aren't we happy? *American Psychologist, 54*, 821–827.

Csikszentmihalyi, M., & Schneider, B. (2000). *Becoming adults: How teenagers prepare for the world of work.* New York: Basic Books.

Damon, W (1977). *The social world of the child.* San Francisco: Jossey-Bass.

Doyle, A. (1982). Friends, acquaintances, and strangers: The influence of familiarity and ethnolinguistic background on social interaction. In K. H. Rubin & H. S. Ross (Eds.), *Peer relationships and social skills in childhood* (pp. 229–252). New York: Springer-Verlag.

Doyle, A., & Aboud, F. E. (1993). Social and cognitive determinants of prejudice in children. In K. A. McLeod (Ed.), *Multicultural education: The state of the art* (pp. 28–33). Toronto: University of Toronto Press.

Epstein, J. L. (1986). Friendship selection: Developmental and environmental influences. In E. C. Mueller & C. R. Cooper (Eds.), *Process and outcome in peer relationships* (pp. 129–160). New York: Academic.

Fabes, R. A., Martin, C. L., & Hanish, L. D. (2003). Young children's play qualities in same–other-, and mixed-sex peer groups. *Child Development, 74*(3), 921–932.

Farver, J. M. (1992). An analysis of young American and Mexican children's play dialogues: Illustrative study no. 3. In C. Howes & C. C. Matheson (Eds.), *The collaborative construction of pretend* (pp. 55–63). Albany: State University of New York Press.

Farver, J. M., Kim, Y. K., & Lee, Y. (1995). Cultural differences in Korean- and Anglo-American preschoolers' social interaction and play behaviors. *Child Development, 66*, 1088–1099.

Farver, J. M., & Shin, Y. L. (1997). Social pretend play in Korean- and Anglo-American preschoolers. *Child Development, 68* (3), 544–556.

Farver, J. M., Welles-Nystrom, B., Frosch, D. L., Wimbarti, S., & Hoppe-Graff, S. (1997). Toy stories: Aggression in children's narratives in the United States, Sweden, Germany, and Indonesia. *Journal of Cross-Cultural Psychology, 28*(4), 393–420.

Fein, G. G., & Stork, L. (1981). Sociodramatic play: Social class effects in integrated preschool classrooms. *Journal of Applied Developmental Psychology, 2*, 267–279.

Finkelstein, N. W, & Haskins, R. (1983). Kindergarten children prefer same-color peers. *Child Development, 54*, 502–508.

Fox, D. J., & Jordan, V B. (1973). Racial preference and identification of black, American Chinese, and white children. *Genetic Psychology Monographs, 88*, 229–286.,

Fox, D. J., & Jordan, V. B. (1973). Racial preference and identification of black, American Chinese, and white children. *Genetic Psychology Monographs, 88*, 229–286.

Garcia, R. L. (1990). *Teaching in a pluralistic society: Concepts, models, and strategies* (2nd ed.). New York: HarperCollins.

Gollnick, D. M., & Chinn, P. C. (1998*). Multicultural education in a pluralistic society* (5th ed.). Columbus, OH: Merrill.

Gonzalez-Ramos, G., Zayas, L. H., & Cohen, E. V. (1998). Child-rearing values of low-income, urban Puerto Rican mothers of preschool children. *Developmental Psychology, 29*(4), 377–82.

Gottfried, A. W., Gottfried, A. E., Bathurst, K., Guerin, D. W., Parramore, M. M. (2003). Socioeconomic status in children's development and family environment: Infancy through adolescence. In M. Bornstein (Ed.), *Socioeconomic status, parenting, and child development* (pp. 189–207). Mahwah, NJ: Lawrence Erlbaum.

Hallinan, M. T., & Teixeira, R. A. (1987). Opportunities and constraints: Black–white differences in the formation of interracial friendships. *Child Development, 58*, 1358–1371.

Howes, C., & Wu, F. (1990). Peer interactions and friendships in an ethnically diverse school setting. *Child Development, 61*, S37–S41.

Huston, A. C. (1991). Children in poverty: Developmental and policy issues. In A. C. Huston (Ed.), *Children in poverty: Child development and public policy* (pp. 1–22). Cambridge, UK: Cambridge University Press.

Igoa, C. (1995). *The inner world of the immigrant child.* New York: St. Martin's.

Jackson, A., Brooks-Gunn, J., Huang, C., & Glassman, M. (2000). Single mothers in low-wage jobs: Financial strain, parenting, and preschoolers' outcomes. *Child Development 71*, 1409–1423.

Johnson, D. W., & Johnson, R.T. (2000). The three Cs of reducing prejudice and discrimination. In S. Okamp (Ed.), *Reducing prejudice and discrimination* (pp. 239–268). Mahwah, NJ: Lawrence Erlbaum.

Katz, P. A. (1976). The acquisition of racial attitudes in children. In P. A. Katz (Ed.), *Towards the elimination o f racism* (pp. 12S–14S). New York: Pergamon.

Katz, P.A. (2003). Racists or tolerant multiculturalists? How do they begin? *American Psychologist, 58*(11), 897−909.

Katz, P. A., & Kofkin, J. A. (1997). Race, gender, and young children. In S. Luthar, J. Burack, D. Cicchetti, & J. Weisz (Eds.), *Developmental perspectives on risk and pathology* (pp. 51–74). New York: Cambridge University Press.

Kivel, P. (2002). *Uprooting racism: How white people can work for racial justice.* Gabriola Island, BC, Canada: New Society Publishers

Kohen, D. E., Brooks-Gunn, J., Leventhal, T. & Hertzman, C. (2002). Neighborhood income and physical and social disorders in Canada: Associations with young children's competencies. *Child Development 73*(6), 1844–1860.

Lambert W. E., & Klineberg, O. (1967). *Children's views of foreign people.* New York: Appleton-Century-Crofts.

Leahy, R. (1983). The development of the conception of social class. In R. Leahy (Ed.), *The child's construction of inequality* (pp. 79–107). New York: Academic.

Leahy, R. (1990). The development of concepts of economic and social inequality. *New Directions for Child Development, 46*, 107–120.

Levine, J. (1994, March/April). White like me: When privilege is written on your skin. *Ms.*, 22–24.

Lott, B. (2002). Cognitive and behavioral distancing from the poor. *American Psychologist, 5*(2), 100–110.

Luthar, S. S., & Becker, B. E. (2002). Privileged but pressured? A study of affluent youth. *Child Development, 73* (5), 1593–1610.

Maccoby, E. E. (1998). *The two sexes: Growing up apart: Coming together.* Cambridge, MA: Harvard University Press.

MacNaughton, G. (2000). *Rethinking gender in early childhood education.* Thousand Oaks, CA: Sage.

McIntosh, P. (1995). White privilege and male privilege: A personal account of coming to see correspondences through work in women's studies. In M. L. Anderson & P. H. Collins (Eds.), *Race, class, and gender: An anthology* (pp. 76–87). Belmont, CA: Wadsworth.

McLaren, P. (1994). White terror and oppositional agency: Towards a critical multiculturalism. In D. T. Goldbert (Ed.), *Multiculturalism: A critical reader* (pp. 45–74). Cambridge, MA: Blackwell.

McLoyd, V. C. (1982). Social class differences in sociodramatic play: A critical review. *Developmental Review, 2*, 1–30.

McLoyd, V. C. (1998a). Socioeconomic disadvantage and child development. *American Psychologist, 53*, 185–204.

McLoyd. V. C. (1998b). Socioeconomic hardship on black families and children: Psychological distress, parenting, and socio-emotional development. *Child Development, 61*, 311–346.

Naimark, H. (1983). *Children's understanding of social class differences.* Paper presented at the biennial meeting of the Society for Research in Child Development, Detroit, MI.

Newman, M. A., Liss, M. B., & Sherman, E (1983). Ethnic awareness in children: Not a unitary concept. *Journal of Genetic Psychology, 143*, 103–112.

Norbis, S. S. (2004). *Different and alike: Diferentes y semejantes: An ethnographic study of language use in a dramatic play center.* Doctoral Dissertation, School of Education, University of Massachusetts, Amherst.

Ogbu, J. U. (1983). Socialization: A cultural ecological approach. In K. M. Borman (Ed.), *The social life of children in a changing society* (pp. 253–267). Norwood, NJ: Ablex.

Ogbu, J. U. (1991). Immigrant and involuntary minorities in comparative perspective. In M. A. Gibson & J. U. Ogbu (Eds.), *Minority status and schooling: A comparative study of immigrant and involuntary minorities* (pp. 3–33). New York: Garland.

Omi, M., & Winant, H. (1986). *Racial formation in the United States.* New York: Routledge & Kegan Paul.

Paley, V. G. (1984). *Boys and girls: Superheroes in the doll corner.* Chicago: University of Chicago Press.

Phinney, J. S., & Rotheram, M. J. (1982). Sex differences in social overtures between same-sex and cross-sex preschool pairs. *Child Study Journal, 12*, 259–269

Piaget, J., & Weil, A. (1951). The development in children of the idea of the homeland and of relations with other countries. *International Social Science Bulletin, 3*, 561–578.

Porter, J. D. (1971). *Black child, white child: The development of racial attitudes.* Cambridge, MA: Harvard University Press.

Quintana, S. M. (1998). Children's developmental understanding of ethnicity and race. *Applied and Preventive Psychology, 7*, 27–45.

Quisenberry, N. & Christman, M. (1979). A look at sociodramatic play among Mexican-American children. *Childhood Education, 56* (2), 106–110.

Ramsey, P. G. (1991a). The salience of race in young children growing up in an all-white community. *Journal of Educational Psychology, 83,* 28–34.

Ramsey, P. G. (1991b). Young children's awareness and understanding of social class differences. *Journal of Genetic Psychology, 152,* 71–82.

Ramsey, P. G. (1995). Changing social dynamics of early childhood classrooms. *Child Development, 66,* 764–773.

Ramsey, P. G. (2004). *Teaching and learning in a diverse world: Multicultural education for young children* (3rd ed.). New York: Teachers College Press.

Ramsey, P. G., & Myers, L. C. (1990). Salience of race in young children's cognitive, affective and behavioral responses to social environments. *Journal of Applied Developmental Psychology, 11,* 49–67.

Rist, R. C. (1970). Student social class and teacher expectations: The self-fulfilling prophecy in ghetto education. *Harvard Educational Review, 40,* 411–451.

Robinson, C. (1978). The uses of order and disorder in play: An analysis of Vietnamese refugee children's play. (ERIC No. ED 1153 944)

Roopnarine, J. L., Lasker, J., Sacks, M., & Stores, M. (1998). The cultural contexts of children's play. In O. Saracho & B. Spodek (Eds.), *Play in early childhood* (pp. 194–219). Albany, NY: State University of New York Press.

Roopnarine, J. L., Shin, M., Donovan, B. (1999). Sociocultural contexts of dramatic play: Implications for early education. In K. Roskos & J. Christie (Eds.), *Literacy and play in the early years: Cognitive, ecological, and sociocultural perspectives.* Mahwah, NJ: Lawrence Erlbaum.

Root, M. P. (Ed.). (1992). *Racially mixed people in America.* Beverly Hills, CA: Sage.

Root, M. P. (Ed.). (1996). *The multiracial experience: Racial borders as the new frontier.* Thousand Oaks, CA: Sage.

Rosenfield, D., & Stephan, W. G. (1981). Intergroup relations among children. In S. S. Brehm, S. M. Kassin, & F. X. Gibbons (Eds.), *Developmental social psychology* (pp. 271–297). New York: Oxford University Press.

Rubin, K. H., Maioni, T. L., & Hornung, M. (1976). Free play behaviors in middle- and lower-class preschoolers: Parten and Piaget revisited. *Child Development, 47* 414–419.

Sadker, M., & Sadker, D. (1995). *Failing at fairness: How our schools cheat girls.* New York: Simon & Schuster.

Schofield, J. (1981). Complementary and conflicting identities: Images and interactions in an interracial school. In S. R. Asher & J. M. Gottman (Eds.), *The development of children's friendships* (pp. 53–90). New York: Cambridge University Press.

Sheldon, A. (1990). Pickle fights: Gendered talk in preschool disputes. *Discourse Processes, 13,* 5–31.

Slaughter, D. Y., & Dombrowski, J. (1989). Cultural continuities and discontinuities: Impact on social and pretend play. In M. N. Bloch & A. D. Pellegrini (Eds.), *The ecological context of children's play* (pp. 282–309). Norwood, NJ: Ablex.

Slavin, R. E. (1995). Cooperative learning and intergroup relations. In J.A. Banks & C. A. M. Banks (Eds.), *Handbook of research on multicultural education* (pp. 628–634). New York: Macmillan.

Sleeter, C. E. (1994). White racism. *Multicultural Education, 1,* 5–8, 39.

Smilansky, S. (1968). *The effects of sociodramatic play on disadvantaged preschool children.* New York: Wiley.

Stabler, J. R., Zeig, J. A., & Johnson, E. E. (1982). Perceptions of racially related stimuli by young children. *Perceptual and Motor Skills, 54*(1), 71–77.

Swadener, E. B., & Johnson, J. E. (1989). Play in diverse social contexts: Parent and teacher roles. In M. N. Bloch & A. D. Pellegrini (Eds.), *The ecological context of children's play* (pp. 214–244). Norwood, NJ: Ablex.

Tatum, B. D. (1992). Talking about race, learning about racism: The application of racial identity development theory in the classroom. *Harvard Educational Review, 62*(1), 1–24.

Theokas, C., Ramsey, P.G., Sweeney, B. (1993, March). *The effects of classroom interventions on young children's cross-sex contacts and perceptions.* Paper presented at the biennial meeting of the Society for Research in Child Development. New Orleans, LA.

Thompson, T. (1992). For the sake of our children: Poverty and disabilities. In T. Thompson, T., & Hupp, S. C. (Eds.), *Saving children at risk: Poverty and disabilities* (pp. 3–10). Newbury Park, CA: Sage.

Thompson, T., & Hupp, S. C. (Eds.). (1992). *Saving children at risk: Poverty and disabilities.* Newbury Park, CA: Sage.

Thorne, B. (1986). Girls and boys together . . . but mostly apart: Gender arrangements in elementary schools. In W. W. Hartup & Z. Rubin (Eds.), *Relationships and development* (pp. 167–184). Hillsdale, NJ: Lawrence Erlbaum.

Tyack, D. (1995). Schooling and social diversity: Historical reflections. In W. D. Hawley & A. W. Jackson (Eds.), *Toward a common destiny: Improving race and ethnic relations in America* (pp. 3–38). San Francisco: Jossey-Bass.

Ulichny, P. (1994, April). *Cultures in conflict.* Paper presented at the annual meeting of the American Educational Research Association, New Orleans.

Van Ausdale, D., & Feagin, J. R. (2001). *The first R: How children learn race and racism.* Lanham, MD: Rowman & Littlefield.

Whiting, B. B., Edwards, C. P., et al. (1988). *Children of different worlds: The formation of social behavior.* Cambridge, MA: Harvard University Press.

28
Parent–Child and Child–Child Play in Diverse Cultural Contexts

JAIPAUL L. ROOPNARINE AND AIMBIKA KRISHNAKUMAR

The knowledge base about the nature and meaning of children's play in different cultures around the world has increased steadily since the publication of Schwartzman's (1978) classic book, *Transformations: The Anthropology of Children's Play*. Several forces from cultural psychology, play research, and early development and education have helped to shape this growing literature. The field of cultural psychology has provided theoretical propositions and research data that have focused on parental ethnotheories or ideas about childhood development, customs, and practices. These perspectives have influenced the work of play researchers. Play researchers also have considered the ecological contexts in which children from different cultures live; the intersection of cultural traditions and modern advances in various world cultures have transformed the nature of play and the social activities available to children (Gielen & Roopnarine, 2004; Shweder et al., 1998; Super & Harkness, 1997; Weisner, 1998). Moreover, in a number of technologically developing societies (Roopnarine & Metindogan, 2006 for a review), there has been an evolving emphasis on play-based early childhood education as an alternative to rigorous academic training. All of these factors have resulted to varying degrees in more indigenous descriptions of the quality and developmental trajectories of children's play, as well as assessments of the importance of play for early development (Roopnarine, Johnson, & Hooper, 1994).

Researchers from different disciplines have recorded children's modes of play behavior with increased accuracy because of more sophisticated methods and culture-specific conceptual frameworks (see Krishnakumar, Buehler, & Barber, 2004; van Vijer & Leung, 1997). These researchers have helped to move forward an understanding of universal play behavior.

This chapter provides a selective overview of children's play in different cultural and ethnic groups around the world. There is a focus on the play patterns of typically developing children from a global context because other chapters in this volume cover much of the extensive play studies conducted with North American and European children. This chapter addresses the following areas of study: (1) the conceptual base for understanding the meaning of play across cultures; (2) parental beliefs or ethnotheories of play; (3) a synopsis of parent–child and children's play in different settings; and (4) the associations between different forms of play and childhood development.

Two basic types of studies that are included are those that have been conducted within specific cultures and those that have used a comparative approach, typically using North American or European children as one of the groups under study. It is fair to say that, while comparative studies are quite informative, they are nonetheless prone to problems of cultural equivalence tied to the conceptualization and measurement of play behaviors (see van Vijer & Leung, 1997 for a discussion of methodological issues and cultural equivalence). For example, researchers who use many translated questionnaires and observational tools do not always assess their validity and reliability, or consider the literacy levels of families, cultural mores, and place of administration. Therefore, the development of culturally sensitive approaches for evaluating various aspects of children's play is as important as the demand for global understanding of children's play.

The Conceptual Base for Understanding the Meaning of Play Across Cultures

Researchers have continually pitched the theoretical notion of cross-cultural generalizations around issues of conceptualization, operationalization, and propositions on play against the need for unique theoretical frameworks and measurement strategies within specific cultures. Play scholars opine that a universally based understanding of children's play provides us with an opportunity to arrive at some common principles about play within and across national, cultural, and linguistic boundaries.

Cross-cultural researchers, however, need to be cautious about accepting only Western explanations for children's play across various cultures. A critical consideration is *conceptual equivalence*, which proposes that the definition and meaning of children's play is similar across cultures. Several theoretical and methodological considerations—functional equivalence, scalar specificity, and operational equivalence—are warranted when implementing investigations of children's play across cultures.

Collectively, a *cultural perspective* views childhood development as the joint effort between parents and children in specific developmental niches (Super & Harkness, 1997; Weisner, 1998). In other words, there is general acknowledgment that children shape and are shaped by experiences within their developmental niches (Super & Harkness, 1997). Along these lines, *interpretive reproduction theory* (Corsaro, 1997) suggests that children actively utilize adult cultural and social "messages" in efficient ways to foster the development of representations of themselves and their social and mental worlds (Stafford, 1995). The point is that children are not passive recipients of adult information about social activities and play. In some cultural communities, play behaviors may be "internally generated"—self-initiated, independent of adult activities (Gaskins, 1999, 2001), or guided by older children rather than adults (Goncu, Mistry, & Mosier, 2000; Maynard, 2004). Thus, play participation in different cultural communities depends, in part, on the adjustments children make to accommodate the childrearing goals and expectations of their parents.

For their part, mothers, fathers, and other caregivers bring to bear their cultural scripts or internal working models regarding the merits of playful activities for childhood development. There is general agreement among child development researchers that mothers and fathers hold beliefs about early childhood care and development that are specific to their culture (see Goodnow & Collins, 1990; Sigel, 1995; Super & Harkness, 1997). Parents have tacit or visible beliefs or cultural scripts about what are important childrearing precursors to the development of cognitive and social skills in children, and about when particular behaviors are likely to emerge during the course of development (Super & Harkness, 1997). Although cultural scripts do vary a good deal within and between cultural communities and by socioeconomic status (Cashmore & Goodnow, 1986; Rogoff, Mistry, Goncu, & Mosier, 1993), they are channeled through childrearing activities to equip children with the social and cognitive skills required to successfully navigate life within specific environments.

Certain cultural scripts about childrearing (e.g., cosleeping) are passed on from one generation to the next (Shweder, 1982), but may change depending on economic and social–cultural circumstances and exposure to competing views about early care and education (McGillicuddy-DeLisi, 1982). For example, Caribbean immigrants in North America may revise their natal cognitive models about the merits of play in the preschool curriculum as they become increasingly immersed in cultural practices about early education in the postindustrialized world. Because they represent internal working models of parenting and education, these cultural scripts assume significant direct or indirect roles that affect intellectual and behavioral development in children, their health, and well being (see review by Sigel & McGillicuddy-DeLisi, 2002).

Beliefs About Play Across Cultures

As was stated already, parental beliefs about childhood development are far from uniform across cultures (see Roopnarine & Metindogan, 2005; Super & Harkness, 1997). The same can be said for parental beliefs about the value of play in childhood development. Jamaican mothers of preschoolers, for example, believed that toys kept children busy or out of trouble and largely disapproved of "messy" play with sand or water. Few recognized the educational benefits of toys and some were indifferent to their use among children (Grantham-McGregor, Landman, & Desai, 1983; Leo-Rhynie, 1997). Yucatec Mayan parents rarely mediated or participated as partners in their children's play activities. In fact, participation in play activities signaled to adults that children were healthy. It also permitted parents to engage in uninterrupted work and social activities (Gaskins, 2001). Similar attitudes toward play have been observed in San Pedro, Guatemala (Goncu et al., 2000), and in India and Thailand, where parents were uncertain about the benefits of different play activities for cognitive and social development in children (Bloch & Wichaidat, 1986; Roopnarine, Hossain, Gill, & Brophy, 1994). Moreover, Sinai Bedouin Arabs parents penalized children for engaging in play (Ariel & Sever, 1980).

These cultural beliefs about play undergo only limited change as some of these groups immigrate to other societies. For example, researchers found that Asian-American immigrants in the United States preferred preacademic activities, such as learning mathematics and the alphabet, over play and attributed far less importance to the value of play than European-American mothers (Parmer& Harkness, 2004). Different from European-American mothers, African immigrant mothers employed visual and verbal cues as opposed to objects during interactions with children (Rabain-Jamin, 1994). English-speaking Caribbean immigrants living in the New York City area (Roopnarine, 1999), and Korean Americans in Los Angeles, also preferred academic activities over play (Farver, Kim, & Lee, 1995). Possibly, parents in these cultural groups believe that play is naturally of intrinsic interest to young children and something children engage in independent of adult guidance (Edwards, 2000).

But even among societies where there is a strong push for academic achievement early in the child's life, there are marked differences in belief structures about the benefits of play for early development. Mothers in Hong Kong saw play as an important tool of early socialization, as an avenue of self-expression, and as educationally beneficial to children (Holmes, 2001). In the *Preschool in Three Cultures* study (Tobin, Wu, & Davidson, 1989), when asked "Why should a society have preschool?" 70% of Japanese, 42% of U.S., and only 25% of the Chinese parents mentioned opportunities to play with other children. However, attitudes toward play may be changing among the Chinese. A recent survey (Ishigaki & Lin, 2000) of the child's right to play indicated that 67.6% of teachers in Japan, 78.5% in Korea, and 56.7% in China endorsed play as a part of the early childhood curriculum. Korean teachers had more positive attitudes about integrating play in the curriculum than either the Chinese or Japanese teachers (Ishigaki & Lin, 2000).

Qualitative accounts of kindergartens in Beijing and Taipei suggest that teachers made provisions for dramatic play (Lin, Johnson, & Johnson, 2001). For instance, in Taiwan, "experimental or exploratory programs," as compared to "efficient schools," where academic subjects are taught in a structured manner, are more inclined to be play-based (Chang, 2002; Johnson & Chang, 2003). The same is true for child-oriented rather than role-oriented preschools in Japan (Holloway, 1999). Flexibility in teachers' beliefs about play in early childhood education has also been noted in "progressive programs" in Malaysia (Miller, 1999), Turkey (Gol-Guven & Krishnakumar, 2003), Singapore (see volume by Honig, 1998; Raban & Ure, 1999), and Jamaica (Morrison & Milner, 2000), and play has been used in early intervention projects in India as a way of advancing the early development of children (Prochner, 2001).

In short, the optimism surrounding the merits of play for children's cognitive and social development in postindustrialized societies (Johnson, Christie, & Wardle, 2005) may not extend to the technologically developing world. In the technologically developing societies, play is still seen as frivolous, an activity that children are drawn to naturally. Parents, through their attitudes toward involvement in play, convey to children the social and cognitive transactions that are important for the acquisition of instrumental competence. They are demonstrating their preferences for socialization practices such as linguistic interactions, sibling relationships, social relations, and the like that may achieve some of the same developmental functions derived from play (e.g., perspective taking, cooperation, sharing; see Maynard, 2004). Once established, these socialization behaviors may set the stage for complex interactions with significant others in society, including playmates. To many adults in technologically developing societies, highly structured competitive educational systems may further accentuate the belief that rigorous academic training early in children's lives improves their later chances to be successful economically and socially. Accordingly, adults may see play as less important to early childhood development.

Parent–Child Play

There is surprisingly little data on the playful activities between parents and children in diverse cultural communities, in spite of all the emphasis placed on responsive, sensitive, and attuned parenting (Collins, Maccoby, Steinberg, Hetherington, & Bornstein, 2000). In many cultures, play partners routinely include nonparental figures, such as grandparents, cousins, siblings, and uncles (Maynard, 2004).

Researchers have noted that only one of their sample mothers in San Pedro, Guatemala assumed the role of "playmate" to toddlers and some mothers laughed at the suggestion of engaging in play with young children (Rogoff et al., 1993). This practice is the opposite of mothers and fathers in the United States who acted as playmates or teachers to their toddlers 47% of the time versus 7% in San Pedro, Guatemala, and 24% in Dohl-Ki-Patti, India, during prescribed episodes (Rogoff et al., 1993). Moreover, when adults in some cultures supervise, dictate to, or prohibit children from engaging in certain types of activities, they are expressing their ideas about what social behaviors they value in their society (see Grantham-McGregor et al., 1993; Rogoff et al., 1993).

Mothers and fathers in middle-income families in technologically developed societies are more likely than parents in less technologically developed societies to provide toys and play materials that facilitate the cognitive, physical, and social development of children. It is uncommon for adults in traditional societies to direct children's play in a positive way (Lancy, 1996). Hence, in many technologically developing countries children's play may be less structured than in the postindustrialized countries and adults may view play more for its amusement than educational value. The section that follows discusses the variations and similarities in three predominant modes of activities between parents and children—rough stimulating play activities, the nature and properties of games, and pretend or fantasy play.

Parent–Child Physical Play

In North America, European–American parent–child physical play is apparent early in the infancy and preschool years before dropping precipitously after age 10 (Macdonald & Parke, 1986). There is an inverse association between physical play and age of parent, and it appears that physical play is more characteristic of the social engagement of fathers and sons than fathers and daughters (Lamb, 2002).

The ubiquity of parent–child physical play (rough-housing, tossing, bouncing, poking etc.) among European-American fathers and children (Lamb, 2002) is not evident in the social activities of parents and children in many other cultures. For example, it does not figure prominently in the parent–child social activities of East Indian families in New Delhi (Roopnarine, Talukder, Jain, Joshi, & Srivastav, 1991); families residing in urban and peri-urban areas of Taiwan (Sun & Roopnarine, 1996); Thai families in Chaing Mai (Tulananda & Roopnarine, 2001); Malaysian families in Kuching, Sarawak (Roopnarine, Lu, & Ahmeduzzaman, 1989); AKA foragers in the Central African Republic (Hewlett, 1987); and Jamaican families in Kingston (Roopnarine, Brownet al., 1995). In all cases, major physical play (e.g., rough-housing) and minor physical play (e.g., tickling and poking) were observed less than one incident per hour or were reported to be absent from social exchanges with young children. Physical play was also less prevalent in the play of families and children in Dhol-Ki-Patti, India, San Pedro, Guatamela, and Kecioren, Turkey, than in Salt Lake City, Utah (Goncu et al., 2000).

There are gender differences in the ways in which adults play with children across cultures. For example, among the AKA, mothers engaged in three bouts and fathers did not engage in any rough play in over 264 hours of observations (Hewlett, 1987). When rough play did occur, fathers were more likely than mothers to engage in physical play in communities in Taiwan and India, whereas mothers more than fathers preferred to engage in object play with children. The gender-differentiated trend seems characteristic of fathers across several societies. Unlike European-American families, though, fathers did not prefer boys over girls as partners in physical play. It is worth mentioning that in the social activities of Swedish (Lamb, Frodi, Hwang, Frodi, & Steinberg, 1982) and Israeli fathers and children (Sagi, Lamb, Shohan, Dvir, & Lewkowicz, 1985), rough physical play occurred at low frequencies as well. Among Italian families, it occurred between adult maternal figures and children (New, 1994; New & Benigni, 1987).

What purpose might physical play serve in human species? Some developmental psychologists (Lamb, 2002) suggest that rough stimulating bouts of play that involve touching and holding may facilitate the development of attachment bonds between fathers and children. As discussed above, physical play is less common outside of North America and it occurs at low rates in other developed societies, perhaps suggesting other epiphenomena (e.g., affectionate displays, duration of holding) in the development of attachment bonds between children and fathers (Tamis-LeMonda, 2004). By the same token, its relative absence in many societies begs the question about an underlying biological function in humans.

Parent–Child Games

Other publications have discussed the types and nature of parent–child games (e.g., MacDonald, 1993; Sutton-Smith, 1976, 2001). Some researchers argue that coplaying in the form of games supports the developmental purposes listed below. Coplaying:

- assists the transmission of cultural information that children internalize (see Bruner, 1972; Vygotsky, 1978);
- contributes to language development (Meacham, 1984; Ratner & Bruner, 1978);
- involves focused interactions that contain the turn-taking rules of social conversations, repetition, and temporal regularities (Roopnarine, Hooper, Ahmeduzzaman, & Pollack, 1993; Stern, 1974);
- offers opportunities for children to receive tactile, visual, and auditory stimulation, and engage in limb or body movements (Johnson et al., 2005);
- and may encourage exploration which helps in the development of self-control (Watson & Ramey, 1972).

With these developmental functions in mind, the next section describes some parent–child games that are more commonly viewed across cultures. During the first few years of life, quite a bit of variation can be witnessed in the nature, frequency, and quality of parent–child games.

Face-to-Face Play

While common in the social exchanges of parents and children in Western industrialized societies (e.g., North America, Europe; Roopnarine, Fouts, Lamb, & Lewis-Elligan, 2005), face-to-face play is rarely witnessed in the mother–infant interactions of Kaluli (Schieffelin, 1991) or Marquesan mothers (Martini, 2005; Martini & Kirkpatrick, 1992) because infants are held facing outward, and others are encouraged to interact with them. However, focusing on the dyadic interactions between mother and infant leaves out other socialization agents. When sibling caregiving was taken into account, Kenyan and American children received about the same amount of face-to-face play (Whaley, Sigman, Bekwith, Cohen, & Espinosa, 2000).

Postural differences also appear in the play of mothers and infants in different cultures as follows:

- Japanese mothers loomed in and out, used tapping to recruit visual attention, held and touched infants.
- White mothers in the United States were more likely than Japanese mothers to use their voices and respond to vocalizations during face-to-face interactions (Fogel, Nwokah, & Karnes, 1993).
- Among East Indians, early parent–child games contained high levels of tactile and verbal stimulation (songs, lullabies, poetry, and rhymes). An in-depth analysis of parent–infant games in India showed that 87% of the time, parents held the child close to the body or massaged the child; 21% of the time, the mother sang to the child; and 52% of the time they engaged in face-to-face interactions, along with elaborate language use (Roopnarine et al., 1994). Indian mothers also tickled, cooed, and played peek-a-boo with their toddlers to express affection, but also teased children, and scared them by growling (Rogoff et al., 1993).
- Parents in Turkey, Guatemala, the United States, and India also engaged in games of touching, patting, hugging, kissing, and dancing (Goncu et al., 2000).

Even among societies where the same game is played, variations do exist. For example, the parent–infant game of peek-a-boo is present in the play of parents and infants in South Africa, Japan, Malaysia, Iran, Brazil, Russia, and Korea. It is likely that other cultures may have parallel games in which parents play hide and seek (Goncu et al., 2000). What is interesting about peek-a-boo is that across cultures the acoustic sounds have different qualities: in South Africa they had a rough and gravely quality while among Tamil and Brazilian speaking parents the exchanges involved use of words beyond nonsense syllables (Ferand & O'Neill, 1993). The different forms of early language use have implications for the complexity of language development later in childhood (Bloom, 1998).

Among older children, adults participate in a wide spectrum of games with their children, from organized sports such as ball games (Johnson et al., 2005, p. 7) to more sedentary activities that entail using strategies (e.g., dominoes, a board game played in different parts of the Caribbean). As children age, the possibility exists that parents in developing societies have less time to play with them because of economic reasons and cultural demands by adults that children make developmental shifts between 5 and 7 years toward subsistence type activities (e.g., tending to animals). It is not that children cease to play. Their games mimic adult activities as play becomes integrated into work. On the one hand, an anthropologist (Lancy, 2001) argues that the toys that adults make in some societies—knives, bows, arrows, and canoes—represent miniature tools, presumably designed to foster participation in future culture-specific adult roles. On the other hand, there is a dramatic decline in mother–child play, from 87% at 12 months to 50% at 48 months (Haight, 1999). With children's increasing social and cognitive competence, the role of parents across societies may gradually shift from that of active participant to that of supervisor of play.

Our observations of parent–child activities in Chaing Mai Province in northern Thailand lend some support for the observation of a decline in adult–child play around the late preschool years.

Over two-hour observation periods conducted during the day, researchers found that Thai fathers engaged in low levels of games with rules with their preschool-aged children (Tulananda & Roopnarine, 2001). Perhaps these parents used other media for playful interactions (e.g., teasing and joking, telling stories) or engaged in other types of electronic games with children during the evening or on weekends. In a related vein, Taiwanese mothers were not very enthusiastic about arranging for their kindergartners to engage in games with rules because they perceived their children to be somewhat immature to participate in such activities. These mothers furnished their children with a variety of toys and permitted them to play between one and two hours per day (Pan, 1994).

Parent–Child Pretend Play

The developmental progression of pretense, the documentation of different modes of pretense, and their presumed functions and benefits are outlined in the present book (see other chapters) and other volumes (Johnson et al., 2005; Roskos & Christie, 2000). During parent–child pretend episodes, there are opportunities to teach communication skills, engage in didactic exchanges, to demonstrate, encourage, and support child-initiated fantasy (Fiese, 1990: Garvey, 1990; Tamis-LeMonda & Bornstein, 1991; Youngblade & Dunn, 1995).

There is abundant evidence of parental participation in fantasy play across cultures. Parental participation in fantasy play with young children has been observed in mother–child and father–child play in Thailand (Tulananda & Roopnarine, 2001), in assessments of differences in mother–toddler play between Japanese and American mothers (Tamis-LeMonda, Bornstein, Cyphers, Toda, & Ogino, 1992), in questionnaire assessments of Korean- and European-American children (Farver et al., 1995), Taiwanese children (Pan, 1994), and Jamaican children (Grantham-McGregor et al., 1983), and during the play of Mexican and Euro-American mother–child interactions (Farver, 1993). In their examination of parent–child play in four cultures, researchers reported that while parents in both Turkey and Utah adopted pretend roles where they entered the play of toddlers as actors (e.g., monsters); this was not apparent in the play of Indian and Guatemalan parents (Goncu et al., 2000).

Generally, the parent as actor during bouts of fantasy play was more characteristic of parents in the technologically developed societies where cognitive development is at a premium. Does this mean then that parents in other cultures are unaware of the potential benefits of engagement in fantasy play? Researchers typically observe children's play transformations with objects or materials and may not be privy to the covert aspects of parents' attempts at facilitating children's transformations of reality. An anthropologist argues cogently that, by observing the nearby adults in traditional non-Western societies, "children gain access to prime script for their make-believe play and, as is widely reported in the literature, parents believe that the primary means for children to acquire the skills of adults is through observation, imitation, and trial and error—not in other words, through adult instruction" (Lancy, 2001, p.56). Moreover, adults in technologically developing societies use stories, tales, and folklore to stimulate their children's imagination (Goncu, 2000), and sibling caregivers assume a central role in conveying cultural and social information to the children in their charge (Maynard, 2004).

Children's Play in Different Settings

Although the research literature provides evidence for children's engagement in a myriad of cognitive and social play activities across cultures, it is limited on the consistency of children's play across cultural communities. It is this issue that we turn to in this segment of the paper. First, some distinguishing features of children's play across cultures are identified before launching into the modes of play and their manifestations in different cultures.

1. Play is mixed with work-related activities in a number of technologically developing societies (e.g., Senegal, Botswana, Tanzania; Bloch & Adler, 1994; Blurton-Jones, 1993). This is more noticeable between 5 and 7 years of age when a developmental shift occurs in parental demands that children participate in subsistence activities (Edwards, 2000; Gaskins, 1990; Lancy 2001; Munroe, Munroe, & Shimmin, 1984).
2. Siblings assume a pivotal role in directing and guiding children's make-believe play (e.g., Mexican; Maynard, 1999, 2004). Elders and other nonkinship members provide ample opportunities for children to imitate and practice future roles (e.g., Kepelle of Sierra Leone; Lancy, 2001).
3. Play often reflects the socialization values and beliefs of a given society. Societies that value collective effort encourage higher levels of cooperative play in children (Martini, 1994), whereas those that embrace individualism and the competitive spirit are more likely than not to invoke such an approach to games (Madsen & Lancy, 1981).
4. Poor physical and emotional health imposes limits on children's play participation. Malnourishment, war, famine, and other "difficult circumstances" have been demonstrated to have negative consequences on children's functioning (see Aptekar, 2004).
5. Children's play occurs in diverse settings such as yards, beaches, near mosques, streets, and alleys, farmland, neighborhood playgrounds, classrooms, in homes, and may involve toys or objects constructed from nearby materials or discarded objects (Lancy, 1996; Roopnarine et al., 1994; Sawada & Minami, 1997). Different characteristics within children's immediate environments can constrain play (e.g., crowding, same-age vs. mixed-age play groups, etc.; Kim, 1993; Liddell & Kruger, 1987). We venture to guess that children's play in traditional societies is less likely to be systematically organized by parents as it is in the postindustrialized world.
6. There is a strong gender cleavage in children's play in traditional societies (e.g., India and Africa). Boys are given more latitude than girls to roam away from living areas. In these societies, playgroups are largely segregated by gender (Edwards, 2000; Lancy, 2001).

With these propositions, what is the nature and level of children's play participation in different cultural communities? One of the most detailed comparative accounts of children's play interactions and responsibilities across societies is offered by the *Six Culture* studies (Edwards, 2000). In a recent reanalysis of the data collected at the six sites—Kenya, Mexico, Philippines, Okinawa, India, and the United States—the presence of creative-constructive, fantasy, role play, and games with rules was identified. Before describing children's play, it is necessary to consider some aspects of their lives in the different settings. In all six cultures, boys between 4 and 5 years of age engaged in more play than girls. With the exception of the United States, girls in the other cultures engaged in childcare and household work, and had more responsibility for infants than boys.

Gender-segregated playgroups were the norm in most cultures. Among the Nyansongo of Kenya, children played with kin members in mixed-age groups, integrating play into work. Games included tag and dirt-throwing, and creative-constructive activity (e.g., building a dam) was the most common form of play observed, particularly among boys. Indian children had few toys and boys played jacks and hockey. Mexican children played simple games with rules such as tag and ball, but showed a preference for role-play and creative-constructive play, especially among girls. Older children in the Philippines taught younger children to play games with rules (e.g., hide-and-seek, tag, drop the handkerchief). These children showed high levels of interest in role-play and fantasy play (Edwards, 2000). Observations of children of the Bamenda Grassfields of the Northern Cameroon showed that they engaged in quite a bit of free play (Nsamenang & Lamb, 1993). A more contemporary study (Goncu et al., 2000) reported that a greater number of toddlers in Salt Lake City, Utah and Turkey engaged in pretend and language play, and games, than in India or Guatemala. Traditional games (see Roopnarine et al., 1998, pp. 205–207, for a more detailed description) have been observed among the Chinese (Pan, 1994), Japanese (Takeuchi, 1994), native people of Australia (Sutton-Smith, 1976), New Guinea (Lancy, 2001), and in different parts of India (Roopnarine et al., 1994). Play may be embedded in festivals and religious celebrations (e.g., Holi in India, the Lantern Festival in Taiwan) and expressed in the "polite arts" (Pan, 1994).

Another play activity that is of interest to child development specialists is pretense. This form of play has been linked to language development, perspective-taking ability, problem-solving abilities, metaplay and comprehension, and the acquisition of a variety of social behaviors and skills (Roopnarine et al., 2000). Complex episodes of pretend play have been observed in India (Roopnarine et al., 1994), Taiwan (Pan, 1994), Sierra Leone (Lancy, 1996), Senegal (Bloch & Adler, 1994), Guyana (Taharally, 1991), the Marquesas (Martini, 1994) and a number of other societies around the world. In some cases, rates of dramatic play are comparable to those in the United States (Pan, 1994), and play themes mirror adult work and roles, and events in their home environments. An account of Kepelle children's play illustrates the kinds of fantasy themes children in one part of Africa employed, as follows: "three toddlers, using found objects, were pretending to hull rice with a mortar and pestle—an adult activity they have witnessed every day of their lives. Games with rules also seem to be rooted in fantasy; thus, while playing 'hopscotch,' children recite a litany of conquest—each square is a 'town'" (Lancy, 2001, p. 56).

Obviously, it would be difficult to describe the entire body of work on children's play in diverse cultures in this chapter. We close this section by describing the play of children in a Polynesian culture (Martini, 1994). The Marquesans exemplify the cooperative spirit in childrearing and engage in the concept of "status-leveling." As might be expected, these socialization practices should encourage high levels of cooperative play. Roughly, 93% of children's play is of a cooperative nature. It has been observed that Marquesan children spent 35% of the time in group object-oriented play (e.g., gathering leaves at the same time), 24% of their time in scripted fantasy (e.g., fishing, hunting), 9% in fighting and negotiating (teasing and status-leveling directed at someone who displays dominance), 18% of their time sitting and talking, 5% of the time in physical play, and some time in organized games.

Links Between Play and Development

What does the cross-cultural research tell us about the links between play and childhood development? Much is implied from descriptive accounts of children's play across some societies with few attempts made to uncover the underlying developmental value of play through cause-effect models. A reasonable explanation for this may be that a good number of sociocultural studies of children's play are bent on recording ongoing social activities. Of course, one cannot underestimate the benefits of role-play and "work-play" in developing societies as preparation for future adult and community activities (Bloch & Adler, 1994; Edwards, 2000). For instance, Nso children who participated in high levels of peer interactions also demonstrated good perspective-taking ability and cooperation (Nsamenang & Lamb, 1993). Nevertheless, the available experimental evidence is rather mixed and supports findings observed among North American and European families and children. A few of the associations between play and childhood development are presented below.

Returning to the observations conducted in Thailand, parent–child symbolic and constructive play were significantly associated with children's social skills in preschool (Tulananda & Roopnarine, 2001). Maternal interaction that involved labeling and pointing to objects, availability of play objects, and involvement in infant games were related to better cognitive outcomes in different samples of Indian infants (Anandalakshmy, 1979; Misra, 1977; Patri, 1988; Prochner, 2001). An intervention study conducted in Guyana, South America suggests that children accrue benefits from fantasy play stimulation; children who played with toys designed to stimulate fantasy for 25 minutes a day for 30 days showed improvements in language scores compared with controls (Taharally, 1991). Cognitive gains were realized in children enrolled in an early stimulation project in rural Jamaica that focused on mother–child interactions that included play and manipulation of objects (e.g., fitting puzzles together, puppetry) (Powell, 2005). Early stimulation as indexed by the provision of play materials and engagement in fantasy play was positively associated with a measure of developmental quotient in another group of Jamaican children (Grantham-McGregor et al., 1983). In yet another region of the Caribbean, Trinidadian children who were enrolled in "developmentally appropriate" early childhood programs that emphasized play (puzzle play, water and sand play, outings, matching and sorting) did not fare better on achievement tests at age 11 compared with children who were enrolled in Montessori programs that do not emphasize learning through play. However, children in the developmentally appropriate program exhibited better social skills with peers than their counterparts in more structured programs (Kutnick, 1994). Early play stimulation in the Sudan had favorable outcomes on children's cognitive functioning and in modifying maternal interaction (Grotberg, Bardin, & King, 1987: Grotberg & Bardin, 1989). By contrast, research carried out on Taiwanese children failed to find significant associations between fantasy play and children's I.Q. and perspective-taking abilities (Pan, 1994).

Taken as a whole, these play-based activities between parents and children and children and their peers in formal settings seem to produce modest intellectual and social gains with no discerned negative effects on children in societies where there is a strong push for rigorous academic training in the early childhood years. These findings, some of which are based on reasonably well-designed experimental studies, hold promise for convincing early childhood personnel in the technologically developing world that play-enriched education may be just as effective in providing children with the requisite skills necessary for school readiness and success as more structured, academically laced programs. What is intriguing are the potential benefits of play stimulation for a majority of the world's children whose lives are not touched by formal institutions of early childhood education.

A word of caution is necessary in interpreting the nature and strength of relationships between play and early development across cultures. On the surface, the salubrious effects of play appear to reflect universal patterns of cultures. However, differences in correlates across cultures reflect meaningful relationships that can only be understood from the cultural values and norms regarding the importance of specific aspects of play to areas of development.

Conclusion

It does appear that play is a universal and essential aspect of childhood in almost all cultures observed to date. The universality of children's play has provided child development scholars with the opportunity to learn about the common characteristics of play across cultures and to share strategies for promoting healthy child development across international boundaries. Since the mid-1990s, several debates on various cultural issues surrounding children's play have been revived because of the increased intermingling among the world's cultures and the multiethnic nature of populations within countries. There is support for the premise that the nature, beliefs, and meanings that specific cultures attribute to play are indeed unique and are more a reflection of a culture's traditions and ethos suggesting an *emic* approach (Gaskins, 2001). At the same time, several characteristics of play are seen across diverse cultures, suggesting that play may be fundamental to human existence and shared among different cultures, possibly transcending the uniqueness of race, culture, and geographic location, and thereby supporting an *etic* approach (Sutton-Smith, 2001).

A key component to understanding children's play is the historical and cultural experiences of individual groups (e.g., technological sophistication; filial piety; religious beliefs; oppression; difficult life circumstances, etc.), and their socialization, beliefs, goals, and expectations of children in a changing global community. These multiple factors may determine how families and children deal with their interpretations of the values, attitudes, and behaviors relating to children's play.

References

Anandalakshmy, S. (1979). Recent research on the young child. *The Indian Journal of Social Work, 40*, 295–309.

Apetkar, L. (2004). The changing dynamics of children in particularly difficult circumstances: Examples of street and war-traumatized children. In U. Gielen & J. Roopnarine (Eds.), *Childhood and adolescence: Cross-cultural perspectives and applications* (pp. 377–410).Westport, CT: Praeger.

Ariel, S., & Sever, I. (1980). Play in the desert and play in the town: On play activities of Bedouin Arab children. In H. B. Schwartzman (Ed.), *Play and culture* (pp. 164–175). West Point, NY: Leisure Press.

Bloch, M., & Adler, L. (1994). African children's play and the emergence of the sexual division of labor. In J. Roopnarine, J. Johnson, & F. Hooper (Eds.), *Children's play in diverse cultures* (pp. 148–178). Albany: State University of New York Press.

Bloch, M., & Wichaidat, W. (1986). Play and school work in the kindergarten curriculum: Attitudes of parents and teachers in Thailand. *Early Child Development and Care, 24,* 197–218.

Blurton-Jones, N. (1993). The lives of hunter–gatherer children: Effects of parental behavior and parental reproduction strategy. In M. E. Pereira & L. A. Fairbanks (Eds.), *Juvenile primates* (pp. 405–426). Oxford: Oxford University Press.

Bruner, J. (1972). Nature and uses of immaturity. *American Psychologist, 27*, 687–708.

Cashmore, J., & Goodnow, J. J. (1986). Influences on Australian parents' values: Ethnicity versus socio-economic status. *Journal of Cross-cultural Psychology, 17,* 441–454.

Chang, P. (2003) Contextual understanding of children's play in Taiwaneese kindergartens. In D. E. Lytle (Ed.), *Play and Educational theory and practice* (pp. 277-298). Westport, CT: Ablex.

Collins, W. A., Maccoby, E., Steinberg, L., Hetherington, E. M., & Bornstein, M. H. (2000). Contemporary research on parenting: The case of nature versus nurture. *American Psychologist, 55*, 218–232.

Corsaro, W. (1992). Interpretative reproduction in children's peer cultures. *Social Psychology Quarterly, 55*, 160–177.

Edwards, C. P. (2000). Children's play in cross-cultural perspective: A new look at the six cultures study. *Cross-Cultural Research, 34*, 318–338.

Farver, J. A. M., Kim, Y. K., & Lee, Y. (1995). Cultural difference in Korean- and Anglo-American preschoolers' social interaction and play behaviors. *Child Development, 66,* 1088–1099.

Farver, J. A. M., Kim, Y. K., & Lee, Y. (1995). Cultural difference in Korean- and Anglo-American preschoolers' social interaction and play behaviors. *Child Development, 66,* 1088–1099.

Farver, J. A. M., & Shin, Y. L. (1997). Social pretend play in Korean- and Anglo-American preschoolers. *Child Development, 68*(3), 544–556.

Ferald, A., & O'Neill, D. (1993). Peek-a-boo across cultures. In K. Macdonald (Ed.), *Parent–child play* (pp. 259–285). Albany, NY: State University of New York Press.

Fiese, B. H. (1990). Playful relationships: A contextual analysis of mother–toddler interaction and symbolic play. *Child Development, 61,* 1648–1656

Fogel, A., Nwokah, E., & Karns, J. (1993). Parent–infant games as dynamic social systems. In K. Macdonald (Ed.), *Parent–child play* (pp. 43–70). Albany: State University of New York Press.

Garvey, C. (190). *Play.* Cambridge, MA: Harvard University Press.

Gaskins, S. (1990). *Exploratory play and development in Mayan infants.* Unpublished doctoral dissertation, University of Chicago.

Gaskins, S. (2001). *Ignoring play: Will it survive?: A Mayan case study of beliefs and behavior.* Paper presented at the Association for the Study of Play Meetings, San Diego, CA.

Gielen, G., & Roopnarine, G. (2004). (Eds.). *Childhood and adolescence: Cross-cultural perspectives and applications.* Westport, CT: Praeger.

Gol-Guven, M., & Krishnakumar, A. (2002). *Evaluation of early childhood classrooms in Turkey.* Paper presented at National Association for Education of Young Children, New York City.

Goncu, A., Mistry, J. & Mosier, C. (2000). Cultural variations in the play of toddlers. *International Journal of Behavioral Development, 24*, 321–329.

Goodnow, J. J., Cashmore, J. A., Cotton, S., & Knight, R. (1984). Mothers' developmental timetables in two cultural groups. *International Journal of Psychology, 19*, 193–205.

Goodnow, J. J., & Collins, W. A. (1990). *Development according to parents: The nature, sources, and consequences of parents' ideas.* Hillsdale, NJ: Lawrence Erlbaum.

Grantham-McGregor, S., Landman, J. & Desai, P. (1983). Child rearing in poor urban Jamaica. *Child: Care, Health and Development, 9,* 57–71.

Grotberg, E., & Bardin, G. (1989). Shifting from traditional to modern childrearing practices in the Sudan. *Early Child Development and Care, 50,* 141–150.

Grotberg, E., Bardin, G., & King, A. (1987). Changing childrearing practices in Sudan: An early stimulation demonstration program. *Children Today, 16,* 26–29.

Haight, W. (1999). The pragmatics of caregiver–child pretending at home: Understanding culturally-specific socialization practices. In A. Goncu (Ed.), *Children's engagement in the world: Sociocultural perspectives* (pp. 128–147). Cambridge, UK: Cambridge University Press.

Hewlett, B. (1987). Patterns of parental holding among AKA pygmies. In M. Lamb (Ed.), *The father's role: Cross-cultural perspectives* (pp. 295-330). Hillsdale, NJ: Lawrence Erlbaum.

Holloway, S. (2000). *Contested childhood: Diversity and change in Japanese preschools.* New York: Routledge Press.

Holmes, R. (2001). Parental notions about their children's playfulness and children's notions of play in the United States and Hong Kong. In S. Reifel (Ed.), *Theory in context and out: Play and Culture Studies* (Vol. 3., pp. 291–314). Westport, CT: Ablex.

Honig, A. (1998). Singapore childcare and early education [Special Issue]. *Early Child Development and Care, 144.*

Ishigaki, E. H., & Lin, J. (1999). A comparative study of preschool teachers' attitudes towards "Children's Right to Play" in Japan, China, and Korea. *International Journal of Early Childhood, 31*(1), 40–47

Johnson, J. (2001). *Taiwanese teacher educators', teachers', and parents,' views about play.* Paper presented at the Association for the Study of Play meetings, San Diego, CA.

Johnson, J. E., & Chang, P. (2003). Teachers' and parents' attitudes about play and learning in Taiwanese kindergartens. Unpublished manuscript, The Pennsylvania State University, PA.

Johnson, J. E., Christie, J., & Wardle, F. (2005). *Play development and early education.* Boston, MA: Allyn & Bacon.

Johnson, J., Johnson, K., & Lin, M. (2001, May) *Dramatic play in Montessori kindergartens in Taiwan and Mainland China.* American Association for the Children's Right to Play, International Conference, Hofstra University, Hempstead, NY.

Kim, Y. A. (2001). Peer relationships and play behaviors of children in three different sized classes over a four-month period. *Early Child Development and Care, 167,* 89–102.

Krishnakumar, A., Buehler, C., & Barber, B. (2004). Cross-ethnic equivalence of socialization measures in European American and African American families. *Journal of Marriage and the Family,* 66, 809-820

Kutnick, P. (1994). Does preschool curriculum make a difference in primary school performance: Insights into the variety of preschool activities and their effects on school achievement and behavior in the Caribbean island of Trinidad: Cross-sectional and longitudinal evidence. *Early Child Development and Care, 103,* 27–42.

Lamb, M. E. (2002). Infant–father attachments and their impact on child development. In C. S. Tamis-LeMonda & N. Cabrera (Eds.), *Handbook on father involvement: Multidisciplinary perspectives* (pp. 93–117). Mahwah, NJ: Lawrence Erlbaum.

Lamb, M. E., Frodi, A. M., Frodi, M., Hwang, C. P. (1982). Characteristics of maternal and paternal behavior in traditional and nontraditional Swedish families. *International Journal of Behavioral Development, 5,* 131–141.

Lancy, D. (1977). The play behavior of Kpelle children during rapid cultural change. In D. F. Lancy & B. A. Tindall (Eds.), *The anthropological study of play: Problems and prospects.* West Point, NY: Leisure Press.

Lancy, D. F. (1996). *Playing on the mother-ground: Cultural routines for children's development.* New York: Guilford Press.

Lancy, D. (2001). Cultural constraints on children's play. In J. L. Roopnarine (Ed.), *Conceptual, social-cognitive, and contextual issues in the fields of play* (pp. 51–60). Westport, CT: Ablex

Leo-Rhynie, E. (1997). Class, race, and gender issues in childrearing in the Caribbean. In J. L. Roopnarine & J. Brown (Eds.), *Caribbean families: Diversity among ethnic groups* (pp. 25–55). Norwood, NJ: Ablex.

Liddell, C., & Kruger, P. (1987). Patterns of activity and social behavior in a South African township nursery: Some effects of crowding. *Merrill-Palmer Quarterly, 33,* 206–228.

Lin, M., Johnson, J. E., & Johnson, K. M., (2003). Dramatic play in Montessori kindergartens in Taiwan and Mainland China. Unpublished manuscript, The Pennsylvania State University, PA.

MacDonald, K. (Ed.). (1993). *Parent–child play.* Albany: State University of New York Press.

MacDonld, K., & Parke, R. D. (1986). Parent–child physical play: The effects of sex and age of children and parents. *Sex Roles, 15,* 367–378.

Madsen, M. C., & Lancy, D. F. (1981). Cooperative and competitive behavior: Experiments related to ethnic identity and urbanization in Papua New Guinea. *Journal of Cross-Cultural Psychology, 12,* 389–408.

Martini, M. (1994). Peer interactions in Polynesia: A view from the Marquesas. In J. Roopnarine, J. Johnson, & F. Hooper (Eds.), *Children's play in diverse cultures* (pp. 73–103). Albany: SUNY Press.

Martini, M., & Kirkpatrick, J. (1992). Parenting in Polynesia: A view from the Marquesas. In J. L. Roopnarine & B. Carter (Eds.), *Parent–child socialization in diverse cultures* (pp. 199–222). Norwood, NJ: Ablex.

Maynard, A. (2002). Cultural teaching: The development of teaching in Mayan sibling interactions. *Child Development, 73,* 969–982.

Maynard, A. (2004). Sibling interactions. In U. Gielen & J. Roopnarine (Eds.), *Childhood and adolescence: Cross-cultural perspectives and applications* (pp. 229–252). Westport, CT: Praeger.

McGillicuddy-DeLisi, A. V. (1982). Parental beliefs about developmental processes. *Human Development, 25,* 192–200.

Meacham, J. A. (1984). The social basis of intentional action. *Human Development, 27,* 119–124.

Miller, L (1997). A vision for the early years curriculum in the United Kingdom. *International Journal of Early Childhood, 29*(1), 34–41.

Misra, N. (1977). Cognitive and motor development of infants (6–12 months): Nutritional and socioeconomic status correlates. Unpublished master's dissertation, University of Delhi, India.

Morrison, J. W., & Milner, V. (1997) Early education and care in Jamaica: A grassroots effort. *International Journal of Early Childhood, 29*(2), 51–68.

Munroe, R. H., Munroe, R. L., & Shimmin, H. S. (1984). Children's work in four cultures: Determinants and consequences. *American Anthropologist, 86,* 369–379.

New, R. (1994). Children's play—una cosa naturale: An Italian perspective. In J. L. Roopnarine, J. E. Johnson, & F. H. Hooper (Eds.), *Children's play in diverse cultures* (pp. 123–147). Albany, NY: State University of New York Press.

New, R., & Benigni, L. (1987). Italian fathers and infants: Cultural constraints on parental behavior. In M. Lamb (Ed.), *The father's role: Cross-cultural perspectives* (pp. 139-167). Hillsdale, NJ: Lawrence Erlbaum.

Nsamenang, B., & Lamb, M. (1993). The acquisition of socio-cognitive competence by Nso children in the Bamenda Grassfields of Northern Cameroon. *International Journal of Behavioral Development, 16,* 439–441.

Pan, H. W. (1994). Children's play in Taiwan. In J. L. Roopnarine, J. E. Johnson, & F. H. Hooper (Eds.), *Children's play in diverse cultures.* New York: State University of New York Press.

Parmar, P., & Harkness, S. (2004). Asian and European American parents' ethnotheories of play and learning: Effects on home routines and children's behavior. *International Journal of Behavioral Development, 28,* 97–104.

Patri, V. (1988). An intervention program of early stimulation in a group of disadvantaged children. Unpublished research report, New Delhi.

Pearson, E., & Rao, N. (2003). Socialization goals, parenting practices, and peer competence in Chinese and English preschoolers. *Early Child Development and Care, 173*, 131–146.

Powell, C. (2005). Evaluation of the Roving Caregivers Programme: Rural family support. Unpublished manuscript, Mona, Jamaica.

Raban, B., & Ure, C. (1999). Literacy in the preschool: An Australian case study. In J. Hayden (Ed.), *Landscapes in early childhood education: Cross national perspectives* (316–329). New York: Peter Lang.

Raban, B., & Ure, C. (2000). Literacy in three language: A challenge for Singapore preschools. *International Journal of Early Childhood, 31*, 45–54.

Rabain-Jamin, J. (1994). Language and socialization of the child in African families living in France. In P. M. Greenfield & R. Cocking (Eds.), *Cross-cultural roots of minority child development* (pp. 147–166). Hillsdale, NJ: Erlbaum.

Rao, N., & Koong, M. (2000). Enhancing preschool education in Hong Kong. *International Journal of Early Childhood, 32*(2), 1–11.

Rao, N., Koong, M., Kwong, M., & Wong, M. (1999, November). Indicators of high quality organization. Unpublished manuscript, University of the West Indies, Mona, Jamaica.

Rogoff, B., Goncu, A., Mistry, J., & Mosier, C. (1993). Guided participation in cultural activity by toddlers and caregivers. *Monographs of the Society for Research in Child Development*. 236(58, Serial No. 8).

Roopnarine, J. L. (1999). *Parental involvement, ethnotheories about development, parenting styles, and early academic achievement in Caribbean-American children.* Paper presented in the Department of Applied Psychology, New York University.

Roopnarine, J. L., Brown, J., Snell-White, P., Riegraf, N., Webb, W., & Hossain, Z. (1995). Father involvement in childcare and household work in common-law dual-earner and single earner Jamaican families. *Journal of Applied Developmental Psychology, 16*, 35–52.

Roopnarine, J. L., Fouts, H. N., Lamb, M. E., & Lewis, T. E. (2005). Mother–infant and father–infant interactions in low-, middle-, and upper-SES African American families. *Developmental Psychology, 41, 723-732.*

Roopnarine, J. L., Hopper, F. H., Ahmeduzzaman, M., & Pollack, B. (1993). Gentle play partners: Mother–child and father–child play in New Delhi, India. In K. MacDonald (Ed.), *Parents and children playing* (pp. 287–304). Albany, NY: State University of New York Press.

Roopnarine, J., Hossain, Z., Gill, P., & Brophy, H. (1994). Play in the East Indian context. In J Roopnarine, J. Johnson, & F. Hooper (Eds.), *Children's play in diverse cultures* (pp. 9–30). Albany, N Y: State University of New York Press.

Roopnarine, J. L. Johnson, J. E., & Hooper, F. H. (1994). (Eds.). *Children's play in diverse cultures.* Albany, NY: State University of New York Press.

Roopnarine, J. L., Lu, M., & Ahmeduzzaman, M. (1989). Parental reports of early patterns of caregiving in India and Malaysia. *Early Child Development and Care, 50,* 109–120.

Roopnarine, J. L., Shin, M., Suppal, P., & Donovan, B., (2000). Sociocultural contexts of dramatic play: Implications for early education. In J. Christie & K. Roskos (Eds.), *Literacy and pretend in the early years: Cognitive, ecological, and sociocultural perspectives* (pp. 205-220). Mahwah, NJ: Lawrence Erlbaum.

Roopnarine, J. L., & Metindogan, A. (2006). Early childhood education in cross-national perspective. In B. Spodek & O. Saracho (Eds.), *Handbook of research on the education of young children* (2nd ed., pp. 555–571). Mahwah, NJ: Lawrence Erlbaum.

Roopnarine, J. L., Shin, M., Jung, K., & Hossain, Z. (2003). Play and early education and development: The instantiation of parental belief systems. In O. Saracho & B. Spodek (Eds.), *Contemporary issues in early childhood education* (pp. 115–132). Westport, CT: New Age Publishers.

Roskos, K. A., & Christie, J. (2000). (Eds.). *Play and literacy in early childhood: Research from multiple perspectives.* Mahwah, NJ: Lawrence Erlbaum.

Sagi, A., Lamb, M. E., Shoham, R. Dvir, R., & Lewkowicz, K. S. (1985). Parent–infant interaction on Israeli kibuttzim. *International Journal of Behavioral Development, 8*, 273–284.

Sawada, H., & Minami, H. (1997). Peer group play and co-childrearing in Japan: A historical ethnography of a fishing community. *Journal of Applied Developmental Psychology, 18*, 513–526.

Schieffelin, B. B. (1990). *The give and take of everyday life: Language acquisition of Kaluli children.* Cambridge, UK: Cambridge University Press.

Schwartzman, H. (1978). *Transformations: The anthropology of children's play.* New York: Plenum.

Shweder, R. (1982). Beyond self-constructed knowledge: The study of culture and morality. *Merrill-Palmer Quarterly, 28*, 41–69.

Shweder, R., Goodnow, J., Hatano, G., LeVine, R., Markus, H., & Miller, P. (1998). The cultural psychology of development: One mind, many mentalities. In R. Lerner (Vol. Ed.), *Handbook of child psychology:Vol 1. Theoretical models of human development* (pp. 865–937). New York: Wiley.

Sigel, I., & McGillicuddy-De Lisi, A. (2002). Parental beliefs as cognitions: The dynamic belief systems mode. In M. Bornstein (Ed.), *Handbook of parenting* (2nd ed., Vol. 3, pp. 485–508). Mahwah, NJ: Lawrence Erlbaum.

Stafford, C. (1995). *The roads of Chinese childhood: Learning and identification in Angang.* New York: Cambridge University Press.

Stern, D. (1974). Mother and infant play: The dyadic interaction involving facial, vocal, and gait behaviors. In M. Lewis & L. Rosenblum (Eds.), *The effect of the infant on its caregiver* (pp. 187–213). New York: Wiley.

Super, C. M., & Harkness, S. (1997). The cultural structuring of child development. In J. W. Berry, P. Dasen, & T. S. Saraswathi (Eds.), *Handbook of cross cultural psychology: Vol. 2. Basic processes and human development* (pp. 1–39). Boston: Allyn & Bacon.

Sutton-Smith, B. (Ed.).(1976). *A children's game anthology.* New York: Arno Press.

Sutton-Smith, B. (2001). Recapitulation redressed. In J. L. Roopnarine (Ed.), *Conceptual, social-cognitive, and contextual issues in the fields of play* (pp. 3–21). Westport, CT: Ablex

Taharally, L. C. (1991). Fantasy play, language, and cognitive ability of four-year-old children in Guyana South America. *Child Study Journal, 21,* 37–56.

Tamis-Lemonda, C. S., & Bornstein, M. H. (1993). Individual variation, correspondence, stability, and change in mother and toddler play. *Infant Behavior and Development, 14,* 143–162.

Tamis-Lemonda, C. S., Bornstein, M. H., Cyphers, L., Toda, S., & Ogino, M. (1992). Language and play at one year: A comparison of toddlers and mothers in the United States and Japan. *International Journal of Behavioral Development, 15.*

Tamis-Lemonda, C. S. (2004) Conceptualizing fathers' role: Playmates and more. *Human Development, 47,* 220–227.

Tobin, J. J., Wu, D. Y. H., & Davidson, D. H. (1989). *Preschool in three cultures.* New Haven, CT: Yale University Press.

Tulananda, O., & Roopnarine, J. L. (2001). Mothers' and fathers' interactions with preschoolers in the home in Northern Thailand: Relationships to teachers' assessments of children's social skills. *Journal of Family Psychology, 14,* 676–687.

Van De Vijver, F., & Leung, K. (1997). Methods and data analysis of comparative research. In J. W. Berry, Y. P. Poortinga, & J. Pandey (Eds.), *Handbook of cross-cultural psychology* (2nd ed., Vol. 1, pp. 257–300). Boston: Allyn & Bacon.

Watson, J. S., & Ramey, C. T. (1972). Reactions to response-contingent stimulation in early infancy. *Merrill-Palmer Quarterly, 18,* 219–227.

Weisner, T.S. (1998). Human development, child well-being, and the cultural project of development. In D. Sharma & K. Fischer (Eds.). *Socio-emotional development across cultures. New directions in child development* (pp. 69–85). San Francisco: Jossey-Bass.

Whaley, S. E., Sigman, M., Beckwith, L. Cohen, S., & Espinosa, M. P. (2000). Cultural differences in caregiving in Kenya and the United States: The importance of multiple caregivers and adequate comparison groups. Unpublished manuscript, University of California, Los Angeles.

Youngblade, L. M. & Dunn, J. D. (1995). Social pretend with mother and sibling: Individual differences and social understanding. In A. D. Pellegrini (Ed.), *The future of play theory: A multidisciplinary inquiry into the contributions of Brian Sutton-Smith* (pp. 221–240). New York: State University of New York Press.

29
Can I Play Too?

Reflections on the Issues for Children with Disabilities

GAYLE MINDES

This chapter explores the concepts of play: the developmental benefits of play, disability, intervention in the lives of children with special needs, labeling, and the meanings ascribed to these phenomena. On the one hand, a psychological perspective supports the idea of intervention in play to increase meaning for the player. On the other hand, variables of mislabeling, sociocultural, and environmental factors interfere and challenge the notion of "normality." Individual reflected meaning for the players, significant others, culture, and the community at large is the third hand. Overall, trying to understand the meaning of play and intervention for children with disabilities requires attention simultaneously to multiple contexts and multiple constructs. The thread that ties this chapter together is the issue of whether play is real for the player, the other, and whose reality is it?

Memories of Childhood Play

Almost everyone can recall a play experience that becomes "not fun" or "not play." Whether a memory of not being chosen for the neighborhood baseball game, being unable to put the ball through the hoop or hit the little white ball sitting on the pin in the green grass, missing the volley at the crucial moment, or maybe even being more interested in the flowers than the action around the soccer ball, the memories are bittersweet. In thinking about these experiences or family stories, the tendency is to shrug and say, "Oh well, it's just one of those things." So many more successful memories of good play crowd to the front of recollection. After all, the marvelous sculptures created from plasticine, the exquisite puns, clever raps, the record setting broad jump, or the story of being the "cutest" turkey in the school play inspire a reservoir of competence.

Nevertheless, what if inept play is a way of life? For children with real or labeled disabilities this may often be the case, whether their own reflections ascribe ineptness or whether others react to them as if the play were "incompetent." Play becomes another failure experience, another instance of nonacceptance, shunning, or inadequacy. So, this chapter struggles with the issues of developmental definitions of play, typical instances of successful play, definitions of disability, challenges for children with disabilities, and interventions to support "better" play, and then suggests another way to construct disability and play and the implications of this alternative view in the age of inclusion of children with special needs in the mainstream.

Developmental Definitions of Play

Often the natural learning medium of the child is play. This is the view from a competence perspective that:

> play is a complex process that involves social, cognitive, emotional and physical elements and relates to an aspect of reality as not "serious" or "real." For the child, this characterization makes it possible to relate to things that might otherwise be confusing, frightening, mysterious, strange, risky, or forbidden and to develop appropriate competencies and defenses. The active solution of developmental conflicts through play thus enables the child to show and feel…competence. (Mindes, 1982, p. 40)

Typical children play, and benefit developmentally, educationally and personally. It is a "win-win" situation; they have fun and grow. Their play activity defines and sustains life (Csikszentmihalyi, 2000; Erikson, 1963; Freud, 1965). For the player the rewards are both immediate—an intrinsic joy—and long term development. At play, whether at home, in the community, or at school, typical children playing alone, by themselves in groups, or under the guidance of adults, grow and gain proficiency (Rubin, 2000).

Competencies Developed Through Play

Child accomplishments developed through play include communication skills, physical agility, independence, social judgment, cooperation, impulse control, and many other skills. Illustrations of the typical developmental sequence of play include the following examples. Babies coo, play with their toes, gaze at interesting patterns of light and color, and gradually begin to jiggle keys, drop rattles, and otherwise move into the world of toys. Toddlers show their growing competence by crawling, walking, using one and two word sentences, imitating the actions of significant people in their environment, and playing beside friends in water, dirt, and sand. Preschoolers add fantasy to play through the imitation of the actions of the world around them, such as lunch at McDonald's. They elaborate on actions of Sponge Bob, Lion King, mom, dad, and the ever present Big Bird. With their greater competence socially, emotionally, cognitively, and physically, preschoolers enjoy many more options for play including table games, blocks, small toys, and rough and tumble. Young children make choices based on interests, settings, and capabilities. They invent playtime for themselves. Older children enjoy games with rules, both those that adults define, like sports and board games, and those that they create, often using codes and special languages. At this 6 to 12 age, children enjoy painting, drawing, music, and acting out "real" plays of stories read and told. It is in this period that lifelong passions for rock collecting, chess, the violin, basketball, sculpturing, or acting may begin (Frost & Wortham, 2005).

By definition, children must internally control the limits and process of play activities. Choices of activity must be free for the child; otherwise, the activity is not play. A parent who is requiring an hour of piano practice is creating work for the child. When the child sits at the piano for hours to enjoy the thrill of mastery of the keyboard and sounds created, it is play. Teachers creating work sheets of turtles marching to illustrate math facts are making material "playlike," but only the child who enjoys repetitive, rote demonstrations of competence will consider this activity "play." For the player the rewards must be inherent.

Environment shapes play opportunities and goals (Hughes, 1999). Swinging on vines across creeks to play Tarzan and Jane is probably only an option for children living in exurbia. Skate boarding up and over trashcans is an option for city slickers. Sledding requires hills, snow, and equipment. Playing at home in front of the television or video game while mom and dad are at work may diminish choices and affect development in artistic and sports ventures. This perspective of aspects and variables of play is from the vantage of typical children. For children with disabilities these and other variables apply depending on the nature and severity of the disability.

Defining Disability

Formal definitions of disabilities include symptoms of developmental differences in motor, language, cognitive, social, emotional, physical, and behavioral performance. These symptoms affect development in complex ways. Sometimes, children cannot produce typical behavior. Often, those who do not believe that the behavior is within the repertoire of a particular child foreshorten that child's opportunities for play.

From birth, or at the age of the diagnosis of the special need, these are the children whose experiences will be "different" lifelong. They will face special challenges. Familial, cultural, social, and educational context will determine opportunity for development, education, and personal growth. Severity, nature, and type of disability will influence opportunity. Trying to make things better for children with disabilities, parents, interventionists, and teachers throw attention toward helping the child with disabilities to blend or fit into the established definition of typical behavior. This practice permits and promotes acceptance by the majority. Children learn early that their disabilities place challenges for them to solve so that they may "fit in."

Play for Children with Atypical Development

Developmental challenges frequently begin at birth. Certainly, the severe and profound difficulties for typical development are present at birth. Parents and others who encounter these babies may foreclose opportunities. They may not encourage play because they are worried about survival, medical equipment, and fragility of the baby with special needs. In turn, these perceptions may contribute to difficult feeding, sleeping, and self-help routines. Thus, in the earliest relationship, synchrony, contingency, play autonomy, and flexibility are missing (Zirpoli, 2005). Other challenges emerge, as found by parents and diagnosticians during the developmental period. Some examples represent the impact of disability on play activities.

Receptive and Expressive Language Delays

Receptive and expressive language delays that make sociodramatic play difficult may cause young children not to play. Instead of playing, they may wander the schoolroom or playground aimlessly, rather than face the stress of competition or the frustration of being misunderstood when trying to communicate. They may skip the story telling and sharing, active listening, acting, and role-playing at home or in preschool situations. During the school years, such children may develop defensive aggressive or passive actions to mask the pain of being forced to compete in verbal situations. If other play activity choices are not available, they may engage in disruptive behavior. Their peers and teachers may perceive them as babyish. These children may develop the reputation for not "going with the program;" that is, being out-of-sync with the rest of the class (Fromberg, 2002).

Attentional Problems or Visual or Auditory Perceptual Difficulties

Attention problems and visual/auditory perceptual difficulties in children with learning disabilities may contribute to "missed chances" for the players. That is, the children may not understand the goals of the play from the vantage of peers or vice versa. These children leave the play, seemingly dissatisfied, destroy the group or individual product, or in another way become nonplayers. For them, stacking blocks, putting together puzzles, remembering the rules to Monopoly, or focusing on one activity may represent "hair pulling" frustration. Such children may never complete model cars or airplanes because the small pieces dumped from the box are overwhelming, particularly when accompanied by the distraction of siblings playing, listening to music, television programming, or radio broadcasting.

Children with Emotional Disturbances or Unique Time or Space Perceptions

Children with emotional disturbances and those with unique time and space perceptions may face difficulty in any social context. Problems in making and keeping friends and in sharing toys may diminish play opportunities for these children. They are not chosen or evaded when they seek out others. Their disruptive behavior may even be frightening to others. In school situations, teachers may devote so much time to trying to control their behavior that both teacher and children are frustrated, locked into power struggles and feelings of failure. In the neighborhood, other children may not invite them to parties or tell them of neighborhood games and activities. Consequently, children with these disabilities may be excluded from typical play opportunities and options, further stunting their development as competent players.

Different Physical Capacities or Sensory Impairment

For those children with differences in physical capacities or sensory impairment, the limitations in the perceptions and realities of opportunities for play by themselves and others are critical. Toys and materials may be unsuitable. Buttons, levers, or blocks may be too small or too close together. Access to some activities may be limited. Shelves may be too high; pathways, too narrow. Playing fields may be too uneven for children in wheel chairs or those using walkers or crutches. One-dimensional toys may lack attractiveness for the child who cannot see or hear. A toddler with sensory hypersensitivities and motor difficulties may find changes threatening, since touch and movement opportunities are unexpected. When such children do not enjoy rough housing, this may lead to stress, overstimulation, and a cycle of miscommunication with the outer world of parents, siblings, and peers (Bailey, Bruer, Symons, & Lichtman, 2001). Children with severe disabilities may have diminished opportunities for play due to time in a hospital, overprotective parents and caretakers, or limitations of medical technology supporting life.

Cognitive Delays and Mental Retardation

Children with cognitive delays and mental retardation often do not "get" the joke or remember the words to plays and poems. Often, they may enjoy activities that their friends have long since given up as babyish. Even at age 7, riding a bicycle may be daunting since they may lack the coordination to succeed with this "typical" activity of childhood. Crucially, for group activities, they may forget "the rules" or apply them rigidly when latitude is an implied norm for the group.

Interventions to Support Play

On a continuum from typical to atypical behavior, teachers, parents and others may see some of these linguistic, physical, cognitive, social, and emotional difficulties in situations with typical children. In typical settings, teachers, peers, and parents frequently intervene to help children in bridging appropriately into an activity. The teacher, peer, sibling, or parent observes a problem, tosses out one or more solutions, and moves on to let the child solve the problem. "Why don't you try it this way: shifting a puzzle piece around?" For children with special needs this approach may not be enough, however.

Children with disabilities may need more support and intervention in play, if they are to be successful community members. They may even need technological assistance. Such children are diagnosed based on individual performance and described in terms of deficits and strengths. Multidisciplinary staffing meetings plan to improve the disability. The goal of intervention is to "normalize" the behavior of the individual with special needs. A frequent consequence is that teachers, parents, peers, and others see children first through the lens of their disabilities and second as children. Sometimes the behavior of children with disabilities is frightening for their siblings, parents, relatives, teachers, and others. Loud cries, self-abuse, kicking, screaming, and biting are all behaviors that are difficult to overlook and understand, so many avoid interactions with children exhibiting these behaviors.

Yet it is too simple to say, "Well, let's forget the disability and let the child grow and evolve typically." By definition, this cannot happen. Thus, those involved in the lives of children with special needs must further hone their skills of intervention in children's play. For these children the experience must be supported play. The line from intervention to intrusion to play for the player is a dotted one, moving through play, intervene, improved play. The result is growth and enhanced personal development. For teachers, parents and others this means using all the tricks in the bag; acting as stage manager, mediator, player, scribe, assessor, and planner (Jones & Reynolds, 1992).

Thus, play facilitators can assist children with linguistic disabilities by the selective use of language:

- mirroring: reflecting a child's nonverbal expressions;
- self-talk: commenting on own actions;
- parallel talk; talking about child's own actions;
- imitation: repeating the child's comments;
- elaborating: introducing new information to build on the child's words;
- corroborating: repeating correctly what the child has said in error; and
- expanding: responding with an corrected, expanded version of child's own words;
- modeling: having conversation without using the child's words (Lindner, 1993).

That is, parents and teachers as assessors must set the stage for play and intervene when the child is unsuccessful. To intervene successfully, parents and teachers must cultivate extended observation skills, such as functional assessment and task analysis (Mindes, 2003). Such skills are directed toward the maintenance of children with special needs in inclusive classrooms that support and encourage independence, creativity, problem-solving skills, mediation skills, and overall growth and development. It is not enough to return children with special needs to the mainstream. Teachers must devote careful planning and ongoing assessment to their adjustment so that children with special needs can flourish in the typical settings. Otherwise, teachers perpetuate negative stereotyping and isolation to the detriment of individual children who "fail" and to the typical mainstream children who persist in a narrow view of acceptable and right behavior. Successful results for inclusion are the growth and enhanced personal development of all the children served. This is not a casual process for the parent or teacher in the assessor role. Overlapping symptoms, complex determinants of behavior, the nature of the child's developmental and sociocultural experience, as well as the social environments of the community and classroom all combine to require detailed parent, child, and teacher assessment.

An additional demand for the assessor is that parents, children, and teachers must accomplish all of this assessment/intervention without disturbing the play-based opportunities in the environment. That is, if the parent or teacher is directing the script by telling the child with special needs what to do and how to do it, it is not "play" but "work" for the child, disguised as "play." "Play" requires internal control, and child determination of the activity agenda. For example, if a teacher or parent says to Bobby, "Let's play Legos" (and the parent or teacher has in mind that this will be good for Bobby's fine motor development), it is not "play" unless Bobby agrees to play and continues with this interest on his own to play, elaborating on the prompt given by the parent or teacher. If Bobby says, "No, I want play doh," and the parent or teacher continues with Legos, the task has become "work" for Bobby. He is not having fun; he is doing what the teacher wants and working on fine motor skills in an activity that is difficult and frustrating for him. With the player as determiner of the agenda caveat in mind, parents and teachers must search carefully in the natural environment to support and enhance the opportunity for successful play experiences for children with special needs (Mallory & New, 1994; Sandoval, McLean & Smith, 2000).

Constructing a Different Paradigm for Disability and Intervention

Successful individuals with disabilities are always examples of those who defy the "handicap" label; for example, singer Ray Charles who was blind, U. S. Representative Patrick Kennedy who skis with a prosthesis, having lost a leg to cancer, Marilee Matlin, who is hearing impaired, in *Children of a Lesser God*, Miss America 1995, Heather Whitestone McCallum, who is hearing impaired, and Tour de France winner and cancer survivor Lance Armstrong. The spirit and drive of these individuals often make individuals without known, visible disabilities accept them, admire them, and expect everyone with disabilities to conform to a conventional and uniform definition of "right" behavior, without regard to prior knowledge of individual experience, cultural values, or individual style.

Flunking softball at home or school is not a joke, for a child who has tried his or her level best and still cannot see where the batter's box really is, judge how fast the ball is moving to catch it, and decide how far to throw it true to home. Individual reaction to this failure may be to forget it, to defy the teacher's or parents' definition of acceptable behavior, to become aggressively nonparticipant, to throw sand in the eyes of others, or to laugh at oneself graciously while inwardly crying. Being labeled a klutz may be okay if a girl accepts the conventional definition that girls aren't good at sports. For a boy, it may cost acceptance with the guys and a loss of face.

At the heart of this issue is the definition of disability and "right" behavior in the home, community, and in the school situation. Individual maladjustment may occur when parents dream of watching their child compete successfully in competitive sports. The child, a chunky, uncoordinated 12-year-old may not consider the 6 a.m. run in the park a joyful experience. Exacerbating the parent–child reciprocal interaction is the feeling of failure on both sides. For the child, the failure is an inability to please the parent; for the parent the failure is the inability to produce the ideal child.

In social situations, definitions of "normal" or "typical" are defined differently in different contexts. "Rule breaking, rule breakers, and those who have considered it their responsibility to react against these have undergone many changes in the history of human societies...the powerful have always decided which behaviors and individuals were "deviant" (Suchar, 1978, p. 7). Definitions of deviance often make a difference in the lives of children. Whether they are regarded as successful players depends on the lens used to describe "normality."

Racism also enters the definitional picture for urban, poor children (Van Ausdale & Feagin, 2001). For example, in African-American culture, aspects of language expressions, that are charismatic and stylistic, are valued more than vocabulary breadth. Play includes verbal rituals, raps, songs, and memorization of messages. "When Johnny can't read, it is suggested that there is an inappropriate match between his level of development and curriculum or instructional strategies. When Willie cannot read, it is suggested that he is culturally deprived and genetically inferior" (Hale, 1994, p. 7) rather than a conclusion that the curriculum lacks saliency (Hale, 2001) .

Thus, miscommunication between teacher and child can begin with ability grouping and the child's response to it. If the teacher ascribes low ability to a child, the child either accepts the label and lives up to it, or fights it and becomes labeled as aggressive, neither of which is a successful adaptation to "school life." If the label is based on soft signs, including academic achievement, it becomes a self-fulfilling prophecy. Sometimes children get out of the system of nonachievement by investing energy in sports, an important marker of cultural success for African-American children. When sports success is limited and a school nonsuccess is accepted, school has contributed in an institutionalized way to the perpetuation of an underclass. (Hale, 1994, 2001)

Children of school age who have social, emotional, and learning disabilities and carry the label of deviant or bad player have particularly painful community and school experiences. Kirk and Kutchins (1992, p. 221) describe the ambiguity of language used to define criteria and procedures in classification manuals that sounds logical and rational. Nevertheless, what does "often loses temper" mean when deciding whether a child possesses a conduct disorder? How often is often? What does temper mean? How often do ordinary children "lose their tempers?"

> The practical solution...may be to embrace ambiguity fully: ...to view the human plenitude without fixed ideational or material goods, evils, heroes, or villains, either to glorify or blame. Whatever else freedom can mean, it must include action to explore, affirm, confront, and transform...truth is plural—endless play of difference. (Luske, 1990, p. 118)

If disabilities are defined in culturally rooted and school-based terms (Gliedman & Roth, 1980), there is always the risk that the times when children have an opportunity to play, to enjoy, to march to their own drum, others will try to shape, mold, and adjust them, thus heightening the pain of the label of acceptable and typical and normal by not respecting or noticing the importance of difference. This is a problem as important in our culture at this juncture as the issues of race, class, gender, and ethnicity; it challenges and has an impact on our concept of "acceptable" and typical. If as a society our value is truly acceptance and promotion of individual growth and personal responsibility, then there must be opportunity for children to play in many ways, and for peers to enjoy differences and expand their understanding of typical and usual; otherwise the doom of pain prevails for children with disabilities.

Fulghum (1991) tells the story of a teacher and children developing the play Cinderella. One boy, who is frequently "not chosen" decides to join in and convinces the teacher that he should be "the pig" who interprets Cinderella. Do we have room for the pigs in our lives? Or must we rely on traditional, conventional definitions of acceptable behavior, tolerable to whom and in which circumstances. To ignore these issues in defining and thinking about disabilities and play is to condemn large numbers of children to lives of pain and isolation. The answer to "Can I Play?" and the deliberate use of the ambiguity of this oft heard child grammatical construction, is how broad are the boundaries to our constructs, how rich are the opportunities for individuals, how skillful is the intervention, and what sociocultural lens constitutes reality? The answer must be kaleidoscopic.

References

Bailey, D. B., Bruer, J. T., Symons, F. J., & Lichtman, J. W. (Eds.). *Critical thinking about critical periods.* Baltimore: PH Brookes.

Csikszentmihalyi, M. (2000) *Beyond boredom and anxiety.* San Francisco: Jossey-Bass.

Erikson, E. (1963). *Childhood and society.* New York: Norton.

Freud, A. (1965). *Normality and pathology in childhood: Assessment of development.* New York: International Universities Press.

Fromberg, D. P. (2002). *Play and meaning in early childhood development.* Needham Heights, MA: Allyn & Bacon.

Frost, J. L., & Wortham, S. C. (2005). *Play and child development* (2nd ed.). Upper Saddle River, NJ: Prentice-Hall/Merrill.

Fulghum, R. (1991). *Uh-oh: Some observations from both sides of the refrigerator door.* New York: Ivy.

Gliedman, J., & Roth, W. (1980). *The unexpected minority: Handicapped children in America.* New York: Harcourt.

Hale, J. E. (1994). *Unbank the fire: Visions for the education of African Americans.* Baltimore: Johns Hopkins Press.

Hale, J. E. (2001). *Learning while black: Creating educational excellence for African American children.* Baltimore: Johns Hopkins.

Hughes, F. P. (1999). *Children, play and development* (3rd ed.). Boston: Allyn & Bacon.

Jones, E., & Reynolds, G. (1992). *The play's the thing: Teachers roles in children's play.* New York: Teachers College.

Kirk, S. A. & Kutchins, H. (1992). *The selling of DSM: The rhetoric of science in psychiatry.* New York: Aldine DeGruyter.

Linder, T. W. (1993). *Transdisciplinary play based intervention.* Baltimore: Brookes.

Luske, B. (1990*) Mirrors of madness: Patroling the psychic borders.* New York: Aldine DeGruyter.

Mallory, B. L., & New, R. S. (Eds.). (1994). *Diversity and developmentally appropriate practice.* New York: Teachers College.

Mindes, G. (1982). Social and cognitive aspects of play in young handicapped children. *Topics of Early Childhood Special Education, 2,* 14.

Mindes, G., (2003) *Assessing young children* (2nd ed.). Upper Saddle River, NJ: Prentice-Hall/Merrill.

Rubin, K. H., Bukowski, W., & Parker, J.G. (1998). Peer interactions, relationships, and groups In W. Damon & N. Eisenberg (Eds.), *Handbook of child psychology: Vol. 3. Social, emotional, and personality development* (pp. 619–700). New York: Wiley.

Sandoval, S. McLean, M. & Smith, B. (2000). *DEC recommended practices in early intervention/early childhood special education.* Longmont, CO: Sopris-West.

Suchar, C. S. (1978). *Social deviance: Perspectives and prospects.* New York: Holt.

Van Ausdale, D., & Feagin, J. R. (2001). *The first R: How children learn race and racism.* Lanham, MD: Rowman & Littlefield.

Zirpoli, T. J. (2005). *Behavior management: Applications for teachers* (4th ed.). Upper Saddle River, NJ: Prentice-Hall/Merrill.

30
Sibling and Peer Influences on Play

SHERRI ODEN

Often with curiosity or concern, parents and educators wonder or worry if their children are learning to express and develop their individualities as they learn to get along with siblings or peers. Are they enjoying positive, constructive relations with their siblings and peers? Parents and educators are often somewhat unsure of their own important roles. While sibling and peer play is interesting, fun, and compelling, it is also sometimes frustrating to contend with or even just to behold. Yet developmental and educational psychologists consider that sibling and peer play make important contributions in the ecology of children's development.

Since the mid-1970s, researchers and educators have observed that as siblings and peers play together, they challenge each other's conceptions of reality and construct their own versions of reality (Dunn, 2002; Ladd, 2005; Rose & Asher, 1999). When we observe children's peer or sibling fantasy play, we see them construct and assume social roles such as teachers, doctors, or parents and routinely enact their own versions of helpers, friends, collaborators, or competitors. In such varied play roles, peers and siblings initiate social relationships and stimulate each other's language and social development, emotional expression, perspective taking, and physical coordination (Oden, 1988).

Many factors influence the focus, content, roles, and processes of children's play. Various settings—homes, neighborhoods, playgrounds, recreational centers, early childhood centers, schools, and places of worship—provide myriad opportunities for a variety of peer relationships, including friends, acquaintances, peer groups, activity partners, and siblings. Each type of setting and relationship contributes different developmental challenges and opportunities. Except for first or only children, siblings are often children's earliest peer influence. Because sibling play is likely to have a unique and powerful impact on children's development, we examine sibling relations first.

Influences on Sibling Play

Unlike friends, siblings do not choose one another, and therein may lie some of the challenges, limitations, and unique sources of influence. While sibling relationships may be exceptionally close, they may also be fraught with conflict; most typically, sibling play includes both intensely positive and intensely difficult elements. It is easy to observe or recall two siblings trying to establish who is the rightful proprietor of a game or toy, or who will be in charge of an activity.

Unlike other types of peer interactions, where children typically choose same-gender and similar-age peer playmates, sibling play has built-in realities. Thus, insights from sibling research may generalize only somewhat to peer play. Studies point to evidence that children's developmental level, birth order, and gender are related to the types of play activities and the various roles that siblings assume as they play together. Furthermore, family members tend to attach privileges and responsibilities according to their children's ages, birth order, and gender. Researchers have examined many factors that influence the characteristics of siblings' play (see Dunn, 2002, for a thorough discussion.)

Birth Order and Development Levels

Researchers have found that first-born siblings are more likely to assume the dominant roles, such as teacher and manager, when playing with a second-born sibling (Stoneman, Brody, & MacKinnon, 1984, 1986). The younger sibling, in turn, is more likely to accept the teaching and managing attempts of the older sibling. The relative developmental levels and ages of siblings exert a strong influence on the roles each child assumes in play, with the older child generally being more directive and controlling. Although conflicts continue, somewhere between ages 3 and 4, a younger sibling typically begins to be more able to cooperate and contribute in joint play with an older sibling (Dunn, 1992; Dunn, Deater-Deckard, Pickering & Golden, 1999).

Is the nature of sibling relationships stable into adolescence and adulthood? Longitudinal research has shown that a fair amount of stability exists in both the positive and negative aspects of sibling relationships (Deater-Deckard, Dunn & Lussier, 2002; Dunn, 1992). An eight-year study of pairs of siblings from preschool to early adolescence assessed sibling interactions through observation and mothers' and siblings' reports concerning positive interactions and hostile behavior such as hitting, teasing, and so on. The study found stability in the nature of the relationships, especially after the youngest sibling had turned 5 years of age (Dunn, Slomkowski, & Beardsall, 1994). Such findings of stability of the relationship pattern may be both encouraging and discouraging to parents.

Gender

Not only can an observer expect to find play roles differing for older and younger siblings, but such differences are likely to be further affected by the genders of the children involved. For example, older sisters have been found to be more positive as siblings than older brothers (Dunn et al., 1999), which may be indicative of the socialization of girls into nurturing or helper roles.

Structure of Play Situations

Just as there are research findings that children's play with peers outside the family can facilitate children's social and cognitive development, different types of sibling play may be more or less conducive to various aspects of development. One study found that older siblings provided opportunities for their younger siblings to join play during activities that included problem solving, artistic skill mastery, social play, and motor experience. However, there was no correlation between such sibling play and the younger sibling's cognitive development (Teti, Bond, & Gibbs, 1988). Nonetheless, on the whole, the body of research suggests that sibling play does offer opportunities for overall social, cognitive, and language development (Dunn, 2002).

Individual Temperament

Children's temperaments are important in influencing the type or quality of interactions and affect both sibling and peer play. Among sibling pairs, for example, one study found that mothers' ratings of their children's temperaments were more predictive of each of their siblings' play and conflict than was their genders or ages (Munn & Dunn, 1989). The study also found that the larger the difference between the temperaments of two siblings, the greater the conflict between them.

Family Life Situations

The tone of sibling play, its positivity or negativity, and the overall ratio of positive to conflictual play can vary for sibling pairs from one day to the next and in general. Parents may take into account factors such as temperaments, developmental levels, birth order, and gender as influences on siblings' play, but they know only too well that these factors do not neatly predict how well a given pair of siblings will get along and play together. Social factors in the family make further contributions to sibling play. Parents' involvement with their children and their reactions to sibling interactions may be affected by numerous social factors that may, in turn, affect sibling relations and differences between siblings (Dunn, Slomkowski & Beardsall, 1994; Herzberger & Hall, 1993; MacKinnon, 1989). Circumstances or status factors in the family at a given time such as divorce, remarriage, or economic stresses affect the family and may affect sibling relations, directly or indirectly. For example, MacKinnon (1989) found that low family socioeconomic status, independent of divorce, correlated with more negativity during sibling play.

Parental Perspectives and Participation

The life circumstances or situations of the family finds each child at a different point in his or her development and may affect each child's temperament somewhat differently. Increasingly, researchers have pointed to the differences between siblings in a family as related to the realities of "nonshared environments" of the individual siblings (e.g., Hetherington, Reiss, & Plomin, 1994; Plomin, Asbury, & Dunn, 2001). On the one hand, therefore, factors of birth order, parental expectations and participation, interpretations of differences and differential parenting and so forth are thought to contribute to different environments for the siblings. On the other hand, parents have been found to see more of the contrasts than the similarities among siblings, even for twins (Saudino, Wertz, Gagne, & Chawla, 2004). Thus, the socializing environment of siblings is both shared by the children and differs for each child. Children also perceive such differential treatment from their parents and may consider some differences to be unfair, which may lead to greater sibling conflict.

Other levels of influences on siblings are experiences outside the home that contribute to the nonshared environments of siblings (Bronfenbrenner & Morris, 1998; Dunn, 2002; Hetherington et al., 1994). For each child, influences outside the family include other adults such as teachers or coaches, and peers, including playmates, classmates, or friends. Even in these outside spheres of influence, however, parents may make contributions. Parents may model or coach their children as they join in on the play and conversations in the home, the backyard, or the playground (Bornstein & O'Reilly, 1993).

Influences from Sibling to Peer Play

Parents may worry that siblings who have many conflicts will lack positive peer relationships in the neighborhood, child center, or school. They wonder if there is continuity between children's sibling play and their peer play. As children increasingly interact and establish relationships with their unrelated peers, they experience many similar types of influences as they do with their siblings. Sibling experiences may provide some degree of structure or predisposition for how children are likely to interact with their peers (e.g., Lieberman, Doyle, & Markiewicz, 1999). Furthermore, the additional and different influences of peer interactions should both challenge and expand the experiences children have had with siblings. In the following, we consider the many influences on peer play and relations.

Influences on Peer Play

There is a large knowledge base pertaining to the various sources of influence on peer play, including factors that contribute to making and keeping friends, peer participation, and acceptance in various situations and settings. (For more extensive discussions of the peer social development research, see Ladd, 2005; Oden & Ramsey, 1993.)

Mixed-Age Play

The content of mixed-age peer and sibling play appears to share many features. An older peer or sibling, for example, may accommodate to the toys, activity interests, and linguistic capabilities of the younger child, perhaps to get or keep the younger child engaged in playing. Thus, on the one hand, the older child may be more authoritative or even controlling, but on the other hand, the older child will compromise and accommodate to what the younger child is capable of playing. Over time, therefore, younger siblings or peers may have an increasing influence over what will be played and how it will be played as they play with their older peers or siblings, thus increasing their ability to interact in peer relationships (see Katz, 1992 for a review.)

Developmental Factors and Progression

During the early childhood years, most children increasingly play with their peers and form relationships as activity partners or friends while their play roles emerge in peer dyads, triads, and groups within growing peer cultures (Leventhal & Brooks-Gunn, 2000; Oden, 1988). The patterns and content of peer play change as children develop. Older friends in upper elementary school, for example, become increasingly focused on sharing their inner selves through secrets and personal feelings, whereas preschoolers and primary school-age children are focused more on activity play and sharing materials, or fantasy role-playing.

Early individual differences in children's responsiveness to peers may predispose a child to potentially long-lasting peer interaction tendencies or patterns (Kagan, Reznick, & Gibbons, 1989). From early peer contacts in the toddler years through the preschool years, most children's peer interactions become more frequent and more complex (Howes, 1988). By the primary and elementary school years, a child's peer status becomes a marker of the child's short-term social adjustment and may predict future social competence or even poor mental health (Buhs & Ladd, 2001; Parker & Asher, 1993).

Gender and Play

Just prior to kindergarten and increasingly throughout the childhood years, children's preferences for same-gender peers increase dramatically (Ladd, 2005; Ramsey, 1991). Boys may be seen to play more frequently in larger groups, often outdoors and involving rough-and-tumble or aggressive play that focuses on competition for dominance. Girls may tend to play indoors, in smaller groups, and focus on forming close friendships. Such typical patterns of play, however, appear to be changing somewhat with expanding opportunities for outdoor group activities such as soccer and other team sports activities for girls and boys, and computer activities that most children play in pairs in the home or school.

Because children readily divide themselves by gender, parents and educators may unintentionally support and reinforce this tendency. There has long been evidence that while preschool boys and girls do play together when specifically reinforced for doing so, they are likely to revert to same-gender patterns when reinforcement stops (e.g., Serbin, Tonick, & Sternglanz, 1977).

Cultural, Socioeconomic, and School Influences

Experiences with peers—rather than siblings who usually share some degree of familial experiences—are likely to both challenge and broaden children's play experience. Community or societal attitudes about race, culture, and social class influence how peers perceive each other and which peers children select for play. Preschool children's play relations with peers shift frequently, and children tend to select friends on the basis of proximity and easily observable characteristics. Thus, as some researchers have pointed out, children who live in the same neighborhood are likely to be from the same social groups and participate in many of the same types of activities, such as music lessons, soccer, basketball, and so forth, both in school and out of school (Leventhal & Brooks-Gunn, 2000; Ramsey, 1991).

The more frequent play that is readily observable between toddler and preschool peers of the same race or ethnic/cultural background also reflects the racial or ethnic patterns in society. Children notice racial differences early in their preschool years, but it is in their early childhood and elementary school years that their perceptions and attitudes about race become more defined (Ramsey & Myers, 1990). In actual practice, preschoolers do not necessarily choose their friends according to race. In racially mixed groups, elementary school children, for example, have long been found to form friendships based on gender rather than race (Singleton & Asher, 1977, 1979).

Compared to children and youths in the upper grade levels, preschool and primary school-age children do not yet grasp the significance of nationality, but they do notice differences associated with a cultural background that differs from their own, such as unfamiliar dialects, interactive styles, dress, and social customs. Cultural customs may influence how a child greets peers, tries to gain entry to a peer group's play activity, and expresses interest in, or familiarity with, certain play activities and experiences, such as specific childhood rhymes, songs, sayings, or story or video characters (Ramsey, 1991).

Playing with peers of a different gender, age, race, or cultural background can foster children's familiarity with a greater diversity of peers. Differences, however, may interfere with communication and cooperative play, especially in areas such as social ability, physical handicaps, and learning styles. In such cases, peers may require guidance from adults, as discussed in the next section. Overall, more experiences with peers who have a greater diversity in adeptness or adaptiveness have the potential to expand children's social development.

Social Competence

Socially competent children, even in preschool, are generally considered by their peers to be friendly, cooperative, attractive, capable, and confident, making them appealing playmates, friends, peer group members, and leaders. Yet other children have persistent problems with peer social ability (Bolvin & Hymel, & Bukowski, 1995; Buhs & Ladd, 2001; Newcomb & Bagwell, 1995; Parker & Asher, 1993). Some children who lack social competence have different learning approaches or abilities and may thereby behave somewhat differently from their peers. Teachers often report frustration with "mainstreaming" or "inclusion" when it does not automatically result in peers playing together (Taylor, Asher, & Williams, 1987). The extent or type of a child's disability or a child's general developmental level, compared to peers, may figure into how well others will accept the child as a play partner.

In general, peers may reject or avoid playing with a child who lacks social competence, although this is less true for younger children. Preschool and primary school-age children tend to be more accepting of a classmate who seems different or has a disability than are older children. The more process-oriented play projects are also less likely to highlight children's differences in ability (Ramsey, 1991).

During the elementary school years, more extreme, persistent social difficulties result from children being rejected for play because they are considered too aggressive, inappropriate, or unengaging. Overly aggressive children, for example, re-create their negative peer status across time and peer groups (Ladd, Herald & Andrews, 2005). Similarly, over the years, highly unengaged children may enter a cycle of withdrawal and rejection (Rubin, Hymel, & Mills, 1989) and thus fail to get the experience they need for social play and peer relationships. A possible contributing factor is that some children are just less socially adept or not well known to their peers (Ladd, Kochenderfer, & Coleman, 1996). We may observe them on the sidelines of peer interactions. Yet these children may be operating less out of choice. Due to individual differences and a lack of opportunities for positive relations in the family, neighborhood or school, they may feel that they lack the ability to participate in play and social relationships.

Parent and Educator Roles

Studies show that parent interventions to coach children can make important contributions to their learning to play in positive ways with peers (Bornstein & O'Reilly, 1993; Lindsey & Mize, 2000, 2001; Mize & Ladd, 1990; Mize, Pettit, & Brown, 1995). Researchers have also found that parents have indirect roles or influences in their children's peer relationships as they set up occasions and activities for their children to play with peers and monitor younger and older children's peer play (Bronfenbrenner & Morris, 1998; Ladd & Hart, 1992; Ladd & Pettit, 2002; Mize & Pettit, 1997; Mize, Pettit, & Brown, 1995). Thus parents may contribute to their children's "connectedness" for playing with peers and making friends (Clark & Ladd, 2000). Researchers also have reported that educators as well as parents can effectively guide or coach children about peers' norms and expectations, helping them to think through the consequences of their actions for others, or alter situations to increase their likelihood of positive play inclusion to offset patterns of peer exclusion or neglect (e.g., Ladd, 1981; Mize & Ladd, 1990; Oden, 1986; Oden & Asher, 1977).

As children become more verbal and more socially competent from toddlerhood through the preschool years, there is less negative peer interaction for most children. But some children may get into a social cycle of peer victimizing or being a victim. Among the considerable research on children who lack positive peer relations, recently, studies have focused more closely on such very harmful pathways of negative peer relations. Due to many factors such as individual characteristics, including physical size and temperament, lack of opportunities for positive parenting, and lack of positive opportunities with peers in the neighborhood or classroom, some children "bully" or harass one or more peers and some peers are more passive and more likely to become victims (Buhs & Ladd, 2001; Kochenderfer-Ladd & Ladd, 2001; Ladd & Kochenderfer-Ladd, 1998).

The Influences of Educational Environment on Peer Play

As more children today experience early childhood care and education, it is important to examine the influences of these settings as well as primary and elementary school influences on children's play opportunities (National Institute of Child Health and Human Development, Early Child Care Research Network, 2000). As peer groups engage in the activities of an educational environment, the teacher, the emerging peer culture and factors in the setting have been found to coalesce to influence young children's early peer interactions (Fernie & DeVries, 1990). Educational and child care environments vary considerably in the opportunities for play outdoors (Hart, 1993), creative activities indoors (Kontos, Burchinal, Howes, Wisseh, & Galinsky, 2002), and after school care activities (Pettit, Laird, Bates & Dodge, 1997). In general, classroom and early child settings that are designed in accordance with the developmental levels of the children are more likely to foster and support positive peer play interactions (Bredekamp & Copple, 1997; Hart, Burts, Durland, Charlesworth, DeWolf, & Fleege, 1998).

Program Approaches

In a comparison of several curricular models, researchers found that constructivist, child-centered approaches, compared to other curriculum approaches, fostered greater cooperative peer play and positive conflict resolution (DeVries, Haney, & Zan, 1991). Some specific curriculum models include the High/Scope approach, which encourages children to plan, take initiative, and carry out activities individually, in peer dyads, and in small and large peer groups (Hohmann & Weikart, 1995). Other curriculum models include the Reggio Emilia model and the project approach. In these curricular approaches, children pursue their interests and collaborate in sustained projects (Helm & Katz, 2001; Katz & Chard, 2000), thus supporting or fostering engaging, positive, and appropriate opportunities for children to play, interact, get to know each other and thereby encourage their social development.

Teacher Roles

Teachers as designers and leaders in childhood care settings and classrooms are central influences on children's play. In addition, teachers' own social abilities are important as they relate to children in their involvement in conversations with the children, get to know the children, guide peer conflict resolutions and nudge children to join peer interaction or activities (Black & Hazen, 1990; Ladd, Birch, & Buhs, 1999). For example, a study of the year-long evolution of "circle time" found that preschool teachers effectively used both modeling and suggestions to guide children in taking turns and responding meaningfully to each other in conversations (Kantor, Elgas, & Fernie, 1989).

Physical Environment

Physical environmental features such as size, design, structure, and available materials can influence the size of peer groups and the type of peer play. In enclosed spaces, children are more likely to engage in cooperative play, but these places may also stimulate more territorial disputes (Ramsey, 1986). Complex materials and well-defined role-play areas usually promote more interactive and imaginative peer play. In art activities, for example, children usually engage in parallel and constructive play; in block activities they also play constructively, but are more likely to interact (Pellegrini, 1984).

Classroom Grouping

The structure of the classroom also influences children's peer contacts and play. First-grade children in one study, for example, were aware of which peers were in the higher and lower reading groups (Rizzo, 1989). These children also played more often with classmates at their own reading levels and tended to tease or reject peers in the lower reading groups. In the intermediate grades, open, flexible physical environmental arrangements that foster children's group interactive learning and problem solving are especially beneficial, as are activities that extend to other areas of the school and community (Bergen & Oden, 1988). Carefully planned, well-run, cooperative activity groups can increase children's academic achievement as well as foster their positive peer relationships and increase the numbers of other-race and mixed-ability peer play partners (Slavin, 1988).

Guidelines for Parents and Educators

Parents are usually interested in learning how to discourage sibling conflict and they wonder what they can do to promote positive sibling interactions and play. Primarily, parents should understand that some degree of sibling conflict, while unsettling, is normal and to be expected. Although many factors influence sibling play and conflict, parents should consider how fair they are in giving attention and listening to each child and in being constructive models for perspective taking, conflict resolution, and play. Beyond that, parents should set limits around sibling conflict so that the children do not harm one another, but too much involvement may prevent children's relationship and conflict resolution development. It is worth remembering that siblings may prepare each other for current and subsequent peer interactions; thus, they may enrich or restrict peer social development. There are many things that parents can do to support the constructive social development of their children, such as:

- Give attention to each sibling or peer to lessen the tendency for children to compete for attention.
- Provide opportunities for siblings to play in structured and unstructured activities in the home.
- Observe a sibling or peer conflict, allowing children the opportunity to find ways to resolve the conflicts and intervening only if there is danger of harm.

- Create opportunities for each child to express and develop individual interests and personalities, thus lessening some children's tendencies to either dominate or accommodate to their siblings or peers.
- Construct occasions for the children to play with other peers to help siblings not get "locked" into roles.

Educators should design educational experiences to support or expand children's peer experiences, taking into consideration that children may carry play roles from their sibling play into their play with classroom peers. One main challenge for educators is to help those children who lack social skills to learn ways to join a group, form friendships, and resolve conflicts without antisocial aggression, bullying, or being a victim. When educators encourage children to develop and express their individual interests, they also help the children to constructively attract peer interest and learn more from and about each other. For example, teachers may assist children in developing individual projects or selecting or creating books on subjects of interest (e.g., insects, animals, sports, music, art). Another major challenge for educators is to set up activities that discourage the stigmatization of children who are different in various ways, such as their ethnic or economic background, language, gender, social ability, or other differences. For example, teachers may assist children in developing projects or selecting books or doing research on customs and languages associated with diverse cultures; the activities of boys and girls and men and women in a diversity of interests and roles (e.g., science, sports, child care); and children and adults with various disabilities who nevertheless achieve in activities such as sports, music, and academics.

While educators should discourage exclusive friendships by providing activities that mix peers together, children should have times in the daily schedule to play and converse with peers to form and sustain friendships and activity partnerships. Through creative planning of activities and situations, educators should develop many approaches to support and facilitate positive and constructive peer interactions and relationships such as:

- Create interesting activities to help children get to know each other in a variety of peer relationships through friendships and activity partners.
- Encourage reticent or quieter children to enter peer activities and converse with peers by coaching them in communication and cooperation skills for resolving conflicts.
- Help children who are locked into a conflict or are becoming harmful to others by asking each child to take the other's perspective and propose solutions, compromises, or accommodations that allow each child to benefit.
- Structure learning situations to offset tendencies for peer stigmatization due to differences in race or ethnicity, social class, gender, or learning styles or skills.
- Structure learning situations to encourage children to play a variety of social roles, including leader, helper, friend, and activity collaborator.

In summary, although both sibling and peer interaction can be conflictual, the conflict is a further opportunity to learn about individual differences and to learn to construct a balance that includes cooperation and compromise, while taking individual desires into consideration. Sibling relationships, somewhat like best friendships, can provide a secure basis for learning about another person with room for individual expression. Care should be taken, however, so that such relationships do not become too exclusive and limiting. Peers and siblings will have conflicts but will also enjoy each other, play creatively, and form unique relationships that allow for individuality. Their play offers major opportunities for children's social development. Parents and educators, therefore, must endeavor to be creative in their planning of activities and situations as they foster and support their children's development of constructive, enriching peer and sibling interactions and relationships.

Acknowledgment

Jennifer Hall made contributions to the section on siblings in the first edition of this book.

References

Bergen, D., & Oden, S. (1988). Designing play environments for elementary-age children. In D. Bergen (Ed.), *Play as a medium for learning and development* (pp. 245–269). Portsmouth, NH: Honeymoon.

Black, B., & Hazen, N. L. (1990). Social status and patterns of communication in acquainted and unacquainted preschool children. *Developmental Psychology, 26*, 379–387.

Bolvin, M., & Hymel, S., & Bukowski, W. M. (1995). The roles of social withdrawal, peer rejection, and victimization by peers in predicting loneliness and depressed mood in childhood. *Development and Psychopathology, 7*, 765–785.

Bornstein, M. H., & O'Reilly, A.W. (Eds.). (1993). *New directions for child development: The role of play in the development of thought.* San Francisco: Jossey-Bass Pfeiffer.

Bredekamp, S., & Copple, C. (Eds.). (1997). *Developmentally appropriate practice in early childhood programs* (Rev. ed.). Washington, DC: National Association for the Education of Young Children.

Bronfenbrenner, U., & Morris, P. A. (1998). The ecology of developmental processes. In W. Damon, & R. M. Learner (Eds.), *Handbook of child psychology: Vol. 1. Theoretical models of human development* (5th ed., pp. 993–1028,). New York: Wiley.

Buhs, E. S., & Ladd, G. W. (2001). Peer rejection as an antecedent of young children's school adjustment: An examination of mediating processes. *Developmental Psychology, 37*, 550–560.

Clark, K. E., & Ladd, G. W. (2000). Connectedness and autonomy support in parent–child relationships: Links to children's socioemotional orientation and peer relationships. *Developmental Psychology, 36*, 485–498.

Deater-Deckard, K., Dunn, J., & Lussier, G. (2002). Sibling relationships and social–emotional adjustment in different family contexts. *Social Development, 11*(4), 571–590.

DeVries, R., Haney, J. P., & Zan, B. (1991). Sociomoral atmosphere in direct-instruction, eclectic, and constructivist kindergartens: A study of teachers' enacted interpersonal understanding. *Early Childhood Research Quarterly, 6*, 449–471.

Dunn, J. (1992). Sisters and brothers: Current issues in developmental research. In F. Boer & J. Dunn (Eds.), *Children's sibling relationships: Developmental and clinical issues* (pp. 1–17). Hillsdale, NJ: Lawrence Erlbaum.

Dunn, J. (2002). Sibling relationships. In P. K. Smith & C. H. Hart (Eds.), *Blackwell handbook of childhood social development* (pp. 223–237). Oxford: Blackwell.

Dunn, J., Deater-Deckard, K., Pickering, K., & Golden, J. (1999). Siblings, parents, and partners: Family relationships within a longitudinal community study. *Journal of Child Psychology & Psychiatry, 40*(7), 1025–1037.

Dunn, J., Slomkowski, C., & Beardsall, L. (1994). Sibling relationships from the school period through early adolescence. *Developmental Psychology, 30*, 315–324.

Fernie, D. E., & DeVries, R. (1990). Young children's reasoning in games of nonsocial and social logic: "Tic Tac Toe" and a "Guessing Game." *Early Childhood Research Quarterly, 5*, 445–460.

Hart, C. H. (1993). *Children on playgrounds: Research perspectives and applications.* Albany: State University of New York Press.

Hart, C. H., Burts, D. C., Durland, M.A., Charlesworth, R., De Wolf, M., & Fleege, P. O. (1998). Stress behaviors and activity type participation of preschoolers in more and less developmentally appropriate classrooms: SES and sex differences. *Journal of Research in Childhood Education, 12*(2), 176–196.

Helm, J. H., & Katz, L. G. (2001). *Young investigators: The project approach.* New York: Teachers College.

Hetherington, E. M., Reiss, D., & Plomin, (Eds.). (1994). *Separate social worlds of siblings: The impact of nonshared environment on development.* Hillsdale, NJ: Lawrence Erlbaum.

Herzberger, S. D., & Hall, J. A. (1993). Consequences of retaliatory aggression against siblings and peers: Urban minority children's expectations. *Child Development, 64*, 1773–1785.

Hohmann, M., & Weikart, D. P. (1995). *Educating young children: Active learning practices for preschool and child care programs.* Ypsilanti, MI: High/Scope Press.

Howes, C. (1988). Peer interaction of young children. *Monographs of the Society for Research in Child Development, 53*(1, Serial No. 217).

Kagan, J., Reznick, J. S., & Gibbons, J. (1989). Inhibited and uninhibited types of children. *Child Development, 60*, 838–845.

Kantor, R. Elgas, P.M., & Fernie, D.E. (1989). First the look and then the sound: Creating conversations at circle time. *Early Childhood Research Quarterly, 4*, 433–448.

Katz, L. G. (1992). Nongraded and mixed age grouping in early childhood programs. *ERIC Digest.* Washington, DC: Office of Education and Research Improvement, U. S. Department of Education. [Available online: www.ed.gov/databases/ERIC_Digests/index/ED351148]

Katz, L. G., & Chard, S. C. (2000). *Engaging children's minds* (2nd ed.). Norwood, NJ: Ablex.

Kochenderfer-Ladd, B., & Ladd, G. W. (2001). Variations in peer victimization: Relations to children's maladjustment. In J. Juvonen & S. Graham (Eds.), *Peer harassment in school* (pp. 25–48). New York: Guilford Press.

Kontos, S., Burchinal, M., Howes, C., Wisseh, S., & Galinsky, E. (2002). An eco-behavioral approach to examining the contextual effects of early childhood classrooms. *Early Childhood Research Quarterly, 17*, 239–258.

Ladd, G. (1981). Effectiveness of a social learning method for enhancing children's social interaction and peer acceptance. *Child Development, 52,* 171–178.

Ladd, G. W. (2005). *Children's peer relationships and social competence: A century of progress.* New Haven, CT: Yale University Press.

Ladd, G. W., Birch, S. H., & Buhs, E. S. (1999). Children's social and scholastic lives in kindergarten: Related spheres of influence? *Child Development, 70,* 1373–1400.

Ladd, G. W., & Hart, C. H. (1992). Creating informal play opportunities: Are parents' and preschoolers' initiations related to children's competence with peers. *Developmental Psychology, 28,* 1179–1187.

Ladd, G. W., Herald, S. L., & Andrews, R. K. (2005). Young children's peer relations and social competence. In B. Spodek & O. Saracho (Eds.), *Handbook for research on the education of young children* (2nd ed.). Mahwah, NJ: Lawrence Erlbaum.

Ladd, G. W., & Kochenderfer-Ladd, B. (1998). Parenting behaviors and parent–child relationships correlates of peer victimization in kindergarten? *Developmental Psychology, 34,* 1450–1458.

Ladd, G. W., Kochenderfer, B. J., & Coleman, C. C. (1996). Friendship quality as predictors of young children's early school adjustment. *Child Development, 67,* 1103–1118.

Ladd, G. W., & Pettit, G. S. (2002). Parenting and the development of children's peer relationships. In M. H. Borenstein (Ed.), *Handbook of parenting* Vol. 5: *Practical issues in parenting* (2nd ed., pp. 377–409). Mahwah, NJ: Lawrence Erlbaum.

Leventhal, T., & Brooks-Gunn, J. (2000). The neighbors they live in: The effects of neighborhood residences on child and adolescent outcomes. *Psychological Bulletin, 126,* 309–337.

Lieberman, A. F., Doyle, A. B., & Markiewicz, D. (1999). Developmental patterns in security of attachment to mother and father in late childhood and early adolescence: Associations with peer relations. *Child Development, 70,* 202–213.

Lindsey, E. W., & Mize, J. (2000). Parent–child physical and pretense play: Links to children's social competence. *Merrill-Palmer Quarterly, 46,* 565–591.

Lindsey, E. W., & Mize, J. (2001). Contextual differences in parent-child play: Implications for children's gender role development. *Sex Roles, 44*(3/4), 155–176.

MacKinnon, C. E. (1989). Sibling interactions in married and divorced families: Influence of ordinal position, socioeconomic status, and play context. *Journal of Divorce, 12,* 221–234.

Mize, J., & Ladd, G. W. (1990). A cognitive–social learning approach to social skill training with low-status preschool children. *Developmental Psychology, 26,* 388–397.

Mize, J., & Pettit, G. S. (1997). Mothers' social coaching, mother–child relationship style, and children's peer competence: Is the medium the message? *Child Development, 68,* 312–332.

Mize, J., Pettit, G. S., & Brown, E. G. (1995). Mothers' supervision of their children's peer play relations with beliefs, perceptions, and knowledge. *Developmental Psychology, 31,* 311–321.

Munn, P., & Dunn, J. (1989). Temperament and the developing relationship between siblings. *International Journal of Behavioral Development, 12,* 433–451.

National Institute of Child Health and Human Development Early Child Care Research Network. (2000). The relation of child care to cognitive and language development. *Child Development, 71,* 960–980.

Newcomb, A. F., & Bagwell, C. L. (1995). Children's friendship relations: A meta-analytic review. *Psychological Bulletin, 117,* 306–347.

Oden, S. (1986). Developing social skills instruction for peer interaction and relationships. In G. Cartledge & J. F. Milburn (Eds.), *Teaching social skills to children* (2nd ed., pp. 246–269) New York: Pergamon.

Oden, S. (1988). Alternative perspective on children's peer relationships. In T. D. Yawkey, & J. E. Johnson (Eds.), *Integrative processes and socialization: Early to middle childhood* (pp. 139–166). Elmsford, NJ: Erlbaum.

Oden, S., & Asher, S. R. (1977). Coaching children in social skills for friendship making. *Child Development, 48,* 495–506.

Oden, S., & Ramsey, P. G. (1993). Implementing research on children's social competence: What do teachers and researchers need to learn? *Exceptionality Education Canada, 3*(1&2), 209–232.

Parker, J. G., & Asher, S. R. (1993). Beyond group acceptance. Friendship and friendship quality as distinct dimensions of children's peer adjustment. In W. H. Jones & D. Perlman (Eds.), *Advances in personal relationships* (Vol. 4., pp. 261–294). London: Kingsley.

Pellegrini, A. D. (1984). The social cognitive ecology of preschool classrooms: Contextual relations revisited. *International Journal of Behavioral Development, 7,* 321–332.

Pettit, G. S., Laird, R. D., Bates, J. E., & Dodge, K. A. (1997). Patterns of after school care in middle childhood: Risk factors and developmental outcomes. *Merrill-Palmer Quarterly, 43,* 515–538.

Plomin, R., Asbury, K., & Dunn, J. (2001). Why are children in the same family so different? Nonshared environment a decade later. *Canadian Journal of Psychiatry, 46*(3), 225–233.

Ramsey, P. G. (1986). Possession disputes in preschool classrooms. *Child Study Journal, 16,* 173–181.

Ramsey, P. G. (1991). *Making friends in school: Promoting peer relationships in early childhood.* New York: Teachers College Press.

Ramsey, P. G., & Myers, L. C. (1990). Salience of race in young children's cognitive, affective, and behavioral responses to social environments. *Journal of Applied Developmental Psychology, 11,* 49–67.

Rizzo, T. A. (1989). *Friendship development among children in school.* Norwood, NJ: Ablex.

Rose, A., J., & Asher, S. R. (1999). Children's goals and strategies in response to conflicts within a friendship. *Developmental Psychology, 35,* 69–79.

Rubin, K. H., Hymel, S., & Mills, S. L. (1989). Sociability and social withdrawal in childhood: Stability and outcomes. *Journal of Personality, 57,* 237–255.

Saudino, K. J., Wertz, A. E., Gagne, J. R., & Chawla, S. (2004). Night and day: Are siblings as different in temperament as parents say they are? *Journal of Personality and Social Psychology, 87*(5), 698–706.

Serbin, L. A., Tonick, I. J. , & Sternglanz, S. H. (1977). Shaping cooperative cross-sex play. *Child Development, 48,* 924–929.

Singleton L. C. & Asher, S. R. (1977). Peer preferences and social interaction among third-grade children in an integrated school district. *Journal of Educational Psychology, 69,* 330–336.

Singleton, L. C. & Asher, S. R. (1979). Racial integration and children's peer preferences: An investigation of developmental and cohort differences. *Child Development, 50,* 936–941.

Slavin, R. E. (1988). *Student team learning: An overview and practical guide.* Washington, DC: National Education Association.

Stoneman, Z., Brody, G. H., & MacKinnon, C. (1984). Naturalistic observations of children's activities with their siblings and friends. *Child Development, 55,* 617–627.

Stoneman, Z., Brody, G. H., & MacKinnon, C. (1986). Same-sex and cross-sex siblings: Activity choices, roles, behaviors, and gender stereotypes. *Sex Roles, 15,* 495–511.

Taylor, A. R., Asher, S. R., & Williams G. A. (1987). The social adaptation of mainstreamed mildly retarded children. *Child Development, 58,* 1321–1334.

Teti, D. M., Bond, L. A., & Gibbs, E. D. (1988). Mothers, fathers, and siblings: A comparison of play styles and their influence upon infant cognitive level. *International Journal of Behavioral Development, 11,* 415–432.

31

A Sociocultural Perspective of Parent–Child Play

WENDY HAIGHT

Parents have long been intrigued by the glimpses into their children's inner lives revealed during pretend play. Consider a mother discussing the spontaneous pretend play between herself and her 3-year-old daughter:

> I have a tendency of watching how she's pretending…to see if she is having any anxieties or worries or…happiness that she wants to share with me that maybe she—at her age—isn't able to come right out and say "I'm scared about this."…I feel like it's important for me to see what's on her mind.…When they pretend you can pick up on what they're feeling and kind of what direction you might need to go in to help them. (Haight, Parke, & Black, 1997)

Many parents not only observe, but become actively involved in the play of their young children (Garvey, 1990). Likewise, some developmental psychologists (e.g., Howes, 1992), early childhood educators (e.g., Paley, 1984), play therapists (e.g., Hellendoorn, van der Kooij, & Sutton-Smith, 1994), and early interventionists (Sheridan, Foley, & Radlinski, 1995) consider pretend play a means through which adults may observe and support children's emotional, social, and cognitive development (Rubin, Fein, & Vandenberg, 1983). In addition, scholars from various disciplines consider pretend play to be a potentially rich context for the creation and re-creation of cultural meanings (Gaskins, 2003; Goncu, 1999; Haight & Miller, 1993; Schwartzman, 1978; Singer & Singer, 1990). In a classic chapter on play, a psychologist discussed two little sisters who pretended to be sisters (Vygotsky, 1978). He noted that in a literal context, children behave without thinking about their role relationships; but in pretending, for example, to be sisters, their actions must conform to the cultural "rules" of sisterly behavior. Thus, "What passes unnoticed by the child in real life becomes a rule of behavior in play" (Vygotsky, 1978, p. 95).

In addition to re-creating existing cultural meanings, however, innovation, creativity, and variability are essential components of play from the earliest parent–infant play (Fogel, Nwokah, & Karns, 1993) to the most elaborate social pretend play in middle childhood (Schwartzman, 1978; Sutton-Smith, 1993). In pretending with particular meanings, for example, of parent–child relations, children not only become more deeply rooted in a system of meanings, they also alter, comment upon, and reinterpret meaning (Schwartzman, 1978). One view argues:

The tension between the myths imposed from without and the exertion of personal control in shaping one's interpretation and use of myths reflects the poles of a dialectic relationship between the individual and his culture. Through play, the child is socialized into a general cultural framework

309

while developing a unique individuality with a distinctly personal matrix of life history and lived meanings. (Vandenberg, 1986, p. 8)

Similarly, pretend play has been characterized as a context in which young children negotiate meanings through borrowing, expressing, and inventing meanings from available social and cultural materials (Slade & Wolfe, 1994). Thus, pretend play is a preface to the ongoing and vital cultural activity of making and remaking meaning.

That play may assist in the transmission and creation of cultural meanings suggests a greatly increased role for adult–child play (Smith, 1994; Trudye, Lee, & Putnam, 1995). During parent–child pretend play, children interact with partners who are more experienced and share an intimate knowledge of their lives. Indeed, play is one of the few contexts in which typically less powerful children interact with their parents on a relatively equal footing around emotionally significant topics of mutual concern such as anger and aggression (Haight & Sachs, 1995). Such interactions can be instrumental in negotiating various cultural meanings, including harmonious interpersonal interactions (Haight et al., 1994), the interpretation and display of emotion (Haight & Sachs, 1995), and literacy (Lightfoot & Valsiner, 1992; Whiting & Edwards, 1988). In the words of one father, "I think it's [pretend play] a good way to … stay in close touch with your 2-year-old … " (Haight, Parke, & Black, 1997).

How Some Parents Facilitate Children's Play

Given the developmental significance of pretend play, as well as its basically social nature, it is important to consider the ways in which parents may facilitate their children's developing pretend play. Research with middle-class, European-American families suggests that parents may support their children's play directly, through teaching them how to pretend, or indirectly, through inspiring within them a love of pretend play.

Teaching Children to Pretend

During interviews, several parents (Haight, Parke, & Black, 1997) spontaneously mentioned that parent–child pretending is important for teaching their 2-year-olds to pretend. In the words of one father, "it's fun to teach him to pretend in different ways, like with the farm … or that he can be a fireman, or he can go to work today. … I like to give him ideas that he wouldn't think of. … " Like this father, many parents spontaneously support their young children's developing pretend play through a variety of direct and indirect methods.

Direct Methods of Parental Facilitation of Pretend Play Parents may exert a powerful direct effect on the development of their children's pretend play. First, parents can introduce the nonliteral, pretend frame to their older infants (Beizer, 1991; Haight & Miller, 1992). During daily routines in the home, some middle-class, European-American mothers spontaneously introduced pretend play to their infants, even though the infants did not yet pretend independently (Beizer, 1991). For example, a mother might animate the peas during feeding, making them greet her 8-month-old.

Second, parents can prompt their young toddlers to pretend. During everyday routines in their homes, some middle-class, European-American mothers prompted their children to pretend (Haight & Miller, 1993). A 12-month-old, for example, vocalized to her teddy bear and her mother prompted, "Say, 'Hi, Teddy-Tie!'"

Third, parents can elaborate upon their toddlers' forays into pretend play. Many mothers extended their young children's pretending by adding new material that was thematically relevant (Haight & Miller, 1992). For example, a 24-month-old child pointed a straw at her mother, waved it, and commented, "Magic." Her mother elaborated, "Oh! You turned me into a frog!"

Consistent with Vygotsky's zone of proximal development (Sutton-Smith, 1993), recent research suggests that parents' direct involvement with their young children facilitates pretending. Children's pretend play with mothers is more sustained (Dunn & Wooding, 1977; Haight and Miller, 1992; Slade, 1987), complex (Fiese, 1987; Slade, 1987), and diverse (O'Connell & Bretherton, 1984) than their solo pretending, and young children incorporate their mothers' pretend talk into their own subsequent pretending (Haight & Miller, 1992). Although research has focused on mother–child pretend play, fathers also support their toddlers' pretending (Farver & Wimbarti, 1995; Haight, Parke & Black, 1997).

Indirect Methods of Parental Facilitation of Pretend Play Parents also may exert a powerful indirect influence on the development of pretending through their arrangement of the physical and social contexts to provide children with ample space, objects, and stimulating partners for play (Haight & Miller, 1992). There is considerable agreement in the literature that objects affect children's pretend play. Authors, for example, describe toys as the "pegs on which to hang our play," and suggest that "because the human imagination is so extensive and complex … children seem to look for solid reference points, as it were, from which to range more freely. Just as language makes subtle and complicated thought possible, perhaps toys do the same for play" (Newson & Newson, 1979, p. 12). By providing children with replica toys suggestive of particular play themes, for example, baby dolls, tea sets, miniature cars, and and action figures, parents may indirectly shape their young children's play.

Considerable cultural variation in the extent to which parents provide their children with replica objects. One study found that the pretend play of North American, middle-class toddlers and pre-schoolers revolved around replica toys (Haight, Wang, & Fung, Williams & Mintz, 1999). In Taipei, however, a sizable proportion of children's pretend play involved no objects at all, but frequently did involve the enactment of social routines such as formally greeting a teacher. Clearly, there is no single way to support children's pretend play. Perhaps children in less materialistic communities "hang" their pretend play on other types of "pegs" such as social routines, or elaborate other forms of play such as physical or language play (Edwards & Whiting, 1993; Goncu, 2003).

Inspiring a Love of Pretend Play

As fascinating as pretend play is for a child, an enthusiastic partner who offers appealing ideas and can put into words the child's depicted actions must inspire pretending (Garvey, 1990). In the words of the mother of a prolific and inspired 2-year-old player (Haight, Parke, & Black, 1997), "I love to pretend play! I mean Frank [husband] has told me that I only had a child so I could have a playmate. … I played with baby dolls up until I was 16 or 17 years old. … " During interviews, one quarter of parents spontaneously cited encouragement of pretend play in explaining why they felt parent–child pretend-ing is important (Haight, Parke, & Black, 1997). In the words of one father, "I want to show her a love for it [pretending]."

In the explorations of adults' memories of childhood play, researchers stress the importance of a key person in the child's life who "inspires and sanctions play and accepts the child's inventions with respect and delight" (Singer & Singer, 1990, p. 4). A.A. Milne, for example, credited his parents, who sanctioned his childhood play, in the creation of his imaginary forest. Vyvyan Holland remembered his father, Oscar Wilde, as a playmate who would go down on all fours and become "a lion, a wolf, a horse" (Singer & Singer, 1990, p. 10).

Indeed, many children and parents apparently derive great pleasure from their joint pretend play. Parent–child play typically is affectively positive (MacDonald, 1993; Singer, 1994) and associated with secure attachment (Sutton-Smith, 1993). By the time children are fluent pretenders in their third year of life, both children and parents actively initiate pretending with one another (Dunn & Wooding, 1977; Haight & Miller, 1992) and generally are responsive to the other's initiations (Haight & Miller, 1993). Interviews of children aged 6 to 12 years revealed that even in middle childhood, many children desire opportunities for pretending with their parents (Otto & Reimann, 1990, as cited in Sutton-Smith, 1993).

Variation in Parental Support of Children's Pretend Play

The extent and ways in which parents support their children's pretend play varies considerably. Within an otherwise healthy parent–child relationship, lack of support for pretend play per se is not a cause for concern. First, cultural communities vary in the types of play forms which children elaborate. The extensive fantasy play typical of many European-American, middle-class children, certainly is not universal (Gaskins, 2003; Goncu, 1999, 2003; Lancy, 1996, 2003). For example, lower-income, urban, African-American children elaborated verbal play such as teasing and complex physical play such as double-dutch (Goncu, 2003). These play forms, no doubt, also support development. They involve imagination, symbolic thought, complex social interaction, and skill development. Within this cultural context, the absence of extensive parent support for pretend play is probably not significant.

Second, some variability in parent support of pretend play is related to social and economic factors influencing child care and work patterns (Edwards & Whiting, 1993). Work requirements or explicit sanctions against playing are evident in communities such as Kenya, Israel, the Andes, and Central America (Sutton-Smith, 1993). Within the Mayan community studied by Suzanne Gaskins (1999, 2003), even young children eagerly participated with adults in everyday work activities. Running errands, helping a parent and contributing to the family income can provide joy, satisfaction and skill building, as well as self-esteem and social integration.

Third, some variability in parent support of pretend play is related to beliefs about play. Parental beliefs, for example, provide a frame of reference within which parents interpret experience and formulate goals and strategies for socializing their children (Harkness & Super, 1992). Their beliefs concerning the relevance of pretense to the development of skills and qualities that parents perceive as necessary for success in their particular communities, and their views concerning the appropriateness of adult participation in children's play, influence their support of their children's pretend play in complex and possibly indirect ways.

Ethnographic research suggests that middle-class parents in the United States (Goncu & Mosier, 1991; Haight, Parke, & Black, 1997), Turkey (Goncu & Mosier, 1991), and China (Haight et al., 1999) generally view play as significant to young children's development, and view themselves as appropriate play partners for their children. The increasing emphasis in Japanese preschools on pretend play (Takeuchi, 1994), for example, has been attributed, in part, to exposure to beliefs in the United States about the importance of play to development. In contrast, Mexican (Farver, 1993) and Italian (New, 1994) mothers do not view play as particularly significant to children's development, and Mayan and tribal Indians (Gaskins, 1999; Goncu & Mosier, 1991) think of play as the child's domain and judge adult participation to be inappropriate. Consistent with these beliefs, naturalistic observations reveal that Turkish, Chinese, and U.S. parents participate in pretend play with their young children, while Mayan, Mexican, Italian, and tribal Indians engaged in relatively little or no pretending.

There also is some evidence that parents' beliefs may account for some of the variation in the quantity and quality of parents' participation in young children's pretending within communities, although such relations are complex and not well understood. European-American, middle-class mothers and fathers who did not differ in the extent and quality of their pretend play, or in their beliefs about pretend play, did differ in the relationships between their beliefs and behaviors (Haight, Parke, & Black, 1997). Fathers who pretended relatively frequently with their children viewed pretend play as enjoyable. Mothers who pretended relatively frequently, however, viewed pretend play as a developmentally significant activity and their own participation as important. The extent to which mothers viewed pretend play as an enjoyable activity was related to the quality of their participation;

for example, mothers who enjoyed pretending typically elaborated upon children's initiations of pretending. These findings suggest that the extent and quality of parents' pretend play is related not only to their beliefs about play per se, but to broader networks of practices and beliefs such as the role of mothers and fathers in the care and development of young children (Haight, Parke, & Black, 1997).

Parent–child pretend play is a potentially rich context for the socialization and acquisition of cultural meanings. Parents may facilitate their children's pretending by teaching them to pretend, introducing the pretend mode to older infants; elaborating upon their toddlers' early forays into the nonliteral; and encouraging an enthusiasm for pretend play. Given the significance of pretend play to children's development, and of parents' contribution to the development of pretend play, advocacy that parent–child play should be encouraged (Sutton-Smith, 1993) seems sound. However, available evidence of cross-cultural and within-cultural variation in the extent and quality of parents' participation in children's pretend play suggests that these activities are complexly related to other systems of practices; for example, the role of mother versus others in the care and development of young children; as well as specific beliefs about and individual preferences for pretend play. Thus, before advocating parent–child play, practitioners must consider the cultural appropriateness of adult–child play, adults' own preferences for interaction with children, as well as other play and nonplay contexts that may promote similar developmental outcomes. After all, the unique benefits of adult–child play can accrue only if the activity truly is play, embedded within a climate of spontaneity and fun (Levenstein & O'Hara, 1993).

References

Beizer, L. (1991). *Preverbal precursors of pretend play: Developmental and cultural dimensions.* Paper presented at the biannual meeting of the Society for Research in Child Development, Seattle, WA.

Dunn, J., & Wooding, C. (1977). Play in the home and its implications for learning. In B. Tizard & D. Harvey (Eds.), *Biology of play* (pp. 45–58). London: Heinemann.

Edwards, C., & Whiting, B. (1993). "Mother, older sibling and me": The overlapping roles of caregivers and companions in the social world of two- to three-year-olds in Ngeca, Kenya. In K. MacDonald (Ed.), *Parent–child play: Descriptions and implications* (pp. 305–329). Albany, NY: State University of New York Press.

Farver, J. (1993). Cultural differences in scaffolding pretend play: A comparison of American and Mexican American mother–child and sibling–child pairs. In K. MacDonald (Ed.), *Parent–child play: Descriptions and implications* (pp. 349–366). Albany, NY: State University of New York Press.

Farver, J., & Wimbarti, S. (1995). Paternal participation in toddlers' pretend play. *Social Development, 4,* 17–3 1.

Fiese, B. (1987, April). *Mother–infant interaction and symbolic play in the second year of life: A contextual analysis.* Paper presented at the meeting of the Society for Research in Child Development, Baltimore, MD.

Fogel, A., Nwokah, E., & Karns, J. (1993). Parent–infant games as dynamic social systems. In K. MacDonald (Ed.), *Parent–child play: Descriptions and implications* (pp. 43–70). Albany: State University of New York Press.

Garvey, C. (1990). *Play.* Cambridge, MA: Harvard University Press.

Gaskins, S. (1999). Children's daily lives in a Mayan village: A case study of culturally constructed roles and activities. In A. Goncu (Ed.), *Children's engagement in the world: Sociocultural perspectives.* New York: Cambridge University Press.

Gaskins, S. (2003). All in a day's work. In *The cultural construction of play.* Symposium at the annual meeting of the Jean Piaget Society, Chicago, Illinois.

Goncu, A. (Ed). (1999). *Children's engagement in the world: Sociocultural perspectives.* New York: Cambridge University Press.

Goncu, A. (2003). Children's play as cultural interpretation. In *The cultural construction of play.* Symposium at the annual meeting of the Jean Piaget Society, Chicago, Illinois.

Goncu, A., & Mosier, C. (1991). *Cultural variations in the play of toddlers.* Paper presented at the biannual meeting of the Society for Research in Child Development, Seattle, WA.

Haight, W, Masiello, T, Dickson, L., Huckeby, E., & Black, J. (1994). The everyday contexts and social functions of spontaneous mother–child play in the home. *Merrill-Palmer Quarterly, 40,* 509–533.

Haight, W,, & Miller, P. (1992). The development of everyday pretend play: A longitudinal study of mothers' participation. *Merrill-Palmer Quarterly, 38,* 331–349.

Haight, W., & Miller, P. (1993). *Pretending at home: Development in sociocultural context.* Albany: State University of New York Press.

Haight, W., Parke, R., & Black, J. (1997). Mothers' and fathers' beliefs about and spontaneous participation in their toddler's pretend play. *Merrill-PalmerQuarterly, 43,* 271–290.

Haight, W., & Sachs, K. (1995). A longitudinal study of the enactment of negative emotion during mother–child pretend play from 1–4 years. In L. Sperry & P. Smiley (Eds.) & W. Damon (Series Ed.), *New directions in child development: Developmental dimensions of self and other* (pp. 33–46). San Francisco: Jossey-Bass.

Haight, W, Wang, X., Fung, H., Williams, K., & Mintz, J. (1999). Universal, developmental and variable aspects of young children's play: A cross-cultural comparison of pretending at home. *Child Development, 70*(6), 1477–1488.

Harkness, S., & Super, C. (1992). Parental ethnotheories in action. In I. Sigel, A. McGillicuddy-DeLisi, & J. Goodnow (Eds.), *Parental belief systems: The psychological consequences for children* (pp. 373–391). Hillsdale, NJ: Lawrence Erlbaum.

Hellendoorn, J., van der Kooij, R., & Sutton-Smith, B. (Eds.). (1994). *Play and intervention.* Albany: State University of New York Press.

Howes, C. (1992). Introduction. In C. Howes (Ed.), *The collaborative construction of pretend: Social pretend play functions* (pp. 1–12). Albany: State University of New York Press.

Lancy, D. (1996). *Playing on the mother ground.* New York: Guilford Press.

Lancy, D. (2003). A development ecology of Kpelle children's play. In *The cultural construction of play.* Symposium at the annual meeting of the Jean Piaget Society, Chicago, Illinois.

Levenstein, P., & O'Hara, J. (1993). The necessary lightness of mother–child play. In K. MacDonald (Ed.), *Parent–child play: Descriptions and implications* (pp. 221–237). Albany: State University of New York Press.

Lightfoot, C., & Valsiner, J. (1992). Parental belief systems under the influence: Social guidance of the construction of personal cultures. In I. Sigel, A. McGillicuddy-DeLisi, & J. Goodnow (Eds.), *Parental belief systems: The psychological consequences for children* (pp. 393–414). Hillsdale, NJ: Lawrence Erlbaum.

MacDonald, K. (1993). Parent–child play: An evolutionary perspective. In K. MacDonald (Ed.), *Parent–child play: Descriptions and implications* (pp. 113–143). Albany: State University of New York Press.

New, R. (1994). Child's play—una cosa naturale: An Italian perspective. In J. L. Roopnarine, J. E. Johnson, & E. H. Hooper (Eds.), *Children's play in diverse cultures* (pp. 123–147). Albany: State University of New York Press.

Newson, J., & Newson, E. (1979). *Toys and playthings.* New York: Pantheon.

O'Connell, B., & Bretherton, I. (1984). Toddler's play alone and with mother: The role of maternal guidance. In I. Bretherton (Ed.), *Symbolic play: The development of social understanding* (pp. 337–368). Orlando, FL: Academic.

Otto, K., & Reimann, S. (1990). *Zur specifik der besiehungen zwischen kindern and erschenen im spiel.* Paper presented at the bienniel meeting of the International Council of Children's Play, Andreasburg, Germany.

Paley, V. (1984). *Boys and girls: Superheroes in the doll corner.* Chicago: University of Chicago Press.

Piaget, J. (1962). *Play, dreams and imitation in childhood.* New York: Norton.

Rubin, K. H., Fein, G. G., & Vandenberg, B. (1983). Play. In E. H. Hetherington (Ed.), *Handbook of child psychology: Socialization, personality, and social development* (Vol. 4, pp. 693–774). New York: John Wiley.

Schwartzman, H. B. (1978). *Transformations: The anthropology of children's play.* New York: Plenum.

Sheridan, M., Foley, G., & Radlinski, S. (1995). *Using the supportive play model: Individualized intervention in early childhood practice.* New York: Teachers College Press.

Singer, D., & Singer, J. (1990). *The house of make-believe.* Cambridge, MA: Harvard University Press.

Singer, J. (1994). The scientific foundation of play therapy. In J. Hellendoorn, R. van der Kooij, & B. Sutton-Smith (Eds.) Play and intervention (pp. 27–38). Albany: State University of New York.

Slade, A. (1987). A longitudinal study of maternal involvement and symbolic play during the toddler period. *Child Development, 58,* 647–675.

Slade, A., & Wolfe, D. (1994). Preface. In A. Slade & D. Wolfe (Eds.), *Children at play: Clinical and developmental approaches to meaning and representation* (pp. v–viii). Oxford: Oxford University Press.

Smith, P. K. (1994). Play training: An overview. In J. Hellendoorn, R. van der Kooij, & B. Sutton-Smith (Eds.), *Play and intervention* (pp. 185–194). Albany: State University of New York Press.

Sutton-Smith, B. (1993). Dilemmas in adult play with children. In K. MacDonald (Ed.), *Parent–child play: Descriptions and implications* (pp. 15–40). Albany: State University of New York Press.

Takeuchi, M. (1994). Children's play in Japan. In J. L. Roopnarine, J. E. Johnson, & F. H. Hooper (Eds.), *Children's play in diverse cultures* (pp. 51–72). Albany: State University of New York Press.

Trudye, J., Lee, S., & Putnam, S. (1995). *Young children's play in socio-cultural context: Examples from South Korea and North America.* Paper presented at the biennial meeting of the Society for Research in Child Development, Indianapolis, IN.

Vandenberg, B. (1986). Beyond the ethology of play. In A. Gottfried & C. Brown (Eds.), *Play interactions: The contribution of play materials and parental involvement to children's development* (pp. 3–11). Lexington, MA: Lexington Books.

Vygotsky, L. S. (1978). *Mind in society: The development of higher mental processes.* Cambridge, MA: Harvard University Press.

Whiting, B., & Edwards, C. (1988). *Children of different worlds: The formation of social behavior.* Cambridge, MA: Harvard University Press.

32
City Play

AMANDA DARGAN AND STEVE ZEITLIN

When John Jacob Raskob and his partners transformed the New York skyline by erecting the Empire State Building, they probably never considered that beneath the tower's express elevators the old Sunfish Creek had once formed a natural swimming hole; nor did they imagine that across the East River in Queens, children would use the switching on of the building's lights to tell the time for coming in from play. Indeed, the architects of cities in the United States did not design stoops for ball games or sidewalks for jumping rope, and no one considered the hazard to kites when they put up telephone wires. As a result of countless design decisions like these, however, a young person's experience of New York gradually changed as streets were paved, buildings grew upward, cars pushed children from the streets, row houses filled once vacant lots, and the increasing density led to rooftop games and cellar clubs.

It is possible to understand an urban setting, such as New York City, by exploring the traditional activities that give it meaning. The tradition of childhood play can imbue harsh and imposing city objects, often made of metal and concrete, with human values, associations, and memories. Play is one of the ways in which children develop a sense of neighborhood in a large city. Play is one of the ways a city street can become "our block."

Barging out of doors with play on their minds, city children confront stoops, hydrants, telephone poles, lampposts, automobiles, brick walls, concrete sidewalks, and asphalt streets. Children leaping from the doorways as He-Man and Sheera, Captain Blood, Superman, or the Knights of the Round Table have at their disposal an array of swords and shields that, to the uninitiated, more closely resemble dented garbage can lids and discarded umbrellas. For the would-be circus performer or ballet dancer, the stoop provides the perfect stage. Those with ball in hand have sewer covers, automobiles, hydrants, and lampposts to define a playing field. Jumping off ledges, using discarded mattresses and box springs as trampolines, or riding bikes up ramps made from scrap wood, children enjoy the dizzying thrills of vertigo. Each element of play—vertigo, mimicry, chance, physical skill, and strategy—has its own city settings and variants (see Callois, 1961; Roberts, Arth, & Busch, 1959).

Play as Transformation

In the crowded, paved-over city, urban dwellers joyfully locate play by incorporating features of the urban landscape into their games. They transform the detritus of urban life into homemade playthings and costumes, and they exert control over their environment by creating and passionately defending private spaces.

The rules of playful transformation, a focused interaction, tell players how the real world will be modified inside the encounter (Goffman, 1961). With the outside world held at bay, players create a new world within. A kind of "membrane" forms around them (Goffman, 1961). They often experience a sense of intimacy, the closeness of sharing a world apart.

Certain kinds of action outside the games, such as an ambulance going by or a building manager yelling out the window, can cause the play scene to "flood out," bursting the membrane (Goffman, 1961). Playing fields exist in such identifiable forms as diamonds, gridirons, courts, and playgrounds, but a playing field can, in fact, be anywhere. It is more akin to an energy field that repels forces outside its domain of interest and envelops the players with a force as powerful as their concentration.

Within play worlds, time has its own measures: "We played until it was too dark to see," many people have recalled. Children play while the last reflection of twilight in the sky still dimly silhouettes a flying ball; they will play while hunger is still possible to ignore. "The heat of the day, the chill of rain, even the pangs of hunger are not sufficient to intrude on the absorption of a child at play" (Biber, n.d., p. 1). Play time often goes by in a split second, metered by the turning of a rope or the rhythm of a rhyme: "Doctor, doctor will I die?/Yes, my child, and so will I/ How many moments will I live?/ One, two, three, four…."

In play, the players themselves define rules and boundaries, such as "This is first base," and so it is. This sidewalk square is jail, this broken antenna is a ray gun, and, through the magic of play, they are. Transformation is the process of recasting the rules, the boundaries, the images, and the characters of the real world within the boundaries of play. Taking a space or an object and devising a new use for it, thereby making it one's own, is at the heart of play.

As they transform the city for play, children manifest a remarkable imagination. A playful order prevails. Hydrants, curbs, and cornices of the city become a game board. The castoffs of city living, such as bottlecaps, broomsticks, and tin cans, become playing pieces. Growing up in an East Harlem tenement, one New Yorker recalls: "The older kids taught the younger ones the arts and crafts of the street…. [A]shcan covers were converted into Roman shields, oatmeal boxes into telephones, combs covered with tissue paper into kazoos…a chicken gullet into Robin Hood's horn, candlesticks into trumpets, orange crates into store counters, peanuts into earrings, hatboxes into drums, clothespins into pistols, and lumps of sugar into dice" (Levenson, 1967, p. 83).

Street toys are not found objects; children need to search for them. A great deal of effort often goes into locating and shaping precisely the right object for play. In Bedford-Stuyvesant, for instance, children filed down a Moosehead Ale bottleneck on the curb to produce a glass ring smooth enough to slide along concrete and serve as a prized cap for the sidewalk game of skelly. In Astoria, the best skelly pieces were the plastic caps from the feet of school desks.

Neighborhoods provide different raw materials. In Chinatown, parents who work in the garment industry provide sought-after items: jacks are often made from buttons, each "button jack" consisting of a set of five or six buttons sewn together. Children use rubberbands hooked together to create a "Chinese jump rope." The elastic is stretched between the feet of two girls while a third does cat's-cradle-like stunts with her legs. Sometimes, the ropes are fashioned from white elastic bands parents bring home from the factories.

"Play is an arena of choice in many contexts where life options are limited" (Kirshenblatt-Gimblett, 1989). In a crowded city with its contested arenas, the freedom to play is hardly regarded as a basic human right. In some parts of the city where space is uncontested, a child can mark the boundaries of a play space with a piece of chalk, and nothing more is needed; children can "frame" their play space with boundaries based on mutual agreement. More often, however, the task of establishing play spaces takes on a different character as young and old battle for autonomy and control. Perhaps the toughness sometimes perceived in city children comes from the human battles they fight to earn and maintain the right to playfully and autonomously transform some space in the city. Through it all, children strive to gain control over their play worlds (Dargan & Zeitlin, 1990). As Alissa Duffy (personal communication, 1985) chanted as she and a friend jumped up and down on a discarded refrigerator box, "We're just kids! I am five and he is three and we rule everything!"

Folklore Study of Childhood Play

The scholarly interest in children's folklore in the United States dates from the work of William Wells Newell (1883/1963), who helped found the American Folklore Society in 1888. Like many of the scholars who documented children's games after him, Newell was primarily interested in traditional games and rhymes that had survived across generations of children. Collecting from both adults and children in Boston, New York, and Philadelphia, Newell believed that "quaint" rhymes of children were "survivals" and "relics" of ancient songs and poetry.

Contemporary folklorists believe that children's rhymes and games are interesting because of the way they comment on the present rather than the past. Nonetheless, through a century of collecting, scholars have emphasized traditional rhymes and games, transmitted through the generations in fixed phrases. The rhymes and games gathered in these works echo one another, and their texts affirm a conservative side of children, who pass on rhymes with small variations from one generation to the next. In New York some of the rhymes have a distinctive urban flavor:

> I won't go to Macy's any more, more, more,
> There's a big fat policeman at the door,
> door, door.
> He'll grab you by the collar
> and make you pay a dollar.
> I won't go to Macy's any more,
> more, more.[1]

> I should worry, I should care, I should marry a millionaire.
> He should die, I should cry, I should marry another guy.
> (L. Senhouse, personal communication, 1987)

> Flat to rent, inquire within,
> A lady got put out for drinking gin,
> If she promises to drink no more
> Here's the key to the front door. (M. Brirenfeld, personal communication, 1986)

Changes in Urban Play

In the 1930s and 1940s, Oscar and Ethel Hale compiled a single-spaced, thousand-page manuscript titled, *From Sidewalk, Gutter, and Stoop*, about traditional games on the streets of New York. They documented hundreds of different games and hundreds of variations of each of those games. They include not only double Dutch, but also double Irish, double dodge, French fried, French Dutch, and double Jewish (Hale & Hale, 1938, p. 77).

Half a century later, researchers did not find anywhere near the number or variety of games played out of doors (Dargan & Zeitlin, 1990). In the 1980s, far fewer blocks preserved that confluence of lifestyle and urban geography that sustains the traditional games and outdoor play. The photographs of Martha Cooper taken on the Lower East Side in the 1970s reveal a life very different from the Leipzig photographs from the 1940s, where Red Rover, ring-aleavio, and Johnny-on-the-pony were played by large groups of children on the sidewalks and streets. Her photographs do not document large groups of children choosing up sides and organizing traditional games. Instead, her pictures have one, two, and sometimes three children on their own in empty lots or on broken sidewalks (Dargan & Zeitlin, 1990).

In the poorer neighborhoods Cooper visited in Harlem and the Lower East Side, children continue to play outdoors and creatively manipulate their environment. In these neighborhoods, interiors are smaller, less comfortable, and often not air conditioned; the street offers open space and fresh air. There is also the concentration of children necessary for group activities. In some neighborhoods, such as Bedford-Stuyvesant's Marcy projects, half a dozen ropes still turn on a hot day. Groups of five or six girls perform cheers, a chanted dance ensemble piece with hand clapping and improvised (often sexual) verses. Groups of girls rehearse in private so that rival groups will not "steal" their cheers, and sometimes they try out their chants on the roaring subways where they can sing at the top of their lungs and hardly disturb their fellow riders.

The changes in city play over the past one hundred years are tied to the changes in city life over the past few generations. In his book, *A History of Children's Play*, Brian Sutton-Smith (1981) offers an extraordinary analysis of some of the complex changes affecting play. Partly because of what he regards as his own optimistic outlook, this New Zealand-born scholar sees many of the changes in play for the better. He suggests that the contemporary forms of play with electronic toys and television are less physically violent than the earlier outdoor games; although the fantasies on television and in video games are all about war, children are not actually bullying each other, as they do on the playground.

These electronic diversions and creative playthings, he suggests, also provide the kind of training that children need today for the world they will inherit. The manual world of the 19th century has been replaced by a world of signs and symbols, in which information systems, particularly television, play a major role. "It is necessary," Sutton-Smith (1981) writes, "to produce generations of children who can be innovative, not in killing birds with catapults but in ideas for use in mass media, advertising, selling, bureaucratizing, computing, education and so on" (p. 288).

Today, when children gather after school and face the recurrent question of what to do, street games are only one possibility that must compete with a range of organized sports and commercial amusements as well as television and radio.

> When life is full of...an ever-changing round of "fads and fancies," ranging from a new record album which one "simply must have," to the reincarnation of Batman at the local movie theater...unrewarded perseverance at the old traditional games may seem pointless....Sports and modern entertainment bring in their train adult interest and encouragement. Traditional games whose only incentive is the enjoyment of playing them cannot compete with these influences. That any such games still persist is testament to the intrinsic importance and meaningfulness of those games to the players. (Sutton-Smith, 1981, p. 249)

Many of the new games that have flourished on the streets of New York bear this out; some, like double Dutch, thrive partly in competitive, adult-run forums such as the annual double Dutch competition at Lincoln Center; even the ghetto-fostered style of gymnastics performed on discarded mattresses and box springs has become a formal adult-sponsored performance with groups such as the Flip Boys. Other activities, deliberately antagonistic to public, polite adult society, thrive on the streets, but have as their purpose engaging the interest and attention, and sometimes the rage, of the adult world. Graffiti, which may appear to be a kind of random vandalism to the uninitiated, is, from the perspective of the graffiti writers, a game played for the "fame" that comes from having one's code name read all over the city by one's peers. Breakdancing, while it has some roots in mock fighting, is largely a performance, played for recognition, for prizes, for prestige, for the money that can come from street performance, and for a ticket out of the ghetto; it is a long way from marbles or skelly played to wile away an afternoon. Similarly, rapping, a street tradition of competitive verbal artistry fostered originally at block and playground parties in black neighborhoods, is now intimately tied to the recording industry that promotes and markets the music.

To a certain extent, Sutton-Smith is correct in his optimism. Children's games and toys, though store-bought, are often creative, and they are well suited to the current time; the same is true of many television programs. However, although bought toys, television, and video games may encourage certain kinds of individual play, they do not create communities. They are placeless; the world they create is on the screen, in the mind, and not on the block. With television, people do not necessarily live where they are (M. Hufford, personal communication, 1988).

The media cannot replace the real experiences of growing up and getting to know a city street; they cannot create a sense of place. In the television-soaked contemporary United States, young people become frustrated with communities and relationships that have none of the glamour of the world depicted on television; advertisements remind them constantly of what they do not have. Ironically, the fear of crime keeps many city residents locked in their apartments, allowing in nothing except television. Thus, local communities become devalued while the constant barrage of the media emphasizes success stories and celebrities.

Children whose lives really turn on the city block draw the most minute distinction in their environment; Hamilton Fish Armstrong (1963) writes about roller skating down his Sixth Avenue block and knowing who lived in each house without looking up; he could tell by the particular buzz created by the pavement on his feet. Other children distinguished between "kite hill" and "vulture's hill" and "dead man's curve," and knew such exotic places as the Casbah, which was a nickname for the railing (the "casbar") leading up to the entrance of P.S. 1 in Long Island City, Queens (Armstrong, 1963, p. 76). The block was a place to be from.

The children who play on the streets of New York not only play together, they often see each other every day in many contexts. They learn how to share spaces together and build relationships and bonds in their neighborhood. Their communities do not revolve around a single interest, such as Little League or bingo. When social interaction moves beyond a single interest, and people become involved in a multiplicity of ways, communities are born; relationships move beyond a simple use and exchange and take on new meaning. As one New York taxi driver put it, a real neighborhood is where the butcher comes to your funeral.

Both adults and children are involved on a day-to-day basis on a patch of urban turf that they come to think of as their own. While there may be an invisible membrane that forms around players intent upon their game (Goffman, 1961), there is another kind of membrane that pulls across the block, that contains the varied groups of children of different ages at their play. It is a membrane created by the adults, a safety net, a web of sociability and unobtrusive vigilance that enables children to create secret societies and play worlds that swell and burst out of harm's way.

The true measure of any city is the degree to which it can nurture and protect this core activity of play. "We must make the streets of our city safe for children because streets that are safe for children are [also] safe for adults" (Edelman, 1987). The quality of playfulness must be cared for, protected, and nurtured. Children and adults need both physical and emotional space to play, to develop their own indigenous arrangements and solutions, and to give their imagination free rein. Sutton-Smith (1981) comments on the "right of free play": "the present record of children's play makes the point that children no less than adults live in order to live vividly, and that their play—and I would add their art—is at the center of such vividness. It seems absurd to me to contrive any future playground or any school or any society in which the pursuit of such vividness is not a major focus of that construction" (p. 297).

Improvisation and Play

Although scholars and laypeople have a longstanding interest in the conservatism of traditional rhymes and games, improvisation has always played a major role in children's play. There is an "apparently paradoxical co-existence of rules and innovation within play" (Hawes, 1974, p. 13). One observer reported that a children's game whose object was to step on all the sidewalk cracks was an exact inversion of another popular neighborhood game, "Step on a crack, break your mother's back" (Hawes, 1974, p. 16). She suggests that "only these cultural items which are susceptible to variation have much chance of survival" (p. 16). Although scholars have noted the improvisatory quality in children's lore, this kind of play has rarely been thoroughly documented, nor has it received the kind of attention paid to traditional children's games.

The research of this chapter's authors (Dargan & Zeitlin, 1990) emphasizes the improvisatory side of children's lore; children may be jumping to the same rhymes and playing the same games, but they are improvising with the materials, negotiating the rules, and imaginatively fitting them into various city spaces. After all, before they can play a game, the players must agree upon the rules; in the city, deciding just how an abstract set of regulations will play in this space at this moment is as important as the game itself. Traditional games and rhymes are testaments to the conservatism of children; but the ways in which they actually play the games at any given moment, the ways they adapt the games to particular urban settings, and the ways they improvise upon them reveals a creativity that is no less important to the legacy. In a similar vein,

> Play as a medium of adventure infuses all aspects of city life.... As "poets of their own acts," players in the city occupy space temporarily; they seize the moment to play as the opportunity arises, inserting the game into the interstices of the city's grid and schedule.... While lacking the kinds of institutions and spaces controlled by the powers that be, players transform the mundane into an adventure by means of a rope, a ball, a dance or a haircut in spaces occupied for the moment. Those adventures lead in many directions. (Kirshenblatt-Gimblett, 1990, p. 194)

The memories of many New Yorkers and other city dwellers, taken together, present a case for the role of play in building multifaceted communities rooted in place; street games contributed to a neighborhood life that made growing up and living in the city memorable. It is probably not possible or relevant to reintroduce games from past times. At the same time, it is probably not productive to simply curse the modern world and paint television and organized games and sports as ogres that would eat children. It may be possible, however, to prevent these forms from becoming the predominant influence on young people. Ultimately, it makes sense to find ways to learn from the indigenous adaptations and transformations of children and adults at play; teachers must learn to encourage free play on school playgrounds; urban planners must learn to build cities that children and adults can use for both work and leisure; and parents must understand the importance of safe havens for play. The current context demands the conscious efforts of individuals, as members of communities, neighborhoods, cities, and nations, to understand what was and is meaningful about their communities, and what about them they can conserve in a changing world.

Note

1. This traditional rhyme is still remembered by many New Yorkers who grew up in the city in the 1930s and 1940s.

References

Armstrong, H. F. (1963). *Those days*. New York: Harper & Row.
Biber, B. (n.d.). *What play means to your child*. Unpublished manuscript.

Callois, R. (1961). *Man, play and games.* New York: Free Press.

Dargan, A., & Zeitlin, S. (1990). *City play.* New Brunswick, NJ: Rutgers University Press.

Edelman, M. W. (1987). *Sermon at the Unitarian Church of All Souls, Manhattan, New York.* Unpublished talk.

Goffman, E. (1961). Fun in games: Two studies in the sociology of interaction. In E. Goffman (Ed.), *Encounters* (pp. 15–81). Indianapolis: Bobbs-Merrill.

Hale, E., & Hale, O. (1938). *From sidewalk, gutter and stoop: Being a chronicle of children's play and game activity.* New York Public Library. Unpublished manuscript, two packages.

Hawes, B. L. (1974). Law and order on the playground. In L. M. Shears & E. M, Bower (Eds.), *Games in education and development* (pp. 12–22). Springfield, IL: Charles M. Thomas.

Kirshenblatt-Gimblett, B. (1989). *Urban play.* Unpublished manuscript.

Kirshenblatt-Gimblett, B. (1990). Afterword: Other places, other times. In A. Dargan & S. Zeitlin, *City play* (pp. 175–194). New Brunswick, NJ: Rutgers University Press.

Levenson, S. (1967). *Everything but money.* New York: Pocket.

Newell, W. W. (1963). *Games and songs of American children.* New York: Dover. (Original work published 1883)

Roberts, J. M., Arth, M. J., & Busch, R. R. (1959). Games in culture. *American Anthropologist, 61,* 597–605.

Sutton-Smith, B. (1981). *A history of children's play: The New Zealand playground, 1840–1950.* Philadelphia: University of Pennsylvania Press.

33
Children's Outdoor Play
An Endangered Activity

MARY S. RIVKIN

Throughout the industrialized world, children have been deprived of safe, accessible, outdoor play spaces (Louv, 2005). No one planned that this should happen, yet children have lost habitat for play, and lost access to those habitats that do exist.

Loss of Habitat

Although the extent of natural habitat for outdoor activity varies in different regions of the United States and throughout the world, overall there has been a strong trend toward loss of such habitat since the mid-1950s. The loss of habitat has three main causes: the dominance of automotive vehicles; the growth in population; and pollution.

Automotive Vehicles and Roads

The dominance of cars and trucks is a major contributor to loss of habitat. Industrialization has increased the dependence of the economy on roads connecting all parts of the landscape, which is unfavorable for children's access to the outdoors. Roads themselves commandeer places where tree-climbing, stream play, playhouses, and other nature-based activities can occur, as well as create barriers to the free ranging of small, slow, vulnerable creatures such as children. By and large, children's movements are heavily restricted by the presence of roads.

The most deadly aspect of roads, however, is the presence of cars and other motorized vehicles, which overpower and endanger children. When vehicles are moving, they can injure or kill children; when they are parked along a street, they block a child's view of danger and conceal children from motorists. One is hard pressed to imagine an invention more unfriendly toward the development of children. While the very young, "knee" and "yard" children, need constant adult supervision, "neighborhood" children (Whiting & Edwards, 1988) ought to be out and about exploring their neighborhood and mentally mapping their home terrain (Moore, 1990). Cars severely inhibit the completion of this developmental task.

Population Increase

More people means less land for children to play on. Land has been turned into roads, houses, parking lots, shopping centers, and other buildings. Vacant lots have been built on or fenced off; streams have been channeled into culverts and vanish from view. In the United States, aided and abetted by a tax code that encourages single-family dwellings, suburban sprawl has minced and privatized the land, restricting and isolating children from access to communal outdoor play spaces (Dargan & Zeitlin, 1990). In the world as a whole, population growth has resulted in the transformation of natural land areas into housing and other facilities to support the increased population.

Pollution

Aside from population growth and short-sighted land use, enormous damage has been done to the landscape by resource depletion and inadequate waste management, further reducing children's access to good outdoor play. Streams and rivers are dirty, the air causes breathing problems, and the ozone layer, thinned in part by modern effluents, no longer protects people from ultraviolet rays. In addition, many chemicals of unknown toxicity are in the environment. Children tend to take in more toxins than adults because they live closer to the ground where many toxins collect, and because "pound for pound, they eat, drink, breathe more than adults" (Greater Boston Physicians for Social Responsibility, 2002). Two positive developments recently have been the banning of arsenic-based pesticide (CCA) in wood used in playgrounds. and an effort to make all schools use Integrated Pest Management (IPM) in order to reduce the quantity of pesticides and herbicides used in and around schools.[1]

Children from low-income households suffer a disproportionate amount of environmental neglect. A study by the United Church of Christ indicated that three of five African-American and Hispanic-American children in the United States live in communities with toxic-waste sites. Furthermore, lead poisoning is endemic in many communities: 55% of African-American children from low-income households have toxic levels of lead in their blood (Commission for Racial Justice, 1987). Lead from car exhaust, paint, and manufacturing lingers in the soil of long-populated cities, never chemically decaying, always poisonous to children playing in the dirt. One of the consequences when cities repair their old bridges, tunnels, and elevated roadways is the release of even more lead into the environment; land near bridges being repainted is particularly hazardous (Levy, 1993).

Reduced Access to Habitat

Children have lost access to outdoor play in their neighborhoods even when habitats for play do exist, such as parks or open, connecting yards unthreatened by busy streets. Five interrelated factors are at work here: the institutionalization of children; an economy requiring most adults to work away from home; an increase in negative social conditions; communications technologies; and, particularly in the United States, a litigiousness that sees children as liabilities to be guarded against.

Institutionalization of Children

As schooling became compulsory for all children over the past century, children gained access to a wider world of knowledge but lost access to their immediate neighborhoods. The institutionalization of children in child care, schools, sports, lessons, and camps—has reduced their time to play outside. In addition, a strenuous pursuit of academic skills has caused many schools in at least 10 states to eliminate recess (Jarrett, 2004) so even the schoolyard is lost to them. Furthermore, simply getting to these various institutions has further restricted children's independent mobility. A study in Great Britain showed that, while in 1971 80% of 7- and 8-year-olds walked or biked to school, in 1990 less than 9% got themselves to school (Hillman, Adams, & Whitelegg, 1990). Children go from building to building confined in vehicles, and almost motionless as a result of the essential use of seatbelts.

Homes without Adults

The current institutionalization is partly a result of another late 20th-century phenomenon of parents, especially mothers, working away from home. This phenomenon has other consequences for children's outdoor play. For example, because parents are not in the neighborhood to supervise or rescue, many children are not allowed out of doors after coming home from school. In addition, many neighborhoods are perceived as dangerous. Indeed, as contemporary chroniclers (e.g., Kozol, 1995) and the urban daily newspapers attest, inner-city neighborhoods, in particular, often are dangerous. On average, eight children a day in the United States are killed by guns (Children's Defense Fund, 2005).

Negative Social Conditions

Even designated public play spaces such as parks are, with justification, perceived as unsafe for play. Drug trafficking, vagrancy, and homelessness, combined with shrunken budgets for upkeep and supervision, contribute to a climate of danger for children, as well as adults. An inducement to inhabitants of some New York City apartments, in fact, is the presence of indoor playrooms for their children, so that families can avoid the problems of outdoor parks. Fear of crime and lack of "neighborly" involvement of other adults in children's activities also add to concerns about giving children free rein in outdoor environments.

Communication Technologies

Television, computers, and electronic games have also eroded the traditional lure of the outdoors for children. Numerous commentators have attested to the deleterious effect of too much "screentime" both for its content and its limited interactivity. There is an apt adjective for such consequences of television and related technologies: iatrogenic, unintended but nonetheless bad.

Legal Suits

Finally, the fear of and fondness for lawsuits, along with a desire for privacy, has caused many landowners in the United States to fence property or otherwise restrict children from access to "attractive nuisances" such as ponds, highly educative though they are. Fear of lawsuits has also led parks and schools to remove equipment that might cause injury (Martin, 1996). Although a wholesome degree of risk taking is desirable for children, the line between risk and hazard is not always clear and depends on a particular child's age and ability. A flowing stream that could safely delight an 8-year-old is of course extremely hazardous to an unsupervised toddler. The usual response is to cover the stream and channel its flow underground. Trees that children might have climbed are removed as hazardous and replaced with climbing equipment. Too often, however, the resilient surfaces that would cushion falls are not installed, or if installed are not well maintained; then using the equipment becomes dangerous, so the equipment is removed.

The Importance of Outdoor Play

Arguments for the importance of outdoor play come from the perspectives of evolution, of human knowledge, of human development, and of cultural transmission.

Children—An Endangered Species?

An axiom of environmental science is that the main cause of species extinction is habitat loss. Human beings may as well consider themselves a species no less on the defensive than the spotted owl or snail darter and regard anxiously the decline of their habitat, particularly for their young. As Darwin observed, humans are an undomesticated species, accustomed to roam at will wherever they consider "home." The human species evolved in the outdoors; senses developed in daylight and moonlight, not electric light; body rhythms are like those of other animals, dependent on light and temperature and other factors only partly understood. Perhaps for fully grown humans, life without much exposure to the outdoors is acceptable, even desirable to some, but is evolution being disturbed when children grow and develop with minimal involvement in the outdoor world?

The "biophilia hypothesis," offered by sociobiologist E.O. Wilson, suggests "a human need, fired in the crucible of evolutionary development, for deep and intimate association with the natural environment, particularly its living biota," and that nature not only supplies material needs but also "aesthetic, intellectual, cognitive, and even spiritual meaning and satisfaction" (cited in Kellert, 1993, pp. 20–21). Humans and nature are linked. Technology cannot replace but only atrophy these links, creating children somehow crippled or limited (Wilson, 1993, pp. 31–32).

The Knowledge Loss

When children are not outdoors, they fail to learn about the outdoors. A study of families from Anglo, Native-American, and Hispanic groups indicated that all children knew far less about nature than the adults, and what they did know they tended to get from television and schoolbooks rather than direct experience (Nabhan & St. Antoine, 1993). Furthermore, they didn't know the cultural meanings of the living things in their own locales, such as myths and legends about them, much less their medicinal or food uses. Unfortunately, when such knowledge is embedded in nontelevision and nonschool sources and conveyed through indigenous languages, it vanishes when the speakers of these languages pass away (Nabhan & St. Antoine, 1993). Furthermore, children learn through television and books by using only the senses of sight and hearing. Such knowledge is pallid compared to that gained through multisensory encounters.

Developmental Issues

No one knows if this generation of children who lack outdoor play will develop "normally," but there are suggestions that certain positive developmental characteristics may be related to outdoor play (Dovey, 1984; Kahn & Kellert, 2002; Moore, 1990; Moore & Cosco, 2004). Thus, an important question is whether children's confinement to buildings and vehicles may be distorting their development.

One area of concern may be children's ability to map out their environment mentally. If children cannot physically explore, at their own pace, how can they grasp the topography of their neighborhoods and, by extension, the rest of the earth's surface? Studies of children's interpretation of space revealed how personal and idiosyncratic children's internal maps are (Hart, 1979; Moore, 1990). Humans are perhaps as territorial as any other species, but how do humans learn about the nature of territories without exploring them?

Another concern is the prevalence of hyperactivity—many children (especially boys) are being judged as too active. This "epidemic" could be partly a cultural disease, evident particularly in indoor settings such as homes and schools (Angier, 1994; Olds, 1980).[2] Distressingly, as Jarrett points out (2004), children in low-achieving schools are especially likely to have no recess, a condition which may contribute to excessive indoor activity. In contrast, Finnish elementary schools, which are highly achieving, schedule children to study for 45 minutes then play outside for 15 minutes, throughout the day (Andersen, 2004). Excessive indoor time and lack of exercise is currently linked with increased rates of childhood obesity and diabetes (Burris & Harrison, 2004; Kaplan, Liverman, & Kraak, 2004)

Another developmental issue is that of satisfactory separation from family, which occurs in late adolescence. This separation might be related to childhood hut building which Sobel (1993) has found across cultures and theorizes is practice for the real separation. Dovey's 1984 research found hut building central to children. While children usually favor natural areas, evidence from urban observations indicates that children, like nesting birds, seek shelter spots everywhere imaginable (Dargan & Zeitlin, 1990). They need time, space, and materials, however, for their constructions.

Finally, there is the question of how children acquire a sense of stewardship for the land if they do not have direct experience with the land as they are growing up. Although it is not well understood how children acquire environmental values (Moore, 1990), Chawla's research indicates that family-based, childhood experiences are key (1995). In another study, of 800 8- to 10-year-olds in Great Britain, experience with vegetation (including playing, eating, mowing the lawn, gardening, hiking, camping, and being allergic to it) was positively correlated with intellectual and aesthetic appreciation of the natural environment (Harvey, 1989). In arguing for children's "need of wild places," Nabhan states, "We need to return to learning about the land by being on the land, or better, being in the thick of it. That is the best way we can stay in touch with the fates of its creatures, its indigenous cultures, its earthbound wisdom. That is the best way we can be in touch with ourselves" (1994, p. 107). Knowledge of the natural world can lead to both environmental activism and knowledge of oneself as a part of nature. Thus, a major question is: How can we get children back "in the thick of it"?

Restoring Children's Habitat

Given the difficulties outlined, the most practical course of action to get children "back in the thick of it" is to rebuild habitats at the one institution dedicated to children, their schools. Movements in Canada, Great Britain, and a few parts of the United States are underway. But for a more substantial restoration of habitats, agencies other than schools must contribute. Both public and governmental cooperation are needed to redirect transportation, housing, recreation, and land-use policies to provide for children's outdoor experiences. In an era of reduced faith in public policy and shrinking budgets for innovation, this is, of course, difficult. Nonetheless, there are notable efforts in such a direction.

Habitat Restoration in the Schoolyard

Most schoolyards are bleakly devoid of good play opportunities. Adults appear to value the ease of maintenance offered by asphalt and mown grass over the play value of woods, meadows, and wetlands. Playground equipment has frequently been imagined as providing primarily gross motor activity, although many newer structures do accommodate social and dramatic play as well. Too often, though, such equipment serves only a fraction of the children on a playground at a time. School recesses, where they exist, for example, are typified by large numbers of children, a small amount of equipment, and the minimum of adult interaction of the sort that might foster good play.

However, since about 1990, the nonprofit Learning Through Landscapes in Great Britain has succeeded in inspiring more than a third of all British elementary schools to undertake schoolyard renovation. While each school has different possibilities and needs, the basics include trees for shade, shelter, and structure, water, places to sit, native plants, and accessibility (Lucas, 1994). A key to the strength of the project has been its tight link to Britain's national curriculum.

One of the most child-oriented schoolyards in Britain, Coombes Infant School, in Arborfield, Reading, Southwest England, began its transformation from bleakness long before the current movement. The asphalt here has been painted with math games, and there are a rowboat for dramatic play, long logs on the edge for climbing and experiencing wood's aging into decay, a tunnel for hiding away, and a dense border of bushes that attracts birds and other wildlife. Beyond the border lies a broad paved path bordered by more bushes, where lunches are eaten on nice days; interspersed are four ponds of various types, with lilies, frogs, and fish. Beyond this are fruit and nut orchards and a willow maze, and wildflower borders. Every year children help decide on a new major project, and every year every child plants a tree. Children do whatever work they can, and the work that only adults can accomplish (e.g., repairing the roof) is closely observed by the children. The library has books with stories, photos, and pictures documenting the events. The result is a densely alive and changing environment to which children feel a commitment. Coombes is an important example of a principal and staff persisting in steadily improving their outdoor environment in the interests of children's pleasure and learning (Humphries & Rowe, 1994).

Several European countries, most notably Scandinavian, have playground improvement groups, and in Canada, the Evergreen Foundation has also undertaken a School Grounds Naturalization initiative. Several hundred schools have had projects to add wildlife habitats to their grounds. In the United States, inspired by the United Kingdom and Canada as well as the pioneering work by Moore and Wong in the 1970s and documented in their *Natural Learning* (1997), numerous groups have promoted natural areas and other improvements in schoolyards. The National Wildlife Federation has sponsored nearly 2000 Schoolyard Habitats; the U.S. Fish and Wildlife Service works with schools in nine states; the National Gardening Association, the Audubon Society, botanic gardens in several cities, state departments of natural resources, soil conservation districts, and arboretums have all been encouraging schoolyard improvements. The Boston Schoolyard Initiative has even put a garden and play equipment on an urban rooftop; Tule Elk Park in San Francisco has transformed a parking lot into a beautiful and active garden/playspace. Most efforts are collaborative. The concept of habitat, now familiar in our thinking about animals, is informing the environments of children.

Other Habitats for Consideration

The recent increase in greenways will help bring play spaces to children. Some envision connecting all schools with greenways, providing pathways for children and small animals for daily intimate use (Lusk, 1994). Efforts to "calm traffic" will also help children play safely. Reducing speeds, adding speed bumps, narrowing passages, and restricting hours all contribute to safer streets. In Northern Europe the practice of creating residential streets, called "Woonerven" in the place of traffic streets provides children with areas where cars are slowed to walking speed, and the addition of plantings, bollards, benches, and removal of curbs increases playability and livability. One study of two German streets before and after becoming Woonerven showed that children played more outside, interacted more with one another and with objects, rode wheel-toys more, and engaged in more fantasy play, music making, and dancing on the Woonerven (Eubank-Ahrens, 1984–1985).

Finally, while many neighborhoods do not support children's play, some progressive communities have planned for children's needs; for example, Columbia, Maryland, Reston, Virginia, and Davis, California (described in Francis, 1984–1985). Too often, however, adults verbalize but do not actualize the resources for children's needs. If children's needs are to be served, adult home buyers must insist that developers provide for children as well as adults.

Lewis Thomas (1975) wrote that if humans would regard themselves as "truly indispensable elements of nature" they would no doubt worry about themselves even more than the rest of the environment. He argued that, if humans did see themselves as part of nature, "movements might start up for the protection of ourselves as valuable, endangered species" (p. 125). Such a movement should start first for the most vulnerable ones in the human species, the children, to restore to them an ancient and indisputable part of their natural habitat, the outdoors.

Notes

1. Consult Children's Enviromental Health Network at http://www.cehn.org, and Healthy Schools Network at http:/www./healthyschools.org for current information on issues of environmental health, and governmental regulations.
2. "There is now an attempt to pathologize what was once considered the normal range of behavior of boys…today Tom Sawyer and Huck Finn surely would have been diagnosed with both conduct disorder and ADHD," according to M. Konner, Emory University professor of anthropology and psychiatry (quoted in Angier, 1994).

References

Andersen, F. O. (2004). *Exploring the roots of optimal learning: A story of successful primary and special needs education in Finland.* Accessed at http://www.legolearning.net

Angier, N. (1994, July 24). The debilitating malady called boyhood. *New York Times* (Northeast ed.), 4, 1.

Burris, K. G., & Harrison, J. B. (2004). *Obesity and children.* Wheaton, MD: Association for Childhood International.

Chawla, L. (1995). *Life paths into effective environmental action.* Paper presented at the annual conference of the North American Association of Environmental Education, Portland, ME.

Children's Defense Fund. Accessed at http://www.childrensdefense.org/data/eachday.asp

Christoffel, K. K. (1995). Handguns and the environments of children. *Children's Environments, 12*(1), 39–48.

Commission for Racial Justice, United Church of Christ. (1987). Toxic wastes and race in the United States: A national report on the racial and socio-economic characteristics of hazardous waste sites (Vol. 14). New York: Commission for Racial Justice.

Dargan, A., & Zeitlin, S. (1990). *City play.* New Brunswick, NJ: Rutgers University Press.

Dovey, K. (1984). The creation of a sense of place: The case of Preshil. *Places*, 1(2), 32–40..

Eubank-Ahrens, B. (1984–1985, Winter). The impact of Woonerven on children's behavior. *Children's Environments Quarterly, 1*, 39–45.

Francis, M. (1984–1985, Winter). Children's use of open space in village homes. *Children's Environments Quarterly, 1*, 36–38.

Greater Boston Physicians for Social Responsibility. (2002). *Out of harm's way: Preventing toxic threats to child development.* Boston: Author.

Hart, R. (1979). *Children's experience of place.* New York: Irvington.

Harvey, M. R. (1989, Spring). Children's experiences with vegetation. *Children's Environments Quarterly, 6*, 36–43.

Hillman, M., Adams, J., & Whitelegg, J. (1990). *One false move...: A study of children's independent mobility.* London: Policy Studies Institute.

Humphries, S., & Rowe, S. (1994). The biggest classroom. In P. Blatchford & S. Sharp (Eds.), *Breaktime and the school: Understanding and changing playground behaviour* (pp. 107–117). London: Routledge.

Jarrett, O (2004). Where have all the players gone? *The Association for the Study of Play Newsletter, 28*(2), 1–4.

Kahn, P. H. & Kellert, S. R. (Eds.).(2002). *Children and nature: Psychological, sociocultural, and evolutionary investigations.* Cambridge, MA: MIT Press

Kaplan, J. P., Liverman, C. T., & Kraak, V. A. (2004). *Preventing childhood obesity: Health in the balance.* Washington, DC: National Academy Press.

Kellert, S. R. (1993). Introduction. In S. R. Kellert & E. O. Wilson (Eds.), *The biophilia hypothesis* (pp. 20–21). Washington, DC: Island Press/Shearwater.

Kozol, J. (1995). *Amazing grace: The lives of children and the conscience of a nation.* New York: Crown.

Levy, C. J. (1993, June 12). Lead levels force closing of parts of two parks. *New York Times*, pp. 23, 25.

Louv, R. (1990). *Childhood's future.* Boston: Houghton Mifflin.

Lucas, B. (1994, August). Grounds for change: The British example. In *Out of the classroom... into the garden.* International symposium on the prepared learning environment, at the Montessori Foundation and the American Horticultural Society, Arlington, VA.

Lusk, A. (1994, July). Let's build 108,000 new garden classrooms for children. *American Horticulturalist.Proceedings from American Horticultural Society National Symposium, 34*–35.

Martin, D. (1996, April 11). That upsidedown high will be only a memory. *New York Times* (Northeast ed.), B1, 4.

Moore, R. C. (1990). *Childhood's domain.* Berkeley, CA: MIG Communication.

Moore, R. C., & Cosco, N.G. (2004). *Developing an earth-bound culture through design of childhood habitats.* Accessed at http://www.naturalearning.org/earthboundpaper.html.

Moore, R. C., & Wong, H. (1996). *Natural learning: The life history of an environmental schoolyard.* Berkeley, CA: MIG Communication.

Nabhan, G. P. (1994). Children in touch, creatures in story. In G. P. Nabhan & S. Trimble (Eds.), *The Geography of Childhood* (p. 107). Boston: Beacon.

Nabhan, G. P., & St. Antoine, S. (1993). The loss of floral and faunal story: The extinction of experience. In S. R. Kellert & E. O. Wilson (Eds.), *The biophilia hypothesis* (pp. 229–250). Washington, DC: Island Press/Shearwater.

Olds, A. (1980, Winter). From cartwheels to caterpillars: The child's need for motion outdoors. *Human Ecology Forum, 10*, 24.

Sobel, D. (1993). *Children's special places: Exploring the role of forts, dens, and bush houses in middle childhood.* Tucson, AZ: Zephyr.

Thomas, L. (1975). *Lives of a cell.* New York: Bantam.

Whiting, B. B., & Edwards, C. P. (1988). *Children of different worlds.* Cambridge, MA: Harvard University Press.

Wilson, E. O. (1993). Biophilia and the conservation ethic. In S. R. Kellert & E. O. Wilson (Eds.), *The biophilia hypothesis* (pp. 31–32). Washington, DC: Island Press/Shearwater.

34
Perspectives on Play and Playgrounds

JOE L. FROST AND IRMA C. WOODS

Organized playgrounds for older children in the United States originated with the outdoor gymnasiums of Massachusetts in 1821 and with the sand gardens of Boston for younger children in 1887. Thereafter, public school and public park playgrounds followed a physical fitness and recreation tradition while preschool playgrounds followed a developmental emphasis. During the 20th century, school and park playgrounds evolved from a traditional pattern of standard equipment, such as merry-go-rounds, see-saws, swings, and jungle gyms, spaced around open spaces fields, to novel equipment such as animal swings and rocket ship climbers. Many child development centers continued to feature swings, climbers, and materials such as sand and water and portable equipment such as wheeled vehicles and toys. Reflecting concerns for child safety, home technology play, and pay-for-play entertainment centers have now begun to supplement or replace outdoor play environments, raising concerns about opportunities for child development through creative play. Issues in playground design and use include safety, developmental appropriateness, provisions for inclusiveness, play leadership, and accessibility. The best playgrounds are never finished but evolve to meet children's changing needs.

Playgrounds for children in a wide variety of settings are a common sight in the United States. They are found in community parks, child care facilities, hotels, hospitals, fast food restaurants, elementary schools and, of course, backyards. Regardless of the setting, playgrounds should be designed to support play and development. The discussion that follows begins with historical perspectives on the development of playgrounds in the United States, explores the developmental benefits of play and playgrounds, discusses the trends in playground safety and the role of adults, considers issues in playground design, and concludes with perspectives on the future of playgrounds.

History of Playgrounds

The outdoor gymnasia founded in Massachusetts in the 1820s were the forerunners of the playground movement. Based on the physical fitness philosophy of Friedrich Jahn from Germany, the first private outdoor gymnasia were founded in 1821 at the Latin School in Salem, Massachusetts (Mero, 1908). The focus of the outdoor gymnasia was not on play or group games, but on individual exercise to keep the body fit and to promote "moral purity" (Cavallo, 1981, p.19). Following the establishment of the first public gymnasia in the United States in 1826, interest waned, and the next 50 years was a dormant period in the playground movement.

In the 1880s, a political leader, Von Schenckendorff, developed play areas in Berlin that consisted of piles of sand bordered by wooden squares called sand gardens (Sapora & Mitchell, 1948). During a visit to Berlin, Dr. Marie Zakrzewska from the United States observed the sand gardens and proposed that they be established in Boston to alleviate the slum conditions for children of the poor (Cavallo, 1981; Mero, 1908). Boston city officials responded and constructed 10 sand gardens in the city's poorest districts in 1887. Trained kindergarten teachers provided supervision (Cavallo, 1981; Mero, 1908). Thus began the first supervised playgrounds in the United States for young children and, coupled with increasing interest in manufactured playground equipment for older children, the true beginning of the American playground movement.

During the late 1800s, vacation schools, housed in public school buildings, led to summer school playgrounds and to year-round play modeled after the school playgrounds of Gary, Indiana (Cavallo, 1981; Frost, 1992a). The principle aim of these early playgrounds was to "overcome lawless tendencies acquired in the street and crowded tenement life" (Mero, 1908, p. 122). Playgrounds were also established to serve as agents of Americanization for the large number of immigrants, especially in the industrial Northeast and in Chicago (Cavallo, 1981).

Playground Association of America

The lack of a well-defined theory of play on the value of playgrounds for the growth and development of children led to the establishment of the Playground Association of America (PAA) in 1906 (Cavallo, 1981). The work of John Dewey and Friedrich Froebel convinced advocates of younger children's play that playground experiences were a means to help children develop cognitive skills, moral tendencies, and social values (Cavallo, 1981; Frost, 1992a). Many reformers, however, held to the belief that the point of organized play was to coordinate the child's psychological and physical apparatus as efficiently as possible (De Groot, 1914). The recapitulation theory of G. Stanley Hall promoted this belief by advocating that morality or strength of character was a direct result of physical fitness (Cavallo, 1981).

From 1906 to 1920 the PAA was responsible for the amazing growth of public and private playgrounds. By 1917, 481 cities operated 3,940 playgrounds and employed 8,748 directors (Cavallo, 1981). These golden years, however, were short-lived. Efforts to broaden its appeal led to changing the name of the association in 1911 to the Playground and Recreation Association of America (Cavallo, 1981; Frost, 1992a). In 1930 the name of the association was changed again to the National Recreation Association and later to the National Recreation and Park Association, which exists today. The removal of the word *playground* greatly reduced the association's active advocacy for children's playgrounds and influenced the physical fitness/recreation emphasis of public school and public park playgrounds to the present time. Preschool playgrounds nevertheless evolved from a developmental emphasis dating back to Froebel and Dewey, and much of this tradition has remained in place.

Playgrounds in the United States

The United States' entry into World War I saw organized play pass primarily to the public school systems as a result of shortage of materials because of the war. A few years later, material to build equipment was again in limited supply during the Great Depression. Franklin D. Roosevelt's New Deal provided funds for the Works Progress Administration to construct playgrounds at schools. Between World War II and about 1980, four major types of playgrounds were popular: traditional, designer or contemporary, adventure, and creative (Frost, 1985). Following the publication of national playground safety guidelines by the U. S. Consumer Product Safety Commission in 1981, interest in safety led to increasing numbers of lawsuits, and older playgrounds in schools and city parks were rapidly replaced by commercial equipment intended to meet the CPSC guidelines. Consequently, playgrounds became increasingly standardized and by the early 2000s the typical school and park playgrounds consisted of a superstructure (composite structure), and a set of swings. Fortunately, child care centers continued to provide a wider array of manufactured and natural materials and equipment to accommodate a wide range of play. During this same period (1980–2005) indoor and outdoor pay-for-play playgrounds and home entertainment centers were rapidly emerging, supplementing or supplanting the traditional community and city public playground concept.

Adventure Playgrounds in Europe

Lady Allen of Hurtwood, a campaigner for children's rights in London, transported the idea of junk or adventure playgrounds from Denmark during the late 1940s. This movement eventually influenced the development of the National Playing Fields Association and the London County Council, which helped organize and support adventure playgrounds. This work was later supported by the organization of the London Adventure Playground Association and the Handicapped Adventure Playground Association. In recent years play provision in England has shifted from the adventure playground model utilizing play leaders to a playcare model utilizing playworkers who pass an extensive playwork study program (Davy, 2001).

The emphasis of the adventure playground is on construction play using a wide variety of manipulative materials. Adventure playgrounds are available to children only when play leaders are present to provide supervision (Vance, 1982). The first adventure playground was developed by C. Th. Sorensen in Emdrup, outside Copenhagen, Denmark. "Often referred to as a junk playground, the adventure playground is a place where children of all ages, with trained play leaders, are free to do many things they can no longer do in crowded urban society: building huts, walls, forts, dens, tree houses, lighting fires and cooking…or doing nothing" (Michaelis, cited in Brett, Moore, & Provenzo, 1993, p.26). "The point of Emdrup is that it was not 'provided' for children. They were allowed to make it themselves" (Lambert, 1992, p. 13). Its developer, the architect Sorensen, upon a visit to the site stated, "Of all the things I have helped to realize, the adventure playground is probably the ugliest: yet for me it is the best and most beautiful of my works" (cited in Lambert, 1992, p. 13).

Adventure playgrounds never gained much popularity in the United States, largely because of their unsightliness, concerns with safety, and lack of well-trained play leaders. Nevertheless, the Houston Adventure Play Association in Houston, Texas, continued to sponsor three adventure playgrounds in the city, and California had three association branches (Shell, 1994). In 2002 the Adventure Playground Association in Houston ceased to exist because of funding difficulties but the movement is still alive in several European countries and in Japan.

The Developmental Benefits of Play and Playgrounds

The evidence that play is a primary vehicle for development, indeed that play enhances development, is clearly and comprehensively documented. Extensive reviews of research show that play promotes cognitive development (discovery, verbal judgment, reasoning, memory, divergent production), language, and social maturity (Berk, 1994; Frost, 1992a; Frost, Wortham, & Reifel, 2005; Rubin, Fein, & Vandenberg, 1983). In addition, play has therapeutic power, allowing children to express and explore feelings, thoughts, and experiences and, consequently, to overcome anxiety and fear (Axline, 1947; Erikson, 1950; Frost et al, 2005; Landreth, 1991). Time for play and rich materials for play are essential for broad based, optimal development.

The benefits of playgrounds for motor development were extensively researched during the early 20th century, and challenging playgrounds were seen as essential to physical or motor development. However, as safety standards became functional, preschool age children were increasingly deprived of a wide range of motor equipment such as challenging climbers and slides, overhead apparatus, balance apparatus, and sliding poles. As early as 1939, an extensive review of playground research on motor achievement of young children, coupled with original research involving 1,973 children ages (Gutteridge, 1939) concluded that children were exhausting the equipment challenges on their playgrounds and had found "no new worlds to conquer" by the age of 4 or 5 years. Young children, ages 2 to 5, demonstrated motor control and proficiency far in advance of the common belief, and steady proficiency was seen throughout the year as they explored playground apparatus. Climbing was well established by the age of 3 with 50% demonstrating proficiency and by age 6, 92% of the children were proficient at climbing playground climbers. The author concluded that playground equipment then provided did "not provide varying opportunities in line with growing abilities" (Gutteridge, 1939, p. 169).

In 2004, an extensive study (Frost, Brown, Sutterby, & Thornton, 2004) generally supported the 1939 findings. Three- to 5-year-old children utilized climbers and overhead apparatus with increasing skill; given appropriate equipment for daily play, most children became proficient, using the equipment in increasingly complex patterns. The only exceptions were obese children who were too heavy to support their weight. Through such studies, the case for recess, extensive time for spontaneous play, availability of natural and creative materials, and challenging playground equipment is strengthened.

Frost, Brown et al. (2004) contains comprehensive reviews of research on the developmental benefits of materials and equipment typically found on playgrounds (e.g., swings, climbers, overhead apparatus, sand, and water) and includes extensive original research on these same features. This work argues against growing standardization of playground equipment resulting in "dumbing down," which affects not only physical development, but also social and cognitive development and overall health and fitness. By 2005, national playground standards committees were questioning the scope and nature of playground equipment standards and were beginning to take steps aimed toward simplification, relevance, and consistency with state safety regulations.

Infants and early toddlers need a wide range of sensory and exploratory opportunities. As they develop into the preschool years, they need playgrounds that provide motor apparatus such as climbers and swings; make-believe or dramatic play areas, such as wheeled vehicles, cars, boats, and play houses; and areas for constructing, stacking, and digging that include tools, dirt, water, and sand. As they approach kindergarten age, an additional element—flat, grassy areas for organized games—often is added, and equipment must be more complex and challenging. Storage facilities on the playground are required to house the 101 loose parts that support play and work–play areas, such as gardens, nature areas, and orchards.

A growing body of research points to the need of children to interact with the environment in diverse and complex ways (Beckwith, 1982; Frost, 1986a, 1992b; Frost, Brown et al., 2004; Frost, Wortham, & Reifel, 2005). Play environments for young children, therefore, need to contain fixed and complex equipment that offers different levels of challenges. Children need to experience raw materials found in nature, such as sand, water, rocks, and soil. Having trees, plants, and gardens in the environment can teach children to see living things as an integral part of the environment and help them to understand how nature supports their lives (Talbot, 1985). Plants also help to create soothing experiences in playgrounds and provide a wide range of sensory experiences (Talbot & Frost, 1990). "Play environments must be powerful enough to sustain children's activity without constant motivational and/or directional assistance from non-players, especially adults" (Gehlbach, 1991, p. 138). Finally, play environments can be beautiful as well as functional, and they should integrate the wonders of nature—trees, gardens, flowering plants, special places, wild places, into children's everyday activities (Goodenough, 2003; Moore & Wong, 1997; Nabhan & Trimble, 1994; Rivkin, 1995).

Contemporary Issues in Playground Design and Use

Issues in playground design and use are much more complex now than even a decade ago. The growing tendency of people in the United States to resolve their problems through lawsuits has heightened public awareness of playground injuries and safety. The growth of violence in inner cities has made many public playgrounds unsafe for children's play and has spurred the development of alternative play places. Accelerating interest in play and play environments among researchers and professionals across the behavioral sciences has heightened awareness and knowledge of the developmental benefits of play and has led to greater interest in playground design and function. The Americans with Disabilities Act of 1990 (PL101-336) influenced, indeed required, that children's public playgrounds be accessible for all children and has stimulated intense study of appropriate means for inclusion.

Several emerging trends are currently affecting the scope and quality of children's play and playgrounds. The spontaneous play of children is declining rapidly due to ill-founded emphasis on high stakes testing in schools, which is favored by politicians and administrators but widely opposed by teachers and professional organizations. Such emphasis is resulting in deletion of recess, destruction of playgrounds, and decline in physical education and the arts. Simultaneously, loss of time for play and increase in sedentary activities such as television, computer games, expanded classroom time and junk food diets are contributing to a growing epidemic of obesity and serious health consequences for children. (Frost, 2004; Frost, Brown, et al., 2004; Sutterby & Frost, 2002; Frost, Wortham, & Reifel, 2005).

The growing threat of litigation is resulting in standardization of playground equipment and a degree of "dumbing down" with respect to children's cognitive, social, physical, and creative development—especially for preschool children. Creative and natural elements of playgrounds, especially for younger children, are eliminated if they do not meet safety guidelines and standards for manufactured equipment or if they are considered too "messy." Such unfounded application of safety standards and short-sightedness removes many rich opportunities for children to engage in creative, spontaneous play and contributes to a growing decline in children's health and fitness along with an increase in childhood obesity.

Playground Safety

Beginning in the mid-1970s the U.S. Consumer Product Safety Commission (CPSC) began to consider the issue of playground safety. This concern was influenced by petitions from citizens, injury data from the newly formed National Electronic Surveillance System, and an increase in playground injury lawsuits. Following several years of study, the *Handbook for Pubic Playground Safety* was published by the CPSC in 1981. Further study led to the publication of revised handbooks in 1991, 1994, and 1997. The American Society for Testing and Materials (ASTM) approved the *Standard Specification for Impact Attenuation of Surface Systems Under and Around Playground Equipment* in 1991 (revised in 1999). In 1993 the ASTM published the *Standard Consumer Safety Performance Specification for Playground Equipment for Public Use* (revised in 1998). The 1991 revisions of the CPSC guidelines were developed for the consumer and the manufacturer, but the more technical 1993 and 1998 ASTM standards were addressed to the manufacturer. Both CPSC guidelines and ASTM standards are voluntary, but they are now recognized as the national standard of care and tend to be very influential in litigation.

Child care center playgrounds are regulated by state departments of human services or equivalent agencies throughout the United States. Most states, however, have very weak regulations that place child care center operators at risk in litigation. A number of professional organizations and agencies have also published weak guidelines or standards that contribute to this problem. Most state education agencies, while responsible for regulating schools, have no regulations or guidelines for school playgrounds. None has guidelines equivalent in quality or scope to the CPSC guidelines or the ASTM standards, yet a growing number of states are making their playground safety regulations increasingly specific and complex. Texas, for example, in September 2003 adopted new regulations for playgrounds of child care facilities, homes, and agencies. These regulations are similar to those of CPSC but the major differences are leading to numerous problems including removal of some equipment that meets CPSC guidelines. This results in additional expense, confusion by designers, manufacturers, and center owners about meeting conflicting state regulations and national guidelines, wasted time, and loss of play challenges for children. Those sponsoring playgrounds need one common set of safety guidelines or standards to guide their work and these guidelines should reflect the need for creative development of new approaches to designing playground equipment.

How serious is the playground safety issue? Two reasons for unsafe play equipment and playgrounds are lack of consumer interest and traditional equipment left unreplaced for decades (Ward, 1987). In litigation involving serious injuries and fatalities on playgrounds, the most common causes of injuries are falling onto hard surfaces, impacting protruding elements of equipment, and entrapment in equipment. Four factors almost always come into play in lawsuits: design of equipment; installation of equipment; maintenance, particularly of resilient surfacing; and adult supervision (Frost, 2001; Frost & Sweeney, 1996). According to recent statistics, over 200,000 injuries occur on playgrounds each year (Frost, Wortham, & Reifel, 2005). Most injuries and some fatalities on playgrounds are the result of falls from equipment onto hard surfaces (Frost, 1990; Tinsworth & Kramer, 1990; U.S. Consumer Product Safety Commission, 1981, 1991/1997). A fundamental tenet that is widely accepted for adults has yet to be understood or accepted for children. Accidents are preventable through the development of strong safety programs but risk is inherent in all play activities. Designers and sponsors of playgrounds must ensure that steps are taken to reduce serious injuries while allowing for challenges essential for healthy growth.

The extent of hazards on playgrounds has been documented in several national surveys (of public schools, community parks, and preschools), three published by the American Alliance for Health, Physical Education, Recreation, and Dance (AAHPERD) (Bruya & Langendorfer, 1988; Thompson & Bowers, 1989; Wortham & Frost, 1990), three by the Consumer Federation of America (Sikes, Fise, & Morrison, 1992; Wood, Fise, & Morrison, 1994) and two by the National Program for Playground Safety (Hudson, Olsen, Thomson, & Olsen, 2004; Hudson, Thomson, & Olsen, 2004).

The AAHPERD surveys published in 1988, 1989 and 1990 revealed that among public school, community park, and preschool playgrounds, public schools were the most hazardous. Generally, playgrounds in all three surveys were antiquated, hazardous, and unfit for children's play. Maintenance was slipshod or nonexistent.

By 2004 national safety surveys of playgrounds were beginning to show improvement in child care, school, and park playgrounds on the National Program for Playground Safety's survey using their SAFE model (Hudson, Thomson, & Olsen, 2004). This was a survey of 3000 playgrounds during on-site visits during 2003. The model elements are: (1) supervision, (2) age appropriate design, (3) fall surfacing, and (4) equipment and surfacing maintenance. Among the four factors in the SAFE model, only supervision was judged to have declined from the earlier survey in 2000, moving from a grade of B- to C. The factors mentioned as needing improvement were movement of supervisors about the playground and the failure to design structures, especially composite or super-structures, for good visibility, thus allowing supervisors to see the children. This, of course, is also an issue of equipment design.

The assigned grade on age appropriate design nationwide increased from a C to C+, yet distinct separation of equipment for 2- to 5- and 5- to 12-year-old children declined between 2000 and 2003 from 41% of play spaces to 29%. Fall surfacing increased from a C to B- with 82% of all playgrounds surveyed using suitable loose-fill or unitary materials under and around playground equipment. The bad news is that only 19% of playgrounds surveyed had maintained loose surfacing at the proper depth. The overall grade for equipment maintenance increased from C+ to B- but concern was leveled at increasing problems with deterioration on metal and wood structures compared to plastic structures. Gaps and head entrapments that threaten entrapment and strangulation continued to be problem areas, and inspection and maintenance of surfacing and equipment continued to be central areas of concern.

The National Program for Playground Safety (Hudson, Thomson, & Olsen, 2004) compared their 2004 survey data for the 12 states that have adopted CPSC in some fashion to those states not adopting CPSC safety guidelines. The overall safety grade for the 38 states not adopting CPSC in the NPPS study was C+ but the overall grade for the 12 states adopting CPSC was B. The overall conclusion was that playgrounds in the states with standards were better designed and maintained than those in states not adopting CPSC, with the exception of separating areas for 2- to 5- and 5- to 12-year-old children.

A dozen states have adopted the CPSC safety guidelines in some form. A prevailing issue is whether mandating safety will have detrimental effects on creativity in design and use of playground equipment. Clearly, design of equipment is only one important factor in ensuring reasonably safe play places for children. Other important considerations are installation of equipment, maintenance and supervision of playgrounds, and the promoting of cognitive and motor skills for children who use playgrounds. Children with poorly developed perceptual-motor skills are at risk on any playground. Making children safe for playgrounds may be as important as making playgrounds safe for children (Frost & Henniger, 1979; Sutterby & Frost, 2002).

Playgrounds for All Children: Inclusion

In July 1990, the Americans with Disabilities Act (ADA) was passed into law. This law mandates that all public services and accommodations, including playgrounds, be inclusive, that is, that they be accessible to all children, regardless of disability. The access board developed accessibility guidelines (ADAAG) for play areas which guide playground sponsors in determining whether their playgrounds are accessible. The guidelines focus on accessibility for wheelchairs, thus providing primarily for children with motor disabilities. This is accomplished in several ways including: providing compact resilient surfacing such as manufactured wood chips or compact rubber surfacing to reach play equipment; providing transfer stations to allow children who are able to leave their wheelchairs to climb to a deck and return to their wheelchair by sliding down a slide and crawling across the resilient surface; providing playing with play elements at ground level, such as game panels and sand tables; and permitting transfer from wheelchairs to special swing seats with back supports.

Such modifications, though useful, do not facilitate imaginative, interactive, dramatic social play at each child's highest level of ability (Malkusak, Schappet, & Bruya, 2002, p. 67). The "accessible playground segregates those with disabilities to one portion of the playground and the 'fun stuff' is located elsewhere" (p. 68). Children want to be in the middle of play in fun places with their friends. One of the present authors visited Lady Allen of Hurtwood's "adventure playgrounds for handicapped children" in London in 1978 (see Allen, 1974; Frost & Klein, 1979). These were the most accessible the author has seen for children with different types of disabilities. In order to improve accessibility and movement, a creative person designed and built a rolling vehicle with some qualities of wagons and tricycles to match each child's disability. This allowed the children to travel an extensive array of roads or tracks to access materials, equipment, and natural features including gardens, sand, and water.

An important criterion for selecting playground equipment and materials is the play value or the degree to which the play materials match the developmental needs of the child (Frost, 1992b; Frost, Wortham, & Reifel, 2005). This criterion includes equipment for children with special needs. Playgrounds need to provide for mobility, accessibility, play options, proximity, sensory-rich materials, and challenges for all children (Arroyo, 1990; Esbensen, 1991; Frost, 1992a; Moore, Goltsman, & Iacofano, 1987).

Children with disabilities need to have the same opportunities as other children to interact with the environment through direct experiences with materials and equipment. Inclusive playgrounds need to provide for interactions among children of all mental and physical capabilities (Arroyo, 1990). Some of the developmental delays in visually impaired children can be attributed to lack of experience, especially in gross motor interactions with the environment (Schneekloth, 1989).Observations of children with disabilities at play indicate that most adults underestimate children's abilities to engage in ever more complex play and to learn from their play. A fundamental tenet regarding children with disabilities is that they can learn and they want to learn.

Play Leadership

Perspectives for the future include the training of play leaders. Perhaps the best play leadership training is modeled after that of the Scandinavian adventure playground movement and the playwork training in England. With all the social issues facing the United States today, play leaders can perform a very important role in supporting the play of children in playgrounds. It is not enough for play leaders to be good supervisors. They need to possess technical expertise and creative curiosity, knowledge of children, a sense of humor, leadership capability, community involvement skills, and basic principles of affirming children's play (Barnet, 1969; Vance, 1982).

A long-time play leader in London described the proper role of a play leader as a person who learns from children, who listens to them, and who understands what they are saying (Lambert, 1992). The attitude must be, "Let's find out!" It is as tough as the play leader discovering what it is like to be a child the second time around. They must be willing to relate well to children, to engage in the adventure of play, and to make available to children the materials and tools they need. The responsibility for the playground must be a shared one so that maintenance and potential vandalism become less of a problem and more of a challenge.

The term *play leader* has been replaced by *playworker* in many European settings, especially in Great Britian. Recognition of playwork as a vocational area gained its own vocational qualification in England, Wales, Scotland, and Northern Ireland as recently as 1992 (Bonel & Lindon, 1996). A readable, practical book by Davy (2001) provides supportive material for playwork courses as well as for all adults responsible for children at play.

Playworkers are adults who support and help children play through providing resources, and an atmosphere of safety and security in environments dedicated to children's play. Playworkers are trained to keep children at the center of the play process, to empower them in their play, to develop relationship with the child's family, to provide equal opportunity, and to extend the child's play world (Bonel & Lindon, 1996, pp. 15–17). In England the Playwork National Vocational Qualification certification requires completion of an extensive series of study units, the development of an extensive portfolio, and on-the-job experience at a play center (Bonel & Lindon, 1996; Davy, 2001).

Fraser Brown, a senior lecturer in the playwork program at Leeds Metropolitan University and Brian Chessman, a course leader at the same university, write that the essential purposes of playwork are: enabling children to pursue their own play agendas; providing opportunities for experimentation and exploration; creating environments that address the effects of play deprivation and bias; responding to children's play cues; helping children develop a sense of self; and introducing flexibility and adaptability into play environments (Brown & Chessman, 2003, p. 4). Frost, Wortham, & Reifel (2005, pp. 377–381) summarized the appropriate roles of playground supervisors, play leaders or playworkers (adults who oversee and facilitate children's play) as follows: The play leader

- studies children;
- ensures that children have access to challenging playscapes;
- prepares the child for risks, challenges, and hazards;
- prepares children for play;
- focuses on the creative aspects of play;
- extends the child's world;
- helps children cope in an increasingly chaotic world; and
- steps aside and lets children play.

One of the most frequently asked questions by child care, school, and park administrators, and one of the most common complaints in litigation refers to the appropriate ratio of adult supervisors to children on playgrounds. A number of guidelines by professional organizations and regulations by states prescribe ratios for child care center classrooms. The regulations typically prescribe the same ratio for playground play (except for field trips and swimming pools which require greater ratios). The National Association for the Education of Young Children, which operates the largest national accreditation program for child care centers, prescribes a ratio ranging from one adult to three infants (birth to 12 months) to one adult to 12 or 15 children (depending on group size) for 9- to 12-year-olds (McCracken, 1999). The National Program for Playground Safety also recommends that the ratio of adults to children on school playgrounds should be the same as the indoor ratio (Thompson & Hudson, 2001, p. 265).

Emerging Alternatives to Traditional Playgrounds

Threats of violence in community parks, absent or working parents, and the poor quality and growing standardization of many existing playgrounds are resulting in the development of alternative playgrounds, particularly in cities. Some educators have proposed a new type of playground, the safe-haven playground (Brett, Moore, & Provenzo, 1993). The safe-haven playground would be supervised by a play specialist, be available year-round from early morning until dark, and provide a wide variety of activities through an informal educational process.

Play specialists have proposed the concept of a temporary playground (Brett, Moore, & Provenzo, 1993; Poole & Poole, 1982). A mobile play unit would take "the playground" to the children. This concept appears ideal for taking raw materials, such as sand and water activities, to playgrounds that lack these opportunities. In England, surplus double-decker buses are used for this purpose. The London Handicapped Adventure Playground Association uses small buses to transport children from all over London to three specially designed adventure playgrounds that employ trained play leaders, provide special safety features, and offer a wealth of challenges for children with disabilities.

Children's museums now located in cities throughout the nation are shining examples of positive, wholesome approaches to alternative places for children's play and learning. In addition, special playgrounds are being developed at special places. Growing awareness of the therapeutic qualities of outdoor play has influenced hospitals to complement indoor playrooms with outdoor playgrounds. Further, commercial agencies are developing pay-for-play places at an unprecedented rate. A number of negative features of these commercial play places must be resolved, however, if they are to win the support of professionals who work closely with children.

Playgrounds at fast food restaurants have expanded rapidly in recent years. They were originally miniature replicas of public playgrounds with modifications for color and appeal. Following a pattern of injuries and litigation, sponsors are replacing original equipment with "soft play" equipment, intended to be ultra safe, yet appealing for large motor activity, follow-the-leader, and chase games. Soft play equipment is enclosed by barriers or nets to prevent falls and is used primarily at fast food outlets because of their expense and small amount of space available. Studies by operators show that these play areas quickly compensate for their cost through customer attraction. The developmental benefits for children are limited, but these play areas help to compensate for the absence of neighborhood play spaces.

Indoor pay-for-play centers are also expanding across the country. They respond to growing concerns about safety, violence, and deprivation of play opportunities for children (Frost & Jacobs, 1995). Pay-for-play entertainment complexes are now at theme parks, gambling casinos, and strip shopping malls. Because of fears of drugs, kidnapping, drive-by shootings, and violence in general, parents are increasingly restricting children from playing in public playgrounds, particularly inner-city playgrounds.

Much of the activity at pay-for-play centers, however, is not spontaneous, creative play. Junk food parties, violent video games, and games of chance in noisy crowded clusters are essentially *entertainment*, which deprives children of time for creative play and constructive time with parents. Such activities often serve as devices for absent fathers who fulfill fathering responsibilities by annual trips to theme parks with their children or an occasional weekend trip to the local pay-for-play entertainment center. Television and video games have also become the entertainment of choice and necessity for many children, thereby restricting active, creative play and consequently, depriving children of social, intellectual, and physical development as well as therapeutic play. In response to these conditions, new playground alternatives are being developed.

The New Generation of Playgrounds

Among the alternatives to common, standardized playgrounds equipped with a superstructure and swings are those created by members of the Community Built Association (CBA; http://www.communitybuilt.com). The CBA is an organization formed in 1989 to promote the transformation of public places by means of such elements as murals, playgrounds, parks, museums, public gardens, sculptures, and historic sites through collaboration between professionals and community volunteers. Their work has expanded to include projects on five continents, including hundreds of playgrounds. Although the members prescribe to high quality professional standards, their creative energy, including extensive input from community workers has led to extraordinary, creative playgrounds surpassing in many respects the standard playgrounds so common at schools and community parks. For example, Rusty Keeler of Planet Earth Playscapes (http://www.earthplay.net) works with communities worldwide to develop play environments featuring free-flowing grassy hills, trees, sculptures, boulders, herbs, sand and water, and more. These are designed to be accessible by all children.

Leathers and Associates, has led hundreds of communities in projects that simulate and intertwine with nature to provide motor, social, and cognitive challenges. Much of their genius is in their extensive involvement of communities, both children and adults, in planning and building. Recently, Bob Leathers and his colleagues designed and constructed a 45-foot high tree house in the Cayuga Nature Center for climbing, simulating the habits of animals, providing educational exhibits, climbing walls, tunnels, and treetop viewing of plant and animal life.

Boundless Playgrounds (http://www.boundlessplaygrounds.com) assists communities throughout the nation in all phases of planning, funding, designing, and building playgrounds that go well beyond the typical ADA accessible playgrounds in providing for the diverse disabilities of children. Whether the disability is motor, sensory (e.g., visual, auditory), or developmental (e.g., autism, Down's syndrome), playgrounds sponsored by Boundless Playgrounds ensure that at least 70% of all play activities can be enjoyed by all children.

Such organizations as those briefly described above are gradually influencing more creative thought about children's playgrounds in child care centers, schools, community parks, zoos, and children's museums. Fortunately, a growing number of playground equipment manufacturers are beginning to search for novel means to meet diverse play needs. The emerging new generation of playgrounds must provide for the broad developmental needs and be accessible to all children. New generation playgrounds must integrate the best of what is known about traditional playground equipment with natural materials and settings, including wild places, gardens, and animal habitats, and they must provide challenging yet reasonably safe havens for children's play.

References

Allen, Lady, of Hurtwood. (1974). *Adventure playgrounds for handicapped children*. London: James Galt.

American Society for Testing and Materials. (1999). *Standard specification for impact attenuation of surface systems under and around playground equipment*. West Conshohocken, PA: The Society.

Arroyo, F. (1990). Designing play for all. *Parks and Recreation, 25*(8), 40–43.

Axline, V. (1947). *Play therapy*. Boston: Houghton-Mifflin.

Barnet, D. (1969). Staffing for socio-educative activities for children. *International Playground Association, 3*(6), 23–25.

Beckwith, J. (1982). It's time for creative play. *Parks and Recreation, 17*(9), 58–62.

Berk, L. E. (1994). Vygotsky's theory: The importance of make-believe play. *Young Children, 50*(1), 30–39.

Bonel, P., & Lindon, J. (1996). *Good practice in playwork*. Cheltenham, UK: Stanley Thornes.

Brett, A., Moore, R. C., & Provenzo, E. F. (1993). *The complete playground book*. Syracuse, NY: Syracuse University Press.

Brown, F., & Chessman, B. (2003). Introduction: Childhood and play. In F. Brown, (Ed.), *Playwork: Theory and practice* (p. 4). Philadelphia, PA: Open University Press.

Bruya, L. D., & Langendorer, S. J. (Eds.). (1988). *Where our children play: Elementary school playground equipment*. Reston, VA: American Alliance for Health, Physical Education, Recreation, and Dance.

Cavallo, D. (1981). *Muscles and morals: Organized playgrounds and urban reform, 1800–1920*. Philadelphia: University of Pennsylvania Press.

Consumer Product Safety Commission (1981). *A handbook for public playground safety*. Washington, DC: The Commission.

Davy, A. (2001). *Playwork: Play and care for children 5–15*. London: Thomson Learning.

De Groot, E. B. (1914). Playground equipment. *Playground, 7*, 439–445.

Erikson, E. H. (1950). *Childhood and society*. New York: Norton.

Esbensen, S. B. (1991, November). *Playground design and mainstreaming issues: Beyond ramps*. Paper presented at the annual conference of the National Association for the Education of Young Children, Denver, CO.

Frost, J. L. (1985). The American playground movement. In J. L. Frost & S. Sunderlin (Eds.), *When children play* (pp. 165–170). Wheaton, MD: Association for Childhood Education International.

Frost, J. L. (1986a) Children's playgrounds: Research and practice. In G. Fein & M. Rivkin (Eds.), *The young child at play* (pp. 195–211). Washington, DC: National Association for the Education of Young Children.

Frost, J. L. (1986b). Planning and using children's playgrounds. In J. S. McKee (Ed.), *Play: Working partner of growth* (pp. 61–67). Wheaton, MD: Association for Childhood Education International.

Frost, J. L. (1990). Young children and playground safety. In S. C. Wortham & J. L. Frost (Eds.), *Playgrounds for young children: National survey and perspectives* (pp. 29–48). Reston, VA: American Alliance for Health, Physical Education, Recreation and Dance.

Frost, J. L. (1992a). *Play and playscapes*. Albany, NY: Delmar.

Frost, J. L. (1992b). *Playground guidelines for school systems* (Report No. PS-021-083). Austin: University of Texas at Austin. (ERIC Document Reproduction Service No. ED353-082)

Frost, J. L. (2001). *Cause and prevention of playground injuries: Case studies*. Wheaton, MD: Association for Childhood Education International.

Frost, J. L. (2004). How adults enhance or mess up children's play. *Archives of pediatrics and adolescent medicine, 158*(1), 16.

Frost, J. L., Brown, P., Sutterby, J. A., & Thornton, C. (2004). *The developmental benefits of playgrounds*. Olney, MD: Association for Childhood Education International.

Frost, J. L., & Henniger, M. L. (1979). Making playgrounds safe for children and children safe for playgrounds. *Young Children, 34*(5), 23–30.

Frost, J. L., & Jacobs, P. J. (1995). Play deprivation and juvenile violence. *Dimensions, 23*(3), 14–20, 39.

Frost, J. L., & Klein, B. L. (1979). *Children's play and playgrounds*. Boston: Allyn & Bacon.

Frost, J. L., & Sweeney, T. B. (1996). *Cause and prevention of playground injuries and litigation: Case studies*. Wheaton, MD: Association for Childhood Education International.

Frost, J. L., Wortham, S. C., & Reifel, S. (2005). *Play and child development* (2nd ed.). Columbus, Ohio: Prentice–Hall/ Merrill.

Gehlbach, R.D. (1991). Play, Piaget, and creativity: The promise of design. *Journal of Creative Behavior, 25*, 137–144.

Goodenough, E. (Ed.). (2003). *Secret spaces of childhood*. Ann Arbor: University of Michigan Press.

Gutteridge, M. V. (1939). *A study of motor achievements of young children*. New York: Archives of Psychology, Columbia University.

Hudson, S., Olsen, Thomson, D., & Olsen, M. S. (2004). The 2004 safety report card. *Today's playground, 4*(5), 18–20.

Hudson, S., Thompson, D., & Olsen, H. (2004). Do the CPSC guidelines make a difference? *Today's Playground, 4*(6), 13–17.

Lambert, J. (1992). *Adventure playgrounds*. (Available from "Out of Order Books" 24 High Street, Winchedon, MA, 01475. 508-297-9729).

Landreth, G. L. (1991). *Play therapy: The art of the relationship*. Muncie, IN: Accelerated Development.

Malkusak, T., Schappet, J., & Bruya, L. (2002). Turning accessible playgrounds into fully integrated playgrounds: Just add a little essence. *Parks and Recreation, 37*(4), 66–69.

McCracken, J. B. (1999). *Playgrounds: Safe and sound*. Washington, DC: National Association for the Education of Young Children.

Mero, E. B. (1908). *American playgrounds: Their construction, equipment, maintenance, and utility*. Boston: American-Gymnasia.

Moore, R. C., Goltsman, S. M., & Iacofano D. S. (Eds.). (1987). *Play for all guidelines: Planning, design, and management of outdoor play settings for all children*. Berkeley, CA: MIG Communications.

Moore, R. C., & Wong, H. H. (1997). *Natural learning: Creating environments for rediscovering nature's way of teaching*. Berkeley, CA: MIG Communications.

Nabhan, G. P., &Trimble, S. (1994). *The geography of childhood: Why children need wild places*. Boston: Beacon Press.

Poole, G. S., & Poole, B. L. (1982). Parks and playgrounds as adjunct classrooms. *Parks and Recreation, 17*(9), 63–66.

Rivkin, M. S. (1995). *The great outdoors: Restoring children's right to play outside*. Washington, DC: National Association for the Education of Young Children.

Rubin, K. H., Fein, G. G., & Vandenberg, B. (1983). Play. In P. H. Mussen (Ed.), *Handbook of child psychology* (Vol. 4, pp. 693–774). New York: Wiley.

Sapora, A. V., & Mitchell, E. D. (1948). *The theory of play and recreation*. New York: Ronald Press.

Schneekloth, L. H. (1989). Play environments for visually impaired children. *Journal of Visual Impairment and Blindness, 83,* 196–201.

Shell, E. R. (1994). Kids don't need equipment, they need opportunity. *Smithsonian, 25*(4), 79–86.

Sikes, L., Fise, M. E., & Morrison, M. L. (1992). *Playing it safe: A nationwide survey of public playgrounds*. Washington, DC: Consumer Federation of America.

Sutterby, J. A., & Frost, J. L. (2002). Making playgrounds fit for children and children fit on playgrounds. *Young Children, 57*(3), 36–42.

Talbot, J. (1985). Plants in children's outdoor environments. In J. L. Frost & S. Sunderlin (Eds.), *When children play* (pp. 243–251). Wheaton, MD: Association for Childhood Education International.

Talbot, J., & Frost, J. L. (1990). Magical playscapes. In S. C. Wortham & J. L. Frost (Eds.), *Playgrounds for young children: National survey and perspectives* (pp. 215–234). Reston, VA: American Alliance for Health, Physical Education, Recreation and Dance.

Thompson, D., & Bowers, L. (Eds.). (1989). *Where our children play: Community park playground equipment*. Reston, VA: American Alliance for Health, Physical Education, Recreation and Dance.

Thompson, D. & Hudson, S. (2001). Children and playground injuries. In J. L. Frost (Ed.), *Children and injuries*. Tucson, AZ: Lawyers and Judges.

Tinsworth, D. K., & Kramer, J. T. (1990). *Playground equipment-related injuries and deaths*. Washington, DC: U.S. Consumer Product Safety Commission.

U.S. Consumer Product Safety Commission. (1997). *Handbook for public playground safety*. Washington, DC: U.S. Government Printing Office. (Original work published 1981, 1991)

Vance, B. (1982). Adventure playgrounds: An American experience. *Parks and Recreation, 17*(9), 67–70.

Ward, A. (1987). Are playground injuries inevitable? *Physicians Sportsmedicine, 15*(4), 162–168.

Wood, B., Fise, M. E., & Morrison, M. L. (1994). *Playing it safe: A second nationwide safety survey of public playgrounds*. Washington, DC: Consumer Federation of America.

Wortham, S. C., & Frost, J. L. (Eds.). (1990). *Playgrounds for young children: National survey and perspectives*. Reston, VA: American Alliance for Health, Physical Education, Recreation and Dance.

35
Play as Ritual in Health Care Settings

LAURA GAYNARD

Children confronted with chronic illness, disabilities, and intense or repeated health care experiences face unique physical, emotional, and mental challenges (Bauman, Drotar, Leventhal, Perrin, & Pless, 1997; LeBlanc, Goldsmith, & Patel, 2003; Sheldon, 1997). From a social–emotional perspective, the process of becoming a hospital patient involves:

- Mortifying experiences involving loss of self-integrity and dignity;
- Unpleasant and frightening procedures involving pain;
- Traumatic separation from family, home, and community;
- Loss of bodily comforts, disruption of routines, intrusive, scary noises, and sleep deprivation;
- Exposure to an overwhelming array of strangers;
- Introduction to a foreign and threatening environment;
- Real or imagined fears about mutilation and death (Clark, 2003; Northam, 1997; Reed, Smith, Fletcher & Bradding, 2003).

This process is frightening and disconcerting for individuals of any age. It is especially difficult for children due to their limited life experience, the immaturity of their information-processing and coping abilities, and the negative impact on their developing self concept (Hanton, 1998; Kain, Mayes, Wang & Hofstadter, 1999; Pless et al., 1994; Sheldon, 1997; Weiland, Pless, & Roghmann, 1992).

The Value of Play in Health Care Settings

To reduce the potential developmental disruption created by childhood hospitalization, health care personnel have implemented and researched the effectiveness of various interventions. Among these interventions are programs centered around play (American Academy of Pediatrics, 2000; LeBlanc & Ritchie, 2001). As the most natural activity of childhood, play in health care environments is an essential element in reducing the degree of threat perceived by children in the new and unfamiliar surroundings (American Academy of Pediatrics, 2000, 2003; Haiat, Bar-Mor, & Shochat, 2003). Play in health care settings functions to optimize children's development, facilitate learning, and promote the expression of feelings. Various forms of play activities can provide young patients with diversion from discomfort, boredom, and pain; and continued development in all domains and peer interactions. Play tends to motivate children to comply with health care regimens, to soothe and comfort young patients and help children cope effectively with their health care experiences (Birch, 1997; Oremland & Oremland, 2000; Rush, 2003; Webster, 2000; Youell, 2001).

The health care professionals who most often facilitate play with children in health care settings are the child life specialists, who are certified members of the pediatric health care team. A central goal of child life programming is to enhance children's ability to cope and feel competent in health care environments, not only to minimize the stresses of illness, injury, and treatment, but ideally to make it a positive, growth-enhancing experience (Child Life Council, 2001; Gaynard et al.,1998; Haiat et al., 2003).

In addition to the benefits of play cited above, it is possible that the play of young patients may serve an additional purpose. Children in health care settings may seek out, and become involved in, play for *ritualistic benefits*. It makes sense that the loss of control and the accompanying stress that young patients experience when confronted with health care challenges, compel them to play in ritualistic ways. Thus, one value of play for young patients is the provision of ritualized behavior that:

- Is self-comforting;
- Increases their perceived sense of control over illness, disability, institutionalization, and their subsequent physical and emotional responses
- Helps prepare them for impending medical procedures.

Ritual, in the play of young patients, can ameliorate the trauma of health care experiences.

The Value of Ritual

Scholars define the term *ritual* as both an established form of conducting a religious rite and as any practice or behavior repeated in a prescribed manner (Flexner, Stein, & Su, 1980). The dictionary defines ritual as an established form of a ceremony; the order of words prescribed for a religious ceremony; a ceremonial act or action (e.g., dance); a customarily repeated series of acts; a performance of actions according to religious law or social custom; or, relating to a rite or rites (Merriam-Webster, 1999). The term *rite* refers to "a prescribed form or manner governing the words or actions for a ceremony or the liturgy of a group" (Merriam-Webster, 1999, p. 1011).

Ritual behaviors may sometimes be ceremonial and connected with religious experiences, or not. The term *ritual* can be applied to individual behaviors as well as group experiences (Brussat & Brussat, 1996; Clark, 2003; Miracle, 1986). Ritual behaviors are peculiar to humans, a universal characteristic of the human animal, and one that has allowed the individuals who performed rituals to survive better than those who did not. In fact, in human evolution the imperative to establish ritual has been more pressing and immediate than the need to produce tools. Yet, the way in which human behavior manifests rituals is directly related to culture; that is, individuals learn specific ritual behaviors. Humans perform ritual and ceremonies deliberately, not instinctively. But, beneath the performance of ritual, some scholars maintain there lies an innate human behavioral tendency that aids survival (Dissanayake, 1992, 2000).

Although rituals vary in form from one society to another, they occur in response to strikingly similar circumstances. All societies observe "rites of passage", which are rituals "associated with a crisis or a change of status for an individual" (Merriam-Webster, 1999, p. 1011). These rites of passage tend to ceremoniously mark states of transition between one significant state and another (e.g., birth, puberty, marriage, death). People also perform rituals to assure prosperity or good fortune in such contexts as hunting, raising crops, curing illness, obtaining absolution, achieving reunification and mediation, and proclaiming allegiances. People perform rites to mark significant changes between seasons, sickness and health, discord and concord, and so forth (Dissanayake, 1992). Ritualistic behavior, in whatever form, is a coping mechanism that humans often practice to deal with uncontrollable situations.

In circumstances that they perceive as threatening, troubling, or uncertain, where strong emotions are stirred up, humans have the tendency not just to fight, flee, or wait, as other animals might, but "to do something." One scholar has referred to this quality as "the imperative to act" (Lopreato, 1984, p. 299).

More than any other living creature, humans deliberately try to do something to affect their own welfare, to influence, forestall, transform, or otherwise control; to bring extreme or untrustworthy situations under control by extraordinary intervention. Control is regarded here as influencing, harnessing, or bringing oneself into alignment in both the social and physical realms. What is controlled, then, in these situations, is oneself, in a manner that is personally (if not socially) satisfying and meaningful. By controlling one's behavior one can feel, by analogy, that the provoking situation is also under control. One is "doing something" about the situation. (Clark, 2003; Dissanayake, 1992). Malinowski (1922), for example, describes how, during a terrifying storm, a group of Trobriand Islanders with whom he lived chanted charms together. Whether or not the gale subsided, the measured rhythm of the chanting and the sense of social unity it provided was more soothing than uncontrolled, noncoordinated, fearful reactions.

Thus, in uncertain circumstances, following the "imperative to act," things are done to bring about desired results and to deal with feelings of anxiety. The effect of ritual actions is surely to make people feel better. Indeed, one might suggest that humans do not so much expect ritual practices to work—though people certainly hope that they will—as to deliver them from anxiety (Clark, 2003; Dissanayake, 1992).

Ritual and Play

Numerous scholars assert that play and ritual serve similar needs in cultural contexts. As previously stated, ritual behaviors are universal, found in every human society, as are play behaviors. The purpose of rituals includes stating and publicly reinforcing the values of a group of people; uniting a group in common purpose and belief; explaining the inexplicable, such as birth, death, illness, or natural disaster; and attempting to control life and make it bearable. People play for similar reasons (Abrahams, 1986; Clark, 2003; Dissanayake, 1992).

As is true of ritual, play includes a special order, realm, mood, or state of being. The penchant for acknowledging an extraordinary realm is inherent in the behavior of both play and ritual, where actions are "not for real." Ritual and play are set off from real or ordinary life. Play is preceded by the acknowledgment by the players that they recognize it as an extra-ordinary dimension of experience. This is also true of rituals, which, by their very nature, are either exceptional kinds of experiences or acts outside the daily routine. Rituals highlight common occasions or make them more significant, such as prayer at mealtime or storytelling before bedtime (Brussat & Brussat, 1996; Dissanayake, 1992, 2000).

Both ritual and play use various means to arouse, capture, and hold attention. Both can serve as a "container" for, and molder of, feelings. Moreover, in both play and ritual the player can manipulate responses. The rhythm and form of play can expand, contract, excite, calm, and release feelings of the involved players (Clark, 2003; Oremland & Oremland, 2000). Ritual also tends to have a similar emotional climate for those involved. In both play and ritual, one or more of the "players" control the script and can manipulate the outcome according to their desires (Jessee & Gaynard, in press).

Ritual Play for Self-Comfort

The self-comforting aspect of ritualized play can be very important to young patients. Humans share with other animals a preference for order rather than disorder. Regularity and predictability are the ways we make sense of our world; understanding or interpreting anything means recognizing its structure or order. A major source of anxiety for children coping with chronic illness and frequent health care procedures is that they feel little control over their lives. It is often difficult or impossible, for example, to predict exacerbations or relapses of illness. Normal daily routines are frequently interrupted for the child and family by treatments, clinic visits, hospitalizations, symptoms from the illness itself, and side effects of medications (Clark, 2003).

When hospitalized, children experience even less predictability about their lives. It is usually impossible to know when procedures and tests will take place, and hospitalized children are forced to interact with an overwhelming number of staff, many of whom are strangers. Young patients are often unable to predict who will come to visit and when. They may be unable to control what and when they will eat or drink, and, in some situations, children even lose control of bowel and bladder due to illness and treatment. In sum, on a daily basis, child patients struggle with a continual lack of control that is exacerbated by regular clinic visits and unpredictable admissions to the hospital. This often results in considerable anxiety.

The literature on human behavior points out that action, in and of itself, can be soothing and reduce stress, and that humans tend to be happier when taking action over their environment rather than when merely waiting passively for events to happen (Csikszentimihalyi, 1997). Activity that is deliberately or actively shaped feels more effective and soothing than uncontrolled random flailing about, and it is a more effective coping behavior. Even non-human animals tend to use action to shape feelings of anxiety or despair. Caged animals sometimes move repetitively in formalized obsessive movements. Male chimpanzees, for example, may rhythmically run about, slap the ground, and vocalize when distressed during thunderstorms. This rhythmic mode is also sometimes present in human behavior. We rhythmically tap toes, drum fingers, and wiggle various body parts as ways of relieving impatience, boredom, or worry (Clark, 2003; Dissanayake, 2000).

In health care settings, the simple, familiar action of play is comforting in itself to both child and parents. Play reduces anxiety because it is a child's familiar medium. Additionally, it allows children to engage actively in interaction or activity that they can control, which is often a rare experience for young patients. Within the hospital setting, for example, children are able to choose where they want to play, who they will play with, what they will play, and for how long. Play is the only activity in the hospital over which children can exercise control, and one of the only experiences to which children can say "No."

During play interactions young patients are able to express energy and anxiety through a multitude of acceptable, fun activities. As is often the case with ritual behaviors, such expressive play helps children shape and channel feelings via a safe, familiar, and soothing behavior that becomes a container for the fear, anxiety, and frustration hospitalized children typically experience (Clark, 2003). Parents, too, tend to experience a decrease in distress as they observe their child engaging in a "normal" activity such as play. As parents and family members are able to interact with their children through the familiar medium of play, they are reassured to see normal play behaviors that had diminished since their child's admission to the hospital. The return of play ritual often leads to decreased distress and an increase in effective coping abilities and feelings of control for both young patients and their parents (Gaynard et al., 1998).

Rhythm and Repetition for Self-Comfort and Self Control

Rhythm and repetition alone are positively enjoyable and have anxiety-reducing, self-comforting properties. Rhythm is the inevitable result of repetition and is a most pervasive environmental fact. In brain waves and circadian rhythms, in lunar and solar cycles, repetition and rhythm characterize animate and inanimate nature. Breathing, sucking, and crying, the infant's earliest repertoire, are all performed rhythmically (Dunn, 2001; Hicks, 1995). Older infants and children, healthy or compromised, respond to both stress and joy by rhythmic, repetitive action, from head banging and rocking to spoon banging and marching. A steady rhythm seems to establish and sustain a predictable ground or "frame" that helps individuals cope more easily with, or even ignore, disturbances caused by the pain and discomfort of illness, injury, and health care. Repetition and rhythm also give shape to time and can increase children's perceived control. There is comfort in simply repeating an action. This process explains how humans can transform obsessive or soothing actions into the movements, chants, and gestures of ritual ceremonies. The repeated individual displacement activities, or "comfort movements" provoked by personal uncertainty and stress, often become ritualized behaviors that reduce distress created in perilous or confusing circumstances (Dissanayake, 1992, 2000).

It is not unusual for children who are stressed or traumatized to engage in "ticlike" self-comforting behaviors that appear to stem from anxiety. Children will pick their noses or their skin, pull out eyebrows or eyelashes, incessantly scratch and rub various parts of their bodies. Other children will rock in their beds or cribs for long periods of time, or cry in a rhythmic manner (Honig, 1993; Lewandowski & Baranoski, 1994; Varley & Furukawa, 1990). Although some of these actions can be considered self-mutilating, they tend to comfort young patients who are observed to engage spontaneously in these ritualized behaviors in a repetitive manner with considerable compulsion.

Young patients sometimes utilize rhythm and repetition to cope with health care experiences during invasive procedures. For example:

John is a renal patient who has needed hemodialysis for most of his 11 years. At the beginning of each dialysis session (3½ hours, three times a week) nurses place two very large needles, one in a vein and one in an artery. Several years ago, John spontaneously began blowing in a rhythmic manner during needle insertions to help himself cope. Just prior to these invasive experiences John closes his eyes, "thinks happy thoughts," and begins slow rhythmic blowing. When John feels the prick of the needle his blowing becomes faster but still maintains a repetitive rhythm. As the pain subsides John's blowing slows, and as the tape is positioned he takes several deep breaths and relaxes. John tells me that his blowing helps him cope effectively with the invasive health care procedures he frequently experiences, and he often requests music (via a personal stereo) with a strong beat which, he reports, "helps me, even more, through the hard part."

Another example of a young patient who frequently uses rhythm and repetition to cope with health care experiences is Cindy, an 8-year-old dialysis patient.

Cindy enjoys painting a great deal and is particularly attracted to this type of activity. When Cindy is hospitalized, she receives hemodialysis in her room, which means she remains in bed for 3½ hours. Child life staff provides play interactions with Cindy during her dialysis time to enhance her coping skills. The staff members have noted that Cindy's art takes on increased intensity and is more repetitive and rhythmic during dialysis. During these times, Cindy draws only scribbles or doodles and becomes totally engrossed in the pulsating beat she creates with her strokes. Cindy repeatedly draws one symbol, totally covering a piece of paper, then moves to another page without missing a "beat." When Cindy begins a new page she draws a different symbol, and she repeats the pattern, rhythmically covering the page, then moving on to the next. Staff notes that when Cindy is drawing in this manner she appears more calm and relaxed than when observed in other play interactions during hospitalizations.

Whether children transform anxiety into repetitive, patterned art movements or ritualized "ticlike" behaviors, rhythmic movement appears to help young patients feel control over their feelings of distress associated with health care. Repetitive play often has a major role in this self-comforting ritual and adults can facilitate its beneficial functions.

Adult-Guided Play with Young Patients

Historically, play theorists have expressed concern that adult-guided play is a contradictory term, that adult-guided interactions and activities cannot be considered true play. Child life professionals, however, have asserted that the intervention-focused play that characterizes many child life programs provides benefits for young patients struggling to make sense of health care experiences. Research regarding the value of adult-guided play with young patients shows that this form of play assists the coping and well being of children in health care settings (American Academy of Pediatrics, 2000; LeBlanc & Ritchie, 2001). What is most important is that young patients have opportunities to experience a variety of forms of play while in hospitals, including both spontaneous and adult-guided forms, and that the play adults facilitate has children's voluntary participation and includes children's intrinsic objectives as well as adult extrinsic objectives.

Preparation Play and Ritual

Because a major source of distress for young patients is the lack of knowledge and understanding about impending medical procedures, many child life programs include psychological preparation through which children and their families are introduced to the circumstances and procedures they will encounter. The value of these programs in reducing emotional disturbance in hospitalized children is well documented in the literature (Claar, Walker, & Barnard, 2002; Hatava, Olsson, & Lagerkranser, 2000; Kolk, van Hoof, & Fiedeldij Dop, 2000; O' Connor-Von, 2000).

Effective psychological preparation for young patients takes the form of adult-guided play during which the child life professional provides information of importance to the child and family in a manner that is comprehensible and age appropriate. For example, the child life specialist often engages young patients in doll play to show them what they will see, hear, taste, smell, and feel during a procedure, and to demonstrate how the medical equipment will be used. The adult then encourages the young patients to play through that procedure on the doll to help them gain a greater understanding and knowledge of forthcoming events (Gaynard et al., 1998).

Adult goals in facilitating these play interactions include:

1. Increasing young patients' sense of predictability regarding a specific procedure or health care experience;
2. Increasing perceived sense of control;
3. Reducing distress from unrealistic fantasies about the procedure;
4. Increasing effective coping;
5. Dispelling confusion and misconceptions (Gaynard et al., 1998; Goldberger, Gaynard, & Wolfer, 1990; Stephens, Barkey, & Hall, 1999).

In addition to achieving these goals, however, preparation play may also provide ritualistic benefits. In general, the practice of preparation rituals marks transitions, assures good fortune or prosperity, satisfies the "imperative to act" when faced with a threatening situation, or increases a sense of control about specific situations. Many children in the United States, for example, leave an offering of cookies and milk for Santa Claus on Christmas Eve in hopes that he will leave many gifts for them under the tree. Similarly, children in Nepal routinely light devotional lamps that represent the Hindu god Narayana in hopes that their household will be protected (Dissanayake, 1992).

Thus the goals of preparation rituals are similar to the goals of all preparation play: control, safety, and mental preparation for an uncertain event. Through this play, young patients can help to shape and understand the information regarding the upcoming medical event that has created anxiety. The event becomes comprehensible and structured, in other words, ritualized, thus becoming less distressing (Clark, 2003; Dissanayake, 1992).

For young patients with chronic illnesses who experience a multitude of health care procedures, preparation play often becomes ritualistically repetitive in idiosyncratic ways. For example:

Nina was a 5-year-old girl with leukemia who was admitted to the hospital every six weeks for chemotherapy and a spinal tap. I would usually meet Nina on admission to the hospital. Subsequent to the start of her IV medicine Nina would announce to me that she needed to perform a spinal tap on her doll in the treatment room. Using actual medical equipment, Nina and I would enact the procedure on her doll in preparation for Nina's spinal tap the following morning. As is typical of many chronically ill children, Nina was meticulous during the preparation play, being very careful to include every detail of the procedure. Nina would also be very vocal when I would do something "wrong" in my role-play as the "nurse."

I observed that, with each admission, the preparation play became increasingly ritualistic. The play always had to be conducted on the evening of Nina's admission, in the treatment room, with a doll as a patient and the use of actual medical equipment. Nina monitored our play so that it included every detail of the actual lumbar puncture, and she protested any variation. Furthermore, Nina was adamant that she "needed" to play through the lumbar puncture with the doll only once each admission, whereas many other children want to engage in endless preparation play. If I was not available to facilitate Nina's preparation play she became highly distressed reflecting a disruption of her preprocedure ritual.

Many pediatric health care professionals have similar anecdotes of young patients' ritualized preparation play behavior. The children have unique play rituals that are most supportive for them in preparing for, and coping with, procedures (Clark, 2003). What all of these children share is the tendency to seek out health care play that is repetitive and ritualistic in their own meticulously similar manner.

Separation Play and Ritual

A significant portion of the distress involved in the process of becoming a young patient can be attributed to separation of the child from home, family, and community. The child is taken out of the home, sometimes due to traumatic circumstances, and delivered to an institution that imposes a whole new set of rules and a standard "patient identity." In the absence of family members, hospitalized children often feel abandoned and experience significant difficulties as they attempt to understand what is happening to them in the hospital and why it is happening (Loranger, 1992; Sheldon, 1997).

Although recent hospital policies typically allow 24-hour visitation for parents, they are usually not able to stay with their child 24 hours a day due to obligations at home or work. Single parents are especially challenged, as are families with numerous children, as well as those with little or no extended family in the vicinity of the hospital. Many children hospitalized in large medical centers come from long distances and are especially disconnected from their home and community.

Even in situations where parents and other caregivers are readily available to the child, the young patient typically experiences the most significant stress points without parental presence. For example, children are usually separated from their caregivers when they experience procedures in the intensive care unit, induction for surgery, and the most invasive health care experiences (Fein, Ganesh & Alpern, 2004; Powers & Rubenstein, 1999; Sacchetti, Guzzetta & Harris, 2003), Thus, the experience of separation is inherent in the process of hospitalization.

Many hospital play programs provide opportunities for children to engage in play specifically planned to reduce the anxiety associated with separation. This form of play includes:

- Reading stories to children that have a separation theme;
- Facilitating symbolic play such as peek-a-boo and going-and-coming-back again games with bubbles, balls, cars, and other toys;

- Hiding-and-finding games, such as finding shapes inside a sorting toy, playing with pop-up toys;
- Pairing separation themes with dramatic play family figures or animal figures to help children play through separation issues (Gaynard et al., 1998).

One of the characteristics that is particularly impressive about separation play is that patients who are 6 years of age or younger often seek out separation play opportunities over other types of play (Gaynard & Bergen, 1986). In the situation described below, it is apparent that the theme of separation is paramount in this child's mind.

Ben was a 4-year-old boy who had been in the hospital for five days. His mother had needed to leave the hospital to care for Ben's siblings at home. Ben was taking a wagon ride around the hospital with one of the child life specialists soon after Mom's departure. As Ben and the child life specialist stopped to view one of the large fish tanks in the hospital the specialist asked Ben what the big blue fish was thinking. "He's sad," reported Ben promptly. "Why is the fish sad?" asked the child life specialist? "He misses his Mommy," responded Ben with certainty. "Where do you think his Mommy is?" inquired the specialist. "I don't know," Ben said sadly, appearing on the edge of tears.

This conversation prompted the child life specialist to take a wagon ride to the playroom where she could engage Ben in play focused on a separation-and-reunion scene with animal figures in which a baby animal is lost and is then found by the Mommy animal. This form of dramatic play with people or animal family figures can be highly therapeutic and reassuring for hospitalized children who are struggling with separation issues. As the baby animal looks for the parent animal the child life specialist has the opportunity to express sadness and fear that the parent will not be able to find the baby in the hospital. As the specialist plays the role of the baby (expressing feelings that the young child is often verbally not capable of expressing) the child usually picks up the parent figure and begins reassuring the baby that they will be found. Playing the role of the mother or father, the child reassures the baby that the parent is merely away from the hospital for a short time and for a realistic reason (e.g., is at work or taking care of siblings). This role reversal is, in itself, valuable for providing much needed assurance that the parent will return in the near future, and that child has not been abandoned. Then, in a matter of minutes, the young patient initiates a joyful reunion with the parent and baby, amidst hugs and kisses, playing out what the child longs to happen. Once again, this also is highly therapeutic and reassuring to the child. To indirectly experience in play what is so greatly desired, and to be able to control and contain that which provokes great anxiety, provides invaluable emotional support for young children in hospital (Gaynard et al., 1998).

As is true in preparation play, children vary in the unique, idiosyncratic details of the separation themes played out. The play takes on a ritualistic characteristic in the compulsion young patients seem to have to repeat this form of play over and over. Separation play also becomes ritualized in the way child patients re-create the play in exactly the same fashion, time and time again. It appears that children find ritualized separation play, in and of it self, calming and soothing. In the case of Ben, once the child life specialist introduced the play with the mommy and baby animals to him he requested to play with them over and over and appeared to want to endlessly play the "animal game." The specialist had to end the play each day, after about 30 minutes, by gently reminding Ben there were other children in the hospital with whom she needed to spend time. Furthermore, after the first couple of times, Ben would play out this theme with meticulous attention to detail, repeating the play sequence each time in the same manner, with the same story line that he reenacted every day. If the specialist added or changed details, Ben was quick to correct her: "No. That's not the way it goes."

Separation play is thus another form of expression that tends to become ritualized in the repetitive manner that young patients play.

Summary

In addition to providing other benefits for hospitalized children, play seems to fulfill their psycho-biological propensity to engage in ritualistic behaviors. Psychologists usually explain that play can be of therapeutic value in that it allows for sublimation and self-expression (Jessee & Gaynard, in press; Kranz & Lund, 1993; Oremland & Oremland, 2000). The reason such play is comforting and healing for child patients, however, has much to do with the fact that play allows them to order, shape, and control a small piece of their world. To repeat and pattern sounds, movements, and events seem to be innate tendencies in humans that provide pleasurable feelings of mastery, security, and relief from anxiety (Dissanayake, 1992, 2000).

It is likely that the play of young patients is a ritualistic coping mechanism similar to many other ritualistic behaviors universally practiced by humans during other times of crisis. As described in this chapter, such health care play can be spontaneous or adults can facilitate it to enhance effective coping responses of young patients. As is true in any environment where children play, however, the opportunities for child patients to control their lives as much as possible is of primary importance. Play and ritual often combine to help them accomplish that.

References

Abrahams, R. (1986). Play in the face of death: Transgression and inversion in a West Indian wake. In K. Blanchard, W. Anderson, G. Chick, & E. Johnsen, (Eds.), *The many faces of play* (pp. 29–44). Champagne, IL: Human Kinetics.

American Academy of Pediatrics. (2000). Child life services. *Pediatrics, 106*(5), 1156–159.

American Academy of Pediatrics. (2003). Clinical report. Selecting appropriate toys for young children: The pediatrician's role. *Pediatrics, 111*(4), 911–913.

Bauman, L. J., Drotar, D., Leventhal, J. M. Perrin, E. C., & Pless, I. B. (1997). A review of psychosocial interventions for children with chronic health conditions. *Pediatrics, 100*(2), 244–251.

Birch, M. (1997). In the land of counterpane: Travels in the realm of play. In A. J. Solnit, P. B. Neubauer, S. A. Abrams, & A. S. Dowling (Eds.), *The psychoanalytic study of the child, 52,* 57–75.

Brussat, F., & Brussat, A. (Eds.). (1996). *Spiritual literacy: Reading the sacred in everyday life.* New York: Touchstone

Child Life Council. (2001). *Child Life Council, Inc. official documents.* Rockville, MD: Author.

Claar, R. L., Walker, L. S., & Barnard, J. A. (2002). Children's knowledge, anticipatory anxiety, procedural distress, and recall of esophagogastroduodenoscopy. *Journal of Pediatric Gastroenterology and Nutrition, 34,* 68–72.

Clark, C. D. (2003). *In sickness and in play: Children coping with chronic illness.* Piscataway, NJ: Rutgers University Press.

Csikszentmihalyi, M. (1997). *Finding flow: The psychology of engagement with everyday life.* New York: Basic Books.

Dissanayake, E. (1992). *Homo aestheticus: Where art comes from and why.* New York: Macmillan.

Dissanayake, E. (2000). *Art and intimacy: How the arts began.* Seattle: University of Washington Press.

Dunn, J. R. (2001). Music and medicine: Clinical applications. An interview with Barry Bittman, M.D. *Psychology Online Journal, 2* (5), 1–6. (http://www.psychjournal.com)

Fein, J. A., Ganesh, J., & Alpern, E. R. (2004). Medical staff attitudes toward family presence during pediatric procedures. *Pediatric Emergency Care, 20*(4), 224–227.

Flexner, S., Stein, J., & Su, P. (Eds.). (1980). *The Random House dictionary.* New York: Random House.

Gaynard, L., & Bergen, D. (1986, March). *Young children's discovery of humorous incongruity in a hospital setting.* Paper presented at the annual conference of the Association for the Study of Play, Tempe, AZ.

Gaynard, L, Goldberger, J., & Laidley, L. N. (1991). The use of personalized dolls with hospitalized children: Techniques and benefits. *Children's Health Care, 20*(4), 216–224.

Gaynard, L., Wolfer, J., Goldberger, J., Thompson, R., Redburn, L., & Laidley, L. (1998). *Psychosocial care of children in hospitals.* Rockville, MD: Child Life Council, Inc.

Goldberger, J., Gaynard, L., & Wolfer, J. (1990). Helping children cope with health-care procedures. *Contemporary Pediatrics, 1*(3), 141.

Haiat, H., Bar-Mor, G., & Shochat, M. (2003). The world of the child: A world of play even in the hospital. *Journal of Pediatric Nursing, 18*(3), 209–214.

Hanton, L. B. (1998). Caring for children awaiting heart transplantation: psychosocial implications. *Pediatric Nursing, 24*(3), 214–218.

Hatava, P., Olsson, G. L., & Lagerkranser, M. (2000). Preoperative psychological preparation for children undergoing ENT operations: A comparison of two methods. *Paediatric Anesthesia, 10,* 477–486.

Hicks, F. (1995). The role of music therapy in the care of the newborn. *Nursing Times, 91*(38), 31–33.

Holden, P. (1995). Psychosocial factors affecting a child's capacity to cope with surgery and recovery. *Seminars in Perioperative Nursing, 4*(2), 75–79.

Honig, A. S. (1993, March). Mental health for babies: What do theory and research teach us? *Young Children,* 69–75.

Jessee, P., & Gaynard, L., (in press). Paradigms of play. In R. Thompson (Ed.), *Handbook of child life.* Springfield, IL: Charles C. Thomas.

Kain, Z. N., Mayes, L., C., Wang, S., & Hofstadter, M., B. (1999). Postoperative behavioral outcomes in children. *Anesthesiology, 90*(3), 758–765.

Kolk, A. M., Van Hoof, R., & Fiedeldij Dop, M. J. C. (2000). Preparing children for venepuncture. The effect of an integrated intervention on distress before and during venepuncture. *Child Care, Health, Development, 26,* 251–260.

Kranz, P. L., & Lund, N. L. (1993). Axline's eight principles of play therapy revisited. *International Journal of Play Therapy, 2*(2) 53–60.

Leblanc, M. & Ritchie, M. (2001). A meta-analysis of play therapy outcomes. *CounselingPsychology Quarterly, 14*(2), 149–163.

LeBlanc, L. A., Goldsmith, T., & Patel, D. R. (2003). Behavioral aspects of chronic illness in children and adolescents. *The Pediatric Clinics of North America, 50,* 859–878.

Lewandowski, L. A., & Baranoski, M. V. (1994). Psychological aspects of acute trauma: Intervening with children and families in the inpatient setting. *Child and Adolescent Psychiatric Clinics of North America, 3*(3), 513–529.

Lopreato, J. (1984). *Human nature and biocultural evolution.* Boston: Allen & Unwin.

Loranger, N. (1992). Play intervention strategies for the Hispanic toddler with separation anxiety. *Pediatric Nursing, 18* (6), 571–575.

Malinowski, B. (1922). *Argonauts of the western Pacific.* London: Routledge & Kegan Paul.

Merriam-Webster (1999). *Merriam-Webster collegiate dictionary* (10th ed.). Springfield, MA: Author.

Miracle, A. (1986). Voluntary ritual as recreational therapy: A study of the baths at Hot Springs, Arkansas. In K. Blanchard, W. Anderson, G. Chick, & E. Johnsen, (Eds.), *The many faces of play* (pp. 164–171). Champaign, IL: Human Kinetics.

Northam, E. (1997). Psychosocial impact of chronic illness in children. *Journal of Paediatric & Children's Health, 33,* 369–372.

O'Connor-Von, S. (2000). Preparing children for surgery—An integrative research review. *AmericanOrganization of Registered Nurses Journal, 71*(2), 334–341.

Oremland, E., & Oremland, J. D. (Eds.). (2000). *Protecting the emotional development of the ill child: The essence of the child life profession.* Madison, CT: Psychosocial Press.

Pless, I. B., Feeley, N., Gottlieb, L., Rowat, K, Dougherty, G. & Willard, B. (1994). A randomized trial of a nursing intervention to promote the adjustment of children with chronic physical disorders. *Pediatrics, 94*(1), 70–75.

Powers, K. S., & Rubenstein, J. S. (1999). Family presence during invasive procedures in the pediatric intensive care unit: A prospective study. *Archives of Pediatric and AdolescentMedicine, 153* (9), 955–958.

Reed, P., Smith, P., Fletcher, M., & Bradding, A. (2003). Promoting the dignity of the child in hospital. *Nursing Ethics, 10*(10), 67–76.

Rush, K. (2003). Restoring control: Medical play can pay off with pediatric patients. *Radiation Therapy Image, 16*(17), 14–15.

Sacchetti, A. D., Guzzetta, C. E., & Harris, R. H. (2003). Family presence during resuscitation attempts and invasive procedures: Is there science behind the emotion? *Clinical Pediatric Emergency Medicine, 4,* 292–296.

Sheldon, L. (1997). Hospitalizing children: A review of the effects. *Nursing Standard, 12*(1), 44–47.

Stephens, B. K., Barkey, M. E., & Hall, H. R. (1999). Techniques to comfort children during stressful procedures. *Advances in Mind–Body Medicine, 15,* 49–60.

Varley, C. K., & Furukawa, M. J. (1990). Psychopathology in young children with developmental disabilities. *Children's Health Care, 19*(2), 86–92.

Webster, A. (2000). The facilitating role of the play specialist. *Paediatric Nursing, 12*(7), 24–27.

Weiland, S. K., Pless, I. B., & Roghmann, K. J. (1992). Chronic illness and mental health problems in pediatric practice: Results from a survey of primary care providers. *Pediatrics, 89*(3), 445–449.

Youell, B. (2001). Recovery from trauma: Identification with the 'octor-montor' (doctor monster)—A description of psychotherapy with a 31/2-year-old boy who had come close to death at 10 days old. *Journal of Child Psychotherapy, 72*(3), 303–317.

36
Clinical Perspectives on Play

KAREN GITLIN-WEINER

In the interest of exploring "normal" and pathological behavior, the field of psychology has gone through many changes in the conceptualization of developmental functioning throughout the life span. Until fairly recently, psychological theorists had a limited understanding of the usefulness and applicability of play and the methods by which play could be used in therapy. Although interest in play began during the 1920s, the significance of the potential power of play as a change agent in treatment was underestimated and not fully examined for decades. Even within the various theories of personality development, scholars discussed the issue of *play* only in relation to a small fraction of human behavior.

Lacking a focused direction and innovative thinking about play, clinicians' interest in it as a method of treatment diminished substantially during the 1960s, 1970s, and first half of the 1980s. Since the mid-1980s, however, clinicians have significantly expanded their play-related theoretical ideas, treatment techniques, and assessment tools. Play is currently recognized as a distinct and valid treatment modality that facilitates adaptive functioning in a variety of areas, such as social, emotional, cognitive, and personality development. Because it is a central experience for children as well as a natural form of communication for them, play provides a unique opportunity to step into their world, as well as to have a positive and direct influence on their adaptive functioning.

Understanding Play

Although play is an essential activity that serves many unique purposes during the life span, the disparity of viewpoints about its meaning has impeded the development of a unanimously accepted definition. Many descriptions of play are too broad or too narrow to be functional or discriminative. Perhaps the concept of play is too complex, diffuse, expansive, and dynamic to allow a singular explanation of its distinctive characteristics and components. Yet researchers continue their efforts to grasp the special elements of play that make it different from other human activities and that allow it to be part of an effective healing process.

Common and Uncommon Definitions of Play

Some of the more common features that adults have associated with play suggest that it is pleasurable, the antithesis of work, free of extrinsic goals, an absorbing process involving the temporary loss of awareness of one's surroundings, nonliteral (having an "as-if" quality), spontaneous, an opportunity to bestow novel meanings onto objects, and an overt expression of wishes and hopes (Cattanach,

1992, 1994; DeMaria & Cowden, 1992; Garvey, 1977; Schaefer, 1993). These aspects are certainly relevant to the play of well-adapted individuals.

Psychologists who have observed the play behaviors of children with emotional disabilities, however, have challenged many of these commonly accepted defining characteristics of play. Children whose functioning has been compromised in other areas may show a variety of features in their play that are not similar to those generally stated, such as inflexibility, concreteness, constrictedness, impulsivity, irrationality, unreliability, inability to engage in or sustain imaginative play, and inability to use play to gain some distance from previously experienced negative and painful emotions (Hellendoorn et al., 1994; O'Connor, 1991). Although the quality of their play is often significantly different from those whose developmental course is on target, these children cannot be described as being unable to "play." For, indeed, their type and quality of play are important keys to understanding the difficulties therapists need to address in assisting the children to return to more appropriate developmental growth patterns.

Functions of Play

In response to this dilemma, some authors suggest that it is more useful for mental health workers to focus on the role of play rather than on its definition (Neubauer, 1987; Solnit, 1987). From this perspective, play therapists assess whether or not their use of play in treatment would serve a specific purpose, rather than assessing whether or not a child was actually engaging in "play" behaviors. This focus becomes even more important when the clinician understands that play alone does not create an effective therapeutic intervention. It is the pairing of the therapist's responses and the quality of the therapeutic relationship with play that promotes change.

There are four primary functions of play: biological, interpersonal, sociocultural, and intrapersonal (O'Connor, 1991). The biological functions include learning basic skills, expending energy, and experiencing kinesthetic stimulation. Practicing and achieving the separation–individuation phase of development and acquiring social behaviors are the categories incorporated under interpersonal functions. Exploring cultural roles and rehearsing individual ones are associated with the sociocultural domain. Especially important to psychological treatment is the intrapersonal function of play, which encompasses mastering of conflicts, learning to negotiate external situations, and meeting a basic need to "do something" instead of remaining idle.

Other authors who have further delineated the intrapersonal and interpersonal functions of play suggest that play promotes the development of problem-solving skills (Knell, 1993; White, 1966), is a source of self-esteem (Lewis, 1993), aids self expression and communication skills (Landreth, 1993), facilitates the definition of personal boundaries (Lewis, 1993; Irwin & Curry, 1993), provides opportunities to become exonerated from guilt feelings (Downey, 1987), and assists in the development of a working understanding of cause-effect relationships, predictions, and consequences (Bretherton, 1984).

Developmental Theories of "Normal" and "Abnormal" Play

Play skills are similar to social and cognitive skills, in that they follow a fairly specific normative pattern of development that moves along a continuum ranging from basic to very complex actions. At each stage, play is essential to the acquisition and mastery of multiple developmental tasks. This information is especially important when working with emotionally challenged individuals. Therapists must have a solid understanding of typical age-appropriate play behaviors in order to identify delays, deviations, fixations, or precocities, as well as to plan and implement effective treatment interventions. Therapists' understanding of how play competencies are achieved permits them to establish realistic expectations for the content of play, choice of play activities, types of toys, continuity of play, ability to differentiate reality and fantasy, and degree of interaction with the therapist. The use of play in treatment is most effective when the type of challenge the therapist presents matches the individual's skills and developmental level of functioning.

The most noted and relevant theories of play development are those of Piaget (1951, 1969), Peller (1954), Anna Freud (1965), Erikson (1977), Ekstein (1966), and Jennings (1990). Piaget's conceptualizaton of play is based on his more elaborate theory of cognitive development; that is, play is viewed as a forerunner to logical thought processes. With regard to play development, he suggests that there are three primary phases: practice/mastery or sensorimotor play; symbolic, representational, or pretend play; and game play with rules. During practice play, the primary focus of activities is on reflex actions, imitation of simple and complex behaviors, and the ability to modify the behaviors being imitated. The goal is to gain mastery over movements. Symbolic play begins when a sense of make-believe becomes part of the child's play at a conscious as well as unconscious level. The child's primary objective is to be able to encode experiences into images that can be recalled and combined. Finally, game play requires the development of concrete operational cognitive skills as well as a number of social skills. The goal is to be able to play cooperatively as well as competitively while thinking more objectively. Play, in each of these phases, assists in the process of assimilating and accommodating new information and experiences. Through play, children "mentally digest" and better understand personal experiences, thereby, assisting in the progress of development. Of particular significance to treatment is Piaget's implied notion that therapists need to match clients' cognitive level to the play therapy techniques they employ in order to have a positive outcome.

Instead of relating play to cognitive development, Peller (1954) describes how the various phases are indicative of an individual's attempts to master specific intrapsychic conflicts. She suggests that the first phase is associated with mastery of anxieties about the body; the second with anxieties about the loss of significant others; the third with anxieties about the loss of love; and the fourth with anxieties about peer relationships as well as those stemming from the superego. During each stage, the content and style of play will reflect the associated themes as well as any difficulties in how well the individual is reacting to and conquering these critical areas of conflict. Peller has provided an initial conceptual framework for using play to gain insight into the inner emotional world of the child.

Rather than focusing on inner discord, Anna Freud (1965) describes the role of play in fulfilling a positive need for pleasure which is obtained from a variety of sources. In the beginning, infants derive pleasure from their own bodies and from their nurturers. Subsequently, the focal point becomes a specific "transitional object," followed by an indiscriminate liking for various toys. Eventually, toys become less prominent after age 3 and fantasy becomes more significant. Finally, children begin to gain satisfaction in seeing the end product of a task. From this point forward, play behaviors dwindle as children delegate their energies to work and gain pleasure through internal constructs, such as the superego and ego ideal, instead of through extrinsic sources. Anna Freud's ideas provide the foundation for the understanding that play is not only an expression of inner conflicts but also serves a positive adaptive function.

Extending his theory of psychosocial development, Erikson (1977) provides a formulation of play development as it relates to how people interact with their external environment. His view outlines stages through which play proceeds, including the "autocosmos" (world of self), which involves the infant playing with her or his own body and eventually with the mother's body. The next stage is the "microsphere" (miniature world) in which play includes a limited number of toys that are employed to maintain contact with a small world of others. Finally, there is the "macrosphere" (shared world), when play actions involve a cooperative effort with a larger group of people. Erikson's work focuses the therapist's attention on the influence that interactions with others through play have on personal development. Additionally, he suggests that within each stage, play can also reflect an individual's attempts to understand and adjust to the effects of traumatic experiences. An important notion discussed by Erikson is that of play disruption which is indicative of a child's inability to cope with specific stressors. Play activities that touch upon these issues tend to stop and remain unfinished until the child achieves a resolution.

Ekstein's (1966) work brings forth yet another perspective. It describes play development as a process involving "deneutralization" of inner energy and an effort to gain the ability to delay impulses while finding adaptive solutions to problems. "Action without delay" is the first phase and is characterized by immediate satisfaction through impulsive efforts. Although play continues to be ruled by primary-process thinking in phase two, "play action," children begin to use language to mediate between the desire for immediate gratification of needs and their actions. The third phase, "fantasy play," results in children's thoughts becoming more functional as substitutes for behaviors; thus, the ability to use internal sources to meet certain emotional needs becomes available. Finally, in "play acting," children show the first signs of attempts to solve problems in various ways by trying them out in role playing. They continue to improve in their ability to delay impulses and to seek alternative solutions in more complex and refined ways through play.

The three developmental stages of play described by Jennings (1990) include embodiment play, projective play, and role play. Embodiment play describes the sensory exploration by the infant of the environment. Stories and narrations are associated with further investigation of objects in projective play. Dramatic play, in which the players restructure life events to gain a better understanding of the self and the world, occurs in the role play phase. During the second two stages, characteristics of the earlier one(s) may be evident. This is a particularly important point that is applicable to all of the theories and is essential for an accurate assessment. Without this knowledge, therapists might mistakenly conclude that temporary regressions are more serious developmental delays.

Evaluating "Normal" and "Abnormal" Play

When evaluating and treating children, therapists must have a practical understanding of normal, deviant, delayed, and precocious development in all areas of child functioning, including play. The theories of play development provide general guidelines, but they lack the specificity therapists need for implementing effective interventions. A wide variety of play assessment tools is now available to delineate details of normative behaviors at different ages; however, these still require study and investigation in relation to children in clinical care.

The current literature regarding normal development indicates that play serves multiple purposes in the growth process, in particular to help children seek adaptive defenses; acquire skills; cope with conflicts, deprivations, or environmental demands; understand the self and the world; learn how to become active in shaping experiences; explore alternatives and possibilities before choosing a solution to a problem; and develop the capacity for relatedness. Children typically exhibit each of these behaviors at different levels of sophistication in various age groups (Cattanach, 1992; Fall, 1994; Gil, 1991; Hellendoorn et al., 1994; Knell, 1993; O'Connor, 1991; Plaut, 1979). Psychologically healthy children spontaneously use such ageappropriate play behaviors in promoting their interpersonal and intrapersonal growth.

Children whose development is problematic, however, may have compromised abilities to spontaneously use these growth-promoting aspects of play. Their attempts to use play in a normative pattern often result in failure and reflect their specific difficulties. Therapists can use play observations to identify children who are temporarily having difficulty negotiating a specific developmental task and design play interventions that help these children reestablish their normal course of development (Crenshaw & Mordock, 2005; Gil, 1998a, 1998b; Kaduson & Cangelosi, 1997; Webb, 1999, Webb, 2004).

Therapists who use play as an intervention with clients who have serious impairments have a goal of assisting them in acquiring their highest possible level of functioning, rather than having them achieve age-appropriate functioning. Because play reflects symptom patterns, the clients often come to treatment with a diagnostic history of ineffective and dysfunctional play behaviors. Children diagnosed as obsessive compulsive, for example, may spend so much time setting up a game or play activity that they have little time left to play. Those children who have attention deficit disorders may begin multiple activities without completing any. Children with conduct disorders may directly express themes of power, sadism, or uncontrolled anger, and show little ability to use fantasy or verbalizations to mediate the intensity of these feelings. Those with borderline personality traits may show magical thinking, narcissistic themes, fear of annihilation, and splitting of the good and bad characters. Children diagnosed as psychotic may have such chaotic play that it is difficult to follow and interpret; these children are often especially unable to use play spontaneously to master conflicts, achieve developmental milestones, or gain understanding of themselves and significant others. As a result of play assessment, therapists more accurately can choose play techniques and treatment goals that meet the children's current level of functioning and projected potential for change (Gitlin-Weiner, Sandgrund, & Schaefer, 2000).

Play Theories and Play Therapies

Therapists who employ psychological treatment interventions use a number of theories that provide frameworks from which they may develop strategies, techniques, goals, and progress evaluations. These theoretical perspectives have grown out of clinical individual observations of adults that therapists have subsequently applied to children. Scholars have proposed modification of traditional theories and developed new theories as their understanding of human behavior has increased. Within each orientation, the global perspectives of a particular set of theoretical assumptions affect the functions they attribute to play.

With regard to treatment intervention, traditional modalities have focused on exposing and resolving troublesome feelings, conflicts, and traumas. More modern treatments have additionally concentrated on promoting positive growth in the personal, family, and social domains. In both, therapists have used play in treatment as a powerful instrument for addressing a wide variety of psychological problems (Bromfield, 1997; James, 1999; O'Connor, 2000; Schaefer, 2003)

The major theories are reviewed here in a simplified format, in which only the significant aspects pertaining to play are described. All of these orientations share the belief that play provides a fundamental forum for connecting with the child in a collaborative effort to resolve the presenting difficulties.

Over numerous sessions, play themes unfold and form into a "play narrative" that describes the child's unique life story. In play therapy, the client learns to develop new "scripts" for use in diminishing confusions, ambiguities, and overwhelming emotions, as well as to gain a sense of self-control and a more realistic sense of self. Because play is a mental process, clients can use it to experience thinking, imagining, pretending, planning, wondering, doubting, remembering, guessing, hoping, experimenting, revising, and working through. One of the most important features of play in treatment is that clients can do what they cannot do outside the therapeutic setting. Children who are overly controlled, for instance, can be spontaneous and free of inhibitions; chronically sad children can experience periods of delight and joy (Mayes & Cohen, 1993).

Psychoanalytic Theory and Play Therapy

The oldest comprehensive personality theory in psychology, psychoanalytic theory, is based on Sigmund Freud's (1953) instinct theory, which posits that the underlying force motivating behaviors is an innate state of excitation seeking tension release. Healthy development occurs when an individual maintains appropriate expression of this tension through the counterbalancing functions of the three structures of the psyche: the id (irrational, impulsive, instinctive features), the ego (rational component), and the superego (moral aspects, conscience). The central goal in this type of treatment is to help an individual gain insight into unconscious conflicts (obstacles that impede development) through the use of interpretation and working through (changing defensive strategies) in order to enable a higher level of adaptive functioning. When working with children, therapists use play activities to provide the opportunity to accomplish this. For each play action, there are multiple levels of meaning that the therapist needs to understand and reconfigure to support positive emotional growth. Each action also plays a part in reconstructing the past by recovering repressed memories associated with intrapsychic conflicts. To this end, the therapist uses play to observe the child, gain information, develop communication, and assist the child in expressing feelings.

Because play is seen as a means of gaining mastery, the child's tendency to repeatedly reenact difficult or traumatic experiences in play ("repetition compulsion") is a spontaneous and healthy effort to gain a sense of inner control. While play is considered to be a way to assist the individual in the pursuit of the "road to reality" (serving the needs of the ego), it is also understood to be guided by the "pleasure principle" (serving the needs of the id).

Anna Freud (1928, 1946, 1965) and Melanie Klein (1932) both believed that play provided a greater opportunity to understand and communicate with children. Freud was more conservative. Play was believed to be an indispensable means for developing a positive therapeutic relationship that helped the therapist connect with the healthier aspects of the child. Additionally, play revealed unconscious themes as well as the discovery of how the client managed conflicts (defense mechanisms). The focus of therapy moved from play to talking as soon as possible.

Klein believed that play was a natural substitute for verbalizations. She viewed the procedures of free association and free play as equivalent. The content of the play itself rather than the verbalizations that accompanied the play was the primary focus in the therapeutic process.

Many others have furthered the understanding of play within the psychoanalytic orientation. It has been suggested that play may be used as a source of wish-fulfillment and need-gratification; as an attempt to imitate others in order to explore new possibilities; and as a process of diminishing the negative impact of unpleasant external situations and traumas (Waelder, 1933). The cathartic function of play allows unvented feelings to be purged through the actions of fantasy characters (Greenacre,1959). Play has been described as an intermediary "space" providing a bridge between the child's inner and outer worlds. Therefore it is not only symbolic but also provides a very "real" and creative experience that is essential to emotional development (Winnicott, 1951, 1968, 1971). Through play, the child may obtain from others or achieve within the self what has not yet been acquired. An opportunity to gain a different perspective on past events by reexperiencing what has been too painful to absorb can be achieved through play. Therapeutic play occurs when the client and the therapist enter into the play in a cooperative effort to help resolve the presenting problems (Winnicott, 1951, 1968, 1971).

In play, employment of "projection" allows the child to cast negative or unwanted self-attributes onto inanimate therapeutic materials. The child can gain some distance from the problem, reconsider it from different points of view, and achieve a sense of self-assurance that it is manageable and not overwhelming. Because the play figures own the problem, the child is able to take on a role of a more objective problem solver (instead of victim) and help the figures learn to more effectively cope with the issues (Lowenfeld, 1939, 1967). A method based on projection, called "the world technique," allows children to play out experiences, thoughts, and feelings through miniaturized figures, thus broadening their self-understanding while working through difficulties that may be impeding healthy development.

> Play…expresses a child's relation to himself and his [sic] environment and, without adequate opportunity for play, normal and satisfactory emotional development is not possible…play [is] an essential function of the passage from immaturity to emotional maturity…"any individual in whose early life these necessary opportunities for adequate play have been lacking will inevitably go on seeking them in the stuff of adult life." (Lowenfeld, 1967, p. 321).

Proponents of ego psychology (Cangelosi, 1995) add that the relationship between therapist and patient, through play, is of critical importance, because it can provide a "corrective emotional experience" as well as support the more adaptive functioning of the individual.

Humanistic, Existential, and Gestalt Theory and Play Therapy

Humanistic, existential, and Gestalt theories view the individual as an integrated whole and each individual as capable of having a basically good, creative, purposeful, and trustworthy core self. Thus, the therapy focuses on enhancing psychological health rather than on correcting pathology. Transforming the basic belief system of humanistic psychology into practice, Carl Rogers (1951) developed client-centered therapy, a nondirective approach to working primarily with individual adults. The fundamental supposition underlying his work is the notion that there exists a universal and innate need for "self-actualization." If there is an imbalance between an individual's functioning level and environmental demands that prevent the gratification of this drive, inaccurate attitudes about the self, others, and the environment will evolve. Therefore, the goal of treatment is to provide the opportunity for clients to modify perceptions, replace symptomatic behaviors with self-acceptance, and achieve a more mature level of emotional development. Therapists with this view provide a nonjudgmental relationship within a permissive setting, expecting clients to use their intrinsic ability to heal themselves.

Virginia Axline (1947) adopted the rationale of client-centered therapy and modified it for work with children. Her framework stresses that the natural activity of play encourages self-expression as well as communication. Play provides a "holding environment" in which children are able to use optimally their internal resources toward achieving positive growth. The therapist reacts to the play in a reflective manner to empower the child with a greater understanding of the barriers preventing progress. Thus, the process of play itself is a therapeutic intervention, not merely an adjunct to another form of treatment (Kranz & Lund, 1993).

The actual experiencing of the "sense of relatedness" during the therapeutic play process is necessary for growth to occur (Moustakas, 1953, 1955, 1959, 1997). The security experienced within the alliance between therapist and client is the key component to a successful play intervention.

There are four stages of change in observable expression during the therapeutic process. The diffuse negative feelings of the first phase emerge into intensely hostile attitudes directed at specific individuals or events in the second phase. Through the experience of understanding and acceptance in the client–therapist relationship, these powerful emotions become less frenzied in the third phase and, at this point, positive emotions begin to emerge with the negative. In the final phase, there is an appropriate balance in feelings that leads to a more accurate perception of the self and the world.

The potential role of the birth trauma is emphasized in preventing an individual from developing adequate interactions with others (Allen, 1942; Taft, 1933). Play therapy assists the child to feel safe enough to experience an intense relationship with the therapist, allowing previous anxieties to diminish and therefore not hinder future relationships.

Gestalt play therapy is a process that provides activities and experiences to assist the child in strengthening the positive aspects of the self that have been suppressed, restricted, or lost (Oaklander, 1993, 1994). Play furnishes a secure setting in which the child is able to establish an adequate level of self-regulation and awareness of what she or he is doing and how it is being done.

Cognitive–Behavior Theory and Play Therapy

Cognitive–behavior therapy is derived from behavior and cognitive therapies, which developed separately before being united. Behaviorism (Bandura, 1969; Skinner, 1938; Wolpe, 1958) is based on the contention that behavior is lawfully determined, predictable, and environmentally controlled. Interventions are directed toward enabling new learning to take place or helping the client unlearn maladaptive habits through the use of reinforcement. Cognitive theory (Beck, 1963; Beck, Rush, Shaw, & Emery, 1979; Ellis, 1962; Kelly, 1963) focuses on internal thought processes (beliefs, assumptions, interpretations, logical distortions, imagery, and attitudes) and how these affect emotional experience, behavior, and personality development. Cognitive therapy aims to alter the underlying assumptions that dictate the client's perceptual views that have led to negative automatic thoughts. These theories have promoted the creation of multiple interventions designed to enhance self-management and self-regulation. Treatment is systematic and goal-directed, and it requires the client to be an active participant.

In cognitive–behavioral play therapy, the therapist is actively involved in selecting the direction of the play by introducing themes and toys in a specific manner that directly addresses the presenting problem(s) (Knell, 1993, 1996). The play, therefore, takes on an educational role. Specific skills, problem-solving strategies, and alternative cognitions or behaviors are modeled as well as practiced. For instance, the act of playing may serve to relax an overly anxious child while the therapist gradually presents the child with the source of the phobia through a systematic desensitization hierarchy.

In a less direct approach, puppets may model appropriate behaviors or coping self-statements to a child who has been socially unsuccessful. Through storytelling, repetitive nonproductive interactions between parent and child may be changed to more adaptive response patterns. In this way, the client can replace maladaptive thoughts, feelings, and behaviors with more functional ones. Play provides the opportunity to try out new ideas through role-playing or to participate indirectly by acting out the alternatives through play characters. In effect, the play acts as an experiment in which the client is able to identify a problem, look at the evidence, test alternatives, examine the consequences, and make choices for personal change by reenacting critical situations in a variety of ways.

Other Theories and Play Therapies

There are a variety of alternative play therapy theories and approaches that treat the child as an individual or within the context of a group.

Individual Child-Focused Approaches

The beliefs of Jungian play therapy (Allen & Levin, 1993; DeDomenico, 1994; McCalla, 1994) fall between the psychoanalytic and client centered approaches. This theory emphasizes the importance of the unconscious belief in development as destiny that moves forward by the search for "wholeness and completion." This theory views personality as the product and container of ancestral history, molded by the cumulative experiences of past generations. Play is an important medium in which clients can gain an understanding of the central theoretical suppositions while transforming their painful selves into healthier ones. Therapists observe patterns of play, which reflect such difficulties as emotional chaos as well as ineffective conflict resolutions, and then use this information to help the clients gain a higher level of functioning. Therapists assume that individuals will automatically choose play activities that are relevant to their personal struggles and developmental concerns. Play with sand using miniature figures, are especially important to this form of treatment. In addition to the standard therapeutic toys, therapists provide many unique items that hold ancestral symbolic meaning.

The first structured therapeutic use of play was based on the principles of release therapy (Levy, 1938) which evolved from work with children suffering from night terrors and posttraumatic stress disorders. Treatment involves repeatedly re-creating the traumatic experience within a secure, structured, and supportive environment until the associated negative thoughts and feelings diminish and become assimilated into nondestructive functioning. Structured play assists the client in managing overwhelming stress and provides time to recover when necessary.

Another structured play therapy approach encourages repeated expressions of powerful, negative emotions such as fear and rage without any negative consequences (Solomon, 1938). Through play, there is redirection of excessive emotional energy into more appropriate play behaviors. The focus is on a specific play situation reflecting the presenting problem. The goal is to work through the critical issue in a more productive manner (Hambridge, 1955). There are eleven preplanned play situations used which address common conflicts, such as sibling rivalry, peer attack, control by elders and separation (Solomon, 1938).

Limit-setting therapy (Bixler, 1949; Ginott, 1959, 1961) involves the process of setting limits as the principal means of effecting change. Maladaptive behaviors are seen as the result of a lack of trust in adults to provide consistency and protection. With limits, the child is able to learn to express intense feelings in more appropriate ways that have positive rather than negative consequences. Play involves having many rules concerning the use of toys. Clients cannot express hostile feelings through the destruction of materials. Instead, therapists encourage them to use the toys appropriately to express the same feelings.

Adlerian play therapists (Kottman, 1993, 1994) believe that there is a basic striving to gain a sense of "connectedness" with others as well as an underlying capacity to make choices and compensate for weaknesses. This form of treatment is based on Alfred Adler's (1927) holistic theory of the individual who is embedded in a social context. Play is used to establish a social interest in others through the relationship with the therapist, to understand inaccurate and inappropriate attitudes toward the self and others, to teach responsibility for setting and achieving realistic goals, to encourage acceptance of strengths and weaknesses, and to convey a sense of hope and encouragement. This theory stresses the importance of working with family members as well as peers within the play context, instead of working alone with the child, because the child constructs and modifies attitudes and behaviors within these relationships.

Involvement of others in play sessions is also part of filial therapy (B. Guerney, Guerney, & Andronico, 1966). The therapist supervises play interchanges among family members instead of directly engaging in play activities with the child The therapist provides instruction to the parents on play therapy techniques and behavioral procedures to enhance child management. This approach serves as a therapeutic medium for the child and a learning laboratory for the parents with the goal of improving parent–child relationships.

Theraplay (Jernberg, 1976; Jernberg & Jernberg, 1993; Munns, 1999) is a treatment modality based on the belief that a deficiency in emotionally positive sensory experiences during infancy has the potential for resulting in psychological difficulties in later life. Theraplay techniques are primarily nonverbal, direct, and physical, with play activities focusing on primitive and nurturing interactions. The therapist emphasizes the development of healthy relationships through lighthearted, empathic, and playful exchanges. Growth is an outcome of having an adult directly attend to the child's narcissistic needs while providing the developmentally appropriate amount of discomfort to foster change. The goal is to provide an intense bonding experience. It is particularly successful with children who have developmental delays and deviations that make them less responsive to more traditional play therapy approaches.

One of the more recent interventions is ecosystemic play therapy, which is a "hybrid model that derives from an integration of biological science concepts, multiple models of child psychotherapy, and developmental theory" (O'Connor, 1994, p. 61). This form of therapy views children's functioning as a reflection of their interpersonal interactions with various systems such as family, school, peer, cultural, legal, and medical. Play is used to promote healthy development during the six phases of treatment: introduction, exploration, tentative acceptance, negative reaction, growing and trusting, and termination. This method attempts to integrate the various functions of play into one inclusive treatment approach.

Group-Focused Approaches

Although many theories and interventions primarily focus on the treatment of the individual, each modality also has the potential to be practiced with groups. Adaptations of these models have resulted in a variety of methods that are specifically applicable to the group play therapy process which focuses on the patterns of interpersonal behaviors between participants and group leaders. (O'Connor, 1991; Rothenberg & Schiffer, 1976; Semonsky & Zicht, 1976; Slavson, 1976; Sweeney & Homeyer, 1999; Van de Putte, 1994). The therapist directs attention to common treatment goals surrounding specific issues such as socialization skills, coping with divorce or surviving abuse. Interventions are based on group dynamics which may fluctuate between supportive responses, catalytic reactions, or even collective negative responses in which the members unwittingly reinforce the pathology of each other.

The central objective of the majority of group play activities, which include role-playing, structured games, and collaborative artwork, is to assist members in developing age appropriate interpersonal skills (Bellinson, 2002; Schaefer & Reid, 2000). Through group play, children learn how their individual problem behaviors have an impact on their relationships with others. Additionally, they can practice corrective modifications of maladaptive behaviors. Many other social skills may be acquired, such as selecting and attending to relevant information, predicting logical sequences of events, anticipating consequences of actions, managing frustration, and learning to relax (O'Connor, 1991, p. 324).

Play-related groups allow children to have experiences that are similar to those they might encounter elsewhere. However, the safety and structure of the group enable them to be more productive in learning how to handle problems by experimenting with behavioral changes in a controlled environment where they can receive constructive feedback. Because these new skills have developed from direct experience, they are more likely to generalize to situations outside of treatment.

Children's play in the context of family therapy can be useful in uncovering and differentiating between dysfunctional and functional familial patterns (Ariel, 1992; Gil, 1994; B. Guerney et al., 1966; L. Guerney & Welsh, 1993; Schaefer & Carey, 1994; Van Fleet, 1994). Observations of play interactions among family members provide rich information on overt and covert communication patterns, individual and group expectations, and the multiple roles each member plays. There is an underlying assumption that the child's symptoms express the family's difficulties. Therapists use play to observe and treat attitudes, alliances, underlying feelings, nonverbal family functioning, goal-achievement processes, and problem solving methods. Interpretations of play behaviors facilitate the understanding of how each member of the family contributes to the presenting problem. There is a variety of family play interventions, ranging from teaching the parents to serve as change agents (B. Guerney et al., 1966; L. Guerney & Welsh, 1993; Kraft & Landreth, 1998; Van Fleet, 1994) to having the therapist play a more traditional role in helping the family members change the family system (Ariel, 1992; Gil, 1994; Schaefer & Carey, 1994).

The play environment provides a supportive place to test the limits and meanings of family relationships as well as to reenact current conflictual patterns at conscious and unconscious levels. Through play, the child becomes a productive and active member of the treatment team who is directly able to contribute to the process of change. The child feels less intimidated in confronting the parents and, therefore, can challenge previously undisclosed issues (family secrets) and resolve them with less anxiety. At the same time, the parents have the opportunity, to see the issues from the child's perspective and are able to experience the problem as being part of a shared systemic development rather than feeling as if they have been the sole source of blame for what has occurred.

The child's comfort with the play format is usually greater than the parents' comfort level. Therefore, the child can help the family become psychologically available to the play therapy process. As treatment progresses, the once difficult child can become the family hero. The family's discomfort is lessened as they learn more productive communication patterns as well as coping strategies through playful experimentation. More appropriate lines of authority are established and destructive power struggles are decreased. Since change occurs through the use of play, and play is a natural activity of childhood, the changes that occur in treatment are likely to be maintained at home, where family members can easily replicate these skills.

The Therapeutic Functions of Play

Since the early 1990s, a variety of formal and informal diagnostic techniques has incorporated play activities and observations. Therapists generally use these procedures as an adjunct to more traditional investigative methods, such as interviews, questionnaires, and standardized testing. Although many of the techniques do not yet have accompanying normative data, the information they glean from the tasks can be vital to confirming or disproving hypotheses about the presenting difficulties. Additionally, play provides the opportunity to assess many factors that are not included in other assessment procedures. Some of the advantages of using play in the assessment process include the ability to detect emerging skills that occur at a low frequency, observe problem-solving skills in action, observe the spontaneous use and integration of acquired skills, determine motivational factors, determine self-regulation and arousal levels, and repeat testing without a learning effect.

Although therapists have realized the importance of play in the therapeutic process, they have rarely identified the actual curative elements that are brought forth through the use of play. In general, they acknowledge that play provides an opportunity for clients to come to a new level of awareness of their individual situation, to experience the self as having choices and being able to try out new behaviors, and to explore the value of making changes. The question remains, however, about what specifically makes play so special in comparison to other forms of child treatment. That is, what are the unique characteristics of play that result in its being such a powerful change agent? Two authors have recently proposed some initial answers to this question.

Change as a Function of the Nature of Symbolic Play

Ariel (1992) focuses on the structural and psychosocial properties of make-believe play. This perspective views symbolic play as a mechanism for regulating the level of emotional arousal when confronting sensitive issues that bring forth intense and potentially overwhelming feelings such as fear, anger, joy, and sadness. Play not only enables clients to address their problems but also provides the framework for repairing inaccurate perceptions or conclusions that they may have developed. These changes occur through a sequence of events. First, the child expresses the problem through play themes that elicit varying levels of arousal. When overstimulation begins to occur, the child can spontaneously and immediately change play characters and themes to introduce more soothing components. Once relief is obtained and the threat of feeling out of control is diminished, the child can return to the original problem. In this way, negative themes can be safely replayed until they no longer elicit powerful feelings. Each time themes are reenacted, the child makes progress toward the therapeutic goal(s), using the processes of habituation, cognitive restructuring, deconditioning, and mastery (Ariel, 1992).

In addition to the function of regulating emotions, there are seven other important properties of symbolic play that make it such an effective treatment tool:

1. *Play framing:* invalid and unconscious attitudes that maintain inappropriate behaviors are challenged and weakened
2. *Owning and disowning the content of play:* inaccurate convictions about self and others are reconsidered and abandoned

3. *Basic duality:* play acts are controlled and observed, revealing conflicts in a safe manner
4. *Symbolism or "arbitrariness of the signifier":* play items can signify something else that has little similarity to the real object (e.g., a crayon or stick may be a sibling)
5. *Covert communication:* an indirect way to exchange messages in order to decrease resistance
6. *Symbolic coding:* representational language instead of objects is used to safely express painful messages
7. *Possible worlds:* exploration of formerly unrealized ways of understanding and solving problems including: actual potentials, unlikely possibilities, or improbable scenarios (Ariel, 1992).

Change as a Function of General Play Factors

Schaefer's (1993) consideration of the aspects of play that make it therapeutically valuable is not limited to make-believe activities. He delineates 14 essential curative play factors.

1. *Overcoming resistance:* play is an interesting and natural activity for children; play is more comfortable than talking; a working alliance is easier to establish; resistance and fears are decreased by expression through play figures instead of direct acting out; increased receptivity to intervention leading to positive change.
2. *Communication:* play increases understanding of the self as well as others; includes a unique type of interchange that is nonverbal and drive-dominated; allows expression of conscious and unconscious thoughts and feelings; increases the probability of critical issues being revealed.
3. *Mastery or competence:* play allows achievement of functional levels of self-esteem; promotes proficiency in all areas of development; "self-motivated activity" that produces a sense of effectiveness; allows practice of appropriate interactions and adaptive responses; decreases feelings of vulnerability; increases ability to take responsibility for own actions.
4. *Creative thinking:* play increases effective problem-solving skills; allows ability to consider multiple possible alternative responses and their consequences before choosing those that will actually be implemented; allows repeated experiencing of successful solutions; supports positive emotional growth; develops divergent thinking in a hands-on experience; allows for a broader range of creativity.
5. *Catharsis:* play provides a safe discharge of emotional tension onto play materials; results in a sense of relief from the motoric expression of intense feelings; increases the understanding of the individual's own emotional energies; increases the ability to move forward and successfully function.
6. *Abreaction:* play allows an intense discharge of affects associated with past stressful life events; uses play materials to replay traumas; mastery is accomplished; reexperiencing results in decreased anxiety; increases ability to imagine a more positive outcome to problems.
7. *Role-play:* play allows experimentation with new behaviors and different emotions; increases understanding of the perspectives of others; allows identification of self as a separate entity; allows the experience of empathy; encourages development of prosocial behaviors.
8. *Fantasy:* play increases a sense of control and compensation for unmet emotional needs and/or weaknesses; increases safe exploration of repressed ideas, feelings, and memories; increases resolution of conflicts; allows practicing of different coping techniques; provides a source of pleasure; promotes healthier levels of functioning; provides a limitless potential to enhance emotional development while overcoming delays or deviations.
9. *Metaphoric teaching:* play promotes the ability to act out play themes through miniature play figures, role-playing, or storytelling characters; provides the opportunity for the therapist to enter the play as a model for adaptation, controlling impulses, reducing excessive negative feelings,

and expressing conflicts in nondestructive ways; provides a sense of hope through collaborative work with the possibility of a positive ending.

10. *Corrective emotional experience:* play allows for the development of an accepting sense of self and pleasure in relationships.

11. *Attachment formation:* play facilitates a bond between the child and therapist.

12. *Relationship enhancement:* play provides a working relationship that is warm, respectful, and connected by mutual feelings of liking each other; considered to be essential to the development of a positive, loving self; minimizes vulnerability to devastating effects of traumas.

13. *Positive emotion:* considered to be a fundamental aspect of play; increases a sense of well-being; counteracts the effects of stressful experiences; provides emotional relief; restores energy as well as persistence needed to resolve problems; helps in "mastering developmental fears"; minimizes anxiety so that it does not impede functioning.

14. *Games:* play facilitates social, emotional, and cognitive development; provides experiences of impulse control, emotional regulation, competitive behaviors, and cooperative interactional skills; enhances the therapeutic alliance, communication, fantasy, catharsis, sublimation, insight, reality testing, ego functioning, recuperation, and adaptive expression of intense emotions (Reid, 1993).

Psychological interest in play has included a focus on descriptions of normal as well as pathological play development; on the role of play in personality development; on the use of play as an assessment tool; and on the therapeutic value of play in treating children with emotional disabilities and their families. Although play itself is difficult to define, many scholars recognize that play, in many variations, has an essential and universal role in the evolution of a well-adjusted and emotionally stable individual.

Although many acknowledge play's healing powers, those who engage in the play therapy process are aware that there still remain many gaps in our understanding of why and how play works. The existing theoretical base of information has only limited supporting empirical data. Even so, play has survived as a vital method of understanding and treating children; in fact, since the mid-1980s, there has been a resurgence of interest in it, which has resulted in a proliferation of new ideas, techniques, and procedures as well as attempts to formally associate play therapy with DSM-IV diagnoses (Landreth et al., 2005). Further exploration of uses of play in therapy is likely to confirm what therapists already know, expand their understanding, and extend their ability to implement playful therapeutic techniques.

References

Adler, A. (1927). *The practice and theory of individual psychology.* New York: Harcourt, Brace and World.

Allen, F. (1942). *Psychotherapy with children.* New York: Norton.

Allen, J., & Levin, S. (1993). "Born on my bum": Jungian play therapy. In T. Kottman & C. Schaefer (Eds.), *Play therapy in action* (pp. 209–244). Northvale, NJ: Jason Aronson.

Ariel, S. (1992). *Strategic family play therapy.* New York: Wiley.

Axline, V. (1947). *Play therapy.* New York: Ballantine.

Bandura, A. (1969). *Principles of behavior modification.* New York: Holt, Rinehart, & Winston.

Beck, A. (1963). Thinking and depression. *Archives of General Psychiatry, 9,* 324–333.

Beck, A., Rush, A. J., Shaw, B. E., & Emery, G. (1979). *Cognitive therapy of depression.* New York: Guilford.

Bellinson, J. (2002). *Children's use of board games in psychotherapy.* Lanham, MD: Rowman & Littlefield.

Bixler, R. (1949). Limits are therapy. *Journal of Consulting Psychology, 13,* 1–11.

Bretherton, I. (1984). Representing the social world. In I. Bretherton (Ed.), *Symbolic play: Reality and fantasy* (pp. 3–41). New York: Academic.

Bromfield, R. (1997). *Playing for real: Exploring the world of child therapy and the inner worlds of children.* Lanham, MD: Rowman & Littlefield.

Cangelosi, D. (1995). Psychodynamic play therapy. In A. Eisen, C. A. Kearney, & C. Schaefer (Eds.), *Clinical handbook of anxiety disorders in children and adolescents* (pp. 439–460). Northvale, NJ: Jason Aronson.

Cattanach, A. (1992). *Play therapy with abused children.* Philadelphia: Jessica Kingsley.

Cattanach, A. (1994). *Play therapy: Where the sky meets the underworld.* Philadelphia: Jessica Kingsley.

Crenshaw, D., & Mordock, J. (2005). *A handbook of play therapy with aggressive children.* NJ: Rowman & Littlefield.

DeDomenico, G. (1994). Jungian play therapy techniques. In K. O'Connor & C. Schaefer (Eds.), *Handbook of play therapy: Advances and innovations* (pp. 253–282). New York: Wiley.

DeMaria, M., & Cowden, S. T. (1992). The effects of client-centered group play therapy on self concept. *International Journal of Play Therapy, 1*(1), 53–68.

Downey, T. (1987). Notes on play and guilt in child analysis. *Psychoanalytic Study of the Child, 42,* 105–126.

Ekstein, R. (1966). *Children of time and space, of action and impulse.* New York: Appleton-Century-Crofts.

Ellis, A. (1962). *Reason and emotion in psychotherapy.* New York: Lyle Stuart.

Erikson, E. (1977). *Toys and reason.* New York: Norton.

Fall, M. (1994). Self-efficacy: An additional dimension in play therapy. *International Journal of Play Therapy, 3*(2), 21–32.

Freud, A. (1928). Introduction to the techniques of child analysis. *Nervous and Mental Disease Monograph, 48.*

Freud, A. (1946). *The psychoanalytical treatment of children.* London: Imago.

Freud, A. (1965). *Normality and pathology in childhood: Assessments of development.* New York: International Universities Press.

Freud, S. (1953). *The standard edition of the complete psychological works of Sigmund Freud* (J. Strachey, Ed. and Trans.). London: Hogarth.

Garvey, C. (1977). *Play.* Cambridge, MA: Harvard University Press.

Gil, E. (1991). *The healing power of play: Working with abused children.* New York: Guilford.

Gil, E. (1994). *Play in family therapy.* New York: Guilford.

Gil, E. (1998a). Essentials of play therapy with abused children. [videotape]. New York: Guilford.

Gil, E. (1998b). Play therapy for severe psychological trauma: The theory and practice of play therapy for trauma. [videotape]. New York: Guilford.

Ginott, H. (1959). The theory and practice of therapeutic intervention in child treatment. *Journal of Consulting Psychology, 23,*160–166.

Ginott, H. (1961). *Group psychotherapy with children.* New York: McGraw-Hill.

Gitlin-Weiner, K., Sandgrund, A., & Schaefer, C. (Eds.). (200). *Play, diagnosis and assessment* (2nd ed.). New York: Wiley.

Greenacre, P. (1959). Play in relation to creative imagination. *Psychoanalytic Study of the Child, 14,* 61–80.

Guerney, B., Guerney, L., & Andronico, M. (1966). Filial therapy. *Yale Scientific Magazine, 40,* 6–14.

Guerney, L., & Welsh, A. (1993). Two by two: A filial therapy case study. In T Kottman & C. Schaefer (Eds.), *Play therapy in action* (pp. 561–588). Northvale, NJ: Jason Aronson.

Hambridge, G. (1955). Structured play therapy. *American Journal of Orthopsychiatry, 25,* 601–617.

Hellendoorn, J., van der Kooij, R., & Sutton-Smith, B. (Eds.). (1994). *Play and intervention.* Albany, NY: State University of New York Press.

Hug-Hellmuth, H. (1921). On the technique of child-analysis. *International Journal of Psycho-Analysis, 2,* 287–305.

Irwin, E., & Curry, N. (1993). Role play. In C. Schaefer (Ed.), *The therapeutic powers of play* (pp. 167–187). Northvale, NJ: Jason Aronson.

James, O. (1999). *Play therapy: A comprehensive guide.* Lanham, MD: Rowman & Littlefield.

Jennings, S. (1990). *Dramatherapy with families, groups and individuals, waiting in the wings.* London: Jessica Kingsley.

Jernberg, A. (1976). Theraplay technique. In C. Schaefer (Ed.), *Therapeutic use of child's play* (pp. 345–350). Northvale, NJ: Jason Aronson.

Jernberg, A., & Jernberg, E. (1993). Family theraplay for the family tyrant. In T. Kottman & C. Schaefer (Eds.), *Play therapy in action* (pp. 45–96). Northvale, NJ: Jason Aronson.

Kaduson, H., & Cangelosi, D. (Eds) (1997). *The playing cure: Individualized play therapy for specific childhood problems.* Lanham, MD: Rowman & Littlefield.

Kelly, G. (1963). *A theory of personality.* New York: Norton.

Klein, M. (1932). *The psychoanalysis of children.* London: Hogarth.

Knell, S. M. (1993). *Cognitive–behavioral play therapy.* Northvale, NJ: Jason Aronson.

Knell, S. M. (1996). *Cognitive–behavioral play therapy.* Lanham, MD: Rowman & Littlefield.

Kottman, T. (1993). The king of rock and roll: An application of Adlerian play therapy. In T Kottman & C. Schaefer (Eds.), *Play therapy in action* (pp. 133– 168). Northvale, NJ: Jason Aronson.

Kottman, T. (1994). Adlerian play therapy. In K. O'Connor & C. Schaefer (Eds.), *Handbook of play therapy: Advances and innovations* (pp. 3–26). New York: Wiley.

Kraft, A., & Landreth, G. (1998). *Parents as therapeutic partners: Are you listening to your child's play.* Lanham, MD: Rowman & Littlefield.

Kranz, P., & Lund, N. (1993). 1993: Axline's eight principles of play therapy revisited. *International Journal of Play Therapy, 2*(2), 53–60.

Landreth, G. (1993). Self-expressive communication. In C. Schaefer (Ed.), *The therapeutic power of play* (pp. 41–64). Northvale, NJ: Jason Aronson.

Landreth, G. et al. (Eds.). (2005). *Play therapy interventions with children's problems: Case studies with DSM-IV-TR diagnoses* (2nd ed.). Lanham, MD: Rowman & Littlefield.

Levy, D. (1938). Release therapy in young children. *Psychiatry, 1,* 387–439.

Lewis, J. M. (1993). Childhood play in normality, pathology, and therapy. *American Journal of Orthopsychiatry, 63*(1), 6–15.

Lowenfeld, M. (1939). The world pictures of children: A method of recording and studying them. *British Journal of Medical Psychology, 18,* 65–101.

Lowenfeld, M. (1967). *Play in childhood.* New York: Wiley.

Mayes, L., & Cohen, D. (1993). Playing and therapeutic action in child analysis. *International Journal of Psycho-Analysis, 74,* 1235–1244.

McCalla, C. L. (1994). A comparison of three *play* therapy theories: Psychoanalytic, Jungian, and client-centered. *International Journal of Play Therapy, 3*(1), 1–10.

Moustakas, C. (1953). *Children in play therapy.* New York: McGraw-Hill.

Moustakas, C. (1955). The frequency and intensity of negative attitudes expressed in play therapy. *Journal of Genetic Psychology, 86,* 301–325.

Moustakas, C. (1959). *Psychotherapy with children.* New York: Harper & Row.

Moustakas, C. (1997). *Relationship play therapy.* Lanfield, MD: Rowman & Littlefield.

Munns, E. (1999). *Theraplay: Innovations in attachment-enhancing play therapy.* Lanham, MD: Rowman & Littlefield.

Neubauer, P D. (1987). The many meanings of play: Introduction. *Psychoanalytic Study of the Child, 42,* 3–10.

Oaklander, V. (1993). From meek to bold: A case study of Gestalt play therapy. In T. Kottman & C. Schaefer (Eds.), *Play therapy in action* (pp. 281–300). Northvale, NJ: Jason Aronson.

Oaklander, V. (1994). Gestalt play therapy. In K. O'Connor & C. Schaefer (Eds.), *Handbook of play therapy: Advances and innovations* (pp. 143–156). New York: Wiley.

O'Connor, K. (1991). *The play therapy primer.* New York: Wiley.

O'Connor, K. (1994). Ecosystemic play therapy. In K. O'Connor & C. Schaefer (Eds.), *Handbook of play therapy: Advances and innovations* (pp. 61–84). New York: Wiley.

O'Connor, K. (2000). *The play therapy primer* (2nd ed.). New York: Wiley.

Peller, L. E. (1954). Libidinal phases, ego development and play. *Psychoanalytic Study of the Child, 9,* 178–198.

Phillips, R. (1994). A developmental perspective. *International Journal of PlayTherapy, 3*(2), 1–20.

Piaget, J. (1951). *Play, dreams and imitation in childhood.* New York: Norton.

Piaget, J. (1969). *The mechanisms of perception.* New York: Basic Books.

Plaut, E. A. (1979). Play and adaptation. *Psychoanalytic Study of the Child, 34,* 217–232.

Reid, S. (1993). Game play. In C. Schaefer (Ed.), *The therapeutic powers of play* (pp. 323–348). Northvale, NJ: Jason Aronson.

Rogers, C. (1951). *Client-centered therapy.* New York: Houghton Mifflin.

Rothenberg, L., & Schiffer, M. (1976). The therapeutic play group: A case study. In C. Schaefer (Ed.), *The therapeutic use of child's play* (pp. 569–576). Northvale, NJ: Jason Aronson.

Schaefer, C. (Ed.). (1993). *The therapeutic powers of play.* Northvale, NJ: Jason Aronson.

Schaefer, C. (Ed.). (1998). *The therapeutic use of child's play* (pp. 569–576). Northvale, NJ: Jason Aronson.

Schaefer, C. (Ed.). (2003). *Foundations of play therapy.* New York: Wiley.

Schaefer, C., & Carey, L. (1994) *Family play therapy.* Northvale, NJ: Jason Aronson.

Schaefer, C. & Reid, S. (Eds.) (2000). *Game play: Therapeutic use of childhood games,* (2nd Ed.). New York: Wiley.

Semonsky, C., & Zicht, G. (1976). Activity group parameters. In C. Schaefer (Ed.), *The therapeutic use of child's play* (pp. 591–606). Northvale, NJ: Jason Aronson.

Skinner, B. F (1938). *The behavior of organisms.* New York: Appleton Century.

Slavson, S. (1976). Activity group therapy. In C. Schaefer (Ed.), *The therapeutic use of child's play* (pp. 577–590). Northvale, NJ: Jason Aronson.

Solnit, A. J. (1987). A psychoanalytic view of play. *Psychoanalytic Study of the Child, 42,* 205–219.

Solomon, J. (1938). Active play therapy. *American Journal of Orthopsychiatry, 8,* 479–498.

Sweeney, D., & Homeyer, L. (1999). *The handbook of group play therapy: How to do it, how it works, whom it's best for.* New York: Wiley.

Taft, J. (1933). *The dynamics of therapy in a controlled relationship.* New York: Macmillan.

Van de Putte, S. (1994). A structured activities group for sexually abused children. In K. O'Connor & C. Schaefer (Eds.), *Handbook of play therapy: Advances and innovations* (pp. 409–428). New York: Wiley.

Van Fleet, R. (1994). Filial therapy with children of alcoholics and addicts. In K. O'Connor & C. Schaefer (Eds.), *Handbook of play therapy: Advances and innovations* (pp. 371–386). New York: Wiley.

Waelder, R. (1933). The psychoanalytic theory of play. *Psychoanalytic Quarterly, 2,* 208–224.

Webb, N. B. (1999). *Play therapy with children in crisis: Individual, group and family treatment* (2nd ed.). New York: Guilford.

Webb, N. B. (2004). *Helping bereaved children* (2nd ed.). New York: Guilford.

White, R. (1966). *Lives in progress.* New York: Holt, Rinehart & Winston.

Winnicott, D. W. (1951). Transitional objects and transitional phenomena. In D. W Winnicott, *Collected papers* (pp. 29–242). New York: Basic Books.

Winnicott, D. W (1968). Playing: Its theoretical status in the clinical situation. *International Journal of Psycho-Analysis, 49,* 591–599.

Winnicott, D. W. (1971). *Playing and reality.* London: Tavistock.

Wolpe, J. (1958). *Psychotherapy by reciprocal inhibition.* Palo Alto, CA: Stanford University Press.

V

Particular Meanings Embedded in Play

Introduction

All play represents meanings that grow out of children's experiences. There are a variety of representational forms that embody varying intensities of play. Among the forms in which children represent their play are imagination, creativity, challenge, humor, and sexuality. Exploration, in contrast, is a step that precedes play (Hutt, 1976). This section focuses attention on some of these forms that represent particular strands that contribute to children's play experiences.

Girls and boys often demonstrate their distinct cultural experiences by the different ways in which they play. Nevertheless, they retain their personal power within their respective forms of play. Children also engage in sexual play. Their playing with sexual content or issues dealing with bodily functions may have considerably less (or more) meaning than an observing adult might infer. It might also be a way to predictably control adult and peer behavior when the child perceives that the meanings will engender negative attention. Sexual play represents children's particular event knowledge, as well as an opportunity to control potentially unacceptable or dangerous ideas in a safe context.

Fantasy, imagination, and risk-taking share with play a sense of empowerment and control. Although play and creativity share the possibility for children to make connections and have some elements of problem solving in common, adults might judge a phenomenon as creative only when a connection or solution is original, elaborative, or useful (Torrance, 1962). For a child, a new connection or solution to a problem may be new or original only to her or him.

Game play is also an important and meaningful activity for children of all ages and the types of games (competitive and cooperative; gaining money or popularity; showing knowledge or strategies) convey much about cultural and family values. Violence in play also reflects both personal and cultural meanings.

These reflections on the meaning of play to children suggest that meanings are specific to a particular personal and social context for each child. To help children feel increasingly competent and supported, adults who have contact with them have a challenging responsibility to continuously learn about the alternative perspectives and meanings that children bring to their play. Some of these understandings can occur when adults study the contexts from which children take their meanings, reserve judgments during sensitive observations, and attempt to try supportive alternative and adaptive responses, while continuing to care about children's meanings.

References

Hutt, C. (1976). Exploration and play in children. In J. S. Bruner, A. Jolly, & K. Sylva (Eds.), *Play—Its role in development and evolution* (pp. 202–215). New York: Basic Books.

Torrance, E. P. (1962). *Guiding creative talent.* Englewood Cliffs, NJ: Prentice-Hall.

37
Fantasy and Imagination

DOROTHY G. SINGER AND JEROME L. SINGER

Fantasy and imagination are two of the most powerful components of human experience. There are various definitions and theories of imagery (Bruner, 1964; Horowitz, 1978; Houtz & Patricola, 1999), computer models (e.g., Kosslyn, Margolis, Barret, Goldknopf, & Daly, 1990), and pioneering experiments on the delay of gratification (Mischel, Ebbeson, & Zeiss, 1972). Within these contexts, it is worthwhile to consider the origins of imagination and fantasy, moving from Piaget's sensorimotor stage to the concrete stage of operations, when the overt pretend behavior and symbolic play of the young child take the form of covert speech and more private imagery. Such observable play has helped scholars to assess imagination and consider the constructive uses of imaginative processes.

What Is Fantasy and Imagination?

When does the capacity for fantasy and imagination begin? One view suggests that 4-year olds are aware of the power of images and thought: "My four-year-old son and I play a game, naming the parts of each other's bodies we like the most.... 'Mama, the part of everyone's body I like the most is their head, what's inside their head—because that's how you think'" (Brickman, 1995, p. 14).

How we think, plan, daydream, imagine, fantasize—all of these processes have intrigued scientists and laypersons alike. One definition of imagery focuses on mental stimulation, or "the capacity to rehearse actions and activities, to explore the possible outcomes of these in the real world.... [I]magery functions in all areas of mental and physical life where adaptation and change are necessary or where there is a need better to understand existing states of affairs" (Marks, 1990, p. 7). Theorists have attempted to discover such origins through both physiological and psychological tests.

Images, according to brain researchers, appear to be associated with the right hemisphere of the brain and its functions, which include visual and auditory imagery, spatial representation, pure melodic thought, fantasy, and emotional components of ongoing thought (J. L. Singer & Pope, 1978). Different components of mental imagery ability, furthermore, might have different neuroanatomic loci (Farah, 1984). One study identified a number of case reports of adult patients who lacked the ability to visualize a mental image from stored long-term visual memory information (Farah, 1984). These patients evidenced damage in the left quadrant of the brain close to the posterior language centers of the left hemisphere. Many of the patients who manifested this particular lesion were unable to communicate their loss of imagery. Image generation per se, according to this study, appears to be a left hemisphere function, while spatial ability and higher visual processing may be a right hemisphere function.

Components of imagery such as kinesthetic/sensory, perceptual or structural, affective, and cognitive may all play a role in the forms of imagery expression. Jerome Bruner (1964) conceptualized three modes of representation of images: the enactive mode, which reflects events through motor responses (a baby waves "bye bye" without the words); the iconic mode, which selectively organizes individual perceptions and images (games such as playing space people); and finally, the symbolic mode, which transforms experience into abstract and complex methods of representation (the words used to describe an image without the physical representation).

Expanding on Bruner's model, Horowitz (1978) conceptualized a system of enactive, image, and lexical representations of conscious expression. Enactive representation is based on memories of motor actions and the retention of imitative behavior of another person's actions. Enactive thought is thinking in action with the tensing of different muscle groups that may signify covert trial actions; both skeletal musculature and visceral neuromusculature are involved. Images, according to Horowitz, are based on perceptions, memories, and fantasies, and are especially effective in yielding information about spatial relationships and forms. Emotional response may be incorporated into images. When human beings inhibit or block image formation, associated emotions may also be delayed. Finally, the lexical mode is the rational one dealing with abstraction and conceptualization.

The notion of two modes of thought has been elaborated and subjected to extensive research by Seymour Epstein in the field of personality psychology (1994, 1999). Epstein proposes that there are two major systems which we can describe in human thought. One of these is a *rational* system and the other is the *experiential* mode. The rational system involves analytic logical thought, the use of abstract symbols, words, numbers, sequences, slower processing, but also great flexibility because it is formulated in abstract terms such as algebraic symbols. It is also characterized often by a sense of control over one's thoughts and it is almost always active at a completely conscious level. It also seems to require greater effort to sustain over any extended period of time and may be most vulnerable to interference by fatigue, anxiety, and brain trauma.

The experiential system is characterized by narrative and emotion. Epstein provides extensive arguments as to why from an evolutionary standpoint the emergence of an experiential system is adaptive along with the rational system. The experiential system is associated more with holistic rather than analytic thought approaches and also with strong emotionality, especially with efforts to experience positive emotion. It is characterized by connections primarily through association rather than through logic and by memories and their emotional correlates with past experience. In the experiential system reality is particularly encoded in concrete imagery or expressed as well through analogy and metaphor or as part of a narrative process. While the processing in the experiential system is rapid because presumably the material has been replayed mentally, and therefore has moved toward greater autonomization, it is also harder to change this type of thinking because of the clarity and vividness of the imagery associated with the narratives formed. There is less subtle differentiation as part of this thought process, more tendency toward broad generalization, occasionally heavy reliance on well-established stereotypes, and a lack of precise integration.

Computer models of image formation have been proposed that suggest that images are similar to displays on a computer screen (Kosslyn, 1983). In this way, we can generate pictures whenever we wish and manipulate them as easily in our minds as when we manipulate information on computers. Researchers suggest further, in a highly technical paper, that subsystems are involved in image formation (Kosslyn et al., 1990). Images are evoked when stored information is activated through input of a particular object. Information is either ignored or selected for further processing through an "attention window."

To test image generation, image maintenance, image scanning, and image rotation, these researchers compared the performance of 5-, 8-, 14-year-olds, and adults on four imagery tasks utilizing those processes that are commonly used in visual thinking (Kosslyn et al., 1990). They found that older subjects were able to scan and rotate images better than younger subjects, and older subjects were better at generating images. There were no differences in maintaining image based upon age. Females, however, were generally superior in generating and maintaining images, but among the 8-year-old group, the males were faster than females in an image maintenance test. These researchers found no evidence to suggest that younger children have fewer processing components; the very youngest are relatively poor at scanning, rotating, and generating objects, but relatively good at maintaining images. Their findings seem to confirm that children are capable of eidetic imagery and can keep these images over time.

Eidetic images, related to photographic memory, are usually under voluntary control of the imager. They are almost as vivid as a perception, can be scanned, may be spontaneous or produced, are externally localized, and may persist for weeks or even years. Whether or not all children have eidetic imagery is still an open question, but most reviews of the literature indicate that about 10 to 15% of children are true eidetics (Morris & Hampson, 1983).

Researchers engaged in psychological rather than physiological studies of image-producing capacity found that the delay of gratification was facilitated when children were able to "think fun," thereby using pleasant cognitive distractions to postpone the receiving of a reward (Mischel, Ebbeson, & Zeiss, 1972). However, when children thought "sad thoughts" or thought about the rewards themselves, the delay time was shorter. If we accept these findings, it would appear that babies thinking about the mother would increase tension and shorten the ability to delay gratification. This is in contrast to Sigmund Freud's notion of delay developing as a result of primary process images. An additional step must be taken before delay is established. The ego must direct energy away from the "mother" image to other images of a pleasant nature less associated with milk, or to some instrumental activity, such as playing with a mobile or rattle or sucking on fingers while awaiting the reward of the milk (Freud, 1911/ 1962; J. L. Singer, 1955).

Developmental Aspects of Fantasy and Imagination

It is difficult to test Freud's assumption that the baby begins to image the mother's face and, through this capacity for imaging and delay of gratification, can move from primary process or id functioning to secondary process or ego functioning. And yet the contours of the caregiver's face must leave an impression quite early in life, as demonstrated by the infant's smile of recognition at about 6 weeks. It is true that the mother or caregiver's odor, touch, and voice also can evoke the smile of the infant, but think how much more effective is the animated face of the adult in achieving the smile response and accompanying global movements.

Developmental psychologists, particularly Jean Piaget, believed that images, the precursors of memory, begin to form in the later part of the sensorimotor period of life, 18- to 24 months of age, at about the time that object permanency develops (D. G. Singer & Revenson, 1996). The baby now can search for objects he or she drops or be upset if the mother leaves the room, because the child's cognitive capacity has matured beyond the perspective that "out of sight" is "out of mind." During this stage of life and perhaps earlier, infants were able to imitate movements of others without seeing the movement on their own bodies, such as opening and closing of eyes and mouth (Meltzoff & Moore, 1983). Infants as young as 9 months manifested a phenomenon of "deferred imitation," in effect, observing an action television one day and then directing their behavior accordingly on another day (Meltzoff, 1988). Piaget describes a six-month-old who would kick in her crib when exposed to a toy across the room, acting as if she remembered kicking at this toy when it was actually in her crib (Piaget, 1952).

Thus, the power of imagery may begin earlier than we had believed during the past two decades. Actually, as 1½- to 2- year-olds become more mobile and begin to use language, they manifest the capacity for symbolic thinking through play, their main mode of activity during the preoperational stage of development, between 2 and 4 years of age.

Gradually, material gets organized into more complex structures and hierarchies through the processes of assimilation and accommodation. If all basic needs are met, an innate curiosity of children motivates them to explore their environment and form scripts or schemata that may or may not be accurate representations. We may laugh at some of the toddlers' antics or mistakes, or remark that what they do is cute or quaint. From the children's perspectives, their responses seem logical and correct. As they develop and gain more control over the complex stimuli that surround them, they begin to reproduce their ideas, thoughts, and experiences through play and imagination. This symbolic representation is what Piaget calls the child's "self-assertion for the pleasure of exercising his powers and recapturing fleeting experience" (1962, p. 131).

Lev Vygotsky (1978) had been an early exponent in the late 1920s and the early 1930s of a critical role for parents and other child caregivers in fostering a variety of forming experiences through playful interactions with children. He was careful to point to the necessity for adults to gear their interventions to the cognitive level of their children. At the same time there is increasing evidence that certain kinds of communications from adults directed to children at extremely early ages may open the ways for expediting not only attachment and mutual enjoyment but also prepare the child for the beginning of symbolic play and the early signs of an awareness of mental activity (Belsky & Most, 1981; Hodapp, Goldfield, & Boyatzi,1984; Kavanaugh, Whittingon, & Cerbone,1983; Slade 1987).

Theory of Mind, Reality and Fantasy

Research evidence suggests that before the age of 4, children often lack a theory distinguishing their own thoughts from those of others. Alan Leslie (1987) proposed that children's imaginative play may have served preschoolers for developing the critical conception of self and others' mental activity. The research of Kavanaugh and Harris (1999) indicates that many 3-year-olds can already recognize that the pretended thoughts and behaviors assigned to play figures are not "real." It may well be that in the course of engaging in pretend games children become aware of their own control of the narrative and, while they enjoy the story and sense of control, they are learning that their inanimate playthings lack any true autonomy.

The research by Elizabeth Meins and her group in England has shown the importance of the parents' treating children as if they have independent mental processes. Their research indicates that when mothers talk to children in their first four years using language that reflects mental activity, the children subsequently show better verbal skills, more awareness of theory of mind, and a richer stream of consciousness in their talk (Meins, Fernyhough, Wainwright, Das Gupta, et al. 2002; Meins, Fernyhough, Wainwright, Clark-Carter, et al., 2003). Secure early attachment is also important. It seems likely that mind-mindedness may be a pattern of adult communication that also stimulates imaginative play. Certainly the research evidence makes it clear that closeness to at least one parent and adult storytelling and reading are all regularly associated with fantasy play. This relationship pattern suggests that warmth and sensitivity of grown-ups' language, their acceptance of children's playful expressiveness, and the sharing of humor and occasionally even of frightening fictional themes, work to increase a sound attachment. Such a relationship pattern also encourages exploration, openness to experience and imagination in the child.

In general, it seems that youngsters who engage in more make-believe play are better able to make distinctions between what is real and what is not real. They also show more ability to grasp a sense of the autonomy of mental attitudes (Rosen, Schwebel, & Singer, 1997; Schwebel, Rosen, & Singer,1999).

Imaginary Companions

Some of the earliest signs of play emerge in the course of older babies' or toddlers' manifestations of what the psychoanalyst Donald Winnicott (1971) termed involvement with "transitional objects." These may be the soft cloth, crib blanket, or plush toy that a child becomes attached to and carries around, clinging to it tenaciously. The transitional objects may soon lead to the personification of the soft toy which is given a name and is treated as a living individual with whom one can converse. Parents often observe the emergence among 3- to 5-year-olds of an invisible playmate or scapegoat, the imaginary companion (D. G. Singer & Singer, 1990; Taylor, 1999). Researchers on imaginary companions of pre-schoolers have agreed to combine vivid personification of some dolls or soft toys along with invisible friends and have found this phenomenon prevalent in between one quarter to more than one half of children in various samples (Gleason, 2002, 2004; D. G. Singer & Singer, 1990). Research indicates that children with imaginary companions fall well within the range of normal functioning. The work of Marjorie Taylor (1999) demonstrates that these children appear to be less aggressive, or impulsive, more self-contained, and more capable of divergent, potentially creative thought.

The Older Child, Imagination and the Electronic Media

As the 2- to 7-year-olds move into the stage of concrete operations, where logical thinking prevails, they still draw on fantasy and imagination, but make-believe goes on privately through imagery and covert speech (Luria, 1932). During and beyond early adolescence, children continue to use their imagination to pretend to be sports heroes in their athletic play, write poetry or short stories, and paint or use photography to express their imaginative capacity. Some children join dramatic clubs and write plays for their peers at school. Children also may manifest creative expression in serious science experiments or in more frivolous activities such as outrageous hair styles, nail polish (each fingernail a different color), wearing funky clothing, or even body piercing, if a parent permits a 12-year-old to emulate a more adventuresome teenager.

Others enjoy watching television or playing computer or video games as part of their imaginative or fantasy experience. Because of the increased complexity of cognitive development, especially the ability to conceptualize, children may begin to play chess, fantasy games such as Dungeons and Drag-ons, or advanced CD-ROM computer games such as Myst. Cognitive psychologists have traced the origins of video games to their earliest prototypes, war and athletic contests, and to their most recent forebears, the mechanical games found in arcades that mirror sports and war scenes, gambling, and fortune-telling (Loftus & Loftus, 1983).

Computer based game-playing can contribute considerably to children's imaginative ability in the object-manipulation manner in games like Tetris (Calvert, 1999; DeLisi &Wolford, 2002; Ko, 2002; Subrahmanyam, Greenfield, Kraut, & Gross, 2001). Henderson, Klemes, & Eshet (2000) showed that when 8-year-olds approached a narratively organized science simulation game as a learning as well as entertainment opportunity, they made strong gains in thinking skills and science language usage. Transfer of such gains to a broader variety of technical or social problems have yet to be shown.

Sandra Calvert (2004) demonstrated that systematic research on how preadolescent children engage in multiuser domain (MUD) play is possible. Under carefully balanced, experimentally con-trolled conditions, the children played a game in which they could choose a name and a character or costumed avatar to represent them in the game. Under particular circumstances boys played with another boy or with a girl, and girls had similar options. Researchers scored variables like the names, characters, and costumes they chose, how active their characters were in their screen movements, and the language used in creating dialogues which appeared as overhead bubbles. They also scored the emotional expressions employed, scene changes, role play which involved pretending and having their characters acting out pretend sequences, and, finally, creating a game in which the avatars or their creators could compete.

Generally, both boys and girls stayed close to real life with apparently some reflection of MTV influences. Boys largely chose to represent themselves in mildly rebellious stances wearing "leather jackets" or with punk identities. Girls seemed more likely to choose soccer costumes as a model of assertiveness. In keeping with findings from studies of gender differences in play, girls used more verbal expression and boys were more playful and engaged in more action. When boy players were pitted against girl players in the MUD, they talked more and were less active. Girls in the mixed gender play also made adjustments, moving their characters more and talking less.

Measures of Fantasy and Imagination

Observing children in their play, and rating them on a scale of imaginative production is useful in attempting to assess preschool children's fantasy productions (D. G. Singer & J. L. Singer, 1990; J. L. Singer & D. G. Singer, 1981). Self-report measures such as journals, diaries, interviews, storytelling, and naturalistic reports also yield information about types and styles of fantasy production. Another form for assessment is a fantasy questionnaire consisting of 45 items that has good validity based on a large sample of first- and third-grade children (Rosenfeld, Huesmann, Eron, & Torney-Puta, 1982). A modification of this measure tested fantasy production of first-graders to assess the relationship between television viewing and imaginal activity (McIllwraith & Schallow, 1982–1983).

Researchers and therapists have used projective techniques in clinical and school settings to assess thoughts and fantasies related to conflict or motives that may not emerge during play therapy, interviews, or observations. These measures include word-association tasks, sentence-completion tests, and tests of storytelling, such as the Children's Apperception Test, the Rorschach inkblots, and drawings of one's family.

Clinicians are trained to note changes in facial expression, breathing, muscle tone, and eye movements when clients are engaged in fantasy reports. Researchers have carried out physiological measures of children's imagery, however, mainly in laboratory experiments, but only rarely. The area of physiological measurement in children needs to be more thoroughly studied. With additional insights, older children and adolescents might learn, then, to become more aware of changes in their physiological state, attach a cognitive label to such changes, and thereby perhaps enable them to lower blood pressure, reduce heart rate, and relax muscle tension.

Constructive Uses of Fantasy and Imagination

Parents need to provide the external conditions of psychological safety and freedom for children to thrive in a creative environment. Children experience psychological safety when they are accepted unconditionally and treated with empathy (Rogers, 1954); they experience psychological freedom when caregivers allow them to express themselves symbolically and with few restraints. When children play in ways that are silly or unrealistic, therefore, parents must not tease or laugh at them. Many educators believe that school experiences can foster creativity and imagination, and they have carried out experiments to demonstrate how imagination training can increase children's cognitive and social skills (Russ, 2004; D. G. Singer & J. L. Singer, 2005.)

In addition to the pretend play of younger children, older children can pass the time through fantasy or daydreaming when they need to wait in places such as airports and doctors' offices. They can also learn to use fantasy to help change their moods and to work out disagreeable encounters with their peers to avoid physical or verbal confrontations. Psychotherapists using relaxation techniques with clients ask them to imagine pleasant scenes as part of sensitivity training or relaxation therapy (D. G. Singer, 1993). Studies of pain similarly indicate that making up a mental story of being in another place at another time is one of the most useful and effective procedures in achieving relief. Coping with fear through the use of narrative thought or imagery is a successful way to alleviate anxiety about such dangers as flying during a storm, being stranded in a snowstorm, and being lost on a mountain trail.

Play therapists have acknowledged the importance of arts and crafts and puppet play as part of their regimen in working with children. Some teachers have been pioneers in helping young people develop imagery skills. These programs are spelled out in step-by-step fashion and use few props and sometimes only imagery methods, movement, and music (Rosenberg, 1987; D. G. Singer & J. L. Singer, 2001, 2005).

Finally, fantasy and imagination help children project their thoughts into the future. Their imagination allows them to think about a variety of possibilities for themselves. Children can play out the notions of "What if?" or "Who can I be?" in internal scripts as a rehearsal for later avocations and even careers. Trying out an occupation in one's mind can convey some semblance of what an actual experience might offer. In a similar way, many athletes use imagery as part of their training. Although there is no substitute for the necessary physical practice, fantasy rehearsal of a particular athletic setting or competitive event seems to give an edge to those athletes who use these methods (Sheikh & Korn, 1984).

Fantasy and imagination fostered through play can be useful to all persons. While fantasy and imagery exploration flourish before puberty, and may well reach their peak by adolescence, this gift continues throughout human life. Through reading, music, education, peer interaction, and the electronic media, as well as an awareness of adult occupation and role models, preadolescents and adolescents are able to envision a vast range of possible futures and possible selves. The seeds of imagination are found in early childhood, when children engage in make-believe play. Through caregivers' acceptance and nurturance of play and fantasy, children may enter the fascinating realm of possibility.

References

Belsky, J., & Most, R. (1981). From exploration to play: A cross-sectional study of infant free play behavior. *Developmental Psychology, 17,* 630–639.

Brickman, H.(1995, July 2). Live and let die (Hers Column). *New York Times*, SM, p. 14.

Bruner, J. S. (1964). The course of cognitive growth. *American Psychologist, 19,* 1–15.

Calvert, C . (2004). *Is all play created equal? How digital culture enhances or impedes children's cognitive development.* Paper presented at Fourth Annual Conference: Playing to Learn, Learning to Play: Why Play Matters for Today's Kids, Washington, DC. (Playing for Keeps, Inc., 116 West Illinois, Suite 5E, Chicago, IL)

Calvert, S. L. (1999). *Children's journey through the information age.* Washington DC: McGraw-Hill.

DeLisi, R., & Wolford, J. L. (2002). Improving children's mental rotation and accuracy with computer game playing. *Journal of Genetic Psychology, 163*(3), 272–282.

Epstein, S. (1994). Integration of the cognitive and psychodynamic unconscious. *American Psychologist, 49,* 709–724.

Epstein, S. (1999). The interpretation of dreams from the perspective of cognitive-experiential self-theory. In J. A. Singer & P. Salovey, *At play in the fields of consciousness* (pp. 51–82). Mahwah, NJ: Lawrence Erlbaum.

Farah, M. J. (1984). The neurological basis of mental imagery: A componential analysis. *Cognition, 18,* 245–272.

Freud, S. (1962). Formulations on two principles of mental functioning. In J. Strachey (Ed.), *The standard edition of the complete psychological works of Sigmund Freud* (Vol. 2, pp. 213–226). London: Hogarth. (Original work published 1911)

Gleason, T. (2002). Social provisions of real and imaginary relationships in early childhood. *Child Development, 38,* 979–992.

Gleason, T. (2004). Imaginary companions: An evaluation of parents as reporters. *Infant and Child Development, 13,* 199–215.

Henderson, L., Klemes, J., & Eschet, Y. (2000). Just playing a game? Educational simulation software and cognitive outcomes. *Journal of Educational Computing Research, 22*(1), 105–129.

Hodapp, R. M., Goldfield, E. & Boyatzi, C. (1984). The use and effectiveness of maternal scaffolding in mother–infant games. *Child Development, 55,* 772–781.

Horowitz, M. J. (1978*). Image formation and cognition.* New York: Appleton-Century Crofts.

Houtz, J. C., & Patricola, C. (1999). Imagery. In M. A. Runco & S. R Pritzker, (Eds), *Encyclopedia of creativity* (Vol. 2, pp. 1–11). New York: Academic.

Kavanaugh, R., & Harris, P. (1999). Pretense and counterfactual thought in young children. In C. Tamis-LeMonda & L. Balter (Eds.), *Child psychology: A handbook of contemporary issues* (pp. 158–176). New York: Garland.

Kavanaugh, R., Whittington, S., & Cerbone, M. (1983). Mothers' use of fantasy in speech to young children. *Journal of Child Language, 10,* 45–55.

Ko, S. (2002). An empirical analysis of children's thinking and learning in a computer game context. *Educational Psychology, 22*(2), 219–233.

Kosslyn, S. M. (1983). *Ghosts in the mind's machine.* New York: Norton.

Kosslyn, S. M., Margolis, J. A., Barret, A. M., Goldknopf, E. J., & Daly, P. F. (1990). Age differences in imagery abilities. *Child Development, 61,* 995–1010.

Leslie, A. (1987). Pretense and representation: The origins of "Theory of Mind." *Psychological Review, 94*, 412–422.

Loftus, G. R., & Loftus, E. E (1983). *Mind at play*. New York: Basic Books.

Luria, A. S. (1932). *The nature of human conflicts*. New York: Liveright.

Marks, D. F. (1990). On the relationship between imagery, body and mind. In P. J. Hampson, D. E. Marks, & J. T. Richardson (Eds.), *Imagery: Current developments* (pp. 1–38). London: Routledge.

Mcllwraith, R. D., & Schallow, J. R. (1982–1983). Television viewing and styles of children's fantasy. Imagination. *Cognition and Personality, 2*, 323–331.

Meins, E., Fernyhough, C., Wainwright, R., Clark-Carter, D., Das Gupta, M., Fradley, E., & Tuckey, M.. (2003). Pathways to understanding mind: Construct validity and predictive validity of maternal mind-mindedness. *Child Development, 74*(4), 1194–1211.

Meins, E. C., Fernyhough, R., Wainwright, M., Das Gupta, E., Fradley, & M. Tuckey. (2002). Maternal mind-mindedness and attachment security as predictors of theory of mind understanding. *Child Development, 73*(6), 1715–1726.

Meltzoff, A. N. (1988). Imitation of televised models by infants. *Child Development, 59*, 1221–1229.

Meltzoff, A., & Moore, M. K. (1983). Newborn infants imitate adult facial gestures. *Child Development, 54*, 702–709.

Mischel, W., Ebbeson, E. B., & Zeiss, A. R. (1972). Cognitive attentional mechanisms in delay and gratification. *Journal of Personality and Social Psychology, 21*, 204–218.

Morris, P. E., & Hampson, P. J. (1983). *Imagery and consciousness*. New York: Academic.

Piaget, J. (1952). *The origins of intelligence in children* (M. Cook, Trans.). New York: International Universities Press.

Piaget, J. (1962). *Play, dreams and imitation in childhood*. New York: Norton.

Rogers, C. R. (1954). Towards a theory of creativity. *ETC: A Review of General Semantics, 11*, 249–260.

Rosen, C., Schwebel, D., & Singer, J. L. (1997). Preschoolers' attributions of mental states in pretense. *Child Development, 66*, 1133–1142.

Rosenberg, H. S. (1987). Creative drama and imagination. New York: Holt, Rinehart & Winston.

Rosenfeld, E., Huesmann, L. R., Eron, L., & Torney-Puta, J. V. (1982). Measuring patterns of fantasy behavior in children. *Journal of Personality and Social Psychology, 42*, 347–366.

Russ, S. (2004). *Play in child development and psychotherapy: Toward empirically supported practice*. Mahwah, NJ: Lawrence Erlbaum.

Schwebel, D., Rosen, C., & Singer, J. L. (1999). Preschoolers' pretend play and theory of mind: The role of jointly conducted pretense. *British Journal of Developmental Psychology, 17*, 333–348.

Sheikh, A. A., & Korn, E. R. (Eds.). (1984*). Imagery in sports and physical performance*. New York: Baywood.

Singer, D. G. (1993). *Playing for their lives: Helping troubled children through play therapy*. New York: Free Press.

Singer, D. G., & Revenson, T. (1996). *A Piaget primer: How a child thinks* (Rev. ed.). New York: Plume.

Singer, D. G., & Singer, J. L. (1990). *The house of make-believe: Play and the developing imagination*. Cambridge, MA: Harvard University Press.

Singer, D. G., & Singer, J. L. (2001). *Make-believe: Games and activities for imaginative play*. Washington, DC: Magination Press.

Singer, D. G., & Singer, J. L. (2005). *Imagination and play in the electronic age*. Cambridge, MA: Harvard University Press.

Singer, J. L. (1955). Delayed gratification and ego-development: Implications for clinical and experimental research. *Journal of Consulting Psychology, 19*, 259–266.

Singer, J. L., & Pope, K. S. (Eds.). (1978). *The power of human imagination: New methods in psychotherapy*. New York: Plenum.

Singer, J. L., & Singer, D. G. (1981). *Television, imagination and aggression: A study of preschoolers*. Hillsdale, NJ: Lawrence Erlbaum.

Slade, A. (1987). A longitudinal study of material involvement and symbolic play during the toddler period. *Child Development, 58*, 367–385

Subrahmanyam, K., Greenfield, P., Kraut, R., & Gross, E. (2001). The impact of computer use on children's and adolescents' development. *Journal of Applied Developmental Psychology, 22*, 7–30.

Taylor, M. (1999). *Imaginary companions and the children who create them*. New York: Oxford University Press

Vygotsky, L. S. (1978). *Mind in society: The development of higher mental processes*. Cambridge, MA: Harvard University Press.

Winnicott, D. W. (1971). *Playing and reality*. Harmondsworth, UK: Penguin.

38
Sociocultural Influences on Gender-Role Behaviors in Children's Play

ALICE STERLING HONIG

Gender Differences in Play Styles

Children have relished play from time immemorial. Indeed, ancient Chinese tapestries show "the hundred games of children," although all the children pictured are males. Theories about play and the "reasons" investigators give for children's play have slighted sex or gender differences to focus on the linguistic, cognitive, and social skill developmental advantages that play offers (Bergen, 1988). Play helps young children clarify and articulate similarities and differences in concepts and categories, including gender. Another major emphasis in studying play has been to observe how peers learn to resolve conflicts through play adjustment and how they learn to understand symbolic uses of materials and toys in creating sociodramatic play scenarios.

Psychodynamic theorists conceptualize play as a way for children to express emotional resonances in their lives. Play helps children express sorrow, anger, and fear. Play opens pathways for them to cope with stress and also serves as a medium to express different worldviews as a function of their gender. Psychoanalyst Erik Erikson (1963) studied dramatic scenes constructed by young children as they freely used blocks and toys. Boys and girls differed significantly in the toy configurations and scenarios they created and recounted. Boys tended to create stories full of bold actions and build tall block constructions. Girls tended to create more peaceful, enclosed domestic scenes.

Gender roles are socially constructed during play. Children invent approaches and patterns of interrelating with other persons (Liben & Bigler, 2002). They imbue activities and objects with values, and think and feel about them in ways that may differ strongly depending on child gender (Slade & Wolf, 1994).

> By the time they enter school, children have long been aware of their basic gender identities, have acquired many stereotypes about how the sexes differ, and have come to prefer gender-appropriate activities and same sex playmates.... During middle childhood... their behavior, especially if they are boys, becomes even more gender-typed. (Sigelman & Shaffer, 1995, p. 307)

This gender typing results in personality traits regarded as stereotypically "masculine" (active, aggressive, ambitions, competitive, dominant, feeling superior, independent and self-confident) and those designated as stereotypically "feminine" (considerate, devotes self to others, emotional, gentle, home-oriented, kind, likes children, and passive). These gender stereotypes, or widely held beliefs

379

about what is appropriately male or female are reflected in everyday gender role behaviors at home, in school, and on the playground.

A summary of decades of play research notes that differences in play styles as a function of child gender have not changed over the years in the following ways: "Girls engage in more doll play and domestic rehearsal, more art activities, and dressing up. Boys play more with transportation toys, with blocks and with carpentry toys. Boys also engage in more aggressive activities and play more in larger peer groups. Girls spend more time talking and spend far more time with teachers than do boys" (Fagot, 1988, p. 134). Preferred play themes differ by gender. Boys have listed preferences for cowboys and soldiers; girls listed playing house and school (Sutton-Smith, Rosenberg, & Morgan, 1963). Children's play with "masculine" toys has been hypothesized to promote the development of spatial skills and interests (Green, Bigler, & Catherwood, 2004).

Sex differences are not found in children's progressively more sophisticated cognitive understandings of *gender identity* (one is a male or a female), *gender stability* (gender identity is stable across time), and finally, *gender constancy* or consistency (one's sex cannot be altered by superficial situational changes such as cross-dressing). Boy and girl toddlers are equally able to label themselves as a boy or girl. Preschoolers may not understand that sex ascription is stable; many still believe that in the future they can carry out biological roles of the other sex.

Roy was visiting with Grandma and playing with his cuddly toy monkey while Mother was in the bedroom nursing the new baby. Roy lifted up his shirt and pretended peacefully to nurse his own furry monkey. Grandma remarked lovingly that his mama had nursed him too when he was a baby. She also explained that boys cannot grow up to make milk and nurse babies. Only girls can grow up to nurse a baby. "Oh yes I will too be able to nurse when I grow up!" Roy asserted indignantly.

Gender constancy does not develop until the later preschool years. By early school age, children across cultures understand that not only is gender classification stable across time, but also across situations (Archer, 1992). Gender will not change because a child wishes to be of a different sex or engages in cross-sex activities. A study of preschool children's gender understanding in divorced versus intact families in Taiwan revealed that in a culture that values males preferentially, older preschool boys in mother custody showed an increased awareness of gender constancy in comparison both with peers in intact families and with children in father custody (Honig & Su, 2000). Thus, family/cultural variables may hasten some young children's understanding that a person's sex does not change. Gender roles, of course, do change, depending on culture and maturity. As rural children in Kenya are socialized by adults into the tasks of their culture group, such as childcare for girls and herding cows for boys, the more rigid gender differences and gender segregation appear (Harkness & Super, 1985).

Early Sex Differences in Play Partner Preference

Sex differences in interactive play styles begin to appear from ten to fourteen months of age and are well established by the time children are 36 months old (Fagot, 1988). The earliest studies of developmental changes in levels of play among preschoolers found that children in two-thirds of the play-groups chose same-sex play partners, and their preferred favorite playmates were usually the same sex as the child (Parten, 1933). A half-century later, other investigators found similar behavior among the solitary and social play of pairs of 33-month-olds in a laboratory playroom (Jacklin & Maccoby, 1978); male and female toddlers were twice as sociable with same-sex as with opposite-sex playmates. Analyzing 20,000 episodes of peer play at a university daycare, Martin & Fabes (2001) noted that sex segregation was very strong and moderately stable over time. Girls tended to be encouraging and supportive.

They tended to play closer to adults and be cooperative with one another. They played house and other games that required more verbal interactions. The researchers suggest that self-segregation in play increases during the preschool and early school years. This increase leads to and intensifies the growth of different sets of social skills, styles, expectations and child preferences, which they call the "social dosage" effect of gender segregation in play.

After years of observing interactions at different schools, Thorne (1993) reported that children's playground choices, defined as "borderwork," effectively emphasized and increased gender separation. Borderwork included single gender chases and wrestling other-sex children to the ground; "rituals of pollution," where boys shouted that girls had "cooties"; and homophobic slurs shouted at boys who showed interest in girls' play activities. Boys groups were large, hierarchically organized, and intensely competitive. Girls often played jump rope or used the climbing bars, and focused more on intimacy and cooperation. Boys invaded girls' play spaces more often than the reverse. Sometimes, when boys asked to join a girls' jump rope game, they had a hidden agenda. The boys turning the jump rope disrupted the game by making the rope go too fast so that the girls got tangled up; then the boys would run away laughing. Boys showed great fear of being teased that they were doing something with "girls" (such as sitting at a lunch table with girls); all children were upset when called "sissies." Thorne perceived that " activities, spaces, and equipment are heavily gender-typed; playgrounds, in short, have a more fixed geography of gender" (p. 44). Boys controlled the large school outdoor play spaces set aside for team sports. Girls had one tenth as much play space! When asked about this, boys explained that girls were not as good at the field games such as soccer, or that they would cry more if knocked down.

Biological Explanations

Almost all reviews of sex differences emphasize that boys show a higher level of activity and engage in more physically vigorous play than girls, whether indoors or outdoors (Hoyenga & Hoyenga, 1979; Rubin, Fein, & Vandenberg, 1983). Baby girls have better hearing than boys and this gap widens with age. Baby girls focus more on details and faces, and baby boys' eyes focus more on actions (Perlman, 2005). Such biological differences may lead to different experiences for boys and girls in classrooms and on playgrounds.

> Some young boys at play on my front lawn were engaged in fairly strong tussling and wrestling holds with each other. "Boys, if you need to fight, you will have to find a place at your own house," I called out. "We wasn't fighting. We was just wrestling!" explained one boy cheerfully as he disentangled from the pile of boy bodies thrashing vigorously around on the grass and stood up to explain boy play fighting.

Researchers across cultures confirm that preschool boys engage in more rough-and-tumble play than do girls (Maccoby, 1990). This phenomenon was found in six cultures among males from 3 to 11 years (Whiting & Edwards, 1973). When they are a few months shy of 3 years old, boy peers playing together are already more likely to play tug-of-war than girl peers playing together or girl–boy pairs who are playing (Jacklin & Maccoby, 1978). Middle-class preschool males who engaged in more same sex rough-and-tumble play on the playground were better liked by peers and rated as more socially competent by their teachers. But they were less liked if they engaged in rough-and-tumble play with girls (Colwell & Lindsey, 2005).

Observing recess play on the playground, Boyle, Marshall, & Robeson (2003) concluded that there is something about the play experiences that reinforces rather than diminishes gender divisions. Both sexes really enjoyed recess playground time. Girls valued relationships and demonstrated positive relationship skills, that included negotiating with laughter, appropriate and frequent use of touch, eye contact, and verbal sharing of inner thoughts. The most striking feature of boys' play was their high level of physical activity. Again, this is a gender difference found biologically in primate studies. The researchers also reported that boys showed their power, by trying to control the use of space, and by finding many ways to challenge authority, which they did more overtly than girls. Observing rural preschool children during free play, Ostrov and Keating (2004) reported the familiar pattern: boys carried out more physical and verbal aggression, while girls displayed more relational aggression than boys.

Even in humorous interactions during play, boys' responses are more vigorous. Young school age boys are more likely to laugh and initiate behavioral and verbal humor than girls. Boys are more likely to clown playfully and throw themselves on the floor (Honig, 1988). Indeed, many researchers hypothesize that the very early tendency of young children from 3 years onward to play in same-sex groups may be particularly attributed to the different play styles of boys and girls (Reifel, 2001) and, possibly, gender differences in fearfulness. There is a tendency for specific fears and phobias to be more frequent in girls at all ages from school entry onward. Feeling more fearful, girls may not be as likely to opt to play an outlaw fleeing a posse or an explorer facing a stampeding herd of wild animals. Since boys show higher levels of active, rough-and-tumble play, toddler females may prefer to play with other girls, whose styles are less bumptious. Thus, the basic biological primate pattern, that males are both more active and more aggressive than females, may in part be responsible for early choices for sex-segregated play.

Cognitive Developmental Explanations

Some theorists suggest that cognitive growth during the early years is deeply implicated in the marked gender separation in playgroups. Children come to understand their own self-definition as a girl or boy as part of a growing ability and active search for ways to understand social relations. Adults are big and children are small. Some children are boys; some are girls. Cook-Gumperz (1991) suggests that "these essentially oppositional categories form part of children's social reasoning from their earliest encounters in the public domain of the…nursery school" (p. 213). Martin and Ruble (2004) reflect that children's awareness of gender identity increases their motivation to be similar to others of their gender in clothing, toy choice, and preferences for members of their own gender group. They also posit that children will develop selective attention to and memory for information relevant to their own sex.

Sex Stereotyping in Toy and Task Preference

The kinds of toys that boys and girls play with differ in infancy, even prior to establishing clear identity as a male or female (Fagot & Leinbach, 1989). Toddlers start segregating themselves by toy preference, so that boys age 14 to 22 months prefer to play with trucks and cars, while girls prefer soft toys and dolls (Huston, 1985; Smith & Daglish, 1977). Preschoolers play more with same-sex than with cross-sex toys (Langlois & Downs, 1980). Cross-cultural researches also report such clear gender differences. In Hong Kong, more primary school boys than girls preferred electronic games and ball games than girls. Girls outnumbered boys in participating in social pretend play with stuffed toys and dolls (Yip, 1999).

Boys often prefer war toys, whereas many girls prefer Barbie dolls (Goldstein, 1994). As children move into the elementary school years, their preferences for toys, as expressed in letters written to Santa Claus, are even more gender stereotyped (Richardson & Simpson, 1982). Far more girls than boys asked for play items that were typed for the opposite sex. Almost 25% of the girls, for example, asked for baby dolls and only .6% of boys. About 15% of the girls and 25%of the boys asked for sports equipment or spatial toys, such as construction sets. Thus, the breadth of toy preference differs for males and females. Girls are far more likely to play with masculine toys than boys with feminine toys. Boys also avoid "girl" toys far more than girls avoid "boy" toys (Rubin, Fein, & Vandenberg, 1983). Researches consistently report such lopsided preference by girls for boys' toys in comparison with boys choosing girls' toys (Etaugh & Liss, 1992).

Boys and girls seem to solve problems differently depending on partner gender. A researcher rated preschoolers who played games with tinker toys and with beads for gender behaviors associated with task success. *Controlling* verbal behaviors were related to task success when boys played together, but *mitigating* verbal behaviors were associated with success when girls played together. In mixed-sex dyads, children used almost twice as many controlling nonverbal behaviors (Holmes-Lonergan, 2003). Girls became more controlling in dealing with boys, and boys were more likely to seek agreement in dealing with girls. Teachers might be able to decrease rigid gender stereotypes by assigning mixed gender groups for class projects.

Moral Development and Gender Differences in Play

Gender bias is not reflected in young children's responses to moral transgressions in play. Preschoolers, whether male or female, respond to violations of moral and ethical imperatives (such as not pulling a child's hair) with explanations of injury or loss. They point to the hurt child's emotional reactions, such as crying. Younger preschoolers are fairly flexible in moral judgments about socially appropriate gender roles. When Damon (1977) asked 4- to 9-year-olds about a little boy named George who insisted he wanted to play with dolls even though his parents told him that dolls are for girls, many of the youngest children believed that doll play and other cross-sex toy play was okay if that was what George wanted to do. By age 6, however, their responses become far more rigid. Children react with intolerance toward those who violate traditional sex-role differences in play. They view transgressions against conventional sex-appropriate behaviors and use of toys very seriously (Nucci & Nucci, 1982). Children entering school affirm stringent beliefs, such as "Boys don't play with dolls. That's girls' stuff," and "Girls should never cuss!"

Thus, 6-year-olds interpret the importance of adhering to gender stereotypes in play as if they are absolute moral imperatives (such as not injuring someone) rather than social conventions (such as wearing party shoes rather than sneakers to a fancy restaurant). Why is this so? Maccoby (1990) suggests that young children must exaggerate gender roles to make them cognitively clear. At Piagetian late preoperational or early concrete operational levels of intellectual functioning, children may view any societal custom or rule as equivalent to a natural law, such as the law of gravity (Carter & Patterson, 1982). By 9 years of age, children are able to distinguish between moral rules that people must obey (such as not deliberately smashing a window) and traditional customs that children could choose to ignore, such as a boy's playing with dolls, but they usually do not, since other boys would then act mean to them (Damon, 1977).

Influence of Peers, Parents, Siblings, and Teachers on Sex-Stereotyped Play

Peers are powerful influences. Whom children are with affects their willingness to play with cross-sex toys. When 3- and 4-year-old boys and girls were left alone with toys, they were more likely to play with cross-sex toys. The lowest probability of such play occurred when they were with an opposite-sex peer (Serbin, Connor, Burchardt, & Citron, 1979). Males particularly discourage cross-sex toy play for other males. They respond quite negatively to boys who choose cross-sex toys or choose to play with girls.

"Daniel, I hate girls! Do you hate girls?" inquired Christopher of his 6-year-old peer who lived down the block and was visiting in Chris's yard. Anxious to please his friend, Daniel hesitantly answered, "Yes. All except Natalie." "Who is Natalie?" asked the frowning Chris. "She's my new baby sister," whispered Daniel bravely.

Male peers impose a more stringent and possibly even menacing meaning at any hint of male peer appreciation or enjoyment of activities and toys perceived as "female." Indeed, Fagot (1988) reports that boys tend to ignore teachers or other girls, but their male peers give them "constant feedback on both appropriate play styles and appropriate playmates" (p. 135). Thus, the gender play preferences of females and their play interaction scenarios are perceived as a *danger* to be avoided by boys who want to be accepted into the world of male peer play.

This massive negative socialization of boys toward activities, toys, and agents perceived as female is troubling. In conjunction with evidence of greater male infant/toddler vulnerability to lack of maternal warmth and support, this negative socialization may well account for later interpersonal difficulties that some males face. When they enter the school system, boys may not have had the wealth of opportunities to learn the sophisticated turn taking, sharing, compromising, adjusting to others' needs, and other subtle socialization skills that females are learning as they play in more domestic spheres in the world of the preschool.

Children often copy a sibling's actions, especially if they revere an older sibling. If sister tells brother that his jacket looks like a girl's jacket, her brother will probably refuse to wear it (Putnam, Myers-Walls, & Love, 2005). Yet, preschoolers from 18 to 47 months who were observed in a playroom, manifested higher levels of play complexity *only* when they played with what are considered female stereotyped toys (Cherney, Kelly-Vance, Glover, Ruane, & Ryalls, 2003). Caregivers can use these findings to create mixed gender playgroups. Teacher may need to focus more attentively on the consequences of toy choice and support for play experiences in trying to implement more equity in the experiences of both boys and girls.

Parental expectations from birth onward provide powerful incentives, both as direct reinforcers and models, for sharply divergent gender-role behaviors (Honig, 1983, 2000, 2002; Schan, Kahn, Diepold, & Cherry, 1980). Parents teach their children what they expect from them, not only for their age but also for their gender. In his anthropological studies, Erikson noted that in Native American families he studied, girls, but not boys, were taught to sit with legs together. Researchers note that fathers strenuously punish the non-gender-stereotyped play of both daughters and sons, but are more punitive with sons for what they perceive as cross-gender play. Mothers, however, actively reward cross-gender play; they "interact with sons when playing with feminine-typed toys" (Golombok & Fivush, 1994, p. 116). Mothers are equally likely to engage in play with daughters regardless of which toy a girl chooses. Thus, boys may be getting mixed and confusing messages from mothers and fathers. Lindsey (2001) observed that mothers and fathers interact with children in ways that are reflected in their observed peer play. He remarks that a father doing yardwork with a male child, but not housework indoors, passes on his own gender schema as his actions define for his children the contexts he believes are more appropriate for boys or girls Mothers who joined in pretend play with their children had children who carried out more pretend play with peers. Fathers gave more demands to boys and boys at play gave more imperatives to peers than girls did. Lindsey's data confirm the importance of parental contextual behaviors:

As families join in to praise or punish cross-sex play, the reinforcements for sexual meanings of play materials and activities are subtle and pervasive (Block, 1983). Parents encourage boys to find out how toys work and how to play in large groups with peers. Fathers of boys tend to play more physical games with infant sons. Fathers provide sons with more vehicles, construction materials, role-enactment toys (such as laser guns and light sabers), balls, and sports equipment, and with fewer dolls and domestic toys.

Families reward girls for learning interpersonal rules that make them easy to keep in close contact with adults. Girls, compared with boys, also engage in different kinds of pretend or sociodramatic role-play. Boys with older sisters are more likely to play house. Older sisters "may be more likely to involve younger siblings in role play than are older brothers" (Ervin-Tripp, 1991, p. 87). Thus, the meaning of sex differences in play becomes profound for promoting divergence in developing interpersonal skills in contrast to skillful manipulation of objects in the physical world. Girls will tend to value and be more adept at the former; boys will value and become more adept at the latter. In elementary school small peer-group settings, Latino/a children oriented to their peer group in a gendered context (Cook-Gumperz & Szymanski, 2001), Their third grade teacher referred to her student groups as "families." The girls in each group adopted the role of facilitating cooperation by peers in their group much as they would as females in their actual families. Gender differences were played out in the milieu of the classroom much as in the home in this bilingual classroom.

Parents and teachers endow boys' and girls' misbehavior during play with different meanings. Caregivers respond significantly more to noncompliant male preschooler responses, although both sexes tend to be mostly compliant with teacher requests (Wittmer & Honig, 1977). Parents read picture books to young children, and often they choose books that emphasize gender stenotypes by the emotional language the characters use (Tepper & Cassidy, 1990).

Swedish researchers observing male and female teachers with preschoolers reported that male preschool teachers exhibit more playfulness and emphasized physical development. Female teachers tended to value calm play and emphasized the importance of social interactions (Sandberg & Pramling-Samuelsson, 2005). Boys and girls, who exhibit differential preferences for high activity physical play may also get cues from teachers that their play preferences are either supported or not approved.

Television's Influence on Sex Roles in Play

Many adults consider television an enlightening force for bringing new ideas to viewers about the range of life roles that men and women can assume. Women are portrayed as doctors as well as nurses, as police officers and business managers as well as secretaries. Research shows, nevertheless, that young children's television diet seems to be cementing even more rigid sex-role conceptions in recent years. In play groups, for example, males are more likely to enact fictional, superhero roles often portrayed on salient television shows (He-Man, Ghostbusters, or Ninja Turtles, for example), while females are more likely to portray familial characters.

In the 1990s particularly, salient television superheroes were the Power Rangers, who average more than two hundred acts of violence per hour, compared with one hundred for the Teenage Mutant Ninja Turtles. The Power Rangers show intersplices footage of real-life actors and settings with special animation effects. This blurring of conceptually clear boundaries between real and film characters may heighten males' tendency to model the violent acts they view. Preschool teachers report that the Power Rangers "encourage more violent play, interfere with imaginative, cooperative play, and...squelch creativity in play" (Levin & Carlsson- Paige, 1995, p. 69). Young children regard the Power Rangers as powerful role models. More than a half-century ago, Bandura, Ross, and Ross (1963) demonstrated that male preschoolers were far more likely than female preschoolers to imitate the aggressive acts of a powerful adult model, particularly an adult male, whether live or televised.

Recently, Japanese anime videos, which mostly portray violent males and big-eyed, big-breasted little girls have sold DVDs for children where helpless females are turned into vicious killers (*New York Times*, 2005). *Gunslinger Girl* appeared in 2003, and portrayed orphan girls who are brainwashed and given cybernetic implants that turn them into "pint-size assassins" for a covert branch of the Italian government. Each girl has her trainer, who teaches her everything. Under the handlers' supervision, the girls then calmly go forth and machine gun criminals. Among the best-selling Japanese anime films of 2005 was *Elfin Lied*, which portrays brutally violent, sexually provocative little girls. The opening image shows a mutilated, twitching hand that Lucy tore off one of her guards. The girls start out helpless, shy, and passive, but are taught to become horrific killers. Television has tended toward widening differences between boy and girl play patterns in the direction of increasing male admiration, and acting out, of violent, antisocial behaviors. Now, TV includes helpless female "victims" coerced into playing the roles of torturers and ruthless killers.

Electronic Games and Gender Differences

Gender stereotypes have been found in educational software recommended for children. There are significantly more male characters than female, and they are more likely than female characters to exhibit masculine-stereotyped traits (Sheldon, 2004). Preschool children of both sexes exhibit equal interest in computer games, but as children mature, investment of interest and time in playing computer games declines for girls and intensifies for boys. Young boys may concentrate intently on play with their "game boy" for hours on end. Children agree that computer games are boys' toys. Yet teachers *can* encourage girls' interest in computers. Agosto (2005) suggests that teachers should select computer games likely to appeal to girls, From her research, she recommends that computer games can be made more female friendly. She suggests specific game content that: does not emphasize the conflict between good and evil; focus on human relationships and girls' common play patterns; feature strong female characters and real-life locales; and center on storylines and character development, rather than competition.

Similar suggestions are given by Laurel (2005) who interviewed playmates who were "friendship pairs". Boys and girls were equally competitive. However, "girls assert social influence and structure relationships while boys seek to dominate and defeat" (p.2). Girls cited their favorite computer pastimes as "role playing games, adventure games, drawing, creative writing programs, skill building or educational games, problem solving and clue-based games.... Girls simply find violence-driven games boring and not complex enough to engage their interests" (p. 2) Laurel advises that adventures for girls should focus on new experiences rather than only on the goal to win, with emphasis on the development of friendships rather than elimination of competitors. Special teacher efforts do work. Elementary school girls in a computer club used digital cameras to take pictures of each other and then, with playful exuberance, inserted the pictures into a word processing program for editing (Dobosenski, 2001).

The Effect of Play Situation on Sex Differences

Sex differences very evident in one setting may not be as noticeable in another setting. Situational factors are particularly evident in mixed-sex settings. Kindergarten and first-grade girls stay closer to an adult than do boys in mixed settings. The girls, however, are willing to go farther from an adult to play with peers when in an all-girl group (Maccoby, 1990). Preschool teachers can use creativity in planning and organizing activities that will minimize strong differentiation in play patterns. Taking down barriers between the housekeeping corner and the block area may make it easier for boys and girls to use construction materials as well as kitchen make-believe appliances in playing "house." Fromberg (1990) has made a passionate plea for preschool educators to sustain the "generative energy and transformational power" of children's creative sociodramatic play into the school years. Indeed, her call for such teacher support promises a deeper understanding and more fulfilling fostering of the needs of all children:

The content of sociodramatic play themes can help to illuminate individual children's emotional development and how they experience contexts and relationships. As a type of syntax that generates changes over time, play has a surface structure and a deep structure. The surface structure consists of what appear to be topics and themes, such as superhero or family play. The deep structure touches on subjective experiences and relationships. (p. 243)

Paley (1986), a teacher-researcher, similarly urges teachers to allow young children to choose and elaborate on their preferred play themes. As they perceptively study the transformational themes in children's sociodramatic play, caregivers gain insights into how to facilitate learning, both in the classroom and in the emotional/social sphere, that will enrich the repertoires of both boys and girls. Teachers can make a significant difference in enlarging the creative, imaginative scope of preschooler sociodramatic play (Smilansky & Shefataya, 1991). Mathews (1981) paired 4-year-olds with a playmate of the same sex. The children mostly enacted the roles of mother and father. Boys playing wife roles suggested that wives are inept and helpless. As fathers, boys enacted leadership roles and did little participation in housekeeping. Girls, in contrast, role-played mothers as nurturant, generous, and highly managerial. They too, however, portrayed wives as helpless and incompetent. Children portray the role of mother as positive in play. The role of wife is not! Active teacher involvement in decreasing negative gender meanings in play is urgently needed.

Sex Play

Sex play begins very early in infancy. Babies focus the earliest sex play, as any other form of play, such as waving hands back and forth or kicking legs vigorously, on their own bodies. Freed of his diaper on a changing table, a baby will often reach for his penis and caress it. Boy babies have erections very early. Little girls have a harder time finding the vulva or clitoris, but they too pat and feel their sexually pleasurable parts in early sex play with their own bodies. One psychiatrist reported that his nearly 3-year-old daughter patted her vulva and shared confidentially as he was snuggling her in her crib at bedtime, "Daddy, this is my best feeling part." Sex play with others often begins as curiosity about the organs that other children have that are similar to or different from one's own.

After toileting time among the 3-year olds, Jerry came over to Lana and lifted up her dress before she had pulled up her panties. The teacher was tense as she turned and saw this. She was sure that Jerry was going to inspect or touch the little girl's sexual parts. Instead he lifted the dress all the way up and gently touched Lana's belly button. Wondrous! She had one too—just like his!

Curiosity about body parts not only can lead to needless teacher tension but also can lead to some comic sequences in terms of sex part disclosures among 3- and 4-year-olds.

Daisy came home from day care and informed her mother in no uncertain terms that she was tired of pulling down her panties in play with boys in her classroom. She had seen their penis enough and they had seen her "gina" (as she called her vagina) enough! Her mama empathized and suggested that she simply firmly tell the boys next time they started the game of "Let's show each other" that she had shown them enough and seen enough. Daisy agreed. She made her announcement with vigor next time the little boys in her playgroup wanted to engage in sex showing. Sex play of this mutually voyeuristic sort then stopped.

Sex play may not always represent simple curiosity about how boys and girls differ. Instead, it can represent a need to engage in what the preschooler already feels is a "forbidden" play experience that must be hidden from adults.

Mr. Stearns noted quietly that Davon and Leroy were always going into the bathroom together and trying to keep others out. Through the partly opened door, he noticed that their sex play involved taking down their pants, looking at and touching each other's genitals. Mr. Stearns walked into the bathroom with other preschoolers and announced cheerfully that if there was something interesting to see, then all the children wanted to see too! Davon and Leroy were surprised. They already had learned in their families that sex was "secret." This open approach to accepting that boys have testicles and penises and that girls have vulvas was not what they had in mind in their furtive play. Calm acknowledgment and open acceptance of sexual anatomy decreased the secretive nature of their sex play and they no longer sought to continue.

Many young boys enjoy the power of their ability to urinate over a distance and to urinate standing up. In play with girls, a boy may tease, "You can't pee standing up and I can!"

Five-year-old Maida protested to the teacher, "I can so pee standing up!" The teacher agreed she surely could try, and after the little girl had straddled the toilet and heroically managed to urinate standing up, the teacher remarked, "Well, you sure showed Robert that you can pee standing up if you want to." The teacher further explained that it surely also felt more comfortable to pee sitting down. Maida could choose whichever way she felt like, not a way that a boy used or teased her about.

Sometimes, children whose parents have not been forthright about labeling sexual parts or matter-of-factly explaining that boys have certain sexual parts and girls have other sexual parts, will move on during the early elementary years to sex play that involves mutual masturbation. Indeed, if sexuality has not been honestly and calmly dealt with in the family, some children seem at young ages to form an early belief that sexual parts are "dirty" and "shameful." They "hide" sex games from adults. They call out tauntingly if a child's pants slip down and sexual organs are bared.

Some caregivers bring their own sexual hang-ups into the classroom. A toddler teacher shook her finger warningly and called out, "Get your hand out of your pants" to a child masturbating dreamily under his blanket at naptime. By their own rejection of the naturalness of masturbation when a child is upset or getting calm at sleep times, some adults confirm lessons from home that sexuality is somehow "bad." Caregivers, of course, can mention that some places and situations (such as nap time) are far more appropriate than others for patting one's genitals. When self-stimulation occurs compulsively and pervasively, teachers will need to find out and ameliorate the source of the child's tensions and also work on increasing a child's feeling of security and interest in play domains. Sexual play that involves dominating or assaulting another child must be firmly forbidden, discussed, and handled by adults who establish clear boundaries and keep children safe from hurt.

A distraught mother came to consult about her son's weekend visits with his father under a joint custody divorce agreement. The father's girl friend and children lived with the boy's dad. The older children tried to put sticks and did force pebbles into the six-year-old's anus. The boy was terrified. He cried and told his mother they had threatened to harm him if he told his dad. She called her ex-husband but he scoffed at her concerns. Since there was joint custody, the mother had been legally told that she and her ex-husband were to work out their own problems; the courts would not intervene. Professional help was urgently needed.

Strong, clear messages about appropriate touches and inappropriate touches need to be given by caregivers, teachers, and parents. Appropriate sexual touching of oneself is fine when a child is in a private space, such as crib or bed. Touching, poking, or hurting sexual parts of another child is not OK. Sexual parts are private. During play, children must not interfere with each other's private parts (Chrisman & Couchenour, 2000).

Easy to understand books are available to help satisfy young children's curiosity about sexual differences (Gordon, 1991). A book that can help parents and teachers explain sexual puzzlements very simply to young children is *Did the Sun Shine Before You Were Born?* (Gordon & Gordon, 1992). The illustrations are gentle and support family closeness. Where children have been brought up with peaceful, matter-of-fact acknowledgment of all parts of the body, including sexual parts, early sex play is likely to be mostly to satisfy curiosity about differences. It does not develop into furtive, compulsive, or hurtful behaviors toward others. Indeed, under such rearing conditions, children take each other's differences for granted.

On the lawn of the child care facility of an Israeli kibbutz, I observed children of varied ages pretending that the large cardboard carton they were playing in was a big boat and they were sailors. One of the younger boys had an itch. He took down his shorts and scratched vigorously under his testicles. None of the other playmates remarked on this, nor did they tease or pay much attention. When the boy finished attending to his itch, he picked up his pants and continued the pretend sailor game with his playmates.

Preschoolers often explore each other's genital and anal regions under the guise of "playing doctor." They may pretend they need to put a thermometer in another child's rectum. They may get another child to undress so they can use the toy stethoscope and get a leisurely inspection of nipples and belly buttons. When children are peaceably reared without shame for their bodies, adults can expect a certain amount of such "doctor play" among preschoolers. But adults must allow no hurting, furtiveness, or coercion. The more that adults accept the naturalness of sexual parts and functions, the more they answer children's sexual questions simply, the less coercive sex play is likely to be. Indeed, early acceptance of children's sensual and sexual selves often leads to their sharing their feelings quite naturally.

> Three-year-old Daniel had just urinated quite carefully into the toilet. "Daniel, you were really careful," remarked Grandma admiringly. "All your pee-pee went right into the toilet." "Want me to tell you how you do it, Grandma?" asked Daniel. "Sure, love," agreed Grandma. "Well, you hold your penis and point it straight down and you rest your testicles on the rim of the toilet, and then all the pee-pee goes straight into the toilet," explained Daniel, proud of his teaching ability and urinary dexterity. His Grandma was mighty impressed also!

The more deeply adults recognize that little children are sexual beings as well as social and physical and thinking beings, the more likely that sex play will involve simple curiosity and sensual self-stimulation for comfort, but not hurtfulness toward others.

Decreasing Gender Differences in Play

Over the past decades, how have caregivers and social institutions fared in decreasing gender differences both in playmate choice and in creation of personal and social meanings through play scenarios?

In the 1970s there were concerted efforts by parents and educators to diminish the gender stereotypes promoted in children's literature, television, film, and children's toys. These were to some degree successful as girls, particularly, began to cross gender lines in their play (Liss, 1986). It became more acceptable for boys to be sensitive and nurturing and for girls to be assertive and independent. But in the next decades, "much of this ground was lost as toy commercials specifically target[ed] children's interest in conforming to social perceptions of gender identity in order to sell more toys" (Van Hoorn, Nourot, Scales, & Alward, 2003, p. 273, citing Shapiro, 1990). TV commercials emphasize that sexual beauty and attractiveness are essential for females; this may make fair treatment of boys and girls even more difficult, even in same-sex groups.

Paley (1992), in a noble attempt to institute a new kindergarten classroom rule, "You can't say you can't play," interviewed third graders for their views on whether acceptance of all children into play could work as a rule. The third graders told her, "Shirley is always rejected." It seems that when this overweight little girl came into the gym, some girls screamed and huddled under a blanket. The children told Ms. Paley that kids tease Shirley and call her names, and no one wants to eat lunch with her. At this point in the discussion, an African-American boy spoke up: " Shirley's not the only one. They reject me too. We're both the ones that they won't play with or anything"(p.51). Rejection, whether because of gender or ethnicity, or any other sociobiological category, is deeply painful and stays long in children's memories. One preschool teacher explained to a group of boys in her classroom that the girls resented being shut out of the block corner. The boys protested that girls don't like to play with blocks. The teacher persisted. The girls indeed wanted to play with blocks. Then boys then came to an agreement and informed the teacher that when they were playing outdoors, then the girls could have a turn at the block corner!

Over a four-month period, Green et al. (2004) read counterstereotyped, nontraditional stories in an attempt to change gender-typed toy play among a group of teacher-identified rigidly gender stereotyped preschoolers. Behavioral change was found for some girls who gradually chose to play more with "boys" toys; however, none of the boys' toy play patterns was changed.

Preschool teachers have tried to encourage girls particularly to increase their command of spatial understandings through more construction activity and motoric play. Typically, girls have chosen activities such as dancing to develop bodily kinesthetic intelligence. Caregivers now encourage both girls and boys to develop fine and gross motor skills in a wider variety of play activities, including building space forts, for example, which formerly would have been predominantly a male play choice. Whether there have been equivalent active efforts by teachers to engage males in learning to articulate strong emotions rather than act them out, and in learning interpersonal conciliation and turn-taking skills, is a challenge for researchers to discover in the next decades. Some teacher training materials engage teachers in *dialogues* about how they would handle situations, such as when a boy is "disruptive, non-attentive, hyperkinetic, and loud" in the classroom (Maher & Ward, 2002, p.20). Such teacher dialogues, if carried out during preservice training, may enhance teacher awareness of how to address issues associated with child gender as well as ethnicity. One suggestion is that schools with wrap-around classrooms, from kindergarten through third grade, could try to enlist the older girls to help younger males enjoy play with dolls and nurturing activities with teddy bears.

Teachers need to be adventuresome in generating and implementing ideas for enhancing gender mixing rather than the rigid separations that school settings seem to perpetuate. Boys who try to sit at a table with girls in a lunchroom are strongly teased. Schlank and Metzger (1997) suggest that the doll corner be renamed the "House Corner" to attract more boys. Names are important. Boys may not want to enter an area that is defined by " girl" toys and activities. They suggest that certain activities, such as acting out theatrical scenes, playing post office, car wash, grocery shopping, or group art and project activities will encourage cross-gender play. The authors provide an extensive annotated bibliography of books for early childhood education teachers to read with children. Daily provision of stories where girls are not always the victims and boys are not always the rescuers and heroes can possibly spark other ways for young children to regard culturally prevalent gender stereotypes.

The increase in single parent, female-headed households, with fewer nurturing male role models who actively demonstrate negotiation techniques and interpersonal cherishing of adult females and their viewpoints, means that young males have fewer opportunities to observe and internalize adult male roles that value the wifely role. Men's ongoing engagement in the interpersonal skills that enrich a marriage and provide powerful observational learning opportunities for young boys needs to be promoted more in families and in child care facilities.

The play world young children construct promotes rigid concepts of sexual differences in play and in the manner in which play activities are carried out. Present efforts to make little girls' play more like that of boys does not hold much promise for helping both boys and girls to become more skilled in empathy and nurturance, compromise and caring, as well as in motor skills and adventuresomeness in play scenarios. Caregivers and parents need to engage in more dialogue about how they can use play-space planning, role-playing, judicious adult participation, and scaffolding of sociodramatic scenarios to enhance play-learning opportunities for children (Honig, 1982, 2000). Teachers may need to assign classroom seating so that mixed gender groupings are arranged. When left to seat themselves, children mostly segregate by gender. Adults need also to accept deeply that children are sexual and sensual beings who will masturbate gently, for example, while listening intently to a long story. Sexual self-play, as a young child gently pats her or his genitals while the teacher is reading, even helps some young children concentrate better on listening to the story!

Children are often curious about sexual similarities and differences between boys and girls. Caregivers need to accept children's urge to know and understand differences and promote diversified play that includes domestic as well as adventurous, and innovative, as well as stereotypic themes. The adults will then promote increased imaginative play and more egalitarian opportunities in play. Adults will be helping young children, regardless of gender, to become creative and skilled at empathic sharing, kindness, intimacy, and win-win negotiations in play, as well as skilled in group teamwork, physical adventuring, and complex symbolic as well as gross motor activities.

References

Agosto D. E. (2005). *Girls and gaming: A summary of the research with implications for practice.* Paper submitted for publication.

Archer, J. (1992). Childhood gender roles: Social context and organization. In H. McGurk (Ed.), *Childhood social development: Contemporary perspectives* (pp. 31–61). Hove, UK: Lawrence Erlbaum.

Bandura, A., Ross, D., & Ross, S. S. (1963). Imitation of film-mediated aggressive models. *Journal of Abnormal and Social Psychology, 66,* 3–11.

Bergen, D. (Ed.). (1988). *Play as a medium for learning and development: A handbook of theory and practice.* Portsmouth, NH: Heinemann.

Block, J. H. (1983). Differential premises arising from differential socialization of the sexes: Some conjectures. *Child Development, 54,* 1335–1354.

Boyle, D. E., Marshall, N. L., & Robeson, W. W. (2003). Gender at play: Fourth-grade girls and boys on the playground. *The American Behavioral Scientist, 46*(10), 1326–1336.

Carter, D. B., & Patterson, C. J. (1982). Sex roles as social conventions: The development of children's conceptions of sex role stereotypes. *Developmental Psychology, 18,* 812–829.

Cherney, I. D., Kelly-Vance, L., Glover, K. G., Ruane, A., & Ryalls, B. O. (2003). The effects of stereotyped toys and gender on lay assessment in children aged 18–47 months. *Educational Psychology, 23*(1), 95.

Chrisman, K., & Couchenour, D. (2000). *Healthy sexual development: A guide for early childhood educators and families.* Washington, DC: National Association for the Education of Young Children.

Colwell, M. J., & Lindsey, E.W. (2005). Preschool children's pretend play and physical play and sex of play partner: Connections to peer competence. *Sex Roles, 52*(7/8), 497–509.

Cook-Gumperz, J. (1991). Children's construction of "childness" In B. Scales, M. Almy, A. Nicolopoulou, & S. Ervin Tripp (Eds.), *Play and the social context of development in early care and education* (pp. 207–298). New York: Teachers College Press.

Cook-Gumperz, J., & Szymanski, M. (2001). Classroom "families": cooperating or competing—girls' and boys' interactional styles in a bilingual classroom. *Research on Language and Social Interaction, 24*(1), 107–130.

Damon, W (1977). *The social world of the child.* San Francisco: Jossey-Bass.

Dobosenski, L (2001). Girls and computer technology: Building skills and improving attitutdes through a girls' computer club. *Library Talk,* 14(4), 12-14,16.

Erikson, E. (1963). *Childhood and society.* New York: Norton.

Ervin-Tripp, S. (1991). Play in language development. In B. Scales, M. Almy, A. Nicolopoulou, & S. Ervin-Tripp (Eds.), *Play and the social context of development in early care and education* (pp. 84–97). New York: Teachers College Press.

Etaugh, C., & Liss, M. B. (1992). Home, school, and playroom: Training grounds for adult gender roles. *Sex Roles, 26,* 639–648.

Fagot, B. I. (1988). Toddlers: Play and sex stereotyping. In D. Bergen (Ed.), *Play as a medium for learning and development: A handbook of theory and practice* (pp. 133–135). Portsmouth, NH: Heinemann.

Fagot, B. I., & Leinbach, M. D. (1989). The young child's gender scheme: Environmental input, internal organization. *Child Development, 60,* 663–672.

Fromberg, D. P. (1990). An agenda for research on play in early childhood education. In E. Klugman & S. Smilansky (Eds.), *Children's play and learning: Perspectives and policy implications* (pp. 235–249). New York: Teachers College Press.

Goldstein, J. H. (1994). *Toys, play, and child development.* New York: Cambridge University Press.

Golombok, S., & Fivush, R. (1994). *Gender development.* New York: Cambridge University Press.

Gordon, S. (1991). *Girls are girls and boys are boys.* Amherst, NY: Prometheus Press..

Gordon, S., & Gordon, J. (1992). *Did the sun shine before you were born?* Amherst, NY: Prometheus Press.

Green, V. A., Bigler, R., & Catherwood, D. (2004). The variability and flexibility of gender-typed toy play: A close look at children's behavioral responses to counterstereotypic models. *Sex Roles, 51*(7/8), 371–386.

Harkness,S., & Super, C. M. (1985). The cultural context of gender segregation in children's peer groups. *Child Development, 55,* 219–224.

Holmes-Lonergan, H. A. (2003). Preschool children's collaborative problem-solving interactions: The role of gender, pair type, and task. *Sex Roles, 48*(11/12), 505–517.

Honig, A. S. (1982). *Playtime learning games for young children.* Syracuse, NY: Syracuse University Press.

Honig, A. S. (1983). Research in review: Sex role socialization in young children. *Young Children, 38,* 57–70.

Honig, A. S. (1988). Research in review: Humor development in children. *Young Children, 43*(4), 60–73.

Honig, A. S. (2000). Psychosexual development in infants and young children: Implications for caregivers. *Young Children, 55*(5), 70–77.

Honig, A. S. (2002). *Secure relationships: Nurturing infant/toddler attachment in childcare settings.* Syracuse, NY: Syracuse University Press.

Honig, A. S., & Su, P. (2000). Mother vs. father custody for Taiwanese preschoolers. *Early Child Development and Care,164,* 79–93.

Hoyenga, K. B., & Hoyenga, K. T (1979). *The question of sex differences: Psychological, cultural, and biological issues.* Boston: Little, Brown.

Huston, A. C. (1985). The development of sex typing: Themes from recent research. *Developmental Review, 5,* 1–17.

Jacklin, C., & Maccoby, E. (1978). Social behavior at thirty-three months in same sex dyads. *Child Development, 49,* 557–569.

Langlois, J., & Downs, C. (1980). Mother, father, and peers as socialization agents of sex-typed play behaviors in young children. *Child Development, 51,* 1217–1247.

Laurel, B. (2005). *How gender differences affect play behavior of girls and boys, ages 7–12. Marketing throughout new media* (pp. 1–3). http://www.tolearn.net/marketing/gender.htm

Levin, D. E., & Carlsson-Paige, N. (1995). The Mighty Morphin Power Rangers: Teachers voice concern. *Young Children, 50*(6), 67–74.

Liben, L. S., & Bigler, R. (2002). The developmental course of gender differentiation. *Monographs of the Society for Research in Child Development* (Serial Number 269), 67(2), 1–47

Lindsey, E. W. (2001). Contextual differences in parent–child play: Implications for children's gender role development. *Sex Roles,* 44(3–4), 155–176. http://www.findarticles.com

Liss, M. B. (1981). Patterns of toy play: An analysis of sex differences. *Sex Roles, 7,* 1143–1150.

Maccoby, E. E. (1990). Gender and relationships: A developmental account. *American Psychologist, 45,* 513–520.

Maher, F. A., & Ward, J. V. (2002). *Gender and teaching.* Mahwah, NJ: Lawrence Erlbaum.

Martin, C. L., & Fabes, R. A.(2001). Time spent playing with peers influences gender-typed behaviors in young children. *Monitor in Psychology, 32*(7), 1–2.

Martin, C. L., & Ruble, D. (2004). Children's search for gender cues: Cognitive perspectives on gender development. *Current Directions in Psychological Science, 13*(20), 65–70.

Mathews, W S. (1981). Sex role perception, portrayal, and preferences in the fantasy play of young children. *Sex Roles, 1*(10), 979–987.

Nucci, L., & Nucci, M. S. (1982). Children's social interactions in the context of moral and conventional transgressions. *Child Development, 53,* 403–412.

Ostrov, J. M., & Keating, C. F. (2004). Gender differences in preschool aggression during free play and structured interactions: An observational study. *Social Development, 13*(2), 255–277.

Paley, V. G. (1986). *Boys and girls: Superheroes in the doll corner.* Chicago: University of Chicago Press.

Paley, V. G. (1992). *You can't say you can't play.* Cambridge, MA: Harvard University Press.

Parten, M. B. (1933). Social play among preschool children. *Journal of Abnormal and Social Psychology, 28,* 136–147.

Perlman, E. (Ed.) (2005). Boys fade; girls shine. *Education Advocate, 6*(2), 1–4.

Putnam, J., Myers-Walls, J. A., & Love, D. (2005). Influences on children' gender development. *Provider–Parent Partnership Retrieved from* http://www.ces.purdue.edu/providerparent/child%Growth-Development/Influences on Gender. htm.

Reifel, S. (2001). *Play and culture studies.* Westport, CT: Greenwood.

Richardson, J. G., & Simpson, C. H. (1982). Children, gender, and social structure: An analysis of the contents of letters to Santa Claus. *Child Development, 52,* 429–436.

Rubin, K. H., Fein, G. G., & Vandenberg, B. (1983). Play. In P. H. Mussen & E. M. Hetherington (Eds.), *Handbook of child psychology: Vol. 4. Socialization, personality, and social development* (pp. 693–774). New York: Wiley.

Sandberg, A., & Pramling-Samuelsson, I. (2005). An interview study of gender differences in preschool teachers' attitudes toward children's play. *Early Childhood Education Journal, 32*(5), 297–305.

Schan, C. G., Kahn, L., Diepold, J. H., & Cherry, E (1980). The relationships of parental expectations and preschool children's verbal sex-typing to their sex-typed toy play behavior. *Child Development, 51,* 266–270.

Schlank, C. H., & Metzger, B. (1997). *Together and equal: Fostering cooperative play and promoting gender equity in early childhood programs.* Boston, MA: Allyn & Bacon.

Serbin, L. A., Connor, J. A., Burchardt, C. J., & Citron, C. C. (1979). Effects of peer presence on sex-typing of children's play behavior. *Journal of Experimental Child Psychology, 27,* 303–309.

Sheldon, J. P. (2004). Gender stereotypes in educational software for young children. *Sex Roles, 51*(7/8), 433–444.

Sigelman, C. K., & Shaffer, D. R. (1995). *Life-span human development* (2nd ed.). Pacific Grove, CA: Books/Cole.

Slade, A., & Wolf, D. P (1994). *Children at play*. Oxford: Oxford University Press.

Smilansky, S., & Shefataya, L. (1991). *Facilitating play: A medium for promoting cognitive, socio-emotional and academic development in young children*. Gaithersburg, MD: Psychosocial and Educational Publications.

Smith, P. K., & Daglish, L. (1977). Sex differences in parent and infant behavior in the home. *Child Development, 46*, 1250–1254.

Solomon, C. (2005, July 17). Mean Girls: These days, anime's most fearsome killers are young and female. *New York Times, Arts & Leisure*, Section 2, p. 4.

Sutton-Smith, B., Rosenberg, B. G., & Morgan, E. (1963). Development and sex differences in play during preadolescence. *Child Development, 34*, 119–126.

Tepper, C. A., & Cassidy, K. W. (1999). Gender differences in emotional language in children's picture books. *Sex Roles, 40*, 265–280.

Thorne,B. (1993). *Gender play: Girls and boys in school*. New Brunswick, NJ: Rutgers University Press.

Van Hoorn, J., Nourot, P., Scales, B., & Alward, K. (2003). *Play at the center of the curriculum* (3rd ed.). New York: Macmillan.

Whiting, J., & Edwards, C. P. (1973). A cross-cultural analysis of sex differences in the behavior of children aged three through 11. *Journal of Social Psychology, 91*, 171–188.

Wittmer, D. S., & Honig, A. S. (1977). Do boy toddlers bug teachers more? *Canadian Children, 12*(1), 21–27.

Yip, C. S. (1999*). A study on play patterns of primary school children in Hong Kong*. Hong Kong: Playright Children's Playground Association.

39

Play and Violence

Understanding and Responding Effectively

DIANE E. LEVIN

The current environment in which children are growing up is permeated with violence in entertainment and news media, and in their own lives (Levin, 2003a). Often children bring this violence into their play and adults have strong reactions to it. In the context of today's world, it is helpful to rethink how we look at and interpret children's play with violence[1] so that we can make informed decisions about how to respond.

Looking at Play with Violence

For the fourth time in 20 minutes, 4-year-olds Wanda and Shelley have made a building with large hollow blocks. Wanda carefully crawls inside and Shelley starts to crash the building down with his fists and feet and yells, "Bang, Pow, Pow, Crash." As he continues kicking and shouting, Wanda, who is now buried under the blocks, yells, "Help me, I'm trapped. My house just blew up on me. I'm trapped. I can't move. Help, Help!" While the first three building demolitions ended with Wanda "dead" under the collapsed building, this time as she calls out for help, Shelley frantically starts pulling blocks off the pile and shouting, "Don't worry, here I come, here I come." Then he enthusiastically pulls a laughing Wanda out of the wreckage. Within minutes they begin rebuilding again.

Jackson picks up his plastic Tyrannosaurus figure and crashes it into other toy dinosaurs, yelling, "I'm smashing your bones, I'm squishing your eyes, I'm gonna grind you up, I'm gonna suck your blood...." As the Tyrannosaurus continues the attack, Jackson frantically hands a dinosaur to a nearby adult, instructing, "Hold this and yell, `Please don't kill me, I don't want to die.'" After several more attacks Jackson has the other dinosaurs capture the Tyrannosaurus in a bloody battle and puts a plastic box over it. Holding a Brontosaurus in his hand, he turns to the other dinosaurs and says, "There, we got it. It's in jail. It won't ever get out of there!" (adapted from Levin & Carlsson-Paige, 2006)

Four- and 6-year-old Mighty Morphin Power Ranger fans Anton and Phil are sitting together on an imaginary airplane using a collection of Power Ranger action figures. They repeatedly push a button on the backs of the figures that "morphs" (transforms) their faces from those of regular high schoolers to Power Rangers wearing masks and back again. Next, the boys take Power Rangers in each hand and begin bumping them against the chairs in front of them with accompanying "Pow, Pow" sounds. Soon, they begin to playfully karate chop each other with the figures. As the figures are put away and the boys get off the plane, they begin using their own bodies to karate chop at each other, making the same "Pow, Pow" sounds.

The children in these three scenarios are involved in play with violent themes. The content from each scenario is in some way connected to violence the children have seen. Anton and Phil's grows out of their exposure to the Mighty Morphin Power Rangers, long popular as violent television shows, movies, and video games, with which a whole line of toys and other products are marketed. Jackson's play occurs soon after he has seen a cartoon about dinosaurs in which a Tyrannosaurus rex violently attacks, kills, and eats other dinosaurs. Shelley and Wanda's play, which occurs the day after the bombing of the federal building in Oklahoma City, seems to grow out of news they have heard about the bombing.[2]

Long-standing discussions and debates about children's play with violent themes have often focused on the origins of such play in children, its role in development and learning, its relationship to violence in society, and how adults should respond to it (Baruch, 1942; Freud & Burlingham, 1943; Goldstein, 1994; Saki, 1914/1988). In recent years, especially as children's exposure to violence in society has increased dramatically and as many children seem increasingly involved in play with violent themes, efforts to resolve these issues have taken on a growing sense of importance and urgency (Carlsson-Paige & Levin, 1990; Levin, 2003; Miedzian, 2002). Such efforts invariably lead to a conundrum of complexities, research, and theoretical and practical questions, which can make it extremely difficult to imagine integrating such issues into a coherent and comprehensive position.

Conventional Views of Play with Violence

Traditionally, practitioners' and researchers' arguments about play with violent themes have tended to fall into two distinct camps—growing out of *either* a developmental *or* a sociopolitical perspective. The separate argument supporting both of these lenses make a great deal of sense. But, using both of these perspectives *together* provides a more powerful lens for helping us understand and respond effectively to play with violence in these violent times than either one alone (Levin & Carlsson-Paige, 2006).

The developmental perspective focuses primarily on children's individual needs and the role of play with violence in helping children meet their needs (Bettelheim, 1987; Freud & Burlingham, 1943; Groves, 2002; Jones, 2002; Singer, 1993; Sutton-Smith, 1986). Adherents of this view have argued that play with violent themes or content helps children work through many important developmental issues, such as feelings of aggression and frustration, a need to feel powerful and strong, and an understanding of the violence they have seen in the media or experienced directly. Adherents also usually hold that children need to be in charge of what they play; their choices reflect their experiences, needs, and interests. If children choose to engage in violent play, then they are showing us what they need to do. Therefore, from this point of view it is generally argued that play with violence is important, serves a useful purpose, and should be allowed. And if children are exposed to a lot of violence of whatever sort, then we might expect them to bring more of such content to their play and have a greater need to work it out through play.

The other dominant point of view, the sociopolitical perspective, has tended to focus more on what the content of play with violence might be teaching children and what messages they are learning about violence and about how people treat each other (Kuykendall, 1995; Miedzian, 2002). Adherents of this perspective argue that children learn antisocial messages and behaviors from engaging in war play and that adults, by allowing it, are tacitly condoning such behavior. They are also concerned that such play contributes to glorification of violence, desensitization to violence, and increases in overall levels of violence in individual children's behavior and, ultimately, in the broader society. Proponents of the sociopolitical perspective usually argue that, whenever possible, play with violent themes and aggressive toys and toy weapons should be strongly discouraged or banned.

There are legitimate reasons for supporting the arguments on both sides of the debate. Children do often bring to their play that which is important to them and what they want or need to work out and master. At the same time, as children play they are working out ideas, resolving issues, and learning (Berk, 1995; Levin, 1995). Thus, if children bring violent content to their play, one could argue that they are bringing it there because they need to. As they play with that violent content, however, they can be learning potentially worrisome lessons about violence (Levin, 1995, 2003b; Levin & Carlsson Paige, 2006).

We are left with a dilemma: How can the strong arguments of both perspectives be reconciled when both make such good sense? How can we help children use their play to meet their developmental needs and work on the increasing amounts of violence they see, while at the same time promote nonviolence and positive social behaviors?

All Play with Violence Is Not the Same

Using the perspectives represented by the two sides of the war play debate to look at the three episodes described above, can lead to a more coherent and comprehensive understanding of play with violence than when either perspective is used alone.

Working Out an Understanding of Real-World Violence

Shelley and Wanda's play grows out of what they have heard about people getting buried when the Oklahoma City federal building was bombed. They are using their block play to reenact the event, including what happened to the people involved. In fact, they reenact the same situation several times. Finally, they change what they do so that, by the end, instead of the scenario ending with Wanda "dead"—one consequence of violence—they have finally figured out a way to have a positive effect: rescuing the victim and making sure she is safe.

From a developmental perspective, while the teacher might wish that these children had not heard about the bombing or brought what they heard to the classroom, the intensity of their involvement and the details of their play suggest that they are working on something that is vitally important to them. It seems that once they did hear about the bombing in Oklahoma City, their play became an important vehicle for working out their understanding, questions, and concerns, and thereby for reaching some degree of resolution and a renewed sense of safety after the bombing.

As Wanda and Shelley play, they focus on those aspects of what they heard that are most understandable at their level of development, the most graphic and concrete aspects of the situation: the people getting buried in the building when it collapses (Levin, 2003a). They use what they already know—for instance, how it feels to be buried under a pile of blocks, what an explosion might be like, how a rescue operation works—as the starting point for working out their understanding. Their considerable skills in using blocks as a play material and in working out a shared play scenario contribute to their ability to use their play to work out the bombing in a meaningful way. Their play also provides adults with information about what the children have heard, how they understand what they have heard, and what else they may need in order to work through their concerns.

From a sociopolitical perspective, we need to ask what the children might be learning about violence and how people treat each other. The excitement of the early scenes seems to glorify and emphasize the violence as Shelley pretends to hurt Wanda while he knocks down the building. The play evolves so that Shelley also becomes the helper and rescuer. The children, therefore, are not left merely with a sense of the excitement that comes from the violence of knocking down a building with no awareness of the consequences that violence can have. Nor are they merely experiencing the sense of helplessness and fear that violence can often instill. Instead, they are working through an understanding of the effects of violence on people and objects, while directly experiencing the empowering and reassuring message that people can and do help in ways they can understand through their own actions. By the end the children are learning positive social messages that are meaningful in their own immediate world.[3]

Working Out an Understanding of Entertainment Violence with Open-Ended Toys

As with Wanda and Shelley, Jackson's play seems to grow out of violence that has come from the media, but, in this case, it comes from entertainment violence (a claymation cartoon) rather than from television news reporting. At the beginning of his play, Jackson uses his toy dinosaur figures to reenact (or imitate) the brutal attacks of the Tyrannosaurus on the other dinosaurs that he had seen in the cartoon. He uses very violent words and actions as he carries out the attacks. As he plays, things gradually evolve into a plot of his own making; he uses his largest dinosaur (the Brontosaurus) as the powerful hero who can rescue the victimized dinosaurs. First, he does this by violent means, "killing" (as he understands it) the Tyrannosaurus several times. By the end of the play, he has come up with a nonviolent solution that creates a safe world for all the dinosaurs by putting the bad Tyrannosaurus in a jail where he "can't ever get out."

From a developmental perspective, Jackson is bringing to his play the violence he has seen in entertainment media because he needs to work out some degree of mastery and control over it. He starts with those aspects of the cartoon that were most dramatic and probably troubling to him and finds a way to re-create them that is based on how he understands them. He then transforms them into something over which he can have control. He uses his collection of toy dinosaurs in the service of these efforts, and he is always in charge of what they do. He is the actor, scriptwriter, prop person, and director. We can learn a lot about him as we watch, including what is upsetting to him, how he understands death and violence, and what play skills he has.

Looking at Jackson from a sociopolitical point of view can lead to additional conclusions about the value and meaning of his play. As he starts out energetically re-creating the violence he saw in the cartoon, he seems to be enjoying and glorifying the violence and destruction. In fact, when the adult observer was given the job of speaking for the dinosaur victims, she reports she was quite conflicted about whether to participate or try to stop the play because of the level of intensity and verbal brutality involved. As Jackson's play continues, he begins to work through and transform the violence he saw. He increasingly takes the point of view of the victims and even gives them a voice ("Please don't kill me…"). He creates a good-guy hero (the big Brontosaurus) who first uses violence and kills the Tyrannosaurus over and over again to keep the smaller victims safe. By the end, the Brontosaurus has found a nonviolent solution, "a jail" made out of a box. The bad guy does not have to be hurt; he can be rendered harmless to never again hurt the other dinosaurs. In these ways, Jackson seems to have tamed the violence in the cartoon and restored the peace by creating a safe environment for his dinosaurs without having to hurt the villain anymore.

Imitating Entertainment Violence with Media-Linked Toys

Anton and Phil are playing with Power Ranger action figures that are highly realistic replicas of the characters on the popular Mighty Morphin Power Ranger television show (Levin & Carlsson-Paige, 1995). They are focusing on those actions that the toys were designed to perform: kicking, karate chopping, and "morphing" back and forth between high schoolers with faces like the actors who play their parts on the television show and Power Ranger superheroes with masked faces. As this scenario changes, it stays focused primarily on the fighting aspects of the Power Rangers; the figures fight with each other, then hit objects around them, and when the figures are put away the boys use their bodies to karate chop each other.

From a developmental perspective, since Anton and Phil are bringing to their play the karate-chopping action that they have seen the Power Rangers do on television, they must need to work it out and understand it in some way, to serve some developmentally useful function. The action figure toys, which are highly realistic replicas of the television characters, however, are used for one thing: fighting. Similar to the other two scenarios, this play begins with the boys imitating the most graphic and dramatic aspects of the violence. Now, however, the play stays focused on the violence from the Power Ranger television show—the karate chops and fighting—with little other content and with little evolution or resolution of the story or violence. As we observe the children's play, we learn little about what the violence means to them or what they are struggling to work out and understand. Compared with the two earlier play scenarios, Anton and Phil seem to be taking a less active role and using less creativity, imagination, or skills to transform what they saw on television into something that is uniquely meaningful to them. The developmental lens leads us to question whether the boys' play is meeting their needs as fully as the play of the previous children. If not, then there is cause for concern because the play is not truly serving their developmental interests.

Using a sociopolitical lens also leads to more worrisome conclusions than from the two previous episodes. Throughout their play, Phil and Anton focus on imitating the same violent actions of the Power Rangers over and over again. They do not seem to explore that violence, its effects on others, or alternatives to it. In this situation, it seems as if they are less likely to be learning the deeper lessons about violence and nonviolence that could counteract the glorification of the violence they saw on the screen.

The Functions and Value of Violence Play

Using developmental and sociopolitical lenses to look at these three play episodes points to the fact that there are fundamental differences in the nature and possible functions of the play. On the one hand, the play in the first two scenarios shows children working on social, moral, and intellectual issues in positive ways (especially given that the children were exposed to violence that they are trying to master). On the other hand, the play in the third episode points to different, potentially worrisome conclusions. Anton and Phil are using their play to focus on violence as exciting and fun, with little else. Are they working on any content that will move toward more positive social attitudes or behavior? Can such play serve a positive role in promoting their development?

Anton and Phil's play with violence is similar to that described by many teachers and parents who have watched children's play in recent years. Teachers say they are seeing much repetitive, one-dimensional play with violence that is becoming harder and harder to limit or control. And some children seem to have few other play interests besides this kind of play. Concerns are expressed most often around play like Anton and Phil's, play which is associated with television shows and the toys that accompany them, like the Power Rangers (Levin & Carlsson-Paige, 1995) and Teenage Mutant Ninja Turtles (Carlsson-Paige & Levin, 1992). But teachers also say that similar play often occurs around whatever violence children have seen, for instance, the World Trade Center tragedy and war against Iraq (Levin, 2003a, 2003b). Looking at war play using the two lenses can help us see how the functions and value of play with violence lie in the nature of the play.

More Violence in Society

There is a great deal of violence in the lives of most children in the United States. In fact, the level of violence some children are exposed to on a regular basis has led some clinicians and researchers to compare growing up in the United States to growing up in a war zone (Garbarino, Kostelny, & Dubrow, 1991). Whether it is violent crime, domestic and child abuse, terrorism, war, or the vast quantities of "just-for-fun" entertainment violence, children are exposed to more and more violence both directly and through the media.

Without considering all the ways exposure to violence can be harmful to them, children now have large quantities of violent content to process and try to figure out and to develop some sense of mastery and control over. They also have many models of violent behavior to try to incorporate into their play. Given this current climate, we would expect them to engage in more and more play of a violent nature. As children are increasingly exposed to violence and are bringing that violent content to their play, however, there are other factors that seem to be undermining their efforts (Levin, 1996, 1998).

Changes in Children's Media and Toys

The children of today are in front of a screen end for an enormous amount of time, spending an average of 6½ hours with media per day (Woodard & Gridina, 2000). During that time they will see a great deal of violence—an average of 8,000 killings and more than 100,000 other acts of violence by the time they finish elementary school (Diamant, 1994). It is young children who are the most vulnerable to the effects of the media violence they see (Bushman & Huesmann, 2001). Yet, 36% of children under 6 years old have a television set in their bedroom where parents have less control over what they see and are not there to help children process the content they experience (Rideout, Vandwater, & Wartella, 2003). Then, when children are not watching television, much of their play time is taken up using media-linked toys that are highly realistic replicas of what they have seen on the screen, many of which are violent.

The wide-scale marketing of toy lines that are linked to media is a phenomenon that began in 1984 when the Federal Communications Commission deregulated children's television. Within two years of deregulation 9 of the 10 best-selling toys had tie-ins with television shows and 7 of those 9 television-linked toys were violent (Carlsson-Paige & Levin, 1990; Levin & Carlsson-Paige, 2006). Once the marketing of violence to children through television and other forms of media became possible, one smash hit after another swept through the childhood play culture, including Masters of the Universe, G.I. Joe, Transformers, Ghostbusters, Teenage Mutant Ninja Turtles, Mighty Morphin Power Rangers, and then, professional wrestling. In addition, blockbuster movies, that often have ratings for older children or adults—like *Jurassic Park*, *Spiderman*, and *Terminator*, have also engaged in wide-scale marketing of realistic toys. Many of these programs and movies have been highly violent. For instance, the Ninja Turtles' program averaged just over 50 acts of violence per half-hour episode and the Power Rangers, has been clocked at just over 100 per episode (Lisosky, 1995). The products marketed with children's media now touch most aspects of childhood culture—with lunchboxes, breakfast cereals, bed sheets, pajamas, thematic birthday party products, and link-ups with fast food chains. One survey of a mass-market toy store by this author and her son found more than 200 products with the Power Ranger logo at the peak of the craze.

Changes in the Quality and Quantity of Violence in Children's Play

Almost immediately after television was deregulated, teachers and parents began to report having problems with children's violent play and toys that have continued up to the present (Levin & Carlsson-Paige, 2006). They said that the play of some children seemed to focus increasingly on violent themes and content. Children were pretending to fight and hurt each other more, and they were making more toy weapons. Teachers thought they were dealing with more instances where children used fighting to resolve their conflicts. They were also seeing more hurt children, which they thought was related to the increases in play fighting. Efforts to ban, limit, or redirect the play were getting more difficult, as adults often found themselves confronted with children who were sneaking around behind their backs and engaging in "guerrilla" wars (Carlsson-Paige & Levin, 1992; Levin & Carlsson-Paige, 1995). These reports continue to today.

Not only did teachers and parents report seeing increases in play with violence and having more difficulty managing it, they were also describing a particular kind of "fighting" play that was similar to what we saw Anton and Phil doing. It is narrow and repetitive, focusing on content and actions that involve fighting, often with children taking on the roles of good guy television characters fighting the bad guys. In one study, after watching such characters on television, children's play and interactions were significantly more aggressive than the play of children who did not recently see such a program (Boyatzis, Matillo, & Nesbitt, 1995). In addition, teachers often reported that the play did not develop or change much over time. One of the most striking aspects of accounts of such play from teachers all over the country was that it sounded pretty much the same everywhere. It did not have the rich variations of play like that of the children in the Oklahoma City bombing or dinosaur scenarios discussed above (Carlsson-Paige & Levin, 1992; Levin, 1996; Levin & Carlsson-Paige, 1995, 2006).

Creative versus Imitative Play

Play with violence, like Phil and Anton's, does not match common notions of play very well, where children are in control and creatively shape what they do to fit their individual needs, experiences, and concerns at their own level of development. Phil and Anton's activity seems more like imitation (Berk, 1995, Carlsson-Paige & Levin, 1990; Levin, 1995, 2003b; Piaget & Inhelder, 1969). In effect, they are trying to replicate salient aspects of the fighting they saw the Power Rangers do. It looks as if they get stuck at that level of action without bringing in any of their own ideas, needs, or skills. Unlike the dinosaur and block play in the first two play scenarios, which the children use in the service of their evolving plot, the Power Rangers action figures seem to show the boys what to do and keep them focused on the fighting.

Play like Phil and Anton's is not what adherents to the developmental side of the debate refer to when they talk about war play that is meeting children's needs. If children are not working on their own ideas in playing about what they have seen, they are less likely to be successful in working out the issues they are bringing to their play in ways that serve their social, emotional, or intellectual development. It will probably be harder for them to resolve the content about violence so they can move on to new issues and content.

When children are primarily imitating the violence they see, as Phil and Anton do, rather than working it through in some more meaningful way, they run the risk of merely assimilating whatever violence they have seen without creating a more realistic view of that violence or transforming it into more positive social solutions. When this happens, they get fixated on the violent and aggressive aspects of what they have seen rather than use their play to develop a repertoire of positive, nonviolent responses to violence (Carlsson-Paige & Levin, 1990; Levin & Carlsson-Paige, 2006).

Reframing the Debate over Play with Violence: Beyond Banning War Play

As parents and educators have struggled to figure out how to respond to the increase in and changing nature of many children's play with violence, many adults have relied on the old paradigm of the two sides of the debate. They are then often frustrated and worried by what might be the resulting conclusions to which either side can lead. Parents, who worry what children learn about violence from their play with violence, have often tried to limit it. They say that they have either thrown up their hands in despair and let their children have control of play because their struggles feel ineffectual or they have converted to a developmental view and decided that it is just a normal part of children's growing up. Many teachers who find this play very hard to control and keep the children safe, worry that it promotes violence, report working harder and harder to try to limit or ban war play from the classroom only to discover guerilla wars springing up. Some say they reluctantly allow it in a specially designated place like the playground and deal with the frequent problems that arise when children get hurt. Such responses are understandable within the context of the conflicting forces that seem to be influencing children's play with violence.

Using a lens that incorporates both the developmental and sociopolitical views, as illustrated in the three scenarios above, can help sort out the dilemma (Carlsson-Paige & Levin, 1990; Levin & Carlsson-Paige, 2006). On the one hand, it appears that simply allowing imitative play with violence leaves children in charge of the lessons they learn from their play with violence without the benefit of adult support and influence. Children also will be left to their own devices to engage in imitative play, without adult help in transforming it into creative, imaginative play that has the potential of meeting their developmental needs.

On the other hand, banning play with violence leaves children who are exposed to violence without a primary vehicle they have for working it out and can leave them frustrated and anxious. Unless adults find alternative channels for play that can help children work through the violence in their lives in some meaningful way (Levin, 2003a), children will be denied an important vehicle for achieving some level of equilibrium and mastery of the violence they have seen. In addition, as many teachers and parents report, a lot of children will simply engage in violent play behind adults' backs, as the ban cuts off adults from having the opportunity to influence the play but has little impact on the influence the play is having on children.

Deciding on an Approach: Meeting the Needs of Children in Today's Society

It is hard to imagine any perfect approach for dealing with children's play with violence in these times (Levin, 2003b). This chapter takes the position that the best approach would be to vastly reduce the amount of violence to which children are exposed. This would include limiting the marketing of violence to children through media and toys, and we can do a lot to work toward this goal.

But as long as children growing up today are seeing vast amounts of violence, many will continue to have a greater need to use their play to work through the violence they see than children in the past. As they do, there is always the risk that they will learn messages that promote and glorify violence. This danger is heightened when children merely imitate what they have seen rather than work it through in creative and personally meaningful play. And, even when children do succeed in working through the violence in their play, it continues to be worrisome to contemplate what they are learning about violence when so much of their playtime and energy is devoted to such violent play.

Adults, therefore, need to develop responses that take into account both the multiple needs of children who are growing up in the midst of violence and the concerns of adults who worry about how play with violence might be contributing to the overall level of violence in society.[4] A dynamic approach, which is forged to match the needs of specific children, families, and classrooms as well as the wider community, is presented here:

- Try to limit young children's exposure to all types of violence as much as possible, even though our best efforts will often feel ineffectual.
- Look for meaningful avenues that will allow children to work through the violence to which they are exposed. In addition to using their play, art, writing, and other forms of creative expression, they need to know they can talk to caring adults who will help them tell their stories in ways that can promote growth and healing.
- Observe children as they engage in play with violence to ascertain the nature of the play. Try to learn more about what specific aspects of violence they have experienced or heard about, what aspects of it they may be working on and how, and what their particular needs may be. Use this information to decide how to help the children better use their play with violence in positive, growth-promoting ways.
- Try to limit children's use of highly realistic media-linked toys that help to keep play narrowly focused on violent content. When they do play with such toys, help them devise more creative and varied uses.

- Encourage the use of open-ended toys, which enhance rather than control play, instead of highly realistic toys that channel children into imitating violent scripts. But remember that children who use a lot of media-linked toys often need help learning how to use toys that do not show them exactly what to do.
- Help children become good dramatic players. Even though most adults trained to work with young children have been taught not to take an active role in children's dramatic play, today many children engage in repetitive, imitative play with violence and need direct help from adults to move beyond that narrow focus (Jones & Reynolds, 1992; Smilansky & Shefataya, 1990). As children become better players, they are more likely to be able to work through the violence they encounter in their play.
- Provide children with appealing, nonviolent content that they can bring into their play. This can reduce some children's dependence on play with violence.
- Help children to keep their play with violence safe. It is very easy for the play to get out of control and children need adults to do such things as: set appropriate limits around safety issues; suggest safer alternatives; gently redirect the play; and help children understand the effects of their actions that can be dangerous (Levin, 2003b).
- Develop strategies for counteracting the messages children may be learning that glorify and promote violence both in and out of their play, and teach them alternatives to that violence (Carlsson-Paige & Levin, 1998; Levin, 2003a). Work in the wider community to change the conditions that are contributing to so much violence in children's lives.

Notes

1. The terms *play with violence*, *war play*, and *superhero play* are used here to encompass the various forms of fighting and aggressive play children engage in than the more common terms, *war* and *superhero play*.
2. Examples of children bringing such news to their play in this way are not unique to these children. I heard many accounts of similar play in the months after the World Trade Center tragedy (Levin, 2003a).
3. Children who directly experience violence also often bring the violent content to their play in a manner similar to how Wanda and Shelley do so. Often it occurs in therapeutic environments, but it also can come up in play with violence at home and school (e.g., Terr, 1990).
4. For examples of teachers successfully working with these complexities see Eric Hoffman (2004), Jane Katch (2001), and Jane Koplow (1996).

References

Baruch, D. W. (1942). *You, your children, and war*. New York: D. Appleton-Century.

Berk, L. (1995). Vygotsky's theory: The importance of make-believe play. *Young Children, 50*(1), 30–39.

Bettelheim, B. (1987, March). The importance of play. *The Atlantic, 259*(3), 35–46.

Boyatzis, C., Matillo, G., & Nesbitt, K. (1995). Effects of the "Mighty Morphin Power Rangers" on children's aggression with peers. *Child Study Journal 25*(1), 45–55.

Bushman, B. J., & Huesmann, L. R. (2001). Effects of televised violence on aggression. In D. G. Singer & J. L. Singer (Eds.), *Handbook of children and the media* (pp. 223–254). Thousand Oaks, CA: Sage.

Carlsson-Paige, N., & Levin, D. E. (1990). *Who's calling the shots?: How to respond effectively to children's fascination with war play and war toys*. Philadelphia: New Society.

Carlsson-Paige, N., & Levin, D. E. (1992). The subversion of healthy development and play: Teachers' reactions to the Teenage Mutant Ninja Turtles. *Day Care and Early Education, 19*(2), 14–20.

Carlsson-Paige, N., & Levin, D. E. (1998). *Before push comes to shove: Building conflict resoluition skills with children*. St. Paul, MN: Redleaf Press.

Diamant, A. (1994). Special report: Media violence. *Parents Magazine, 69*(10), 40–41, 45.

Freud, A., & Burlingham, D. T. (1943). *Children and war*. New York: Ernst Willard.

Garbarino, J., Kostelny, K., & Dubrow, N. (1991). *No place to be a child: Growing up in a war zone*. Lexington, MA: Lexington Books.

Goldstein, J. (Ed.). (1994). *Toys, play, and child development*. New York: Cambridge University Press.

Groves, B. M. (2002). *Children who see too much*. Boston: Beacon Press.

Hoffman, E. (2004) *Magic capes, amazing powers: Transforming superhero play in the classroom*. St. Paul, MN: Redleaf Press.

Jones, E., & Reynolds, G. (1992). *The play's the thing: Teachers' roles in children's play*. New York: Teachers College Press.

Jones, G. (2002). *Killing monsters: Why children need fantasy, Super heroes, and make-believe violence.* New York: Basic Books.

Katch, J. (2001). *Under deadman's skin: Discovering the meaning of children's violent play.* Boston: Beacon Press.

Koplow, L. (1996). *Unsmiling faces: How preschools can heal.* New York: Teachers College Press.

Kuykendall, J. (1995). Is gun play OK here? *Young Children, 50*(5), 56–59.

Levin, D. E. (1995). Media, culture and the undermining of play in the United States. In E. Klugman (Ed.), *Play, policy, and practice* (pp. 175–184). St. Paul, MN: Red Leaf.

Levin, D. E. (1996). Endangered play, endangered development: A constructivist view of the role of play in development and learning. In A. Phillips (Ed.), *Playing for Keeps.* St. Paul, MN: Redleaf Press.

Levin, D.E. (1998). *Remote control childhood? Combating the hazards of media culture.* Washington, DC: National Association for the Education of Young Children.

Levin, D. E. (2003a). *Teaching young children in violent times: Building a peaceable classroom* (2nd ed.). Cambridge, MA: Educators for Social Responsibility.

Levin, D. E. (2003b). Beyond banning war and superhero play: Meeting children's needs in violent times. *Young Children, 58*(3), 60–66.

Levin, D. E., & Carlsson-Paige, N. (1995). Mighty Morphin Power Rangers: Teachers voice concern. *Young Children, 50*(6), 67–72.

Levin, D. E., & Carlsson-Paige, N. (2006). *The war play dilemma: What every parent and teacher needs to know!* (2nd ed.). New York: Teachers College Press.

Lisosky, J. M. (1995, March 12–16). *Battling standards worldwide—"Mighty Morphin Power Rangers" fight for their lives.* Paper presented at the World Summit for Children and Television, Melbourne, Australia.

Miedzian, M. (2002). *Boys will be boys: Breaking the link between masculinity and violence* (2nd ed.). New York: Lantern Books.

Piaget, J., & Infielder, B. (1969). *The psychology of the child.* New York: Basic Books.

Rideout, V. J., Vandwater, E. A., & Wartella E. A. (2003, Fall). *Zero to six: Electronic media in the lives of infants, toddlers and preschooler. A Kaiser Family Foundation Report.* Accessed at: http://www.kff.org/entmedia/upload/22754_1.pdf

Saki. (1988). Toys of peace. In *The complete works of Saki* (pp. 393–398). New York: Dorset. (Original work published 1914)

Singer, D. G. (1993). *Playing for their lives: Helping troubled children through play therapy.* New York: Free Press.

Smilansky, S., & Shefataya, L. (1990). *Facilitating play: A medium for promoting cognitive, socio-emotional and academic development in young children.* Gaithersburg, MD: Psychosocial and Educational Publications.

Sutton-Smith, B. (1986). *Toys as culture.* New York: Gardner.

Terr, L.C. (1990). *Too scared to cry: Psychic trauma in childhood.* New York: Harper & Row.

Woodard, IV, .E., & Gridina, N. (2000). *Media in the home 2000. The fifth annual survey of parents and children.* The Annenberg Public Policy Center of the University of Pennsylvania. Survey Series No. 7. Accessed at: http://www.annenbergpublicpolicycenter.org/

40
Attaining the Protean Self in a Rapidly Changing World
Understanding Chaos through Play

KAREN VANDERVEN

Chaos now presages the future as none will gainsay. But to accept the future one must renounce much of the past (Gleick, 1987).

It seems that the very experiences these children seek out are ones we avoid: disequilibrium, novelty, loss of control, surprise. These make for a good playground... (Wheatley, 1992).

With the 21st century underway, rapid change is the hallmark in all modes of human endeavor. The economist Eamonn Kelly describes how the world is "increasingly messy, complex and interconnected": and that we are now living in a "change of age" that will "demand an openness of mind and an openness of heart that do not come readily" (2006, p. x.). Given these challenges of modern life, then, how do early childhood educators help young children grow up to be adaptable and productive contributors to such a turbulent world? The concept of a Protean self, as predicated on Proteus, the Greek sea god of many forms (Lifton, 1993) who is able to adapt readily to a rapidly changing context, while still being able to maintain an internal sense of direction, may offer a helpful metaphor to express these necessary human qualities.

During their play, young children demonstrate their capacity to function in such Protean ways. Therefore, I propose that play, as affirmed for its dynamic qualities (Fromberg, 2002; Smilansky, 1990) is an ideal medium to help us understand complex and chaotic aspects of the world. After all, "Complexity...is the unavoidable accompaniment and indeed prerequisite of progress.... the world we live in is an enormously complex system" (Rescher, 1998, p. xiii). For this compelling reason, play not only should be accepted as a legitimate educational activity in early and primary grades, but also should be a featured curricular component (although not necessarily excluding traditional instruction) for the most powerful impact of all. Thus focusing primarily on play, this chapter will:

- Provide an overview of chaos theory and its basic tenets most relevant to play;
- Describe the characteristics of play that relate to a chaos perspective;
- Show how play with its chaotic features contributes toward the attributes that comprise the Protean self needed for the future.

Applying a new conceptual framework to a phenomenon can refresh more entrenched viewpoints. No perspective expresses better than chaos theory the transformation in both world changes and worldviews, and helps us understand and relate to those changes.

As new worldviews so often do, chaos and complexity theory emanate from conceptual and empirical advances in the physical sciences. However, challenging the classical scientific view of the world as orderly, rational, predictable, and controllable, chaos theory is concerned with disequilibrium, interconnectedness, and unpredictability. In fact this transformed perspective is so compelling that we are urged to view the reality of the world as essentially chaotic (Goerner, 1994). If the reality of the world is indeed chaotic, then certainly the task of adults is to help young people learn to understand, adapt to, and live in such a world, or to develop a Protean self.

Chaos Theory

For purposes here the term *chaos* refers to the chaotic and complex processes that characterize all change (Butz, 1997). It is easiest perhaps to understand chaos theory if one considers it in contrast to the mechanistic worldview of classical theory in the physics of the 16th into the 20th century in which lawfulness, precision, linearity, predictability, stasis, and reductionism held sway (Gleick, 1987; Goerner, 1994; Penrose, 1994). This mechanistic approach to thinking about the world led to belief in technique—precise interventions that produce precise, predictable, controllable results. We get the kind of thinking that says, if I apply this technique to my children they will grow up happy (Goerner, 1994, p. 15).

With the advent of quantum theory, a theory of uncertainty, indeterminism, and mystery (Penrose, 1994, p. 150), a new worldview was ushered in. In 1987 James Gleick published the book *Chaos* that brought the concept into the public eye. Chaos theory began with the notion of "sensitive dependence on initial conditions"—that a small input into a system may lead over time to a much larger effect or output, Since then chaos theory has come to embody many other phenomena that have been applied to various social phenomena with the goal of increasing understanding of their chaotic and dynamical aspects.

With the advent of chaos theory has also come complexity theory (e.g., Gell-Mann, 1994; Kauffman, 1995). Complexity theory like chaos theory is often used as a lens for viewing and understanding social phenomena. If the original premise of chaos theory was sensitive dependence on initial conditions, the major focus of "complexity theory" is the complex adaptive system, referring to an open system that gathering information over time, undergoes significant change as it integrates and acts upon or adapts to, this information. Perhaps the connecting factor between chaos and complexity theory is the notion of the edge of chaos (Kaufmann, 1995): that an information laden system about to transform into a chaotic state has an outcome that is not predictable. At the same time, a system on the edge of chaos is the most amenable to change. As this chapter will discuss, play has both chaotic and complex aspects, that is, it functions as a complex adaptive system, and reflects many chaotic phenomena. To avoid confusion, the term *chaos theory* will continue to be used throughout to refer to both the chaotic and complex aspects of play.

The following description of some of the major features of chaos theory will outline its main features of nonlinearity, interdependence, and unpredictability, specific chaotic concepts, and the complexity theory concept of the complex adaptive system.

Nonlinearity, Interdependence, and Unpredictability

Nonlinearity is a fundamental concept in chaos theory. Nonlinearity means that not everything in the world is organized or proceeds in a logical or easily recognized order, with one entity following another sequentially. Thus linearity implies singular causation. One occurrence or phenomenon in the sequence causes the next in a proportional way: Whatever an input is into a phenomenon, the output will be directly proportional. Nonlinearity, in contrast, implies multiple causation and disproportionality: a small input may have a huge impact or a large input may have a small effect.

However, much linear thinking that espouses that one cause yields one effect is frequently utilized in education. For example, if Johnny is acting differently today, one might assume that he is upset "because something is going on at home," rather than consider that he may be affected by occurrences in any number of other systems or settings that could also affect him, in an ever evolving transactional process.

Similarly, the "more is better" thinking (VanderVen, 1994) that is commonly applied in education would suggest that children will absolutely learn more in school by lengthening the day—simply adding on more hours. Those who use nonlinear thinking recognize the inverse relation of input and output, and might suggest that children may actually learn less if the additional time were spent doing more drill and passive occupations, because the children would become even more disengaged with learning when they were in school for a shorter period of time.

Interdependence refers to the effect of multiple variables of a system in interaction with each other. The ecological theory of child development (Bronfenbrenner, 1977) holds that the child functions within a hierarchy of systems that interact among each other and are multidirectional. This theory is an early, powerful example of interdependence. Thus, causality is extremely complex. Therefore, if one wishes to encourage change, an effective intervention needs to address all aspects of the systems that cause the particular situation.

Unpredictability refers to chaos theory's notion of sensitive dependence on initial conditions: that in a "chaotic" world, one input (even a very small one) may lead to an output that is not only disproportional to the input, but also to one that is unexpected or unpredictable. For example, one might contend that using a "behavior modification" program that includes taking points away from children who misbehave, that we will be able to control children's actions in a desired way. Imagine the consternation of those who utilize these practices when they find that behavior is worse than ever and even harder to control (VanderVen, 1994). In chaos theory unpredictability is sometimes considered to be reflected by novelty, surprise, and paradoxical (unexpected) occurrences.

Complex Adaptive Systems

Complex adaptive systems are open and unbounded, and evolve over time. Such systems establish a recognizable and describable pattern of complex behavior that leads to the frequent acknowledgment that "there is order in chaos" (Goerner, 1994). As complex adaptive systems acquire information from their interaction with the environment they feed this back into themselves, demonstrating "learning" and defined regularities or schemas. They then continue to act on the world based on these schemas (Gell-Mann, 1994). Complex adaptive systems thus are both emergent—and evolutionary. One system may spawn a new one which in turn, over time, evolves into a new, but coherent, complex form, and the cycle of creation and recreation continues. Complex adaptive systems are found in all aspects of the world, living and inanimate, and as will be contended, are central to the rationale for the power and significance of play.

Specific Concepts of Chaos Theory

Within the overarching definition of chaos theory are specific concepts describing chaotic phenomena that can exist within dynamic systems. A listing of those concepts that are most pertinent to play, education, and the goals and dynamics of human development is as follows (This is an integration of earlier definitions from VanderVen, 1994; and from Gell-Mann, 1994; Gleick, 1987; Goerner, 1994; Wheatley, 1992):

- Determinism. The notion that a particular system can be determined (defined specifically) and yet have paradoxical or unexpected outcomes as it evolves over time.
- Weak chaos, Edge of chaos: A system that is about to enter a phase transition or bifurcate into a reorganized state can be said to be at the edge of chaos, demonstrating increased apparent turbulence (Kaufman, 1995). The introduction of a small amount of chaos into a system can keep it dynamic and amenable to change.
- Bifurcation: A transformation from one state into a reorganized or completely different, new state; a bifurcation may result in surprise, due to the rapidity and nature of the change.
- Sensitive Dependence on Initial Conditions: When a very small input into a system may yield widely disparate results, in form and quantity.
- Recursion. Information from a system is fed back on itself, thereby changing the nature of the system, affecting the initial condition. Often recursion effects are responsible for unanticipated or paradoxical outcomes.
- Entrainment. The joining of two or more systems into a larger, synchronous system; the synchronization of two or more rhythmic systems into a single pulse (Nachmanovitch, 1990, p.99) Entrainment thus embraces a "combinatory" notion: that separate entities become juxtaposed or connected hence forming new combinations and coherent patterns.
- Disequilibrium: Condition representing a system capable of change.
- Self-Organization. The spontaneous reemergence of a turbulent, disequilibrious system into patterned, computational (purposeful) behavior—a feature of a complex adaptive system.
- Fractal: Self-similarity, in which iteration (replicating itself additively) reproduces the same pattern at different levels of scale, over and over.
- Attractor: That which drives a system into a certain behavior, and to which the system refers as it continues to evolve, even with apparent disorder.
- Phase portrait. A geometrical, topological representation of the dynamics of a system; phase portraits or phase space portraits enable the "mapping of possible states (the) system can go through" (Goerner, 1994, p. 206).
- Fuzzy logic. Reasoning with nonabsolute or dichotomous quantities or concepts (Kosko, 1993). It relates to the mental processes that enable understanding of chaos.
- Pattern. The emergent and coherent forms that continually evolve and emerge in the natural world (e.g., Conforti, 1999).

Human Development, Play, and Chaos

Recent changes in developmental theory that represent chaotic aspects further support the framing of play as a complex adaptive system that has chaotic features. Furthermore, play is a crucial component of development.

Human development throughout the life span is no longer viewed as a sequence of invariant stages in which the person moves linearly and sequentially from one to the next. Rather it is seen as a complex, recursive, dynamic process (Kegan, 1982) in which new complex capacities emerge as a result of individuals making meaning of their experiences, and using this meaning to construct a new sense of self in a constantly emergent and lifelong evolutionary process. This shift in the conceptualization of development "from entity to process, from static to dynamic, from dichotomous to dialectical" (p. 13) and in which "a lifelong process of evolution or adaptation is the master motion in personality" (p. 113) has a strong chaos flavor. The view of human development as a dynamic process supports the examination of more specific components of development, such as play, so that the components can be integrated within these contemporary perspectives.

Human development itself is like play, a complex adaptive system in which the player takes in information and integrates it with existing information (Kegan, 1982). This integrative process, in which children construct or create new and meaningful knowledge out of their own experience, a process of constructivism, that results in the formation of new internal schemas which become entrained with other schemas. Experiences during play provide feedback that has chaotic aspects. For example, motor skills development is essential for increasingly complex forms of play. At the same time, play contributes to the development of motor skills. The chaotic aspects of motor skills have characteristics of "non-equilibrium dissipative systems" (Thelen, 1995, p. 83) that gain and lose energy as they evolve over time.

We may thus view play as having a special integrative and mediating function. Play supports and modifies development by helping children to synchronize and have self-similar experiences with fractal qualities.

Play is a significant systemic component of chaos theory. We can proceed to establish the relationship between play and chaos theory by showing how play is a complex adaptive system; and how many of the characteristics of play reflect some of the specific chaos concepts as described above.

The following section will offer a chaotic and complexity analysis of play functions, characteristics, facilitation, and development, weaving in the concepts already described.

Play Development as a Complex Adaptive System

Despite the fact that everybody seems to "know play when they see it," play is not a unitary or fixed construct, with one definition and one meaning. This crucial attribute of play is underscored by Sutton-Smith (2001), who in *The Ambiguity of Play* describes the "complexity and variability" of play and also refers to Gleick's concept of play as chaos (p. 219). Thus the "fuzzy" unbordered aspect of play allows it to be viewed as a complex adaptive system that is constantly evolving into more intricate forms and patterns, and showing other attributes of a complex adaptive system.

To show how play functions as a complex adaptive system that develops as children grow, it is helpful to review some of the commonly recognized forms and developmental sequences of play. The forms of play appear in Sara Smilansky's (1990) model, as follows: functional, or exploratory play, a sensorimotor approach in which a child learns the nature of his or her surroundings; constructive play, in which pieces or entities are combined, such as block play; dramatic play, which entails pretending; sociodramatic play, dramatic play with more than one player, and with the players interacting within a theme, and a time trajectory over which the play continues and evolves; and games-with-rules.

As a child grows, functional play allows children to import information mentally and add it to their behavioral repertoire. As this repertoire expands, and as children select anew from their physical environment and with interact with others, new forms of play emerge. As children connect and then integrate their experiences with each other through entrainment, the play becomes more complex. Thus, children combine "individual action sequences [into] multischeme combinations" (Fromberg, 1992, p. 57).

Sociodramatic play, particularly as it develops out of combinations of other forms of play, embraces interdependence and complexity (Smilansky, 1989). Thus, it may be the most "chaotic" of the established play forms. As new play themes emerge, previously combined forms may entrain again into more combinations. For example, when the teacher adds constructive play and other play forms, sociodramatic play may emerge into projects. In this process, not only may the play be bifurcative, moving into a transformed state, but also may increase the number of connections among various aspects of the play. This process leads to cooperative play, one of the most important functions of play, because it enables the formation and use of already existent connections, both with objects and with persons. As a complex adaptive system, play is open ended with multiple available pathways, forms, and options or, in a chaos framework: bifurcative, recursive, and hence unpredictable. It can go in one direction, or take another, at any time! In this way, of course, play encourages divergent thinking—the compiling of a response to a problem out of multiple sources rather than simply providing one answer, thereby bringing out and enabling the expression of creativity (Baer, 1993; Russ, 1993).

If we apply the concepts of nonlinearity and recursion to the development of play then the emergence of new forms of play listed above is actually not a straight trajectory. Instead, the functions of play follow a more recursive unfolding and regeneration that is aligned with chaos theory and contemporary theories of human development (Kegan, 1982). Precursor behaviors become entrained into more complex and synchronous forms, and then the form, like a fuzzy image becoming focused, surfaces visibly.

Games can serve as an example. Game playing begins during infancy and does not suddenly emerge as games-with-rules during the school years. Such simple games as patty cake and peek a- boo promote the anticipation of another's actions and may serve to bring them forth, thus containing game aspects. This phenomenon functions as games-with-implicit-rules. Children then engage in games with informal rules prior to the introduction of the more formal rules of many games. Children who engage in game- with-informal-rules adapt their own responses to nominal guidelines, but with less, or no, emphasis on winning and losing as is characteristic of games-with-rules which evolve from this dynamic sequence. The dynamic aspect of games, in all forms, requires children to anticipate the moves of others, to adapt, and cooperate. Thus, games are significant in preparing children for adult life, and also for their ability to reflect dynamic, chaotic aspects of systems (Sigmund, 1993). In fact, this "chaotic" analysis suggests to me that game activity may appropriately be utilized in early childhood programs earlier, and more explicitly, than it is now. Games can be adapted by simplifying rules, themes, formats, and the like.

As children grow older and continue to play more formal, complex games, they may implicitly learn approaches to adaptation, such as how to take a particularly entity, be it a game or something else, and identify specific components of it that can be altered or tweaked to make it more readily fit into a particular context and need. Through their exposure to play (including games) throughout childhood, children acquire information, connect with others as they adapt to the parameters of evolving play scenarios, and develop the crucial quality of self-regulation (Berk & Winsler, 1995). The active experience of playing helps children to begin to develop a sense of themselves as having multiple capacities that they can apply in different situations, a strong developmental precursor to the adult Protean self.

Chaotic Characteristics of Play

The following discussion briefly considers how play reflects and represents chaotic concepts. Thus, players enact and implicitly understand chaotic concepts. The characteristics of play that make it playful and reflect its chaotic capacities, include the features listed below. Play is:

- Nonlinear, representing the chaos concept of sensitive dependence on initial conditions. Play's nonlinear aspects are obvious to the observer of children's play. The outcome of many spontaneously forming and rapidly shifting play episodes is unpredictable. A small input into a play situation may yield a completely different and nonproportional output. For example, a child may suggest a new prop for a dramatic play situation that will alter the content, roles, pace and outcomes of the play. Many play materials express nonlinear components. For example, the old childhood trick of lining up dominoes in a long curving line and gently knocking the first one over, represents the attaining of an output that is disproportional to the input.
- Connectionist. There are connectionist, or entraining, aspects to many play forms. Constructive materials make connections between the various parts and pieces. Players can add smaller constructed components to larger ones in order to change the configuration of the construc-

tion. Sociodramatic and project-oriented play require players to make meaningful connections between various components of the play, not to speak of the connections that play enables the players to make among themselves.

- Recursive. Because play is constructivist, in that children construct play activity out of their own experience, play is recursive. Play feeds back into itself information that it creates and therefore changes the nature of the player(s) and the evolving nature of the play.
- Entraining. Playful activity can represent entrainment as players may take two disparate elements, combine them, and enable them to function together integratively and harmoniously. For example, a play episode may begin in one area, as players embark on enacting a theme, and then entrain into itself.
- Disequilibrious. Children actually initiate play as a result of an internal feeling of disequilibrium. The act of play addresses that feeling and brings a sense of mastery and inner harmony. Disequilibrium does not always have to be a negative situation to be resolved; curiosity can also create a sense of disequilibrium. When a play episode results in a perception of inner equilibrium, another area of meaning may then emerge.
- Fractal. Many play materials have fractal qualities in that they are similar in form no matter what their size. Unit blocks are just one example.
- Sensitive dependence on initial conditions. In play, a minor or apparently insignificant occurrence can have extensive and influential outcomes. For example, the simple, perhaps even casual act of an adult or player suggesting that a certain object stand for a theme-related concept, can initiate a dynamic and expansive play episode that may last for days, even weeks and months. Thus, a small input leads to a large output.
- Bifurcative. A play episode can grow in intensity and complexity, and suddenly bifurcate, change in form and content, with new subsystems emerging. For example, children can be carrying out one theme when suddenly the idea emerges for a new, related theme. A group of players may separate at the bifurcation point in order to carry out and develop the new theme while the old one continues.
- Attractor-driven. The goal of the play, or the theme, serves as the attractor or driving point around which the play revolves and evolves. The dynamic nature of play implies that goals and themes can shift and, as they do, so will the attractor. These changes may be gradual or transformational, and then be governed by a periodic or even "strange" attractor.
- Self-organizing. As play evolves into a complex adaptive system, it is self-organizing, developing its own pattern of coherence. For example, children may identify a theme, "Let's play hospital," quickly assign roles, and decide what will stand for what. As the scenario evolves, the players will demonstrate elements of self-organization.
- Patterned. Play, particularly with certain materials, enables patterns to be created or to emerge from a more fluid situation.

With these capacities and chaotic features of play, it is crucial to consider that the play itself must be rich and dynamic, therefore necessitating attention to how to facilitate play.

Play Facilitation

Just as some policy makers and teachers resist the inclusion of play as a legitimate educational component of the school curriculum, there also has been some resistance to the suggestion that teachers and caregivers might take an active role in enabling good quality play to occur. However, there is research evidence that children with gaps in their development and experience need more active facilitation; and such facilitation can result in both higher level play and other developmental outcomes. Among facilitation strategies are the following:

- suggesting a theme;
- suggesting a use for an object;
- taking on or assigning a role;
- adding a player;
- introducing a new object; or
- changing the physical environment (Smilanksy, 1990).

Another strategy is to create a web, in which players brainstorm various notions around a topic or theme (Katz & Chard, 2000). The web helps to bifurcate play into higher, more complex levels that take on new significance in a chaos analysis. Despite research findings, however, the role of adult facilitation in play is a debated issue. Several chaos concepts are particularly relevant to justify play facilitation, as follows:

- Determinism. With this paradoxical concept (a system can be determined and have unpredictable outcomes) play facilitation strategies, such as setting the stage for play or suggesting a theme, need not be viewed as dampers on the play, since their outcomes may not be totally predictable.
- Weak chaos. Any play facilitation action injects weak chaos into the system, and keeps it dynamic: changing, moving, evolving, especially when the play as complex adaptive system is in equilibrium, or begins to show entropy.
- Bifurcation. To extend play, the facilitator may encourage a bifurcation, a transition into a new form or state. The Vygotskyan concept of scaffolding (Berk & Winsler, 1995) is pertinent; in effect, scaffolding a child toward a higher level of development is analogous to creating a bifurcation. Given "sensitive dependence on initial conditions," any facilitation can encourage such a bifurcation.
- Attractor. As play settles into a stable pattern and then begins to run down, facilitation may alter the attractor to reconfigure the play into another more novel focus that engages the children's energy and attention.
- Phase portrait. The phase portrait is a geometric, topological representation of the dynamics of a system. Phase portraits or "phase space portraits" enable the mapping of possible states (the) system can go through (Goerner, 1994, p. 206). The process of webbing—which graphically maps the extensions, existent knowledge, and related themes of a given concept—can be considered the childhood analogy of a phase portrait; indeed a well-done web, with its varied patterns and connections, is a dynamic representation of connections between concepts.

Connecting Play and the Protean Self

When considering the significance of play in the development of the Protean self, its specific functions in development are key. A synthesis of research and scholarship on play (Fromberg, 1992; 2002; Smilansky, 1990a, 1990b; VanderVen, 2004) tells us that play promotes the following understandings and abilities which will be related later to the attributes of the Protean self:

- Representational/Symbolic. Play allows the player to let one thing stand for another, in effect, the use of symbols to represent his or her perception of the world through both symbolic and nonsymbolic use of various media. (There will be a discussion below about play as an ideal medium for representing, and hence experiencing, chaotic content and concepts.)
- Making meaning. Play is personally meaningful because the player can connect various elements of experience. A constructivist context enables players to make meaning out of their experience through combining, or entraining, various aspects of their experience into larger configurations.

The patterned aspect of a complex adaptive system is relevant here in that the play enables the player to gain an experiential sense of meaningful patterns.

- Dynamic. The very nature of play, as it develops and evolves in the growing human being, and as any particular theme or material use shifts from moment to moment, its oscillatory quality (Fromberg, 2002), embraces continual change. Thus play demonstrates the capacity of children to convey the dynamic, changing, and interactive aspects of a phenomenon or situation.
- Connectionist. Play enables children to make connections among themes, situations, and persons, especially in cooperative play. Thus, play is an ideal medium for understanding interdependence.
- Referential. Play has a focus at any particular time. This may be in the form of a theme, or a frame of reference that gives the play itself a purpose. Thus, in addition to process for its own sake, play encourages goal-oriented or computational behavior.
- Regulatory. Play has been recognized for years as a form of self-expression that enables the integration, and hence mastery, of diverse and perhaps puzzling, experiences. In this way, play helps to develop self-regulation. Play enables children to integrate and deal with disequilibrious experiences, which often serve as the energizing force to sustain play.
- Creative. The combinatory, integrative, aspects of play both develop and reflect divergent thinking. Play enables children to creatively construct new patterns and configurations. In fact, as children elaborate and modify the themes of their play, they are in line with the contention that creativity in essence is a variation on a theme (Hofstadter, 1983).
- Informational. As a dynamic system in constant evolution, play creates information. Children develop abstractions, and knowledge of attributes of both objects and persons. Through entrainment, they incorporate new information into older constructs.

Attaining the Attributes of the Protean Self Through Play

It is quite apparent that play is a phenomenon that comprehensively reflects the meaning of chaos in the context of the human life span when life itself is a chaotic undertaking. The characteristics of play actually enable representation and observation of chaotic phenomena. Furthermore, the concept of the Protean self is an ideal metaphor for focusing the connection of chaos and play, and to develop the attributes for living effectively and adapting to the reality of a chaotic world.

Thus, from the experience of good quality, facilitated childhood play, opportunities to experience, to represent, and hence experience chaotic dynamics, we could expect that the emerging mature thinker and contributing member of society would have the following Protean capacities:

- Self-regulation: to maintain one's center and focus in a shifting context;
- Representation: to use multiple ways to represent one's world in ways that can express its complexity;
- Systemic thinking: to recognize interdependence among components of a situation or phenomenon; and to recognize how a certain phenomenon, entity, or situation can evolve over time from the simple to the complex;
- Integration: to see patterns across formally bounded situations and occurrences;
- Improvisation and creativity: in the context of creativity conceived as making new combinations out of disparate elements or components;
- Anticipation and flexible responsiveness: anticipation and flexible responsiveness to unpredictability, sudden change, and surprise;
- Reflexive: to be able to look at one's experience and utilize it in planning one's next actions;
- Anticipation of paradoxical outcomes: apparently logical interventions into ordinary situations lead to unexpected results;

- Acceptance of ambiguity: to accept the inherent fuzzinessof many concepts and situations;
- Proactive: to construct one's own life and meaning, thereby creating weak chaos and contributing to the continued evolution of humankind. The human being, not only nature, is a vital player in determining what happens in the future (Darling, 1993);
- Utilization of metacognition: to be aware of one's own thinking processes and actions in order to develop and apply them (Fromberg, 1995; Perkins, 1992).

If we can consider the compelling argument for play in education that is reinforced by the tenets of chaos and the needs for persons who can relate productively to a chaotically driven world, then what do we need to do to encourage it in human service and educational programs that still seem primarily linear?

Toward the Future: Beyond Chaos

First of all, we must be careful not to take an either–or approach to our thinking about play, chaos, and linearity, just as we no longer view play and work as dichotomous (VanderVen, 2004). As we make the case for play as preparation for the future, just as Sara Smilansky (1990) made the case for sociodramatic play as preparation for school, we do not have to completely eliminate the linear, the predictable, and the precisely defined. Thus, classical scientific reasoning and knowledge would still be included in educational experiences.

Similarly, as we plan to expose children to play activities of various kinds that represent chaotic phenomena, we need to make sure that we offer them a way that recognizes what they may have experienced. This involves encouraging metacognition. To develop metacognition, knowledge of the strategies for knowing that one uses, and knowing what one knows, may need to be confirmed by more academic, information-oriented instructional approaches that name them. To be able to reason, even fuzzily, in any particular field, one must have core knowledge of its concepts and their characteristics and be able to use the language of that particular field. The issue is how clearly adults organize, present, and explain information so that it is conceptually accurate, explicit, meaningful, and sequenced (Perkins, 1992, p. 46).

Finally, we may need to find ways to enable those who both question the value of play and the significance of chaos theory as it enhances understanding of development, to experience play and its dynamical, chaotic aspects directly. This may involve addressing the increasingly recognized significance of adult play, which is the ability of adults to play and to reconnect with their childhood playing selves. The contention that the rare but successful adult is one who can truly be "childlike" (Hoare, 2002, p. 137, citing Erik Erikson) gives further support for the encouragement of play in both children and adults. Similar support exists in the contention that being able to play as a mature adult is a criterion for a successful and creative postcareer life (Valiant, 2002).

Armed with an integrated experience of playful experiences that are connected to relevant concepts and knowledge, encouraged and facilitated by playful adults, children may thus truly emerge as Protean selves, equipped to master the challenges of an uncertain and definitely complex and chaotic future.

Reference

Baer, J. (1993). *Creativity and divergent thinking: A task-specific approach.* Hillsdale, NJ: Lawrence Erlbaum.

Berk, L., & Winsler, A. (1995). *Scaffolding children's learning: Vygotsky and early childhood education.* Washington, DC: National Association for the Education of Young Children.

Bronfenbrenner, U. (1977). Towards an experimental ecology of human development. *American Psychologist, 33*(7), 513–532

Butz, M. (1997). *Chao and complexity: Implications for paych.ological theory and practice.* Washington, DC: Taylor and Francis.

Conforti, M. (1999*). Field, form and fate. Patterns in mind, nature and psyche.* Woodstock, CT: Spring.

Darling, D. (1995). *Equations of eternity*. New York: Hyperion.

Fromberg, D. (1992). A review of research on play. In C. Seefeldt (Ed.), *The early childhood curriculum: A review of current researcresearch* (3rd ed.). New York: Columbia University Teachers College Press

Fromberg, D. (1995). *The full day kindergarten*. New York: Columbia University Teachers College Press.

Fromberg, D. (2002). *Play and meaning in early childhood education*. Boston: Allyn & Bacon.

Gell-Mann, M. (1994). *The quark and the jaguar*. New York: W.H. Freeman.

Gleick, J. (1987). *Chaos*. New York: Viking.

Goerner, S. (1994). *Chaos and the evolving ecological universe*. Langhorne, PA: Gordon & Breach.

Hoare, C. (2002). *Erikson on development in adulthood*. Oxford: Oxford University Press.

Hofstadter, D. (1985*). Metamagical themas: Questing for the essence of mind and pattern*. New York: Basic Books.

Katz, L., & Chard, S. (2000). *Engaging children's minds: The project approach* (2nd ed.). Stamford, CT: Ablex.

Kauffman, S. (1995). *At home in the universe*. Oxford: Oxford University Press.

Kegan, R. (1982). *The evolving self*. Cambridge, MA: Harvard University Press.

Kelly, E. (2006). *Powerful times. Rising to the challenge of our uncertain world*. Upper Saddle River, NJ: Wharton School Publishing.

Kosko, B. (1993). *Fuzzy thinking*. New York: Hyperion.

Lifton, R. (1993). The protean self. New York: Basic Books.

Nachmanovitch, S. (1990). *Free play*. Los Angeles: Tarcher.

Penrose, R. (1989). *The emperor's new mind*. New York: Oxford University Press.

Perkins, D. (1992). *Smart schools*. New York: The Free Press.

Rescher, N. (1998). *Complexity: A philosophical overview*. New Brunswick, NJ: Transaction.

Russ, S. (1993). *Affect and creativity: The role of affect and play in the creative process*. Hillsdale, NJ: Erlbaum.

Sigmund, K.(1993). *Games of life*. New York: Oxford University Press

Smilansky, S. (1989). Significance of creative materials and pretend activities as a medium for the development of cognitive, academic and socio-emotional abilities and skills of young children. In B. Po-King Chan (Ed.), *Early childhood toward the 21st century. A worldwide perspective*. Hong Kong: Yew Chung Education Publishing.

Smilansky, S. (1990). *Facilitating play: A medium for promoting cognitive, socio-emotional and academic development in young children*. Gaithersburg, MD: Psychological and Educational Publications.

Sutton-Smith, B. (2001). The ambiguity of play. Cambridge, MA: Harvard University Press.

Thelen, E. (1995). Motor development: A new synthesis. *American Psychologist, 50*(2), 79–95

Vaillant, G. (2002). Aging well. Boston: Little Brown.

VanderVen, K. (1994). Preventing second-generation child abuse: Applying chaos theory to reframe interventions. *The Child and Youth Care Administrator, 6*(1), 27–34.

VanderVen, K. (2004). Beyond fun and games to a meaningful theory of play: Can a hermeneutic perspective contribute? In S. Reifel & M. Brown (Eds), *Social contexts of early education, and reconceptualizing play. Advances in Early Education and Day Care* (Vol. 13, pp. 165–206). Oxford: Elsevier.

Wheatley, M. (1992). *Leadership and the new science*. San Francisco: Berrett-Kohler.

Epilogue

Emerging and Future Contexts, Perspectives, and Meanings of Play

DORIS BERGEN AND DORIS PRONIN FROMBERG

As a member of the World Future Society, Doris Bergen attends conferences and avidly reads the organization's journal. She remains very interested in how contemporary events can be used in future forecasting. The most important thing she has learned while trying to answer such questions as, "How do you think children will be playing in the year 2050?" was that there are numerous factors existing at any one time that have the potential to affect the future and that the weight given to these factors by various future forecasters differs greatly.

Futurists take the trends that appear to be evident at one particular time and project them into future years to decide what their eventual impact might be. What appears as only a slight trend, if projected using existing probability formulas, may be predicted as a major influence on future conditions. (This slight-into-massive transformation parallels the chaos theory concept of sensitive dependence on initial conditions.) What is most intriguing about the programs of future-oriented conferences is that the presentations seem to be evenly distributed between those that predict dire consequences and those that envision glowing possibilities. Many times the futurists use similar present-day data to make these negative and positive predictions!

What does this mean for those persons who are trying to predict the future of play? While many factors that may affect play remain to be identified, two present trends can be cited that have the potential to be major influences in the future. One is the increase in sophisticated and emerging technology, which is making it possible for human beings to have more leisure (either chosen or forced by economic change), communicate more intensely with others throughout the world (through computers and television), travel more widely (through faster transportation options), and expand the possibilities of action and thinking (with CD-ROM, DVD, virtual reality, and video games). The other explosion of knowledge is in psychobiology, which is opening up windows of opportunity in health (genetic evaluation and repairs, as well as new medications), cognitive science (understanding, memory, and other information-processing domains), and social-personality psychology (enhancing mental health, understanding social attractions, and conflict).Each of these trends, if carried forward, enables us to make either a very positive or a very negative prediction about the future of children's play.

First, the positive: Play will become so valued by adults, who will have the leisure, health, and technological resources to engage in more play themselves, that the value of play for children will be more widely recognized. Children will be encouraged to play with all aspects of their learning, to use new play materials and processes, and to interact regularly with adults in intergenerational and intercultural play. Both males and females will be encouraged to play with many media and in cooperative as well as competitive ways. Instead of having actual warring conflicts, disagreements will be handled in symbolic games and conflict resolution will be managed in a low-risk context; thus children will learn through their play to resolve social as well as cognitive problems. Health will improve, the value of play for information processing will be recognized, and technologically enhanced creative thinking will be promoted.

Now the negative: Play will be taken over by adults, who will appropriate for themselves all of the growth-enhancing value of play. These adults will require children to earn the right to play, after they have mastered some authoritatively determined body of knowledge. Because the population as a whole will be older, the needs of adults will be even more preeminent than they are now; thus children's ideas and actions will seem less important and their need to play will not be considered of great importance. The gender divisions seen today in children's play will continue to be encouraged by the media, resulting in even greater competitive, adult-directed, sports-games demands, especially on boys, and stereotyping of fashion and shopping play, especially for girls. Technological development will not lead to the resolution of conflict through symbolic games but rather will result in more sophisticated methods of destroying other cultures and peoples. The children's play that is permitted will increasingly mirror a violent society, with the toys that now provide these models becoming pervasive.

The most important point to remember in predicting the future is that the actions taken in the present can promote or diminish the trends that will affect the future. If policymakers decide what should be the play opportunities for children in the future and they act to influence the present society in ways that strengthen the trends that can lead to these outcomes, then it is possible to envision a positive future in which adults will recognize play as important for all people, and will encourage children to reach their full play potential. To create these conditions, adults need to realize that the future of children's play depends on everyone.

There are some strategies that committed adults might employ in implementing actions that promote children's right to play in the contemporary world. There already is a policy statement, which was adopted by the United Nations (1989). Article 31 of this document confirms the child's right to play, culture, and the arts. (The United States is the only Western nation, and only one of a few nations overall, that has never ratified this document.) The International Association for the Child's Right to Play also published a document, *The Child's Right to Play* (1979/1990). The proponents of this document have stated, "If the future of play for children is to be assured and play considered a guaranteed right of every child, there is much work to be done. In the next millennium, society owes children 'the best it has to give,' which includes the right to play" (Guddemi, Jambor, & Moore, 1998, p. 528).

The contexts, perspectives, and meanings of play will continue to be influenced by a postmodern world. Readers may take up the issues as well as the conclusions regarding play raised in this book as a basis for many future discussions.

New Contexts for Play in a Postmodern World

During an era that is both rooted in the hierarchical linear determinism of the factory model and in transition to an emerging postmodern, self-organizing system, play is in a paradoxical position. This paradox is confounded by the impact of technology through the mass media, such as television and computer communication. Technology has created two major accessibility dichotomies, one of which is seen in the contrast between the general access to varied technologies by the "haves" and the lack of access to most technologies because of the daily economic realities of the "have-nots." The other dichotomy exists in the knowledge gap between the same mass media messages presented on television, the most commonly accessible technology to people of all cultures in the United States, and the specific nontechnical event knowledge beyond the media that is multicultural and individualistic. These accessibility differences create a dynamic that cuts across most general trends cited as indicative of postmodern social systems.

Influences of Technologically Based Play

The influence of a postmodern world in which roles, agents, relationships, functions, materials, lifestyles, and advocates may become delineated in fresh ways is not likely to repress children's play, although these influences may suggest different directions and opportunities, especially for children with more or less access to technology. The play of children whose technology access is limited to television has already been greatly affected by that medium of information. With the advent of these new media and the mediation of direct experiences that they bring, a shift in forms of play has begun for those children with access to these technologies.

For example, studies conducted by such disparate groups as the Sporting Goods Association, the Kaiser Family Foundation, and the Centers for Disease Control have found that elementary school children during the past decade have engaged in significantly less outdoor play and more sedentary activity with computers, video games, and watching television (Cauchon, 2005). Moreover, when present college-age students report memories of their childhood play, they are more likely to say it was solitary rather than with peers and indoors with technology-related toys/games rather than being active outdoor play. This is in marked contrast to the play memories of adults who grew up 10 to 15 years earlier (Bergen, 2003). Today, young children seem to have more structured, solitary, and technology-related play than these college students report. Recently, even babies are being exposed to technology toys and media, which may infringe on the time they have to gain access to parent–child play interactions.

Computer Networks and Games

There is increasing access to the Internet in elementary schools and homes. Although at the present time this access is unequally distributed, it is likely that all children and adults in the technologized world will eventually have access. For children who have access to computer technology, the Internet has replaced the library and books as sources for school research. Indeed, some teachers of children in the intermediate grades are requiring some nonelectronic library-based, book-based references in homework. Some textbooks have become available to children on-line, so that they do not have to carry heavy textbooks. Some teachers post homework and class information on line, a way to bring school and home closer, because parents also can access such information.

The Internet, with its various "rooms" and specialized subjects, can be the social approximation of "hanging out" with friends. The Internet also has been used for quilting (Louie, 1995), formerly a social leisure activity for older girls and women that had its historical roots in practical necessity. At the same time, "[h]omemade goods, which involved play and imagination as well as hard work, were 'inefficient' in the modern era but are being rediscovered in the post-modern era" (Elkind, 1991, p. 9). On the one hand, the capacity of networking with computers, when freely chosen, can feel playful and can add to the possibility for children to engage in cooperative and constructive projects. On the other hand, beyond entertainment, the freewheeling industry that communicates through computer networks raises the issue of children's exploitation by adults, whether for extended commercial gain, prurient interests, sexual abuse, or exposure to extreme violence. Computerized games and video games have replicated some aspects of board games or games that engage physical skills with balls, sticks, blocks, or balance.

It is worth noting that players in a new generation of video games not only learn to play the games but can continue to learn from the characters and situations within the play (Gee, 2005; Shaffer, Squire, Halvorson, & Gee, 2005). Consider, for example, the Electronic Arts games such as the *Sims Online* selections that also offer an opportunity to interact with other players. Another example is *The Geometer's Sketchpad* software that supports mathematical learning while permitting aesthetic representation in playful ways. The growth of Lego Robotics team competitions in the United States is a particularly potent intellectual, physical, and social play phenomenon; teams of intermediate age children compete in constructing actual representations that solve particular physical problems by using computerized Lego materials. It is noteworthy that girls as well as boys are present on the Lego Robotics teams. Thus, participating children are engaging in a motorized form of block play. Children, in a sense, are playing in advance of development as they need to use their knowledge in order to play and learn from the collaborative effort, a dynamic process that parallels the dynamics of sociodramatic play.

A postindustrial interpretation of *postprogressive* education references the development of computer software that engages players in simulations (Shaffer, 2005). Just as sociodramatic play reflects a particular grammar of experience, interactive computer-based simulation games represent an underlying structure. In both instances, the event knowledge of the players and how they use the play contributes to the relative wholesomeness of the experience. The central play issue in the players' use of new technologies is that the experience remains self-selected and meaningful.

The technology offers increasingly accurate voice recognition and realistic voice synthesis that provides additional feedback and "friendly" use. In such transformations, there is a redistribution of physical involvement and social contact, as well as different levels of access for people of varying ages and abilities. Children can enter into play frames that contain the potential for them to ask "What if…?" and behave "as if" play is possible. For example, the game format of "Microworlds," developed by the MIT Media Lab Learning and Common Sense Group (2005), permits players to generate new connections beyond simulations; Starlogo 2.2 (2005) also permits interactive play. It is apparent that the computer offers some parallels with play that can be seductive because it is intrinsically motivating, usually basically risk-free, empowering, and satisfying. The boundaries of play or the playground, however, exist in a different medium. The issues to raise in the face of electronic frames and toys is the degree to which direct experience and child empowerment trade off for varied implementations. For the physically challenged child, for example, the assistive technology of finger or voice control through a computer becomes empowering.

A related development has been the evolution of the IPOD and cell phone, instant messaging (IM), and instant webcam communication (interactive video-camera and microphone). Children also "direct connect" with their friends and send photos without e-mail or instant messaging with pictures. Children as young as 6 years of age have begun to engage in Instant Messaging (IM) with other children (Personal communication, 2005).* The development of IM has, in turn, reduced the use of e-mail among children in the elementary school. Along with the use of both e-mail and IM, there has developed a system of abbreviated spelling that has become national in scope; for example, G2G=got to go; BRB=be right back; TTYL=talk to you later; LOL=laughing out loud; GN=good night; GM=good morning; BIE='bye; CUZ=because; 2=to, two, too; WEN=when; WER=where; SUM1=someone; beta=better; sumthin=something. Language is always changing, as is apparent with the streamlining of spelling since Chaucer's time. Some adults, however, have expressed concern about their children's use of standard spelling because of phonetic IM spelling. It is worth considering,

---

*The Kravitz family of Manalapan, New Jersey and the Janis family of Baton Rouge, Louisiana provided helpful information.

though, that the development of IM is a playful form of social interaction that children voluntarily seek out. Children play with the freedom and power of changing their IM screen names. Children also playfully decorate their cell phones with covers or dangling toys.

Some issues to consider in the context of these technological play forms include the speed of communication and access as well as the disparity of access. First, children who have their own computers or cell phones as compared with children who share a computer or cell phone at home have different opportunities. In turn, those children who have no such access are outside of these interactive opportunities beyond school or public library settings. The speed of communication and nearly constant access to one another might impact on the relative time available for contemplation, personal fantasy, and independent, creative connection-making. Thus, in some ways, technological advances bring us closer to others but, perhaps, in both more and less intense ways. Thus, there is an opportunity for research on the impact of speed and electronic contact on the nature of play, socialization, communication, and learning.

Virtual Reality

A power shift takes place, however, when virtual reality laboratories and playgrounds program their simulated range of play opportunities. "Instead of using screens and keyboards, people can put displays over their eyes, gloves on their hands, and headphones on their ears. A computer controls what they sense; and they, in turn, can control the computer" (Aukstakalnis & Blatner, 1992, p. 7). Participants can feel, smell, see, hear, zap, and experience velocity changes "as if" they were real. For example, the participant can recreate some of the vicissitudes of watching a slapstick comedy or horror film; in watching either film, there is a thrill of suspense, relief, and sense of empowerment in risking the adrenalin rush without danger of humiliation, damage, or destruction. Virtual reality technology also has been used to reduce anxiety, as a type of play therapy (Schare & Scardapane, 2005).

The multisensory nature and three-dimensionality of virtual reality technology can affect tacitly held assumptions about play and learning. Public school education in the United States, for example, historically has afforded primacy to the two-dimensional visual domain by emphasizing written skills. By marginalizing the strong oral skills in which children are competent before they begin formal education, many children become immediately handicapped. The strong heuristics in the oral tradition of human beings offer valuable ways of encoding and retrieving experiences (Egan, 1988). Sociodramatic play, in particular, rests heavily on oral skills. By marginalizing these skills, therefore, schools may contribute to the disempowerment of children in additional ways that subtly influence their creative and social competence as well as their capacity to play. It is possible that virtual reality technology can "readjust the ratio, moving the auditory back into parity with the visual…and potentially all other modes of sensation as well" (Moulthrop, 1993, p. 80). To the extent that this readjustment occurs, it is possible that such technology can provide a better balance in schools than is currently the case. For example, educational games in the Active Worlds Educational Universe software, provide virtual environments that are interactive (Active Worlds Universe, 2005).

Regardless of the range of options, virtual is still not real; the impressive array of options has limits. The consumer can construct and create only information that programmers can translate into digital form (Wexelblat, 1993). The programmers' imaginations, connection-making options, and aesthetic sensibilities may also close down children's unique connection-making and problem-solving processes before they have a chance to become engaged. Television programming, in itself, markets particular ideologies and attitudes toward people based upon gender, class, race, and abilities. By reaching more deeply into and touching human sensory experiences, it is certainly possible that, as access to virtual reality technology expands, it can become equally influential. Of course, influence has the potential to broaden as well as narrow one's social perspectives and personal possibilities.

Among recent developments in schools are "virtual trips" to other locations. Another innovation is an interactive and participatory "virtual" dissection of a frog or other life form. Children can interact with virtual film characters. For children who live in locations that are distant from trip locales, or for schools that do not fund field trips, the virtual trip may serve as a bonus. However, each region has unique offerings that, nevertheless, offer important possibilities for underlying learning and play. There needs to be caution not to substitute the virtual for the real, and to provide plenty of opportunities for social interaction through play.

Now that there is a recursive relationship among toys, television, and stories in books, with commercial interests transforming any one medium into the others, the notion of immersing children in the simulated three-dimensional environments of virtual reality technology invites speculation concerning both the best and worst case scenarios that might result. At the same time, it is apparent that among the services of virtual reality technology are the possibilities to entertain, educate, and empower (Moulthrop, 1993). The capacity of human beings to entertain multiple mental models helps to make virtual reality possible. As another mental model, virtual reality builds on the shared awareness that makes scripted play possible. As is the case within the play continuum, the stages of virtual reality include passivity (person cannot control), exploration (person attempts to find out how things work), and interaction (person can interact and change events) (Wexelblat, 1993, p. 23): "[T]he technology is simply a tool" (p. 14). As with any tool or medium, providing balance in children's access and use of time becomes an important consideration. Perhaps it is helpful to consider computers, CD-ROM (voice and motion picture synthesized), and virtual reality technologies as additional playground sites. Virtual reality technology may develop into the broadly available, ultimate, mediated experience that can transport participants into sensing other times, places, and physical experiences.

The process of balancing simulation with real experience remains the challenge of the future. To maintain this balance, children need to have opportunities for authentic play experiences. There have been many voices raised to promote attention to "real-life" experiences for children, even as the virtual world becomes more prominent. There also are signs that adults are attempting to balance their vicarious experiences with more authentic pastimes. If the current surge of interest in pursuing more and varied authentic activities—ranging, for example, from pick-your-own apples to climbing real rocks, hiking through and clogging national parks—is a prologue to the future, then it is possible to be optimistic about meeting the challenge of a balanced life. The postmodern world is, after all, focused on the situation-specific, individual perspective and experience. Such a focus coalesces with the nature of play as a context-based pastime that can empower the player. It will be very important, however, for advocates of play to monitor the contexts that children will inhabit in the future so they can assure that the balance of real and virtually real is a healthy one for children. With a redistribution of technology in the twenty-first century, provision for play and support for the meaningful development of creative educational forms in schools is worthwhile. Indeed, the notion of moving beyond the "information age to the conceptual age" (Pink, 2005) supports the need for advocacy about play and meaning as integral to a post-modern education for children.

Influences of Psychobiologically Based Play

In this century, technology will continue to develop, whereas the biology of the human brain will not be much changed. Because biological evolution is much slower than cultural evolution, humans are "forced to grapple with current social and environmental issues using a brain that biological evolution has tuned to the far different cognitive challenges of 30,000 years ago" (Sylwester, 1995, p. 27). Humans have designed technological innovations to serve as another layer of brain, a "technological brain" that senses what humans cannot directly sense, moves bodies through the air in ways that humans cannot move, and infuses into the human brain unhumanlike experiences for which meaning must be sought by the brain's existing emotional and cognitive processes. Sometimes, human coping with these technologically induced experiences is breathtakingly positive, but, more often, technological innovation creates new problems that require creative and flexible uses of human biological and psychological capacities. Fortunately, one part of the human brain, the frontal lobe, has evolved with the "extra power" to enable humans to cope with situations requiring such problem solving and critical thinking.

These capacities of the brain, which have always been needed to cope with environmental and creature-induced crises, enabling humans to figure out ways to survive in emergency situations, are available for other uses when survival issues are not prominent. To keep these abilities functioning optimally, humans have "invented social and cultural problems to keep them continually stimulated and alert. The arts, games, and social organization provide pleasant metaphoric settings that help to develop and maintain our brain's problem-solving mechanisms. They are not trivial activities" (Sylwester, 1995, p. 53). Rather, they enhance the brain's effectiveness in rapid processing of "ambiguities, metaphors, abstractions, patterns, and changes" (p. 53). In particular, the prefrontal cortex, which is the last part of the brain to mature in adolescence, enables humans to "plan and rehearse future actions, to take risks in our brain's mental world rather than in the real world" (p. 54); that is, it is the site of the human capacity to play with ideas. It is conceivable that, in the future, the technological brain will take over many more of the mundane aspects of human thought, thus releasing an even greater portion of the higher brain centers for playful activity and "music, art, drama, invention, and a host of other human experiences that open us to the broad exploration of our complex world" (p. 54). Virtual reality and other recent technological innovations also point to the possibility of finding other worlds of currently unperceived sensory experiences for human exploration. If this seems an impossible dream, it is only necessary to remember a time when such phenomena as radio waves and X-rays did not exist in human thought or experience. It may be that the human capacity to play is only beginning to be demonstrated!

This playful brain power, which has been present in humans for centuries, also results in "behavioral plasticity ... which is the ... ability to change at a faster rate than can be driven by the gradual evolution of the gene pool" (Ellis, 1988, p. 24). It is likely that rigid predictability of behavior, which prevents adaptation to changing conditions, is not a major quality of human behavior because over the course of many centuries those individuals who could adapt to new situations, learn quickly, demonstrate flexible actions, and meet challenges by using risky new behaviors were more likely to be the ones who survived. From this perspective,

> Whenever the environment is changing it selects for playful individuals.... Playfulness is thus stabilized and enhanced from generation to generation by the genes.... [Therefore,] ... play is never `just play' ... it is during play that humans are most human. They learn to extend the limits of human experience and to develop the capability to deal with the unknown.... [Therefore, play ... will be the basis for our future adaptation to the unpredictable future. (Ellis, 1988, p. 25)

When looking at the future of play from a psychobiological perspective, consider the distinction between what defines an Olympic sport and what is "just a game." As a spectator at the 1996 Olympic Games in Atlanta, Doris Bergen was able to admire the marvelous human physical and emotional feats displayed in Olympic events while admiring the human species as a whole. Humans have invented so many other play/game/sport activities that could conceivably be included as Olympic events in the future. In 1996, beach volleyball and mountain biking made the list; in 2006, snowboarding and curling were added; perhaps next time Frisbee or bowling or golf or line dancing or Roller Blading might be included. The human capacity to invent and play games is phenomenal, as is the human capacity to accept challenge, risk failure, and strive for excellent performance. If the plethora of "new" play/game/sport activities evident in present culture is any indication, the future of physical and game extra play is very healthy.

Visitors to "space" museums (e.g., a *Star Trek* exhibit) often see an interesting intermingling of the "real" and "could-be-real." Exhibits from episodes of television or movie adventures "pretend" technology artifacts that might eventually be "real" artifacts used in space or even in everyday life. For example, versions of the robots portrayed in space war movies are now sold to parents of pre-schoolers, and the "shoe phone" of a fictional "smart" spy is not too dissimilar from present day cell phones! Over 400 years ago, Galileo created a sensation with playfully serious ideas that subsequently changed the view of humans' place in the universe. The world of 400 years in the future might be even more unusual than that of the world portrayed by the imagination of fiction writers and scientists today. The "as-if" mode of space adventure holds a very powerful attraction for humankind. It does not seem to be very different from the "as-if" mode of 5-year-olds' pretense and, indeed, it may serve very similar purposes. "In the same way that play provided a medium for invention in other centuries, it encourages the thinking and dreaming that are needed for survival now" (Bergen, 1988, p. 301). From the vantage point of the year 2006, those who hope that pretend play will continue to be valued in the future seem to have little to worry about. The big question is whether children will lose much of their opportunities to play imaginatively while the adult world continues to gain greater and greater access to playful experiences.

Although the technology shown in many fictional space epics is very advanced, the human inter-actions are still very primitive. Such behaviors as competitiveness, jealousy, pride, greed, hatred, and deceit are shown to be the motivators of behavior, just as they are in our present society The human character does not appear to be at all improved; these traits are merely more likely to be demonstrated through more powerful technological means. Because "our prefrontal cortex (with its strong limbic system connections) also regulates important elements of our emotional life-feelings of empathy, compassion, altruism, and parenting" (Sylwester, 1995, p. 53)—it may be that, as technology takes on more of the mundane parts of our planning, predicting, and worrying, our brain will be able to play with ideas that envision a new world of motive and behavior as well. "Perhaps, in the future, war games will be played on a computer or in a stadium with symbolic weapons so that we can even leave the crazy `reality' of war's pain and destruction behind us" (Bergen, 1988, p. 301) and perhaps replace war itself. Today, soldiers are being trained to fight with computer-generated war games; the games have not yet replaced war itself. If adults of all ages, within many cultural contexts, embracing differ-ing perspectives, and realizing varied meanings, can use technology to improve human motivations and empathy, a true technological breakthrough will occur.

In the meantime, we must "convey to children our knowledge that a life playfully and actively lived is worth the risk" (Bergen, 1988,, p. 301), so that the future of play remains secure. When adults play more worldwide, as they are freed by expanded technology from the tedium of daily survival, children also should be able to continue to imagine the possible and the now impossible, and by us-ing play to engage in social negotiation and self-empowerment, experience the unalloyed joy of these transcendent experiences.

References

Active Worlds Universe (2005). http://www.activeworlds.com/tou/asp

Aukstakalnis, S., & Blatner, D. (1992). *Silicon mirage: The art and science of virtual reality* (E. Ross, Ed.). Berkeley, CA: Peach-pit.

Bergen, D. (1988). Play, technology, and the authentic self. In D. Bergen (Ed.), *Play as a medium for learning and development* (pp. 299–301). Portsmouth, NH: Heinemann.

Cauchon, D. (2005, July 12). Children leave behind days of outdoor play. *Albany Times Union,* A1, A7.

Egan, K. (1988). *Primary understanding.* New York: Routledge.

Elkind, D. (1991, June). Postmodern play. *Readings, 8–11.*

Ellis, M. J. (1988). Play and the origin of species. In D. Bergen (Ed.), *Play as a medium for learning and development* (pp. 23–25). Portsmouth, NH: Heinemann.

Gee, J.P. (2005). What would a state of the art instructional video game look like? *Innovate 1* (6). http://www.innovateonline. info/index.php?view=article&id=80

Guddemi, M., Jambor, T., & Moore, T. (1998). Advocacy for the child's right to play. In D. P, Fromberg & D. Bergen (Eds.), *Play from birth to twelve and beyond: Contexts, perspectives, and meanings* (pp. 519–529). New York: Garland.

International Association for the Child's Right to Play (1979, 1990). *International Play Association declaration of the child's right to play,* rev. ed. Malta: Author.

Louie, E. (1995, May 11). Quilting: Artistry over the Internet. *New York Times,* C1.

Massachusetts Institute of Technology (2005). Microworlds. www.umcs.maine.edu/~larry/microworlds/microworld.html

Moulthrop, S. (1993). Writing cyberspace: Literacy in the age of simulacra. In A. Wexelblat (Ed.), *Virtual reality: Applications and explorations* (pp. 77–90). Cambridge, MA: Academic.

Pink, D. H. (2005*). A whole new mind: Moving from the information age to the conceptual age.* New York: Riverhead Books.

Schare, M. L., & Scardapane, J. R. (2005, Spring). Virual realtiy technology (VR) as treatment for anxiety disorders. *Hofstra Horizons,* 8–12.

Shaffer, D.W. (2005). *Multisubculturalism: Computers and the end of progressive education.* Madison, WI: Author.

Shaffer, D.W. Squire, K.R., Halvorson, R., & Gee, J.P. (2005). Video games and the future of learning. *Phi Delta Kappan 87*(2), 105–111.

Sylwester, R. (1995). *A celebration of neurons: An educator's guide to the human brain.* Alexandria, VA: Association for Supervision and Curriculum Development.

United Nations (1989). *Declaration on the rights of the child.* New York: Author.

Wexelblat, A. (Ed.). (1993). *Virtual reality: Applications and explorations.* Cambridge, MA: Academic.

Contributors

Melanie Ayres is a Ph.D. candidate in developmental psychology at the University of California at Santa Cruz when she is not kickboxing, going to live concerts, painting, or wrestling with her cat. She has been studying late adolescent girls' perceptions of gender discrimination, and their coping skills with discrimination, with an emphasis on intersectionality. Through it all, she has discovered that the key to stress reduction is one heaping scoop of Marianne's homemade Maltball Fudge ice cream. Prior to graduate school, Melanie graduated with a B.S. in psychology from the University of Oregon and later, worked at the Oregon Social Learning Center where she enjoyed conducting interviews with children and their parents.

Donna R. Barnes, a historian and philosopher of education at Hofstra University, is fascinated with the ways children have always learned eventually to take on adult roles in their communities and societies. She has been studying collections of children's toys in museums in Europe and the United States for more than a decade, and teaches a graduate course on "Toys and Games: Play and Learning in Historical and Cross-Cultural Perspectives." She sees play, games, and toys as important building blocks for developing children, and later adults, blessed with imagination, knowledge, skills, and values. With interests that are historical, aesthetic, culinary, artistic, and multicultural, she plays at re-creating food, meals, and menus from around the world. Other adult play activities include travel, reading, word games, and attending musical concerts, ballets, and theater performances.

Doris Bergen (coeditor) is professor of educational psychology at Miami University, where she served as department chair and director of the Center for Human Development, Learning, and Teaching. She is a past president of the National Association of Early Childhood Teacher Educators and editor of the *Journal for Research in Childhood Education*. For most of her academic career she has studied and written about children's development and especially about play as a medium for development and learning. Of late, she has been looking at the way children's sense of humor develops. Although, as a lover of play, she has chosen scholarly interests that are fun to explore, most of her life is spent working. Even then, however, during much of her work time she experiences the "flow" that is really like play. Her most recent "work as play" activity has been serving as a consultant in the production of a children's television series. Her "official" play activities as an adult are reading, theatergoing, and gardening. She also runs, but that is definitely work!

Elena Bodrova received her Ph.D. from the Russian Academy of Education and conducted research at the Institute for Preschool Education, which has implemented Vygotskian ideas in the early childhood classroom for over 40 years. She currently teaches at Metropolitan State College of Denver. She and Dr. Deborah Leong have written a book, *Tools of the Mind: The Vygotskian Approach to Early Childhood Education* (Prentice-Hall/Merrill) and a film on the Vygotskian approach for early childhood educators. Dr. Bodrova enjoys playing with her 13-year-old son, Andrei.

James F. Christie is a professor at Arizona State University, where he teaches courses in reading and early childhood education. He is the author of numerous books and articles on play, especially on how play can function as a medium for emerging literacy development. His favorite play pursuits include growing arid-climate plants in his garden (it must be play because there are few tangible outcomes) and messing around with computers.

Robert J. Coplan is an associate professor of psychology at Carleton University, Ottawa, Ontario. He received his Ph.D. in developmental psychology from the University of Waterloo. His general research is in the area of children's social development and peer relations, with a particular focus on the development of shyness and social anxiety. He has published extensively in the area of young children's play behaviors in natural settings (i.e., preschool, kindergarten), and is most interested in children who tend to "play alone" in the presence of peers. When not working, he plays piano in a local blues band.

R. Hays Cummins received his Ph.D. in oceanography from Texas A&M. He is a professor of interdisciplinary studies at Miami University, director of Discovery-Oriented Science Instruction in the School of Interdisciplinary Studies, and science editor for *Dragonfly*. Most of his research is in the areas of ecology and paleoecology, and he teaches a wide variety of subjects, including field courses in tropical ecology in Costa Rica and the Bahamas. Dr. Cummins plays sports with his friends and children, especially basketball and racquetball. He enjoys all outdoor pursuits and explorations on land and sea. He also plays a mean game of poker.

Amanda Dargan is director of the Center for Folk Arts and Education at the Bank Street College of Education in New York City. For 13 years, she served as folk arts program director for the Queens Council on the Arts. Among her publications is *City Play* (with Steve Zeitlin), which won the 1992 American Folklore Society Opie Award for the best book on children's folklore. She earned her Ph.D. in folklore and folklife from the University of Pennsylvania. When she is not working, she plays with her two children, Ben and Eliza.

Jane Ilene Freeman Davidson (deceased) has been a master teacher at the University of Delaware Laboratory Preschool and a lecturer in the Department of Individual and Family Studies. She authored two books, *Children and Computers Together in the Early Childhood Classroom* (1989) and *Emergent Literacy and Dramatic Play in Early Education* (1996). Teaching 4-year-olds allowed her to play even as she worked. She particularly enjoyed the pretend play of young children and its more adult version, the theater. When playing without children she did puzzles, logic games, and other forms of play that require the manipulation of language and ideas. She enjoyed playing at Torch Lake with her children, Lily and Michael, and her husband, Jeff.

Rheta DeVries is director of the Regents' Center for Early Developmental Education and professor of curriculum and instruction at the University of Northern Iowa. A former public school teacher, she received her Ph.D. in psychology from the University of Chicago and did postdoctoral work at the University of Geneva, Switzerland. Previous publications include *Constructivist Early Education: Overview and Comparisons with Other Programs* (coauthored with Lawrence Kohlberg) and *Group Games in Early Education* (both coauthored with Constance Kamii). She enjoys playing the piano.

Greta G. Fein (deceased) retired as a professor of education and psychology at the University of Maryland. She had been a student of play since the early 1970s, making her debut with the chapter on play that appeared in *Day Care in Context,* her first book on early child care. Her own play took two forms: one on the tennis court, playing a game to which she was addicted; another, playing with one or both of her grandsons, another addiction that yielded many hours of pleasure.

Leanne C. Findlay is completing her Ph.D. at Carleton University, Ottawa, Canada (her supervisor is Dr. Robert Coplan). Her dissertation deals with childhood shyness and sports participation as a potential protective factor for shy children. Her research interests also include the self system and social–emotional adjustment in childhood. In her spare time, she is a figure skating coach and loves to do things in the great outdoors.

George Forman, currently retired from the University of Massachusetts, earned his Ph.D. in 1967 in developmental psychology from the University of Alabama. He has studied children at play since 1968, when he left the university laboratory for the playground. He has studied children putting together jigsaw puzzles, building with geometric blocks, and drawing with markers. He has watched children use computer animation to make their own stories and microworlds. He has videotaped children in India, Japan, Korea, and especially in Italy, as they built designs using many different art and construction media. He has published books on the use of play in early education, the use of blocks in the curriculum, and the educational use of video replay. He has invented toys, puzzles, the Gravity Wall, and a water works exhibited at the Kohl Children's Museum in Chicago. His own playground is his digital video editing suite, where he produces educational videotapes to explain the competence children express when they play. In 2003 he retired from teaching to found Videatives, Inc. in order to create digital video resources to help teachers "see what children know."

Valeria J. Freysinger is an associate professor of leisure studies and lifespan development in the Department of Physical Education, Health, and Sport Studies at Miami University. She received her doctorate from the University of Wisconsin, Madison. Her research interests include leisure as a context for and means of development and the impact of gender on experiences of leisure, work, and family. When she was a child, seven siblings provided ready-made playmates for physical and outdoor activities; a love of reading and baking was picked up from her mother and great-aunt. Hiking, camping, reading, and ethnic cooking continue to be favorite leisure pursuits today.

Doris Pronin Fromberg (coeditor) is a professor of education and chairperson of the Department of Curriculum and Teaching, Hofstra University. She has served as a teacher and administrator in public and private schools, as well as director of Teacher Corps projects. She is past president of the National Association of Early Childhood Teacher Educators (NAECTE) and past-chair of the Special Interest Group on Early Education and Child Development of the American Educational Research Association. She was recipient of the 1996 Early Childhood Teacher Educator of the Year Award from NAECTE/Allyn & Bacon. Among her publications are *Play and Meaning in Early Childhood Education* (Allyn & Bacon, 2002), *The Full-Day Kindergarten: Planning and Practicing a Dynamic Themes Curriculum* (Teachers College Press, 2nd ed., 1995) and *The Encyclopedia of Early Childhood Education* (coedited with L. R. Williams, Garland, 1992). When not working playfully, she enjoys romping with the family dog, jogging, rock climbing, folk dancing, and imagining novels with alternative nonarchetypical heroines.

Joe L. Frost is Parker Centennial Professor Emeritus, University of Texas. He spent his childhood in the fields and hills of the Fourche River valley of the Ouachita Mountains in central Arkansas. He directed a major research project on children's play and play environments over the past three decades. He has published 18 books and more than 100 articles, reports, and chapters. His latest books, with coauthors, are *Play Development* and *The Developmental Benefits of Play*. He is past-president of the International Play Association/IPA, the Association for Childhood Education International (ACEI), and the 2006 recipient of the ACEI Patty Smith Hill Award. He continues to write, design play environments, speak at conferences throughout the United States and other countries, and spend play time in the hills of his childhood. A special passion is collecting old and rare volumes on children's play and play environments for inclusion in the Joe L. Frost Research Collection at the University of the Incarnate Word in San Antonio.

Barbara P. Garner retired as a faculty member of Louisiana Tech University. Her doctorate in child development is from the University of North Carolina at Greensboro. She has been director of a program for infants and toddlers, a teacher, and a supervisor of teachers, and designed an infant and toddler caregiver training institute that has been presented throughout the southeastern United States. As a child, Dr. Garner's favorite play activity was with baby dolls; as an adult, her interest has developed into play with babies, especially her grandbabies.

Laura Gaynard received her doctorate from the University of Pennsylvania. She has done research and published works on child hospital play. She is currently child life manager at Primary Children's Medical Center in Salt Lake City and an adjunct faculty member at the University of Utah. Downhill skiing is her favorite form of play and the reason she moved to Salt Lake City. Other play that she enjoys includes camping, hiking, tennis, and just hanging out with good friends. Of course, she plays at work with young patients and their siblings (which is also great fun).

Karen Gitlin-Weiner is a licensed psychologist who works with emotionally troubled adolescent girls and maintains a private practice focused on children, adolescents, and their families. Dr. Gitlin-Weiner has conducted many training seminars on play assessment and play therapy and worked as a special educator, consultant, and psychologist for emotionally, behaviorally, and learning-disabled youngsters. She is coeditor of the book, *Play Diagnosis and Assessment.* In her childhood she enjoyed both solitary and interactional play activities and appreciates her family's influence in showing her the various roles that play can have. She learned from them that a sense of playfulness can infuse any situation, even very difficult and potentially conflictual ones, and that commercial play materials are not necessary to engage in playful behaviors. She believes that it is within the power of our own minds to use the world of play and playfulness in our own best interest.

Michelle Glick Gross is Research Assistant Professor and the Associate Director of Research at the University of Miami's Debbie Institute, an early intervention center for young children with special needs. She received her Ph.D. in applied developmental psychology from the University of Miami. As the Principal Investigator of the Miami site of Legacy for Children, a parenting intervention and research study, she has enjoyed helping parents of young children at-risk learn about the importance of parent–child play to promote optimal child development. She spends most of her free time playing blocks and doing puzzles with her very active toddler son and dress-up with her 5-year-old daughter.

Wendy Haight is associate professor and Ph.D. program director in the School of Social Work at the University of Illinois, Urbana-Champaign. Her doctorate in developmental psychology is from the University of Chicago. She has done much of her research on adult–child interactions in pretend play and on sociocultural issues in child development. Her recent research focuses on vulnerable children and families involved in protective services.

Linda Homeyer is an associate professor in the Professional Counseling Program of the Department of Educational Administration and Psychological Services at Texas State University-San Marcus. She is a registered play therapy supervisor and is actively involved in play therapy relationships with children. Her research on the play behaviors of sexually abused children is extensive and resulted in a unique instrument for assessing sexually abused children. Dr. Homeyer is the recipient of the 1995 Graduate School award for Who's Who in American Universities.

Alice Sterling Honig is professor emerita of child development at Syracuse University. Her numerous articles, chapters, and books focus particularly on caregiving, teaching, and parenting young children. For many years, Dr. Honig directed the annual Quality Infant/Toddler Caregiving workshop at Syracuse University. As a licensed clinician, she works with families to help them resolve child-rearing problems. Dr. Honig serves as North American editor for the British journal, *Early Child Development and Care*. Dr. Honig's play preferences are eclectic: they include solving double acrostic puzzles, giving folk song concerts in many languages, reading stories to grandchildren, writing poetry, exploring neolithic cave art, gardening, avid museum visiting, and e-mail exchange with friends across the world.

James E. Johnson is professor-in-charge of early childhood education in the Department of Curriculum and Instruction in the College of Education at Pennsylvania State University. He is past president of The Association for the Study of Play and serves on the National Board of Directors of Playing for Keeps. He coauthored *Play and Early Childhood Development* (with James Christie and Thomas Yawkey) and coedited *Play in Diverse Cultures* (with Jaipaul Roopnarine and Frank Hooper), among numerous publications in the areas of socialization, early education, and children's play. He grew up in Warren, Michigan, and remembers war and adventure play in natural environments near his home, where he later organized baseball, football, and hockey teams. He was Michigan's Junior Chess Champion one year in the 1960s. He remains an avid chess enthusiast and teaches chess at his son's charter middle school.

Yasmin B. Kafai is an associate professor at the UCLA Graduate School of Education and Information Studies. Before coming to UCLA, she worked at the MIT Media Laboratory and received her doctorate from Harvard University. She was one of the first researchers to establish the field of game studies with her work on children's learning as designers and players of educational software and games. Her research has been published in *Minds in Play: Computer Game Design as a Context for Children's Learning* (Lawrence Erlbaum, 1995) and *Constructionism in Practice: Designing, Thinking, and Learning in a Digital World* (coedited with Mitchel Resnick, Lawrence Erlbaum, 1996). She also has been active in several national policy efforts, among them the AAUW report, "Tech-Savvy Girls" (2000) and "Under the Microscope: A Decade of Gender Equity Interventions in the Sciences" (2004). She lives, works, and play in Los Angeles.

Constance Kamii is a professor of early childhood education at the University of Alabama at Birmingham. She received her Ph.D. in psychology and education from the University of Michigan and subsequently studied under Jean Piaget off and on for 15 years. She worked closely with teachers for more than 30 years to use Piaget's theory for curriculum development at the preschool level as well as in primary mathematics. She and coauthor Yasuhiko Kato have worked together for more than 20 years on curriculum development, along with colleagues in Japan, with an emphasis on young children's moral development and their development of logico-mathematical knowledge.

Yasuhiko Kato is a professor in the Department of Early Education at Chugoku Gakuen University in Okayama, Japan. He has led this department toward basing its teacher education program on Piaget's constructivism. With Constance Kamii, he continues to study Piaget's theory and to develop the preschool curriculum that she has been building since the 1980s. His most recent contribution to early childhood education in Japan is his introduction of "big books" in Japanese and a holistic approach to beginning reading and writing.

Aimbika Krishnakumar is associate professor in the Department of Child and Family Studies, Syracuse University. She received the Ph.D. from the University of Tennessee-Knoxville. Her research interests include family dynamics, child and adolescent development, and developmental transitions. Her play interests include badminton and tennis.

Garry Landreth is a Regents professor in the Department of Counselor Education and director of the Center for Play Therapy at the University of North Texas-Denton. He is a registered play therapy supervisor and is actively involved in play therapy relationships with children. He trains parents to be therapeutic agents in the lives of their children by using child-centered play therapy procedures in structured play sessions in their own homes. Dr. Landreth has published numerous journal articles and books, including *Play Therapy: The Art of Relationship*. He is past-chair of the board of directors of the International Association for Play Therapy and has conducted training workshops on play therapy throughout the United States, Europe, Canada, and China. He is the recipient of the 1995 Virginia Axline Award for Professional Contributions. He notes that experiencing a child's play is a wonderful time of relationship building and discovery: a time of *being with* that transcends the limits of time and space. It is a time to experience being fully accepted and to make exciting discoveries. He believes such times for him are among the most meaningful of his life.

Deborah J. Leong is professor of psychology at Metropolitan State College of Denver. She has coauthored many articles on play and the impact of play on the development of self-regulation. She is also coauthor with Dr. Elena Bodrova of *Tools of the Mind: The Vygotskian Approach to Early Childhood Education* (Prentice-Hall /Merrill, 1996) and four educational videos (Davidson Films), one on play. She is coauthor with Dr. McAfee and Dr. Bodrova of the *Basics of Assessment* (National Association for the Education of Young Children, 2004), and with Dr. McAfee, *Assessing and Guiding Young Children's Development and Learning* (4th ed., in press).

Leslie D. Levé received her doctoral degree in developmental psychology from the University of Oregon. She is currently a research scientist at the Oregon Social Learning Center (OSLC), which is known worldwide for its innovative research with families and children. Her developmental research has been published in over a dozen papers, including several that focus on adoptive and birth families. "Infant Temperament, Pleasure in Parenting, and Marital Happiness in Adoptive Families" (*Infant Journal of Mental Health* with Scaramella and Fagot, 2001) is one example of this work. For the Early Growth and Development Study, Dr. Leve is responsible for supervising the interview team.

Diane E. Levin is professor at Wheelock College in Boston, where she has taught courses in early childhood education and human development. She is the author of *Teaching Young Children in Violent Times: Building a Peaceable Classroom* and *Remote Control Childhood? Combating the Hazards of Media Culture*. She has coauthored four additional works, including *The War Play Dilemma: What Every Parent and Teacher Needs to Know*! She is founder of Teachers Resisting Unhealthy Children's Entertainment (TRUCE; http://www.truceteachers.org) and the Campaign for a Commercial-Free Childhood (CCFC; http://www.commercialfreechildhood.org). She is a senior adviser for three PBS Parents websites including, "How to Talk to Kids about War and Violence" (http://www.pbs.org/opb/thenewheroes/parents).

M. Lee Manning teaches in the Department of Educational Curriculum and Instruction, Darden College of Education, Old Dominion University, Norfolk, Virginia. His doctorate is from the University of South Carolina. As a child, when he lived around other children, he skated and rode bikes and pretended to be cars or planes; when he lived several miles from others, he played alone as he roamed creeks, gullies, and hills pretending to be an explorer. Whether playing alone or with other children, he usually had a "secret lab" where he conducted experiments and thought of inventions.

Today, similar to previous "exploring," his play includes exploring beaches, roaming mountains in the western United States, and sailing his boat.

Gayle Mindes is professor of education at DePaul University. She is a graduate of Loyola University of Chicago with a major concentration in early childhood completed at the Erikson Institute. Throughout her career, she has taught undergraduate and graduate courses in early childhood and elementary education. Dr. Mindes has served in a variety of leadership capacities in the field of early childhood education in Illinois. She also has served as a consultant for Head Start, child care agencies, public schools, and state agencies. Books include *Assessing Young Children* (3rd ed., Prentice-Hall/Merrill, forthcoming*); Teaching Young Children Social Studies* (Greenwood, forthcoming), *Secondary and Middle School Methods* (2nd ed., with Allan C. Ornstein, Allyn & Bacon). She is coauthor of *Planning a Theme-Based Curriculum* (with Carla Berry, Delmar, 1993). She serves on the editorial board of the National Association for the Education of Young Children and as a consultant to Anthology-Preface and Heinemann-Raintree for the development of text materials for children and adolescents. She enjoys playing with recipes and viewing movies, plays, and contemporary art. More actively, she walks and enjoys travel, particularly service trips that take her from the coke ovens of West Virginia to Montana and the first dude ranch—OTO Ranch.

Shirley K. Morgenthaler is Distinguished Professor of Education and coordinator of graduate and undergraduate studies in early childhood education at Concordia University, River Forest, Illinois. Her doctorate is in early childhood education and curriculum development, and she teaches courses in those areas. She directs the Children in Worship research study in her role as the director of the Center for the Study of Children's Ethical Development. She is also Director of the KidFaith Institute, a national training initiative for congregational development of appropriate children's programming. She is past president of the Illinois Association of Early Childhood Teacher Educators. Her own favorite play with objects involves the challenge of riding the movement of water and tube behind a speeding boat. Her continuing play with objects also involves doing crossword puzzles and using fishing poles. The challenges of cognitive play, strategy play, and pragmatic play are well represented in her life!

Mary Morrison is a doctoral candidate at the University of North Texas in the Counseling Department where she is Assistant Director of the Center for Play Therapy, the largest play therapy training program in the world. She teaches courses in play therapy at UNT and provides supervision for masters and doctoral interns. Her dissertation research investigates the effectiveness of training and supervision of Head Start teachers in play therapy principles and procedures to be used in the classroom as an early mental health intervention. She is a nationally certified counselor and a registered play therapist. She has most fun playing with her niece, Stella.

Christopher A. Myers received his Ph.D. in ecology and is a professor in the School of Interdisciplinary Studies at Miami University. He teaches on ecology-related themes, with a particular interest in participatory science and human rights. As a director of Project Dragonfly, he is trying to prove that scientists and kids can actually have fun together. His personal play life includes visiting ecosystems with his wife, Lynne Born Myers and daughter, Mickey; writing stories for children; as well as general shenanigans, monkeyshines, and tomfooleries.

Patricia Monighan Nourot is professor emeritus of education and coordinated early childhood education programs and graduate programs in the School of Education at Sonoma State University, Rohnert Park, California. She retired from university teaching in fall, 2004 and has returned to classroom teaching with young children, a multiage primary class in a public charter school. She is the coauthor of three books on play in childhood, *Looking at Children's Play: A Bridge between Theory and Practice* (1987), *Play at the Center of the Curriculum* (4th ed., 2005), and *First Class: California's*

Guide to Early Primary Education (1999), and has written several articles and chapters concerning the role of play in learning and development. When "at play" she is cooking, hiking in the Napa Valley, or reading detective novels.

Sherri Oden is a professor in the Department of Human Development and Child Studies at Oakland University where she coordinates the doctoral program in early childhood education. She has conducted research on children's peer relations and methods of coaching social skills to assist children who lack positive peer relations. She also has conducted research on child development in educational programs such as Head Start and the Cleveland Opera program in elementary school classrooms. She received a Ph.D. in human development and educational psychology from the University of Illinois. She enjoys many activities with her nieces, Kirsty and Rebecca, and her nephews, Mathew and Riordan help her to rediscover the joy of true play.

Anthony D. Pellegrini received his Ph.D. from Ohio State University in 1978 and works at the University of Minnesota as a professor of educational psychology. He has studied many aspects of children's and adolescents' play, including symbolic play and rough-and-tumble play, and has authored numerous articles, book chapters, and books on these topics. He has worked on a project examining the role of recess in the primary school curriculum. In the middle of most work days, he takes a break to engage in Nordic skiing-related exercise.

Patricia G. Ramsey is a professor of psychology and education at Mount Holyoke College in South Hadley, Massachusetts. She has published a number of articles and chapters reporting her research on children's early attitude development and their friendship patterns. Among her books are *Teaching and Learning in a Diverse World: Multicultural Education for Young Children* and *Making Friends in School: Promoting Peer Relationships in Early Childhood* (both published by Teachers College Press). She loves playing sports (for fun), day dreaming, writing silly poems, and telling funny stories.

Mary S. Rivkin is a professor in the early childhood education program at the University of Maryland, Baltimore County. She received her Ph.D. from the University of Maryland. She has taught in inner-city and suburban classes of 3-year-olds through graduate school. She is the author of *The Great Outdoors: Restoring Children's Right to Play Outside*. Observations as a mother, teacher, and urban/suburban householder inspired her research into the changing outdoor environment for children. She grew up in a small city in the Pacific Northwest, playing outside as much as possible, particularly liking to climb trees, make mudpies, explore flowers and bushes, and simply mess around.

Jaipaul L. Roopnarine received his Ph.D. from the University of Wisconsin. He is professor of child development at Syracuse University. His research interests include father–child relationships across cultures; Caribbean immigrant families and schooling; early childhood education in international perspectives; globalization and convergences in childrearing and early socialization, and children's play across cultures. He has published extensively in the areas of developmental psychology and early childhood education, and has served on several editorial boards in the psychological sciences. His recent books are *Families in Global Perspectives* (Allyn & Bacon, 2005), *Approaches in Early Childhood Education* (4th ed., Prentice-Hall/Merrill, 2005), and *Children and Adolescents Across Cultures* (Praeger, 2004). He plays cricket and dominoes.

Kenneth H. Rubin is Director and Professor, Center for Children, Relationships, and Culture in the Department of Human Development, University of Maryland. He received his B.A. from McGill University and his M.S. and Ph.D. from the Pennsylvania State University. He is a fellow of the Canadian and American Psychological Associations and has been a recipient of both a Killam Research Fellowship (Canada Council) and an Ontario Mental Health Senior Research Fellowship. He has twice served as an associate editor of *Child Development* and is past president of the Society for the Study of Behavioral Development. His research interests include the study of children's peer and family relationships and their social and emotional development. He is the senior author of chapters that have appeared in *The Handbook of Child Psychology—Play* (1983) and *Peer Interactions, Relationships, and Groups* (1998, 2006), the *Handbook of Parenting* (1995, 2002), and the *Handbook of Childhood Social Development* (2002). He is also the author of *The Friendship Factor* (2002), a book for parents that received the Gold Award in 2002 from the National Parenting Publications Award.

Steven B. Silvern is a professor of early childhood education at Auburn University. His doctorate is in child development from the University of Wisconsin-Madison. He teaches introductory and advanced courses on Piaget, as well as language development, construction of number, early childhood curriculum, and program evaluation courses. He has been studying children's play and learning for many years and is the author of multiple articles and chapters on the subject. When not playing with words or heads, he plays at golf.

Dorothy G. Singer is codirector of the Yale University Family Television Research and Consulting Center. She is also senior research scientist in the Department of Psychology. She received her doctorate in psychology from Columbia University. Her interests include research on the effects of television on children's cognitive, social, and emotional development. She has authored over 120 articles and 20 books. She coauthored *The House of MakeBelieve: Play and the Developing Imagination*. Among her books is *Playing for Their Lives: Helping Troubled Children through Play Therapy* and *Imagination and Play in the Electronic Age* (with Jerome L. Singer). Her current work has been in the area of developing curricula to help preschoolers learn readiness skills for school entry. She is an exceptionally playful grandparent.

Jerome L. Singer received his doctorate in clinical psychology from the University of Pennsylvania. He is professor of psychology at Yale University, where he served as director of the graduate program in clinical psychology and director of graduate studies in psychology. He is codirector, with Dr. Dorothy G. Singer, of the Yale University Family Television Research and Consultation Center. He is a specialist in research on the psychology of imagination and daydreaming. Dr. Singer has authored more than 200 technical articles on thought processes, imagery, personality, and psychotherapy as well as on children's play and the effects of television. He has written or edited more than 15 books, including *The Inner World of Daydreaming; The Power of Human Imagination; Television, Imagination and Aggression: A Study of Preschoolers; The House of Make-Believe: Children's Play and the Developing Imagination; The Parents' Guide: Use TV to Your Child's Advantage;* and *Imagery Methods in Psychotherapy and Behavior Modification*. He also has written (with Dorothy G. Singer), *Imagination and Play in the Electronic Age*. Tennis, bird watching, and listening to opera are his main modes of "play." He is an exceptionally playful grandparent.

Jeffrey Trawick-Smith is a professor of education at Eastern Connecticut State University and has conducted and published research on young children's play. He received his doctorate from Indiana University. This research interest did not emerge by accident: he has been an expert player from his earliest days. Among his more impressive make-believe roles of childhood were The Wolverine, a role he invented while browsing pictures in an encyclopedia and one he enacted with all of the ferocity that he lacked in real life; The Flying, Invisible Minister, a role that blended the spiritual qualities of a religious leader with the more practical crime-fighting talents of Superman; and The Groom, a role he played reluctantly with his older sister, who as The Bride never tired of formal weddings. As an adult he engages in utter, unbound silliness with his two sons and writes novels. He also writes playful and controversial chapters about play.

Karen VanderVen is professor of child development and child care at the University of Pittsburgh and a 1995–1996 visiting scholar at Harvard University Graduate School of Education. Her special interests include play and activity, professionalization of early childhood education, and human service applications of chaos theory. She is editor of the *Journal of Child and Youth Care Work,* on the editorial board of five other journals, and author of over 150 publications. She is a frequent presenter on play topics at the annual conferences of the National Association for the Education of Young Children. In her "spare" time, she is a certified scuba diver, dives for new additions to her extensive collection of Florida and Caribbean seashells, plays basketball, watches birds, enjoys her cats, collects Florida mystery books, and practices juggling. She is interested in innovation and invention, and utilizes her shelf of varied toys and playthings to generate new ideas.

Nancy W. Wiltz received her Ph.D. in curriculum and instruction from the University of Maryland. She teaches courses in human development, and supervises student teachers in early childhood education. She also serves as the early childhood liaison between the Department of Human Development and the Office of Laboratory Experiences. As a former preschool teacher and the mother of two, she intuitively knew that children loved to play, but she did not become a "student of play" until she became a graduate student and discovered the magnitude and depth of play as a serious research topic. In her spare time, she enjoys playing with her husband. This is her first publication.

Christopher R. Wolfe is professor of Interdisciplinary Studies at Miami University, director or Quantitative Reasoning and Instructional Computing for the Western College Program, and an affiliate of Miami's departments of psychology and educational psychology. He is president of the Society for Computers in Psychology, codirector of Miami's Center for Human Development, Learning, and Teaching, and holds a Ph.D. in learning, developmental, and cognitive psychology from the University of Pittsburgh, where he worked in the Learning Research and Development Center. In addition to playing with his children, Michael and Patrick, he enjoys reading, fishing, and camping.

Irma C. Woods grew up in the hot, humid, but breezy climate of a coastal South Texas town; trees were a luxury, and as a child she delighted in playing in their cool, cozy shade. Today, she continues to enjoy the outdoors, particularly canoeing, camping, and gardening. She is a former first grade teacher and social worker of a state agency and teaches in the Early Childhood Department at Del Mar College in Corpus Christi, Texas. Her doctoral work at the University of Texas focuses on the influence of culture on play and developmentally appropriate practice in the care of young children.

Steve Zeitlin received his Ph.D. in folklore from the University of Pennsylvania. He is the director and cofounder of City Lore, an organization dedicated to the preservation of New York City's living cultural heritage. Zeitlin served as a regular commentator for the nationally syndicated public radio show, *Crossroads* (frequently rebroadcast on *Morning Edition).* Prior to arriving in New York, he served for eight years as a folklorist at the Smithsonian Institution in Washington, DC, and taught at George Washington University and American University. He is coauthor of a number of books on American folk culture, including *A Celebration of American Family Folklore; The Grand Generation: Memory, Mastery and Legacy;* and *City Play.* He is currently completing a book on Jewish stories for Simon & Schuster. He has also coproduced a number of award-winning film documentaries, including *Free Show Tonite* on the traveling medicine shows of the 1920s and 1930s. He considers all of his work a form of play.

Index